Markets, Money and Capital

Sir John Hicks (1904–89) was a leading economic theorist of the twentieth century, and along with Kenneth Arrow was awarded the Nobel Prize in 1972. His work addressed central topics in economic theory, such as value, money, capital, and growth. An important unifying theme was the attention to economic rationality 'in time' and his acknowledgment that apparent rigidities and frictions might exert a positive role as a buffer against excessive fluctuations in output, prices, and employment. This emphasis on the virtue of imperfection significantly distances Hicksian economics from both the Keynesian and monetarist approaches. Containing contributions from distinguished theorists in their own right (including three Nobel Prize-winners), this volume examines Hicks's intellectual heritage and discusses how his ideas suggest a distinct approach to economic theory and policy-making. It will be of great interest to scholars and students of economic theory and the history of economic thought.

ROBERTO SCAZZIERI is Professor of Economics at the University of Bologna, a Senior Member of Gonville and Caius College and Life Member of Clare Hall, Cambridge.

AMARTYA SEN is a Nobel laureate and Professor of Economics and Philosophy at Harvard University.

STEFANO ZAMAGNI is Professor of Economics at the University of Bologna and Adjunct Professor of International Economics at Johns Hopkins University.

Markets, Money and Capital

Hicksian Economics for the Twenty-first Century

edited by
Roberto Scazzieri,
Amartya Sen
and
Stefano Zamagni

CAMBRIDGE
UNIVERSITY PRESS

CAMBRIDGE UNIVERSITY PRESS
Cambridge, New York, Melbourne, Madrid, Cape Town,
Singapore, São Paulo, Delhi, Tokyo, Mexico City

Cambridge University Press
The Edinburgh Building, Cambridge CB2 8RU, UK

Published in the United States of America by Cambridge University Press, New York

www.cambridge.org
Information on this title: www.cambridge.org/9780521188791

First published 2008
First paperback edition 2011

A catalogue record for this publication is available from the British Library

Library of Congress Cataloguing in Publication data

Markets, money and capital : Hicksian economics for the 21st century / edited by
Roberto Scazzieri, Amartya Sen, and Stefano Zamagni.
    p.   cm.
Includes index.
ISBN 978-0-521-87321-5
1. Hicks, John, 1904–1989.   2. Economists–Great Britain.   3. Economics.
4. Capital.   I. Scazzieri, Roberto.   II. Sen, Amartya.   III. Zamagni, Stefano.
HB103.
H47M37   2008
330.092–dc22

                                                                        2008027703

ISBN 978-0-521-87321-5 Hardback
ISBN 978-0-521-18879-1 Paperback

Contents

List of figures   page viii
List of tables   x
List of contributors   xi
Preface and acknowledgments   xiii

Between theory and history: on the identity of Hicks's
economics
ROBERTO SCAZZIERI AND STEFANO ZAMAGNI   1

Part I The Intellectual Heritage of John Hicks

1   Hicks on liberty
    AMARTYA SEN   41

2   An economist even greater than his high reputation
    PAUL A. SAMUELSON   49

3   Hicks's 'conversion' – from J. R. to John
    LUIGI L. PASINETTI AND GIANPAOLO MARIUTTI   52

4   Dear John, Dear Ursula (Cambridge and LSE, 1935):
    eighty-eight letters unearthed
    MARIA CRISTINA MARCUZZO AND ELEONORA
    SANFILIPPO   72

5   Hicks and his publishers
    ANDREW L. SCHULLER   92

6   Hicks in reviews, 1932–89: from *The Theory of Wages* to
    A Market Theory of Money
    WARREN YOUNG   109

Part II Markets

7 Hicks and the emptiness of general equilibrium theory
CHRISTOPHER BLISS   129

8 Hicks versus Marx? On the theory of economic history
PIERLUIGI CIOCCA   146

9 Hicks's notion and use of the concepts of fix-price and flex-price
MARCELLO DE CECCO   157

10 On the Hicksian definition of income in applied economic analysis
PAOLO ONOFRI AND ANNA STAGNI   164

Part III Money

11 Historical stylizations and monetary theory
ALBERTO QUADRIO CURZIO AND ROBERTO SCAZZIERI   185

12 Hicks: money, prices, and credit management
OMAR F. HAMOUDA   204

13 Core, mantle, and industry: a monetary perspective of banks' capital standards
RAINER MASERA   225

14 A suggestion for simplifying the theory of asset prices
RICCARDO CESARI AND CARLO D'ADDA   252

Part IV Capital and Dynamics

15 'Distribution and Economic Progress' after seventy years
ROBERT M. SOLOW   277

16 Flexible saving and economic growth
MAURO BARANZINI   287

17 The economics of non-linear cycles
PIERO FERRI   309

18 A perspective on a Hicksian non-linear theory of the trade cycle
KUMARASWAMY VELA VELUPILLAI   328

19 Capital, growth, and production disequilibria: on the
    employment consequences of new technologies
    HARALD HAGEMANN   346

20 Capital and time
    ERICH W. STREISSLER   367

21 Sequential analysis and out-of-equilibrium paths
    MARIO AMENDOLA AND JEAN-LUC GAFFARD   382

    References   405
    Name index   433
    Subject index   441

Figures

10.1   Ratio of expected to actual inflation, 1970–2005   *page* 167
10.2   Household disposable income with and without Hicksian
       correction (percentage change), 1971–2004   167
10.3   Rate of profit and real rate of return on financial assets
       associated with industrial fixed capital, 1951–2003   171
10.4   Rate of profit and real cost of capital, 1951–2003   173
10.5   Real rate of return on financial assets and real cost of capital,
       1952–2003   174
10.A1 Household consumption: error correction representation (a),
       1971–2003   177
10.A2 Household consumption: error correction representation (b),
       normalized residuals, 1971–2003   178
10.A3 Household consumption: error correction representation
       with disposable income partially adjusted *à la* Hicks (a),
       1971–2003   179
10.A4 Household consumption: error correction representation
       with disposable income partially adjusted *à la* Hicks (b),
       normalized residuals, 1971–2003   180
12.1   Hicks's model in *Capital and Growth*: traverse I   213
13.1   Equity as a percentage of assets for US commercial banks,
       1840–1993   233
13.2   Aggregate supply with exogenous wage rates   234
13.3   Credit and market risk: frequency distributions   239
13.4   Portfolio credit losses   244
13.5   Capital/asset ratios of banking system in the United States,
       the United Kingdom, and Switzerland, 1830–2000   245
17.1   The endogenous fluctuations of the economy   318
17.2   Endogenous cycles with bounded rationality   321
18.1   Multiple equilibria in *A Contribution to the Theory
       of the Trade Cycle*   332
18.2   The Goodwin characteristic   339
18.3   Stable limit cycle for the Goodwin characteristic   339

19.1   Effects of technological progress on the marginal product
       of labor (without displacement)   358
19.2   Effects of technological progress on the marginal product
       of labor (with displacement)   358
19.3   The fix-wage path   364
21.1a The evolution of the economy with a decreasing growth rate
       of 'take-out': the overall growth rate and productive capacity   393
21.1b The evolution of the economy with a decreasing growth rate
       of 'take-out': unemployment and productivity   394
21.2a Increasing investment and monotonically decreasing
       growth rate   396
21.2b Increasing investment and increasing distortion
       of productive capacity   396
21.3a The evolution of the economy with an increasing growth rate
       of 'take-out'   397
21.3b The evolution of productivity and real wages with
       an increasing growth rate of 'take-out'   398
21.4a The evolution of the economy with coordination
       mechanisms and a decreasing growth rate of 'take-out'   400
21.4b The evolution of productivity with coordination mechanisms
       and a decreasing growth rate of 'take-out'   401
21.5a The evolution of the economy with coordination
       mechanisms and an increasing growth rate of 'take-out'   402
21.5b The evolution of productivity with coordination mechanisms
       and an increasing growth rate of 'take-out'   403

Tables

10.1   Rate of profit, real return on financial assets, and real
cost of capital (percentage values), 1951–2003   *page* 171

10.A1 Household consumption: error correction representation   175

10.A2 Household consumption: error correction representation
with disposable income partially adjusted (0.4) *à la* Hicks   176

13.1   A simplified model of financial markets   234

17.1   The impact of the accelerator parameters on the fluctuations   319

17.2   Consistent expectations   322

Contributors

MARIO AMENDOLA Professor of Economics, University of Rome La Sapienza.

MAURO BARANZINI Professor of Economics, Università della Svizzera Italiana, Lugano Campus, Lugano, Switzerland.

CHRISTOPHER BLISS Nuffield Professor of International Economics, University of Oxford, and Fellow of Nuffield College, Oxford.

RICCARDO CESARI Professor of Financial Mathematics, University of Bologna.

PIERLUIGI CIOCCA Former Deputy Director General, Bank of Italy.

CARLO D'ADDA Professor of Economics, University of Bologna, and Past President, Italian Economic Society.

MARCELLO DE CECCO Professor of Economics, Scuola Normale Superiore, Pisa.

PIERO FERRI Professor of Economics, University of Bergamo, Italy.

JEAN-LUC GAFFARD Professor of Economics, University of Nice, France.

HARALD HAGEMANN Professor of Economic Theory, Hohenheim University, Stuttgart, and Life Member of Clare Hall, Cambridge.

OMAR F. HAMOUDA Professor of Economics, York University, Toronto.

MARIA CRISTINA MARCUZZO Professor of the History of Economic Thought, University of Rome La Sapienza.

GIANPAOLO MARIUTTI Assistant Professor of Economics, University of Verona.

RAINER MASERA Adjunct Professor of the Economics of Financial and Monetary Institutions, University of Rome II.

PAOLO ONOFRI Professor of Economics, University of Bologna.

LUIGI L. PASINETTI Emeritus Professor of Economic Analysis, Catholic University of Milan; Honorary Fellow of Gonville and Caius College, Cambridge; Past President, Italian Economic Society and European Society for the History of Economic Thought.

ALBERTO QUADRIO CURZIO Professor of Economics, Catholic University of Milan, and Past President, Italian Economic Society.

PAUL A. SAMUELSON Emeritus Professor of Economics, Massachusetts Institute of Technology (MIT); Nobel Laureate; Past President, International Economic Association.

ELEONORA SANFILIPPO Research Fellow in the History of Economic Thought, University of Rome La Sapienza.

ROBERTO SCAZZIERI Professor of Economic Analysis, University of Bologna; Senior Member of Gonville and Caius College, Cambridge; Life Member of Clare Hall, Cambridge.

ANDREW L. SCHULLER Former Economics Editor, Oxford University Press.

AMARTYA SEN Professor of Economics and Philosophy, University of Harvard; Former Master, Trinity College, Cambridge; Nobel Laureate; Past President, International Economic Association.

ROBERT M. SOLOW Emeritus Professor of Economics, Massachusetts Institute of Technology; Nobel Laureate; Past President, International Economic Association.

ANNA STAGNI Professor of Economics, University of Bologna.

ERICH W. STREISSLER Emeritus Professor of Economics, University of Vienna, and Past President, European Society for the History of Economic Thought.

KUMARASWAMY VELA VELUPILLAI Fellow in Economics, Girton College, Cambridge and Professor of Economics, University of Trento.

WARREN YOUNG Professor of Economics, Bar-Ilan University, Ramat Gan, Israel.

STEFANO ZAMAGNI Professor of Economics, University of Bologna, and Adjunct Professor of International Economics, Johns Hopkins University, Bologna Center.

Preface and acknowledgments

This volume is the result of interaction within the invisible college of former colleagues and pupils of John Hicks. In our view, its scope reflects both the breadth of his approach to different research traditions in economics and the lifelong coherence of his commitment to the understanding of a well-defined set of issues centered upon the relationship between rationality and equilibrium, history and time.

Early drafts of all the chapters were presented at the international meeting 'John Hicks: One Hundredth Anniversary Workshop,' which was hosted by the Cassa di Risparmio in Bologna on October 10–11, 2004.

It is in the recollection of those days of intense intellectual exchange that we wish to express our gratitude to all the institutions that made both that meeting and the publication of this volume possible. In particular, we are grateful to Banco San Paolo IMI, Turin, and Cassa di Risparmio in Bologna for their enlightened support. We are also grateful to the Department of Economics of the University of Bologna for its research facilities during the preparation of this volume.

Preface and acknowledgements

Between theory and history: on the identity of Hicks's economics

Roberto Scazzieri and Stefano Zamagni

Hicks's economic theorizing

John Hicks was one of the most influential economists of the twentieth century. His contributions have shaped the core theories of rational choice and human welfare, value and money, capital and growth. At the same time, Hicks's contributions often address contentious issues, and sometimes suggest unconventional and controversial points of view. In John Hicks, we see economic theorizing at its most fundamental, almost formative, stage. In his writings, economic theorizing strives to achieve, and succeeds in maintaining, a balance between the requirements of analysis and the explicit recognition of the relevance of history and institutions. In short, Hicks's contribution to economics belongs *both* to the so-called 'mainstream' and to its critique.

This characteristic feature of Hicks's work derives from a seemingly simple, but in fact highly sophisticated, approach to the construction of economic theory. Hicks takes theories to be the product of a particular 'concentration of attention' (Hicks, 1976a: 209). Theories are focusing devices that may be effective in bringing to view certain causal patterns, while leaving other (possible) causal patterns aside. This makes theories essential to economic analysis (as some concentration of attention is a necessary condition for the identification of a causal relationship). The same approach makes *multiple* theories possible, however. Indeed, the possibility of distinct theoretical frameworks is a most natural consequence of changes in the concentration of attention (see Scazzieri, 1993b). Moreover, such changes are often necessary to preserve the relevance of theories vis-à-vis historical or institutional changes.[1] In Hicks's view,

---

[1] The view of economic theories as frames suggesting certain patterns of causality, while leaving other patterns aside, is reinforced by Hicks's belief that 'many of the terms that are used by economists are derived from business practice' and that 'a good part of what is called economic theory is best regarded as a criticism of those concepts, finding out what adjustments have to be made to the business concepts in order that we may use them as instruments of more general thought' (Hicks, 1986a: 99).

1

particular (almost context-dependent) theories are at the same time essential and dispensable tools of investigation. In one of his late writings (*Causality in Economics*; 1979a), Hicks maintains that economics 'if it is on the edge of the sciences...is also on the edge of history' (1979a: 4). His approach to economic theorizing as a scholarly pursuit is accordingly multifaceted. Hicks did not belong to any specific 'school' of economic thought. He would have certainly subscribed to the well-known sentence by Johann Wolfgang Goethe: 'Every school of thought is like a man who has talked to himself for a hundred years and is pleased with his mind, no matter how stupid it may be' (Goethe, 1976 [1821]: 39).

Hicks was especially skilled in identifying similarities and points of convergence among distinct theoretical frameworks. His interest in the Walras–Pareto formulation of economic equilibrium and in Alfred Marshall's analysis of markets was combined with a deep knowledge of Austrian and Swedish capital theory, and of John Maynard Keynes's macroeconomics. Hicks's view of the subject matter of economic theory is at the root of his highly distinctive approach to the relationship between pure economics and institutional economics. In his contribution, economic theorizing *includes* the consideration of the conditions that make specific theoretical frameworks outdated. In this connection, Hicks maintained that recognition of the *limits* of economic theory might be an important source of theoretical innovation. In this sense, we may say that Hicks was a standard-bearer of the idea that there cannot be a unique theory at the center of economic discourse.

The intellectual agenda of John Hicks shows a remarkable mix of continuity and change (see also Baumol, 1972). This is partly due to the tolerant disposition that was characteristic of Hicks as a theorist. The varied course of economic history may require changes in the theorist's concentration of attention. Hicks, however, always preferred 'to combine elements from different theoretical systems rather than deduce his conclusions from a set of consistent hypotheses' (McKenzie and Zamagni, 1991: xxix). It is interesting that this approach has a precise counterpart in Hicks's attitude to the identification of causal relations in history. In this case, as noted by Peter Bauer, Hicks uses a combination of two distinct methods: 'First, inferences from statistical uniformities of some aspects of his historical events, and, second, examination of the implications of particular phenomena to deduce how one situation leads predictably to another' (Bauer, 1971: 175–6). Hicks's analysis of the 'rise of the market' in his *Theory of Economic History* is a case in point, for he suggests that one should identify a critical phenomenon, or watershed, in history and then look into 'what logically follows from it' (1969a: 7–8). Economic theory is necessary to this analytical exploration of history, but, according to Hicks, the relevance of particular theories is likely to change as we move from one set of historical circumstances to another. Similarly, attention to historical record is necessary, but this does not imply that the theorist should be unduly restrained by statistical uniformities. As a matter of fact, Hicks requires only that the analysis of the logical implications of historical events should not clash 'with the largest and most obvious facts' (1969a: 8). In short, he is acutely aware of the importance of hierarchical structures both among theoretical concepts and among facts. The success of any attempt to identify 'intelligible reasons for which one [economic state of society] should give way to another' (1969a: 6; as quoted in Baumol, 1990: 1712) ultimately depends upon the analyst's ability to identify meaningful associations between theoretical concepts and facts – that is, associations appropriate to the specific context under consideration.

This approach is highly characteristic of Hicks, and paves the way to Hicks's propensity to go back to past concepts in order to highlight new and sometimes radical changes in economic institutions and patterns of behavior. Hicks is well known for his willingness to recognize that views (or theoretical frameworks) that he had previously endorsed ought to be discarded due to the need to switch to different concentrations of attention. At the same time, there is in Hicks a surprising continuity underlying an intellectual output of more than sixty years. This is especially clear if one looks at the linkage between decisions and time, and at the related issue of the stage structure of the production process. These features emerge as a critical element in the analysis of the 'repercussions which *must* take time to work themselves out – which are delayed, not by slowness of communication or imperfect knowledge, but by the technical duration of productive processes' (Hicks, 1974a [1939]: 283). The same themes are taken up again in Hicks's discussion of the methods of economic dynamics (1956a, 1985a), in his analysis of the traverse from one steady state to another (1973a), and in his discussion of the causal structure of decision-making (1979a).

One important theme running through Hicks's contributions is the idea that, at any given time, the space of possible outcomes open to individual choice is bounded by physical or historical constraints (often arising from past choices), and that such constraints causally link events along temporal sequences. Such complementarities over time are central to Hicks's understanding of money, capital accumulation, and economic dynamics. In Hicks's conceptual framework, human choice is free and historical inevitability is rejected. This means that choice is seen as the ultimate determinant of actions, even if the actual outcome of any given choice reflects a 'structure' of possible events that is, to a large extent, independent of human deliberation (see Scazzieri, 1993a, 1993b). Choice, in Hicks's terms, presupposes a difficult balancing act between the pursuit of a particular objective and the representation of a specific set of intertemporal constraints. In this way, historical inevitability is questioned on two different grounds. First, human goals and decisions reflect not only the state of the world when the decision is taken, but also the unfolding set of constraints met by any given decision in the course of its realization. Second, constraints are associated with loopholes that make human decisions central to the actual course of events. That is why, according to Hicks, the widespread practice of reducing time to a mere dimension of space cannot be accepted as wholly satisfactory in economics.

Hicks's intellectual output shows a surprising continuity in what he came to recognize as the distinctive features of his identity as an economist. The causal structure associated with decision-making and with the implementation of decisions has been central to his theoretical work. In this connection, the relationship between time and economic decisions provides the background to contributions ranging from value and welfare theory to the theory of capital, from monetary economics to the methods and theories of economic dynamics (see Hamouda, 1993).

John Hicks was primarily a theoretical economist, but he never turned his interest in abstract concepts into one-sided attachment to any particular scheme of theory. He was, as Robin Matthews has noted, 'a conceptualiser' (Matthews, 2004: 32; see also Matthews, 1989). Indeed, he was 'more a toolmaker than a tool-user' (Matthews, 2004: 32). He never allowed any particular point of view to conceal the *variety* of possible theoretical frameworks, however. In spite of having 'in his own mind a consistent system of thought' (*ibid.*), he was ready to accept the provisional and contingent character of specific economic theories. At the same time, he was convinced that theoretical schemes are essential to the understanding of economic reality. Hicks acknowledged the need for theoretical pluralism. He was not an eclectic economist, however. He adopted a pragmatic view of theorizing (Hicks, 1985b, 1988). This led him to think that theories are context-dependent and that the switch from one situation to another may sometimes require the introduction of a different theoretical framework.

Hicks's view of economic theories as 'blinkers' that induce a selective concentration of attention (1975a, 1976a) made him look at theories as local devices. The switch from one context to another could make a previously accepted theory (and causal structure) no longer useful under the different conditions.

This explains the persistence of fundamental theoretical schemes in the midst of changing circumstances (and academic paradigms). This is possibly the reason why 'the relationships of Hicks to modern economic orthodoxy are ambiguous and complex... An architect of such an orthodoxy, Hicks distances himself from it more and more as his career proceeds' (Benetti *et al.*, 2001: 8; see also Dostaler, 2001: 21–2). It is this peculiar way of doing economics that makes Hicks's work so influential with so many authors of different schools and methodological approaches.[2]

Choice, time, causal structures

One important premise of Hicks's theoretical framework is the distinction between the structure of reality and the purpose-oriented arrangement of human actions. There are reasons to believe that, at an early stage of his development as an economist, Hicks came across the distinction between an 'order of being' and an 'order of doing,' as discussed by Maffeo Pantaleoni (Pantaleoni, 1925). As a matter of fact, Pantaleoni (in a passage carefully read and annotated by Hicks) had written:

Ancient logicians distinguished between a *causa fiendi* and a *causa essendi*, then between an *ordo fiendi* and an *ordo essendi*. In modern language, we have reserved the term *cause* to phenomena related to one another by a necessary order of occurrence in *time*, and the term *joint occurrence of conditions* to phenomena of *necessary and contemporaneous co-ordination*. A causal process is not a reversible one. On the contrary, a system of co-ordinated conditions may be looked upon starting from any one of its points; it has no order; it shows simultaneity. Now, economic phenomena show sometimes the former, sometimes the latter property. In any practical case, it will be easy not to get lost. (Pantaleoni, 1925: 71–2)

Pantaleoni's dissection of causality concepts continues with the discussion of alternative classes of phenomena:

There are...amongst phenomena associated with an *ordo fiendi*, that is, phenomena associated with a causal connection, many in which we cannot overlook the *reaction* that the effect generates upon the conditions from which it was born, reaction such that a new *effect* has the above reaction as one of its causes. The following may be a scheme of such an order of phenomena: let all circumstances A, B, C be such that effect α can be produced; once α has been produced, the circumstances that *now* will produce a new effect β will *not only* be A, B, C – as beforehand – but A, B, C, *plus* what is due to a modifying or additional factor, that is we shall have to consider $A, B, C, + d$ as concurrent causes of β. And this process will continue... To sum up, we shall have three classes of phenomena: (i) phenomena that present us only with an *ordo essendi*, in which it is out of place to speak of cause–effect relationships; (ii) phenomena that present us with an *ordo fiendi* of

---

[2] Hicks is almost unique among contemporary economists in the recognition received across the full spectrum of academic economics. See, for example, the three collective volumes edited respectively by Wolfe (1968), Hagemann and Hamouda (1994), and Puttaswamaiah (2001).

the simple kind, in which the relationship of cause to effect is not difficult to disentangle; (iii) phenomena that also present an *ordo fiendi*, but in which it is necessary to account for the reaction that the effect produces upon its generating causes, thereby modifying such causes in their subsequent operational phase. (Pantaleoni, 1925: 72)

Hicks carefully read the chapter of Pantaleoni's *Erotemi di economia* in which the above argument is to be found, and noted the importance of the distinction between 'an order of being and an order of doing – the latter, in economics being complicated by interdependence' (Hicks, manuscript notes, presumably 1920s).[3] The distinction between order of being and order of doing is a distinctive feature of Hicks's approach to economic decisions in their relationship with economic causality. Indeed, it may be argued that, according to Hicks, such a distinction is precisely the critical element explaining why economics is at the edge of history and science. This epistemic structure leads to an interesting implication as to the history of economic theory. For, as Hicks acknowledged, '[e]conomics is more like art or philosophy than science, in the use that it can make of its own history' (1976a: 207).[4]

Hicks went back to an explicit discussion of this issue in the lectures he delivered in Oxford in Trinity term 1979 and published in *Causality in Economics* shortly afterwards (1979a). There he discussed 'old causality' (causal relations based upon responsibility) and 'new causality' (the Humean view of causal relations in terms of generalizations and 'laws') (see Hicks, 1979a: 1–11). In particular, Hicks noted that, in spite of the explicit commitment of economics to new causality (at least since Adam Smith), 'the relationship of economics to the New Causality is nevertheless rather special' (1979a: 9). The reason is that 'economics is concerned with actions, with human actions and decisions, so there is a

---

[3] Manuscript notes, in Hicks's handwriting, inserted in his personal copy of Pantaleoni's *Erotemi*. John Hicks presented his copy of Pantaleoni's *Erotemi* to one of the editors of this volume (Roberto Scazzieri) in December 1987.

[4] Hicks elaborated this point on many different occasions. In particular, in his 'Capital Controversies' essay (1977d: 149–50), he writes:

Economics is a social science, and a particular kind of social science, in that it is concerned with the rational actions, the calculated actions, of human beings, and with their consequences. This has the result that those whom we study can hear what we say. We may speak to each other in our private languages, but private conversations are no more than goods in process: while we speak only to each other we have not finished our job. The ideas of economics, the powerful ideas of economics, come from the market-place, the 'real world', and to the 'real world' they go back. [...] In the course of the dialogue ideas acquire associations; they cease to be free ideas, which can be defined at choice... We cannot escape associations, but we can try to understand them, so as to be masters of them. That is what, in my view, the history of economics is for. We need to know the history of our concepts in order to know what it is that we are handling.

way in which it comes nearer to the Old Causality than the natural sciences do' (*ibid.*). Hicks is noting the close relationship of this issue with 'the struggle between free will and determinism' (*ibid.*). In a brilliant twist of his argument, however, he also maintains that 'in economics we find a solution' due to the 'relativity of time' that the analysis of economic decisions brings to light.[5] In Hicks's view, the relativity of time in economics is simply due to the fact that a 'double vision' is needed. Economic decisions at dates other than the present are taken when decision makers 'have different pasts behind them and futures before them' relative to the pasts and futures they have in the current period (1979a: 10). Hicks's concept of a double vision is related to his distinction between two different types of causality. Causality as interdependence (or causality as joint occurrence) makes identification of responsibility difficult (see above). On the other hand, causality as sequential determination may conceal the possible joint determination of outcomes (as any given outcome may follow from a plurality of causes). In other words, old and new causality are often intertwined to such an extent that to privilege one type of causality over the other may obscure the causal processes at work in any particular situation.

The double vision advocated by Hicks could be seen as a partial solution to the above problem. This is because human beings take decisions starting with a specific set of pasts and futures (see, for instance, Hicks, 1979a: 10). As a result, different positions in time are likely to be associated with different decisions and different patterns of sequential causality. Identification of sequential causality is often too demanding in terms of the amount and quality of the information required, however. For example, we may lack adequate knowledge of the causal loops that can turn intermediate effects into reinforcing or mitigating influences relative to the original cause. The dual vision allows the economist to switch from the pasts and futures from the agents' point of view to the pasts and futures from the point of view of the causal process under investigation. The *ex ante* approach to causality deals with decisions not yet made. This makes *ex ante* causality closer to the identification of the joint occurrence of conditions than to the reconstruction of a historical sequence of events (see Hicks, 1962a). As a result, *ex ante* causality may be useful when adequate historical information is missing, so that we are bound to the fiction of the joint (or simultaneous) occurrence of causes and effects (Hicks's contemporaneous causality). *Ex post* causality presupposes detailed historical knowledge, and is less concerned with the existence

[5] Hicks acknowledges that this is 'a much more elementary sense of relativity...than Einstein's' (1979a: 10).

of a 'virtual' causal space (Hicks's sequential causality). Hicks's double vision implies the analyst's ability to switch from the understanding (*Verstehen*) of human decisions *in time* to the description and explanation of causal linkages as they unfold *through time*.[6] In Hicks's view, economic thinking is on the edge of science and history precisely as a consequence of such an interplay between two different views of causality (see also Zamagni, 1991: 264).

In short, there are a plurality of ways in which time can be conceptualized in economics, and each one answers peculiar cognitive questions. It follows that there will be a multitude of different methods, each one able 'to cast some light upon some aspect of the phenomena' (Hicks, 1965: v). This implies that *the* dynamic method does not exist. Indeed, there are two wide varieties of dynamics: 'expectational' and mechanical. In the former, expectations play a fundamental role in explaining the economic process – i.e. in dealing with the specific role of history in economic affairs. This is not so in mechanical dynamics models, where change consists only of 'locomotion' – that is, is an analogue of a simple change of place. It is within such a cognitive frame that one can understand the specific meaning of Hicks's traverse analysis. By drawing attention to deviations between the actual position of the economic system and its corresponding long-period (steady-state) position, the study of traverse provides a case for the *counterfactual* approach to sequential causality – the cause being a change in technology occurring at a certain point of time (the 'impulse'), the effect being the entire difference between the traverse path and the path the economy would have followed in the absence of such a disturbance.[7] In this connection, it may be interesting to note what Keynes wrote in the passage of the *Treatise on Money* where he first mentions causal processes: 'The real task...is to treat the problem dynamically, analysing the different elements involved, in such a manner as to exhibit the causal process by which the price level is determined, and the method of

---

[6] The classical distinction between human deeds (*res gestae*) and the corresponding narrative (*historia rerum gestarum*) is relevant in this context.

[7] It is interesting that traverse analysis is especially useful in explaining patterns of change that have to take time to unfold themselves. This is clearly shown by the relationship between Hicks's *Theory of Economic History* (1969a) and his *Capital and Time* (1973a). The former discusses in an informal way the idea that economic processes may be analyzed by examining the logical implications of discontinuous change (for example, the switch to a different method of production, or to a different institutional set-up). The latter introduces a theoretical framework for the investigation of this type of shock. As it emerged in Hicks's work after *Capital and Time*, the distinctive feature of traverse analysis is not the investigation of possible convergence to a new steady state, but 'the concept of an impulse, a shock which can be traced through a sequence of consequences flowing from the potential of a major new invention' (Helm, 1984: 19).

transition from one position of equilibrium to another' (Keynes, 1971 [1930]: 120). Keynes's argument runs in terms of deviations of actual magnitudes from long-period counterparts – a conceptual exercise very close to Hicks's sequential causality.

Irreversibility and freedom of choice

Isaiah Berlin's distinction between negative and positive freedom is well known (Berlin, 1958).[8] Hicks's analytical contributions may be considered an attempt to solve Berlin's duality by taking advantage of the special epistemological status of economics (see above). According to Hicks, human beings are to a large extent free from *binding* constraints if we consider them as rational economic agents. Here Hicks is close to the standard view that, under given conditions, economic choice may be defined as a deliberation about how to use available means when a variety of different alternatives are feasible. Nevertheless, Hicks's attitude to freedom of choice entails not just the recognition of the (negative) freedom associated with the ability to make use of available resources according to the agent's best judgment. It also entails recognition that the (positive) freedom associated with the actual options that any given agent may be able to choose is bounded by past choices and by their outcomes. In particular, past choices do not only influence the agent's choice set at any given time; they also influence the causal processes associated with any given choice at different time periods. Actions a_t and a_{t+1} (selected from choice set **A** and such that $a_t = a_{t+1}$) are likely to produce different outcomes ($e_t \neq e_{t+1}$) as long as actions a_t and a_{t+1} have a different past. This time asymmetry – which lies at the bottom of both path-dependent phenomena and lock-in effects[9] – is central to Hicks's view of economic action, and is at the root of his interest not only in the pure logic of choice but also in the particular conditions making any given choice causally different depending on its particular timing.

---

[8] Berlin maintains that there are two central senses of freedom or liberty (1958: 6–7):

> The first…, which I shall call the 'negative' sense, is involved in the answer to the question 'What is the area within which the subject – a person or group of persons – is or should be left to do or be what he wants to do or be, without interference by other persons?'. The second, which I shall call the 'positive' sense, is involved in the answer to the question 'What, or who, is the source of control or interference, that can determine someone to do, or be, one thing rather than another?'. The two questions are clearly different, even though the answers to them may overlap.

[9] This is because, once a state of affairs has been achieved, it is difficult to escape from it.

An early recognition of the time-dependent character of economic choices *as causes* may be found in the treatment of complementarity over time in Hicks's *Value and Capital*: 'Initial equipment will consist, to a large extent, of goods at the intermediate stage of production; work has already been done on them with the object of converting them in the end into a certain kind of product; if this process is at all far advanced, the degree to which its ultimate object can be changed will be limited' (1974a [1939]: 211). Agents may be equally rational and subject to similar (or altogether identical) resource constraints. Nonetheless, the outcomes associated with their choices may be radically different as long as any given choice has a *different past* and is thus inserted in a different set of causal connections over time. This time dependence of economic causality has an interesting implication as to the irreversibility of economic actions. This is because choices may be reversible as long as the same individual (or group) is subject to broadly similar boundary conditions. The principle of substitution works on that basis. In Hicks's words, 'If the price of a particular factor A rises, and is expected to remain constant at the higher level, the total planned input of that factor must be reduced' (*ibid.*).

All the same, 'there are reasons...for supposing that the effect on the inputs planned for the more remote future will be greater than the effect on current input and input of the near future' (*ibid.*). This qualification suggests that the reversibility of economic actions is limited, and is consistent with Hicks's 'pragmatic attitude' to the principle of substitution (see Paul Samuelson's contribution in this volume). The near future is more closely influenced by the immediate past, and in particular by the 'specific character of the initial equipment' (Hicks, *ibid.*). Limited reversibility points to the causal determinacy of economic choices under conditions of freedom of choice. This means that, according to Hicks, choices are neither inevitable nor completely reversible. History (not only economic history) is shaped by human freedom to choose; but the causal influence of any given choice is specific to its timing and to the causal processes initiated in its past. To conclude, agents may choose the same alternatives, and yet the outcome of their choice may be radically different from one agent to the next depending upon their past choices and complementarities over time. This point of view is a unifying thread of much of John Hicks's theoretical work, from the dynamic explorations in parts III and IV of *Value and Capital* to the traverse analysis of *Capital and Time*. In this way, Hicks's dynamic theory 'emerged as a recognisable theory of a process' (Hahn, 1990: 541), which has roots in the Swedish tradition (see, in particular, Lindahl, 1933, 1939) and stimulated modern developments in the analysis of sequence economies and temporary equilibria (see Radner, 1972, and Grandmont, 1976, 1977).[10]

Twentieth-century science witnessed the dropping of Pierre Simon Laplace's rigid determinism. Werner Heisenberg's principle of indetermination, emphasizing the impossibility of obtaining, simultaneously, accurate measurements for two different magnitudes (in his case, the position and speed of a particle), placed a strong limitation on the possibility of making exact forecasts. On the other hand, on a macro scale, unpredictability may stem from the turbulence of a phenomenon, resulting in errors being amplified due to the complexity of the dynamics. These aspects explain the failure of classical deterministic theories, the result being that equilibrium analysis, so central to economic discourse, is nowadays disputed by a growing number of economists. It is fair to acknowledge that Hicks, as early as *Value and Capital*, had anticipated such a conclusion. To be precise, in chapter 17 of that book ('Interest and the Production Plan') he expressed strong doubts regarding the adequacy of the equilibrium method, while favoring a more historically oriented approach to economics.[11]

Liquidity, money, and macroeconomics

Hicks's attitude to economic theorizing is characterized by unwavering interest in the relationship between human choices, actions, and causal processes (see above). In that connection, lags and reserves, liquidity, and complementarities over time are central to his view of the economic system. This may explain Hicks's interest in monetary theory throughout the full span of his intellectual life.

The Hicksian reflection on money and macroeconomics effectively never ceased in his exceptionally long academic career. It is not by mere chance that Hicks's very last book and last essay – both of which appeared posthumously – dealt with these subjects: *A Market Theory of Money* (1989a) and 'The Unification of Macroeconomics' (1990). Toward the end of the 1920s at the London School of Economics – where Hicks had arrived in 1926 to learn his 'trade as economist' – the predominant belief was that, in the absence of obstacles, spontaneous market mechanisms are capable of ensuring rapid convergence to equilibrium. Hicks's

---

[10] It is interesting to note that L. M. Lachmann found *Capital and Time* especially important in its recognition that the 'fundamental issues' debated by economists in the 1960s could not be answered 'within the orbit of the Ricardian or Marshallian "long period"' (Lachmann, 1989 [1973]: 271).

[11] This was 'one of the less-read chapters' of *Value and Capital*, as Hicks kept on repeating.

first important work, *The Theory of Wages* (1932), testifies that he too shared such a vision at that stage. Such a belief would not have endured for long, however – so much so that, by the 1970s, he did not hesitate to distance himself completely from the theses on the functional distribution of income contained in that book.

Indeed, as early as 1935, in his well-known article 'A Suggestion for Simplifying the Theory of Money' (1935a), Hicks kept at a distance from traditional laissez-faire positions, arguing that competing economic systems tend to be unstable and, since the source of instability is largely of a psychological nature, the degree of instability increases, in general, when imperfections and frictions are eliminated – a proposition that helps us understand Hicks's subsequent thinking on matters of monetary policy. In the 1935 article, three points are noteworthy. First, the demonstration that it is not possible to build up a credible monetary theory without taking uncertainty into proper consideration. Second, the statement that demand for money is demand for a stock, and as such it pertains to the more general problem of asset composition. Finally, the idea that uncertainty lies at the core of the instability of modern monetary economies.

It is no wonder, therefore, that when *The General Theory* appeared the next year (Keynes, 1936) Hicks was already 'prepared' to welcome Keynes's message. The two reviews that he wrote in the following few months serve to mark the successive evolution of macroeconomics. In his celebrated IS-LM model – a model of temporary general equilibrium – Hicks showed how macroeconomic equilibrium can be reached simultaneously in the money and savings markets. It is precisely this model that played such an important role in the diffusion of Keynesian thought and that represented the core of the 'neoclassical synthesis' in the 1950s and 1960s. In spite of Keynes's own judgment about Hicks's review article – 'I found it interesting and I don't think I have anything to say from the viewpoint of criticism' – it is a fact that Hicks was never convinced that his model would have been able to capture the whole of Keynes's message. As it appears explicitly in *The Crisis in Keynesian Economics* (Hicks, 1974b) and *Economic Perspectives* (Hicks, 1977a), Hicks has two fundamental reasons to criticize the reductionist stance of his IS-LM model. The first one is that the role played by liquidity preference, as Keynes intended it, in the determination of the dynamics of employment cannot be adequately explored within a static temporary equilibrium model. The second reason is that it makes no sense to determine the macroeconomic equilibrium by means of two curves, one of which, the IS curve, conveys a condition of flow equilibrium while the other, the LM curve, conveys a condition of stock equilibrium.

The later macroeconomic writings of Hicks are significant mainly because, with his 'fix-price method,' Hicks laid down the theoretical bases of the new Keynesian macroeconomics of the 1980s. The fix-price approach, originally expounded in *Capital and Growth* (Hicks, 1965, especially 76–83), goes well beyond the traditional argument that Keynesian results depend on the abandonment of the assumption of perfect competition. Such an approach also moves beyond the observation that most Keynesian macroeconomic modeling, beginning from the theory of the multiplier, implicitly presupposes the fix-price assumption. Hicks's objective was much more ambitious. He wished to reject the neoclassical theory of price formation under competitive conditions, a theory that needed the assumption of an imaginary auctioneer to account for the process of price-setting. To Hicks, it is only in particular markets – the speculative ones – that the traditional flex-price hypotheses make sense. In industrial goods markets, by contrast, prices are set by the agents themselves, who modify them by responding to economic signals such as variations in wages and other prices. This implies that prices in industrial markets, even if not completely rigid, do not change as rapidly as traditional theory would lead us to believe. The main consequence is that it is essential to reject the widespread prejudice of Marshallian origin (even though Marshall himself was not a theorist of the auctioneer), according to which price variations predominate in short-run adjustments, and quantity variations in long-run adjustments. Hicks's interest in a *differentiated* time structure of lags and adjustments suggests a reformulation of Keynes's arguments that goes far beyond what would have been possible within the Marshallian theoretical framework adopted (for this particular issue) by Keynes himself.

Perhaps it is fair to say that the most innovative contribution to monetary theory by the 'later' Hicks was the realization that, even at a time when the monetarist counter-revolution and the new classical macroeconomics justified unexpected enthusiasm for spontaneous market mechanisms, laissez-faire policies are subjects to limits and snares. As recent research has convincingly shown (against Robert Lucas's argument), endogenous reactions of the economy to systematic changes – such as major economic policy decisions – may be such that economic systems are *not* insensitive to the enforcement of those policies. This is a proposition that Hicks always adhered to, and that was strongly reaffirmed in *A Market Theory of Money* (Hicks, 1989a).

In a heated argument on the use of alternative methods in historical research, the British historian Thomas Southcliffe Ashton is reported to have said: 'The debate whether we should use quantity or quality to argue in history is juvenile. It is like arguing whether one should hop on the left leg or on the right. People with two legs find they make better progress if they walk on both' (Ashton, 1971 [1946], as quoted in McCloskey, 1990: 300). Perhaps Hicks would have given the same type of answer to the old question of whether market forces should be left to their own or not.

The structure of the book

The purpose of this volume is to assess the intellectual achievement of John Hicks, to highlight the features of Hicks's contribution that are more closely associated with his distinctive approach to economic analysis, and to identify promising lines of future research that may be pursued on that basis. Early drafts of all chapters were presented and discussed at a workshop held at the University of Bologna in October 2004 to celebrate the 100th anniversary of John Hicks's birth. We believe economics owes a lot to John Hicks. His work not only teaches; it also inspires. The contributions in this volume testify to the fact that almost every branch of economic theory continues to use his work as a foundation for conceptual and analytical innovation.

Markets, money, capital, and dynamics are the research areas more directly connected with the central interests of John Hicks as a theorist. Markets provide the institutional and 'material' background of value theory. In particular, markets introduce intertemporal linkages (through expectations and the carry-over of physical stocks) and, at the same time, make available buffers that may reduce the sensitivity of economic systems to internal or external disturbances. Money and liquidity allow economic agents to separate buying and selling decisions and to distribute them along the time dimension. Capital accumulation calls attention to 'the technical duration of productive processes' and thus to 'those repercussions which *must* take time to work themselves out' (Hicks, 1974a [1939]: 283).[12] Markets, money, and capital provide a vantage point for the assessment of Hicks's contribution to economic theory. In particular, they call attention to the role of causal structures working themselves out in historical time, and to the specific features of the economic agents' double vision (*ex ante* and *ex post*). In Hicks's view, it is primarily through markets, liquidity, and durable production processes that the different pasts of economic choices become causally relevant (so that choices bring about different consequences depending on their timing).

Part I of this volume ('The Intellectual Heritage of John Hicks') explores the philosophical underpinnings of Hicks's economic thought,

---

[12] As we have seen, Hicks distinguishes the repercussions arising from 'slowness of communication or imperfect knowledge' (1974a [1939]: 282) from those due to the necessary duration of production activity.

his position relative to the central traditions of economic theorizing in the twentieth century, and the internal evolution of his research framework. Amartya K. Sen, in his chapter 'Hicks on liberty,' examines the relationship between freedom and efficiency in Hicks's thought. According to Sen, there are two distinct, but closely interrelated, strands in Hicks's analysis of the 'efficacious functioning' of a market economy, for Hicks's pioneering work in *Value and Capital* on the welfare properties of competitive equilibrium is complemented by attention to 'the diverse functions of transactions and markets in society and the enabling opportunities they could generate.' In Sen's view, Hicks came to question the reasonableness of the emphasis on 'the efficiency features of economic arrangements,' and became 'deeply involved in the social importance of liberty and freedom.' The first part of the chapter examines Hicks's contribution to social choice theory, and calls attention to Hicks's analysis of majority rule. A characteristic feature of Hicks's thinking is his emphasis upon the possible arbitrariness of majority rule, and, more generally, of any one 'particular way of counting outcomes, ignoring other procedures.'

In particular, Hicks calls attention to how small variations in voting criteria may lead to very significant differences in social choice outcomes. This is because, in Hicks's view, each particular voting system is bound to overlook relevant information. Sen points out that it is precisely Hicks's attention to the 'social deafness' of voting procedures in a democratic society that makes his contribution interesting in a discussion of liberty and minority rights. In this connection, the chapter brings to attention how, according to Hicks, majority rule could be less or more arbitrary depending upon the depth of divisions among spheres of interest within the social body. In a sufficiently homogeneous society, voters are likely to find themselves among the majority, although perhaps at different stages of their respective lives. In a strongly heterogeneous society, however, there would be a significant likelihood of majority rule turning into social deafness and oppression. In the latter part of his chapter, Sen highlights the relationship between Hicks's approach to majority rule and the same author's view that markets should primarily be judged in terms of 'the freedoms they can generate,' rather than in terms of 'their implications for what is often called "economic efficiency."' The field of policy-making is one in which Hicks's views on freedom and efficiency are especially relevant, as Hicks's concern with the social deafness of any specific voting procedure or criterion for efficiency comparison leads him to argue that economic advice should be associated with practical reason rather than with the single-minded pursuit of any particular technical rule.

Paul A. Samuelson, in his chapter 'An economist even greater than his high reputation,' asks why Hicks never seems to have gained full recognition of his theoretical contribution, in spite of the enormous influence of his writings. Samuelson argues that part of the answer is Hicks's independence of established traditions and his stance as a solitary scholar. These same features, in Samuelson's opinion, may explain the originality of some of Hicks's views, such as his attention for markets as a central organizing theme of economic history, and his pragmatic attitude to the principle of substitution. In this connection, Samuelson makes reference to an 'off-the cuff intervention' of Hicks at the 1958 Corfu conference on capital theory, in which Hicks had noted (in paraphrase): 'Do realize that in between two neighboring items listed in the order catalogue of a toolmaker, there are a plethora of intermediate items that the supplier will offer if only they are confronted with a critical demand for such an offering' (Hicks as quoted by Samuelson). In Samuelson's view, Hicks's remark suggests a middle way between 'Clarkian neoclassical marginalism with an uncountable infinity of alternative techniques' and 'a von Neumann technology with only a finite number of alternative techniques.'

The following chapter, by Luigi L. Pasinetti and GianPaolo Mariutti ('Hicks's "conversion" – from J. R. to John'), considers the intellectual evolution of Hicks from his early phase ('from the beginning of his career in the 1930s to the end of the 1960s') to his late phase ('from the 1970s onwards'). Starting with Hicks's well-known 'change of name' (from J. R. Hicks to John Hicks), the authors ask whether this change 'was…a whimsical caprice of a successful economist or…a meditated choice.' In their reconstruction and evaluation of Hicks's change of name, the authors focus on the specific characteristics of the change of mind from the young to the old Hicks. The early phase of Hicks's thought is relevant in this connection, especially if one considers Hicks's essay 'A Suggestion for Simplifying the Theory of Money' (1935a) and his emphasis upon the theory of liquidity. The subsequent balanced review of Keynes's *General Theory* (Hicks, 1936a) was followed by the well-known IS-LM paper (1937a), in which Hicks outlined a formal representation of the *General Theory* in terms of simultaneous (rather than recursive) equations. Pasinetti and Mariutti point out that Hicks's change of mind was not an abrupt switch to an altogether different theoretical framework. It was, rather, a process in which Hicks started with the reconsideration of methods of dynamic theory, moved through the acknowledgment of the special relationship between monetary theory and monetary history, and eventually 'left aside equilibrium and steady-state positions, and began to look at economies as systems that change over time in quantitative as well as in qualitative terms' (Pasinetti and Mariutti). Hicks's concluding works (starting with *Capital and Time*, 1973a) are to be seen as recognition of the central need of a theoretical framework in which time and history are taken seriously. Nonetheless, Hicks considered '[r]evolutions in economic thought' not 'like political coups d'état,' for he 'felt that economics could be more at ease with slow evolution of thinking rather than with sudden turmoil' (Pasinetti and Mariutti).

In the following chapter of this section, 'Dear John, Dear Ursula (Cambridge and LSE, 1935): eighty-eight letters unearthed,' Maria Cristina Marcuzzo and Eleonora Sanfilippo examine an important phase of Hicks's intellectual development through the eighty-eight letters exchanged between John Hicks and Ursula Webb (later Hicks) in the period September 1935 to December 1935 (that is, in the months immediately preceding their marriage on December 17, 1935). Marcuzzo and Sanfilippo draw attention to the rich web of intellectual relationships and exchanges described in the correspondence, especially as the letters were written in a relatively short time span (Michaelmas term 1935) and in the period of intense discussions preceding the publication of Keynes's *General Theory*. In particular, the correspondence illuminates the seminar network in which discussions took place. A central position in the correspondence is reserved for the 'Cambridge Graduate Seminar' (also called 'Sraffa's seminar'), which was conceived from the very beginning as a meeting ground between Cambridge economists and economists from the London School of Economics (LSE). The chapter calls attention to the pattern of intellectual proximities (as well as distances) that the correspondence highlights. For instance, Hicks enjoyed discussing with Arthur Pigou, but at the same time he mildly distanced himself from him when noting (regarding Pigou) 'what a general equilibrist is at bottom' (letter of John Hicks to Ursula Webb, October 14, 1935). The correspondence also highlights the proximity between Hicks and Dennis Robertson, as well as the meeting of minds between Hicks and Piero Sraffa. It also provides evidence of the intellectual distance between Hicks, on the one hand, and Richard Kahn and Joan Robinson on the other.

The chapter 'Hicks and his publishers,' by Andrew Schuller, explores the still uncharted territory of the relationship between John Hicks and the publishing world. The early relationship between Hicks and Macmillan is discussed through correspondence about *The Theory of Wages* involving Lionel Robbins (who highly recommended the book for publication), Keynes, Harold Macmillan, Robertson and Hicks himself. In spite of a negative report from Keynes and a somewhat guarded recommendation from Robertson, 'Macmillan were bold' and accepted the book. Schuller notes that the decision-making process was fast (the book was published 'six months after the typescript was first submitted for consideration') and from the very beginning had an international character – so much so that the possibility of an Italian translation had already been envisaged by Gustavo del Vecchio at Bologna even before Macmillan's final decision. The relationship between Hicks and Macmillan continued well after the publication of *The Theory of Wages* and Hicks's move to Cambridge. Until 1937 Hicks kept Macmillan informed about the progress he was making on *Value and Capital*, but he finally decided (in spring 1938) to accept an offer from Oxford University Press. Schuller speculates on the reasons that might have induced the switch to the new publisher, such as Hicks's awareness that *Value and Capital* was going to be 'academically weightier than *The Theory of Wages*,' 'Keynes's closeness to Macmillan,' and Robertson's influence 'in guiding him to Oxford.'

This move started a relationship with Oxford University Press that went on to last for fifty years. Schuller examines Hicks's time as an Oxford University Press author, drawing attention to the fact that Hicks 'introduced carefully' to his publisher his 'book-length scholarly works.' In so doing, he often came to portray his contributions in a sharp and effective way. For example, he described *Capital and Growth* (1965) as a volume that would 'sail pretty much into the middle of the current controversy,' and *Capital and Time* (1973a) as 'a modernization not only of the Austrians but also of the English classics – Ricardo and Mill' (Hicks, as quoted in Schuller). Schuller also considers Hicks's 'move to Blackwell' and his subsequent 'return to OUP' by noting that '[t]here does not seem to be any specific irritating incident, let alone a major rift between OUP and Hicks.' Hicks's relationship with Blackwell continued with *Causality in Economics* (1979a), and the three volumes of *Collected Papers in Economic Theory* published between 1981 and 1983. Hicks eventually returned to Oxford University Press, however, for his last two books (*Methods of Dynamic Economics*, 1985a, and *A Market Theory of Money*, 1989a) – a move possibly induced by colleagues' advice and perceptions of ongoing change in Blackwell's publishing policy.

In the chapter 'Hicks in reviews, 1932–89: from *The Theory of Wages* to *A Market Theory of Money*,' Warren Young examines the reception of Hicks's writings by his contemporaries by critically assessing and systematizing the initial reviews of his books, from *The Theory of Wages* (1932) through *Value and Capital* (1939a) to *A Market Theory of Money* (1989a). The chapter introduces a taxonomy for the evaluation of the reviews based on the dual distinction between (i) *purposive* as opposed to *substantive* reviews and (ii) reviews associated with an *external* as opposed to *internal* focus. (Young relates the latter distinction with Stephen Toulmin's discussion of 'the institutional and personal history of a scientific discipline,' as against the history of the 'intrinsic importance' of its contributions.) The reviews of Hicks's *Theory of Wages* are distinctly different depending on whether one considers the mixed reception of the first edition (1932), or the widespread positive response to the second edition (1963). Hicks's *Théorie mathématique de la valeur en régime de libre concurrence* (1937b) was carefully reviewed by Arthur Lyon Bowley in *The Economic Journal* (1938), while the reviews of *Value and Capital* 'ranged from highly complimentary (Lerner) to highly critical ([Oskar] Morgenstern)' (Young). A characteristic feature of *Value and Capital* is that it also became the object of partial reviews, such as Abba Lerner's review of Parts III and IV, and Fritz Machlup's review of 'Hicks' Statics' (as quoted in Young).

The chapter surveys the principal reviews of all books published subsequently by Hicks, and calls special attention upon some of them. For example, Young mentions Richard Goodwin's 'positive and insightful review' of *A Contribution to the Theory of the Trade Cycle* (Hicks, 1950a), together with more critical reviews of the same book by Lerner and Nicholas Kaldor, which are primarily mentioned for their remarks about the role of expectations in trade cycle theory. Frank Hahn's and Robert Solow's reviews of *Capital and Growth* (Hicks, 1965) are discussed, as is Robert Clower's review of the *Critical Essays in Monetary Theory* (Hicks, 1967a). The chapter then devotes special attention to Solow's and Thomas Rymes's reviews of *Capital and Time* (Hicks, 1973a), and to Geoff Harcourt's and Axel Leijonhufvud's reviews of *Economic Perspectives* (Hicks, 1977a). Young notes that important reviews followed the publication of all subsequent books by Hicks, such as Alan Coddington's review of *Causality in Economics* (Hicks, 1979a), or David Laidler's and Robert King's appraisals of *Money, Interest and Wages* (Hicks, 1982a). Moving on to *A Market Theory of Money*, Young recalls Hahn's critical appraisal, but also his acknowledgment that 'not to understand Hicks may mean that one does not understand economics' (Hahn, as quoted in Young). The chapter concludes by pointing to the general consensus among Hicks's reviewers concerning 'the connection between the central message or messages of Hicks's works…and what *was*, or *was to become*, the mainstream of economic inquiry and analysis.'

Part II ('Markets') focuses upon markets as one of the central organizing themes of Hicks's theoretical contribution. This part has been conceived with the twofold aim of assessing the role of markets in the development of Hicks's thought and of exploring a number of research lines suggested in Hicks's writings but not yet fully explored in economic literature.

The first chapter of this part is by Christopher Bliss, on 'Hicks and the emptiness of general equilibrium theory.' This contribution starts with an assessment of John Hicks's statement (in *Value and Capital*) concerning the sterility of static general equilibrium. To pursue Hicks's point of view further, Bliss asks what follows from proofs of the existence or the stability of general equilibrium prices and quantities. In particular, Bliss investigates Hicks's claim that 'it is dynamics that gives life to the otherwise empty general equilibrium theory' (Bliss). In Bliss's view, an important clue as to Hicks's economics is given by his belief that 'Walrasian statics needed to be reinforced by a better dynamics than the unsatisfactory dynamics that Walras had provided,' and that one could use Marshallian ideas to that purpose. The starting point of Hicks's *Value and Capital* was interest in the 'interrelations of markets' (Hicks) and awareness that Marshall's theory was possibly superior to Léon Walras's and Vilfredo Pareto's if one were to build a theory of economic dynamics. Hicks considered 'the general equilibrium of markets as the central defining model of pure economic theory,' according to Bliss. At the same time, Hicks thought that a theory of capital was 'the greatest prize to be obtained from his investigation.' In pursuing the latter line of research, Hicks turned his attention to Marshall's period analysis 'for the partial equilibrium of a market served by many firms' and 'adapted it to treat of dynamics and comparative statics in a simultaneous equilibrium model' (Bliss). Hicks adopted Marshall's method of lagged factor input adjustment, and turned it into a method of 'lagged adjustment of out-of-market prices.' Hicks approached economic dynamics from the point of view of capital theory and Marshall-type period analysis.

This point of view makes his contribution distinctly different from the Arrow–Debreu theory of forward markets and contingent goods, as Hicks's attention (following *Value and Capital*) was directed to 'patterns of complementarity and substitutability between inputs and outputs,' and to the treatment of capital theory in terms of 'the asymmetry between different contemporaneous goods, as opposed to current versus dated goods' (Bliss). Hicks also called attention to the intertwining of the time structure of capital with the way in which agents' expectations evolve over time. This points to the need of 'theory of a qualitatively different character to address that problem,' as 'expectations are seldom formed in an atomistic manner' (Bliss).

The following chapter, by Pierluigi Ciocca ('Hicks versus Marx? On the theory of economic history'), addresses Hicks's contribution to the understanding of markets and their historical dynamics. Ciocca's starting point is the belief that Hicks's 'celebrated contributions to pure economic theory can be seen as propaedeutic to the highly ambitious attempt made in *A Theory of Economic History*.' Hicks's contribution was at the time little understood, either in Oxford or in the reviews that followed its publication. In spite of that, one must be aware that 'theories of economic history do not abound.' Nevertheless, 'they are…useful for analytical purposes, as general schemes for ordering one's thoughts and asking oneself relevant questions' (Ciocca). In Hicks's view, a theory of economic history is neither a 'history of single events' nor a 'philosophy of history.' It is, rather, 'the history of averages and norms. It is the history of the permanence and evolution of structures, whether gradual or revolutionary' (Ciocca).

The chapter calls attention to a number of specific points raised in Hicks's book. One is the analysis of the internal structure and evolution of the 'custom and command' economies (with prevalence of custom over command – or vice versa – depending on the relative weight of routine over emergencies). Another is the causal process leading from markets to institutions (markets as the breeding ground of new institutional arrangements). Yet another is the relationship between markets and production, and the view that (in Hicks's words) markets' function is primarily the 'creation of traders and subsequently financiers, not of farmers or artisans' (which suggests a fundamental distinction between market and production coordination). Ciocca draws attention to the flexibility of Hicks's taxonomies, and notes that such a flexibility 'avoids a loss of capacity to analyze various historical situations.' The chapter also highlights the fact that, in spite of Hicks's awareness of the radical novelty represented by the rise of capitalism, *A Theory of Economic History* is characterized by emphasis upon the market as a dynamic principle (the market as an 'agent of transformation'). Ciocca notes that this point of view clearly differentiates Hicks's theory of economic history from that of Karl Marx. He also notes that market advantages may turn into mere reallocations of existing resources unless production and technical change make new resources available.

Hicks's interest in 'out-of-market prices' and in the asymmetries between goods that are simultaneously exchanged is at the root of his distinction between fix-price and flex-price markets. The chapter by Marcello de Cecco ('Hicks's notion and use of the concepts of fix-price and flex-price') examines such a distinction and its relationship to Hicks's view of how economic theory reflects developments in economic history. De Cecco calls attention to Hicks's discussion of fix-price and flex-price markets in his early essay 'A Suggestion for Simplifying the Theory of Money' (1935a), and notes that Hicks points out there the critical role of slowly adjusting markets in absorbing 'the occasional turbulence taking place in flex-price markets.' In Hicks's view, fix-price markets are to some extent inherited from pre-capitalist times (or modes of organization) and may be essential to introduce some degree of stability, as the latter is not 'one of the essential features of pure capitalism' (de Cecco). Hicks's view is thus far removed from that of 'market fundamentalists' (de Cecco). This is because, according to Hicks, '[t]ransaction cost removal policies may kill the flywheel that keeps capitalism stable and in the end prevents it from self-destructing' (de Cecco).

22   *Roberto Scazzieri and Stefano Zamagni*

The chapter also considers Hicks's use of the fix-price/flex-price distinction in the expectation framework of *Value and Capital* (1939a) and draws attention to Hicks's view that 'the way in which a population is divided' with respect to the sensitivity of price expectations (Hicks, 1974a [1939]: 271) may be essential to the short-period stability considered in temporary equilibrium analysis. De Cecco concludes his chapter with a discussion of how Hicks's analysis of fix-price and flex-price markets relates to the argument put forward in Hicks's own *Theory of Economic History* (1969a). In particular, de Cecco notes the roots of Hicks's interpretation of economic history in Henry Sumner Maine's analysis of the progress of human society 'from Status to Contract.' De Cecco also points out, however, that Hicks clearly took a less positive view of such a progress, thereby attaining a balanced understanding of the instability of capitalism, and of the complex mix of flexibility and rigidity that is required for it to achieve some degree of permanence over time.

Hicks's analysis of markets is characterized by close attention to those 'rough approximations, used by the business man to steer himself through the bewildering changes of situation which confront him' (Hicks, 1974a [1939]: 171).[13] In this context, Hicks gave much attention to the analytical representation and measurement of income. The main reason for this is stated in *Value and Capital*. There Hicks maintains that 'income' and other macroeconomic concepts such as 'saving' or 'investment' lack logical precision as there is 'too much equivocation' in their meaning (1939a). Hicks acknowledged the need of such concepts from a pragmatic point of view, however. The chapter by Paolo Onofri and Anna Stagni ('On the Hicksian definition of income in applied economic analysis') addresses Hicks's problem from the point of view of the necessary approximation of (theoretical) economic concepts when the statistical measurement of quantities is considered. Indeed, '[t]he "true" definition of income is a subjective *ex ante* measure, but statisticians can produce only objective *ex post* measures' (Onofri and Stagni). The chapter assesses Hicks's 'approximation to the central meaning of the concept of income' (Hicks, 1974a [1939]: 175), such that income is considered as 'the maximum amount of money which the individual can spend this

---

[13] It is interesting that, at a relatively early stage of his theoretical development, Hicks thought that business accounting could provide a route for the development of dynamic economic analysis: 'If the consumer's (or the producer's) budget is considered as an instance of income accounting (or of profit and loss accounting), we are carrying out the type of "static" analysis most familiar to Walras and Pareto; if we interpret such a budget as a balance of positive and negative activities at a given time, we may use it as the foundation of a very general theory of capital and interest' (Hicks, 1937b: 55).

week, and still expect to be able to spend the same amount *in real terms* in each ensuing week' (*ibid.*: 174).

In particular, Onofri and Stagni examine the feasibility of Hicks's above definition of income in its application to the measurement and evaluation of household disposable income. The authors point out that, if one were to follow Hicks's suggestion, one should subtract from monetary income 'the loss in the purchasing power of the accumulated stock of wealth due to inflation.' A model allowing for this 'Hicksian correction' is empirically tested considering Italian data over the sample period 1970 to 2003, and it is found that consumers' perception of the influence of inflation upon the purchasing power of their wealth 'is not negligible, but incomplete' (Onofri and Stagni). The authors conjecture that a reason for that may be changes in sensitivity to inflation over the period under consideration, and the introduction of correction devices different from the Hicksian one, such as attempts to avoid the fiscal illusion attached to public debt in recent decades. The chapter also explores the implications of Hicks's income concepts for the evaluation of the financial wealth of households and firms. In this connection, Onofri and Stagni point out that Hicks's definition should be adjusted to the specific class of phenomena one is considering. In particular, they note that, differently from households, firms are likely to evaluate their financial wealth in terms of the prerequisite of 'maintaining capital intact.' The chapter concludes that Hicks's 'third' definition of income, if suitably differentiated for different categories of income receivers (households and firms), highlights the non-neutrality of inflation and the existence of a wedge 'between return to the household claims on the capital of the firms and the return to capital for the firms.' This suggests a clear-cut separation, stemming from Hicks's analytical framework, between saving and investment decisions.

Hicks's view of economics as a discipline on the edge of history and science made him especially interested in the analysis of monetary issues, as these are issues in which the 'dual vision' implied by economic decisions is most clearly in view (see also 'Choice, time, causal structures' above). Part III of this volume ('Money') focuses in particular on the relationship between monetary theory and monetary history, the role of buffers in financial intermediation, the formation of portfolio decisions resulting from the demand of financial characteristics associated with regarding assets as bundles of characteristics, and the working and governance of monetary markets.

The chapter by Alberto Quadrio Curzio and Roberto Scazzieri ('Historical stylizations and monetary theory') explores the implications of Hicks's contention that monetary disturbances are a source of monetary theory. The starting point of this chapter is the eighteenth-century discussion on monetary disturbances, and the theory of imaginary money associated with that discussion. Quadrio Curzio and Scazzieri note that the monetary disturbances literature makes reference to a particular case of Hicks's 'dual money system,' in which account money is kept separate from transaction money. In particular, the chapter outlines the institutional set-up of imaginary money and investigates the relationship between the latter set-up and the general features of the dual money system. Special attention is given to historical realizations of imaginary money in particular contexts, such as the bank moneys of Amsterdam and Venice in the seventeenth century. The utilization of a unit of account that was not itself traded allowed people to engage in monetary transactions without confusing the need for a fixed standard of value with the idea that effective currencies should be of constant value.

This system was the expression of a rational economic need. Its implementation through history has been marred by an abuse of sovereign power and sluggish monetary policy, however. The separation between a particular monetary technique (the dual money system) and the vicissitudes of its implementation is a distinctive mark of the literature on ideal or imaginary money. Quadrio Curzio and Scazzieri call attention to the fact that the effective management of internal exchange rates (between imaginary money and transaction money) is a necessary condition for the working of a dual monetary economy. This is because the separation between abstract money and effective money could lead either to stability in the general price level and the foreign exchanges, or to monetary disturbances and the collapse of trade. The chapter argues that the general principles and objectives of imaginary money are surprisingly close to some of the central monetary developments of the second half of the twentieth century. The conception of imaginary money and its manifold historical applications provide an intellectual benchmark for the analysis of current developments in monetary institutions and practices, and a significant guideline for monetary reform.

In the following chapter ('Hicks: money, prices, and credit management'), Omar F. Hamouda draws attention to Hicks's special attitude to monetary institutions and monetary governance. In particular, Hamouda notes that Hicks 'stood in between the two poles [intervention and laissez-faire], envisaging an institutional framework in which monetary information emanates through "rings" of financial players…to industry, the borrowing sector, which makes its own decisions.' Hamouda reconstructs the evolution of Hicks's thoughts on money and credit as an instance of such a distinctive approach to laissez-faire and governance. In particular, his chapter examines Hicks's view of credit in relation to the real economy and calls attention to Hicks's belief that 'there was...enough empirical evidence and theory to link alterations in the quantity of available credit to potentially undesirable or desirable events' (Hamouda). This led Hicks to emphasize the need of monetary management 'by a central bank, whose operations must be determined by judgment and cannot be reduced to procedure by a mechanical rule' (Hicks, as quoted by Hamouda). In particular, Hicks came to favor a governance set-up in which 'a "centre," aided by close consultation with intermediaries,' would have the primary goal 'to narrow the gap between the monetary interest rate and the rate of return on marginal investment, in an effort to maintain the economy in a state of monetary equilibrium' (Hamouda). In its conclusion, the chapter emphasizes the originality of Hicks's view of monetary policy, particularly as Hicks was aware of the need for active monetary management but, differently from Keynes, was also convinced of the principal role of the central bank in the governance of a credit economy.

The chapter by Rainer Masera ('Core, mantle, and industry: a monetary perspective of banks' capital standards') assesses the analytical framework behind the current revival of policy interest in the relationship between capital and risk. In particular, Masera calls attention to the role of banks' capital under conditions of credit distress and examines past financial history in order to put into perspective the new international capital standards for banks (the standards associated with the Basel Capital Accords). Masera's analysis is carried out in terms of the analytical framework formulated by Hicks in his 'Monetary Experience' essay (1977b). In that essay, Hicks considers a decomposition of the economic system into three broad sets of activities: the banks (called the 'core'), the financial system (called the 'mantle'), and the rest of the economy (this latter set of activities, which Hicks called the 'industry', includes the enterprises, the households, and the government). Masera highlights the fact that risk absorption and risk management are very important features of banks. He also argues that there is an important difference between market risk and credit risk, and that credit losses, which are in general relatively low, can sometimes be very large (especially when the economic cycle enters a truly recessionary phase). Bank capital acts as a buffer to absorb future unidentified losses – that is, losses that are not expected on average. The chapter argues that Hicks's theory of capital, and in particular his distinction between a 'fundist' and a 'materialist' conception of capital, can be a useful analytical benchmark in the investigation of banks' capital funding as a buffer against risk. In particular, Hicks's approach entails the view of capital as a fund that 'appears on the liabilities side of the balance sheet,' whereas plant and machinery would appear 'on the assets side' (Hicks, 1977d: 154). According to Masera, this suggests the idea of a 'trust fund' that could 'invest in fresh capital of the banks at the time of impending major systemic risk.'

In the chapter 'A suggestion for simplifying the theory of asset prices,' Riccardo Cesari and Carlo D'Adda take up Hicks's suggestion that one could deal with portfolio selection by looking 'at the regular statistical parameters of the prospect, considered as a probability distribution – not just the first moment (E) but other moments also' (Hicks, 1967b: 106). The authors argue that this approach avoids reference to expected utility and greatly simplifies the equilibrium theory of asset prices. In particular, it is argued that the relevant probability distribution is expressed by a number of different parameters and that such parameters are 'quantities of joint products directly priced by the market.' In particular, the authors focus on two principal characteristics (moments) of financial assets (mean and standard deviation) and maintain that such characteristics may be considered as 'joint products' accruing to the asset owner. Indeed, it is argued that 'these two parameters are much like goods and services: they may be measured, have their own market price, and are to be thought of as arguments of an *ordinal utility function.*' Any asset or portfolio is associated with a given probability distribution, and may be described by 'a bundle of different characteristics (moments)' (Cesari and D'Adda). The chapter outlines on this basis a moment pricing theory, which includes the intertemporal general equilibrium asset pricing model. The authors emphasize that their approach to asset pricing presupposes only ordinal utility and does not presuppose any independence axiom. This feature allows a solution to well-known paradoxes (such as the St. Petersburg, Allais, Kahneman–Tversky and Tversky–Kahneman paradoxes). In conclusion, the chapter argues that, when one is facing situations in which 'many people behave according to the expected utility theory and many others do not,' a reasonable approach is to strive for 'a generalized approach that encompasses both behaviors and is liable to empirical measurement and test.'

Part IV ('Capital and Dynamics') addresses Hicks's contribution to the theory of an economic system in which 'repercussions of economic change' cannot be contained within the single period (Hicks's 'week'). In Hicks's view, this is the field of 'a pure theory of economic dynamics' (1974a [1939]: 283), in which capital accumulation (or decumulation) are central features.

The first chapter of this part is by Robert M. Solow ('"Distribution and economic progress"' after seventy years'), who examines Hicks's early study (in his *Theory of Wages*, 1932) of 'how...economic progress affect[s] the distribution of the national income among the broad factors of production' (Solow). In the relevant chapter of *The Theory of Wages*,

Hicks examines an economic system characterized by 'increases in working population and the stock of capital goods' and also by 'invention, the advance of technology' (Solow). In particular, says Solow, Hicks addresses the questions of 'what is likely to happen to the equilibrium distribution of income as capital intensity…rises through time' and also 'how can one classify inventions to highlight their distributional effects.' In Solow's view, Hicks's analysis of such issues broke new ground at the time and nowadays suggests a useful avenue to fresh theoretical work. The concept of 'elasticity of substitution' suggested a way to discuss the response of the relative distributional shares of capital and labor to changes in the (macroeconomic) ratio of capital to labor. Solow emphasizes that Hicks took a broad view of the elasticity of substitution (which he did not simply see as a parameter of the production function). For instance, he did not conceive of substitution between capital and labor simply as a shift along the production function, but also as the result of induced invention or as the consequence of a changed composition of final demand (this would normally be a compositional shift away from the goods that are more intensive in the productive factor that is becoming more costly).

Solow emphasizes that 'the demand-function side' of the adjustment 'can be as important as the production-function side,' even if the process is not clearly in view when the investigation is carried out in terms of a one-good economy. Multisectoral analysis may be useful in separating off the two components of economy-wide elasticity (supply-side and demand-side), and in highlighting the possibility of 'substitution-driven growth' (growth associated with factor substitution in the absence of technical change). The chapter examines the distributional consequences of the latter growth pattern when substitution 'is occurring over and above technological progress,' so that 'the share of capital must be increasing as the capital/labor ratio rises' (Solow). A discussion of the implications of alternative assumptions on the distribution of capital ownership along a substitution-driven growth path concludes the chapter.

Whereas Solow's contribution examines the distributional consequences of capital accumulation in the flexible prices set-up of *The Theory of Wages* (Hicks, 1932), Mauro Baranzini, in his chapter ('Flexible saving and economic growth'), addresses capital accumulation in the fix-price model of Hicks's *Capital and Growth* (1965: chaps. 7–11). In this analytical set-up, as Hicks points out, 'an economy which has been in long-term equilibrium…cannot adjust to a change in its desired growth rate, unless the propensity to save is varied, or the capital–output ratio is varied' (1985a: 131). An important consequence of this set of assumptions is that the existence of differences between the propensities to save out of different types of income, or between the propensities to save of different groups of earners, turns income distribution into a means to achieve the required adjustment. Baranzini calls attention to Hicks's analysis of this issue in *Capital and Growth*, and especially to the composition effects that a broad disaggregation of overall savings highlights, due to the different saving or bequest behavior of different socio-economic groups (classes).

In particular, the chapter examines the consequences of a differentiated rate of growth across sectors of the economy and the consequences of a different rate of return on investment for different groups of savers. Different rates of capital accumulation for different groups (and different rates of return on savings) 'may indeed open up new horizons in the field of steady-state growth analysis' (Baranzini). The above theoretical framework allows investigation of a balanced growth path of the economic system 'where each class maintains a constant relative economic strength and a constant share of the capital stock' (Baranzini). The author then examines the case in which the economic system leaves the balanced accumulation path as a result of capitalists having 'a too low propensity to pass on bequests to their children,' or of workers having 'a much stronger desire...to transmit intergenerational wealth.' The latter analytical set-up is considered to be especially promising, as it provides an insight into the dispersion (or the concentration) of wealth, and thus into 'the formation, persistence, and dispersion of socio-economic classes.'

A characteristic feature of Hicks's dynamic analysis is the combination of attention to long-term growth paths and to medium-term changes of economic magnitudes. As early as *Value and Capital* Hicks was examining what follows from an initial increase in 'the rate of investment by entrepreneurs' (1974a [1939]: 295), and associated it with the identification of a number of adjustment phases that are distinct, sequential and temporarily circumscribed. The method of temporary equilibrium, which Hicks developed in *Value and Capital* (see particularly chapters 20 and 21), draws attention to 'what happens in a particular "week" – that is to say, [to] those repercussions of economic change which might take place immediately, if people were sufficiently alert, and if communications between markets were good enough' (1974a [1939]: 283).

Nevertheless, 'in practice even these repercussions take some time to work themselves out' (*ibid.*), and there are 'repercussions which *must* take time to work themselves out – which are delayed, not by slowness of communication or imperfect knowledge, but by the technical duration of productive processes' (*ibid.*, emphasis in original). The time taken by repercussions of economic change to work themselves out is a central feature in Hicks's analysis of capital accumulation.[14] For example, 'in a process of capital accumulation where the construction period [of new capital goods] is at all long, where output begins to expand at a much later date than input expanded, income will increase perceptibly before output increases. [...] The natural thing to expect is that a period of active investment will witness an increase in expenditure while the capital goods are being constructed, so that little is left to offset the depressing effect of the increased output when it materializes' (1974a [1939]: 286–7). In other words, 'increments in output and increments in income need not correspond at all closely' (286).

The likely mismatch between the rates of variation of different economic magnitudes is at the origin of the sequential pattern followed by economic dynamics in the medium term. An example may be found in the changes of 'the relative prices of goods and services which are brought about by capital accumulation' (*ibid.*: 288).[15] In this case, it is possible 'to follow through the effect on real wages of a process of accumulation,' provided we assume 'a sufficient degree of rigidity in expectations to maintain the stability of the system' (*ibid.*). In the first phase 'new capital goods are being produced but are not yet completed,' and there is 'an increased demand for those resources which are needed to make the capital goods' (*ibid.*). This situation is likely to be beneficial to wage-earners (due to rising employment). In the subsequent 'middle phase' 'the expenditure of entrepreneurs (and profit-receivers in general) may run ahead of the additional output of commodities' and the 'tendency for an improvement in labour's position may be reversed' (*ibid.*: 289). Finally, in the late phase the output of consumption goods is likely to run ahead 'of the expenditure of entrepreneurs,' and their prices are likely to fall in terms of other prices. This means that 'the effect on real wages is at first sight necessarily favourable,' even if 'employment may be decreased' (*ibid.*). This adjustment sequence is likely to take place 'if ordinary substitution relations [between capital and labor] hold throughout' (*ibid.*: 290). This effect will be dampened if 'early input and late input are complementary' (*ibid.*). Hicks thinks it unlikely, however, that 'early and late input will be so complementary that they increase in the same proportions' (*ibid.*). Even limited substitutability, in Hicks's view, entails

---

[14] In *Value and Capital*, Hicks describes capital accumulation as a situation in which 'some of the inputs of the first week have been used, not merely to maintain in the future the first week's rates of output and input, but in order to make it possible to produce larger outputs (or employ smaller inputs) in later weeks than in the first week' (1974a [1939]: 284).

[15] Hicks maintains that 'it is these relative prices which determine real incomes, and it is real incomes which are important from the point of view of economic welfare' (1974a [1939]: 288).

a 'falling off in the demand for labour in the later stages of the plan relatively to the early stages' (*ibid.*).

The above sequential framework is the analytical background of Hicks's early treatment of the trade cycle in chapter 24 of *Value and Capital*. There Hicks distinguishes between: (i) a 'period of "preparation,"' in which both 'a small increase in the demand for factors' and 'a small increase in the demand for money' are likely (*ibid.*: 295); (ii) a 'second phase,' in which 'a start is made with the physical construction of the new capital goods,' and 'the increase in the demand for factors becomes much more considerable' (*ibid.*); and a possible 'third phase,' which may be characterized 'by nothing else but a gradually spreading elasticity of expectations' and a further fall in unemployment (*ibid.*: 296). In the third phase 'the boom waxes fast and furious,' but 'there are several ways in which it may get into trouble' (*ibid.*). In particular, Hicks calls attention to the fact that '[t]here are...at least two quite different ways in which a general boom can be brought to an end; it may be killed by credit restriction or it may die by working itself out' (*ibid.*: 297).[16]

Hicks subsequently developed trade cycle theory in a way that combines his early interest in the stage structure pattern of economic repercussions (see above) with closer attention for strictly macroeconomic principles of causation. This he clearly expresses in chapter 1 of his *A Contribution to the Theory of the Trade Cycle* (1950a), in which he concentrates upon 'the greater variability (over the cycle) in the demand for investment goods [relative to that for consumption goods]' (*ibid.*: 134), while referring to 'the "macrodynamic" theory, compounded out of Keynes and [Ragnar] Frisch' (5–6), and to Roy Harrod's 'insistence on the propriety, indeed the necessity, of approaching the business cycle as a problem of an expanding economy' (8). This combination of an aggregate approach to dynamic impulses and a 'structural' decomposition of the economic system was to remain a distinctive feature of Hicks's later work. Indeed, Hicks spent much time in discussing the relative merits of alternative representations of an economic system, and in disentangling the relative weights of horizontal and vertical bottlenecks on the medium-term evolution of the economy (as in his *Methods of Dynamic Economics*; Hicks, 1985a).

The concluding set of chapters in this volume address the theory of uneven economic dynamics by pursuing one or the other of the different methods explored by Hicks. The macroeconomic approach followed by Hicks in his model of the trade cycle based upon the identification of

---

[16] The latter possibility arises because 'the mere lapse of time' may shift entrepreneurial expectations downwards (Hicks, 1974a [1939]: 296).

'ceilings' and 'floors' (1950a) is investigated by Piero Ferri ('The economics of non-linear cycles'). In his chapter, Ferri emphasizes the distinctive features of Hicks's trade cycle theory, and in particular Hicks's attention to the endogenous dynamics associated with a medium-term perspective. Ferri highlights the two 'main sources of endogeneity' in the medium-term dynamics of the economic system: (i) the determination of cash flows and debts, which are shown to exert 'a powerful influence on investment'; and (ii) bounded rationality and learning (with the associated properties of time dependence). Ceilings and floors are considered to be useful theoretical constructs in order to 'check explosive patterns... otherwise implied by linear difference equations,' and to generate dynamic paths 'more consistent with historical experience' (Ferri). The chapter discusses a number of different economic interpretations as to the nature of ceilings and floors, and suggests that such boundary conditions point to the 'interplay between the structural economic forces represented by the model and the role of institutions in checking their dynamics.'

It is shown that the economy undergoes endogenous fluctuations as a result of interaction between the labour market and investment activity. In particular, the chapter argues that the expansion would be associated with 'an increase of both investment and debt,' which eventually brings the upward phase to a standstill, whereas the opposite takes place during the recessionary phase. The introduction of bounded rationality and learning affects the dynamic profile of the business cycle, making it more consistent with historical data. The chapter concludes that the main strength of Hicks's ceiling and floor model is its ability to interpret dynamic states of the economy that are distinct both from short-run fluctuations and long-run tendencies. Hicks's approach allows the interaction of structural 'forces' and institutional constraints. This makes a Hicksian theory especially useful when assessing policy effectiveness in specific contexts.

The following chapter, by Kumaraswamy Vela Velupillai ('A perspective on a Hicksian non-linear theory of the trade cycle'), undertakes a reading of Hicks's *A Contribution to the Theory of the Trade Cycle* (1950a) that leads him to argue that Hicks's treatment contains 'insights and suggestions that seem to have escaped formalizations by earlier students of the book.' According to Velupillai, Hicks was aware that his complete trade cycle model was one of multiple equilibria, such that 'a locally stable equilibrium' coexists with 'a separate unstable equilibrium.' In particular, Hicks suggested that 'the discovery of a new investment opportunity...in a period of depression' may speed up recovery and make the economy move toward its ceiling more quickly if the expansionary incentive is large enough, or if it comes late enough (*ibid.*: 121–2). On the other hand,

Hicks maintained that, if 'the hump is only a small one,' the expansion would 'look like a weak boom – an expansion in output which fell away again without reaching the ceiling' (122). Velupillai suggests that Hicks's conjecture should be assessed against the background of the standard interpretation of the ceiling and floor model, and could be modeled through 'serious reconsiderations of the original non-linear investment function.'

In particular, it is maintained that it would be necessary to modify the classical formalization of the Hicks model, which 'consisted only of the induced part of investment, to which autonomous investment...was tagged as an additive component' (Velupillai). The chapter suggests that, if one wants to answer some of the criticisms raised against Hicks's distinction between induced and non-induced ('autonomous') invest-ment, a possibility would be to introduce a 'multiplicative assumption' and to include autonomous investment 'inseparably in the functional form $\psi(.)$' [the functional form for the induced part of investment]. Velupillai then examines some specific criticisms of the ceiling and floor assumptions in Hicks's trade cycle theory, and considers in particular Richard Goodwin's view that there might be justification only for the assumption of a ceiling associated with the full employment barrier (but not for the assumption of a floor associated with a 'dead' accelerator and its revival). This chapter concludes with an assessment of Hicks's attitude to historical context and its implications for economic theorizing.

Hicks's discussion of the methods of dynamic analysis came to be associated, in his later work, with the comparative appraisal of distinct representations of economic interdependencies. The chapter by Harald Hagemann ('Capital, growth, and production disequilibria: on the employment consequences of new technologies') examines Hicks's treat-ment of economic systems in a state of transition, and more particularly on the 'traverse' from one steady-state growth path to another. This investigation is undertaken by considering 'the employment consequen-ces of a different, more mechanized method of production' (the so-called 'Ricardo machinery effect'). The chapter explores Hicks's view that mon-etary disorders may be 'superimposed upon other disorders; but the other disorders are more fundamental' (Hicks, as quoted by Hagemann). From this point of view, Hicks's attitude is close to that of Adolph Lowe, who opposed Friedrich Hayek in debates about the causes of the business cycle and argued for the primary importance of technological change relative to money and credit. Hagemann suggests a comparative assessment of two different approaches to the analysis of technological disequilibria, which are respectively associated with vertical and horizontal representa-tions of the production system. In particular, he notes that the horizontal approach highlights 'the consequences of process innovations on sectoral structures.' The vertical approach is better equipped in dealing with product innovations (such as the introduction of new capital goods), however.

The chapter explores the employment consequences of mechanization by assessing the earlier contributions of David Ricardo and Knut Wicksell against the analytical background of Hicks's theory and his back and forth move between vertical and horizontal schemes of production. In this connection, Hagemann draws attention to the different views as to the possibility of technological unemployment expressed by Hicks in *The Theory of Wages* (1932) and in his late writings. In his earlier contribution, Hicks denies that the introduction of new machinery can result in a fall of gross income, whereas in his later contributions Hicks admits the possibility of such an outcome. The chapter argues that Hicks's standpoint in fact shows more long-term consistency than it may at first appear, since as early as *The Theory of Wages* Hicks had noted that inventions increase the 'total dividend' (that is, gross income) only if 'a successful compensation process has taken place.'

Further discussions of Ricardo's 'machinery problem' (such as those associated with the contributions by Kaldor, Emil Lederer, and Hans Neisser in the 1930s) point to the central role of compensation effects and suggest that different compensation processes may be associated with dissimilar technological structures. Hicks's reformulation of production theory in *Capital and Time* grafts his earlier classification of technical inventions ('neutral,' 'labour-saving,' and 'capital-saving') onto a time structure view of the production process (see also the final two chapters in this volume). Hagemann suggests that Hicks's case of 'strongly forward-biased' invention (this would be an invention in which cost saving at the utilization stage dominates cost saving at the construction stage of the production process) is the most suitable analytical set-up for the understanding of temporary technological unemployment.

In the years following the publication of *Capital and Growth* Hicks became increasingly dissatisfied with the investigation of transitional paths constrained by 'horizontal' interdependencies and bottlenecks (across mutually related and simultaneously operated processes). This led him to envisage a different method of transitional dynamics, in which interdependencies connect different time periods, and bottlenecks are of the 'vertical' type (in this case, causal linkages follow the historical chain from the state of the economy at time t to the state of the economy at time $t + k$). This approach made Hicks increasingly interested in economic causality through historical time, and is associated with Hicks's description of production processes as a sequence of fabrication stages following one another in time (the flow input/flow output version of Austrian theory he developed in *Capital and Time*).

Erich W. Streissler, in his chapter, 'Capital and time,' examines the foundations of Hicks's theory of time in economics going back to Hicks's early work of the 1930s. In particular, the chapter maintains that Hicks's essay 'A Suggestion for Simplifying the Theory of Money' (1935a) is 'probably the most "Austrian" of Sir John's essays.' This is especially attributable to Hicks's interest in 'the relevance of the variance in returns for behavior toward risk,' which 'had actually been prefigured in Böhm-Bawerk's thesis of habilitation' (Streissler). Streissler notes that Hicks's monetary essay is remarkably close to 'the most important and most relevant ideas of Hayek,' such as the relevance of money to the equilibrium of the real economy not only in the short run, and the importance of expectations. Hicks came to consider money principally a disequilibrium phenomenon, and excluded it from *Capital and Time* (which is considered 'mainly an equilibrium theory').

Streissler also notes that Hicks's theory of real capital is characterized by a combination of fixed and circulating capital that makes it significantly 'un-"Austrian."' Certain features of *Capital and Time* are close to some classical Austrian themes, however, such as Carl Menger's interest in the time structure of production. In general, though, Hicks appears to be distant from Menger's view that the consideration of errors should be central to the analysis of the time structure of production. Also, Hicks did not share the basic structure of Eugen von Böhm-Bawerk's theory of capital and interest, especially as, for Böhm-Bawerk but not for Hicks, the fundamental reasons for the explanation of the rate of interest (both in a capitalist and a socialist economy) are 'subjective valuations on the part of the final consumers' (Streissler).

The second part of this chapter discusses Hicks's 'Austrian trilogy.' In 'The Hayek Story' (1967c), Hicks examines the lag structure implicit in Menger's and Hayek's sequence from capital goods to final consumption and calls attention to the fact that Hayek's dynamics is a theory of traverse rather than of trade cycle. In the subsequent essay, 'A Neo-Austrian Growth Theory' (1970), Hicks introduces his analysis of transitions associated with lag structures and makes it clear that, in his view, the ability to deal with transitions ought to be considered 'a main strength of the Austrian theory' (267). Finally, in *Capital and Time* (1973a), Hicks goes back to Hayek's theme that capital is a multidimensional magnitude, and outlines on that basis his analysis of traverse paths. In this connection, the chapter suggests that Hicks relied too much on the assumption of given technical and economic characteristics for any given technique, thus overlooking Adam Smith's insight that one should not separate 'given production functions and technical advances,' and that it would be more appropriate to think 'of an inseparable mixture of both.'

Streissler's chapter calls attention to the critical role of the 'ruling rate of interest' in determining adaptations of the production structure (rather than the other way around). In this way, this author suggests that monetary and institutional considerations should take center stage in the analysis of economic dynamics. The relationship between the monetary and the technical features of production along sequential adjustment paths is examined by Mario Amendola and Jean-Luc Gaffard in the concluding chapter of the volume ('Sequential analysis and out-of-equilibrium paths'). The authors argue that the central issue to be addressed in this context is that of the harmonization of the construction and utilization phases along the adjustment path. The reason for this is that the viability of such a path may be hampered when the terminal collection of capital goods is not the required one. This is especially the case when it is impossible to reduce the adjustment process to 'a sequence that can be fully traced out *ex ante*' (Amendola and Gaffard). The authors maintain that the analysis of economic change under the above set of conditions requires the explicit consideration of a monetary economy. The main reason for this is that a central economic function (liquidity) may now be associated with a specific magnitude (money), so that it becomes possible to distinguish between liquid reserves and material goods.

The chapter investigates adjustments of productive structure in a sequential and out-of-equilibrium context, with the aim of identifying sources of distortions of productive capacity and conditions for their absorption. Actual investment is usually constrained by available resources, so that actual productive capacity is usually different from the desired one. The out-of-equilibrium analysis suggests that a 'Smithian' increase in the saving rate ('hoarding') does not induce an automatic and immediate increase in the rate of growth (due to distortion of productive capacity and the possibility that disequilibria be 'handed down the sequence'). Similarly, a 'Keynesian' reduction in the saving rate implies a contraction of productive capacity and eventually a falling wage fund (that may in turn induce excess supply and strong economic fluctuations). In both cases, specific coordination policies are required. For example, an increasing saving rate may induce a higher growth rate (after 'the initial period of turbulence') only if additional labour resources are available (for instance through immigration). On the other hand, a contracting saving rate may be compatible with a constant (or increasing) growth rate as long as the emergent distortion of productive capacity is made good by a suitable ('accommodating') monetary policy, and external financial resources are made available. The chapter suggests that a 'Hicksian' approach to economic policy turns attention away from a single-minded association between instruments and goals, and points to the need for external intervention in order to make 'the expansionary process associated with a structural modification' a viable one.

There are economists who do not like to 'think in the open.' They publish theorems but never conjectures, and if a result is capable of diverging interpretations they limit themselves to exposing them in a neutral manner. For these authors, only what is or can be definitively assessed in formal terms is worth being written. Differently from them, Hicks always thought 'in the open.' Thus, he did not prevent us from benefiting from his disquieting reflections, from his openness to 'all that has not been seen yet.' Clearly, this is a risky road, but Hicks took it, convinced as he was that '[e]conomics, surely, is a social science. It is concerned with the operations of human beings, who are not omniscient and not wholly rational; who (perhaps because they are not wholly rational) have diverse, and not wholly consistent, ends. As such it cannot be reduced to a pure technics and may benefit by being distinguished from a pure technics' (1960a: 707).[17] Hicks was a humanist in the most honorable sense of this word. In raising a question, he envisaged not only its analytical side but also its social and human side, never forgetting that economic relationships are, basically, relations among human beings living in society. Hicks's aim was always the demolition of the commonplace, to make his interlocutor free from the fatal illusion created by the belief that knowledge was acquired once and for all. He was never a doctrinaire, and he never wanted to destroy one hierarchy to the advantage of another.

---

[17] This point of view made Hicks critical of any attempt at achieving conceptual integration through the identification of merely 'formal' connections across different bodies of theory. For example, Hicks noted that '[t]hough the Minimax theorem is usually stated as a theorem in Game theory...it is not necessary to state it that way. It can easily be stated in a more abstract manner – as a pure property of numbers that are arranged in a rectangular matrix...What von Neumann's Minimax theorem states is that there is a process of "enlarging" the matrix by which the gap between minimax [the minimum of row maxima] and maximin [the maximum of column minima] (if it initially exists) can be so reduced that it ultimately disappears... What I want to emphasize is that this enlargement is a purely abstract operation, which can be given all sorts of meanings, that have nothing but a formal connection with one another' (1960a: 708–9). Hicks's criticism of the treatment of social issues as 'matters of technique' goes back to his relatively early essay on 'Education in Economics' (1941a: 6). There, Hicks notes that a purely technical attitude to economic theorizing 'is subject to a real danger of Machiavellism,' and would make it impossible to consider social problems 'as facets of the general search for the Good Life.'

Just as, with the sea, there are waves and changing tides, so there are periods when the influence of Hicks has been more apparent and less apparent, more vigorous and less vigorous. We may conjecture that this pattern will continue to manifest itself even in the future. Indeed, this is the destiny of a great thinker, of somebody who has accomplished a decisive step in intellectual development, and has shown the path of further progress to future generations of scholars.

Part I

The Intellectual Heritage of John Hicks

1   Hicks on liberty

Amartya Sen

Questions

John Hicks is often taken to be the apostle of economic efficiency who taught us how to think about markets and prices and their efficacious functioning. That diagnosis is not mistaken, especially given the role of *Value and Capital* (1939a), which is one of the defining books of contemporary economics and a pioneering exposition of what an equilibrium in a competitive market achieves. There is another part of Hicks's thinking, however, that made him worry about whether the focus on efficiency could capture adequately the diverse functions of transactions and markets in society and the enabling opportunities they could generate. He also wondered whether efficiency is all that economists should be interested in and whether economists are right to base their policy recommendations so heavily on the efficiency features of economic arrangements. In looking for a different – and in some ways more radical – interpretation of the role of economists, Hicks was deeply involved in the social importance of liberty and freedom.

Hicks did, in fact, address these issues explicitly, and yet the general understanding of him among economists tends, by and large, to be based on neglecting these parts of his work and commitment. This chapter is an attempt to assess Hicks's concerns about values other than efficiency, including his appreciation of problems of economic evaluation and the reach and relevance of social choice theory.

Social choice and majority rule

Was Hicks really interested at all in social choice? It is not hard to detect a certain reluctance on his part to go into that subject, even after Arrow's pioneering departure in 1951. Eventually, when Hicks published his collected essays in the early 1980s, he did include in the first volume (entitled *Wealth and Welfare*; 1981a) an essay – I believe it had not previously been published – called 'The Rationale of Majority Rule' (1981b). I will comment on it presently, but I might also take this opportunity of expressing my personal frustration earlier on in not being able to get Hicks to tell us what he thought of social choice problems even when the subject matter of his investigation seemed to demand such an engagement.

My frustration had, I must confess, something of a personal background, which I now – at the risk of some self-indulgence – mention here. My early education in economics was for two years in Presidency College in Calcutta, and I emerged from those beginning years of economic study with an overarching admiration for Hicks's writings (I was encouraged to read him particularly by Bhabatosh Datta and Tapas Majumdar, two of my teachers at Presidency, and strongly supported by another great teacher I was privileged to have, Amiya Dasgupta, who was then based at the Banaras Hindu University, in Varanasi).

I had also developed a firm view on how rapidly one learned economics if one could find and read an essay by Hicks on the subject. At my second location of economics education – Cambridge University – I encountered a rather frosty atmosphere in relation to Hicks and his economics, however: many of the Cambridge theorists who lectured to us tended to dismiss the significance of Hicks's contributions with a rapidity that I found truly astonishing (even though, happily for me, in my own college, Trinity, Hicks did have admirers, both among economists who basically agreed with him, particularly Dennis Robertson, and those who were pursuing altogether different approaches, especially Piero Sraffa and Maurice Dobb). As it happens, my Calcutta-originated adulation of Hicks's excellence survived well enough despite the Cambridge dismissals.

When I resigned from my job in Cambridge in 1963 to go to Delhi University to teach, I wanted a firm break from the work I had been mostly doing in Cambridge, in particular growth theory, development economics and capital theory (a decade later I would write an essay – Sen, 1974 – that reflected my strong sense of skepticism of the reach and relevance of Cambridge capital theory). I wanted to work, inspired by Kenneth Arrow, on social choice theory (I had started that pursuit in a very preliminary way as an undergraduate in Calcutta ten years earlier but had effectively abandoned it in Cambridge), and, naturally, I wondered whether Hicks had written anything on it.

I could not, alas, find anything that even touched on social choice theory, and when I happened to see Hicks personally (this would have been, I think, at the annual meeting of the American Economic Association in December 1963), I asked him why he didn't give any evidence of being interested in social choice theory. Hicks told me that, on the contrary, he was extremely interested in the subject. Indeed, he added, I would see this in his next book. So it was with great expectations that I opened his next book, *Capital and Growth* (Hicks, 1965), but the index did not give any indication that

I might be on to something. There was nothing, of course, on social choice, nor anything on crucial institutions for social choice such as majority decisions, or voting rules, or other methods of going from individual preferences to social decisions. Nor did I find anything on liberty, and the sole reference to 'social welfare function' by Hicks led me to a very brief – and rather anodyne – statement that seemed to say extremely little.

Being at a loss, I thought I would look up 'Arrow' (I hoped that Hicks would have said *something* at least on the Arrow paradox and the famous impossibility theorem), and my excitement was great when I found an index item that referred to 'Arrow, paradox of.' Now at last, I told myself, I would know what Hicks made of the impossibility theorem. The reference to 'Arrow paradox' turned out, however, to be an allusion not to the paradox of social choice by Kenneth Arrow, but to the paradox of 'the moving arrow' by Zeno – to wit, that at each indivisible instant the moving arrow could, on Zeno's reasoning, neither be in motion (for then the instant would not be indivisible) nor at rest (for then the arrow could not be moving at all, since time is made up of an aggregate of such moments). While I enjoyed the element of absurdity in the anticlimactic end of my search, I was really sad to be so completely frustrated in not being any wiser on Hicks's take on social choice theory.

Comfort did eventually come plentifully to me, however, when I was able to read his manuscript 'The Rationale of Majority Rule'; this was in 1980, when that unpublished essay was being placed for inclusion in Hicks's *Wealth and Welfare* (1981a), to be published in the following year. The paper is indeed very engaging, and in many ways insightful. This is not because Hicks says anything very interesting, in that essay, on the central content of the social choice difficulty captured by Arrow's impossibility theorem,[1] but because he has other interesting things to say about problems of social choice.

Hicks's discussion of the arbitrariness – going beyond mere inconsistency – of majority rule is both insightful and important (and it certainly involves a different focus of attention from that in the consistency-centered impossibility theorem of Arrow; 1951a). Indeed, the arbitrariness to which Hicks was pointing can be seen both (i) in the general light of showing how capricious it may be to rely on one particular way of counting voting outcomes, ignoring other procedures, and (ii) in the special light of identifying the problems this

---

[1] Hicks makes only a passing reference to Arrow's result, contrasting it with some substantive problems Hicks himself had identified in voting rules. Indeed, after inviting the reader to 'compare' his finding with 'the "Impossibility Theorem" of Arrow,' he merely makes the enigmatic observation (correct as it is): 'My proposition, however, though related to his, is not the same' (1981b: 289).

arbitrariness can create for the liberty and freedom of minority groups and others not in the empowered mainstream. While Hicks also discusses, with an example, the cycles of indecision based on pair-wise majority votes (1981b: 289–91), the real interest in his analysis lies, rather, in his demonstration – and far-reaching discussion – of the immense variability of the social choice outcome of voting procedures depending on what may initially look like small variations in the exact voting rules.

To exemplify, Hicks considers a preference profile of the individuals over three alternatives *a*, *b*, and *c* (1981b: table 13.1, 288–9) such that:

  (i) *a* will win if the highest vote-getter is chosen when each person votes for one alternative only and goes for his or her top choice (Hicks calls this 'plurality voting' – *a* will have plurality but not majority);

 (ii) *b* will win if the alternative with the smallest support from voters in plurality voting is eliminated, leading to a pair-wise contest between the two top vote-getters (this procedure is sometimes called a 'run-off' in political polls in a number of countries for selecting the president of the country, such as France; in this case *c* will be eliminated, and then *b* will defeat *a* and have a majority of supporters among all voters);

(iii) *c* will win in pair-wise majority voting, defeating *a* and *b* respectively in standard pair-by-pair contest.

Hicks not only notes the arbitrariness of the process of selecting an outcome depending on how votes are counted to arrive at the social choice, but also points out how each system ignores some types of possibly relevant information. For example, plurality voting, by which *a* is chosen, looks only at everyone's first preference and pays no attention to the second preference, and its 'rationale' (Hicks notes) must lie in 'an assumption that second preference…can be taken to be randomly distributed' (1981b: 289). These issues relate to those that had been discussed in the eighteenth century by French mathematicians, particularly the Marquis de Condorcet and Jean-Charles de Borda, in comparing majority voting of different types with positional voting, such as the 'rank-order' procedure associated with the name of Borda (generalized in the 1970s by Gardenfors, 1973, and Fine and Fine, 1974a, 1974b). As in every field, however, Hicks's lucid discussion is a good way of understanding the underlying problems that are involved in these outcome variations.

Liberty, minority rights and the relevance of empirical features

Hicks goes on from there to discuss the implications of these problems for liberty and minority rights. In fact, it is to the *excluded* information (just discussed), or what can be called selective 'social deafness,' that Hicks turns to note that any voting rule can be not only arbitrary, but also in some sense oppressive. In discussing the varying seriousness of this problem, Hicks makes an important point about the likelihood of a tyranny of majority rule in some kind of societies, but not in others, thereby bringing an empirical consideration into a largely analytical investigation.

I take the liberty of quoting rather extensively Hicks's assessment that there is the very real possibility that majority rule may be an instrument of oppression, depending on the empirical characteristics of the diversity of the population involved (Hicks, 1981b: 298–9):

> Majority rule is often defended on the ground that it does at least provide a basis for decision, as compared with the opposite, which is to be found (I suppose) in the 'liberum veto', where any elector can prevent a decision; that is of course a strong point. Decisions can nevertheless be biased; and biased decisions, which are such that they continually show the same bias (our 'cumulative skewness'), are clearly oppressive. There is thus a sharp distinction between the application of majority rule to a homogeneous body of voters – homogeneous in the sense that any voter can expect that in a good proportion of the issues that come up during his life time (or during his 'planning period') he will find himself among the majority – and its application to a body which is more permanently divided. [...] The case is very different when the division is one of colour, of race, of religion or perhaps of language. In a community that is strongly divided in one of these ways, simple majority rule is only too likely to mean Oppression.

If the social-choice-theoretic essay on majority rule brings out Hicks's analysis of arbitrariness of different kinds of voting rules, it also points firmly to his interest in minority rights and personal liberty. This is, of course, a classic issue of the freedoms of individuals and of outvoted groups. Hicks's distinction between different kinds of social divisions (his talking in particular of the diversity 'of colour, of race, of religion or perhaps of language') shows the relevance of empirical features that influence the contingent practical seriousness of a general conceptual difficulty in political philosophy.

Economic efficiency, social freedoms, and the role of economists

Hicks's discussion of majority rule certainly gives us reason to believe that he took liberty and minority rights seriously. Is it possible, though, that he took the view, which many economists do, that problems in mathematical politics are of little relevance to economics in general and to welfare economics in particular? It is one thing to bring out the limitations of majority rule and of other voting procedures for political decisions, and it would be quite another to try to bring into the analysis of standard economics – markets, prices, and so on – the relevance of liberty and freedoms. Isn't the lack of interest in the dimension of liberty in *Value and Capital* a good indication of where Hicks stood on these economic matters?

In fact, there is considerable evidence that this would be an altogether wrong reading of Hicks. He went into this question explicitly in two publications in 1959 (1959b, 1959c), giving considerable pride of place to his rejection of that possible line of reasoning in his collection of essays *Wealth and Welfare*. Indeed, he chastises economists, including himself (through using a first personal plural 'we': Hicks, 1959c, 1981a: 138):

> The liberal, or non-interference, principles of the classical (Smithian or Ricardian) economists were not, in the first place, economic principles; they were an application to economics of principles that were thought to apply to a much wider field. The contention that economic freedom made for economic efficiency was no more than a secondary support. [...] What I do question is whether we are justified in forgetting, as completely as most of us have done, the other side of the argument.

Judging markets by the promotion of freedom to choose would be, in Hicks's understanding, a return to an old, classical tradition in economics. If Hicks is critical of the abandonment of that tradition, it is because he continues to believe that the case for markets rests very substantially on the freedoms they can generate, rather than on only their implications for what is often called 'economic efficiency.'

In a paper called 'Markets and Freedoms' (Sen, 1993), I have tried to show that a consequential analysis of markets in terms of freedoms generated, rather than incomes or utilities only, can be obtained through an analytical extension of general competitive economics (see Hicks, 1939a, Arrow, 1951b, Debreu, 1959, and Arrow and Hahn, 1971).[2] This is not the occasion to go into the particular extensions that were obtained (and the identification of those parts of the earlier results that could not be so extended), but I should mention that my inspiration to pursue this possible extension came very substantially from being impressed by Hicks's clear-headed assessment of what had to be done and what he thought classical political economists were really aiming at, in defending a competitive market mechanism (my essay is in fact a revised text of my 'John Hicks Lecture' given at Oxford, in 1992).

Given Hicks's interest in different kinds of problems that are relevant in their own right, there could be a tension between what Hicks himself

---

[2] One part of the connection between competitive equilibrium and economic efficiency, namely that the former entails the latter (with suitable assumptions), goes through without much problem, but the converse is deeply problematic (on this, see Sen, 1993).

actually did and what he recognized as being important. As it happens, though, in his work in pure economic theory Hicks did not see any real tension. He could work on economic efficiency and the 'welfarist' results of standard economic analysis and regard these to be worthy exercises, without assigning to them an overarching importance that would sink our reasons for being interested – rather profoundly – on issues of liberty and freedom. He puts his general attitude to what might initially look like a major tension in the following way (Hicks, 1959c, 1981a: 139):

Much of the concentration of power in the hands of large organisations, which is the major threat to freedom within Western societies, is technological, not socio-logical, in its origin. I have accordingly no intention, in abandoning economic welfarism, of falling into the 'fiat libertas, ruat caelum' which some latter-day liberals seem to see as the only alternative. What I do maintain is that liberal goods are goods; that they are values which, however, must be weighed up against other values. …we can recognise these limitations, and still feel that these ends are worthier ends than those which are represented in a production index.

One does not have to reject – or, indeed, celebrate – Hicks's conclusions about working rules for economist theorists (particularly for himself), and the reasoning that led him to decide to stick to 'economic welfarism' in his own work, to see that he did regard liberty and freedom to be extra-ordinarily important, no matter how exactly that importance is pursued and incorporated in the social sciences.

It is in the realm of policy-making that Hicks urged economists to go well beyond the results of deliberately constrained pure economic theory. Even as economists we have to recognize that there are critically important concerns that economic arguments fail to take into account adequately, and even as an economic adviser a professional economist could not brush his or her hands off from those other – allegedly 'non-economic' – concerns.

I end this chapter with Hicks's firm statement on what he took the duties of a professional economist to be when it comes to policy-making (Hicks, 1959c, 1981a: 136–7; emphasis in original):

I cannot therefore now feel that it is enough to admit, with that very moderate Welfarist Sir Dennis Robertson, that 'the economist must be prepared to see some suggested course of action which he thinks would promote economic welfare turned down – his own judgement consenting, perhaps not – for overriding reasons. This is still no more than an admission that there are 'parts' of welfare that are not included in Economic Welfare, and that the two sorts of ends may conflict. The economist, as such, is still allowed, and even encouraged, to keep within his 'own' frontiers; if he has shown that a particular course of action is to be recommended, *for economic reasons*, he has done his job. I would now say that if he limits his function in that manner, he does not rise to his responsibilities. It is impossible to make 'eco-nomic' proposals that do not have 'non-economic aspects', as the Welfarist would call them; when the economist makes a recommendation, he is responsible for it in the round; all aspects of that recommendation, whether he chooses to label them economic or not, are his concern.

To conclude, our understanding of economic efficiency may have been profoundly enriched by Hicks's work, but no one acknowledged with greater clarity the confined and contingent reach of that understanding. Liberties, distributions of freedoms, minority rights, and other such concerns are not only important, in Hicks's assessment, but they are subjects into which economists have a responsibility to enter. He discussed with great force and lucidity the reasons why the discipline of economics cannot ignore the relevance of liberty and its far-reaching implications on the assessment of economic understanding and policy.

No matter whether – or how well – economists can accommodate this enduring relevance and its implications in their pure economic theory, they cannot abstain from taking into account – to the best of their abilities – their bearing on the decisions on which they, as economists, have to pronounce. There is no way of keeping these broader social choice concerns out of the 'practical reason' that economists have to undertake, for which economic epistemology, important as it is, will be, as Hicks argued, an altogether inadequate foundation. Hicks's understanding of the methods as well as of the substance of economics remains deeply relevant today.

2 An economist even greater than his high reputation

Paul A. Samuelson

In print I have told the story more than once how my University of Chicago tutor, Eugene Staley, answered my naive beginner's question, 'Who's the world's greatest economist?' Without hesitation he answered, 'John Maynard Keynes (rhymes with "brains").' That was a good call, especially since it was made before the classic 1936 *General Theory* and just after the disappointing two-volume *Treatise on Money*.

Once not bitten, twice non-shy. After arriving at the Harvard Graduate School I asked a lively assistant professor there, John Cassells, 'Who is the world's best young economist?' 'John Hicks,' he said. I came to verify this on my own, from reading Hicks's 1932 *Theory of Wages*. My reason for particularly mentioning this is because Hicks in his characteristic way disclaimed in middle life that his first book had been a good one. We authors cannot be trusted in evaluating our own brainchildren.

Neither can award committees be trusted in awarding honors. In the fourth year of the Bank of Sweden's new Alfred Nobel Prize in economics, the Stockholm Committee of the Royal Swedish Academy of Science made two qualitative misjudgments: they gave only one-half a Nobel to each of Sir John Hicks and Kenneth Arrow. In my considered judgment, Arrow deserved two Nobel Prizes in economics: one for his *Social Choice* classics and one more at least for his novel theory of complete stochastic markets. Hicks himself, meanwhile, certainly deserved an early full prize for his large corpus of important contributions. At the time I suspected that punctilious Swedish resentment against an English scholar who was cavalier in recognizing and documenting the related publications of contemporary researchers – as when Hicks learned a lot about non-linear business cycles from Richard Goodwin, a less appreciated economist – persuaded a committee majority to pair the names of Hicks and Arrow. Certainly, it was a stretch to justify the pairing by pointing out that both had contributed to general equilibrium theory. That they did do. But what each did was quite different. Arrow and Gerard Debreu, or Arrow and Lionel McKenzie, would have made better sense.

Within the United Kingdom itself, Hicks's home country, in my calibration he never did quite receive his full measure of recognition. For one thing, he was not primarily in the tradition of 'pope' Alfred Marshall. No capital offense, since at the LSE Hicks drifted more into the better tradition of the Swedish Knut Wicksell. Second, Hicks was an Oxford undergraduate during lean seasons there. Third, without being a Mt. Pelerin conservative such as Friedrich Hayek or Milton Friedman, centrist John Hicks was not quite 'politically correct' by contemporary leftish Oxbridge standards. It may be no mortal sin in academia to be a bit Napoleonic, but sometimes it will be held against you.

The purist economist Tjalling Koopmans was against fine writing by scientists: it gave, he believed, undeserved weight to your views. If it is criminal to be a facile writer, few economists need fear indictment. Hicks was an exception. He wrote understandable prose and, being satisfied with his thoughts, he never suffered writer's block. R. G. D. Allen, Hicks's more mathematical comrade at the LSE, told me that, when Hicks asked about the theory of determinants and quadratic forms, Roy Allen lent him Eugen Netto's little book on the subject. 'And in a few months, John came back with his 1939 *Value and Capital*.' William Makepeace Thackeray declared that *Vanity Fair* was a novel without a heroine. I declare that the Oxford University Press first edition of *Value and Capital* was without improvements, without resetting a single page. Although Allen and Hicks's articles (1934a, 1934b) were written without knowledge of the wartime Italian classics of Eugen Slutsky, their papers did essentially complete Vilfredo Pareto's quest for the testable structure of consumer's demand theory. It says something for Hicks's good judgment that, while G. C. Evans (1930), Allen (1932), Nicholas Georgescu-Roegen (1936), and Samuelson (1947) allocated considerable space to non-integrable demand structures, Hicks fairly early on concentrated on the more relevant case of integrable demand structures. Along with H. Hotelling (1932, 1935) and M. Allais (1943), Hicks wrote sure-footedly about generalized consumers' surplus.

When Hicks was an early reviewer of Keynes's *General Theory* he seemed to think that he and Keynes were competing rivals to arrive at the North Pole, where the Holy Grail of a new paradigm was to be found. I never quite understood that belief. Later, Hicks's famous 1937 graphical model of intersecting IS and LM curves did become a classroom workhorse to exposit Keynes's paradigm. There was nothing that I remember in Hicks's 'A Suggestion for Simplifying the Theory of Money' (1935a) that implied *those* curves, however. In any case, very much of 1937 Hicks (1937a) was derived from Roy Harrod, who had himself earlier commuted from Oxford to Cambridge to join the famous Kahn–Robinson–Meade–Harrod 'circus' that helped generate, in 1932–5, Keynes's 1936 *General Theory*.

We must accept great scholars as they are, warts and all. In 1962, a decade after Harry Markowitz (1952, 1959) had published the much-used quadratic programming mean:variance approach to optimal portfolio construction, Hicks published that same approach. If Hicks had already worked it out for himself beforehand and independently, it would still have been inexcusable to submit this to *The Economic Journal*. Alas, more likely Hicks and the peer reviewers of this one-time world-beating learned journal were so out of touch with the frontier of modern finance theory that they were still unaware of Markowitz's Nobel-calibre contributions.

I need to admit explicitly that being Napoleonic can itself contribute to important scholarly progress. It led Hicks to nominate as an important organizing theme for economic history the origins and evolution of the market mechanism. Although his suggestion may not have caught on with history-trained experts in economic history, I believe that economics-trained experts would do well to explore Hicks's lead further. Interestingly, no large society has been known to achieve progressive growth and a high standard of living with prolonged life expectancies without considerable reliance on supply-and-demand market-clearing mechanisms. Utopian reformers, impressed by self-sufficient biological families and occasional kibbutz-like small groups, have favored socialist regimens. (Albert Einstein was one such. Perhaps Noam Chomsky, the famous linguistics innovator and formidable polemicist, is another. We are not preprogrammed from birth to answer such questions by *a priori* thought alone. Analytical sifting of relevant evidence can alone balance the imponderables concerning this conundrum.)

Indulge me to add one further example of Hicks's sage judgment. In 1958 the annual meeting of the International Economic Association (IEA) was held on the Greek island of Corfu. Sir Austin Robinson had scheduled it there to trap Piero Sraffa into attending. The mountain was brought to Mohammed, but that did not coax Sraffa into uttering any memorable words on capital theory. Still, nature abhors a vacuum, which Nicholas Kaldor helped fill with *two* late papers: along with the draft the Kaldor commentator was handed on the day of the Kaldor lecture, was the stenographer's different text of what came out of the Kaldor mouth. The published 1958 IEA volume was a vintage issue. All the same, the single remark that has stayed with me longest was an off-the-cuff intervention by Hicks, saying (in paraphrase): 'Do you realize that, in between two neighboring items listed in the order catalogue of a toolmaker, there are a plethora of intermediate items that the supplier will offer if only he is confronted with a critical demand for such an offering.' To the degree that this is correct, the gulf between (i) Clarkian neoclassical marginalism, with an uncountable infinity of alternative techniques, and (ii) a von Neumann technology, with only a finite number of alternative techniques, becomes importantly narrowed.

3 Hicks's 'conversion' – from J. R. to John

Luigi L. Pasinetti and GianPaolo Mariutti

Introduction

How many Hickses do we know? Looking at the signatures of his papers, and hence at his bibliography, one suspects that there have been at least two: *J. R. Hicks*, from the beginning of his career in the 1930s to the end of the 1960s, and *John Hicks*, from the 1970s onwards. Was this change of name a whimsical caprice of a successful economist, or was it a meditated choice? An answer comes from Hicks himself. In 1975 (Hicks, 1975b: 365) he emphatically writes: 'J. R. Hicks…[is] a "neoclassical" economist now deceased… John Hicks [is] a non-neo-classic who is quite disrespectful towards his "uncle."'

Hence, Hicks changed his name because he changed his mind. John, the 'nephew,' came to develop different ideas about economic theory from J. R., the 'uncle.' This is a startling and intriguing occurrence; to be fair, though quite unique in the form, it is not entirely in the substance.

In the natural sciences in particular, where eager attention to new evidence is most keenly paid, changes of mind are not exceptionally rare events. Even in economics, one can cite several cases of a sharp change of mind. The most clamorous of all is, of course, the one of John Maynard Keynes, who – after leading an entire bright career within the stream of traditional economics, culminating with the two-volume *Treatise on Money* (Keynes, 1930), expected to be his *magnum opus* – just a few months after publication dramatically repudiated the book, and concentrated all his efforts on a radically new theory: *The General Theory of Employment, Interest and Money* (1936).

At least superficially, Hicks would seem to belong to the same family of scientists. His change of mind was certainly not due to a desire to gain new glory. When John Hicks, the 'nephew,' decided openly to distance himself from his 'uncle,' J. R., he was a very well-known and successful economist; so much so as to be awarded the Economics Nobel Prize, in 1972, for his 'pioneering contributions to general economic equilibrium theory and welfare theory' – i.e. the pillars of neoclassical economics, which, as J. R., he had contributed to establishing. If he had been so successful along these lines of research, why did he decide openly to repudiate them?

This chapter deals with this question. We are not suggesting a parallel with Keynes. The two cases are quite different. Hicks's change of attitude is softer and more cautious. It lacks the suddenness and the drama of Keynes's 'revolution.' Many economists might even have found it almost imperceptible; and this may offer a hint at why he decided to mark it with a sharp signal – a change of name. Despite this difference of attitude, the eye of the cyclone in Hicks's tortuous intellectual journey points at Cambridge, and at the kind of economics that grew there out of Keynes's revolutionary book.

Those who are patient enough to follow the plot of the present chapter will probably realize that economics is not a subject spared by the irony of history. Hicks is widely perceived as the economist who – with his IS-LM model – offered the tools to take the sting out of the revolutionary spirit of the *General Theory*. Nonetheless, this did not prevent its author from developing growing skepticism toward his own original analytical tool, while paying increasing attention to the relevance of Keynes's new approach to economics.

Before 1936

Hicks graduated in Oxford. As he writes in his biography (1979b), it was just by chance that he took economics as a major subject. 'It was easier to find a job,' he was advised. In fact, at the age of twenty-two, he started his career as an economist at the London School of Economics. The LSE was already at that time a place of international renown, very open toward the ideas, and the presence, of Continental economists – an attitude, as Hicks recalls, largely missing in other English universities.

From the tendency of its studies, the LSE was generally considered as strongly pro-market. It was the place of Hayek and, since 1929, of Lionel Robbins, who became the head of the economics department. The skills of Robbins as a leader and organizer were widely recognized. He was able to aggregate around himself a discussion group, which gathered the best young economists of the LSE. Hicks later used to recall with nostalgia that experience, as one of the most fruitful phases of his intellectual life.

Not surprisingly, Hicks became 'a standard LSE product.' His first significant 'theoretical achievement' arrived in 1932 with the publication of *The Theory of Wages*. This was his first book – 'thoroughly "neoclassical."[1] It achieved widespread success, above all in the United States, where even in the following decades it remained the book for which Hicks was most generally known. The 'theoretical achievement' of the book was due to several novel concepts of his, such as the elasticity of substitution and the notion of the neutrality (or non-neutrality) of technical change with respect to distributive shares, and, moreover, to his clever reformulation of earlier discoveries, such as Eugen Slutsky's distinction between income and substitution effects. These were all concepts absorbed as staple results of neoclassical theory, and decades later they became perfectly integrated into mainstream economics.

Frankly, the publication of the book could not have happened at a worse time. The analytical apparatus on which it was based relied entirely on the free market mechanism and full employment, precisely at a time when the Great Depression was under way. This contrast between the assumptions of the theory and economic reality rebounded on the author himself. While the book started to make some good inroads into the learned journals, receiving a mixture of praise and criticism, Hicks seriously began to doubt the foundations on which it was based. On reflection, the free market solution appeared to him far from being the perfect mechanism that he had assumed it to be. The book 'had nothing to do with the state of the world at the time when I was writing,' Hicks was to write forty years later, and he continued: 'I had diagnosed a disease, but it was not the right disease. The unemployment of 1932 was of quite a different character from what I had supposed' (1977a: 5).

Hicks, though 'completely innocent' of the ideas that were being put forward in other places at the time (particularly in Cambridge and in Sweden), became increasingly skeptical about an economic framework based exclusively on free market competition. It was his awakening to these doubts that made him become a potential Keynesian economist, or, to use his own words, a 'semi-Keynesian' economist (1973d).

Hicks, in isolation, at the birthplace of *The General Theory*

Among economists, the conviction has become widespread that Hicks's 'suggested interpretation' of 'Mr Keynes and the "Classics"' (1937a) offered the back door through which neoclassical economics 'digested' Keynes's *General Theory* and eventually neutralized Keynes's 'revolution.'

---

[1] The quotes refer to Hicks's own comments, as reported in his biography (1979b), and later reprinted in Hicks (1984a: 281, 283).

This is true, if not in terms of the intentions, then certainly in terms of the effects that the Hicksian IS-LM model produced. To understand how this happened, it is necessary to look carefully into the historical connections of the two protagonists – Hicks and Keynes. We start to look in this section at the origin of this relationship, leaving to the next section what happened once *The General Theory* came out.

Between Keynes and Hicks there was a generation of difference. Keynes was born in 1883, Hicks twenty-one years later, in 1904. Their relationship began in the early 1930s. In those years Keynes was a powerful intellectual figure, a *deus ex machina* in the economics circles of Cambridge, and the editor of *The Economic Journal*. From King's College, his influence on academia was formidable, and he also played a powerful role as government adviser in London and as a publicist on the national and international press. The star of Keynes was shining on the international scene, just when the star of the young Hicks was starting to light up, from the LSE to the outside academic world.

Keynes came to know J. R. Hicks through the several articles that the latter was sending (with mixed success) to *The Economic Journal*. As has been said, the Great Depression was raising increasing doubts in Hicks as to the method he had followed in his *Theory of Wages*. His weakening faith in the free market mechanism, which was so popular among his colleagues at the LSE, was making him more and more aware of the need for different approaches to economics. This induced him to look elsewhere, particularly to some foreign authors. He claims to have read Pareto in Italian, but it was in the Swedish school that he found the less sympathetic views on laissez-faire principles that he was seeking (Hicks, 1984a: 282–4). The climate of intellectual curiosity, which was present at the LSE and which led him to the examination of new ideas (even of a socialist nature), let him pursue his explorations without formal blame.

All this produced a quite interesting result from the point of view of the present investigation. The attitude of J. R. Hicks started to transform into an approach to economics not that dissimilar from the one Keynes was promoting at the beginning of the 1930s among his pupils of the 'Cambridge circus.' By 1934 Hicks felt that his separation 'from the faith in the free market' had become explicit, as he worked on his paper 'A Suggestion for Simplifying the Theory of Money' (1984a: 285). He felt and feared that his colleagues at the LSE would become, in reading it, 'aware of what was happening, but ... the atmosphere at LSE was tolerant, and I have been able to keep them among my friends' (286). An LSE colleague of his, Barrett Whale, advised Hicks that the topic he was discussing reminded him of Keynes's *Treatise on Money* (Keynes, 1930). Hicks, who had not read it carefully, went back to it and then made some changes to his paper, before sending a third draft to Keynes and another copy to *Economica* for publication (Hicks, 1935a).

In discussing what was going to become known as the theory of 'liquidity preference,' Hicks defined himself 'more Keynesian than Keynes' (1935a: 3). For his part, Keynes, who had classified Hicks as a young man 'committed to the dogmatism of the LSE stable,' received the paper and replied to it quite happily: 'I like it very much. I agree with you that what I now call "Liquidity Preference" is the essential concept for Monetary Theory' (Postcard from Keynes dated 24 December 1934 addressed to J. R. Hicks, as reported in Hicks, 1973d: 7). In an earlier version (1933) he had commented: 'As you suppose, there is a good deal with which I do not agree, but it is now clear that our minds are no longer moving in opposite directions' (as again reported in Hicks, 1973d: 7).

It seems that their views were beginning to converge. Hicks no longer considered himself a pure product of the LSE. Some of his ideas (though not all) were overlapping with those of Keynes. In fact, not only their views but their lives as well started to converge. After the publication of the article in *Economica* in 1935, Hicks decided to seize upon an invitation by Arthur Pigou to apply for a post at Cambridge, in Keynes's place! Hicks met Keynes for the first time in the interview that preceded his arrival. Once accepted, he remained in Cambridge for four years, from 1935 to 1938. Thus, when *The General Theory* saw the light of day, Hicks was teaching in its birthplace.

Keynes was at Cambridge what Robbins was at the LSE: an inspiring figure, a great organizer, and the master for many of the pupils who were working around him. Thus many young colleagues of Hicks, at Cambridge, were openly Keynes enthusiasts. They gathered in a select group, with the purpose of scrutinizing and discussing the ideas of Keynes. Hicks, despite physically being at Cambridge, and despite his incipient convergence toward Keynesian topics, never became part of Keynes's entourage. The economics faculty at Cambridge was already, by the 1930s, divided into two camps: the pro-Keynesians and the anti-Keynesians. Hicks was perceived as part of the anti-Keynesians. His friendship with Dennis Robertson and the invitation to apply for a Cambridge post, having come from Pigou, 'the Professor' at that time, were both considered as evidence that he was (and for Keynes's pupils this actually remained the case) an outsider.[2] In any case, Hicks was not keen, by predisposition, to be involved in academic battles between opposite camps.

---

[2] The detailed, biographical, first part of Hamouda's book (Hamouda, 1993: 20) suggests that, on the issue of appointments, Hicks's application was received with favor by those who wished to keep Joan Robinson out of the faculty.

Therefore, the exclusion from the Keynesian group did not particularly hit him. His timid and introverted character and his independent mind did not suffer particularly from what occurred. He was a fellow of Gonville and Caius College (not King's! – Keynes's college) and being left out of Keynes's circle was not perceived by him as a great loss. After all, he wanted to concentrate on his own research. His aim in coming to Cambridge was to use this period to put his notes in order and collect them in a book, which was to be published in 1939 as *Value and Capital*. His marriage, right at the beginning of his Cambridge period, to Ursula Webb (another standard product of the LSE) helped him. Hicks's isolation from Keynes's direct pupils became a further incentive to concentrate on his own work, though he confessed, from time to time, that he missed the lively discussions at the LSE.

1936 and afterwards: Hicks's 'reformation' of *The General Theory*

The General Theory eventually came out in 1936, and in Cambridge (and elsewhere) it was like a bolt from the blue. The fact that Hicks was perceived as an outsider was, indirectly, an advantage for him. While the book was still in press Keynes asked Hicks, to the latter's great surprise, to review it for *The Economic Journal*. Hicks was flattered, and, obviously, delighted to accept the invitation. His review even preceded the reviews by the members of Keynes's entourage. He was given only three months (from January to March 1936) to prepare what became a fifteen-page-long review article (1936a). It was, in Hicks's own words, no more than a 'first impression' (1980: 140). Despite this, one can find in it several interesting hints at what was to come. Hicks called the article 'Mr Keynes's Theory of Employment,' and placed the problem of mass unemployment right at the center of Keynes's analysis.

How could one interpret this, undoubtedly new, theory of employment? According to Hicks, there are two different standpoints. The first is to look at the book as a break from tradition, by accepting 'directly Mr Keynes' elaborate disquisitions about his own theory, and its place in the development of economics; praising or blaming the alleged more than Jevonian revolution' (Hicks, 1936a: 238). The second is to adopt a more accommodating point of view, and 'investigating these disquisitions, and tracing (perhaps) a pleasing degree of continuity and tradition, surviving the revolution from the *ancien régime*' (*ibid.*).

Between the two options, Hicks – at least on the face of it – preferred not to choose, while trying to judge the new theory on its own merits. In so doing he was able to assess the importance of the interweaving, in

Keynes's book, between the theory of output and the theory of money. Despite being quite sympathetic with *The Treatise on Money* (Keynes, 1930), Hicks acknowledges that the new book is not only about money, but appears as a 'superior re-formulation' that 'breaks away from the whole of this range of ideas.' It is 'primarily...a theory of employment; but before the book is ended, both author and reader are convinced that it is not only a theory of employment. It is sometimes presented as a theory of "output in general"; sometimes as a theory of "shifting equilibrium"' (Hicks, 1936a: 238). Truly well-deserved words! All in all, the review article is well balanced, and thorough in highlighting the novelties of *The General Theory*. Hicks does not mention explicitly the principle of effective demand, but he does deal at length with the marginal efficiency of capital, the role of expectations in triggering investments, the new interpretation of the interest rate, and, above all, the dynamic frame that he sees embodied in *The General Theory*, as compared with the static stand of traditional analysis. In this review, however, there is no attempt to simplify the message, even though it was obvious that the book needed a sort of 'portable' version to make its contents more acceptable both to economists and to policy-makers.

Attempts to squeeze from Keynes's book a simple and manageable model were in fact under way in the work of many young economists. A seminar (organized by the Econometric Society) that took place in autumn 1936 at Oxford, eight months after the publication of the book, became the main arena for presenting such efforts. Hicks participated in it, after having carefully read the papers that Roy Harrod and James Meade were going to present on the same occasion.[3] Hicks's, Harrod's, and Meade's papers all had the same aim, of outlining a formalized model squeezed out of Keynes's novel work. Indeed, at some level of abstraction, all three papers do have something in common that recalls what nowadays is presented in the textbooks as the IS-LM apparatus. Hicks was rewarded with more success than the other two, however.

He arrived at Oxford with the aim of framing the *General Theory* into a simpler, manageable, not too disruptive model. The paper was later published (1937a) with the title 'Mr Keynes and the "Classics": a Suggested Interpretation.' And it is from this work that what we nowadays call 'the neoclassical synthesis' developed and made its way as the most popular interpretation of Keynesian economic theory.

What did Hicks do? As the title suggests, he proposed a 'little apparatus to elucidate the relation between Keynes and the classics,' where the

---

[3] They were later published respectively in Meade (1937) and Harrod (1937).

classics are in Hicks's (and in Keynes's) language the predecessors of Keynes. Hicks produced a mix of equations and graphs (his original SI-LL curves), which later became known as the IS-LM Keynesian model. Markets (both the goods and the money markets) were connected and an equilibrium was always guaranteed.

It was a kind of simple 'hydraulic' interpretation of *The General Theory*. Following its inclusion in later editions of Samuelson's textbook on *Economics* (1948), its didactical success has become irresistible. Some further refinements of the neoclassical synthesis[4] have turned this model from a suggested into the accepted interpretation of Keynes's *General Theory*. To explain the extent of this success, there is more than one reason.

To begin with, the IS-LM skeleton, as compared with Keynes's book, was indeed simpler, avoiding all the complexities of language and inter-pretations of *The General Theory*.[5] Moreover, contrary to what Keynes believed, the use of formalized models and graphical representations was congenial to the current development of economics teaching and research, since it allowed and stimulated further model-building.

The story of the reactions to Hicks's paper is quite well known. Keynes received a copy from Hicks himself, and left it for a long while in his in tray. Eventually he replied to it, after almost seven months. His opening few lines, at face value, could be classified as falling somewhere between formal appreciation and indifference: 'I found it very interesting and I have next to nothing to say by way of criticism' (Keynes, 1937b: 79). This reply remains puzzling. What is certain is that Keynes's published article in *The Quarterly Journal of Economics* (1937a), in which he explains the essence of his new *General Theory*, stands in sharp contrast with the theory captured by the IS-LM model. In fact, Hicks's central aim – as he explicitly pointed out – was to reframe the *General Theory* in terms of Walrasian general equilibrium. This operation did not destroy Keynes's 1936 book, but it certainly deformed it, precisely in the way of neutralizing its revolutionary spirit. This notwithstanding, the IS-LM apparatus has been perceived ever since as a true piece of Keynesian economics.

The big question, which is still not fully answered, is why Keynes and his pupils at Cambridge did not react to Hicks's apparatus, right from the start, much more firmly than they did. The answer remains to a large

---

[4] The term 'neoclassical synthesis' itself appears in the fourth edition (1958) of Samuelson's textbook, published ten years after its first edition.

[5] A survey by Weintraub (1979) almost three decades ago counted no fewer than 4,827 different interpretations of Keynes's masterpiece. Hence, the problem of which one of them to pick is not a trivial one.

extent open to different explanations, which may be classified along three lines.

First, the 'public relations' argument. Keynes and the Keynesians did not react strongly to the IS-LM model because they thought it was needed to make at least some of the novel ideas of the 'Keynesian revolution' palatable to the profession. In this sense, the IS-LM model could represent a solid bridge between the old (the classic) and the new (the Keynesian) economics.

Second, the economic policy argument. Keynes wrote *The General Theory* with the same spirit in which Karl Marx wrote *Das Kapital*: to affect the world, not just to describe it. At that time the world was indeed in a bad shape, with mass unemployment disrupting the economics of all the advanced countries. Policy-makers, and policy advisers in general, needed a quick, ready-to-use recipe for taking (or suggesting) decisions concerning fiscal and monetary policy. The IS-LM was an excellent tool for these purposes. The mind can readily understand from it what happens from raising money supply, cutting taxes, or shifting public spending: curves move and a new equilibrium is reached. The economic policy revolution that Keynes was propounding – if not the revolution in economic theory – found in this manageable apparatus a justification.

Third, the underestimation argument. Keynes never thought of humility as a virtue in economics or among economists. After the publication of *The General Theory*, his main aim was to popularize it as much as possible.[6] In this view, any interpretation, above all one made by the younger generation, would be well received. There was the obvious danger of misinterpreting *The General Theory*, but the difference in stature between him and his interpreters would have counterbalanced things in the correct direction. Accordingly, Hicks was not perceived as a serious danger. Keynes probably never achieved a deep understanding of what Hicks was doing, at root, with his book, and never devoted much effort to attempting to go any further. The impression he probably had was that Hicks was a systematizer more than an original thinker.[7] In this interpretation, therefore, Hicks could have helped to popularize the message of the book without reversing the destiny of the Keynesian revolution.

Ex post that turned out to be a big mistake. The IS-LM interpretation, consolidated into the textbooks and with the help of other contributors (Alvin Hansen, Franco Modigliani, James Tobin), became the staple way of presenting Keynesian economics. What prevailed, in fact, was not

---

[6] It is by now well known that he pressed the publisher to keep the price low, so as to encourage sales of the book.

[7] See the interview of Robert Skidelsky in Snowdon and Vane (2005: 91 ff.).

Keynes's economics but what became known as the neoclassical synthesis of 'Keynes and the classics' (Hicks, 1937a).

How could Hicks achieve this? He accepted Keynes's stance that there can be equilibrium of aggregate demand and supply without full employment. In so doing, he set himself in opposition to the orthodox view (including Pigou's: 1933), according to which only frictional and voluntary unemployment could exist in equilibrium. Hence Hicks could rightly claim that he was not an anti-Keynesian. He was, rather, an un-Keynesian.

He accepted Keynes's identity of aggregate income as being equal to consumption plus investment,[8] but then he proceeded to develop the investment function, where he made the first subtle but fundamental change. Contrary to Keynes, who made investment dependent on the expected profitability of projects and the interest rate, Hicks introduced the traditional marginal productivity of capital. He shifted to the complement of the consumption function – that is, to the saving function – which is not, as it is in Keynes, simply dependent on aggregate income, but is also *instantaneously* dependent on the interest rate. Finally, he slightly modified the interest rate function itself by introducing income, alongside the falling liquidity preference schedule. In this way, consumption (although he says savings) is a function not only of income but also of the rate of interest, and demand for money is made to be dependent not only on the rate of interest but also on income. At the end of this, apparently innocuous, manipulation, Hicks had in fact broken up Keynes's basic chain of relations, which were thereby turned into a system of *simultaneous* equations – i.e. precisely the opposite of what Keynes intended to do. Hicks exploits his procedure twice over by scolding Keynes for considering only what in his simple apparatus appears as a 'particular case' of a 'more general' model, namely the particular case of a surreptitiously more general model, where the newly inserted variables have no influence.[9] The result is that a simple graph with the final criss-cross of two curves was all that was needed to express the Keynesian message that unemployment is compatible with equilibrium. The Keynesian theory was made to find its accommodating stay within the Walrasian framework, and Keynes's theoretical 'revolution' was practically over. At least, for the time being.

The dawning of doubts

It has already been said that Hicks's (1937a) 'Suggested Interpretation' of Keynes constituted the skeleton on which the neoclassical synthesis

---

[8] Surprisingly enough, in *The General Theory*, government expenditure is not made explicit.
[9] For further details, see Pasinetti (1974: 45–8).

matured and established itself in the economic profession, at least from the 1950s onwards. It looks natural to think of Hicks as the founder of this line of research; but this is not the case. Hicks was neither the founder nor (at least apparently) an official supporter of these neoclassical developments. Their architects should be looked for elsewhere.[10] They did indeed use Hicks's 'Suggested Interpretation' as a starting point. Hicks himself during those decades was working on other subjects. In 1939 he published *Value and Capital* – a work on value, much nearer the interests being pursued at the LSE than those being pursued at Cambridge. No doubt he did not like the American approach to economics, but neither did he like the Cambridge attitude.

Before the outbreak of the Second World War Hicks moved to Manchester, remaining there throughout the conflict (1938–46), and the central subjects of his research became the so-called 'new welfare economics.'[11] At that time, in the United Kingdom, the temples of economics were Cambridge, Oxford, and the LSE. Everywhere else was considered peripheral. After the war Hicks clearly perceived the remoteness of Manchester, and he looked around for a new place. In 1946 he was able to leave his professorship at Manchester University and return, with a tenured post, to Oxford, his alma mater. Before settling there, however, he made his first visit to the United States.

After so many years of blackout, he 'found out what had been happening' (1984a: 287) on the other side of the ocean. He was surprised to find that his *Theory of Wages* and *Value and Capital* were so popular among graduate students and professors, and that their author was rather well known and respected among them. Even more surprised was he to discover that he was thought to be the founder of what was becoming known as the 'neoclassical synthesis.' Amazingly enough, he was not at all happy to learn this. What American economists liked of his books and 1937 article was connected with their static settings. In fact, he discovered that the second part of *Value and Capital* – concerned with dynamics – was far less popular. When he met the cream of American economists (including the then younger and promising generation, such as Arrow, Friedman, Patinkin, and Samuelson), he tried to convince them that 'my Walrasian–Wicksellian approach (more fully developed in *Value and Capital*, but already represented in *The Theory of Wages*)' was too static. He realized, however, that 'it was on this kind of thing that the Americans themselves

---

[10] A small sample of them may be the following: Modigliani, James Duesenberry, Lawrence Klein, Tobin, James Meade, Don Patinkin, Paul Samuelson, Robert Solow.
[11] The works of reference here are more numerous: Hicks (1939b, 1941b, 1942b, 1944, 1945b); see also Hicks (1950a, 1950b, 1950c, 1950f).

were building [their theories]' (Hicks, 1963: 312). He left the United States without much sympathy for the way the American economists were doing economics: 'I did not know them...but they did know me. I am afraid I disappointed them; and have continued to disappoint them. Their achievements have been great; but they are not in my line' (Hicks, 1984a: 287).

His lines of interest were broadening in several directions, and at least a few of them continued to overlap with those that were so dear to the Cambridge Keynesian school. Hicks went on to publish his contributions on trade cycle theory (1950a) and on growth and capital (1965), touching subjects such as fluctuations, economic growth, and capital theory that were central to the works of people such as Michał Kalecki, Harrod, Richard Kahn, Nicholas Kaldor, and Joan Robinson, who were convinced of the necessity of pushing ahead with Keynes's revolution. The treatment of Hicks was still largely based on his earlier simplifying apparatus, however. In writing his *Contribution to the Theory of the Trade Cycle* (1950a), he had been inspired by reading and reviewing (Hicks, 1949) Harrod's *Towards a Dynamic Economics* (1948). Hicks's book exploited the interaction between the multiplier (present in *The General Theory* and proposed by Kahn, 1931) and the accelerator mechanism (Harrod, Kalecki, Kaldor, Samuleson). He tried to constrain the extreme instability of Harrod's model by introducing a *ceiling* and a *floor*, thereby groping for an explanation of the coexistence of fluctuations and growth.[12]

Capital and Growth was a further step forward (Hicks, 1965). Hicks purposefully avoided getting directly in touch with the Cambridge Keynesians, however, and even more getting involved with the capital controversy between the two Cambridges, although at some point he wrote about it (1965, 1973b, 1974c). He was clearly conscious that he was moving toward fields of investigation in which Kaldor and Robinson had been working. He avoided getting into any discussions with them, however. After *Capital and Growth* he decided to bring together all his works on money in a single volume – *Critical Essays in Monetary Theory* (Hicks, 1967a), adding some essays that were completely new. One of them was particularly relevant, 'Monetary Theory and History: An Attempt at Perspective' (1967a: 155–73). Money and history! The mix was explosive in Hicks's evolving thought. A storm of excruciating doubts was gathering. At this stage, J. R., the uncle, was irretrievably retreating. A wide space was opening up, favoring the birth and growth of John, the nephew.

---

[12] For an attempt at systematizing this family of models, see Pasinetti (1960).

'Conversion'

The arguments that Hicks came to develop on money and history are simple, but disruptive. In monetary theory 'the question is not merely analytical, it is also historical' (1967a: 155). In other words, a good monetary theory should be 'less abstract than most economic theory; it cannot avoid a relation to reality, which in other economic theory is sometimes missing. It belongs to monetary history in a way that economic theory does not always belong to economic history' (156).[13] This call for history stands in complete contrast to the mainstream attitude of looking at an economic system in a static and logical time setting, where the future simply reproduces the past.

This interest in connecting history and theory, in opposition to equilibrium, was one of the first notable signals characterizing the emergence of John, the 'nephew.' It may be worth mentioning that a similar connection and opposition emerged in the writings of Keynes, *before* his 'revolution.' In 1923 he wrote: 'Economists set themselves too easy, too useless a task if in tempestuous seasons they can only tell us that when the storm is long past the ocean is flat again' (Keynes, 1923: 88). The flat ocean did not satisfy Hicks either. Quite coherently, he began in 1967–9 to shift his research considerably toward the study of economic theory *with* economic history (Hicks, 1969a).

To be fair, the interest in history was not new in Hicks. His father, Edward, had initiated young John at the age of seven in the study of the Greeks and Romans. The novelty, though, in the 1960s, consisted in a theoretical economist (and a successful one) moving toward this subject when very few economic theorists would ever write a paragraph on economic history. Hicks wrote a book as a the result of his Gregynog lectures at the University of Wales, in 1967, on 'economic theory and economic history.' His subject matter bore a resemblance to the method of the classical economists and of the Keynesian school of economics, in that it was looking at the evolution of economic systems in historical time rather than in a logical time.

It must be said, however, that, despite this big step made by Hicks, his conception of the relationship between history and theory was not exactly coincidental with that of the classical economists or of the Keynesian school. Especially with respect to the latter, Hicks was on a 'traverse,' in more than one sense. 'My theory of history,' Hicks argues at the beginning of his book (1969a: 2) 'will...be a good deal nearer to the kind of thing

---

[13] A detailed analysis of Hicks's monetary theory and history has been carried out by Giuseppe Fontana (2004).

that was attempted by Marx, who did take from his economics some general ideas which he applied to history, so that the pattern which he saw in history had some extra-historical support.' A scholar of Marx would probably argue that the author of *Das Kapital* produced his theory *after* having interpreted history, and not the other way around.

Nevertheless, the novel feature is the close connection (in Hicks, 1969a) of theorization and historical evolution. In comparison to the previous Hicksian works, *A Theory of Economic History* is in a league of its own. It is the starting point of what may well be regarded as the 'conversion' of Hicks. The crucial and distinctive element that made this book different from the earlier ones was that Hicks left aside equilibrium and steady-state positions, and began to look at economies as systems that change over time in quantitative as well as in qualitative terms.

The book that followed, *Capital and Time* (1973a), goes even further and deeper in this direction. By this stage it belongs – as Hicks explains – to the collection of John, the nephew. It is a purely theoretical work, which takes seriously the unorthodox Austrian approach, according to which economic variables, and capital in particular (i.e. that factor of production peculiar to the industrial age), cannot be theorized without a proper conceptualization of the time dimension. The next year, just to mark his change of interests, Hicks published his Yrjo Jahnsson Lecture on *The Crisis in Keynesian Economics* (1974b), touching on three main topics of extreme relevance: investments and the multiplier effect, money and liquidity preference, and wages and inflation.

Hence, when Geoffrey Harcourt, in organizing a symposium for *The Economic Record* on a 'Revival of Political Economy,' traced the path of research of various neoclassical authors – Hicks included – as a long continuum of smooth development, the consequence was to trigger Hicks's reaction (1975b: 365):

Clearly I need to change my name. Let it be understood that *Value and Capital* was the work of J. R. Hicks, a 'neoclassical' economist now deceased; while *Capital and Time* – and *A Theory of Economic History* – are the work of John Hicks, a non-neoclassic who is quite disrespectful towards his 'uncle.' The latter works are meant to be read independently, and not be interpreted, as Harcourt interprets them, in the light of their predecessor. They themselves do however belong together. They are both of them fruits of a historical approach. In *A Theory of Economic History* this is explicit (and developed much further than the economists whom Harcourt admires have ever developed it); in *Capital and Time* it is implicit, and no doubt less obvious. Yet the purpose of *Capital and Time* can still be explained in terms which historians could understand. For it is now widely accepted, among them, that the course of events in history can only be explained by what they call counter-factual analysis; by supposing that something which did happen did not happen, and asking what difference that would have made to the course of events.

His 'conversion' is thereby made public. Time and history are coming to change Hicks's conception of the way economic theory should be pursued. His distancing himself from the lines of research of the neoclassical school (recall his visit to the United States) becomes, by the 1970s, a definite and explicit break. Almost forty years after his 'Mr Keynes and the "Classics"' – as Joan Robinson wrote with disrespectful sarcasm – 'John Hicks noticed the difference between the future and the past and became dissatisfied with IS/LM, but (presumably to save face for his predecessor, J. R.) he argued that Keynes's analysis was only half *in time* and half in equilibrium' (Robinson, 1978b: 13).

In the fifteen years following his 'confession' Hicks's research interests were clearly converging toward those topics that were so dear to the Cambridge pupils of Keynes, while he distanced himself further and further from the followers of the Walrasian method, mainly located on the other side of the Atlantic. One must hastily add, however, that, despite these changes, Hicks did not become part of the Cambridge Keynesians. He remained Hicks, in the sense that his independent mind always refused to be part of any school of thought.

In the 1980s he declared his 'dissatisfaction' with the IS-LM apparatus most openly (1980).[14] His repudiation of what had become the standard way of presenting Keynes's ideas is without reservation, but – one must add, to be meticulous – not crystal-clear either. It looks as if the author has already moved miles away from the positions of J. R., the uncle, so as to need no pleading to be believed or to be convincing.

The sociology-of-science view of these events adjusted accordingly. The Cambridge Keynesians cheered the courage of John, the nephew – a Nobel Prize-winner who, at the height of his professional success, had the courage to make his turnabout public.[15] On the other side, the American neoclassical colleagues did not like 'Sir John.' Their reactions were a mixture of indifference and disappointment, if not outsight opposition. They continued to think that the real Hicks was J. R., the 'uncle,' and they continued to study and celebrate the earlier, rather than the later, Hicks. Solow made the point explicit in a friendly but firm way, in delivering the first Oxford Lecture dedicated to Hicks (Solow, 1984).

Neither group, however, discussed openly the motivations that induced Hicks to change his mind. To avoid the same criticism, let us gather at

---

[14] The precise words are: 'I have myself become dissatisfied' (1980: 139).

[15] Some indication that Hicks did not put too much credence in the official reason given for his Nobel Prize, jointly awarded to him with Kenneth Arrow, was that his Nobel lecture in 1972 was devoted to economic growth, and not to 'general equilibrium and welfare economics,' for which the Prize was awarded.

least a short list of reasons (we shall mention five) that may explain why John, the nephew, could no longer associate himself with J. R., the 'deceased' uncle.

First, Hicks realizes that, in a production monetary economy in which there is division of labor, merchants and producers no longer coincide, and there is no guarantee that they behave in a way compatible with an economic equilibrium, let alone a stable one. In these conditions, unemployment is a realistic possibility, since markets may not clear. This means that the classical notion of equilibrium is out of place in the study of a modern economy – 'a deliberate violence to the real world,' which is 'a nonsense,' as he writes (Hicks, 1977a).

Second, Hicks concedes that in modern (industrial) markets the adjustment mechanism of demand and supply is reliant on quantities more than on prices. Therefore, any attempt to apply a Walrasian model to modern economies becomes questionable right from the start.

Third, John, the nephew, is convinced that the modern economic system should not only be studied in dynamic terms, but also placed in historical time – acknowledging the irreversibility of the past and the uncertainty of the future, and that the past and the future may be qualitatively different.

Fourth, in the analysis of a production economy, stocks and flows coexist but should not be mixed up, as erroneously happens in the Walrasian model. In a growth model, one should keep the analysis of flow equilibrium (or, for the matter, disequilibrium) separate from that of stock equilibrium (or disequilibrium).

Fifth, adopting historical time in economics brings serious consequences for the modeling of a monetary economy. Money cannot simply be thought of as a means of payment; it should also be thought of as a store of value, in which credit and debt contracts are the norm rather than the exception. In this situation, money becomes a key tool to deal with the uncertainty of the future, making a simultaneous Walrasian trading model – or, for that matter, any model that treats money as a simple veil of the real economy – entirely obsolete and unsuitable.[16]

William Baumol, who also wrote about the mismatch of J. R. and John, contended that taking into account all the objections made by John, the nephew, would be tantamount to making it impossible to have any economic theory at all, at least in the traditional way that we know (Baumol, 1990). This is correct, but it is precisely the point that Hicks's 'conversion'

---

[16] Hicks (even 'uncle' J. R.) always considered the monetary part of *The General Theory* as truly set in dynamic terms, and therefore as taking a genuinely novel approach with respect to anything previously known (see Hicks, 1982a).

is raising: not the need to abolish economic theory altogether, but the need to find a different way to carry it on – less abstract, more history-friendly, less technical, more concerned with real economic phenomena, less reductionist, and more open to taking advantage of the contributions coming from other social and moral sciences (Hicks, 1984b). Even at first glance, one realizes that all these points are the very ones that motivated many followers of Keynes to pursue a different – indeed, an alternative – way of doing economics. The question to be answered is: has John, the nephew, ended up adhering to this alternative approach to economic theory, or, if not, what else?

What sort of conversion?

The tormenting thoughts and doubts about the genuineness of any important 'conversion' have provided a classic locus throughout world literature. In this vein, it is natural to wonder whether Hicks's 'conversion' from J. R. to John was a truly genuine one. We can safely say that it was, in one sense, but that, in another, it was not.

It was certainly genuine in the negative sense that Hicks became *increasingly* dissatisfied with the way the works of the first part of his career had been used – as building blocks to strengthen and expand mainstream theory, from which he distanced himself at a certain point, both in substance and in method. This meant that Hicks disagreed on the instrumental use of his works to pursue certain objectives. Even more, he disagreed on the selective use of his work that left some parts of them – from his point of view equally important – in total oblivion. Hicks never wrote with the purpose of serving a particular school of thought. When he realized that the content of some works of his opened the way to strengthening a particular approach to economics, he reacted critically, no matter how crucial his contributions were supposed to have been to the foundations of those developments.

When Hicks put history and money at the center of his interests (this occurring, as we have seen, at the end of 1960s) he realized the extent of the unrealism, abstraction, and reductionism that had characterized his previous work, and even more the unrealism, abstraction, and reductionism that his colleagues had made of his previous work. Hence his new position on the dynamic nature of industrial economies, the centrality of money in running them, the need to look more at chains of causation (that is, to look at the processes of evolution) rather than to equilibrium: all this was indeed strongly and genuinely felt. Moreover, his firm criticism and rejection of the use of the production function apparatus (Hicks's Nobel lecture; 1973c); his rejection of the IS-LM equations as central to explaining macroeconomics and to interpreting Keynesian economics; his refusal to accept ad hoc hypotheses in open contrast to reality, such as the decreasing returns to scale (1989b); his considering money and time as weak, if not missing, points in the neoclassical framework were all equally authentic (1989a).

All the same, it would be unjustified to regard all this as a full 'conversion,' in the positive sense of having underwritten a well-defined theoretical framework, as an alternative to, and in opposition to, the one followed by mainstream economists. Throughout his life Hicks continued to maintain a sort of scientific relativism (1979a, 1984b). His opinion was – and remained – that phenomena in the social sciences are too variegated to be captured by a unique economic paradigm. To put it differently: there is room in economics for theories of production as well as for theories of exchange. He kept his distance from his earlier works, but more for the use that others made of them than for the ideas he developed himself. In other words, John's disrespect for his uncle, J. R., did not go so far as to disclaim him as a relative.

He never dared to state explicitly a clean fracture between old and new Hicksian views. Revolutions in economic thought, for him, were not like political *coups d'état*. He felt that economics could be more at ease with slow evolutions of thinking rather than with sudden turmoil. He accepted, by the way, that the evolution of thinking could go in the wrong as well as in the right direction. Indeed, he did not agree with the direction followed by the majority of his colleagues in the twentieth century. That was not enough for him, however, to embrace an opposing school of thought. Hicks, the nephew, though sharing, late in life, the views of the more sanguine and faithful followers of Keynes, never embraced the idea of becoming part of their group. In this sense, he never abandoned the uniform of a school of thinking, because he had never dressed in one in the first place.

Final remarks: the Hicks dilemma

Hicks was, and remained, an independent thinker. He paid a high price for this independence, by being surrounded by an atmosphere of solitude both in Cambridge and in Oxford – the two places that housed him in the critical moments of his academic life. The companionship of Ursula and the friendship of many (often Italian) colleagues and students who visited him regularly at his home provided some counterbalance against academic isolation.[17]

---

[17] The editors of this book were among the best examples of this kind.

It is in fact not surprising that, unlike many of his colleagues, Hicks did not claim to belong to a specific school of thought; even less that he should aim at founding one. This was in line with his introverted character, and even more so with his methodological stand. He has left us a remarkable example of scientific honesty in not hiding the 'structural break' that took place in his way of doing economics.

This chapter has focused on this break, in an attempt to uncover the reasons that lay behind it and the lessons that, in general, may be drawn from it. For the supporters of J. R., the neoclassical uncle, there seems to be very little, if any, to be learned from John, the nephew. For those who do not belong to mainstream economics and look with interest at alternative theories, however, the lessons to be learned are significant, though not always simple.

To begin with, Hicks makes us reflect on the technicalities of the economic profession. Any technicality, but in particular the technicalities adopted in the social sciences, should not be allowed to become so invasive as to superimpose themselves on the scientific agenda. In our case, if economists have paid a good deal of attention to the issue of equilibrium and very little to the issue of historical evolution, this is not because the former is more relevant than the latter, but because it has appeared better in terms of the toolbox that economists have been accustomed to use. In this way, the analytical tools that should serve the profession become the masters, however, and the economic topics that should be the masters of our research become the servants.

Second, Hicks, the nephew, explicitly invokes an economic discipline that is not blinkered and closed in on itself. To be relevant, an economist needs a continuous dialogue and confrontation with other social scientists, and with other disciplines too. There is no real room for a reductionist approach in economics. In natural science (as in physics) things may be different; but all this means is that to go on uncritically to study economics as we study physics cannot be right.

Third, on a more specific issue, Hicks warns us that money, on the one hand, and historical time, on the other, break up the Walrasian system in a way that cannot be fixed. Economics needs to deal with these two issues in a very different (if not in an alternative) way. Going back to his own IS-LM apparatus, what is the point of persisting in using it if we know that the two curves continue to move, to change shape, to shift at any swing of each variable? What is the point of sticking with something that – as a macroeconomic generalization – is proved to be defective?

These are really worrying points. It is not difficult to realize that Keynes would have been pleased to hear all of them. They are not an irrelevant part of the reasons why he advocated a 'revolution in economics,' both in theory and in policy. The same remarks that Hicks made against some hesitancy in *The General Theory* about accepting in full the theoretical consequences of the points stated above may be shared by several followers of the Cambridge Keynesian school of economics. Indeed, this is why they have persisted in their conviction of the necessity to pursue and accomplish Keynes's revolutionary research program.

Admittedly, looking back at the difficulties that such a 'revolution in economics' has caused for the profession, some justification may be found in Hicks's more flexible attitude and in his cautious stand with regard to drastic changes in economic theory. This may well be understandable, but we have to admit that it is also questionable. Supposing that we share the views of John, the nephew, does that mean that we should not go beyond the critique of the dominant approach? Or does it mean that we should also be constructive in offering a clearly alternative theory to mainstream economics? This is the dilemma that Hicks has left unanswered. Those of us who in the past few decades have adhered to the belief that there exists an alternative theory, consistent with, and in fact more suitable to, Keynes's conception of a *monetary production economy*, will try to use their efforts and John Hicks's remarks in order to solve the dilemma in a positive way.

4   Dear John, Dear Ursula (Cambridge and LSE, 1935): eighty-eight letters unearthed

Maria Cristina Marcuzzo and Eleonora Sanfilippo

Introduction

Eighty-eight letters were unearthed while sifting through the Hicks papers at the library of the University of Hyogo, Japan, in December 2003.[1] They had been written between September and December 1935, when John Hicks left the LSE[2] for Cambridge, having being appointed university lecturer and fellow of Gonville and Caius College, while Ursula (then Webb) was at the LSE, where she had been a student from 1929 and was currently a member of the staff. The letters cover the three months preceding their wedding, which took place in London, on December 17, 1935.

It is a daily exchange, with just the odd interruption marking the days when they would visit each other (mostly at weekends) either in Cambridge or in London. It is a portrait of a marriage in the making, a picture of an academic milieu and a glimpse into British society in the 1930s.

It may be objected that making them public is barely justified by the copyright permission obtained with purchase of the papers, but we

We would like to thank Irini Liakopoulou, Alexandra Saunders, and Emiliano Vendittelli for invaluable research assistance; and Mauro Baranzini, Roger Backhouse, Daniele Besomi, Victoria Chick, Guido Erreygers, Omar Hamouda, Donald Moggridge, Nerio Naldi, Tiziano Raffaelli, Alessandro Roncaglia, and Annalisa Rosselli for comments, suggestions, and help in clarifying various matters. We are also particularly indebted to Sue Howson for her precious help in reconstructing the events and circumstances referred to in the letters. For the relevant information about the people whose names are mentioned in the chapter, we drew extensively on Besomi (2003a), Howson (2005), and Moggridge (1992). An earlier version of this chapter, together with the eighty-eight letters between John and Ursula, can be found in Hirai *et al.* (2005).

[1] The research was undertaken by M. C. Marcuzzo and A. Rosselli as part of a joint project with the Japanese group on Cambridge economists, in collaboration with T. Hirai, Y. Hakamata and T. Nishizawa (see www2u.biglobe.ne.jp/~olympa/cambridge/hyoushi/), who made possible access to and digital reproduction of the letters. The letters were later catalogued, indexed and transcribed by E. Sanfilippo. Copyright of the correspondence between John and Ursula Hicks is with the University of Hyogo.

[2] Hicks taught at the LSE from 1926 to 1935 (Hicks, 1982b: 5).

sincerely hope that disclosure of them will be accepted as a tribute to – rather than an intrusion into – their relationship.

A few words of justification are also needed on the relevance of the correspondence in reconstructing ideas as well as facts. Most of our understanding of the past is heavily dependent on the sources we have access to. The failure to grasp concepts and debates occurring in more or less remote times is due to our reliance on contemporary language and mindset, and to a lack of knowledge sufficient to place those concepts and debates in their context.[3] Correspondence offers the opportunity to approach opinions, ideas, and feelings in the appropriate setting; it also opens the way for us to retrieve information long wrapped in oblivion. And, of course, it satisfies curiosity – a form of indulgence that is nevertheless the prime mover of any historical investigation.

Cambridge and the LSE

What were Cambridge and the LSE like in the mid-1930s? Much has been written about the rivalry between the two economics faculties, divided by style of teaching, intellectual climate, theoretical approaches, and politics. Above all, perhaps, it was a matter of personalities: the domineering influence of John Maynard Keynes and his pupils on the one hand, and Lionel Robbins and Friedrich Hayek with their supporters on the other. The way discussion was organized between students and staff is also worth comparing. First of all there were the two seminars, Robbins's on Monday afternoon (Howson, 2005: 22) and Keynes's every other Monday in the evenings during term time.[4] According to one of the accounts by a contemporary, A. K. Dasgupta:

Lionel Robbins would allocate papers on subjects topical because of some important publication...to about eight research students [and] teachers would also be present. The papers would be read, then 'cyclostyled' and discussed in a kind of second-reading debate a week later. Over tea, groups would be formed to discuss a particular paper further in considerable detail. Sometimes one paper remained on the seminar agenda for several weeks, with Robbins in the Socratic role...In the end, Robbins would turn to the teachers. 'Hicks, do you have anything to say?' Sometimes he did, and sometimes he did not. (Dahrendorf, 1995: 298)

---

[3] Personal papers are among the most important archival sources for historians. It is a shame to disperse them in separate batches. The Hicks papers – like the Harrod papers, which were sold in seven batches (see Besomi, 2003: xxxi) – are, sadly, a case in point. They are at present divided into two batches, one held at the University of Hyogo, the other at the Hicks Foundation in Oxford.

[4] Robbins's seminar started in 1929 (Robbins, 1971: 131; Howson, 2005: 3) and Keynes's seminar yet earlier, around 1909 (Skidelsky, 1992: 5).

74   *Maria Cristina Marcuzzo and Eleonora Sanfilippo*

Keynes's political economy seminar ('Keynes's club') was run in a different fashion. According to Lorie Tarshis, who was a student there in 1935:

Kahn [was] invariably present with a sprinkling of other faculty members... Sometimes academics from outside Cambridge attended too [and] there was a contingent of students, a very few research students amongst them and perhaps ten or twelve undergraduates. [A paper was read by Keynes or a distinguished visitor, and students whose slips had been drawn were expected to stand up and comment on it; see Plumptre, 1947: 370–1; Moggridge, 1992: 189; and Skidelsky, 1992: 5.] After the students had made their remarks, we all were served tea and fruit cake. Then Keynes asked each of the faculty members and distinguished visitors present whether he wished to speak. And after that Keynes stood up. [...] Sometimes – I guess usually – the paper and the discussion that followed it were merely the spring-board from which after gentle criticism and encouragement for the students who had participated, he jumped into any or many related topics – with a wit, a grace and an imagination that were a joy to experience. (Patinkin and Leith, 1977: 50–1)

From the many accounts and recollections (see Robbins, 1971; Coase, 1982; Hicks, 1979b, 1982b; Kaldor, 1986b; Thirlwall, 1987; Shehadi, 1991; Hamouda, 1993; Dahrendorf, 1995; and Hayek, 1995 [1963]) we can infer that Robbins's seminar was more cosmopolitan, attracting mostly Continental scholars and visitors passing through London, while Keynes's seminar was much more imbued with the clubby atmosphere that permeated Cambridge societies and colleges. Moreover, the two theoretical approaches favored at the LSE and Cambridge could not be farther apart. Hicks recalls of himself and his LSE colleagues:

[W]e seemed, at the start, to share a common view point, or even a common faith. The faith in question was a belief in the free market, or 'price mechanism' that a competitive system, free of all 'interferences,' by government or monopolistic combinations, of capital or of labour, would easily find an 'equilibrium.' [...] Hayek, when he joined us, was to introduce into this doctrine an important qualification – that money (somehow) must be kept 'neutral,' in order that the mechanism should work smoothly. (Hicks, 1982b: 3)

By contrast, Austin Robinson's account of the making of the Keynesian revolution brings to light the loss of faith in the market mechanism, neutrality of money, and laissez-faire. In particular, he writes: 'We learned to distinguish very clearly...between those propositions that are universally true and those propositions that are only true in conditions of full employment...[What we learned] was really the integration of value theory and monetary theory into what we now call macroeconomics' (Robinson, 1985: 57).

In the mid-1930s the clash between the two faculties of economics was in full spate, with some people totally integrated, others – such as Nicholas Kaldor and Abba Lerner – on the verge of leaving one camp for the other, and yet others – Dennis Robertson, to name but one – already feeling misplaced in their own territory. Meetings between economists from London and Cambridge and academic seminars were more frequent than ever before, providing an arena for confrontation and challenge.

Besides Robbins's and Keynes's seminars there were the much older 'London Political Economy Club,' founded in 1822 (Skidelsky, 1992: 22; see also Moggridge, 1992: 172), and the 'Economic Club,' attended by people from the LSE and Cambridge and, more generally, economists working in London. The latter was founded in 1891 and was held for a period of time at University College London (*Twenty-eighth Annual Report of The Economic Club* and letter from B. Lander to J. Mair, October 10, 1923, in BEV[5] papers Suppl. 376; see also Moggridge, 1992: 175). In 1923 – while William Henry Beveridge was president – the Economic Club moved to the LSE[6] (letter from B. Lander to J. Mair, October 12, 1923, in BEV papers Suppl. 376). To these should be added at least three more, extensively referred to in the correspondence between John and Ursula – as we shall see: the so-called 'Joint Seminar,' which started in November 1935, involving mainly research students (but also senior economists) from the LSE and Cambridge; the 'Cambridge Graduate Seminar' (known as 'Sraffa's seminar'), which also saw the occasional participation of people from London; and 'Hayek's seminar,' addressed specifically to Hayek's students.[7]

Let us now look more closely at this environment, where our two characters will be seen living, working, and loving each other, exchanging between themselves accounts of their feelings.

The meeting grounds

Since the early part of 1933 the younger generations from Cambridge and the LSE had been seeking a meeting ground 'to get together behind the

---

[5] References to the Beveridge Papers are given as BEV, according to the classification of the catalogue of the London School of Economics Archives, London.

[6] According to the 'rules' of the club, '[I]ts object...[is] the study of Economics' and the 'Club meetings are held on the Second Tuesday in each month at 8 p.m.' The list of the members in 1922 included, for example, Beveridge (president from 1922 to 1924), Harold Laski, and Marjori Tappan Hollond from the LSE, Keynes, Herbert Foxwell, and Alfred Marshall from Cambridge, and members of the Treasury such as Ralph Hawtrey and Henry Higgs (*Twenty-eighth Annual Report of The Economic Club*, in BEV papers Suppl. 376). In November 1935 – when John and Ursula corresponded – Hayek was elected as president of the 'Economic Club,' and Hicks had just resigned as one of the honorary secretaries. In 1936–7 some of the members, besides Hicks and Beveridge, were Lionel Robbins, G. L. S. Shackle, and Nicholas Kaldor, and also R. G. D. Allen, Hugh Dalton, and Evan Durbin (*Forty-first* and *Forty-second Annual Report of The Economic Club*, in BEV papers Suppl. 376).

[7] For a reconstruction of the seminars that took place in that period at the LSE, see also McCormick (1992: 29).

backs of their embattled seniors' (Robinson, 1951: viii). In October 1933 a new journal was launched – *The Review of Economic Studies*: the 'children's magazine,' as it was referred to in the correspondence between Keynes, Joan Robinson, and Richard Kahn (see, for example, the letter from J. Robinson to Keynes, September 28, 1937, in JMK[8] papers CO/8/232-5, and the letter from J. Robinson to Kahn, September 13, 1933, in RFK papers 13/90/1/253-5). According to Kaldor, '*The Review* was conceived as an outlet for young writers. Its continuance depended on the extraordinary energy of two people, Abba Lerner and Ursula Webb, who organized printers, produced estimates, read all the proofs and recruited subscribers' (Kaldor, 1986b: 41).

The most colorful account of one of the meetings of the group behind *The Review* is by Joan Robinson:

[A] weekend meeting was arranged at an inn half-way between London and Cambridge. Cambridge was represented by Kahn, Austin Robinson and myself, and James Meade who had been back in Oxford for a year... Abba Lerner brought three contemporaries (none of whom remained in the profession). It was agreed that there should be no appeal to authority; every point must be argued out on its merits. At the first session, James explained the multiplier; Kahn, who came later, went over it again. Then it was the turn of London. They said that before they could discuss employment they must analyse what would happen if everybody confidently expected that the world was coming to an end in six months' time. [...] The point was to distinguish what capital goods could be consumed in six months, by ceasing replacements from what would have to be left. [...] Next day, Abba asked to go over the multiplier argument. With some help, he repeated it correctly and seemed to be convinced. His companions were quite shocked and were seen afterwards walking him up and down the lawn, trying to restore his faith. (Robinson 1979: xv)

Quite rightly, Ursula commented to Joan Robinson: 'There is something at work emotional or extra-economic, hindering a clearer understanding I really think' (letter from Ursula to J. Robinson, November 13, 1933, in JVR papers vii/201/1).

The confrontation between the two camps was felt as a threat to either group's identity, which had been built up under the spell of Robbins and Keynes. While Cambridge people, notably Keynes, Kahn, Joan Robinson, and Piero Sraffa, each of them with his or her own agenda, were attacking traditional economic beliefs and customs, the LSE people, Hayek, Robbins, Hicks, Allen, and Kaldor were establishing an orthodoxy, based on general equilibrium and intertemporal analysis, highly formalized, and derived from first principles.

---

[8] References to the Keynes, Kahn, Kaldor, J. Robinson, and Dennis Robertson papers are given as JMK, RFK, NK, JVR, DHR respectively, according to the classification in their respective catalogues at King's College and Trinity College, Cambridge.

There were, in particular, two dividing issues. The first was whether it was legitimate to analyze imperfect competition within a partial equilibrium approach, with no consideration for strategic interaction among agents, as Joan Robinson and, to some extent, Kahn were prepared to do, against which Hicks and Kaldor were raising objections (Rosselli and Besomi, 2005).

'I think the problem of imperfect competition is harder, and less important than you do,' wrote John Hicks to Joan Robinson three months after the publication of *The Economics of Imperfect Competition* (Robinson, 1933) (letter June 15, 1933, in JVR papers vii/200/1). He maintained the same point later, when writing to her reviewing the matter for his monopoly article (Hicks, 1935b): 'I think the real difference between us is that you are more optimistic than I am about the application of the theory of imperfect competition, just because you think that theory is simpler than I do' (letter February 28, 1935, in JVR papers vii/200/25).

The second dividing issue related to the direction of causality between saving and investment and whether it should be reversed when money was explicitly taken into account. Again, it was Ursula who neatly summarized the 'differences' between the two lines of approach:

I think all the younger people at the school [the LSE] are prepared to admit that saving doesn't directly lead to investment in a monetary economy and that this may have important deflationary effects *at least when uncertainty is rampant* – but this doesn't convince us that investment is not made via monetary saving. (letter from Ursula to J. Robinson, November 13, 1933, in JVR papers vii/201/2: emphasis in original)

By the autumn of 1933 Keynes had abandoned the approach taken in the *Treatise* and was rapidly moving toward that of *The General Theory*, pressed by criticisms and help by Kahn and, to some extent, Joan Robinson and Sraffa (Marcuzzo, 2002). Discussion outside the 'inner circle' continued to revolve around the *Treatise*, whose approach had not been greeted favorably by Hicks: writing to Joan Robinson he bluntly remarked, 'I don't like the *method* of analysis [of the *Treatise*]' (letter July 12, 1933, in JVR papers vii/200/12: emphasis in original). Not surprisingly, Hicks's dislike 'for the method of fundamental equations' (letter August 16, 1933, in JVR papers vii/200/19) was shared by Robertson, who was finding in him an ally against the upsurge of the Keynesian revolution.

When his appointment to a lectureship to Cambridge was finalized,[9] however, Hicks was looking forward to the 'improving facilities for thrashing

---

[9] From the Faculty Board Minutes: 'The Appointments Committee meeting of Monday 18th February 1935 unanimously agreed to offer the vacant lectureship to Mr J. R. Hicks as

out our differences,' as he wrote to Joan Robinson, adding – with a degree of wishful thinking – that they were 'in any case tending to diminish' (letter February 28, 1935, in JVR papers vii/200/23).

As from November 1935 the Joint LSE and Cambridge Seminar crossed the *Review* board meetings, providing a further outlet for confrontation between the two groups. The Joint Seminar crossed, in particular, with Ursula's activity around *The Review*, organizing the issues and attracting people.[10] In a letter dated November 12, 1935, Ursula wrote to John: 'The following weekend we must have Pearsall[11] on the Sat.[urday] 23, as we are having Douglas [Allen][12] and possibly Maurice Allen[13] on the Sun.[day] (It is the Review weekend).' And on November 13 she wrote to him: 'I had a most friendly note from Hitch,[14] congratulating us. He is evidently very pleased to be asked to join the Review Board...and he wants to bring in Oxford to the Joint Seminar, which would be excellent.'[15]

The move to Cambridge

According to Robbins's *Autobiography*, 'Beveridge's insensate hostility to pure theory' forced John in 1935 to leave for Cambridge (Robbins, 1971: 129).[16] Hicks, typically, put it rather differently, writing – almost forty years afterwards – that '[b]y 1935, I got so much [from the LSE, where he had been member of staff since 1926] that I needed to go away to put it together. Thus when an opportunity arose for moving...I took it' (Hicks, 1972).

from October 1st 1935, and to recommend to the General Board that the probationary period of 3 years be waived in Mr Hicks's case, in view of his academic standing and teaching experience in the University of London' (FB Mins. V. 118, 27).

[10] Kaldor confirms that these seminars were reserved to research students and sometimes coincided with a meeting of *The Review* board (Kaldor, 1986b: 41).

[11] Charles William Pearsall (1880–1939), economist from South Africa.

[12] Sir Roy George Douglas Allen (1906–83), economist and mathematician.

[13] William Maurice Allen (1908–88), economist.

[14] Charles Johnston Hitch (1910–95), economist.

[15] According to a contemporary witness, 'subsequently "Oxford" was added to the seminar's title [London and Cambridge Economic Seminar] and it sometimes met there' (Brown, 1988: 36). An indirect confirmation of it can also be found in the oral recollection of Elizabeth Durbin, reported in Ebenstein (2001).

[16] This dislike of theoretical economics is confirmed by Beveridge's comments on the activities of the economics department at the LSE, quoted by Robbins in his 'Note on the Director's Reflections' (probably of November 1935), in which Beveridge is reported as saying: 'The academic developments [theoretical and mathematical] of the school within the range of my special interests [economics] have not been those which I myself should have favoured' (NK papers 2/31/102).

The opportunity[17] was a post as lecturer at the faculty of economics in Cambridge,[18] for which Pigou warmly invited him to apply.[19] It has been argued (Hamouda, 1993) that Hicks had been appointed, under the influence and initiative of Robertson and Pigou, to rein in Joan Robinson, who was all too obsessively propagating the Keynesian creed. This circumstance – according to Omar Hamouda's interpretation – would explain the coldness that Robertson apparently showed toward Hicks when he arrived at Cambridge, as Robertson wanted to avoid any public appearance of being particularly close to Hicks.

On the question of obstructing Joan Robinson's career, the evidence is that, when Keynes stepped in to prevent her proposal to give a course on money for two terms from being turned down (letter from Keynes to C. R. Fay, March 5, 1935, in JMK papers UA/14.2), Pigou supported him and a compromise was reached.[20]

What seems more likely is that Pigou, eager to maintain a certain degree of 'academic pluralism,'[21] favoured Hicks's election in the interest of achieving readjustment between the different orientations within the economics faculty, as well as counteracting Robertson's growing isolation

---

[17] From the Faculty Board Minutes: 'The Appointments Committee meeting of Friday 23 November 1934 unanimously agreed to advertise in the Reporter that the Committee expect shortly to appoint to a University Lectureship, covering economics, economic history, or political science. Applications to be submitted by 1st February 1935' (FB Mins. V. 118, 13).

[18] As from October 1, 1935, the list of members of the Cambridge faculty of economics was as follows: A. C. Pigou (professor of political economy), D. H. Robertson (reader), P. Sraffa (assistant director of research), Joan Robinson (faculty assistant lecturer); lecturers: L. Alston, C. G. Clark, M. Dobb, C. W. Guillebaud, J. R. Hicks, M. Hollond, R. F. Kahn, E. A. G. Robinson, J. Rowe, G. F. Shove, W. Thatcher (*Cambridge University Reporter*, October 1, 1935: 5).

[19] Forty-four years later Hicks gave this explanation of his move to Cambridge: 'I went there in consequence of an invitation from Pigou, and it was because of the friendship I had already formed with Robertson that I was attracted' (1984a: 285).

[20] In March 1935 Joan Robinson proposed to the faculty board (which Robertson chaired at the time) to lecture a two-term course on money for second-year students, while Robertson gave the lectures to the third-year students on the same subject. Robertson firmly opposed Robinson's lecturing: he feared, not without grounds, being ridiculed by her before his own students. Fay intervened in order to defend Robertson's point of view (letter from C. R. Fay to Keynes, March 2, 1935, in JMK papers UA/14.2). Keynes sided most decidedly in favor of Robinson, however, and in the end she taught a two-term course: applications of monetary theory (two hours per week in Michaelmas and Lent terms) followed in Easter term by a course on some problems of economic theory. The courses taught by Robinson were, however, included in the list of lectures for part II of the Economic Tripos, so that neither of them appeared as preliminary to Robertson's course on money (Moggridge, 1992; Naldi, 2005).

[21] A similar preoccupation would be expressed by Pigou a few years later, in 1938, about the editorial policy of *The Economic Journal*, which led him to a clash with Keynes (Bridel and Ingrao, 2005).

(see Sanfilippo, 2005). What is certain is that Robertson felt psychologically supported by Hicks's arrival in Cambridge, and it appears no coincidence that both decided to leave Cambridge at more or less the same time, in the autumn of 1938 (Hicks for Manchester University and Robertson for the LSE).

On the question of the supposed coldness shown toward Hicks by Robertson when they were both at Cambridge, the correspondence between John and Ursula suggests that contact between them was fairly regular: there are several references to Hicks's coming to visit Robertson, discussing with him his papers and work, and being invited by him to a Trinity feast (see, for example, the letters from John to Ursula, October 9 and 28).

Robertson's attitude may be interpreted not as coldness but as the intention to protect Hicks against the growing climate of hostility surrounding him because of his staunch opposition to *The General Theory*. This interpretation finds support in an interview with Hicks in 1983: 'The feud between Keynes and Robertson had already erupted. And they had already sort of cut the relationship, and Robertson kept out of Hicks's way. Hicks told me that was very sweet of Robertson, because Robertson thought that if he was seen associating with Hicks it would be held against him' (N. Shehadi, 'Interview to John Hicks,' 1983, History of LSE Archive, 5).

What is unquestionably true is that, in Cambridge, Hicks felt 'much closer to Robertson than to any other economists' amongst his seniors (Hicks, 1982d: 127), not only from a theoretical point of view but also at a personal level, so that he felt himself 'to be temperamentally much closer' to Robertson 'than to the Keynesians' (*ibid.*).

Hicks supervised about eighteen students of Gonville and Caius College (John to Ursula, October 8), his favourites among them being an American, M. F. Millikan,[22] and a Hungarian, P. T. Bauer.[23] He had a more or less covert agenda, as far as teaching was concerned, with the intention of 'spreading what I think to be sound doctrine among research students here.' He wrote enthusiastically that 'apparently they are already having a prolonged battle about the measurability of utility!' (John to Ursula, November 11).

---

[22] On November 7 he wrote to Ursula: 'My Mr Millikan brought me an essay this evening on the theory of interest, which was really excellent. I was tremendously cheered by it.' And again, on November 11: 'He does continually go up in my estimation.' He was a research student – not registered for a degree – whom Hicks supervised for one year (May 20, 1935, FB Mins. V. 118, 64).

[23] P. T. Bauer took a first in part I of the economic tripos in 1935.

His interest in 'spreading the sound doctrine' is attested by his willingness to do extra teaching, besides lecturing and supervising: 'I fixed up at the lecture to take a private class of half a dozen of the more promising people coming to my lectures; they want to discuss Indifference Curves, and it will be just as well for me to get to know them' (John to Ursula, November 12). Ursula, of course, endorsed the project and provided the necessary encouragement: 'The process of making Cambridge take notice is really progressing very nicely' (Ursula to John, November 12).

While in Cambridge (1935–8) Hicks lectured on the principles of economics,[24] labor problems,[25] and some leading Continental economists,[26] and was examiner in the tripos for three years.[27] His teaching in the Cambridge faculty left Keynes with a somewhat negative impression. On June 15, 1939, the year after Hicks's departure for Manchester University, Keynes wrote to Pigou:

I am just at the end of the Tripos examining. The general standard is lower than anything I have previously struck for Part II...The appalling ignorance of even the more intelligent candidates must be partly, I think, due to the breakdown of the curriculum last year through illness and leave of absence. And Hicks's teaching of the Principles has, I think, definitely confused the men and put them further back than as if they had had no such instruction.[28] (In JMK papers EJ/1/6/5–7)

Let us now turn to the issues that were topical in Cambridge and the LSE while the correspondence between John and Ursula was in course.

The issues debated during Michaelmas term 1935

During Michaelmas term 1935 *The General Theory* was going through its final stage. The previous June Keynes had sent the second proofs to Harrod, Hawtrey, Kahn and Joan Robinson. A few of their comments survive, but Hicks is not mentioned in any of the correspondence they exchanged.

---

[24] Michaelmas and Lent terms 1935, 1936, 1937 (on leave in Lent term 1938).

[25] Easter terms 1936, 1937.

[26] Easter term 1937.

[27] In 1934 Hicks had been appointed as external examiner in part II of the economic tripos, when R. Bryce and L. Tarshis took firsts. He was examiner in part II for 1935, when D. Bensusan-Butt, S. Dennison, R. Stone, and R. Simon took firsts. He was also examiner for the preliminary exam in economics in 1936. He was also appointed as examiner for part II in the tripos 1937 (October 19, 1936, FB Mins. V. 118) but he resigned at the beginning of 1937 'owing to pressure of work' (January 25, 1937, FB Mins. V. 118). He was examiner in part I for 1938.

[28] Keynes's negative opinion did not concern only Hicks's teaching. On *Value and Capital* a few months earlier Keynes wrote to Kahn: 'I don't think I have ever read a book by an obviously clever man, so free from points open to specific criticisms, which was so utterly empty' (letter from Keynes to Kahn, 11 April 1939, in RFK papers 13/57/411).

Moreover, in the letters between John and Ursula there is no reference to the process of the final drafting of Keynes's book.

Hicks must surely have been a total outsider as far as the genesis and evolution of Keynes's ideas from *The Treatise* to *The General Theory* were concerned, which does not, however, mean that their theories (as developing in the spring of 1935) were entirely devoid of points of contact. On the contrary, this letter from Keynes to Hicks, dating to April 2, 1935, clearly testifies a theoretical convergence between their researches, at least on the matter of expectations:

> Your point about the effect of the expectation of the future on current readiness to invest[29] has not yet been published, to the best of my belief, and is on rather similar lines, as I said, to what I shall be publishing in the autumn. I should rather like you to get this on record before my book[30] comes out in the autumn. (Catalogue of the Hicks papers at Oxford, 63)

While writing *The General Theory* Keynes found enthusiastic support in Cambridge from his 'inner circle' (Kahn, J. Robinson, and, much later, Harrod) but strong opposition from his otherwise close friends Sraffa and Robertson. The beginning of 1935 saw Robertson and Keynes engaged in extensive discussion of the first proofs. After reading them Robertson made a swingeingly forthright remark: 'A large part of your theoretical structure is still to me almost complete mumbo-jumbo' (letter February 10, 1935, in Moggridge, 1973a: 506).

In particular, three main analytical points underlay the controversy that saw Keynes and Robertson on opposite sides. First of all, there was the question of method. Robertson was accustomed to using a kind of sequential analysis as the only way to address the problems of economic fluctuations, cycle, depression, and, generally speaking, dynamics. He found it hard, for example, to accept Keynes's approach whereby the current level of saving was seen as a function of current income without any reference to the past level of savings – as, indeed, it was hard for him to imagine a theory of investment in which the latter was not linked to the saving decisions made in the previous periods. For the same reason, he had some doubts about the mechanism of the multiplier of investment and, in general, the short-period method, both of which Keynes derived from Kahn. He could not understand how the effect of the multiplier on income could prove instantaneous. Nor was he able to see how Keynes

---

[29] Keynes was probably referring to 'A Suggestion for Simplifying the Theory of Money' (Hicks, 1935a).
[30] *The General Theory*, which in fact appeared only in January 1936.

could speak of differences between effective demand and aggregate demand without using any kind of intertemporal method.

The second question concerned the rate of interest. Despite Keynes's arguments to the contrary, Robertson (as in his article in *The Economic Journal*: Robertson, 1931) continued to consider the rate of interest as the price bringing the demand and supply of loanable funds into equilibrium, and to consider money like every other good from the point of view of the determination of its price, pointing out that Keynes's theory of liquidity preference put undue emphasis on the speculative motive, at the expense of the transaction motive, for demanding money.

Third came the question of cycle versus long-term stagnation. Keynes was above all concerned with the problem of the tendency of contemporary capitalist economies toward a condition of persistent underemployment of resources, while Robertson, on the other hand, remained ever preoccupied with the 'old' question of business cycle. On at least two of these points (the first and the third), Hicks would surely have been on Robertson's side rather than Keynes's (see, for example, Hicks 1936a, 1956a, and 1973a).

As from March 1935 Robertson's position in Cambridge became rather difficult. There is an interesting exchange between Robertson and Hicks in 1936 showing just how badly the situation had deteriorated. Robertson, commenting on Hicks's review of *The General Theory* (Hicks, 1936a), wrote to Hicks:

It will be a comfort to find somebody who thinks there is a great deal in this book [*The General Theory*] and with whom nevertheless one can discuss – for *entre nous* my trouble is that with the author and his more whole-hearted disciples I can no longer discuss but only be made to feel obsolete and pig-headed for not having seen the light! (Letter May 20, 1936, in DHR papers C4/1.7)

Hicks replied: 'Indeed, I think our differences are less formidable than I feared they might be. I am in whole-hearted agreement with you about the critical view of the book. It is quite nonsense to pretend it is as new as it pretended' (letter May 21, 1936, in DHR papers C18/29.1–2).

Robertson also accused Hicks of having forgotten – together with Keynes – that Pigou and Marshall, in their works, had already dealt with the crucial role of expectations in the economy; Hicks defended himself, writing: 'I am particularly sorry that I should have led you to suppose that I had joined the ranks of the forgetters' (*ibid.*; see also Mizen and Presley, 1998).

In Michaelmas 1935, however, there might have been at least one possible point of convergence between Hicks and Keynes, the latter having, in the meantime, become very appreciative of Knut Wicksell. He had solicited Kahn's translation of Wicksell's *Interest and Prices*, still in the proof stage at the time. Keynes wrote to Kahn: 'Old Wicksell comes out of it, I think, extraordinarily well. Even at this time of day there are very few dull pages, and he is wonderfully on the right track. It's odd how little influence it has had, and how little progress along these obviously fruitful lines was made in the 30 years after he published it' (letter September 8, 1935, in RFK papers 13/57/137). Hicks would have been pleased but hardly in agreement with this statement, as he had been one of the first to take notice of the Swedish approach (see Hicks, 1979b; Thirlwall, 1987: 25; and Hamouda, 1993).

Another admirer of the Swedish economists was Gottfried Haberler, who was on a short visit to the United Kingdom.[31] A controversy had raged between him and Kahn the previous year, and was probably renewed during his visit to Cambridge, as it is hinted at in Hicks's account to Ursula: 'Haberler come to tea, after what I should imagine was a stormy encounter with Kahn at lunch. Our discussion was not at all stormy; we had some pleasant talk about cycle *policy*, where I don't think we had any strong disagreement' (John to Ursula, October 22).

The controversy between Haberler and Kahn (also involving Harrod and, to some extent, Robertson) ran basically on different definitions of saving and the role of inequalities between saving and investment in explaining the cycle. Haberler was closer to Hayek on this, considering saving as a prerequisite for investment; Kahn, on the contrary, had accepted Keynes's reversion of the causality between saving and investment implicit in the multiplier mechanism (Besomi, 2000: 359–65). Ursula also showed acceptance of the Hayekian framework of Haberler's analysis:

We had quite an interesting discussion with Haberler at Hayek's seminar – mostly on the point as to whether a 'horizontal maladjustment'[32] would cause a cumulative

---

[31] Haberler, then working at the League of Nations in Geneva on his *Prosperity and Depression* (Haberler, 1937), asked for leave permission from October 14–18 to go to London to give a series of four lectures on business cycle research, present situation and future outlook. He also asked for two more days of leave to go to Cambridge and Oxford to visit 'competent economists' (League of Nations, Haberler personal file; we are indebted to Daniele Besomi for this information). From the correspondence between John and Ursula we learn that Haberler gave the first of his lectures at the LSE on October 14 (letter from Ursula to John) and that, during his stay, he went for one day to Cambridge (letter from Ursula to John, October 16).

[32] In a letter from Robertson to Hicks dated November 13, 1934, when Hicks was still at the LSE, discussing the different conceptions of equilibrium that Keynes, Gunnar Myrdal, Erik Lindahl, Hicks, Hayek, Haberler had, together with their different conceptions of the adjustment mechanisms (horizontal or vertical), Robertson wrote: 'I'm depressed by the hardness of it all, and the lack of fundamental agreement between the people' (in DHR papers C4/1.3).

deflation – he basing the argument that it would, on the time lag necessary before new investment could take place in other lines, and hence a contraction in the demand for credit and factors would first occur. (Ursula to John, October 23)

Finally, in the autumn of 1935, Joan Robinson was busy writing some 'riders' (Robinson, 1979: 185–6) from *The General Theory* and debating with Sraffa whether the rate of interest can actually be negative in a monetary economy (letters December 9 and 11, 1935, in JVR papers vii/43/10–13). The point is related to her 'The Long-period Theory of Employment' and its companion piece, 'The Concept of Zero Saving,' which was included in her *Essays in the Theory of Employment* (Robinson, 1937). Once again, it is noteworthy that Hicks – who had just published his 'Suggestion for Simplifying the Theory of Money' – was apparently not consulted by Joan Robinson, and certainly was not cited.[33] It was obvious that Hicks was not going to get a good hearing from Keynes's pupils.

The letters

This correspondence helps fill in the picture of the events and circumstances referred to above. This new evidence comes to us in the form of fragments that can be used to fit in a missing element or fill a gap in the story. For instance, we now have a better understanding of how seminars were organized and their relevance as meeting grounds for young people from Cambridge and the LSE.

There was a proposal, referred to by Ursula, to schedule the 'Cambridge Graduate Seminar' for Sunday 2.30–4.00 to 'give the London people a chance to attend when they liked' (Ursula to John, October 16). It was called 'Sraffa's seminar,' thought it is not clear whether – as was the case with the Cambridge 'circus' (Robinson, 1978a: xii) – he had been the initiator ('Lerner says Sraffa has promised to be sort of unofficial chairman'; Ursula to John, October 16), or it was related to his being the newly appointed assistant director of research (Marcuzzo, 2005), or simply because he was appreciated also by people at the LSE, since – according to Kaldor – his 1926 article had been much discussed at Robbins's seminar (Kaldor, 1986b: 39).

We also have Ursula's reports of the other seminars, mentioned above. In a letter by Ursula to John, dated November 8, she wrote:

---

[33] Later, Joan Robinson did cite Hicks in her *Essays* (1937); in one case, however, Keynes suggested 'a slight modification of what you say about Hicks' (Moggridge, 1973b: 147).

We had the first Joint Seminar tonight – 26 turned up, of which from Cambridge [David] Champernowne, Bensusan-B[utt],[34] Stone, Singer,[35] Lamberti.[36] We got Fleming[37] to lead off *faut de mieux* at short notice, and a rather technical discussion arose on the imputation of output to various input functions. I think we shall probably do better to stick to monetary theory. But there is no doubt we have got some very good people.

On the London 'economic club' she wrote: 'The Economic Club was quite fun (You are to be made an Honorary Member) – the discussion mostly went on the usefulness of Tintner's[38] assumption that demand depended on price and the rate of change of price. [...] Edelberg[39] once more demonstrated that he had more unknowns than anyone else' (Ursula to John, November 13).

In general, Ursula was anxious that Hicks should attend seminars: 'Will you come to the Joint Seminar Sun.[day]? Hayek will probably be there and probably Sraffa. We shall have to finish up discussing Fleming's article, and then Cambridge must have a look in. We think of "What fixes the rate of interest"' (Ursula to John, November 12). Hicks was reluctant: 'I am a bit shy of turning up at the Sunday seminar without being asked from this end. Do you really think one ought?' (John to Ursula, November 13). Hicks was not too keen on seminar-hopping. On one occasion, he had even failed to realize 'that there was an Economic Club meeting,' wondering 'who was speaking, and what happened' (John to Ursula, November 13). He was more at ease in conversation with selected interlocutors.

As for Hicks's relations with colleagues in Cambridge, we have some interesting accounts. With Pigou he had found it easy to talk economics:

The thing to do is never to press him, or argue with him; just throw out a remark to see if it tempts him. Then I said to him that I thought the Stationary States [Pigou, 1935][40] would be easier to read if he had used more geometry; he said he didn't like geometry, because it was always making you leave out important variables; again he instanced Joan's book as a case in point. It is funny what a general equilibrist he is at bottom! (John to Ursula, October 14)

---

[34] David Miles Bensusan-Butt (1914–94), economist.
[35] Hans Wolfang Singer (b.1910), economist.
[36] Mario Lamberti Zanardi (1900–45), economist.
[37] Albert Grant Fleming (1887–1943), economist.
[38] Ursula is probably referring to the paper 'The Theory of Monopoly, with Reference to Time,' which Gerhard Tintner (1907–83) presented at the session of November 13, 1935, of the Economic Club (*Forty-second Annual Report of The Economic Club*, in BEV papers Suppl. 376).
[39] Victor Gregory Edelberg, economist.
[40] Hicks reviewed the book for *The Economic Journal* (Hicks, 1936d).

With Sraffa he seems to have hit it off from the outset: 'Sraffa has been showing me some of his Ricardo treasures' (John to Ursula, October 23). He also reported that they 'were in precise agreement' (John to Ursula, October 24) about the paper presented by Joan Robinson at the Political Economy Club meeting on October 21 (see below).

With Kahn and Joan Robinson it was a different story. They had taken upon themselves the task of disseminating Keynesian ideas and launched a campaign of 'tutorage,' whether they were requested to do so (as in the case of Kahn and Harrod; see Besomi, 2000: 360–7) or out of proselytizing passion (as in the case of Robinson; see Rosselli and Besomi, 2005). This brought strong reactions from people in Cambridge and outside; some we already know very well (for instance, the reactions of Robertson, Pigou, Robbins, and Hayek), and we can now add John and Ursula to the list. The day after Joan's performance at Keynes's club, John reported to Ursula:

It was one of the indigestible papers[41] – whole series of rather complex propositions read out rather rapidly – and it left most people pretty bewildered. As far as I could make out – and this is due to subsequent reflection, it was really a fantasia on the Robertsonian theme of satiability of wants, decked out in Keynesian colours, and culminating in a fantastic world where you increased employment 'in the long period' by raising the rate of interest in order to decumulate capital. As a matter of fact, Keynes' own contribution was much more sensible than that of his disciple. He concluded that even if these anticipated perils of too much equipment materialise, and obviously he didn't regard them as very pressing, there were really dozens of things you could do to prevent them becoming serious. (John to Ursula, October 22)

Keynes's opinion of the paper was strikingly different (as was Lerner's[42]). He wrote to Joan Robinson: 'I thought your paper at the [Political Economy] Club was crystal clear and extremely interesting' (letter October 24, 1935, in Moggridge, 1973a: 652).

Ursula's reaction was attuned to John's:

We had a discussion on Joan's paper, at Department tea – on the basis of what Tintner and Lerner had gathered (which didn't agree very well) and what Haberler and I had gathered from you. I loved your description. It doesn't seem to worry either Joan or Kahn that their assumptions are entirely fantastic and in this respect they are on a par with Lerner: one set of assumptions is as worthy of discussion as another. (Ursula to John, October 23)

---

[41] The paper was on the 'The Long-period Theory of Employment.'
[42] 'Lerner reports very well of Joan's paper,' Ursula wrote to John on October 22.

In the case of Joan Robinson, one cannot help feeling that some misogyny on the part of her colleagues was also at work. It has been noted elsewhere that Robinson

> brought a touch of novelty, her intellectual vitality, temperament and looks attracting attention unknown to the tradition of Cambridge economists. Marshall's wife, who died four years before women were officially accepted in the University of Cambridge in 1948, offered the model of the woman economist who remained a wife in the shade of her husband. Robinson also expressed those unconventional attitudes and social criticism that had Cambridge overlapping with Bloomsbury (although this was very much the reserve of King's and Trinity men) [in its] rejection of conformism lapsing into eccentricity. (Marcuzzo and Rosselli, 2005: 12)

Pigou's reaction to their getting married is also revealing of the attitude toward women: 'He showed considerable interest in our affairs,' wrote John to Ursula, on October 14; 'we had really maligned him previously. The truth was that the idea of a female economist at once suggests Joan to him. He is really very attached to Austin, and very sorry for him! I assured him that my future wife has a wider range of conversational subjects.' Ursula's reaction shows how she herself thought that a woman economist should behave: 'The poor creature [Pigou] has simply no defences against a woman like Joan. If he can be brought to talk to me I shall try and win his heart by talking about mountains or something like that' (Ursula to John, October 14). At the same time, her approach to women's issues and feelings was awkward: 'The Review sends you its best congratulations on the daughter,' she wrote to Joan Robinson after the birth of her first child. 'It must be a tremendous relief to have all the bother *over*, or terrific fun speculating on the child's capacities and future' (letter July 7, 1934, in JVR papers vii/201/5).[43]

Ursula's style and personality made it particularly difficult for her to penetrate Cambridge diversity. She had not a clue about Sraffa: 'I am sure if one could only get at him he would be most congenial. It is just he wants a quiet life, so doesn't say out loud when he disagrees' (Ursula to John, October 25). At the same time, she was intimidated and annoyed by Joan Robinson.[44] Moreover she was aware that that there was some special bonding among Cambridge people from which she was excluded: 'Dennis

---

[43] Another interesting glimpse into British society is provided by the correspondence between Ursula and John (letters of November 26–7), which give us an idea of how an educated couple faced sexual issues in the 1930s: by reading a book on sex written and recommended to Ursula by a gynecologist after a medical check-up just before their marriage. Through these exchanges we also learn that they planned to have children, although none ever materialized.

[44] To John she wrote: 'It was very satisfactory not only to have a good talk with Joan but to convince her that someone else may be right' (Ursula to John, November 12).

Robertson turned up at tea' – she reported – 'and I had a very good talk with him, he was much more oncoming than ever before, almost as one Cambridge person to another' (Ursula to John, November 19).

Cambridge was so different that Robertson invented an adjective to describe it: *Cambridge-y*. In a previous work (with A. Rosselli) one of us describes it thus:

> More than in a shared theory, the identity of this group is rooted in motivations, values and habits: perhaps it is common lifestyles and work styles that most aptly and tellingly express these aspects. By work styles we mean the importance attached to correspondence and oral discussion in the process of forming ideas and drawing up texts – authoritativeness and authority founded on an internal hierarchy that does not necessarily reflect seniority in terms of age or academic qualification. By lifestyles we mean the importance ascribed to personal relations, affording a framework for scientific intercourse, which explains how so many theoretical divisions left ample safe ground for reciprocal respect and affection. (Marcuzzo and Rosselli, 2005: 15)

For the Hickses, 'belonging to Cambridge' was never a goal, but perhaps – we may conclude – it was never an option either.[45]

A marriage in the making

'Their marriage was a marriage of opposites. He was shy, she was outgoing; she was direct, he was subtle. She protected him and organized their lives. Their loyalty to each other was unswerving.' So Robin Matthews (1994: 13) depicts the enduring and 'ever-green' union between John and Ursula.

Many personal recollections by generations of scholars from all over the world who had the opportunity to become acquainted with the Hickses directly and visit their house (see, for example, Hamouda, 1993; Samuelson, 2001; and Simkin, 2001) reflect the image of a couple still much involved in each other and very well suited. We cannot read into the letters, which were exchanged during the three months before their marriage, the secret recipe of so fortunate a relationship, which belongs entirely to the protagonists and their capacity for renewing their mutual interest over the years, but we can glean some of the ingredients of their successful encounter.

First and foremost, it was a matter of intellectual companionship: she was evidently fascinated by John's brilliance of mind, and he was attracted by her energy and determination, as well as her capacities. They were both stimulated by the opportunity to share in depth their interest in

---

[45] 'He [Hicks] didn't enjoy Cambridge at all,' according to Shehadi ('Interview to John Hicks,' 1983, History of LSE Archive, 5).

economics.[46] This was not all, though. They had much in common:[47] their passions for poetry (see, for example, the references to Dante Alighieri and John Donne, in the letters they exchanged on October 9 and 10), literature in general, and theater, as well as their interest in political affairs. They also shared the same curiosity about visiting other countries and finding out about different cultures, which saw them traveling far and wide around the world.

In addition to all this, they held genuine physical attraction for each other. They shared their existences profoundly and in all respects, participating in each other's family events and professional successes or failures. Ursula never missed a chance to let him know how very proud she was of him and his scientific and academic achievements.[48] He, too, took a close interest in the development of her career, as for example when Ursula wrote to him (letter December 3) that her teaching job at the LSE would not be renewed,[49] and he replied: 'I am so sorry to hear...about your lectures. [...] I hope you are not too disappointed. But let us comfort ourselves by the thought that it would anyhow have been only a temporary arrangement, and the main job of seeing that you do in the future get some teaching, will certainly have to go in other directions' (John to Ursula, December 4).

She was also protective and supportive toward him in a manner and to a degree that could not simply be put down to the fact that she was eight years his senior.[50] She genuinely liked taking care of him, well aware of his real needs, intelligently reinterpreting without actually questioning the traditional role of a wife of the times.

From the letters we also know that she was in charge of all their financial affairs; she also took care of all the details in fitting out their house, called

---

[46] Their professional partnership was particularly intense in the 1940s and 1950s (Hicks, 1984a: 287–8), leading to some joint articles and other work.

[47] They each expressed this concept differently. Ursula wrote: 'What a new meaning all the poems and the songs one has loved take on when there's somebody really to attach them to, at least when the somebody is you. It's just wonderful to feel that we can be together, not just through lots of ordinary interests but right through all of us' (Ursula to John, October 11). John, in his own way, wrote: 'It is nice that we can be partners in economics..., but thanks heaven it is not only that!' (John to Ursula, October 24).

[48] For instance, in the letter of November 13 she wrote to John: 'Laski drew me aside this afternoon and said "I want to tell you I have been hearing such golden opinions of John at Cambridge"...specifically the opinion [of graduates and undergraduates] was that you were making things that had never been clear before, suddenly stand straight by showing their connections and real significance. Isn't it nice? (But no more than I suspected).'

[49] Ursula spent seven years at the LSE, as a student from 1929 to 1932, then as a PhD student in economics, and finally as a lecturer (though only for a brief period) in 1935 (obituary of Lady Hicks, *The Times*, 18 July 1985; David, 1973).

[50] When they married she was thirty-nine and he thirty-one.

Campden,[51] which they had just bought in September 1935, and of organizing their wedding party. She guided him in all practical questions, and he seemed perfectly happy to follow her directions scrupulously. For all these reasons we can well imagine the aching loneliness John must have experienced when she died in 1985, four years before him.

Concluding remark

The sheer richness of this correspondence, greatly enhancing our knowledge of the Cambridge and LSE environment of the period, has helped us – as indeed we hope it will help our readers – to overcome the feeling of a breach of privacy, of intimacy violated. It confirms the importance of primary sources in dealing with historical matters and therefore of the invaluable worth of personal archives. They should be preserved and made public, to record the past and to foster knowledge, as best we possibly can.

---

[51] It was the last house on the west side of Trumpington Road, just within the southern boundary of Cambridge.

5   Hicks and his publishers

Andrew L. Schuller

Introduction

In commissioning this contribution on John Hicks and his publishers the editors of this volume sought insights on a number of issues: how Hicks presented his work to publishers – i.e. the extent to which he tried to relate each new book proposal to his previous work; what he felt about the work of others, and especially Erik Lindahl and Knut Wicksell; and why he occasionally published with other publishers. What follows sheds some light on the first and last of these issues but, apart from the passing 1936 comment about the Swedes quoted below, no light at all on the Scandinavian issue.

Hicks's first book, *The Theory of Wages*, was published in 1932 by Macmillan. By 1939, however, Hicks had turned to Oxford University Press (henceforth OUP) for the publication of *Value and Capital*, and OUP published most of his subsequent books, though there was an interlude in the 1970s and early 1980s when Basil Blackwell published some Hicks titles. In total Hicks published twenty books, including three volumes of *Collected Essays*. *The Theory of Wages* and *Value and Capital* both went into second editions and *The Social Framework* had four editions, as well as separate American and Indian editions, a Japanese version, and a Japanese translation of the English version. That amounts to a substantial output, and OUP, who published the majority, can reasonably claim to be Hicks's main publisher.

Macmillan

Be that as it may, Hicks's publishing history started with Macmillan. On April 12, 1932, Lionel Robbins of the London School of Economics sent the typescript of *The Theory of Wages* to Harold Macmillan. Robbins's covering letter recommended the book in the strongest terms; 'absolutely of the first order of excellence' was how he described it. Not only did Robbins predict that the book would 'become a standard work among professional economists,' he also thought that it would appeal to 'men of affairs' and to 'any educated and disinterested person.' Unfortunately, I have not been able to track down the 'explanatory letter' from Hicks that accompanied the typescript. The first letter from Hicks himself in the Macmillan archive in the British Library is dated May 19, 1932, and asked politely for a decision about his book. On May 20 Harold Macmillan explained to Hicks that, because the manuscript had been submitted to more than one reader, it had taken rather longer than usual to evaluate.

What had happened, in fact, was that Macmillan had immediately asked John Maynard Keynes to advise on the Hicks proposal. By April 27 Keynes had provided a very equivocal report. He was not impressed at all:

[T]he method is to me so unsympathetic that I find it very difficult to be fair to him. It is a highly theoretical book, the serious and careful work of an unoriginal but competent mind. It fills something of a gap in the subject and...the treatment is probably fairly good of its kind and would, I think, meet with exceedingly favourable reviews in many quarters...But to me personally the book is extremely boring, and I feel that the author is incapable of adding to my knowledge or understanding of the subject, or of getting anywhere near a satisfactory solution, because he is using traditional technique for a problem which experience shows it is incapable of solving. I find the author's very indefinite and jejune conclusions a confirmation of my general expectation.

Keynes was, however, honest enough to recognize his own prejudice, and did not advise outright rejection. Instead he suggested a second reader, and pointed Macmillan to Dennis Robertson, also at Cambridge. On May 19 Macmillan acknowledged Robertson's report, in which he, too, expressed some concern about the book, partly because it was a 'product of the extreme school of laissez-faire individualism which...is now dominant at the LSE and with which I find myself a good deal out of sympathy' and partly because chapter 6, which Robertson saw as the most original part of the book, depended heavily on the mathematical appendix, on which Robertson thought he was 'ill-equipped to pronounce.' Nevertheless, Robertson recommended strongly that the book be published.

Given the tenor of the two reports, it is interesting to speculate how the Delegates at Oxford University Press would have voted had the book been submitted to them. Macmillan were bold, however, accepting the book at their publishing meeting, and wrote to Hicks on May 26 inviting him to meet Harold Macmillan in the office to discuss the comments of one of the advisers (Robertson) and offering a choice of contractual terms: either a profit-sharing arrangement or a royalty. Hicks chose the latter. On June 3 he sent the typescript, amended to accommodate some, though not all, of Robertson's comments. On October 4 *The Theory of Wages*, an academic monograph by a twenty-seven-year-old at the beginning of his career, was published, six months after the typescript had first been submitted for consideration. In contrast, on September 14, 1963, twelve months after Hicks had delivered the additional material for the second edition of *The Theory of Wages* (1963), he received advance copies, but publication had to be delayed until October 17 because the printer had omitted the last page of text and the book ended in mid-sentence.

Not only was the publishing process in the 1930s fast, it was also already international. Hicks's original request for a decision was prompted by the possibility of an Italian translation, and, when he asked that copies be sent for review to specific German and Italian journals, he apologized for suggesting what he assumed his publisher would be doing anyway. The Italian translation suggested by Professor Gustavo del Vecchio was already under way in 1933, starting a long association between Hicks and economists in Bologna.

Author and publisher were pleased with the book, and on November 14, 1936, prompted by being alerted about the need for a reprint, Hicks made the first set of suggestions for a new edition. This was not, however, followed up with immediate rewriting, and Hicks's position on why he was or was not ready to deliver a new edition evolved over the years. Various revision plans were made and let slip in the 1930s. By June 9, 1939, Hicks was suggesting that his revision plans were extensive enough to merit a new title and publication as a new book, but on March 11, 1940, he admitted that he had made no progress and it was agreed that *The Theory of Wages* could go out of print. On October 15, 1945, Hicks admitted to a want of any enthusiasm for a new edition and concluded that 'it had better stay dead.' Eventually, in 1962, prompted by a request from an Indian publisher to reprint the original 1932 version, Hicks concluded that it would be silly not to reprint it in the United Kingdom if the book was still available in the United States (a special reprint in 1948), Japan, and India. Furthermore, he wrote on May 5, the economic scene at the time made the 1932 analysis more relevant. So he suggested a reissue with a new preface and two new articles. On May 9, 1962, Tim Farmiloe of Macmillan told Hicks that his directors suggested a complete rewrite, but Hicks did not want to embark on this, preferring to leave the book essentially as it was, albeit adding some responses to criticisms. On July 20 Hicks told Macmillan that he was following his usual working method – i.e. 'to rough the thing out in manuscript and then do a fair copy for myself on the typewriter.' He delivered the typescript at a meeting on September 20.

The second edition papers contain more correspondence about the progress of the book through the press than the first edition file. Hicks did not like the draft of the jacket copy (November 14, 1962). Macmillan accepted this objection but Farmiloe responded sharply to Hicks's complaint about the layout of the new material and told him he was being 'unfair' (January 25, 1963). When Hicks complained that Blackwell, the bookshop in Oxford, had no copies in stock (January 14, 1964) Farmiloe retorted that they had taken nineteen. While writing (April 30, 1964) to say that he was 'gratified by the amount of royalty,' Hicks took the opportunity to mention that he had seen no reviews. He grumbled about the royalty rate on American sales but accepted it in order not to delay publication any further. The American edition was published on February 5, 1964, by St. Martin's Press (Macmillan's partner firm), which agreed to take an edition of 500 after negotiations that also involved Macmillan Inc. (a separate company) and the University of Indiana Press. When they reordered before the end of that year the royalty rate was raised. There was much discussion as to whether to issue a paperback, Hicks (December 1, 1964) writing: 'I have never yet gone into a paperback – I am not really convinced that it is worthwhile.'

This account of the history of the second edition of *The Theory of Wages* makes a chronological leap but it illustrates Hicks's behavior concerning the publication of his books. He was keen to explain how he saw his work in the light of what he – and others – had written previously; and he conducted a polite but watchful and certainly not supine correspondence about practical publishing matters.

Between the first and second editions of *The Theory of Wages* Hicks had changed publisher. What the papers I have seen do not reveal is how *Value and Capital* came to be published by Oxford University Press. I have not seen the OUP file for the first edition but it is reasonable to assume that OUP took the initiative in establishing contact. On February 8, 1937, John Mulgan, then the OUP editor responsible for economics, wrote to C. J. Hitch, an American Fellow in economics at the Queen's College (who later went on to be president of the University of California), asking: 'Who is J. R. Hicks ...?' Mulgan was planning a trip to Cambridge, and, since Hitch told him the following day that 'J. R. Hicks is the ablest theoretical economist extant,' we can assume that Mulgan met Hicks and started the OUP relationship. We do not know how Mulgan came across Hicks's name. Nor do we know whether anyone at Cambridge University Press thought of approaching Hicks, who had, after all, spent the three years 1935–8 in Cambridge writing the book.

We do know that Hicks had been informing Macmillan for some time about the new book he was working on. On November 14, 1936, he told Macmillan that he was two-thirds of the way through a new book: 'In the second part I combine my own new method with the new Swedish manner of approaching dynamic problems. (This latter has not been used in any English book before, though Keynes sometimes gets near it.) I shall be interested to hear what you think about it. I am afraid it sounds rather formidable from some points of view.' In 1937 the correspondence indicates a mutual expectation that Macmillan would publish the new book, which Hicks hoped to complete in September of that year. On May 21, 1938, however, Hicks announced not only that the new book was nearly finished but also that 'I have had an offer for it from Oxford University Press, which, all things considered, I feel I should like to accept. I don't think you will feel that I am in any way committed to publishing with you as a result of our correspondence. But I think I ought to inform you before I decide to publish elsewhere.' By return Harold Macmillan wrote to 'Dear Mr Hicks' at Cambridge to say: '[W]e naturally feel some disappointment...though we recognize that your letters did not commit you to publishing it with us,' and made an excellent counter-offer 'to an author whose work we hold in particular esteem,' but Hicks had made up his mind. On May 26 he acknowledged the offer but went on: 'I think I would still prefer to do as I said so will you please excuse me.' Macmillan's response was rather frosty, addressed to 'Dear Sir' and signed 'We are yours faithfully.'

In fact Macmillan swallowed their disappointment, and the relationship remained open. Hicks continued to provide advice, submitting prompt and pragmatic reports. On November 26, 1954, he took a realist's view of the prospects for an IEA symposium volume: 'I cannot see many individuals buying the book when its price would be inflated by so much chaff. On the other hand there is a considerable library market, and most libraries would need to have it for the good papers which it would contain.' Macmillan, for their part, valued their connection with the United Kingdom's leading economist. Tim Farmiloe was swift and warm in congratulating Hicks on his knighthood in 1964, and in 1966 both John and his wife Ursula were invited to one of Maurice Macmillan's parties.

Moving to OUP

Nonetheless, it must have been irritating to have lost Hicks, especially when he seems to have offered no explanation for his move to OUP. What could his reasons have been? Perhaps there is a clue in his 1936 warning that the book was going to be 'formidable'; he might have felt that his new book would be academically weightier than *The Theory of Wages* and would sit most appropriately on a university press list. Perhaps he was worried that Keynes's closeness to Macmillan would militate against him; or he did not want to be the number two to Keynes on the Macmillan list; or Robertson had some influence in guiding him to Oxford. Whatever, with the publication of *Value and Capital* Hicks was linked to OUP in a relationship that lasted for fifty years.

As early as 1939 (March 22) he was taking pains, from Manchester, to recommend Ragnar Frisch to OUP. By the time he arrived in Oxford in 1946 he had published two more books with OUP (*The Taxation of War Wealth* and *The Social Framework*) and was clearly on good terms with his publisher. By March 22, 1939, he was addressing his editor as 'Dear Mulgan' and by 1941 (April 3) the Secretary to the Delegates was addressing him as 'My dear Hicks' and involving him as an adviser. In 1949 Hicks wrote requesting that the annual retainer of £50 that OUP was paying him for advice should cease, since he did not feel that he was doing enough to merit it. In 1951 plans were being laid for the re-establishment of a series of Economics Faculty Monographs (essentially D.Phil. theses), which had been launched in 1936 with financial support from the university but had lapsed during the war. Hicks was involved in the planning and was one of four editors appointed after the proposal was accepted by the Delegates in 1952, the year that Hicks himself became a Delegate.

The OUP structure and Hicks

At this point it is worth clarifying some technical terminology about OUP and explaining its relationship with the university, since Hicks's relations with the Press were given a distinctive character by virtue not only of his membership of the university from 1946 but also of his service as an OUP Delegate. The Press is simply a department of the university and is wholly owned by it. The Delegates are the board of Oxford academics 'delegated' by the university to oversee the affairs of the Press, and they have to approve all the books published by OUP. There are now about twenty Delegates, though there were only half that number when Hicks arrived in Oxford. Finance Committee is a subcommittee of the Delegates with special responsibility for the financial and commercial health of the Press. The Secretary to the Delegates is the chief executive. Hicks was both a Delegate and a member of Finance Committee, so, in effect, he was on the board of his own publisher – unusual for an author–publisher relationship.

A number of Hicks's books were accepted by the Delegates for publication while he was himself a Delegate; six titles during this period was a prolific output relative to that of his fellow Delegates. There is a convention that, when a book by a sitting member of the Delegacy is being considered, the Delegate concerned leaves the Delegates' Room in the Clarendon Building, where the meetings are held. Hicks, doubtless, conformed to the convention. Books written by wives of Delegates are rarely submitted to OUP, but in 1964 Ursula Hicks's book *Development Finance* was being considered by the economics editor. He asked Hicks whether he would like to see 'an outside opinion.' On April 17, 1964, Hicks claimed that, though he had 'heard a lot about it,' he had 'not, myself, read what she has written.' He was going to think about the issue of an outside reader. The book was duly accepted at a Delegates' meeting six months later at which Hicks was not present, but the file does not reveal whether an outside report was ever commissioned.

In the course of his fifty-year relationship with OUP Hicks dealt with many people. Early Secretaries such as Kenneth Sisam and Thomas Norrington, who steered the Press through the Second World War and its immediate aftermath, were fully aware of his standing as an author. In 1946 Sisam wrote: 'Hicks is such an important writer for us (his books sell extraordinarily well) and is so well known in America ...' Secretary Roberts's tenure (1954–74) coincided almost exactly with Hicks's Delegatorial years, from 1952 to 1971. In 1965 Roberts laid on a large dinner party for John and Ursula Hicks to celebrate the remarkable fact that the Press had, that year, published a book by each of them. When Hicks stepped down as a Delegate in 1971, as a result of a new governance regime that limited Delegates' terms of office, he was succeeded by George Richardson. Richardson was not only an economist but had had Hicks as an undergraduate tutor for the economic theory paper in the politics, philosophy and economics (PPE) degree at Oxford and as a graduate supervisor. It was Hicks who encouraged Richardson to leave the Foreign Office, return to Oxford, and buy a house in Hicks's village in the Cotswolds; and Hicks's support surely helped Richardson's successful application for a fellowship at St John's College at Oxford. Richardson's 1960 book *Information and Investment* had been approved by Hicks as a Delegate even though it took an approach fundamentally different from Hicks's own. Hicks, by the way, would not accept Richardson's original title for the book; *The Economics of Imperfect Knowledge* would have sent a much more appropriate and interesting signal to potential readers. When Richardson himself became secretary in 1974 he was – subject ultimately to the Delegates – in a position to control the oeuvre of his former mentor. Thus, Hicks's relations with his main publisher were considerably closer and more complex than is usual.

Hicks as OUP author

What does one expect an author–publisher relationship to be? The most important elements are the publisher's understanding of what his or her author is trying to achieve with his/her book, and the author's sense that his/her publisher has this understanding and is doing all he/she can to further the book's chances of success. Within that, there is enormous variation: the publisher can be proactive, suggesting projects to his/her author, or reactive, accepting whatever is offered; the publisher can be demanding and want his/her author to comply with tight house rules and procedures, or he/she can be lax; the author may want control over details of production, design, and marketing; and he/she can behave like a prima donna, or a publishing novice, or a sensible collaborator; or he/she can be suspicious. 'Now Barrabas was a publisher,' wrote Lord Byron, and *Now Barrabas* was the title of a book by one of the United States' leading publishers of the 1960s and 1970s, whose Harcourt Brace building in Manhattan was once buzzed by an irate author in a small plane.

Hicks's relationship with OUP, as with Macmillan and Blackwell, seems to have been sound and steady – no need to buzz the Press buildings. As an author, Hicks certainly tried to make it easy for his publisher to understand what he was trying to achieve with each book. *The Social Framework* (1942c), as a pure textbook, was in a category of its own. Hicks thought his expository approach was radical. He intended to write a series of six 60,000- to 70,000-word books. This he described (April 15, 1941) as 'breaking the subject into a series of topics issued in the order most suitable for present-day teaching in contrast to the "classical" teaching of economics which introduces subjects in the wrong order.' *The Social Accounts*, as it was originally to be called, aimed to provide a 'map' of the whole economic system 'before the student had undertaken the effort of abstraction involved in analysing its working.'

The book-length scholarly works were also introduced carefully. When, on June 4, 1964, Hicks gave OUP a progress report on *Capital and Growth* (1965) he wrote:

It is a serious work, in my view more important than anything I have done since my *Trade Cycle* book in 1950. Indeed with that book and *Value and Capital* it will make something of a trilogy. People have often said to me that the approaches that I used in those two earlier books were so different that they did not see how I squared one with the other. I have long felt that I should like to make an effort to answer that question and that is one of the things that I am doing in this book. It is moreover mainly concerned with the different approaches made by the economists (including those at Cambridge and MIT) who have been having quite a dog-fight recently. It will therefore sail pretty much into the middle of the current controversy.

A marketing blurb, presumably drafted by Hicks himself, described *Capital and Time* (1973a) as follows:

This is the third book that the author has written about Capital. *Capital and Growth* was a largely expository work which sought to reduce the extensive writings on the subject by others to some sort of order; the present volume is more constructive. It takes up the approach that was peculiar to the Austrian School of 1890–1930; an approach which has been abandoned by most economists because of an obstacle it failed to surmount. It is shown that the obstacle can be surmounted and the method restored to vigour. Several principal results which have been reached by other methods can be reached by this method rather simply and expeditiously; it can then be developed to deal with other problems, which to the other methods were rather out of reach. What results is a modernization not only of the Austrians but also of the English classics – Ricardo and Mill.

With *Essays in World Economics* (1959b) a pattern starts: Hicks making books by putting together previously published papers. On May 27, 1958, he wrote:

I have thought of putting this volume together because these papers, being written for particular occasions, will never get their substance included in books, as I always go on hoping with my theoretical papers and yet, being essays in diagnosis, rather than recommendations for policy, they do go on being of some use. I think of reprinting them as they originally appeared, which I think is the fair thing to do, but of adding some explanation (perhaps in a general introduction) of places where subsequent events or additional information, or criticism that has been offered by others, have made me feel that particular passages are in need of amendment. It would not take very long to do this.

He recognized that this might cause some difficulties. 'I do have the gravest doubts whether a book of this sort should be a CP book [Clarendon Press, OUP's scholarly imprint].' Why this reticence? Because then, as now, OUP has taken the line that its resources should be allocated to the publication of original scholarly or pedagogical material rather than the republication of what is already available, and it might have looked bad if a Delegate were asking the Press to disregard this convention. The issue was discussed internally, and, happily, the Delegates took the view that this collection represented the work of a scholar of great distinction and would sell very well. Once that decision had been made, there was further correspondence about which papers to include, the various extra sections of explanation and expansion that had to be written, and the title to settle on.

This pattern was repeated. On June 11, 1965, he showed plans for two volumes of essays 'adding some notes or commentary indicating changes of view and relation to contemporary or subsequent work of other people.' In spite of being familiar, 'they will gain very much by being set in the context in which I plan to place them.' This was published in 1967 as a single volume, *Critical Essays in Monetary Theory* (1967a). In 1975 what was published later as *Economic Perspectives* (1977a) arrived as a synopsis and a note claiming that it would take only a month to prepare. Interestingly, in a discussion about whether to include a paper that had been published only in German, Hicks noted on October 15, 1976, that the paper 'shows how far it was possible to get three years before Keynes's

General Theory to move a good way in Keynes's direction, though starting from a very different line of thought.' Similarly, in 1985 *Methods of Dynamic Economics* (1985a) was essentially a cut-and-change version of *Capital and Growth*, prompted by his feeling that, in the second part of that book, he had made a serious error of classification.

All this provides some idea of how Hicks saw his own books as he introduced them to the Press. I suspect that his descriptions that I have quoted above locating his intellectual positions will not surprise readers. Although he did refer a number of times to contemporary work that related to his own, there was very little detail. I could find only the one specific reference to the Scandinavians that I quoted above, in the context of *Value and Capital*.

Everything in the publishing relationship seems to have been smooth. OUP recognized Hicks's quality early on and gave his books priority treatment, especially when paper was in short supply during and immediately after the war. Royalty rates were generous; the offers were consistent and never seem to have been questioned, though, as with Macmillan and paperbacking *The Theory of Wages*, Hicks was somewhat concerned about the effect on his royalties of selling cheap editions, be they within the English Language Book Scheme (government subsidies to publishers to price books cheaply in developing countries) or low-priced paperback series. In the files there is quite a lot of prosaic business correspondence about production matters and the selling of foreign rights. A grumble about the marketing of *Critical Essays* prompted a full report on what had been done to promote the book, which turned out to be a great deal. A review in *The Economist* that had dismissed *Capital and Growth* because it was 'of no practical use' irked him. No one could blame the Press for that, though. When he objected to the 1977 proposal to put *Trade Cycle* out of print OUP relented and reprinted.

The move to Blackwell and the return to OUP

Why, then, did Hicks defect to Blackwell? There does not seem to have been any specific irritating incident, let alone a major rift between OUP and Hicks. I suspect that a conjuncture of factors was at work.

(i)   In 1971 Hicks ceased to be a Delegate.

(ii) The Jahnsson Lectures were, as a series, contracted to Blackwell, so *The Crisis in Keynesian Economics* (1974b) had to be published by them.

(iii) This gave Hicks a fresh publishing experience. Blackwell were, at that time, very dynamic and aggressive, and treated him as an honored newcomer to their list, while OUP may have been giving him the impression that they rather took him for granted. René Olivieri, who, while still at MIT Press, had had experience of co-publishing with Blackwell, had been urging Blackwell to target Hicks as a potential supplier of collected papers.

(iv) Dieter Helm, another young and dynamic figure, was in Oxford, was close to Olivieri, and was prepared to act as amanuensis for Hicks.

So, no great dramatic divorce, though OUP was not pleased. I myself was certainly disappointed, since I had been suggesting a complete edition of his works to Hicks in the late 1970s. Hicks returned to the fold for his last two books, however. OUP was always keen to have him back and maintained contact with him, consulting about reprints and paperback cover design. Hicks, himself, approached Richardson about OUP publishing *Methods of Dynamic Economics*. Amartya Sen, who was by then the OUP economics Delegate and had remained close to his predecessor as Delegate and as Drummond Professor at All Souls, may have felt that OUP would be a more appropriate publisher at that time than Blackwell. Tony Courakis, who had been Hicks's graduate student and remained closely involved in his work, certainly felt the same. Moreover, Blackwell may no longer have been so keen on Hicks's later works; after all, in *Methods of Dynamic Economics* (1985a) and *A Market Theory of Money* (1989a), Hicks's references to recent work by others in the same field were strikingly few, and Blackwell was anyway moving away from publishing scholarly monographs.

No one can say, at this remove, which of these factors was most important, but all parties seemed satisfied with the outcome. Perhaps Hicks, who was not immune to vanity, had enjoyed his 'affair' with the younger, more flattering, and lively Blackwell, but was happy to return, in due course, to his 'marriage' to OUP.

Hicks as OUP Delegate

So much for Hicks the author. What of Hicks the Oxford University Press Delegate? Robin Matthews's entry in the *Dictionary of National Biography* records that Hicks was a 'very active Delegate' (Matthews, 2004). Without reading more Delegatorial files than I have, I cannot expand much on that, and it would be a different exercise to try to assess fully what, if any, impact Hicks had on OUP's economics publishing during the twenty years of his term as a Delegate. Books by Michio Morishima, Walt Rostow, Robert Solow, I. M. D. Little, and Hla Myint appeared during those years, and the presence of Hicks's own books on the Oxford list could have made it attractive to other economists, but it would be difficult to claim that Oxford was publishing a majority of the internationally most prestigious books of the day. Hicks was proactive in steering authors to Oxford, most notably Harry Johnson. In early 1965 Hicks initiated and continued to be involved in negotiations between Johnson and OUP about the lectures that were very successfully published as *The World Economy at the Crossroads* (Johnson, 1965). In 1959 Hicks had introduced David Miles Bensusan-Butt to OUP. He was also very supportive of several books that turned out to be solid additions to the OUP list, for example Marjorie Grice-Hutchinson's *The School of Salamanca* (Grice-Hutchinson, 1952) and Walter Newlyn's *Theory of Money* (Newlyn, 1962). He was, interestingly, cautious about committing OUP to publishing the *Glasgow Edition of the Works of Adam Smith* when the proposal was first submitted in February 1962; indeed, he was rather skeptical about the need for another edition at all and took pains to consult his peers at the Royal Economic Society about the project.

Hicks also offered strategic advice. For instance, in 1952 he urged OUP to jump at a proposal made by Dudley Seers and David Henderson on the grounds that it was important to catch bright young economists early in their careers, and in 1955 he wrote of a proposal from Henry G. Aubrey: 'I think we ought to be prepared for works of this kind...we shall be performing a public service.' On a more practical level, Hicks was prepared to give OUP editors his views on the market for economics books, as he had in his reports for Macmillan. In the context of intermediating between Harry Johnson and OUP, on February 18, 1965, he told John Cordy of OUP that publishing Johnson's book would be 'an excellent opportunity of demonstrating to economists that we can get things out quickly – a point on which we still have something to live down.' How Hicks's activities compared with those of his fellow Delegates is difficult to judge, but his position on Finance Committee would have given him an intimate knowledge of his publisher's financial position that few other authors had. Since he traveled so much, he also had a more personal knowledge of the various OUP branches around the world than most of his fellow Delegates.

Personal memories

I met Hicks in February 1970, shortly after I had first joined OUP in Oxford. In those days relations between a young commissioning editor and a Delegate were very different from what they are now. Delegates were distant figures of authority, handing down judgments, rather than colleagues engaging in discussion. Nevertheless, before Hicks retired from the Delegacy in 1971 I had a number of meetings with him in which I outlined my, often naive, views about what textbooks were needed in the subject. I had no formal training in economics but was commissioning textbooks. Through the smoke from his pipe, Hicks's blue eyes expressed amused tolerance of the egregious errors I was making in expounding my view of the subject. Later, during the 1980s, I visited Hicks a number of times, both at his house in the Cotswolds and in hospitals in Oxford. I felt privileged to be working with such a figure. More importantly, on a personal level it was heartening to observe how it was the life of the mind that kept Hicks going. He would summon up his energies for a spell in the middle of the day, which included sherry and lunch, and would sparkle as he explained his current work (this was mainly about *A Market Theory of Money*) and reminisced about intellectual debates of the past. 'Sprightly' is how my diary describes his demeanour at a lunch in December 1979. He lived for his economics.

I have one final quotation to offer as an envoi. In a typed letter dated May 20, 1989, the day of his death, Hicks wrote: 'I am trying to make arrangements to what should happen after I am gone. One problem is the royalties from my books. I would like to give the whole lot to the Secretary of the Delegates. I think this would be the most suitable.' That, surely, is the sign of a successful author–publisher relationship.

Note on sources

When the OUP archivist told me that he had seventy Hicks items in the archive I excitedly imagined that I would find a lot of meaty material. Alas, the fare was generally pretty meager – and the file for the first edition of *Value and Capital* (1939a) is missing. I have read the OUP files that are still active or findable in the archive. The quotations from Hicks's letters to OUP are from the following files: CP/ed/000167 (Frisch); OP321/1982, *The Social Framework*; OP318/1959, *Capital and Growth*; 0198772866, *Capital and Time*; OP314/1928, *Essays in World Economics*; OP318/1956, *Critical Essays in Monetary Theory*; 0198284079, *Economic Perspectives*; OP1037/7728, *The World Economy at the Crossroads*; OP318/1958, U. Hicks, *Development Finance*. These, and other Hicks quotations, are reproduced by kind permission of Anthony Courakis, Sir John Hicks's literary executor. The quotation from Sisam is reproduced by permission of the Secretary to the Delegates of Oxford University Press.

I have also consulted the Macmillan Archive in the British Library. It contains the Letterbooks, the Manuscripts Received Ledger, the Agenda Books, and Readers' Reports. The archive is catalogued and the relevant papers begin at Add.MSS 55723. The quotation from Keynes's report on *The Theory of Wages* is published in D. E. Moggridge (ed.), *The Collected Writings of John Maynard Keynes*, vol. XII, *Articles and*

Correspondence: Investment and Editorial, London, Macmillan, 1983, and is reproduced with the permission of Palgrave Macmillan. I thank the OUP archivist, Martin Maw, the Macmillan archivist, Alysoun Sanders, and the staff at the British Library, Jamie Andrews and Elizabeth James, for their assistance. I am also grateful to Verity Andrews at the University of Reading Library for sending me a copy of Robbins's letter recommending Hicks to Macmillan, and the rights departments at OUP, Macmillan, and Blackwell for information about translations of Hicks's books. There are some unresolved inconsistencies between my list of translations and the information in the bibliography compiled by Irini Liakopoulou for *The Letters between John Hicks and Ursula Webb September–December, 1935,* edited by M. C. Marcuzzo and E. Sanfilippo with T. Hirai and T. Nishizawa, Working Paper no. 207 for the Institute for Economic and Business Administration Research at the University of Hyogo, Tokyo (Hirai *et al.,* 2005).

Unfortunately, it appears that Blackwell have no record of their dealings with Hicks. Nor have I had the opportunity to peruse Hicks's own papers or his files on his various books. I have spoken to George Richardson (who described Hicks's objection to his book's first title), Anthony Courakis (to whom I owe the speculative suggestions about Hicks's motives for publishing *Value and Capital* with OUP), and a number of other people who were involved in Hicks's publishing: Tim Farmiloe of Macmillan, René Olivieri of Blackwell, John Cordy, my predecessor at OUP, and Dieter Helm, who edited the Blackwell collections of Hicks's work. I thank them for their observations.

Appendix

Books by Hicks (published by Oxford University Press except where noted)

The Theory of Wages, 1932; 2nd edition 1963 (Macmillan).
Value and Capital, 1939; 2nd edition 1946.
Taxation of War Wealth (with U. Hicks and L. Rostas), 1941; 2nd edition 1942.
Social Framework, 1942; editions 1952/1960/1971, US editions 1945/1955, Indian edition 1984.
The Problem of Budgetary Reform, 1948.
A Contribution to the Theory of the Trade Cycle, 1950; 2nd edition 1961.
A Revision of Demand Theory, 1956; paperback 1986.
Essays in World Economics, 1959.
Capital and Growth, 1965; paperback 1987.
Critical Essays in Monetary Theory, 1967; paperback 1979.
A Theory of Economic History, 1969; paperback 1969.

Capital and Time, 1973; paperback 1987.
Crisis in Keynesian Economics, 1974 (Blackwell).
Economic Perspectives, 1977.
Causality in Economics, 1979 (Blackwell).
Wealth and Welfare, 1981 (Blackwell).
Money, Interest and Wages, 1982 (Blackwell).
Classics and Moderns, 1983 (Blackwell).
Methods of Dynamic Economics, 1984; paperback 1987.
A Market Theory of Money, 1989.

Translations of Hicks's books

Translation	Publisher	Date published
The Theory of Wages		
Italian	Utet	1936
Japanese	Oriental Economist	1952
	Toyo Keizai	1965
Spanish	Editorial Labor	1967
Value and Capital		
Spanish	Fondo de Cultura	1940; 3rd edn. 1968
Japanese	Iwanami Shoten	1951; 2nd edn. 1972; paperback edn. 1996
Italian	Utet	1954
French	Dunod	1956
Korean	Donggoog Monwhasa	1958
English reprint Japan	Maruzan	1960
Hindi	Hindi Samiti	1964
Kannada	Institute of Kannada Studies	1972
Polish	PWN	1975
Urdu	University of Karachi	1976
Hungarian	Kozgazdasag	1979
French, reissue	Bordas	1979
Portuguese	Abril	1984; 2nd edn. 1990
Russian	Progress	1988
German, 2nd edition	Wirtschaft	1998
The Social Framework		
Indonesian	PT Peru-bangunnan	1952
Hindi	Motilal Banarsidass	1954
Korean	Tamgudan (1st and 2nd edn.); Changmoonkag (3rd edn.)	1955; 2nd edn. 1959; 3rd edn. 1972
German	Rowohlt	1956

Translation	Publisher	Date published
Italian	Einaudi	1956; 4th edn. 1970
Chinese	China Culture	1960
Sinhalese and Tamil	Sri Lankan government	1964
Portuguese, 4th edition	Zahar	1971
Indian, 4th edition	OUP Delhi	1972
Japanese, 4th edition	Dobunkan Shuppan	1972
Spanish, 4th edition	Fondo de Cultura	1974
The Social Framework of the Japanese Economy		
Japanese	Dobunkan Shuppan	1976
A Contribution to the Theory of the Trade Cycle		
Japanese	Iwanami Shoten	1951
Italian	L'Industria	1954
Spanish	Aguilar	1955
A Revision of Demand Theory		
Japanese	Iwanami Shoten	1958
Spanish	Fondo de Cultura Economica	1958
Essays in World Economics		
Japanese	Iwanami Shoten	1965
Spanish	Tecnos	1966
Capital and Growth		
Spanish	Bosch	1967
Japanese	Iwanami Shoten	1970
Italian	Il Saggiatore	1971
Polish	PWN	1978
Serbian	Centar	1989
Critical Essays in Monetary Theory		
Italian	Etas-Kompass	1971
Spanish	Ariel	1971
Japanese	Toyo Keizai	1972
A Theory of Economic History		
French	Du Seuil	1970
Spanish	Aguilar	1970
Swedish	Bonniers	1970
Italian	Utet	1971
Japanese	Nihon Keizai	1971
Portuguese	Zahar	1971
Norwegian	Gyldendal	1972
Spanish, pocket edition	Orbis	1984
Japanese	Kodansha	1996
Korean	Saenul	2000

Translation	Publisher	Date published
Capital and Time		
Japanese	Toyo Keizai	1973
Italian	Gruppo Editoriale Fabbri	1974
French	Economica	1975
Spanish	Fondo de Cultura Economica	1976
Economic Perspectives		
Portuguese	Zahar	1978
Italian	Etas Libri	1980
Japanese	Iwanami Shoten	1985
Polish	PWN	1988
Causality in Economics		
Italian	Il Mulino	1979
Methods of Dynamic Economics		
Spanish	Fondo de Cultura Economica	1989
A Market Theory of Money		
Italian	Il Mulino	1991
Japanese	Toyo Keizai	1991
Portuguese	Dom Quixote	1992
Portuguese	Record	2003
Money, Interest and Wages		
Italian	Il Mulino	1982
Spanish	Fondo de Cultura Economica	1982

6   Hicks in reviews, 1932–89: from *The Theory of Wages* to *A Market Theory of Money*

Warren Young

Introduction

For over half a century, from the 'years of high theory,' through the decline of Keynesianism and rise of monetarist and new classical alternatives, John Hicks made fundamental contributions to economics. In this chapter I survey the reception of his books, from *The Theory of Wages* (1932), through *Value and Capital* (1939a), to *A Market Theory of Money* (1989a). I do so in order to gauge the initial reactions to his path-breaking work, which range from high praise to harsh criticism: if critical, depending upon the intellectual traditions some reviewers were 'defending' against Hicksian insights; if supportive, depending on the degree to which they identified with his analytical methods.

The medium of the book review has a peculiar place in the history of economics, especially with regard to reviews of Hicks's work, many of which have been overlooked. To reassess *all* reviews of Hicks is not my object. Indeed, that would be a Herculean task. What I do try to present is a *systematic* way of dealing with reviews of his work, by surveying what I consider to be *key* reviews of Hicks.

In order to accomplish this, I distinguish between *purposive* reviews, critical or supportive, as against *substantive* reviews, dealing with an essential central message. Such a demarcation between 'types' of review can be complemented by reference to their 'focus.' Stephen Toulmin (1972: 307–13) distinguishes between 'external' and 'internal' analytical focus. In his view, 'external' focus is on the institutional and personal history of a scientific discipline, whereas 'internal' focus is on the intrinsic importance of contributions in the discipline as the basis for 'take-off' into further self-sustained theoretical development. Hicks's published volumes consisted of three types: original monographs, lectures, and collected essays. While the specific central message can be identified in his monographs, the other types of volumes – lectures and collected essays – need a unifying scheme. This can be accomplished by identifying major, minor, and integrating themes in them. I use the classificatory framework outlined above to deal with reviews of his books.

The Theory of Wages (first and second editions)

Gerald Shove's 'famous review' (Shove, 1933), as Melvin Reder put it (Reder, 1965: 88), of the first edition of *The Theory of Wages* (Hicks, 1932) in the September 1933 issue of *The Economic Journal* was not the first review of the book. Henry Clay, in the August 1933 issue of *Economica*, had reviewed it in positive terms overall, and even suggested (Clay, 1933: 332) that Hicks extend his approach from static to dynamic analysis. This is something that Hicks undertook over the years after *The Theory of Wages* was published, as manifest in 'Wages and Interest: the Dynamic Problem' (Hicks, 1935c), and which culminated in *Value and Capital* (1939a). Shove's critical review essay on Hicks's book is well known and will not be discussed in detail here. What is interesting to recall, however, is that, in the second edition of the book (Hicks, 1963), not only did Hicks include Shove's review of the 1932 edition but a long 'commentary,' which, as Reder put it in his review of the second edition, attempted 'to present a Shove-proof argument' (Reder, 1965: 88).

Hicks's 1932 book was also reviewed in two leading American journals, *The American Economic Review* and *The Journal of Political Economy*. In his *American Economic Review* review, L. A. Morrison took issue with Hicks's application of 'marginal productivity theory' to wage determination, but did not go further in his criticism (Morrison, 1933: 687). In his February 1935 *Journal of Political Economy* review, on the other hand, Aaron Director was more forthright, when, in effect, he 'damned' the book with 'faint praise.' According to Director, there was not 'much that is new' in the first part of the book, although he still found it 'precise and judicious.' Moreover, while Director wrote that 'Hicks' conclusion that labor-saving inventions will predominate' was 'ingenuous,' he also said it was 'hardly convincing' (Director, 1935: 109–10). Director then described the second part of the book as 'not of equal merit.' He wrote that Hicks's 'theoretical consideration' regarding the 'consequences of wage regulation' was 'to be congratulated' for 'thoroughness,' and went on to criticize Hicks for 'his further suggestion' regarding the applicability of Eugen Böhm von Bawerk's approach to capital theory ('time structure' or 'period of production') as being 'quite unsatisfactory'. (*ibid.*: 110–11).

The reputation of the *Theory of Wages*, however, was rehabilitated in the reviews of the second edition, especially in those of Reder (1965) and Arthur Kruger (1965). Although critical on some points, Reder concluded: 'All in all, *The Theory of Wages* has been an important book that continues to exert an influence on economic thought' (90). In his review of the second edition in the *Canadian Journal of Economics and Political Science*, Kruger wrote:

On re-reading the original volume one is struck by the mixture of the pioneering and the archaic, which it contained. However, there is still much that economists, and in particular a labour economist, can learn here... This book should interest most economists. Not only do we have here a reprint of a classic in its field, but we are also provided with a view of the intellectual growth of one of the great economists of this generation.

Value and Capital and its mathematical appendix

In my survey 'The Early Reactions to *Value and Capital*' (Young, 1991), I dealt with reviews of *Value and Capital* by Ralph Hawtrey (1939b), G. G. Firth (1939), B. F. Haley (1939), Roy Harrod (1939b), Kenneth Boulding (1939), Abba Lerner (1940), and Oskar Morgenstern (1941). These reviews ranged from highly complimentary (Lerner) to highly critical (Morgenstern). Two important reviews that I did not deal with in my 1991 survey were Arthur Bowley's (Bowley, 1938) September 1938 *Economic Journal* review of Hicks's *Théorie mathématique de la valeur en régime de libre concurrence* (1937b), which eventually appeared as the mathematical appendix to *Value and Capital*, and Fritz Machlup's 1940 *Quarterly Journal of Economics* review essay on the first part of *Value and Capital* (Hicks, 1939a), which he called 'Professor Hicks' Statics.' I did this because, at the time, I was focusing upon Lerner's review essay on the dynamic part of the book, which appeared in the same journal volume immediately after Machlup's treatment of Hicks's statics (Young, 1991: 299).

Because of the importance of Bowley's *Economic Journal* review of Hicks's 1937 work (Bowley, 1938) I deal with it at length here, and also provide a translation of the only sentence on dynamics in Hicks's 'booklet' (published in French). Bowley started by placing Hicks's 1937 'booklet,' the title of which, when translated, is *The Mathematical Theory of Value in a Free Competition System*, in historical context. As he wrote (513–14), it was

in principle a preliminary study to a forthcoming work by the same author on *Value and Capital*. [...] [W]e find here a development of the very important methods initiated in 1934 by Hicks and Allen in *Economica* under the title 'A Reconsideration of the Theory of Value'. [...] The earlier articles related to one individual with a complex of preferences for any number of goods, the formulae being worked out for three goods only. But now we have the analysis extended to include any number of goods (Chapter I), any number of consumers (Chapter II) and any number of producers (Chapter III). [...] It is to be hoped that in his larger work the author will justify these processes.

Bowley continued (514): 'Generally the treatment here makes great demands on mathematical knowledge and owing to compression sometimes fails in lucidity. In the new work there may be a place for the more exact definition of the mathematical theorems used, with proofs where it is not possible to give reference to easily accessible textbooks.' He then wrote (514–15):

The declared object of this work is not, however, the generalization of earlier formulae, but to break completely new ground. The system of equations developed by Pareto went no further than the description of a position of statical equilibrium, without further reference to its stability. Nevertheless, knowledge of the conditions and nature of statical equilibrium tell us the effect of small changes only. If equilibrium is stable, a body will remain at or near its position, till larger or continued disturbances take place, and then we are faced with dynamic problems. It is perhaps important to make clear that here there is no treatment of dynamical economics.

Bowley then cited (515) what he called Hicks's 'tentative' statement on dynamics that appeared on page 53 in the 1937 'booklet,' the translation of which is: 'Then, by assuming that these conditions are still valid in the neighbourhood of the equilibrium condition, we can arrive at some formal conclusions regarding the price mechanism system.' In any event, while Hicks's 1937 'booklet' formed the basis for the mathematical appendix to *Value and Capital*, it remains to be translated!

Machlup's February 1940 *Quarterly Journal of Economics* review essay 'Professor Hicks' Statics' consisted of a long and detailed survey of parts I and II of *Value and Capital*, which he described (Machlup, 1940: 277) as 'a great book.' Machlup opened his survey by stating that, for Hicks, 'all economic theory is equilibrium theory.' When presenting Hicks's analysis of consumption 'as a function of income and a function of price,' Machlup correctly noted (282, note 8) that in his 1937 'booklet' Hicks had already 'dealt with the effects of price changes in terms of elasticities.' Machlup also noted (284–5, note 2) that he had corresponded with Hicks on a specific point in the book due to problems in clarity, and continued on to describe other points made by Hicks as 'complicated' and 'paradoxical,' until the reader of *Value and Capital* 'discovers at some inconspicuous place the assumption from which everything follows' (285). Indeed, it would be interesting to analyze the Machlup–Hicks correspondence, if it could be found. In any event, Machlup then proceeded to deal with possible criticisms of the book (293–7), and concluded (297): 'The study of Professor Hicks's work has cost me more effort per page than any other book I have read in economics. But it was well worth it. I believe that this book is certain to become a "classic."'

The Social Framework

Hicks published *The Social Framework* in 1942 (Hicks, 1942c), and the book was well received in both its first (1945a) and subsequent adaptations and second edition (1952). Hicks's approach in the book was original, as it was, in effect, the first textbook based on what he termed 'social accounting.' In his *Economica* review, C. W. Guillebaud praised Hicks for 'breaking new ground' (Guillebaud, 1943: 191). In the December 1943 issue of *The Economic Journal*, Austin Robinson compared Hicks's approach to that in Boulding's *Economic Analysis*, which he reviewed in the same piece. Robinson made the cogent point that 'Boulding's book represents the American approach' (Robinson, 1943: 387), and went on to criticize it when counterpointed to Hicks's approach in *The Social Framework*. Robinson praised Hicks's 'originality' in taking an 'applied economics,' rather than a theoretical, approach (390–2).

Taking a lead from the adaptation of James Meade's *Economic Analysis and Policy* (Meade, 1936) to the American market by Meade and Hitch (1938), Hicks and Albert Gailord Hart published *The Social Framework of the American Economy* in 1945. Albert L. Meyers reviewed it in the June 1946 issue of *The Journal of Political Economy*. Interestingly enough, in his mostly favorable review, Meyers pointed out that 'the introduction as given is equally suitable for a Keynesian or non-Keynesian subsequent treatment' (Meyers, 1946). G. P. Adams reviewed the Hicks–Hart volume very favorably in the June 1947 issue of *The American Economic Review*, saying that it 'strikes a beautiful balance between simplicity and subtlety' (Adams, 1947: 428). The second edition of *The Social Framework* was also favorably reviewed in the November 1952 issue of *Economica*, especially in light of the two supplementary chapters Hicks had added to it.

A Contribution to the Theory of the Trade Cycle and A Revision of Demand Theory

In his review essay on Hicks's *Trade Cycle*, in the August 1950 issue of *The Quarterly Journal of Economics*, James Duesenberry dealt critically with this 'very concise volume,' which he described as 'ingeniously contrived and urbanely expressed' (Duesenberry, 1950: 464). As he wrote (466), 'Hicks's theory is an elegant one, but if we look at it closely its validity seems doubtful. There are a number of weak points in the theoretical structure. In addition there is considerable doubt about the empirical validity of some of fundamental assumptions.' In his concluding remarks, however, Duesenberry toned down his criticism somewhat (476).

In the November 1950 issue of *The Review of Economics and Statistics*, Richard Goodwin published a review essay on Hicks's *Trade Cycle* book (Goodwin, 1950). Goodwin's article is a prime example of a substantive review with internal focus. Goodwin's positive and insightful review placed the book in the perspective of the treatments of the cycle that preceded Hicks, and Hicks's contribution, which formed the basis for much subsequent work – both theoretical and empirical – in the field of business cycle analysis.

Lerner also reviewed Hicks's book in the October 1951 issue of *Econometrica*. One of the most important points made by Lerner is that regarding the treatment of expectations in the book – or lack of it. As Lerner noted (Lerner, 1951: 473), 'Still more surprising is the absence, in a book by the inventor of the "elasticity of expectations," of any discussion of different expectations in the determination of either investment or consumption.' In a prescient conclusion, Lerner wrote (473–4):

What is clearly demonstrated by this important work is the infinitely greater returns to be expected, at this stage, from top-level economic theorizing than from the exponential accumulation of statistics. And if this is true for the theory of the trade cycle, it is even truer for the theory of achieving and maintaining economic stability and prosperity in a free society, where complex lags and reactions in consumption and investment may be difficult to manage. It is hoped that Hicks and his pupils throughout the world will now apply themselves more directly to this task, for which the theory of the trade cycle is an excellent training ground, even if it should yield no directly applicable results.

Nicholas Kaldor's December 1951 *Economic Journal* review essay on Hicks's *Trade Cycle* book was constructively critical with an external focus. Indeed, like Lerner, Kaldor lamented the fact that 'on the subject of expectations, to which Mr Hicks made such distinguished contributions in the past, the present work is remarkably silent... It is very much to be hoped that the distinguished author of *Value and Capital* will return again to that field...which he seems for the present to have forsaken' (Kaldor, 1951: 839, 846). Kaldor ended his review essay by saying: 'I have devoted so much space to what appeared to me the unsettled issues, that I must have failed to convey an adequate appreciation of the many brilliant and original pieces of analysis with which Mr Hicks's latest work abounds' (847).

G. J. Stigler reviewed Hicks's *A Revision of Demand Theory* (1956b) critically in the April 1957 issue of *The Journal of Political Economy* (Stigler, 1957). In his review, Stigler wrote (169):

On the one hand, the volume elicits strong admiration, for it is a superb peda-gogical performance: lucid, orderly, and ingenious in the exposition of modern utility theory. On the other hand, the volume is of little substantive interest: its chief purpose is to teach well known theorems by the use of elementary tools. One is compelled to question the significance of the task while admiring the performance.

Stigler went further when he remarked critically (*ibid.*): '[T]he scope of "demand theory" is narrowly defined...the literature dealing with interdependence of utility functions of different persons is also brushed aside.' Stigler did recognize, however, that the book was 'a halfway bridge to a promised volume on welfare economics' (170). It must be recalled at this point, though, that Stigler may have perceived Hicks's book as a competitor to his own *Theory of Price* text (1946 1st edn.; 1952, 2nd edn.).

Essays in World Economics

This book (Hicks, 1959b) was reviewed by C. J. Stokes in the June 1960 issue of *The American Economic Review*, by Harry Johnson in August 1960 in *Economica*, and by A. J. Brown in the *Economic History Review* in May 1960. Stokes reviewed it favorably and focused on its implications for US economic policies, calling it 'one of the most powerful condemnations' of US polices 'that has yet appeared,' albeit something that Hicks 'would be first to deny' (Stokes, 1960: 485). Johnson was somewhat disappointed in the volume, which he said was composed of Hicks's 'more popular "policy" pieces of the bank review and tourist lecture type' (Johnson, 1960: 279). Johnson described Hicks's approach as problematic and criticized his views on 'government economic control' and his treatment of 'exceptions' in his 'simple models' and 'generalizations' (279–80). Brown, meanwhile, reviewed Hicks somewhat more objectively, focusing upon his treatment of inflation (Brown, 1960: 304).

Capital and Growth

In his 1965 volume *Capital and Growth*, Hicks returned to themes raised in his seminal '*Value and Capital* growth model' paper (Hicks, 1959a), and went beyond them. Reviews of the book included those by F. H. Hahn in the March 1966 issue of *The Economic Journal*, Davis Dewey in the September 1966 *Journal of Finance*, and Robert M. Solow in the December 1966 issue of *The American Economic Review*. While sympathetic in general to Hicks's central message, reviewers were critical, in places, of the way he tried to put it across. Hahn, for example, praised the 'quality of exposition' and 'lucidity of thought' exhibited in part I of the book, which Hicks called 'Methods of Dynamic Economics,' and thought part II ('Growth Equilibrium') to be 'an extremely skilful exposition.' Hahn had reservations, however, regarding some sections of part III ('Optimum Growth'), especially that dealing with 'optimum savings,' and part IV ('After Growth Theory'), due to Hicks's omission of literature references and detailed discussion of certain issues such as the 'aggregation problem' (Hahn, 1966). Despite this, Hahn concluded: 'For a first-rate progress report on the state of play in current growth theory (which may yet prove abortive), go to Hicks's' (87). Dewey, on the other hand, was critical of many aspects of Hicks's book, especially its literary style and 'form of argument,' accusing Hicks of writing 'like a graduate student's caricature of an Oxford economist' (Dewey, 1966: 568). What Dewey seemed to forget, however, was that the contributions of Oxford economists, from Francis Edgeworth through Hicks, are at the core of modern economics (Young and Lee, 1993).

Solow opened his review of *Capital and Growth* by saying that the book was 'unmistakably Hicks' (Solow, 1966: 1257). He started his analysis of the substance of the book by reference to part II, dealing with growth equilibrium, which he called 'the best part of the book.' In his discussion of Hicks's treatment of 'saving behaviour,' Solow utilized Karl Shell's distinction between 'non-steady-state' and 'steady-state' behavior. He then linked the nature of the assumption of a fixed wealth–income ratio to expectations. As Solow put it, 'In such models, the assumption that expectations are fulfilled generates paths that diverge from the steady state,' but, citing Shell, he went on to say: 'If producers maximize present value and savers maximize utility, full competitive equilibrium leads to the steady state' (1258). In other words, as early as 1966 Solow was saying that, given the conditions of rational expectations and perfect competition, under neoclassical assumptions, such an economy would converge to a steady-state equilibrium accordingly. Solow then turned to parts III and IV of the book, and said that the former made 'accessible the whole range of difficult and important modern theory' (1259). To sum up, Solow's position was that 'anyone who wants to introduce himself or his students to the large volume of recent work on the structure of equilibrium growth will turn to Hicks. This is exposition made into a fine art. And it is more than that; there are some interesting ideas as well. One could hardly expect otherwise' (1258). When Solow's balanced piece is counter-pointed to that of Dewey's, one immediately distinguishes between the *substantive* as against *purposive* types of review of Hicks's work.

Critical Essays in Monetary Theory

Brian Tew (1968), Don Patinkin (1968), Edward Kane (1969), and Robert Clower (1970) reviewed this volume. In his March 1968 review for *The Economic Journal*, Tew focused upon Hicks's 1966 LSE lectures on the subject of the theory of the demand for money. Patinkin, for his part, *purposively* utilized his December 1968 *American Economic Review* piece to continue his ongoing debates with Hicks. First, he took issue with Hicks's treatment of 'liquidity preference.' Patinkin then returned to his earlier debate with Hicks regarding the implications of price flexibility. He wrote that the 'the basic message of Hicks's 1937 paper' – which it shared with the contemporary interpretations of Harrod, Meade, Brian Reddaway, and Oskar Lange (Young, 1987) – was 'that the Keynesian system should be reviewed as a specific instance of a general equilibrium model.' He went on to say, however, that Hicks's emphasis 'on the "liquidity trap" as the distinguishing feature of Keynes's theory of unemployment' was 'less justified' (Patinkin, 1968: 1435). With regard to price flexibility, Patinkin wrote that Hicks's well-known review of *Money, Interest and Prices* for *The Economic Journal* (Hicks, 1957), which was reprinted in Hicks's volume, failed to deal with 'unemployment in terms of a *dis*equilibrium system,' which he had advocated from 1956 onwards (Patinkin, 1968: 1436; emphasis in original). Indeed, here Patinkin was once again defending his 'patrimony,' as in his rejoinder to Hicks's review of *Money, Interest and Prices* (Patinkin, 1959). Finally, Patinkin took issue with Hicks's attempt to relate the 'traditional' with the 'Keynesian' classificatory scheme regarding the characteristics and functions of money (Patinkin, 1968: 1436–8).

Kane reviewed Hicks's *Critical Essays* in the February 1969 issue of *The Canadian Journal of Economics*, asserting that some of them were written as if Hicks '*were* back in the 1930s' (Kane, 1969: 142; emphasis in original). Nevertheless, Kane did recognize that, while, in his view, Hicks may have failed in 'his attempt to reconcile the two triads...the book contains much that is new,' and deserves 'to be read, and read carefully' (144).

Clower's review of *Critical Essays* appeared in *The Journal of Political Economy* in 1970 (Clower, 1970). He opened his review by saying (608): 'No living economist has done more to shape contemporary modes of economic analysis than Sir John Hicks. With regard to monetary theory and Keynesian economics, it would hardly be an overstatement to say that Hicks's ideas have dominated and directed developments in both fields for more than three decades.' His review is a good example of the *substantive* type with *internal* analytical focus, for in it Clower attempted to go *beyond* 'Hicks' conception of a money economy' (608).

A Theory of Economic History

Hicks's 1969 volume *A Theory of Economic History* (1969a) was well received, not only in leading economics journals, such as *The Economic*

Journal and *The Journal of Economic Literature*, but in leading history journals, including *The English Historical Review* and *The American Historical Review*, and *The Journal of Interdisciplinary History*. Brian Mitchell, in his June 1970 review for *The Economic Journal*, wrote that there was 'much that is wise and admirable' in his book (Mitchell, 1970: 350), noting Hicks's special emphasis on 'the growth of specialization' as the driving force in his analytical classificatory system (351) – something that the other reviewers dealt with at length. In his September 1970 *Journal of Economic Literature* review, Frederic Lane, for his part, dealt with Hicks's classificatory and general 'scheme of social evolution within which different forms of economic life may be distinguished' (Lane, 1970: 821).

D. C. Coleman reviewed the book for *The English Historical Review* in July 1971. He concluded that Hicks's volume offered 'little encouragement to modern enthusiasts' of what was then called 'new' or 'quantitative' economic history (Coleman, 1971), which is now called 'cliometrics.' William Parker, in his review for *The American Historical Review*, was somewhat critical of Hicks's writing style, but not of the substance of the book itself. He wrote that Hicks 'has produced not a theory of economic history, but a theorist's economic history – a different, but a more human and interesting thing' (Parker, 1972: 1087), going on to note that Hicks deliberately omitted dealing with technology as he excluded it 'in his definition of things economic' (1088).

Jonathan Hughes, in his 1972 review essay on the book for *The Journal of Interdisciplinary History*, wrote that, while Hicks's object was 'to create a theory about *all* of economic history,' it was '*not millennial.*' Thus, it was not deterministic, nor were there any 'inexorable historical forces' involved. As he noted, 'Hicks uses stages as a classification scheme, but *they are not historically irreversible*' (Hughes, 1972: 271–2; emphases added). Hughes went on to counterpoint Hicks as 'theorist' to Hicks as 'historian' (272). Peter Bauer and Alexander Gerschenkron wrote other notable reviews. In a critical vein, Bauer noted that '[i]n general, in Hicks's account the causal relationship runs almost exclusively from economics to the other social fields, and not in the reverse direction' (Bauer, 1971: 166). Similarly critical, though 'inextricably combined with admiration,' was the review by Gerschenkron, who noted that 'in several respects...the author's stress on the merchants as the promoters of economic progress appears to this reviewer exaggerated and one-sided' (Gerschenkron, 1971: 666).

Capital and Time: A Neo-Austrian Theory

Some reviewers have dated Hicks's interest in Austrian economics, and thereby his book *Capital and Time* (1973a), from his 1970 attempt at developing a neo-Austrian growth theory (Hicks, 1970). Hicks himself dated his interest in Austrian capital theory to Friedrich Hayek's LSE seminars over the period 1931–5. Two important reviews of Hicks's treatment of capital from a 'neo-Austrian' perspective in his 1973 book are that of Solow in *The Economic Journal* and Thomas K. Rymes in *The Canadian Journal of Economics*.

Solow, in his March 1974 review for *The Economic Journal*, called the book 'illuminating' and a combination of 'lucidity and depth' (Solow, 1974: 189, 192). Solow accepted Hicks's interpretation of the 'Austrian model' with regard to the transition between steady states. Indeed, he found it 'enlightening' insofar as 'it says that a capital-using innovation is one whose cost-savings and productivity gains are concentrated late in the process' (191). On the other hand, he was critical of 'the Austrian model' when it dealt with processes 'outside the steady state' – that is to say, 'in disequilibrium' (*ibid.*).

Rymes, for his part, in his November 1974 *Canadian Journal of Economics* review of the book, focused upon what Hicks called 'the principal proposition,' which Hicks thought 'perhaps the most important' in the book. This involved the assertion 'that substitution over time slows the rise in real wages that accompanies technical improvement,' but also extends 'the rise through time so that a larger rise is ultimately achieved' (Rymes, 1974: 705). Like Solow before him (Solow, 1974: 191), however, Rymes criticized Hicks's 'key assumption of static expectations' as 'especially brittle' (Rymes, 1974: 705).

The Crisis in Keynesian Economics, Economic Perspectives, and Causality in Economics

The Crisis in Keynesian Economics

Hicks's volume *The Crisis in Keynesian Economics* (1974b) was reviewed by a number of prominent monetary theorists who were not in the 'Keynesian camp.' The reviewers included Johnson, A. L. Marty, and Karl Brunner, among others, and reviews appeared in the leading journals, including *The Journal of Economic Literature*, *The Economic Journal*, and *The Journal of Money, Credit and Banking*, with *two* reviews in *The Journal of Political Economy*: that of Johnson in 1975 and that of Brunner in 1981. Johnson's review in the June 1975 issue of *The Journal of Political Economy* was *purposive* and very critical. Johnson attacked Hicks for 'undue deference to Keynes and the Cambridge Keynesians' and he called the book 'disappointing' (Johnson, 1975: 672). Philip Bell, in the March 1976 issue of *The Journal of Economic Literature*, focused upon what

I called above the '*integrating theme*' in his review, which, as he put it, was that 'the whole book was telling us to stop dealing solely with macro-economic generalities and to start disaggregating and looking more at *particular* markets and market situations and structures' (Bell, 1976: 70; emphasis added). Michael Posner, in his March 1976 review for *The Economic Journal*, saw the volume as consisting of 'interesting and thought-provoking essays in the Keynesian spirit' (Posner, 1976: 123).

In his substantive, albeit somewhat critical review in the May 1980 issue of *The Journal of Money, Credit and Banking*, Marty used an internal focus in his attempt to deal with the central message of the lectures 'in turn' (Marty, 1980: 253). With regard to the first lecture, he suggested replacing the wage-unit deflator with a price deflator (254). When discussing the second lecture, Marty explained how Hicks differed from the monetarist position via reference to Hicks's definition of 'the price of money as the "rate of interest" rather than the reciprocal of the general price level' (254). With regard to the last chapter, which he termed the 'most cryptic and controversial,' Marty showed that Hicks implicitly rejected 'the natural rate hypothesis' (255). In contrast to this, in his October 1981 review for *The Journal of Political Economy*, Brunner thought the last chapter to be 'particularly informative and suggestive' (Brunner, 1981: 1053). Brunner's comments also indicate an internal focus when he wrote 'The attention given by Hicks to the comparative durability of market relations seems particularly promising for a useful approach to the explanation of wage behaviour. Such reasoning would link the labour market phenomena with evolutions on the output market' (1053–4).

Economic Perspectives

Economic Perspectives (Hicks, 1977a), was reviewed by Geoffrey Harcourt in the March 1979 issue of *The Economic Journal* (Harcourt, 1979), and by Axel Leijonhufvud in the June 1979 issue of *The Journal of Economic Literature* (Leijonhufvud, 1979). Harcourt's focus was external, and he dealt with the evolution of Hicks's ideas as manifest in the essays reprinted in the volume. Leijonhufvud's review, on the other hand, had an internal focus. He first made the distinction between 'Hicks the younger' and the 'elder Hicks' (*ibid.*: 525). The internal focus of Leijonhufvud's review is seen in his discussion of Hicks's essay 'Monetary Experience and the Theory of Money,' which made its first appearance in this volume. Leijonhufvud identified what he called the '"Hicks curve", a locus summarizing the feasible long-run combinations of inflation and real growth rates' (526), although this curve has remained *overlooked* up to now. Leijohnufvud also noted the fact that Hicks's 1969 *Journal of Money*,

Credit and Banking paper 'Automatists, Hawtreyans and Keynesians' (Hicks, 1969b), reprinted in *Economic Perspectives*, contained analysis that included 'endogenous expectations dependent on government choice of policy' (Leijonhufvud, 1979: 527). Both of these points remain to be investigated by the present generation of historians of economic thought.

Causality in Economics

In 1979 Hicks published *Causality in Economics*. The volume was reviewed by Alan Coddington in *The Economic Journal*, Charles Kindleberger in *The Journal of Economic Literature*, and Lawrence Boland in *The Canadian Journal of Economics*. In his June 1980 review for *The Economic Journal* (Coddington, 1980: 396), Coddington noted that, while

Hicks is interested in the identification of causes insofar as they contribute to, or function as, explanations…, an alternative way of looking at this monograph is a very discursive review of, and postscript to, Keynes' *General Theory*, in which the opening chapters provide the preamble and the necessary apparatus for this re-working of a task to which Hicks has repeatedly returned.

Coddington thought (397) that Hicks's 'central message' in the book was a program of 'ambitious theoretical reconstruction,' enabling the identification of 'phenomena' requiring 'a more elaborate analytical framework in order to permit the work of causal explanation.' Kindleberger, for his part, in his September 1980 *Journal of Economic Literature* review, noted that Hicks's 'discussion of causality…penetrates deeply into the philosophical riddles of causation in history as well as contemporary economic decision-making' (Kindleberger, 1980: 1087).

Boland, in his November 1980 *Canadian Journal of Economics* review, took Hicks's 'central message' to be 'that the methodology and causal precepts of physics are inappropriate for economics' (Boland, 1980: 741). In his substantive review, Boland took an internal focus on the volume, relating Hicks's position on causality to his view of economics in general.

Collected Essays on Economic Theory (volume I, Wealth and Welfare; volume II, Money, Interest and Wages; volume III, Classics and Moderns)

Tibor Scitovsky reviewed *Wealth and Welfare* in the September 1982 issue of *The Journal of Economic Literature*. The focus of his substantive review was internal, and he related Hicks's papers as reprinted in the volume to the development of economic theory in general, and what he called 'the new welfare economics' in particular (Scitovsky, 1982: 1063–4).

Harcourt, David Laidler, and Robert King reviewed *Money, Interest and Wages*. In his March 1983 *Economic Journal* review, Harcourt's focus was external, dealing with a historical development of the papers in the volume and the ongoing evolution of Hicks's thought (Harcourt, 1983: 215–16). The focus of Laidler's August 1983 review for *The Journal of Money, Credit and Banking*, on the other hand, was internal. Laidler linked a number of Hicks's papers to modern developments, such as Hicks's anticipation of the 'modern analysis of wage contracts as a means of sharing risk between firms and their employees,' as manifest in Hicks's 1931 *Economica* paper 'The Theory of Uncertainty and Profit,' reprinted in the volume. Laidler also illustrated the relationship between the models of Hicks and Robert Lucas on the one hand, and those of Hicks, Clower, and Leijohnifvud on the other (Laidler, 1983: 386).

In his important December 1983 *Journal of Economic Literature* review of *Money, Interest and Wages*, King raised the thematic issue regarding the collection of Hicks's essays, and, at the same time, provided a wide-ranging internal focus regarding the volume's contents, going so far as to identify some of Hicks's work as the basis for such progressive research programs as 'perfect foresight dynamic equilibrium' and 'dynamic general equilibrium models' of growth and the business cycle (King, 1983).

Hahn reviewed *Classics and Moderns* in the December 1984 issue of *The Economic Journal*. Hahn's review had external focus, and he related the development of Hicks's thought via an overview of papers in the volume and what he called Hicks's 'intellectual inclinations' (Hahn, 1984: 960–1). Brian Scarfe, in his *Journal of Economic Literature* review, published in the same month, dealt with the 'integrating theme' in the volume, which he took to emanate from 'the important first chapter on revolutions in economics' (Scarfe, 1984: 1634).

A Market Theory of Money

Hicks's final book, published in 1989 (Hicks, 1989a), was reviewed in 1990 by Tony Cramp in *The Economic Journal* and in 1991 by Hahn in *Economica*. In his March 1990 *Economic Journal* review, Cramp started from what could be called the 'cognitive dissonance' of Hicks 'the monetary theorist' and Hicks 'the value theorist', and proceeded by focusing his review, in external terms, on the 'tension' between 'the monetary Hicks' and 'value theorist' accordingly (Cramp, 1990: 251). Cramp concluded his short but insightful review by saying (252): 'Monetary economists will do well to keep listening, on both method and content, to an economist, who is dead but far from defunct.'

Hahn's August 1991 *Economica* review provided an external focus on Hicks's last book. Regarding the first part of the volume, as Hahn put it (Hahn, 1991: 410), 'Much of what Hicks has to say is well known and yet is persistently ignored.' As for the second part of the volume, Hahn wrote (411): 'There is much in this part of the book that is arresting (and crying out for formalisation).' He then turned to the third part of the book, which in his view 'has a very fine chapter on Wicksell's credit economy and a very good one on international financial matters,' while the 'best' was the chapter on inflation. Hahn concluded, however, that he could not detect a 'unifying theme' between the parts of the book. As he put it (*ibid.*), 'I could not detect a unifying theoretical framework, only a series of often very penetrating chapters on various aspects of money, finance and markets. The Marshall in Hicks has defeated me. Others may do better. Certainly they should try, since experience tells us that not to understand Hicks may mean that one does not understand economics.'

Conclusion

The development of modern economics has been called 'the age of Hicks.' As Leijonhufvud noted, however, Hicks changed his views over the course of his career, and the reviews of some of his later works reflect the reaction of some reviewers to his shift in interest from what they considered the 'mainstream.' Summing up the reviews surveyed in this chapter, however, attests to the fact that, even in his later works, Hicks's contributions were recognized as thought-provoking, and in many cases original and insightful. Moreover, whether the reviews of his work surveyed here had an internal or external focus, in only a few cases were the purposive reviews critical, and, even when critical, they recognized that the issues Hicks raised needed to be addressed.

Most of the substantive reviews surveyed in this chapter recognized the connection between the central message or messages of Hicks's works – that is, of his research program – and what *was*, or *was to become*, the mainstream of economic inquiry and analysis. As an illustration of this, we can recall King's insightful review, in which, basically, he said that Hicks's ideas from 1931 onwards influenced the development of modern economics – ranging from Arrow–Debreu through Muth–Lucas, and up to and including Kydland–Prescott and Long–Plosser varieties of research programs (King, 1983: 1498–9). In retrospect, then, let us paraphrase Hahn's conclusion in his review of Hicks's last book: in order to understand *future* developments in economics, one must understand Hicks.

Appendix

Reviews of Hicks's books cited (by title and chronological order)

The Theory of Wages (1st and 2nd editions)
1st edition
1933: Clay, H., *Economica*, new series 41 (August), 329–32.
1933: Shove, G. F., *Economic Journal*, 43 (September), 460–72.
1933: Morrison, L. A., *American Economic Review*, 23 (December), 686–7.
1935: Director, A., *Journal of Political Economy*, 43 (1, February), 109–11.
2nd edition
1965: Reder, M. W., *Economica*, new series, 32 (February), 88–90.
1965: Kruger, A., *Canadian Journal of Economics and Political Science*, 31 (1, February), 164.

La Théorie mathématique de la valeur en régime de libre concurrence
1938: Bowley, A. L., *Economic Journal*, 48 (September), 513–15.

Value and Capital and its mathematical appendix
1939: Hawtrey, R. G., *Journal of the Royal Statistical Society*, 102 (2, April), 307–12.
1939: Firth, G. G., *Economic Record*, 15 (June), 68–73.
1939: Haley, B. F., *American Economic Review*, 29 (3, June), 557–60.
1939: Harrod, R. F., *Economic Journal*, 49 (2, June), 294–300.
1939: Boulding, K. E., *Canadian Journal of Economics and Political Science*, 5 (4, October), 521–8.
1940: Machlup, F., *Quarterly Journal of Economics*, 54 (2, February), 277–97.
1940: Lerner, A. P., *Quarterly Journal of Economics*, 54 (2, February), 298–306.
1941: Morgenstern, O., *Journal of Political Economy*, 49 (3, June), 361–93.

The Social Framework (1st and 2nd and American editions)
1943: Guillebaud, C. W., *Economica*, new series, 10 (May), 190–1.
1943: Robinson, E. A. G., *Economic Journal*, 53 (December), 387–92.
1946: Meyers, A. L., *Journal of Political Economy*, 54 (3, June), 275.
1947: Adams, G. P. Jr. *American Economic Review*, 37 (3, June), 428–9.

A Contribution to the Theory of the Trade Cycle and A Revision of Demand Theory
1950: Duesenberry, J. J., *Quarterly Journal of Economics* 64 (3, August), 464–76.
1950: Goodwin, R. M., *Review of Economics and Statistics*, 32 (4, November), 316–20.
1951: Lerner, A. P., *Econometrica*, 19 (4, October), 472–4.
1951: Kaldor, N., *Economic Journal*, 61 (December), 833–47.
1957: Stigler, G. J., *Journal of Political Economy*, 65 (2, April), 169–70.

Essays in World Economics
1960: Brown, A. J., *Economic History Review*, new series, 13 (2, May), 303–4.
1960: Stokes, C. J., *American Economic Review*, 50 (June), 483–5.
1960: Johnson, H. G., *Economica*, new series, 27 (August), 279–80.

Capital and Growth
1966: Hahn, F. H., *Economic Journal*, 76 (March), 84–7.
1966: Dewey, D., *Journal of Finance*, 21 (3, September), 568–9.
1966: Solow, R. M., *American Economic Review*, 56 (December), 1257–60.

Critical Essays in Monetary Theory
1968: Tew, B., *Economic Journal*, 78 (March), 108–10.
1968: Patinkin, D., *American Economic Review*, 58 (December), 1435–8.
1969: Kane, E. J., *Canadian Journal of Economics*, 2 (February), 141–4.
1970: Clower, R., *Journal of Political Economy*, 78 (3, June), 608–11.

A Theory of Economic History
1970: Mitchell, B. R., *Economic Journal*, 80 (June), 350–2.
1970: Lane, F. C., *Journal of Economic Literature*, 8 (3, September), 821–3.
1971: Bauer, P., *Economica*, new series, 38 (May), 163–79.
1971: Coleman, D. C., *English Historical Review*, 86 (July), 596.
1971: Gerschenkron, A., *Economic History Review*, new series, 24 (4, November), 653–66.
1972: Parker, W. N., *American Historical Review*, 77 (4, October), 1087–8.
1972: Hughes, J. R. T., *Journal of Interdisciplinary History*, 2, (3, Winter), 263–80.

Capital and Time
1974: Solow, R. M., *Economic Journal*, 84 (March), 189–92.
1974: Rymes, T. K., *Canadian Journal of Economics*, 7 (4, November), 705–6.

The Crisis in Keynesian Economics
1975: Johnson, H. G., *Journal of Political Economy* 83 (3, June), 671–3.
1976: Bell, P. W., *Journal of Economic Literature*, 14 (1, March), 68–70.
1976: Posner, M. V., *Economic Journal*, 86 (March), 122–3.
1980: Marty, A. L., *Journal of Money, Credit and Banking*, 12 (2, March), 253–5.
1981: Brunner, K., *Journal of Political Economy*, 89 (5, October), 1052–4.

Economic Perspectives
1979: Harcourt, G. C., *Economic Journal*, 89 (March), 144–6.
1979: Leijonhufvud, A., *Journal of Economic Literature*, 17 (2, June), 525–8.

Causality in Economics
1980: Coddington, A., *Economic Journal*, 90 (June), 395–7.
1980: Kindleberger, C. P., *Journal of Economic Literature*, 18 (3, September), 1086–8.
1980: Boland, L. A., *Canadian Journal of Economics*, 13 (4, November), 740–3.

Collected Essays on Economic Theory, vol. I, Wealth and Welfare
1982: Scitovsky, T., *Journal of Economic Literature*, 20 (3, September), 1062–4.

Collected Essays on Economic Theory, vol. II, Money, Interest and Wages
1983: Harcourt, G. C., *Economic Journal*, 93 (March), 215–17.
1983: Laidler, D., *Journal of Money, Credit and Banking*, 15 (3, August), 385–9.
1983: King, R. G., *Journal of Economic Literature*, 21 (4, December), 1497–9.

Collected Essays on Economic Theory, vol. III, *Classics and Moderns*
1984: Hahn, F. H., *Economic Journal*, 94 (December), 960–2.
1984: Scarfe, B. L., *Journal of Economic Literature*, 22 (4, December), 1633–4.

A Market Theory of Money
1990: Cramp, T., *Economic Journal*, 100 (March), 251–2.
1991: Hahn, F. H., *Economica*, new series, 58 (August), 410–11.

Part II

Markets

7   Hicks and the emptiness of general equilibrium theory

Christopher Bliss

The ontology of general equilibrium

In his great classic work *Value and Capital*, John Hicks claims that static general equilibrium theory is somewhat sterile (see Bliss, 1994: 87–8). What did he mean by that, and how did he propose to deal with the problem? Before elaborating Hicks's particular answer to my question – which answer, I argue is not correct – I exposit a broader account of the emptiness of general equilibrium theory.

Bologna, which hosted the Hicks anniversary conference, was the home of some of the finest medieval philosophy. And a good starting point for me is the famous ontological proof of the existence of God. Put very simply, this argument claims that there must exist a perfect being – identified as God – because non-existence would be an imperfection, for which reason God must exist. I cannot detail here the numerous problems with the ontological argument. Thomas Aquinas was unconvinced. Bertrand Russell pointed out decisively that existence is not a predicate. It is not a property of an entity, as having one horn is for the unicorn, despite that poor creature being poorly endowed where existence is concerned.

I want to focus here on a secondary difficulty with the ontological proof. Even if one were to accept the proof, we are not told much about the God whose existence is demonstrated. He (though it might be she, or neither he nor she) is perfect, which is hard to visualize, and – that apart – exists. If all we get is existence, we do not get much.

The situation is very much the same where general equilibrium theory is concerned. If one starts with the basic axioms of the theory – convexity, maximization, the Walras identity, etc. – what follows rigorously and generally from those axioms? The answer is simple and clear. *The existence of at least one general equilibrium follows, and nothing else.* It gets worse. Suppose we assume that we have a dynamically stable general equilibrium, although there is no proof in existence for such an equilibrium; what can we infer then? Again, the answer is a disappointment. Nothing follows; not uniqueness, not specific comparative statics results. General equilibrium theory is like the ontological argument: it gives us existence but tells us nothing about what it is that exists. This is detailed formally in two fine papers by Hugo Sonnenschein, 'Market Excess Demand Functions' (1972) and 'Do Walras' Identity and Continuity Characterize the Class of Community Demand Functions?' (1973) (see also Kirman, 1989).

Stability, comparative statics, and the correspondence principle

To people with a training in physics, my claim that assuming the stability of an equilibrium does not give us anything may come as a surprise. In mechanics, stability is critical in obtaining definite results. The principle of virtual work applied via the tensor calculus works only for a stable equilibrium. Here the fundamental underlying principle is energy conservation in a closed system, and energy conservation and maximization are almost the same. William Rowan Hamilton's great contribution is his establishment of a precise equivalence between the two.

Unfortunately, economics is not physics. Many agent market equilibrium systems do not conserve anything – at least, not anything that it is much help to take into account. That is a major explanation for the emptiness of general equilibrium theory. We cannot leave the matter there, however. Any inquiring student will surely ask: are there interesting special cases in which market equilibrium systems are like mechanical equilibrium states? It is through the answer to that question that we can best appreciate what John Hicks achieved, and also see the difference between his approach and the distinct but somewhat parallel work of Paul Samuelson (see also Bliss, 1987).

To put it simply, Hicks believed that it is dynamics that gives life to the otherwise empty general equilibrium theory. To say, as I have already done, that this is not quite correct is not to deny that dynamic analysis may be the most challenging and interesting application of general equilibrium techniques. That said, dynamics is harder than statics. For the general equilibrium of competitive markets there is more or less only one way of formulating the model. The dynamics of the model can be formulated in numerous ways, each with some plausibility, each perhaps capturing an important feature of reality. As usual, Hicks was ingenious and creative in the way he did his dynamic analysis. So, even if he did place too much faith in what dynamics can do for us, what he did retains an extraordinary interest.

Where John Hicks came from

Many who met Hicks will think that it is scarcely possible to imagine anyone more English. One could argue, however, that what made Hicks uniquely important and distinctive is that his economics education was to a considerable extent not English. It spared him the insular schooling in Marshallian economics that was the norm in the United Kingdom in the early decades of the twentieth century. Alfred Marshall had done great things, but his tradition had become stale and unproductive by the 1920s.

Hicks's years at the London School of Economics, early in his career, while he was still learning economics brought him into contact with powerful scholars who were well acquainted with the thinking of continental European economists, notably Lionel Robbins and Nicholas Kaldor. The difference that these influences made is immediately evident from reading the introduction to and part I of *Value and Capital*. Its author takes the general equilibrium of markets to be the leading problem of economic theory. Marshall's *Principles of Economics*, which supposedly discusses everything, has nothing on that fundamental problem.

Hicks was not ignorant of Marshall's economics, nor did he discard it completely. Rather, he used Marshallian ideas to argue that Walrasian statics needed to be reinforced by a better dynamics than the unsatisfactory dynamics that Léon Walras had provided. This mixing of the English with the unEnglish refreshed both traditions. As is often the case with intellectual exchanges, the whole is more than the sum of the parts. This, as well as its author's powerful mind, accounts for the greatness of *Value and Capital*.

There is no need to unravel further the intellectual influences that feed into *Value and Capital*, for the author lays it all out clearly in the introduction (Hicks, 1939a: 3–5). He starts with an unMarshallian definition of the fundamental problem of value theory, the general equilibrium of many markets. He leaves no doubt, moreover, concerning the economists who have inspired him. He writes (*ibid.*: 4):

What we mainly need is a technique for studying the interrelations of markets. When looking for such a technique we are naturally impelled to turn to the works of those authors who have specially studied such interrelations – that is to say, the economists of the Lausanne school, Walras and Pareto, to whom, I think, Wicksell should be added. [...] Our own work is bound to be in their tradition, and to be a continuation of theirs.

A continuation is required only if the end has not been reached. What was it that Hicks regarded as missing from the work of the Lausanne school to which he had to add? He refers to 'a certain sterility' about the approach of Walras (60). Again, the introduction to *Value and Capital* provides the answer as to what it was that he found to be missing.

Vilfredo Pareto's work is limited by a lack of attention to capital and interest. Knut Wicksell's work, which is certainly not deficient in that regard, suffers from the limitation that, lacking as it did a knowledge of Pareto's contribution, which his own work pre-dated, Wicksell could not take his analysis beyond what Hicks calls 'the artificial abstraction of a stationary state.'

In communicating with a readership that he presumes to be English, familiar with Marshall, and unfamiliar with the works of the Lausanne school (not at that time available in the English language), Hicks explains his proposed course in words that capture perfectly his English and not so English position (Hicks, 1939a: 5):

I shall summarize such parts of their [the Lausanne school's] work as I need in the course of my own argument. I shall take for granted not Pareto's value theory but the more familiar value theory of Marshall; and this will have some advantages, since I do not regard Pareto's theory as being superior to Marshall's in all respects. One of the things we have to do is to fill out Pareto's theory in those respects where it is defective compared with Marshall's.

There is more below on the respects in which Pareto's theory suffered from problems, and Marshall's was possibly superior.

The map of pure economic theory

As has been noted already, Hicks regarded the general equilibrium of markets as the central defining model of pure economic theory. That, however, provides less than a complete plan of how theory – or, rather, various interrelated economic theories – hangs together. The reader of *Value and Capital* is left in no doubt that its author regards a theory of capital as the greatest prize to be obtained from his investigation. Nonetheless, he goes at the pursuit of that prize indirectly, first working through the building blocks of a general equilibrium model. As he puts it (Hicks, 1939a: 3):

That is why I have to ask the reader to control his impatience to be reading about Saving and Investment, Interest and Prices, Booms and Slumps; and to be content to go back to school with Marginal Utility. Roundabout methods, it has been said, are sometimes more productive than direct methods; it is perhaps fitting that we should discuss the theory of capital in a setting which illustrates that famous principle.

A contemporary reader is likely to find this passage disorientating. We are so used now to receiving our economics neatly packaged in parcels labeled 'macro' and 'micro' that Hicks's flagrant disregard of the boundary between general equilibrium and macro/money theory cannot fail to seize our attention. This is not an old approach, long established and long forgotten. It was fresh and radical when it was written, very much a product of a particular time, the second half of the 1930s, and of Hicks's encounter with the John Maynard Keynes of *The General Theory*.

Hicks read Keynes, and it hit him like a 'road to Damascus' conversion. His thinking could never be the same again. He could easily have abandoned his researches into the general equilibrium; or he could have pursued that research as a self-contained exercise, not worrying about the new issues. Those would both have been simple paths to take. Instead, he chose a more bold and risky course: to take the Lausanne school general equilibrium of markets and to make it respond to Keynes's questions.

It is no contradiction to say that this enterprise was less than entirely successful, and that what Hicks did achieve was of monumental importance. He did more than apply the general equilibrium model. He first refined it and gave it a modern specification. Then he extended it to encompass capital theory. Hicks was not content with the static long-run view of capital that he found in Wicksell, however, and he used an unstated axiom that courses through the pages of *Value and Capital*: capital equals dynamics.

At first sight this position seems to be odd. A static theory of capital may be limited, but it is surely a natural starting point. We know now, as probably Hicks did not fully appreciate, that we can even have a meta-static capital theory, with all the Arrow–Debreu markets for forward and contingent goods present. I suspect that it is not just that Hicks did not consider these points but, rather, that he would have had no patience with them had he done so. With his head buzzing with Keynes's ideas, he wanted to bring expectations in, and with them a less formal treatment of uncertainty than we get from the Arrow–Debreu model. Then dynamics really do become rewarding and equilibrium theory will no longer be empty.

Value and Capital is divided as follows. The titles are due to Hicks, but the interpretations in brackets are my own.

Part I: Subjective Value (demand from ordinal utility);
Part II: General Equilibrium of Exchange (given life by stability conditions);
Part III: Foundations of Dynamic Economics (general equilibrium through time);
Part IV: Workings of a Dynamic System (expectations in intertemporal dynamics).

One question may be answered straightforwardly. How does this schema relate to what had gone before? The answer is simple. There had never been anything like it before. What made Hicks's contribution important is not the answers that he provides to classic questions, although there are some of those. Rather, it is the development of entirely new questions and new ways of viewing the fundamental issues of economic theory. There, even when his answers are far from perfect, Hicks effectively redefined the field.

Subjective value

In part I of *Value and Capital*, we find a Hicks developing older ideas, especially his joint work with Roy Allen (Allen and Hicks, 1934a, 1934b), on lines that owed nothing to the new thought of Keynes. What Hicks does, though, is powerful, original, and hugely important. He takes the concept of the indifference curve, conceived by Pareto but never properly developed by him, and shows how the entire theory of consumer demand can be derived from ordinal utility alone. Obviously, what follows later in *Value and Capital* is of greater ultimate importance. Even so, in observing how Hicks handles this problem we learn a great deal about his philosophy and technique. In summary, he covers the existence of a solution, but is far from satisfied by it. The meat of a theory, as he sees it, is comparative statics, which in turn depends upon dynamics. This requires, first, the convexity of indifference curves – quasi-concavity of preferences, as we would now say – and then depends ultimately upon patterns of complementarity and substitutability between goods.

The general equilibrium of exchange

Equipped with his theory of consumer demand, Hicks applies it at once to the most basic general equilibrium of markets model: pure exchange between consumers involving only goods and personal services. Hicks is soon able to show that stability is problematic. In particular, price changes cause income effects, and these can, in principle, do anything. To resolve these issues, Hicks requires a method for treating stability in a general multiple commodity market system.

Although he does not state it directly in the introduction to *Value and Capital*, it is evident what Hicks found to be missing from the Lausanne school ideas from which he started. His criticism of Wicksell captures it. He takes the view that static general equilibrium theory is somewhat sterile (see Bliss, 1994: 87–8). His idea parallels the thinking in Paul Samuelson's doctoral thesis (published as Samuelson, 1947), while being completely independent of it, for Hicks was unaware of Samuelson's work until much later. Samuelson's correspondence principle says that only comparative statics results give substance to economic theory; and only stability conditions yield comparative statics results. Therefore, statics needs at least local dynamics to give it life.

Feeling the need for dynamics, where was John Hicks to turn? There were three natural routes, which I list in more or less decreasing order of plausibility. Hicks entirely neglected the first; examined the second but found it unsatisfactory; and built an elaborated theory from the third. Attaching personal names to all three routes, so that they have memorable labels, I call them:

(i)   Galileo and Newton;
(ii) Cournot; and
(iii) Marshall.

The first item on the list is labeled 'Newton' to indicate the obvious point that Hicks might have drawn on the huge body of scientific knowledge concerning dynamics that already existed in his time in a highly developed form; that had existed in its essentials in the over two centuries going back to Isaac Newton's *Principia*; and that originated with Galileo Galilei, who understood that rates of change are the magnitudes for which physics should seek to account. That this was a highly possible route is proved by the fact that Samuelson followed it and was able to elucidate the basics of economic dynamics as well as anyone has ever done. That Hicks did not do likewise may be explained by the fact that he did not have Samuelson's high level of mathematical training.

If he was to find his starting point closer to economics, Hicks had a less rich store on which to draw. A little economic dynamics had been developed by older writers, however. The second label indicates the contribution of non-English economists, notably Augustin Cournot, whose approach was closest to physics and the best. Walras also had a dynamics, which Hicks rightly found to be unsatisfactory.

Summarizing Walras's argument crudely, but not unfairly, he reasoned as follows. Market equilibrium solves a complicated mathematical problem. Complicated mathematical problems can be solved by successive approximations. Price adjustments in markets should be seen as successive approximations to the solution to the complicated mathematical problem of market equilibrium.

We now know that this sequence of steps is invalid. Existence and stability cannot be equated. In truth, we cannot explain how the mathematical problem of simultaneous market equilibrium is solved. Indeed, it is highly likely that in reality nothing that could be so described happens. The train hits the same buffers in Samuelson's *Foundations* (1947). When equilibrium entails a single maximizer, that author obtains beautiful thermodynamic-style comparative statics results. For other equilibrium models, however, the same is not true. Samuelson, a born-again Keynesian as much as Hicks, illustrates this with a simple Keynes-style equilibrium model.

The third route was to look for an economic dynamics from the work of English-language economists. There was even less material there than for the case of the non-English-language economists, but there was some. In particular, Alfred Marshall had developed a pseudo-dynamics in the form of his period analysis for the partial equilibrium of a market served by many firms (see Marshall, 1920, book V). As it stood, this model was not at all what Hicks required. It was partial equilibrium with no obvious means of extending it to general equilibrium. Hicks repaired that problem. He borrowed the method and adapted it to treat of dynamics and comparative statics in a simultaneous equilibrium model.

There was another, deeper, difficulty, however. Marshall's dynamics was not genuine dynamics. Not, that is, in the sense that Newton's dynamics is genuine dynamics – i.e. a set of mathematical equations that determine the rates of change of the system variables; or, at least, that only for a very special case. Marshall's model applied to a market initially in long-period equilibrium that receives a permanent shock – say a sudden and permanent rise in demand.

Three defining model variables are assumed to adjust at such sharply differential rates that three different types of equilibrium are reached successively according to whether one, two, or all three of these variables have adjusted to the post-shock state, or have not adjusted at all. The variables at issue, in decreasing order of adjustment speed, are: market price; output or fast-adjusting factor input; and capital stock or slow-adjusting factor input. Then the successive equilibria are respectively: the market-period equilibrium; short-period equilibrium; and long-period equilibrium.[1]

Hicks took this model and adapted it brilliantly to general equilibrium analysis by replacing the lagged adjustment of factor inputs by the lagged adjustment of out-of-market prices. The method is most easily understood via the figures shown on page 68 of *Value and Capital*. The curves drawn in price space each show various combinations of prices that equilibrate one market or the other. The dynamic adjustment process is of a successive adjustment of prices to equilibrate first one market and then the other. Such a description of price adjustment, as Samuelson pointed out, is artificial and does not correspond to true dynamic (i.e. differential equation) stability. This valid point turned out not to matter as much as one might expect, however. The point is that general stability does not have usable implications. We are always forced, therefore, to consider special cases.

---

[1] Hicks exposits this model and criticizes it on pages 119–22 of *Value and Capital* (1939a).

It happened that Hicks's Marshallian method captured the crucial special cases. In particular, Hicks found that substitution effects need to dominate if the system is to be well behaved, and that own-price effects should be larger than cross-price effects. These findings paved the way for later mathematical economic modeling using gross substitutability and diagonal dominance.[2]

I would like to add a retrospective note to the above discussion of the various approaches to dynamics. It is tempting, yet wrong, to suppose that the simple differential-equation approach is always the best method of doing economic dynamics. Economics has gained greatly from the use of the maximum principle of Lev Pontryagin (see Pontryagin et al., 1962). That technique has state variables driven by a system of differential equations, and constrained by fixed initial conditions. The control variables, however, behave differently. They are piecewise continuous and unconstrained except by boundary rules.

That distinction between what might be called differential-equation variables and jump variables appears again in Rudiger Dornbusch's famous overshooting model. There the exchange rate is a jump variable, although not an optimal control (see Dornbusch, 1976). Can something along the lines of Marshall's period method be made mathematically precise? Probably not, as a period analysis will always be somewhat artificial.

The remainder of Part II of *Value and Capital* looks at production, extending similar techniques to that case. The differences are clear. With constant returns there is no equivalent to the income effect. On the other hand, the presence of both inputs and outputs allows for more complex patterns of complementarity and substitutability than can appear in a model of consumption in which all goods are like inputs to consumption.

Dynamics, temporary equilibrium, and income

In view of his expressed dissatisfaction with Wicksell's capital theory, the definition of economic dynamics with which Hicks opens part III of *Value and Capital* comes as a surprise (1939a: 115).

---

[2] Daniel McFadden (1968) shows that Hicks's stability method is valid in precisely those cases in which partial equilibrium analysis constitutes a valid approximation. Those cases, in turn, are the only ones in which general equilibrium stability and comparative statics results can be rigorously shown. In that exact sense, partial equilibrium analysis is all that we have.

I call Economic Statics those parts of economic theory where we do not trouble about dating; Economic Dynamics those parts where every quantity must be dated. For example, in economic statics we think of an entrepreneur employing such-and-such quantities of factors and producing by their aid such-and-such quantities of products; but we do not ask when the factors are employed and when the factors come to be ready.

This seems to be mistaken. Even when Hicks was writing *Value and Capital* it was known that dated products and factors can be treated in a manner parallel to goods and services in an entirely static model. The device that achieved this equivalence was the classical stationary state. Later, Kenneth Arrow and Gerard Debreu showed how the technique could be extended to non-stationary-state applications via the assumption of complete forward markets.

The 1930s Hicks knew nothing of that, and, indeed, he pioneered the approach in *Value and Capital*. He did not follow the exact path of Arrow and Debreu, however, and one can see why. He did know about the classical stationary state, and what the passage quoted above, and the following text in the same chapter, indicate is that Hicks was so impatient with the pseudo-dynamics involved in treating dated goods exactly as if they were current goods in a static equilibrium that he wasted little time on it.

He does make his position clear on pages 116–17 of *Value and Capital*. In particular (117), he writes:

Either we have to face up to the difficulty, and allow deliberately for the fact that supplies (and ultimately demands too) are governed by expected prices quite as much as by current prices; or we have to evade the issue by concentrating on the case where these difficulties are at a minimum. The first is the method of Marshall; the second (broadly speaking) is the method of the Austrians.

Hicks's non-Austrian intertemporal economics is quickly constructed and explained. For the prices of future goods that markets do not provide, agents are given expectations. To be exact, this means that agents have inside their heads prices that they treat as if they were definite data, although they are in fact subjective and can be incorrect and biased in any manner. To employ modern terminology, price expectations are point expectations but they are not rational.

Hicks notes that treating uncertain values as if they are definite cannot be absolutely right, and he mentions the possibility of adjusting point expectation prices upwards or downwards to correct for their dispersion, without developing this idea of certainty-equivalent prices formally. Did he sense that he would run into serious problems if he were to attempt the complete simultaneous definition of the certainty-equivalent levels of a number of different prices?

A similar problem was encountered by Keynes in *The General Theory* (1936), where expectations are treated in an exactly parallel manner and suitable adjustments to their values are supposed to reflect both the presence of subjective risk and possibly variable willingness to undertake it. No doubt Keynes is the source of Hicks's conception. Even supposing that to be the case, however, Hicks applies the idea of subjective price expectations in a different manner from Keynes, in a way that may be categorized as less Marshallian. He looks at the implications of subjective price expectations for the general equilibrium of current markets and thus derives one of his great contributions to economic theory: *temporary equilibrium*.

An essential difference between Hicks and Keynes is that the latter constructed a fix-price model in which not all current markets clear, while in Hicks's temporary equilibrium current markets are in equilibrium each period (see Hicks, 1939a: 131), despite the fact that the demands and supplies that are thus equated are derived from expectations of future prices that may be wrong, and perhaps absurd and unreasonable. Embedded in this construction is the special case in which price expectations are correct and the world unchanging, so that the same expectations continue to be valid.

Hicks's discussion of temporary equilibrium takes him easily and naturally into the discussion of interest in chapter 11. He concentrates on money loans and money rates of interest, although the principles are general. The strict temporary equilibrium case in which only current goods are traded for current goods, although those trades reflect expectations concerning the relative prices at which trades will take place in the future, is reinforced by the presence of a subset of futures markets in which trades involving future deliveries take place today, in the present period.

In markets for current goods, some evident, although not very interesting, arbitrage conditions apply. The relative price of potatoes in terms of carrots multiplied by the relative price of cabbages in terms of potatoes must equal the relative price of cabbages in terms of carrots. With many money rates of interest for loans of different duration, similar conditions yield an arithmetic relation between long rates and short, period-to-period, rates. Where the system of loan markets is incomplete expectations again fill the gap.

Chapter 12 addresses for the first time what might be regarded as the fundamental question of capital theory: the determination of the rate of interest. Hicks distinguishes two separate issues.
(1) Is the rate of interest determined entirely by the real economy?
(2) Insofar as money markets influence the rate of interest, is it flow equilibrium or stock equlibrium that does the work?

Hicks regards the first issue as genuine, and firmly takes the view that monetary influences do matter for the determination of the rate of interest. He holds the second issue to be a false one, because flow equilibrium and stock equilibrium are simply two ways of looking at the same general equilibrium of markets. Did Keynes agree with him? The footnote to page 162 of *Value and Capital* indicates otherwise.

The final chapter of Part III examines a field in which Hicks made some of his most important and distinctive contributions. The measurement of income is the central problem of economic measurement. It is impossible to measure income without measuring the depreciation of the capital stock; and it is impossible to measure the depreciation of the capital stock without measuring capital. Once capital is measured, true measures of net investment and saving follow automatically (see Hicks, 1961b).

Here Hicks gives us a bold and powerful concept, what we now call Hicksian income. This is the level of real income that an individual, or a firm or a society, could spend in perpetuity. Naturally, this is a much more permanent concept of income (to borrow Milton Friedman's term) than a current net cash flow measure. That makes it more useful than a simple current accounting measure; but also, because it embodies so many forward-looking and speculative values, much more difficult to estimate.

Conceptually useful though it is, Hicks's measure of income can give rise to paradoxes. To see this, consider first a simple Solow growth model with exogenous technical progress and – to make the example simple – stationary population. If consumption is to remain constant, capital must be disinvested at exactly the right rate to offset the output-boosting effect of technical progress. Holding capital constant, which is the same as holding consumption constant, implies less and less K as time proceeds. Then, what looks like disinvestment if one focuses on the weight of the capital stock turns out to be holding capital constant.

Worse brain-teasers arise when production depends upon a finite and irreplaceable natural resource – call it oil. This can be run down optimally or non-optimally. If it is genuinely irreplaceable, however, and if technical progress cannot indefinitely lower the quantity required to produce a unit of output, there will be no positive level of consumption that can be sustained indefinitely. Hicksian income will be zero, despite the fact that positive consumption levels will be sustainable for a very long time.

The working of the dynamic system

It is in part IV of *Value and Capital*, the title of which is the same as the above section heading, that we find for the first time material that would be classified from an orthodox perspective as capital theory. In confronting the classic questions of capital theory, however, Hicks was in a most curious position. This is because he simply did not accept the ground rules for constructing a theory of capital as they had been understood previously. He was not willing to contemplate any kind of long-run or perfect equilibrium model. As he puts it (1939a: 191):

The only laws we can expect to find, in the first place, are the laws of the working of the price-system in any particular 'week'; and that is only the beginning of what we should like a dynamic theory to tell us. (However, even temporary equilibrium analysis of this sort yields several important and rather surprising conclusions when it is carefully carried out.) To penetrate beyond this point is very difficult; but we shall make an effort before concluding to see what can be said about the laws of the development of the price system through time.

The method is clear: to analyze a sequence of temporary equilibria, one following another. Evidently, moreover, the chief problem to be overcome in order to do that is to model how price expectations are adjusted from one period to the next in the light of experience.

Although this method cannot be identified with any classical approach, it brings the argument close enough to classical territory to allow comparisons to be made with older ideas. Why that is important to Hicks is explained shortly (*ibid.*: 192):

Even to-day, the great name in this department of economics is the name of Böhm-Bawerk. This is so, not because his doctrine is generally accepted (it was not generally accepted even in his own time, and it has still fewer supporters in ours), but because it is a challenge that has somehow to be met. Nearly every one who comes to the study of capital falls a victim to Böhm-Bawerk's theory at some stage or other.

One senses that Hicks himself had been such a victim at one time. He found the idea of Eugen von Böhm-Bawerk that capital is equivalent to waiting as intriguing as Wicksell before him had done. Hicks must have loved the idea, and later he was to explore it systematically and to celebrate it in *Capital and Time* (1973a). He loved the Böhm-Bawerk idea – but he could not accept it. Hicks had created an exceedingly broad framework, and within that framework Böhm-Bawerk was clearly exposed as a very special case: a fascinating special case, perhaps; but a special case without doubt.

Hicks's model of intertemporal production planning is the generalization of static production planning, via net value maximization, to time in the form of many periods, and the generalization of inputs and outputs to dated inputs and outputs. In its strictest formal realization, which is the Arrow–Debreu general equilibrium model, this approach reduces the list of goods and services to an itemized list with $N.T$ entries: the product of the number of goods distinguished by type, and the number of time periods. For many purposes, however, it makes sense to preserve the structure of goods and periods that reminds us that corn available in 2008 stands in relation to corn available in 2009 in a different regard from the way in which corn available in 2008 stands in relation to meat available in 2008.

That distinction was of even greater importance for Hicks, because his conception of equilibrium is profoundly asymmetrical with regard to goods and time. Present goods are united in all having definite prices, whereas most future goods have prices that are manifest in the first period only as subjective expectations. It is allowed that one good – call it 'money' – can be traded at definite prices between present and future periods. Even in that case, speculation plays a role. That is because, even if rates are quoted today for loans of all durations, the levels that short rates will take in future periods are not known for certain. For this reason, an agent needing to borrow long may choose to speculate that short rates will fall, and borrow short, planning to refinance the loan by means of subsequent short borrowing. That this strategy is risky, because short rates may not fall as expected, and may indeed rise, is obvious from theoretical consideration. It is also the lesson of practical experience, for it is the story of the international debt crisis of the 1980s.

Many of Hicks's insights come from applying his static apparatus of production theory, augmented by its stability conditions, to the 'dynamic' intertemporal case. Consider a static production model. The price of one input falls. In general, every magnitude in the optimal value-maximizing plan may be affected. What exactly happens depends, as Hicks shows, on patterns of complementarity and substitutability between inputs and outputs. When these techniques are applied to the intertemporal model, various kinds of complementarity and substitutability relations may exist.

For instance, if the wage rate is lower, current capital inputs may be lower: current capital is a substitute for current labor. In addition, however, nearer outputs may tend to rise and more distant (in time) outputs fall. Nearer outputs are complements to labor; more distant outputs are substitutes. This last case is in harmony with Böhm-Bawerk's view of capital accumulation. Hicks's model makes it plain, however, that Böhm-Bawerk's case, in which substitutions are all between time periods for the same good, is a special case.

The goods-plus-time-periods special structure further manifests itself when interest rate changes are taken into account. A change in the rate of interest alters the whole structure of relative prices in a manner that has no analogue in the static model. Even more marked are the differences that arise when Hicks runs the model as a sequence of temporary equilibria.

Initially relative prices are set by expectations, and could in principle take any values. In fact, they are restricted by the condition that they must not allow for unbounded plans to take advantage of strange price values.

As time moves on, agents experience current prices, and revise their expectations in the light of their experiences. This gave Hicks the opportunity to elaborate one of his finest intellectual constructs: *the elasticity of expectations*. He shows that, for a sequence of temporary equilibria to be well behaved, the responsiveness of price expectations to current experience must not be too large.

Hicks's apparatus is brilliantly effective. Because it might happen that price expectations are more or less correct, it covers the perfect or long-run steady-state equilibrium that had been the main focus of the type of analysis conducted by Böhm-Bawerk and Wicksell. It does much more as well. When price expectations are badly wrong, it provides a method for describing what happens. Finally, allowing money to be the good that directly bridges time periods, because there are active forward markets for lending and borrowing money, permits Hicks to construct a theory of the demand for money. To put it simply, what happens is that uncertainty concerning future relative prices encourages the holding of money, for which the own rate of return is given for certain by the money market, against the productive holding of other goods, which are subject to return uncertainty.

Postscript: beyond empty general equilibrium theory

Having started out with the grand conclusion that general equilibrium theory is empty beyond the ontological demonstration that an equilibrium exists, how to account for the wide and rich developments that John Hicks gave to us? It is crucial that Hicks recognized that general equilibrium theory leads nowhere, and he wanted to look at general equilibrium systems with the awkward income effects chained. With that freedom he developed general equilibrium theory beyond the static stationary state special case, to give it life via dynamics. Dynamics can mean many things, and most importantly for Hicks it means a dynamic capital theory based on the asymmetry between different contemporaneous goods, as opposed to current versus dated goods.

After the pre-war years and *Value and Capital* John Hicks's thinking never stood still. *Capital and Growth* (1965) was the product of afterthoughts concerning, and continuing discontents with, *Value and Capital*. It was forged in intellectual interchanges with Michio Morishima during the latter's visit to All Souls College; see Morishima (1994). In two particular respects it springs from *Value and Capital*: in one case via the rejection of a

Value and Capital assumption; in the other case via an extension of a *Value and Capital* technique.

The rejection involved putting aside the assumption that current markets at least always clear. Instead, Hicks now considered the fix-price economy, in which all or many current prices are fixed at arbitrary levels. Despite being strongly influenced by Keynes in the 1930s, Hicks had rejected the assumption of sticky prices, which was why his temporary equilibrium, for all its evident non-optimality, was not Keynesian in character. On the other hand, fix-price general equilibrium is notoriously difficult to analyze. If *Capital and Growth* is not a huge success, this is partly because it offers that great reasonableness plus a certain vacuity which is all too easily the product of fix-price reasoning.

The other problem was the new dynamics. Hicks created the concept of the traverse, being the path followed by an economy as it moved from one steady state to another. It is a clever construct, the transfer taking the form of the successive adjustment of different and broader classes of variables. The old question reasserted itself, however: is this genuine dynamics? To judge by the profession's response, measured by how influential Hicks's contribution was, the answer was 'no.' Growth modeling at that time was making use of Newtonian – i.e. differential equation – dynamics, and that corresponded better to the taste of the time.

There remained Böhm-Bawerk. Surely Hicks had laid his ideas to rest in *Value and Capital*? It seemed not. In *Capital and Time* (1973a), he returned to the consideration of those old, wrong-headed, yet ever-nagging ideas. What he provides is a neo-Austrian theory, so-called because he greatly generalizes the special cases considered by Böhm-Bawerk and Friedrich Hayek. This was now the time when capital paradoxes and reswitching were high fashion. By examining intertemporal processes, in which dated inputs and outputs are jointly produced, Hicks created an elegant technique and some fine results. For example, terminable processes, which can be cut off at any time, behave differently from non-terminable processes.

Although this appears to be completely new, the root ideas are already there in *Value and Capital*. As has been remarked already, a change in an interest rate alters a number of relative prices simultaneously, and this affects the complementarity and substitutability consequences. The attack employed in *Capital and Time* places its emphasis on the intertemporal substitution effects of those price changes. That those are not the only consequences of price changes is clear, of course, because the capital model of *Value and Capital* demonstrates exactly that point.

There remains what is perhaps the most important thing that John Hicks failed to do, although little has been done on it subsequently. If dynamics is king, and expectations are essential to the proper treatment of dynamics, we need a theory of the dynamics of expectations formation. We do not find it in Hicks, and Keynes gives us hand-waving. One problem among many is that expectations are seldom formed in an atomistic manner, so it needs theory of a qualitatively different character to address that problem.

8 Hicks versus Marx? On the theory of economic history

Pierluigi Ciocca

On theory and history

After more than two centuries of theoretical – and, perhaps above all, empirical – analysis since Adam Smith's *Wealth of Nations* (1776) we have to acknowledge that we now know a great deal about the capitalist market economy, the system that has gradually taken root in more and more countries since the Industrial Revolution started in the United Kingdom.

Let us distinguish between *structure* and *performance*.

As far as *structure* goes, the allocation of resources and the distribution of the fruits of production are entrusted to prices and markets; production, now consisting chiefly of industry and services, is effected by powerful machinery operated by a labor force that is also bought and sold in a (special) 'labor market'; workers are employed by firms that are owned and financed by capitalist-rentiers, run by manager-entrepreneurs, and administered internally according to principles of custom, cooperation, and command far more than on the basis of market transactions and relative prices. The mode of production and exchange that Smith and David Ricardo theorized for London and its surroundings now applies to virtually the whole world. The main difference nowadays is that workers, too, save and own assets. In the days of Smith and Ricardo they 'subsisted' and property was concentrated in a few hands. In an 'average' economy, such as Italy's, three-fourths of personal wealth and over two-thirds of personal financial assets are owned by households headed by employees or pensioners.

As for *performance*, thanks to an empirical tradition ranging from Gregory King and John Graunt to Simon Kuznets, up to Angus Maddison and François Bourguignon, we now have a stylized framework covering the whole world since the start of the nineteenth century. World *gross output*

I am grateful to Stefano Fenoaltea for his comments. The usual caveat applies.

has increased sixtyfold and *per capita output* tenfold, while the *population* has jumped from 1 billion to over 6 billion. This formidable growth (which was even faster in the twentieth century than in the nineteenth) has been combined with profound transformations in production; it contrasts sharply with the Malthusian stagnation and very slow gains in per capita income of earlier centuries.

Economic activity has been highly *unstable*, however. In the last two centuries world output has deviated from trend – peak to through – by as much as 20 percent on five or six occasions and by 4 to 5 percent on ten to twelve. Though kept at bay by policies and institutions, instability is in fact a deeply entrenched, incurable feature of our economies.

Finally, the personal *distribution* of income among the citizens of the world has become less and less equal over the last two centuries. The Gini and Theil indexes are now a third to two-thirds higher than at the beginning of the nineteenth century. Income inequality worldwide has increased *between* countries, while diminishing *within* them, particularly among the first-comers in development. The problem of distribution thus largely coincides with that of the persistent economic backwardness of most of the world's nations.

A link between capitalism and history *before* capitalism

There are a number of economic theories available to us. Often they can be refuted empirically, in terms of their forecasting ability and the realism of their assumptions; some lack logical coherence. These theories are in some respects conflicting; they propose alternative ways of linking structure and performance, and they suggest different policy measures. We do not find them entirely satisfactory. Nonetheless, political economy has made enormous analytical progress. This was very appropriately recognized when the Nobel Prize was extended to the discipline.

Sir John Hicks made a fundamental contribution to this body of theory and empirical analysis. And he did more.

Hicks was very earnestly engaged in establishing a link between the past 200 years and the logical and chronological time (centuries and millennia) before modern capitalism. He did so, in particular, in an extraordinary book, which I believe to be one of his most important works, especially if we read it in conjunction with *Causality in Economics* (1979a) and his last book, *A Market Theory of Money* (1989a). His celebrated contributions to pure economic theory can be seen as leading to the highly ambitious attempt made in *A Theory of Economic History* (1969a), from which all the quotations are taken.

I attended Hicks's special classes at Oxford in 1967–9, when he no longer taught ordinary courses. Robin Matthews, my supervisor, had replaced him as Drummond Professor of political economy. I was not actually a student of Hicks's, therefore, although I had other occasions, nearly until his death, to listen to him and learn from him. These included his frequent visits to the Bank of Italy, where I spent my entire career cultivating, among other things, a dilettante's interest in economic history.

I had the great good fortune to hear him expound the content of this book, just before its publication, in four seminars at Oxford in 1968, before a large audience of distinguished economists and historians. The audience showed little enthusiasm. As sometimes happens with special works of unique value, Hicks's was not immediately understood, either around All Souls or in the reviews by specialists – mainly historians – that followed (Frederic Lane, Brian Mitchell, Peter Bauer, Rolf Henriksson, D. C. Coleman, William Parker, Jonathan Hughes, Edoardo Grendi).[1] The historians quibbled over single events or points of fact, sometimes of secondary importance. The economists found it hard to swallow the sharp switch from theorems to the broad sweep of history. Nor has the book been accorded much recognition in the subsequent literature.[2]

History has made a great, though often indirect and mediated, contribution to the best economic theory from Smith to Paul Samuelson.[3] In turn, economic historiography has borrowed heavily from economic theory, and increasingly so in the past thirty years.

Theories of economic history do not abound, however. They are rare, though this is not the only reason they are precious. I believe they are also useful for analytical purposes, as general schemes for ordering one's thoughts and asking oneself relevant questions.

One relevant question is: how did the capitalist market economy in which we live come to be, and is it here to stay? In other words, in what sense is this economic form itself 'historical'?

---

[1] Of the reviews by historians, the most critical was that of Grendi (1971), who rejected the book en bloc, calling it 'a trite, conventional little treatise, with nothing new or stimulating to say,' and one that, 'neglecting the theory of economic growth, …showed no opening to unorthodox disciplines.'

[2] Neo-institutionalists such as Douglass C. North and Robert Paul Thomas (1973) measure themselves against the Marxists and Henri Pirenne, not against Hicks. Sir John himself reviewed North and Thomas in a critical vein (Hicks, 1974e).

[3] See Ciocca (2002), which includes essays by Sylos Labini, Giacomo Becattini, Marcello De Cecco, Milton Friedman, Samuelson, and Luigi Pasinetti.

Only a few great thinkers – and very few economists – have ventured an answer. Hicks was among them. It is important for us to go back and reflect upon the answer he gave. It is in this spirit that I again offer it up for consideration.

Markets and capitalism: two approaches

Hicks's answer falls somewhere between the two basic approaches, which have long stood in opposition.

One approach recognizes that the form of the capitalist market was preceded by others and that it coexisted and coexists with others. In the preceding forms the first constituent elements of the market economy emerged, however, leading to its establishment through a clear though not necessarily linear process. In this view, as it steadily grew and spread, the market economy was completed, generalized, and consolidated into a sort of terminal stage – that of the capitalist market – that is held to be irreversible because it is 'superior.'

Many historians – Pirenne is one – virtually equated the market economy with capitalism. They traveled back through the centuries to follow the early forms of organized market – precursors of the modern market economies (of which money is an integral part) – as they developed and spread in a sort of crescendo. These lines of research share the conviction that, by nature, man is and always has been *Homo œconomicus*: rational in calculating cost-benefit and profit at every turn. Exchange (including barter), markets, and money represent clear and precise modes that conform to such rationality. Either they exist or they do not exist. As soon as they 'appear' they expand and take root, though not necessarily without momentary backsliding, in the 'rise' of the exchange and monetary economy (Postan, 1944). A discontinuity, which can be dated back far into the past, and a determinable start are followed by a permanent progression toward the perfect markets of Léon Walras and Vilfredo Pareto, or toward those of Kenneth Arrow and Gerard Debreu, whose only limit is access by agents to 'full and symmetrical' information.

According to the opposing approach, the market system is historical – capitalism even more so – not only because it was preceded by and coexists with other systems, but also in another twofold sense. The difference with respect to the other systems, including non-capitalist economies with market elements, is deeper: not of degree but of kind. Trading of rations in a prisoner-of-war camp with cigarettes used as money does not represent a capitalist economy (Radford, 1945). Moreover, a capitalist economy allows scope for considerable variations. Above all, it *can* be followed by other forms as different from itself as were those that went before it. History does not tend to an end, and does not end.

Averages and norms: Hicks's theory of economic history

Hicks liked history. He proudly recalls his exchanges with G. D. H. Cole, Eileen Power, Michael Postan, and S. Ashton. History was more than erudition, though: it nourished his economic theory. I mention, merely as an example, his contributions to the labor standard theory, the theory of money, the theory of central banking, as well as to the history of economic analysis (William Thornton, for instance, as much as Ricardo).

Given these premises, what, according to Hicks, is a 'theory' of economic history? It is not the history of single events. It is not philosophy of history. It is the history of averages and norms. It is the history of the permanence and evolution of structures, whether gradual or revolutionary.

In view of this definition, if throughout his lifetime Hicks measured himself, in (macro)economic theory, chiefly against John Maynard Keynes, in the theory of economic history his first term of comparison could only have been Karl Marx.

Hicks dismisses grand designs *à la* Arnold Toynbee or Oswald Spengler as 'more aesthetic than scientific' (1969a: 2). He discards Weber–Troeltsch-style theories of capitalism inspired by a 'spirit' with factual arguments, such as that modern banking preceded the Protestant Reformation by a couple of centuries ('It was practice that made the Ethic, not the other way round'; *ibid.*: 79).

He makes explicit reference to Marx: 'My "theory of history" ... will be a good deal nearer to the kind of thing that was attempted by Marx. [...] It does ... remain extraordinary that one hundred years after *Das Kapital* ... so little else should have emerged.' 'An alternative version' can be for-mulated on the basis of all the developments in economic analysis, as well as in anthropology, that have taken place since Marx's time (2–3).

Hicks's research plan is extremely clear (6):
  (i) to 'classify ... economic states of society';
 (ii) to 'look for intelligible reasons for which one such state should give way to another'; and
(iii) to sketch 'a sequence not altogether unlike the "Feudalism, Capitalism, Socialism" of Marx,' albeit 'less deterministic,' and solidly grounded in modern economics, in addition to the classical political economy of Smith and Ricardo, which was familiar to Marx.

Hicks's approach to the problem of modes of production is similar to the question of the pre-capitalist *Formen* posed by Marx and in the more articulated later Marxian categories: 'Asian, ancient, feudal, modern bourgeois,' or 'slave, feudal, and bourgeois' modes of production. Like Marx, Hicks intends to analyze 'the Economic History of the World as a single process' (7), and refers to a 'trend to which we may be willing to give the name of "progress"' (6–7): economic growth or development according to Hicks, man's emancipation from nature according to Marx.[4]

Hicks's writing is so synthetic and readable that there is no need for a summary. Two sets of brief considerations, based on references to Hicks's text, suffice to refocus attention on a book that has been largely underrated. The first highlights the book's contributions on specific topics that can be relevant even for readers who are not interested in, or do not agree with, its more general propositions. Second, this precious book contains analytical gems that are invaluable in themselves and continue to be so even in the light of subsequent developments and the current state of economic analysis and historiography.

World economic history 'as a single process'

One specific analytical contribution relates to 'non-market organizations' (9) that preceded the market economy, but also those – such as 'the factory *in its internal structure*' (10; emphasis in original) – that coexist with it. The rules governing these 'custom and command' organizations can derive, in various combinations, from above or below. The predominant combination will depend, as Hicks shrewdly points out, on the prevalence of routine ('belowness' of the rules) and the frequency of emergencies ('aboveness' of the rules) in each historical context. For example, feudalism is a 'command economy' when the original military despotism is founded on attack and plunder; it becomes a 'customary economy' when the element of defense is permanent and 'regular income' (16) is needed to finance it.

The causal nexus from markets to institutions

A second insight concerns the relationship between a market economy and institutions: money, credit, and law. The institutions often exist before the market and are a prerequisite for it. Hicks underscores even more forcefully, however, the causal nexus from market to institutions, to the evolution of their forms, and even to changes in their nature. Trade

---

[4] From an economist's and a historian's point of view, these aspects of Marxian analysis are best put into perspective by Eric Hobsbawm (1964). For an anthropologist's point of view, see Maurice Godelier (1970).

and market, even if confined to the exchange of products, offer enormous advantages, but – and this is the key point – 'the growth of the trade would narrow the profit' (45). 'The Mercantile Economy may go into a decline' (59). The solutions to this 'tendency to diminishing returns' (45) include 'constant improvements in organization' (56). State money becomes bank money; credit can be created and multiplied; money *or* credit becomes money *and* credit; the law – at least, commercial law – ceases to be an expression of the Roman Empire and becomes law expressed and enforced by merchants, *lex mercatoria*.

The relationship between market and production

The third point is one of method. It concerns the relationship between market and production, which is seen as radically different from that between market and products. According to Hicks, production means 'Factors of Production, Land and Labour,' as well as 'Forms of Production, Agriculture and Industry' (100) – all with capital letters. In Hicks's view, 'The Market, as a form of organization, is the creation of traders and subsequently financiers, not (or not at all to the same extent) of farmers or of artisans. The commodity markets and the financial markets are the places where the market system is at home; when it proceeds to the formation of factor markets, land and labour markets, it is penetrating, or "colonizing," relatively refractory territory' (*ibid.*). As a result, 'there was a struggle, which begins very early, and continues (though in forms which are undergoing significant charges) into our own day' (*ibid.*). 'Struggle' is a strong, indeed, a quasi-Marxian, word.

Hicks sets the abolition of the 'lord and peasant system' – of which feudalism is only a part – and the various, contradictory ways in which it took place within the framework of a bilateral monopoly. The services exchanged were the support offered by the peasant and the protection and settlement of disputes offered by the lord. Nevertheless, 'the terms of exchange are "indeterminate"; settled ... by the will of the stronger' (106) – another ringing word.

Finally, there is the most delicate transition, from the sale of people (slavery) or of rights over people (serfdom) to the sale of their labor (wage proletariat). The Church played no role in this: 'It was concerned with the soul of the slave, but not with his status' (131). According to Hicks, the fact is that 'free labour was cheaper,' though not necessarily more efficient (*ibid.*), as a number of factors combined to maintain the supply and contain the price of the services provided by the 'urban proletariat' to incipient manufacturing. Regarding the formation of the proletariat and society's polarization into capitalists and wage workers, Hicksian and

Marxian analysis (such as that of Maurice Dobb) coincide in some points but diverge in more (Dobb, 1946).

The second order of considerations relates to the whole of Hicks's scheme, viewed both in itself and in relation to that of Marx, which served as Hicks's point of departure.

The role of non-market organizations

The crux of Hicks's theory of history taken as a whole is summed up in this statement: 'There is a *transformation* which is antecedent to Marx's Rise of Capitalism, and which, in terms of more recent economics, looks even *more fundamental*. This is the Rise of the Market...' (7).

The market, according to Hicks, is the solvent that washes away the encrustations inherited from history and forges new forms, although its rise is not continuous or free from contradictions.

The market precedes modern capitalism – which Hicks calls 'Industrialism' (8) or 'Modern Industry' (141). It also precedes 'the reaction against the Market which has followed upon it' (8) – a reaction that Marx calls class struggle between capital and labor.

Hicks classes pre-capitalist modes of production in the category of 'non-market organizations.' This negative definition is more general than Marx's modes of production. Meanwhile, by separating non-market organizations into customary and command economies, with different combinations of *aboveness* and *belowness*, Hicks avoids a loss of capacity to analyze various historical situations. Hence, Hicks's scheme appears at the same time more general and more flexible than Marx's.

The crucial issue continues to be the relationship between feudalism and capitalism, the transition from one to the other, and the historical nature of the capitalist market economy as defined here. Hicks's position lies somewhere between the two basic approaches that have long stood in opposition, but perhaps closer to the second than to the first: closer, that is, to Marx than to Pirenne.

He acknowledges the discontinuity that occurs in the spread of the 'Exchange Economy' and the 'Rise of the Market' (which had been gradual until then) with the Industrial Revolution in the United Kingdom. For Hicks and Marx alike, the pre-capitalist economy is very different from the capitalist market economy.

There was and is no difference between craftwork and trade: 'The artisan buys to sell again, in a different form from what he buys' (141). The artisan's capital, like that of the tradesman, is 'mainly working or circulating capital, capital that is turned over' and can be stored in 'containers' (142).

Modern industry differs – the difference is of degree, but so great as to verge on a difference in kind – in the much greater weight of 'fixed capital' and the 'range and variety of the fixed capital goods' (142–3). Labor that is bought and sold for a wage is combined in factories with means of production – machines – that provide high and increasing productivity.

According to Hicks, there were basically two mainsprings of the sharp rise in the ratio of fixed capital to working capital and labor. The first was 'financial development,' which took place in the United Kingdom, as well as in the Netherlands and France, in the eighteenth century and made it possible 'to *sink* large amounts of capital' (144; emphasis in original). The second was technical progress: more accurately, it was 'science,' which cut costs and increased the precision of the 'machines made by machines' (145).

For Hicks as well as Marx, the other crucial break with centuries of history was the 'class consciousness' (154) of industrial workers. Unlike the old urban proletariat, when they are employed they are 'regularly employed.' No longer are they 'casual labour' incapable of using complex and durable machinery (155). 'The industrial worker was not rootless: he was a member of a group'; as such, he was capable of protection, organization, and bargaining power, and able to hold strikes and form trade unions and political parties (156).

The excess supply of labor resulting from the reserve army of farm laborers, population growth, and the fact that, following Ricardo, 'machines do, very often, displace labour' (149 and the splendid appendix on 'Ricardo on Machinery') meant that until about 1830 real wages lagged far behind productivity. The tension in income distribution fueled the incipient class consciousness, spurring a motive for wage claims and industrial conflict. That motive remains. It has spread among the circle of countries outside the industrial first-comers.

To complete the comparison between Hicks and Marx, on which I have perhaps insisted too much, I think that if Marx had had Hicks at his disposal he would have made great use of him, as he did of Ricardo.

Apart from this supposition, what Hicks meant when he said that the 'Rise of the Market' was 'more fundamental' than the 'Rise of Capitalism' should now be clear. The capitalist market economy, or 'Modern Industry,' differs radically *on the production side* – (fixed) capital, (wage) labor-cum-class struggle, land (a liquid asset) – from the previous economic forms (various combinations of custom and command, including not irrelevant mercantile elements). This was true for Hicks as it had been for Marx. Nonetheless, this is a comparison between states and stages, an exercise in comparative statics. The difference emerges when we turn to dynamics, to the 'traverse' from one state to another, and to the 'reasons for which one state gives way to another.'

The rise of the market as an agent of transformation

Hicks believed that the 'Rise of the Market' was the most important 'transformation,' or, rather, *agent of transformation* – more important than the mechanism envisaged by Marx: the dialectical contradictions inherent in each mode of production. For John Hicks, author of *A Theory of Economic History* (1969a), no less than for J. R. Hicks, author of *Value and Capital* (1939a), modern economic theory – Hicks's theory – can better codify the decisive role of the economic advantage implicit in exchange and trade as a source of change (see chapter 3, by Pasinetti and Mariutti, in this volume).

The important qualification, from the point of view of the performance of the economy, is that trade, exchange, and the market increase the wealth of nations by improving the allocation of *existing* resources in a static sense, a one-off jump in logical time. In a radically different fashion, industry and production for the market, using fixed capital and wage labor, increase the wealth of nations by *augmenting* resources, in a cumulative and possibly never-ending process. This process no longer entails one-off changes but rates of change over time (Pasinetti, 2002).

The economic superiority of this second mode of production is evident. It is the intrinsic force of seeking advantage in the market through exchange and trade, however, that drives society toward the mode of production in which we live.

Hicks's book concludes by opening a perspective on the future that now, nearly forty years later, is history. The extraordinary material progress of the nineteenth century and, in particular, the twentieth century – measured by Simon Kuznets and others in macro-statistics on *modern economic growth* – really can make 'insiders' of the untold millions (Hicks says more than half a billion) of 'pre-industrial proletarians' in the developing world. 'The rate of expansion that is needed is certainly no greater than that which has been achieved hitherto' (Hicks, 1969a: 159). If this Herculean task is not accomplished, the system will be at risk.

Hicks thus appears to be saying that the basic contradiction – the coexistence of capitalism and backwardness, of wealth and poverty – can be overcome. He, cautions, nevertheless, that it is not a sure thing that it will be. The mechanism of progress – the spread of international trade and industrialization – is in motion, but there are also grounds for pessimism. In any case, it will be no easy matter.

'I am afraid there are hindrances,' he says (*ibid.*: 159). For one thing, there are nationalism and differences (precious, too) of religion and culture in the developing countries, which resist the 'melting pot.' On the other side we find the reluctance of the developed nations to forfeit their relative economic advantage, their tendency to oppose the spread of free trade and industrialization by resorting to a new, more subtle, and more dangerous form of protectionism.

In the end, both are *political* issues. Given that 'mobility of labour is not perfect' (165), the economist can call only for 'forms of direct investment less wounding to national pride' (166) to circumvent the obstacles. 'The path may be cleared' (*ibid.*), but the battle – to escape from underdevelopment, to achieve a more equal distribution of income among the world's citizens – is under way. The outcome is uncertain.

Had he been able to witness what has occurred since his pen stopped writing in 1989, Sir John would have found confirmation for his theses at least in these developments.

 (i) China has nearly tripled the per capita income of 1.3 billion people and built up some $700 billion in foreign exchange reserves, mainly thanks to foreign direct investment inflows.

 (ii) The per capita income of the other developing countries has risen by more than 50 percent.

 (iii) The meeting of the World Trade Organization in Cancún in 2003 provided graphic evidence of how hard it is to sweep away protectionism.

 (iv) Faith-drenched politics (but also wealth and income inequalities, fanaticism, and violence) have triggered conflicts in Afghanistan, Iraq, and Palestine and such terrorist attacks as those on the World Trade Center in New York and Atocha station in Madrid.

I imagine that our economic thoughts would be different, and better, if Hicks's book were more widely studied, fully understood, and subjected to more constructive criticism.

Marcello de Cecco

The coexistence of fix-price and flex-price markets

It is generally accepted that John Hicks attached great importance to the distinction between fix-price markets and flex-price markets. He was by no means the first to notice the existence of these two types of markets, but he was more insistent than most economists in stressing the frequent coexistence of both markets and in trying to model it. More than that, he maintained that flex-price markets needed fix-price ones to survive in the long run. While leaving the theoretical aspects of this issue to people more conversant than I am with theoretical economics, I intend in this chapter to go over Hicks's own use of this notion in the space he dedicated, in his published work, to the analysis of real-life economies, and of economic history.

Fix-price, flex-price, and sticky wages

Hicks noticed the coexistence of the two types of markets in the first important work he produced, his 1932 book *The Theory of Wages*. Labor markets – he notes there – did not behave in many cases like Marshallian markets. Money wages were sticky, relativities mattered, and – at least in a highly unionized labor market such as the British one, where the union movement was fragmented, by historical reasons, according to the many trades coexisting under the same factory roof and thus given to frequent demarcation disputes – wage-fixing was based mainly on the perception of the need by each trade to maintain a fixed place between adjoining trades. In the language of physics, we may say today, trade unions behaved like 'spin glasses,' adjusting only to movements by their near neighbors.

As to the upward stickiness of wages compared to the prices of commodities and manufactures, Vilfredo Pareto noticed this phenomenon in his *Corso di Economia Politica* (Pareto, 1943, vol. I: 236) and pointed it out as an important reason why the burden of inflation was borne chiefly by wage-earners. He did not live in the first industrial country, however, and was not likely to give the same importance that Hicks, and later John Maynard Keynes, would attribute to relativities in the wage-fixing process, to explain in particular the downward stickiness of money wages.

The distribution of monetary assets and the 'probable differences in the reactions of different members of the community'

It is in 'A Suggestion for Simplifying the Theory of Money' (Hicks, 1935a) that Hicks first generalizes his notion of fix-price and flex-price markets, extending it to markets different from the labor market. In the concluding section of that paper, he provides a sketch view of the dynamics of late capitalism (which he called by its German name, *Spaetkapitalismus*).

It is perhaps useful to quote in full what he had to say on the matter (1935a: 18–19):

The assumption which seems to me most plausible, most consistent with the whole trend of our analysis, and at the same time to lead to results which at any rate look realistic, is one which stresses the probable differences in the reactions of different members of the community. We have already seen that a considerable proportion of a community's monetary stock is always likely to be in the hands of people who are obliged by their relative poverty to be fairly insensitive to changes in anticipations. For these people, therefore, most of the incentive to reduce their demand for money when events turn out more favourably will be missing [...] But we must also allow for the probability that other people are much more *sensitive* – that an increase in wealth is not particularly likely to increase their demand for money, and may very well diminish it. If this is so, it would follow that where the sensitive trade together, price-fluctuations may start on very slight provocation; and once they are under way, the rather less sensitive would be enticed in. Stock exchange booms will pass over into industrial booms, if industrial entrepreneurs are also fairly sensitive; and, in exactly the same way, stock exchange depressions will pass into industrial depressions. But the insensitive are always there to act as a flywheel, defeating by their insensitivity both the exaggerated optimism and the exaggerated pessimism of the sensitive class. [...] If it is the insensitive people who preserve the stability of capitalism, people who are insensitive...largely because for them the costs of transferring assets are large relative to the amount of assets they control, then the development of capitalism, by diminishing these costs, is likely to be a direct cause of increasing fluctuations. It reduces the costs in two ways: by technical devices (of which banks are only one example) and by instilling a more 'capitalistic' spirit, which looks more closely to profit, and thus reduces subjective costs. In doing these things, capitalism is its own enemy, for it imperils that stability without which it breaks down. Lastly, it seems to follow that when we are looking for policies which make for economic stability, we must not be held aside by a feeling that monetary troubles are due to 'bad' economic policy, in the old sense, that all would go well if we reverted to free trade and *laisser-faire*. In so doing, we are no better than the Thebans who ascribed the plague to blood-guiltiness, or the supporters of Mr Roosevelt who expect to reach recovery through reform.

In the long passage quoted, it is precisely the interplay between fix-price and flex-price markets that leads to trouble, in the crucial money and financial markets, if it leads to the gradual but inexorable destruction of the slowly adjusting markets that absorb the occasional turbulence taking place in flex-price markets.

The dynamics of capitalism and the interplay of fix-price and flex-price markets

Hicks's paper is usually read as a foundation of neoclassical monetary theory and a forerunner of portfolio selection theory. Undoubtedly, it is both things. Its concluding passages, however, as quoted above, show that it is something else, besides and – in my view – beyond that. There Hicks postulates a view on the dynamics of capitalism that has been held before and was also put forward by a contemporary of Hicks, Joseph Schumpeter. Nonetheless, the path to self-destruction that, in Hicks's view, capitalism inevitably takes if left to its own devices is different from other paths drawn by philosophers, political scientists, and economists. It is traced, as we have seen, by the interplay between fix-price markets, which are inherited from pre-capitalist times, and flex-price markets, whose number and efficiency increase as capitalism advances, until they displace fix-price markets altogether. Stability not being one of the essential features of pure capitalism, the ballast represented by fix-price markets is gradually thrown overboard, by the ever more efficient working of flex-price markets, until the boat, by now completely deprived of its keel, capsizes under the instability imparted to it by the working of flex-price markets.

The last passage I quoted from Hicks's article indeed anticipates some conclusions that Keynes reached in *The General Theory*, and could be taken as a theoretical basis for James Tobin's 'sand in the wheels' argument for a tax on international short-term capital movements. It is necessary to appreciate how far removed Hicks's view on this particular topic is from what we hear these days from market fundamentalists: that there are not enough markets and that the existing ones are not perfect enough, and that, as a consequence, the remaining rent factors are themselves the cause of the instability of capitalism. This is precisely the view against which Hicks wrote the passage I quoted. Rent removal policies, transaction costs removal policies, may kill the flywheel that keeps capitalism stable and in the end prevents it from self-destructing.

The optimum mix of fix-price and flex-price markets

The lesson Hicks wants to convey is, therefore, that there is an optimum mix of flex-price and fix-price that keeps capitalism on a stable growth path. Fix-price markets are inherited from pre-capitalist times but are as essential to the latter's survival as flex-price markets are to the continuation of its growth. More than that, some markets are by nature fix-price, and attempts to transform them into flex-price ones may be severely counterproductive.

In the same decade as Hicks's article appeared, Ronald Coase came to very similar conclusions at the end of his inquiry into the interplay between firms and their antinomy, markets (Coase, 1937). Firms emerge as a command response to the incapacity of markets to perform efficiently when there are transaction costs. Obviously, world economic events of the 1930s induced the most gifted and perceptive economists of the time to ask those questions and to give those answers.

A reiteration, and generalization, of the notion of the coexistence of fix-price markets and flex-price markets is contained in Hicks's best-known theoretical book, *Value and Capital* (1939a, 1946). There we read (1946: 265):

So far we have been assuming that all prices are perfectly flexible, so that it is possible for *all* prices to move together, under the free play of supply and demand [...] This assumption must now be dropped, for it is of course highly unrealistic. In most communities there are a large number of prices which, for one reason or another, are fairly insensitive to economic forces, at least over short periods. This rigidity may be due to legislative control, or to monopolistic action (of the sleepy sort which does not strain after every gnat of profit, but prefers a quiet life). It may be due to lingering notions of a 'just price'. The most important class of prices subject to such rigidities are wage-rates; they are affected from rigidity from all three causes. They are particularly likely to be affected by ethical notions, since the wage-contract is very much a personal contract, and will only proceed smoothly if it is regarded as 'fair' by both parties. But, for whatever cause rigidity occurs, it means that some prices do not move upward or downward in sympathy with the rest – they may consequently exercise a stabilizing influence.

After noting that Keynes put wage rigidity at the heart of his *General Theory of Employment, Interest and Money*, Hicks states that, 'while his [Keynes's] way of putting it has many advantages for practical application, it seems to me that the more fundamental sociological implications are brought out better if we treat rigid wage-rates as merely one sort of rigid prices. It is hard to exaggerate the immediate practical importance of the unemployment of labour, but its bearing on the nature of capitalism comes out better if we look at it alongside the unemployment (and even the misemployment) of other things' (*ibid*.: 266).

Hicks then goes on to suggest a theoretical method to deal with price rigidities in one market, but just a little later returns to dwell on the theme he had advanced in his 'Suggestion for Simplifying the Theory of Money', in the long passage that I have quoted:

We must give the system sufficient factors of stability to enable it to work; but we must not assume that these forces are so powerful as to prevent the system from being liable to fluctuations. There must be a tendency to rigidity of certain prices, particularly wage-rates; but there must also be a tendency to rigidity of certain price-expectations as well, in order to provide an explanation for the rigidity of these prices. [...] Indeed we should do better to assume a good deal of variation in different people's elasticities of expectations. [...] Of course the way in which a population is divided with respect to this sort of sensitivity will vary very much in different circumstances. [...] We have to be prepared to deal with a range of possible cases, varying from that of a settled community, which has been accustomed to steady conditions in the past (and which, for that reason, is not easily disturbed in the present), to that of a community which has been exposed to violent disturbances of prices (and which may have to be regarded, in consequence, as being economically neurotic). (271–2)

Hicks then concludes by noting that sensitivity also depends on the length of time the analysis encompasses. The formation of price expectations, he says, is composed of past experience and present experience. If we make the past long and the present short, past experience will determine expectations more than present experience. While, if we make the present experience long enough, this by itself will make expectations more volatile, whatever the community's previous or present experiences, because a very short present cannot disturb the normality of the past sufficiently. Normality, of course, may mean great price volatility in the past, so that a return to stability in a short present cannot influence expectations strongly enough.

As a result, Hicks argues that we need not be afraid 'of falling into [the] conclusion' that 'while any system (excepting the most neurotic) is stable in the short period, it is bound to become unstable in the long period' (272). The reason for this is that 'the longer the period over which our "week" is taken to extend, the less satisfactory an approximation to reality we know it becomes. There are things that lie outside Temporary Equilibrium analysis, and some of these things ought to be taken into account before we can make any generalisations about long periods' (*ibid.*).

Hicks, however inadequate he came to consider the temporary equilibrium method, never renounced in subsequent decades the *Weltanschauung* he had obtained by the use of that method, even when so many of his colleagues came to the conclusion that capitalism was a self-stabilizing system, and also the most efficient possible one in terms of growth, and even of the distribution of resources between people and countries. He went on using his fix-price/flex-price model, ever refining its theoretical and historical underpinnings.

From status to contract

I leave it to others, as I have said, to analyze this decades-long progress from the point of view of theory. In the rest of this chapter, I intend to concentrate on the explanation Hicks gave in his *Theory of Economic History* (1969a) of how the fix-price/flex-price model came about. In that splendid little book, Hicks did not quote the intellectual grandfather of his approach, a quintessentially English jurist who obtained worldwide fame by a very similar historic-theoretic construct. His name, of course, is Henry Sumner Maine, best remembered precisely for having traced a path of progress for human society, from status to contract (Maine, 1905 [1861]). In his book on economic history, Hicks adopted exactly the same dynamic model to trace society's economic progress. He refrained, however, from embracing the positive view of that process that Maine, the eminent Victorian, held. Hicks came of age after the First World War, which wrought the dissolution of the European equilibrium. This perhaps explains the difference in outlook. Nor did Sir John refer to Max Weber or to his pupil, Karl Polanyi. Still, some of the issues Hicks faced in both the article I quoted and in his *Theory of Economic History* are germane to those that Weber and Polanyi grappled with, and Hicks's solution is rather akin to theirs.

In all cases, according to Maine, Weber, and Polanyi, a mercantile system grows from being the periphery of a society based on status and custom, where prices are very far from containing all the information pertaining to demand and supply, to one in which markets become the core of society, and prices contain all information. Indeed, market society becomes a sum of individuals. Here it finally meets its own undoing. For all these writers, with the exception of Maine, a market society organized exclusively on flex-price markets run for the benefit of, and by, individuals cannot survive its own volatility. When markets finally conquer the center of the stage, having destroyed all rival institutions, they are destroyed by their own oscillations, as all the pre-existent social shock absorbers are now missing.

In his theory of economic history, Hicks attempts a historical reconstruction of how this process unfolds throughout the ascent of capitalism. In his more professional writings as well, though, even in the most highly theoretical among them, he is at pains to show his awareness of the complexity of reality, of the need to model it as realistically as possible, all the time trying, of course, to achieve realism without a loss of generality.

An economist's explanation of the instability of capitalism

The fix-price/flex-price model is an answer to this methodological need. While it is certainly true that the three above-mentioned predecessors on this line ploughed the same field, the tools used by Hicks are very much his own, and peculiarly suited to the job. The fix-price/flex-price model is, in fact, elegant and evocative. It reduces the picture to essentials, which is the mark of a good model, and is powerful enough to lend itself to misuse if consigned to hands less skilled than those of its inventor. The fix-price/flex-price model is the product of the mind of a theoretical economist. It is an economist's explanation of the instability of capitalism, and it is enough to contrast it with the explanations given by Weber, Polanyi, and Maine to see the difference of the approaches. Even in his theory of economic history, the tools Hicks uses are those of the economist.

Consider, for instance, his explanation of the apprenticeship system as it had developed in medieval times, which survived them and still lingers on in parts of the capitalist system. Although the derivation of the system from custom and command is openly acknowledged by Hicks, he goes into a masterful demonstration as to why a young man of low birth and small means will voluntarily apprentice himself to an artisan, and why the artisan will accept him, even though he knows that in the end he will become his competitor by using the skills learned from him. Here the argumentation Hicks uses is altogether that of economics, and, ideally, we can build a link between the 1969 demonstration given by the mature Hicks and that contained in the *Theory of Wages* of thirty-five years earlier. Clarity and elegance have increased, but the way of reasoning has remained the same.

This is, in fact, one of the most striking features in John Hicks's work. From beginning to end he uses the same box of tools. Although his collected essays contain prefaces to each article in which he is at pains to explain in what ways his views have changed over the years, the reader is struck by the compactness of his thought, by its homogeneity in time. The fix-price/flex-price method, which he began to use in his youth, as I hope 1 have shown in this chapter, and kept as a reference model throughout his professional career, constitutes an excellent example of this consistency. And it is a consistency that has paid off in the long run, if we can still find inspiration in that model and use it as a frame to address some of the important economic issues with which we are faced today.

10 On the Hicksian definition of income in applied economic analysis

Paolo Onofri and Anna Stagni

Introductory remarks

In the preface to the first edition of *Value and Capital*, Sir John Hicks acknowledges that he 'profited from the constant reminder which [he] had from [Ursula's] work, that the place of economic theory is to be the servant of applied economics' (Hicks, 1939a: v). There are several aspects of applied economics that benefited from the theoretical analysis that Hicks developed. One of the least noticed was the distinction between flex-price and fix-price markets, and their influence in the shaping of econometric models. We aim to focus on an even narrower question, which raised quite a lot of theoretical discussions in the 1930s and 1940s, but lay dormant in applied economics till the great inflation of the 1970s: the definition of income.

It was not the rate of inflation in that decade that brought the question to life; it was its persistence. The persistence of inflation, as Hicks on many occasions noticed, changed the 'normal' long-run rate of interest, making it diverge from the long-run real return to capital. Households started realizing that, had they consumed their total comprehensive income, they might have eaten up part of their wealth. Measuring the propensity to save and the true burden of the public debt became a problem in macroeconomic analysis. It was during those years that household disposable income started being calculated with the so-called 'Hicksian correction.' The usual quotation was drawn from *Value and Capital* (chap. 14), where Hicks states, as a central meaning of the concept of income, that 'we ought to define a man's income as the maximum value which he can consume during a week, and still expect to be as well off at the end of the week as he was at the beginning' (1939a: 172). He supplies three approximations to this concept.

We would like to thank Mariagiulia Folloni (Prometeia Associates) for her valuable contribution to the econometric part of the chapter.

Income definition no. 1
'The maximum amount which can be spent during a period if there is to be an expectation of maintaining intact the capital value of prospective receipts (in money terms)' (*ibid.*: 173). What happens if interest rates are expected to change, however? This question led him to the second approximation.

Income definition no. 2
'The maximum amount the individual can spend this week, and still expect to be able to spend the same amount in each ensuing week' (174). What happens, though, if prices are also expected to change? Hence the third approximation.

Income definition no. 3
'The maximum amount of money which the individual can spend this week, and still expect to be able to spend the same amount *in real terms* in each ensuing week' (*ibid.*).

The economic quantity that economists are looking for is the third one, but of course it is not the quantity the statisticians can measure; they would need interest rates expectations, price expectations, and each individual's (or firm's) prospect for the future. The 'true' definition of income is a subjective *ex ante* measure, but statisticians can produce only objective *ex post* measures to be aggregated at the social level. To approximate the economic concept, the work of statisticians should be integrated with the work of econometricians in order to estimate time series expectations: the futures of the past.

In what follows we apply the Hicksian definition of income to the evaluation of household disposable income and to the definitions of the return of both financial and real capital assets; all time series refer to the Italian economy.

Household disposable income

The disposable income corrected *à la* Hicks (Y_d^*) is defined as follows:

$$Y_{dt}^* = \bar{Y}_{dt} + (r_t^e - \dot{p}_t)W_{t-1} \qquad (10.1)$$

where $\bar{Y}_d$ is the disposable income net of the return to financial assets, r_t^e is the return to financial assets expected at the beginning of time t for t, $\dot{p}_t$ is the expected consumer price inflation for t, and W_{t-1} is the value of financial wealth at the end of the previous period.

The traditional statistical data simply define disposable income as

$$Y_{dt} = \bar{Y}_{dt} + r_t W_{t-1} \qquad (10.2)$$

Comparing the two definitions, we can infer that considering expected instead of actual yields of financial wealth does not change substantially the value of the disposable income, unless expectations errors are extremely high. The relevant correction is the one that allows for the burden of maintaining the purchasing power of wealth intact, obtained by subtracting from income the loss in the purchasing power of the accumulated stock of wealth due to inflation. Hicks's suggestion is to use the *ex ante* inflation rate, on the assumption that, at the beginning of the period, the consumer needs an estimation of his or her expected budget constraint.

To obtain an estimate of household disposable income corrected according to Hicks's definition,[1] we use statistical data over the time period 1970 to 2004. As regards personal income flows and taxes, we use historical data, implicitly assuming that households behave as if they had perfect foresight of their personal incomes and taxes at the beginning of the year. For interest income flows from financial wealth, we use expected values, both for the nominal return on financial wealth (bonds) and inflation rates.

The expectations estimates are based on autoregressive rolling sample models of the two variables. The results appear quite different. The forecast errors for interest revenues are definitely stationary and appear randomly distributed, at least in the last decade. The same does not hold for the forecast errors of inflationary expectations over the whole sample, even if they are reverting toward the end of the sample (see figure 10.1). At the beginning of the inflationary process of the 1970s agents underestimated inflation for a short period of time. The subsequent years are characterized, in contrast, by a persistent overestimation of inflation. If we assume that our autoregressive model for expected inflation is the true model, this seems to suggest a data-generating process that works as if agents assign a higher cost to underestimating than to overestimating inflation.

In any event, the effect of forecast errors on the size of the adjustment of disposable income is moderate, as is apparent in figure 10.2, which compares observed data with two adjusted time series, computed using both expected and actual inflation.

In either case the Hicksian correction produces a very strong increase in the variance of disposable income, thus strengthening the *excessive smoothness paradox* in the relation between the variance of the consumption dynamics implied by the theory and the empirically observed variance of

---

[1] Careful investigation into the relevance of the Hicksian correction for Italian households was carried out within the Bank of Italy's econometric model. See Ando, Guiso, and Visco (1994) and Zollino (2001).

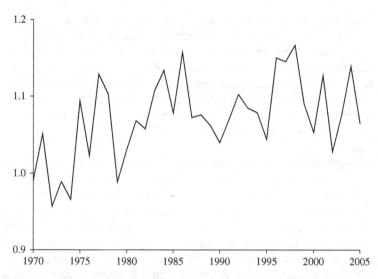

Figure 10.1 Ratio of expected to actual inflation, 1970–2005

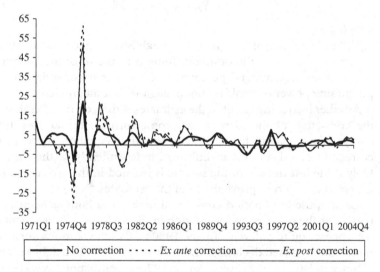

Figure 10.2 Household disposable income with and without Hicksian correction (percentage change), 1971–2004

aggregate consumption. Of course, the impact of the corrections is much stronger in the period of higher inflation than in the other periods.

It is interesting to investigate whether consumers' decisions actually take into account the Hicksian corrections. The empirical test was performed using the aggregate consumption function included in the quarterly econometric model of the Italian economy built by Prometeia. The original equation, reported in the appendix, was estimated over the sample 1970–2003 using the official definition of household disposable income.

Surprisingly, the first result is that the Hicksian correction of household disposable income worsens the fit of the econometric equation, both with the *ex ante* and with the *ex post* version of the correction. Nonetheless, this does not necessarily imply that consumers ignore the Hicksian correction. They might grasp that there is a source of variability in their disposable income that depends on the size of their wealth and on the rate of inflation, without being able to define its exact impact. This might imply that consumers behave as if they have in mind a notion of disposable income resulting not from a full Hicksian correction but from a partial correction, according to the following definition:

$$Y_{dt}^* = \bar{Y}_{dt} + (r_t^e - \gamma \dot{p}_t) W_{t-1} \tag{10.3}$$

with $0 \le \gamma \le 1$.

Different values of γ were used, establishing that values within the interval 0.3–0.5 give the best contribution to the fit of the equation. In other words, consumers' perception of the impact of inflation on the purchasing power of wealth is not negligible, but incomplete.

Another intriguing result of the estimates is that, on the overall sample, the correction of the disposable income through the *ex post* inflation always improves the fit of the consumption equation more than the correction based on *ex ante* inflation, independently of the value of γ. Only if the last decade of the sample is isolated in the estimate does the expected inflation improve the fit of the estimates.[2]

Clearly, the long period considered here is not homogeneous, and in particular the role played by inflation in the 1970s and subsequent decades appears quite different. By the 1980s inflation was not a surprise any more, and it started declining, while the weight of public debt kept rising.

Since inflation was a surprise in the 1970s, the inflation tax was high and public debt remained virtually stable over the whole decade. The Hicksian correction significantly affects disposable income, as inflation remained in

---

[2] Documentation of the whole set of data and estimations are available from the authors: paolo.onofri@unibo.it and anna.stagni@unibo.it.

the double-digit range for most of the time. The role played by the Hicksian correction in the 1970s might have been substituted in subsequent decades by other factors, such as an effort to avoid the so-called 'fiscal illusion' attached to the size of the public debt, as Amilcare Puviani defined it in 1903 (see Puviani, 1973 [1903]), seventy-one years before Robert Barro (see Barro, 1974).

Hicks's correction allows a redefinition of households' propensity to save, taking into account the wealth redistribution between the whole government sector and the household sector produced by inflation. On the other hand, the value of the households' wealth might be distorted by a wrong perception of the value of the claims the households hold on both the ownership and the debt of firms. Unfortunately, with the available time-series data it is not possible to measure this kind of perception. Moreover, the imperfections of the capital markets are such that the present value of a firm is not independent of the composition of the ownership and debt claims, as the Modigliani–Miller theorem would suggest. These imperfections and misperceptions introduce a divergence between the return to the claims and to real capital. We turn to this topic in the next section, and use the Hicksian correction to uncover the divergence.

The rate of return to capital[3]

As Hicks suggested, it is necessary 'to keep in mind the relation of every definition to the purpose for which it is used' (Hicks, 1942a: 175). The analogy with the arguments of the preceding section suggests that, according to the Hicksian correction, the return on financial assets must be defined at a constant purchasing power of wealth.

On the other hand, the Hicksian suggestion implies that, from the point of view of the firm, the profit on fixed capital has to be defined evaluating corporate income at constant productive capacity – that is, 'maintaining capital intact.'

It is easy to compare the points of view of households and firms, deriving the definitions relevant in the two cases. For households, the flow of income R obtained from holding an asset – adjusted *à la* Hicks – is defined as follows:

$$R_t = E_t + (\dot{p}_{vt} - \dot{p}_t)V_{t-1}$$

---

[3] The contents of this section replicate some of the arguments developed in Onofri and Stagni (1984).

where E is the flow of earnings from the asset, V is the value of the asset, p_v is the price of the asset, and p the consumer price. Dotted variables denote proportional rates of change. The corresponding rate of return is

$$r_{vt} = \frac{E_t}{V_{t-1}} + \dot{p}_{vt} - \dot{p}_t \tag{10.4}$$

Usually the expression above is meant to represent the real rate of return as opposed to the nominal one, while in the Hicksian strict sense it represents the only meaningful notion of return. In discrete time the precise definition of the rate of return in real terms $\bar{r}_v$ is the following:

$$\bar{r}_{vt} = \frac{E_t}{(1 + \dot{p}_t)V_{t-1}} + \frac{\dot{p}_{vt} - \dot{p}_t}{(1 + \dot{p}_t)} \tag{10.5}$$

For firms, income defined in the Hicksian sense must be consistent with the maintenance of the existing productive capacity. It is therefore necessary to subtract from gross profits the depreciation allowances valued at the end-of-period prices, and the rate of return to physical capital (r_c), or the rate of profit, must be defined as follows:

$$r_{ct} = \frac{PR_t}{C_{t-1}} - \delta(1 + \dot{p}_{ct}) = \frac{E'_t}{C_{t-1}} - \dot{p}_{ct}\delta \tag{10.6}$$

where C is the value of capital stock, δ is the proportional decay during the current period of production, PR is the flow of firm gross profits (revenues net of current cost of production), E' is the corresponding flow of profits net of depreciation (valued at the costs of the preceding period), and $\dot{p}_{ct}$ is the rate of change of prices of physical capital. The last term in the expression above represents the Hicksian correction relevant in this definition. In this case, inflation affects the real rate of profit only with reference to the scrapping of fixed capital.

Since we are interested in investigating the empirical relevance of the Hicksian corrections, we have to calculate the time series consistent with definitions (10.5) and (10.6). To make these two data series comparable, some qualifications are necessary. In particular, the financial assets variable V of equation (10.5) must be representative of the capital stock of industrial firms; therefore, it includes both equity and bonds used to finance the capital stock of the industrial sector. Since the model for expected inflation does not appear very satisfactory, we always compute the Hicksian corrections using *ex post* observed inflation data instead of expected inflation. Moreover, all the variables represent pre-tax values.

The data obtained both for r_c and $\bar{r}_v$ are reported in figure 10.3. The rate of profit over the last fifty years has been 12.6 percent on average,

Table 10.1 *Rate of profit, real return on financial assets, and real cost of capital (percentage values), 1951–2003*

	1951–79		1980–2003		1951–2003	
	Average	Standard deviation	Average	Standard deviation	Average	Standard deviation
r_c	10.4	2.7	15.2	1.5	12.6	3.2
$\bar{r}_v$	3.4	13.7	8.0	21.6	5.6	17.9
$\bar{p}$	3.4	2.7	3.3	1.0	3.3	2.1

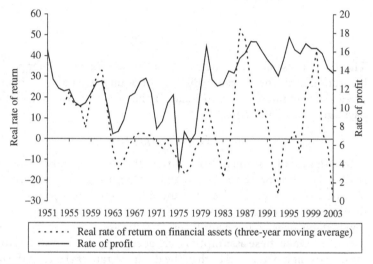

Figure 10.3 Rate of profit and real rate of return on financial assets associated with industrial fixed capital, 1951–2003

compared with the average real return on financial assets for households of 5.6 percent (see table 10.1). The Hicksian correction accentuates the variability of the return to financial assets; the standard deviation of $\bar{r}_v$ is almost six times the standard deviation of the rate of profit (17.9 and 3.2, respectively). Both variables show similar behavior in the two subperiods (1951–79 and 1980–2003) included in the sample. During the first period both the rate of profit and the real rate of return on financial assets are declining steadily; in the second period they look more stationary, with higher average values and higher variability, in the case of the real return on financial assets. As for the rate of profit, in the second period a sharp increase in the average value is accompanied by a slightly lower standard deviation.

The comparison of these two returns is not relevant for investment decisions, since the *ex post* measure of the income perceived by a representative holder of a portfolio of securities cannot be considered an estimate of the opportunity cost of capital for the firm. The opportunity cost of capital is the market capitalization rate of a stream of expected future earnings, thus involving the concept of *ex ante* income obtainable from the new capital goods. It is commonly accepted that the cost of capital (ρ) could be defined as the ratio between the expected return from current assets (X) and the sum of the market value of shares ($p_A A$) and the market value of firm's debt ($p_B B$):

$$\rho = \frac{X}{p_A A + p_B B} G \tag{10.7}$$

The term G is an adjustment factor for special growth opportunities incorporated in the market valuation of equity. Using r_B to denote the average rate of interest on bonds, and Y the expected profits net of interest payments, we could write

$$X = Y + r_B p_B B$$

In order to infer some information on the cost of capital from available market data, however, we need to make some strong assumptions. First of all, one has to assume either that there is no retention of profits, or that dividend payments are proportional to expected profits and the proportion is stable over time. Secondly, it has to be assumed that G is also stable over time. Once these assumptions are accepted, we can proceed to define the cost of capital in terms both of the dividend rate (r_A) and of the interest rate on bonds. That is to say,

$$\rho = w_A r_A + w_B r_B \tag{10.8}$$

where w_i are the weights of shares and bonds, respectively.

Since inflation is not neutral, we also need to express the cost of capital in real terms. If we still assume that shareholders are capitalizing correctly the effects of inflation on share values, it follows that r_B will be swollen by inflation, unlike what happens to r_A. If inflation affects the purchasing power of the sole debt component, the real cost of capital ($\bar{\rho}$) can be defined as follows:

$$\bar{\rho} = r_A w_A + \frac{r_B - \dot{p}}{1 + \dot{p}} w_B \tag{10.9}$$

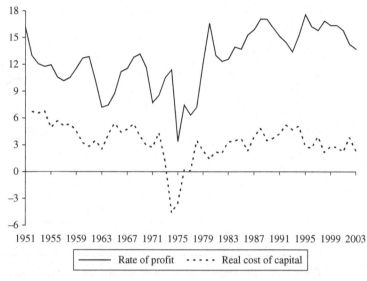

Figure 10.4 Rate of profit and real cost of capital, 1951–2003

where $\dot{p}$ is the proportional change of the price deflator of the value added of the industrial sector. Once the effect of inflation on the real burden of the corporate debt is included, the real cost of capital is no longer increasing in the 1960s and 1970s as nominal rates do. In fact, it becomes negative in the middle of the 1970s. On the overall sample, it shows a slightly declining trend (see figure 10.4).

The cost of capital, as defined above, shows an impressive stability in the long run, both in the average level and the standard deviation; unfortunately, shareholders are unable to perceive the change – favorable to them – that inflation causes in firms' asset accounts. In principle, the fall in the purchasing power of the outstanding debt securities should be counterbalanced by the capitalization by the shareholders of the resulting reduction in future debt burden. In the event, though, no conclusive test can be used to prove whether Italian shareholders had this perception. What is indisputable, however, is that in the 1970s there was a deterioration in the prospects for firms' growth that has more than balanced the real financial leverage effect. Indeed, in the subsequent decades the improvement in firms' growth prospects has compensated for the return to positive values of real interest rates on corporate debt.

Under the circumstances mentioned above, it goes without saying that the behavior of the cost of capital does not coincide with that of the rate of return on financial assets. A comparison between $\bar{r}_v$ and $\bar{p}$ (figure 10.5 and

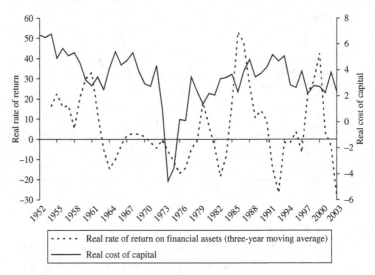

Figure 10.5 Real rate of return on financial assets and real cost of capital, 1952–2003

table 10.1) shows how different the variance of the two time series is throughout the half-century under investigation. In other words, it shows how strong the redistribution process between households and firms has been during those decades. A quick look at figure 10.5 is sufficient to see that there is no definite drift in the redistribution process. The rate of return for holders of financial assets has been higher than the cost of capital in the years of low inflation, and it has fallen to a greater extent than the cost of financing for firms during the double-digit inflation period (1974–84). Ultimately, all this does is stress the separation between decisions as to the uses of savings (portfolio allocation) and investment decisions. The definition of the rate of return to capital both for firms and households according to the Hicksian correction emphasizes that financial and real assets are even more imperfect substitutes.

Conclusions

We have followed John Hicks's suggestions for correcting the definitions of income for households and firms. The non-neutrality of inflation that the Hicksian correction allows to emerge is reflected in the divergence between the return to household claims on firms' capital and the return to capital for the firms. In other words, the Hicksian correction of the definition of income may shed light on the divergence between investment and saving decisions. Of course, this is not the whole story (as Sir John would say). The divergence is also related to how much households are able to see through the two veils that separate their wealth either from the value of the assets of the firms they own, or from the value of the public debt they hold in their portfolio. But that is another story.

Appendix

The consumption function of the Prometeia quarterly econometric model of the Italian economy

The long-run relationship is the following (standard errors in parentheses):

$$\text{Log}(C^*) = 0.71477 \quad \text{Log}(Y^*) - 4.5108 \, R^* + 0.2173 \, \text{Log}(W^*)$$
$$(0.065441) \qquad\qquad (0.74804) \quad (0.023753)$$

where C is households' consumption of non-durables (* stands for long-run levels), Y is the unadjusted household disposable income, W is households' net financial wealth, and R is the real rate of return of households' financial portfolio. All the variables are at constant prices.

Co-integration analysis, performed over a sample from the third quarter of 1970 to the fourth quarter of 2003, points to the stability of the long-run relation between the propensity to save and wealth.

The dynamic path of consumption toward the long-run values follows an error correction model (ECM). The error correction term is the discrepancy between actual (C_t) and desired long-run consumption (C_t^*).

The estimation results of the dynamic relationship are presented in table 10.A1.

Table 10.A1 *Household consumption: error correction representation*

Dependent variable: ΔLC

Method: Least squares
Sample (adjusted): 1971:2–2003:4
ECM $= 1.0LC^* - 0.71477LY^* + 4.5108R^* - 0.2173LW^*$

Variables	Coefficient	Standard error (SE)	t-stat	t-prob
Constant	0.0045729	0.00085563	5.345	0.0000
$\Delta\text{Log}(C(-1))$	0.19571	0.080026	2.446	0.0159
$\Delta\text{Log}(C(-2))$	0.096596	0.074947	1.289	0.2000

Table 10.A1 (*cont.*)

Variables	Coefficient	Standard error (SE)	t-stat	t-prob
ΔLog(Y)	0.10471	0.022914	4.570	0.0000
ΔLog($Y(-1)$)	0.044674	0.023246	1.922	0.0570
ΔLog($R(-4)$)	−0.11269	0.067537	−1.669	0.0978
ΔLog(W)	0.022670	0.014005	1.619	0.1082
ΔLog($W(-1)$)	0.019577	0.013408	1.460	0.1469
ΔLog($W(-2)$)	0.032147	0.013376	2.403	0.0178
ΔLog($W(-3)$)	0.040529	0.014033	2.888	0.0046
ECM(-1)	−0.052453	0.010277	−5.104	0.0000
R-squared	0.556784	F-statistics		13.59
SE of regression	0.00390981	Prob(F-statistics)		0.000000
Sum squared residual	0.001819	Durbin–Watson statistics		1.93

Table 10.A2 *Household consumption: error correction representation with disposable income partially adjusted (0.4)* à la *Hicks*

$$\text{Log}(C^*) = 0.82442 \, \text{Log}(Y^*) - 5.1659 \, R^* + 0.15251 \, \text{Log}(W^*)$$
$$\quad\quad (0.071932) \quad\quad\quad (0.74345) \quad (0.026875)$$

Dependent variable: ΔLC
Method: Least squares
Sample (adjusted): 1971:2–2003:4
ECM $= 1.0LC^* - 0.82442LY^* + 5.1659R^* - 0.15251LW^*$

Variables	Coefficient	Standard error (SE)	t-stat	t-prob
Constant	0.015756	0.0027590	5.711	0.0000
ΔLog($C(-1)$)	0.18537	0.078421	2.364	0.0197
ΔLog($C(-2)$)	0.094514	0.073675	1.283	0.2020
ΔLog(Y)	0.095932	0.018746	5.117	0.0000
ΔLog($Y(-1)$)	0.022646	0.018559	1.220	0.2248
ΔLog($R(-4)$)	−0.12349	0.066736	−1.851	0.0667
ΔLog(W)	0.016915	0.013290	1.273	0.2056
ΔLog($W(-1)$)	0.016900	0.012909	1.309	0.1930
ΔLog($W(-2)$)	0.027684	0.012972	2.134	0.0349
Δ Log($W(-3)$)	0.037441	0.013599	2.753	0.0068
ECM(-1)	−0.057929	0.0091041	−6.363	0.0000
R-squared	0.58163	F-statistics		15.04
SE of regression	0.00379864	Prob(F-statistics)		0.000000
Sum squared residual	0.00171713	Durbin–Watson statistics		1.96

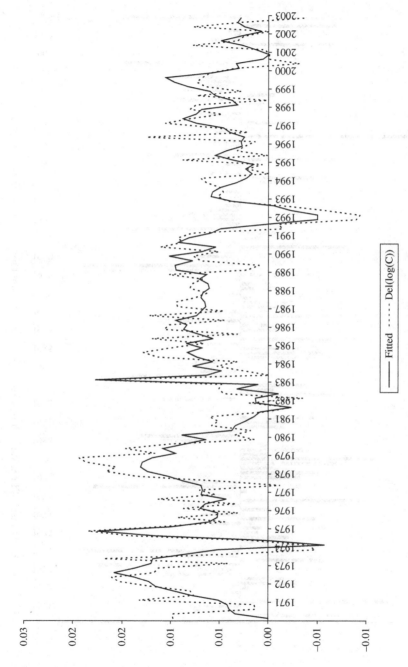

Figure 10.A1 Household consumption: error correction representation (a), 1971–2003

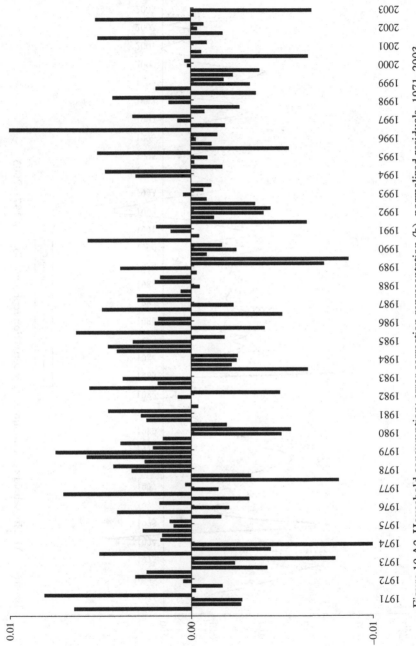

Figure 10.A2 Household consumption: error correction representation (b), normalized residuals, 1971–2003

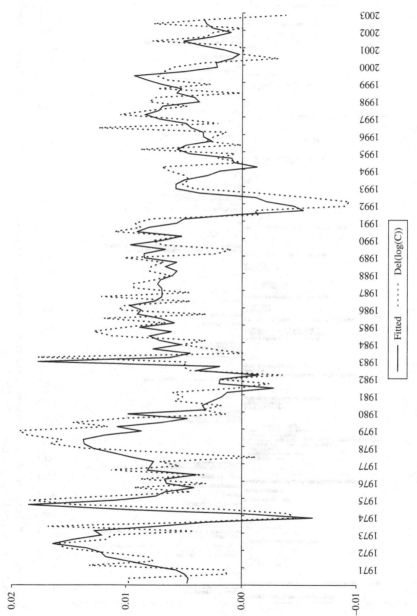

Figure 10.A3 Household consumption: error correction representation with disposable income partially adjusted *à la* Hicks (a), 1971–2003

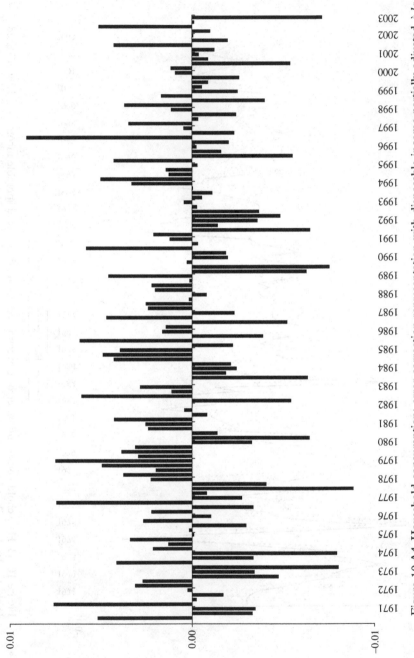

Figure 10.A4 Household consumption: error correction representation with disposable income partially adjusted *à la* Hicks (b), normalized residuals, 1971–2003

Statistical sources

Expected inflation: our own rolling sample autoregressive estimation on the consumer price index, Istat.

Household wealth: Bank of Italy.

Households' disposable income: Istat.

Households' national consumption: Istat.

Rate of decay of the capital stock: Italian Confederation of Employers.

Profits, interest payments, and depreciation for industrial firms: Istat, and Italian Confederation of Employers.

Dividend yield, yield on bonds, and financial assets: Datastream, Bank for International Settlements (BIS).

Part III

Money

11 Historical stylizations and monetary theory

Alberto Quadrio Curzio and Roberto Scazzieri

Introduction

John Hicks maintained that 'a large part of the best work on Money is topical. It has been prompted by particular episodes, by particular experiences of the writer's own time' (Hicks, 1967a: 156). The reason for this is that the principal goal of monetary theory is not 'general understanding' (that is, the discovery of principles uniformly applicable in a variety of times and places) but 'particular understanding – an understanding directed towards a particular problem, normally a problem of the time at which the work in question is written' (*ibid.*).

This focused character of monetary theory brings out an important association between monetary theory and monetary disturbances:

Monetary theories arise out of monetary disturbances. This is obviously true of the *General Theory*, which is the book of the Great Depression – the World Depression – of the nineteen-thirties; it is also true of Keynes's other version, the *Treatise on Money*, which differs from the *General Theory* quite largely because it is directed at a different contemporary problem. Though the Treatise was published in 1930, after the Depression had begun, it must largely have been written earlier. Its world is not the world of the Depression, it is the world of the Restored Gold Standard. Its problem is how the Restored Gold Standard is to be made to work. (156–7)

The topical character of monetary theory makes it especially sensitive to changes in monetary arrangements and institutions. Developments in monetary theory may reveal a special insight into the roots of monetary disturbances, and thus allow the discovery of principles that may have passed unnoticed beforehand. In this way, monetary disturbances may suggest not only useful explanatory criteria for the existing arrangements, but also guidelines for a change in monetary institutions (monetary reform).

The purpose of this chapter is to explore the implications of Hicks's approach to monetary disturbances as a source of monetary theory. We do so by examining some contributions to the eighteenth-century discussion on monetary disturbances. This discussion highlights fundamental principles of the underlying conceptual and institutional system (the set-up of *imaginary money*, in which the unit of account is distinct from the monetary means of transaction and payment). The chapter is arranged as follows. The first section describes a specific eighteenth-century monetary disturbance: the monetary disorder (*disordine monetario*) that engulfed the Habsburg-ruled state of Milan in the mid-eighteenth century. The next section considers the most important theoretical contributions that were put forward with the purpose of explaining the Milanese monetary disturbance. In particular, this section examines the monetary essays by Cesare Beccaria and Pietro Verri, and illustrates the general principles that Beccaria and Verri were led to discover through the analysis of a specific monetary disturbance. The following section discusses technical features of the 'dual money' system, especially the relationship between imaginary money and bank money (a relationship often emphasized in classical analyses of this issue). The final section brings the chapter to a close by suggesting that the topical character of monetary theory calls attention to the role of imaginary money as an ideal standard against which to explain specific monetary disturbances, and as an heuristic tool for the identification of effective rules in the field of monetary policy.

Monetary disturbances in a multi-currency economy

This chapter considers developments in monetary theorizing stimulated by monetary disturbances in the multi-currency economy of the Milanese state of the mid-eighteenth century.[1] Monetary transactions were carried out by means of twenty-two gold currencies and twenty-nine silver currencies. Only two Milanese currencies were used; all the others were currencies of foreign states. Monetary contracts were stipulated in a unit of account (called *lira*) that was not used in actual transactions. Real payments were carried out not through the unit of account but through one or the other of the currencies in circulation. For example, as Luigi Einaudi has noted, whoever 'had sold a house or a field for 25,000 lire, would have to exchange contracts with a seller who would give him 10,000 gold scutes of the sun as payment' (Einaudi, 1936a: 8). This type of monetary economy could simultaneously allow the persistence over time

---

[1] Our reconstruction of the monetary discussion that took place in the Milanese state during the 1760s is based on previous collaborative research (Quadrio Curzio and Scazzieri, 1986, 1992). The present chapter explicitly addresses the connections of that historical episode with the theory of dual money systems and with the relationship between bank money and imaginary money (see below).

of monetary obligations and the flexibility of payment arrangements. Contracts were expressed in a unit of account (the lira as 'imaginary money') that no longer existed as a real currency. As a result, and for this very reason, contracts could have an immutable structure and be independent of changes in the purchasing power of real currencies. At the same time, the same monetary obligation could be fulfilled by making use of multiple currencies.

This set of arrangements presupposed certain necessary conditions. In particular: (i) currencies of equal gold or silver content should exchange for one another on a 1:1 basis; (ii) gold currencies should exchange for silver currencies according to a ratio expressing the scarcity of gold relative to silver and the content of metal in each currency; and (iii) the production costs of different currencies should not be a relevant factor in determining the exchange rate of one currency for another. If the above conditions are satisfied, any given amount of imaginary money corresponds to the same quantity of gold or silver in different currencies. Monetary disturbances arise when the exchange rate between any two currencies does not match the ratio between their gold or silver content. In his essay *Del disordine e de' rimedi delle monete nello Stato di Milano nell'anno 1762* (Beccaria, 1986 [1762]), the first edition of which was published in 1762, Cesare Beccaria notes that the first condition above was not met in the Milanese state: 'I have computed how much gold content is to be found in one hundred lire expressed in different currencies, and the outcome of my computations is that such a ratio is different in each currency' (78). The mismatch between official exchange rates (between imaginary money and real currencies) and market exchange rates (between currencies in circulation) meant that speculative currency flows became possible. For example,

If we take among the silver coins the lira of Savoy and the lira of Genoa, foreign nations can exchange one for the other and gain to our expense 10 lire, 8 sols and 4 dinars for one hundred lire; and if we consider gold coins, the foreign countries having trade with us may exchange the double of Genoa with the zecchin of Savoy and draw a gain of 16 lire, 9 sols and 8 dinars for one hundred lire, thanks to the mistake of our official exchange rates. (220–1)

Another monetary disturbance is associated with the mismatch between the exchange rates of gold and silver coins and the overall proportion between the gold and silver metals. If that is the case, as Beccaria notes, the system of legally fixed exchange rates between metal currencies and imaginary money allows 'the nations trading with us to extract 16 ounces of pure silver for 12 ounces they send to us, and thus to continue the detrimental trade with us at the great loss of 25 per cent' (85).

Finally, the mismatch between the legally fixed proportions among Milanese currencies and the corresponding metal contents brings about another type of monetary disturbance. For example, the 'enormous disparity between the Philip and the 5 sols coin of Milan' is such that, for the sum of 100 lire, '[t]he sols give 6000 silver grains, whereas the Philip gives about 6926' (86).

To sum up, the primary source of monetary disturbance is the mismatch between different value systems. Contracts expressed in terms of imaginary money cannot be fulfilled unless real currencies are traded. This discrepancy opens up the possibility of speculative specie flows with a drain upon the national resources of certain countries: 'The scarcity of money brings about the increase in the interests of capital, and with it debts, then bankruptcies and the loss of public faith, whose course is followed by the collapse of trade' (71).

The theory and management of imaginary money

The Milanese monetary disturbances discussed by Beccaria are a particular instance of a widespread European phenomenon. Its roots lie in the separation between different functions of money, especially the distinction between money as unit of account and money as means of payment. Such a distinction is a characteristic feature of monetary transactions in medieval and early modern Europe up to the end of the eighteenth century. Luigi Einaudi describes as follows that type of monetary economy (1936a: 7–8):

There was...a monetary unit that was useful for contracts, obligations, accounts, and this was the accounting lira, or imaginary, numéraire, ideal lira. People computed and made contracts, drew accounts, established permanent rents, incomes and taxes in lire, sols and denars. At the time of Malestroit and his *Paradoxes* (1565), people would contract a unit of velvet for 10 lire, a measure (*muy*) of wine for 12 lire, a pair of shoes for 15 sols, a work day of a journeyman for 5 sols, the annual rent of a nobleman at 500 lire, a house or a field at 25,000 lire. If it was possible to contract and compute through imaginary lire, it was obviously impossible to make use of them for payments, since they had not been coined for centuries in any of their subdivisions. Payments were made through real and effective currencies, which were coined in gold, silver, billon (a mixture of silver and copper), copper... Malestroit's contracting agent would make his payments as follows: the unit of velvet purchased at 10 imaginary lire by delivering 4 golden scutes of the sun at the exchange rate of 2 lire and 10 sols per scute; the measure of wine purchase at 12 lire by delivering 20 silver testons at the exchange rate of 12 scutes per teston; the pair of shoes purchased at 15 sols by delivering 15 *douzains* of billon at the exchange rate of 12 denars per *douzain*. The journeyman, who had contracted his work day for 5 sols, was happy to receive 5 *douzains* at the rate of 12 denars per *douzain*; the nobleman would cash, for his 500 lire of annual rents and incomes, 200 golden scutes of the sun; whoever had sold a house or a field at 25,000 lire was expected to acknowledge completion of contract if the purchaser delivered 10,000 golden scutes of the sun.

The above set of monetary arrangements is one in which 'A just sells to B against B's promise to pay, B to C against C's promise to pay, and so on' (Hicks, 1967a: 8). There is in such a market 'some unit of account in which the promises to pay are expressed...but that unit of account is not a means of payment, nor is it an object of exchange at all' (*ibid.*). A monetary economy in which 'money is simply a unit of account' but 'it is not one of the traded commodities' (10) is an economy in which 'there is...no supply–demand equation to determine its value [the value of money]' (*ibid.*). The demand and supply equations for traded commodities 'are sufficient to determine relative prices, prices (that is) in terms of one of the traded commodities taken as numéraire; but this numéraire *is not the money in terms of which calculations are made*' (*ibid.*; emphasis added). As a result, in this type of monetary economy 'absolute prices – money prices – are indeterminate' (*ibid.*).

Hicks's argument calls attention to the possibility of 'partial' monetary economies – that is, of economies in which money performs some but not all the functions usually associated with it. In particular, Hicks discusses a stylized case that is close to the historical setting of imaginary money, although not identical to it. This is because Hicks's case is one of indeterminate monetary prices, whereas the imaginary money described by Seigneur de Malestroit, Beccaria, and Einaudi coexisted with multiple currencies and allowed (in principle) a multiplicity of monetary values for any given commodity or contract. Hicks's theoretical argument examines an abstract possibility and suggests a relationship between the system of imaginary money and a pure credit economy (an economy in which money is not used as a means of payment). Einaudi examines real monetary transactions carried out in a multi-currency economy against the benchmark of imaginary money. His historical reconstruction makes clear that imaginary money could be conceived as a way to make monetary arrangements stable over time. At the same time, he calls attention to the possibility of speculative specie flows in a multi-currency economy (see Einaudi, 1936a, 1936b, 1937; see also Loria, 1936).

The Milanese monetary disturbances stemmed from the mismanagement of the 'dual money' system. Disturbances arose in particular from the different speeds at which private and public decisions were made. The multi-currency system of payments allowed currency-trading to lead to speculative gain precisely as a result of the slow adjustment of 'internal' exchange rates (the legal exchange rates of any given currency relative to the abstract money that was used as the unit of account). In spite of the monetary disturbances (which were relatively frequent) and the associated collapse of public trust and trade, the dual monetary system could also lead – if it was well managed – to the achievement of a number of important goals. In particular, abstract or imaginary money allowed stability of the general price level in the midst of changes in the internal exchange rates between abstract money and the various currencies in which payments were made: 'Let us assume that the price of bread increases from 1 to 2 lire per kilo; if, at the same time, the exchange rate of the scute relative to the lira goes up from 2 to 4, the price of bread remains fixed at half a scute' (Einaudi, 1936a: 18).

Another important achievement of a well-managed 'dual money' system is the stability of foreign exchanges. This result may be obtained by fixing *ex ante* the gold or silver content of national currencies, so that the foreign exchange rates will be constant or variable solely as a result of the gold or silver content of those currencies. In this case, there may be fluctuations in the *internal* exchange rates between abstract money and the national currency. As long as abstract money is a purely internal accounting device, however, it will be clear that 'fluctuations of exchanges' are 'wholly an internal affair' (Einaudi, 1937: 264). As a matter of fact, if foreign exchanges are fixed in specie terms, fluctuations in the value of foreign currencies derive from changes in the domestic exchange rate between these and the national currency. In short, internal decisions are assigned the central role in determining the fluctuations in the purchasing power of any given currency in each country.

The 'European proportion' and the 'Minister of Money'

The conceptual system of abstract money outlined in the previous section has the remarkable property of introducing topicality right at the core of monetary theory. This is because the separation between abstract money and effective money could alternatively lead to stability in the general price level and foreign exchanges, or to monetary disturbances and the collapse of trade. The effective management of internal exchange rates is a necessary condition for the working of a dual monetary economy. This explains why monetary policy is central in this system, and why the governance of internal exchange rates acquires a distinctively contingent character. The discussion between Beccaria and Verri as to the best policy to avoid monetary disturbances under the system of abstract money hints at the flexibility of monetary policy rules with this type of economy. Monetary management requires effective utilization of the following policy instruments: (i) a uniform criterion should be used in order to fix the correspondence between abstract money and real currencies (so as to remove discrepancies between the intrinsic and the 'numéraire' value of real currencies); (ii) the exchange rates between gold and silver currencies should reflect both the respective metal content of the currencies and the relative scarcity of gold and silver in a suitable economic space; and (iii) the exchange rates of gold to silver currencies should react promptly to shocks affecting the relative scarcity of the two metals.

Beccaria outlines a monetary reform whose goal is to remove the causes of monetary disturbances and to achieve the effective working of the dual money system. The principal components of Beccaria's plan are the following: (i) the utilization of a 'European proportion' in establishing the exchange rates of gold to silver currencies; and (ii) the introduction of a 'Minister of Money' who, 'having a close look at the internal exchange rates of all nations, would be able to detect changes in the proportion, and with this measuring rod could reform, if necessary, the price of currencies in circulation' (Beccaria, 1986 [1762]: 94). The 'European proportion' is at the core of Beccaria's argument, as it points to the instrument to be used in order to identify internal exchange rates between gold and silver currencies. It is worth noting that, precisely in this connection, Verri expresses a different view and notes that the 'proportion' between gold and silver currencies should be established by attaching greater weight to a particular country 'the closer and more involved in trading with that country is' (Verri, 1986b [1772]: 124; see also his previous discussion in Verri, 1986a [1762]).

Beccaria finds this proposal unconvincing: '[If] the neighbouring countries are in line with the rest of Europe...it would be good to govern ourselves on their basis, not because they are our neighbours but because they are following a right standard, and we must be in line with them' (Beccaria, 1986 [1762]: 87). The 'European proportion' benchmark is a fundamental aspect of Beccaria's monetary proposal. It derives from his belief that the dual money system is workable only if one can remove monetary disturbances arising from exchange rates between gold and silver currencies different from the overall exchange values between gold and silver metals in any given monetary space. Beccaria identifies such a space with Europe, as it is in Europe that discrepancies between intrinsic and numéraire values of currencies can easily be detected and exploited (due to the density of trade linkages and the magnitude of specie flows).

Account money, bank money, and imaginary money

Their analysis of monetary disturbances led Beccaria and Verri to pinpoint the central features of the dual money system and the strategy that monetary policy should follow so as to ensure stability of the general price level and foreign exchanges. The reconstruction of this eighteenth-century discussion led Luigi Einaudi to discuss the ideal features of the dual money system *and* the possibility of monetary reform based upon the separation between money as unit of account and money as means of payment (Einaudi, 1937). The features of this 'modern' dual money economy are described as follows (260):

Let us suppose that a country, or the most important commercial countries of the world, adopted the following monetary system: a) The unit of money of account is called a 'dollar'. The dollar is not coined, nor will it ever be coined; nor will paper notes ever be issued in dollars. The dollar is merely an instrument of accounting or pricing... b) The mint will coin gold pounds, platinum, guineas, and silver florins, all of them weighing 120 grains each... No legal connection ought to be established or otherwise maintained between pounds, guineas, and florins. c) The printing press of the central bank will issue notes payable in so many gold pounds, platinum guineas, and silver florins. It will be the duty of the central bank to issue notes against gold, platinum, and silver and to pay precious metals of the required species against notes... As dollars are an imaginary money of account, pound, guinea, and florin coins and notes will be the money of effective payment. The wages of a railway man will be fixed at so many dollars a day and paid in so many pounds or florins. All that is needed to make the system work is an initial proclamation, to be followed in due course of time by successive proclamations, fixing the connection between the money of account (dollar) and the species of effective moneys of payment, let us say, gold pounds... Thenceforward the system will work in part automatically and in part by proclamation.

The fixing of prices, contracts, and other monetary obligations in a unit of account that is not also a means of payment allows the persistence of multiple currencies, the stability of the general price level, and the stability of foreign exchanges. The three results are closely related. For there would be no room for Gresham's law to operate once the unit of account is excluded from circulation: 'Debtors, customers, and employers who are in debt so many dollars will pay indifferently, in gold, platinum, or silver coins or notes, according to the ruling market rate' (Einaudi, 1937: 261–2). The settling of monetary obligations could take place through a variety of means of payment and there would in principle be no reason why the utilization of a particular means of payment should give economic agents an advantage over agents using alternative means of payment. Stability of the general price level is achieved through changes in the internal exchange rate between the money of account (the 'dollar') and the money of payment (say, the gold pound):

Suppose that prices had fallen 16.66 per cent. All that is required, under the system, is a proclamation increasing the rate of exchange between the money of account (dollar) and the money of payment (gold pound) from 5 dollars = 1 pound to 6 dollars = 1 pound. [...] Without a change in the amount of effective coins and notes in circulation, or in the weight and fineness of coins, the circulation of the money of account is increased 20 per cent by fiat. People and banks find their pocket money and their till notes increased by 20 per cent in dollar valuation. Prices which, with gold pounds at 5 dollars, had sunk from 100 to a level of 83.33 will tend to rise again to 100 with gold pounds at 6 dollars. (*ibid.*: 262–3)

A constant general price level (and a constant purchasing power of money) may be obtained through appropriate monetary policy. Changes in the purchasing power of money would pinpoint a failure of monetary management. Finally, external exchange rates (rates of exchange between foreign currencies) will be constant as long as: (i) 'effective money, in coins or bars, [is] the only money accepted for settling international accounts' (264); (ii) there is no change in the 'weight and fineness' of coined metals (*ibid.*); and (iii) there is no change in the internal exchange values of the different currencies relative to the money of account. Fluctuations in the relative values of different currencies on each internal market will be associated with changes in the exchange values of given currencies relative to the money of account, so that 'fluctuations of exchanges will be wholly an internal affair' (*ibid.*).

Beccaria outlined a theory of imaginary money (a set of 'theorems' and 'corollaries') in order to make sense of monetary disturbances in a specific context. His theory allowed him to identify a set of general principles for monetary governance as well as a set of specific policy proposals (the 'European proportion' and the 'Minister of Money'). Taking inspiration from Beccaria's (and Verri's) analysis, Einaudi investigated the abstract possibility of a dual money system in contemporary setting: 'Can the old two-money system offer nothing useful to contemporary practice? Must the idea of a money which cannot be coined, which cannot even be issued in the form of representative paper, a money which is a mere "ratio", be discarded without examination?' (*ibid.*: 268). In other words, the exploration of an old monetary disturbance allows the reconstruction of an even older set of monetary ideas, and these suggest the (abstract) possibility of a monetary practice entirely at variance with contemporary institutions and rules but not necessarily irrelevant to contemporary problems.

To take up Hicks's ideas about monetary disturbances and monetary theory, one could argue that monetary history suggests a collection of 'idealized' problem sets (see Hicks, 1975c). Any given set of problems is context-specific but likely to have an analogue under different historical conditions. The analogue may be associated with different institutional and technical conditions, and thus be open to policy alternatives that could not originally be conceived. Stylized monetary history may inspire critical thinking as to the principles of money and monetary reform. For example, the vicissitudes of the dual money system are a clear instance of a sophisticated institutional device embedded in a yet undeveloped set of monetary institutions. The dual money system introduced a clear distinction between money as a unit of account and money as a means of payment:

> [P]eople in the Middle Ages and in the times before the nineteenth century could see, much better than our contemporaries, that money is a negotiable commodity, just like any other commodity. Since we are used to trade money at the border, modern money does appear, at least within any given country, as a super-commodity whose value is constant. [...] People of past times, through imaginary money, could every day swap and estimate the florins, scutes, doubles, testons, zecchins they received and gave as payment. (Einaudi, 1936a: 31)

The utilization of a partial money (a unit of account) that was not itself traded allowed people to engage in monetary transactions without confusing the need for a fixed standard of value with the idea that effective currencies should be of constant value. The system was the expression of a rational economic need. Its implementation through history, however, has been marred by abuse of sovereign power and sluggish monetary policy. The separation between the *formal structure* of a particular monetary technique (the dual money system) and the vicissitudes of its implementation is a distinctive mark of the literature on ideal or imaginary money. This literature suggests that the dual money system was, to a large extent, the outcome of a lengthy historical process independent of sovereign decisions.

For example, writers such as the Genoese legal theorist Raffaele De Turri or the economists Pompeo Neri and James Steuart explicitly linked the introduction of imaginary money with trade fairs and other international transactions. In particular, De Turri argued that the imaginary money commonly used on such occasions was introduced so that, 'since at market fairs manifold people of different places and provinces get together, a kind of measure common to everybody and with everybody would be available, a measure upon which all deliberations of merchants would be based' (De Turri, as quoted in Jannaccone, 1954 [1946]: 41).[2] Neri too emphasized the connection between trade and imaginary money, and added the distinction between 'bank imaginary money and current

---

[2] '*Cum in feriis convenirent plures diversarum partium et provinciarum gentes, adesset quaedam veluti communis gentibus omnibus mensura et apud omnes eadem, ad quam veluti scopum dirigerentur vota omnia mercatorum.*' Pasquale Jannaccone acknowledges Wilhelm Endemann for an earlier quotation of the same passage (see Endemann, 1874–83).

imaginary money. Bank imaginary money was a wise device that could restore to the contractual degrees of economic value the certainty they had lost as a result of faulty standards of measurement' (Neri, 1804 [1751]: 153). Value could be fixed 'with the names of those imaginary moneys that were called bank lire or scutes These values were regulated by a standard independent of civil laws and public disasters [...] [They] made contracts unambiguous, and the degrees of value constant and unalterable, so that it was very convenient to measure and value any type of commodity and any type of real money' (*ibid.*).

Carlo Antonio Broggia, in his *Trattato delle Monete* (Broggia, 1743), explicitly described the abstract properties of imaginary money as account money (see also Natoli, 1937):

The other Nations, also of an Industrious nature, which established themselves after the Romans, ...introduced the *Imaginary* money, which, as to its denomination, would not have any substance, but would only have it as to the Price, that is, as to Extrinsic [...] They convened that such an account money, or money for private contracts, would be *Ideal*, and not *Real*, as to its Denomination and Intrinsic silver content. (Broggia, 1743: 286)

Broggia also referred to the Banco of Venice and to the Bank of Amsterdam as important institutional arrangements showing how far imaginary money might go in achieving an effective dual money system. For the Venetian case, Broggia quoted from, and commented upon, an earlier treatment by Jacques Savary, who had written that

the Republic of Venice has established itself as the perpetual Cashier to its inhabitants: it has taken from the one and from the other the money needed to make bulk purchases of commodities, as well as of letters of exchange, and to achieve that objective it has established by decree that the payment of such bulk commodity purchases and letters of exchange could not be made except through the Banco [...] In this way the Republic of Venice, without troubling the freedom of commerce, has become the owner of the money of its inhabitants. (Savary, 1749 [1679])

In this way, Broggia adds, 'if the Republic of Venice gives to anybody the Freedom to withdraw his money from the *Banco* through the Cash Counter at the *Banco* itself; yet the need to pay letters of Exchange, and to make bulk purchases of commodities, through the *Banco*, assigns to it at any time the Property of Funds, and the Possession of all Liquid Cash' (Broggia, 1743: 395).

The Amsterdam Bank was established upon similar principles.[3] A decree of the States of Holland of January 31, 1609, had established that

---

[3] Broggia refers to a description of the Bank of Amsterdam to be found in the 'Traité de la Banque d'Amsterdam,' published as an appendix to Jean Pierre Ricard's French

all transactions in excess of a certain sum (300 florins) could not be carried out through the transfer of cash but would require the transfer of letters of exchange drawn on private deposits at the Bank of Amsterdam. All transfers of liabilities within the bank were carried out in terms of an imaginary money of constant value (the florin banco), whereas any exchange of florin banco for cash would allow the Bank of Amsterdam to charge an *agio* in excess of the official value of the florin banco itself (see Broggia, 1743: 412–13). Broggia considered such an *agio* as not

born from the bank itself, but...from the increase in the current price of Moneys. [...] Due to Account Money, which always must keep the same and immutable Price, the imaginary Florin was established, and it was decided to fix its value at 20 sols; it was also decided to increase the current Florin to 21 sols, which makes a 5 per cent difference. Thus, if Money would further increase in Amsterdam, we may be sure that also the Bank Agio would correspondingly increase (*ibid.*: 413)

The special connection between imaginary money and banking transactions is also central to the monetary theory of James Steuart. Steuart too emphasized the role of the Amsterdam Bank as a central clearing house regulating the value relationships between imaginary money and the real (metal) currencies at the international level. In particular, Steuart considered the Amsterdam Bank, and the network of financial intermediations around it, to be a prototype dual money system with a successful record of internal price stability. To understand Steuart's argument, it is useful to examine his own definition of money (based upon a sharp distinction between unit of account and means of payment):

The first thing...to be done in treating of money, is, to separate two ideas, which, by being blended together, have very greatly contributed to throw a cloud upon the whole subject. Money, which I call of account, is no more than *an arbitrary scale of equal parts, invented for measuring the respective value of things vendible*. (Steuart, 1966 [1767]: 408; emphasis in original)

The practical viability of the dual money system is shown by its utilization by the Bank of Amsterdam:

translation of an earlier Dutch essay by Johannes Phoonsen on the 'laws and customs' of exchange between different monetary units (see Phoonsen, 1715). There it was pointed out that, at the Amsterdam Bank, 'all payments are made by a simple transfer of credit, and whoever is a debtor on the Bank's books, ceases to be such as soon as he has transferred his due upon somebody else. This latter is considered to be debtor in his place, and in this way consecutively from the ones to the others: claims are simply changing denomination, and no real and effective payment is required' (318–19).

A florin banco has a more determinate value than a pound of fine gold, or silver; it is an unit which the invention of men, instructed in the arts of commerce, have found it. This bank money stands invariable like a rock in the sea. According to this ideal standard are the prices of all things regulated; and very few people can tell exactly what it depends upon. The precious metals with their intrinsic value, vary with regard to this common measure, like every other thing. A pound of gold, a pound of silver, a thousand guineas, a thousand crowns, a thousand piastres, or a thousand ducats, are sometimes worth more, sometimes worth less of this invariable standard; according as the proportion of the metals of which they are made vary between themselves. No adulterations in the weight, fineness, or denominations of coin have any effect upon bank money. These currencies which the bank looks upon as merchandize, like every other thing, are either worth more or less bank money, according to the actual value of the metals they are made of. All is merchandize with respect to this standard; consequently, it stands unrivalled in the exercise of its function of a common measure. (413)

The most remarkable consequence of the Amsterdam system of account money is that it became feasible to make any change in commodity prices independently of the value of the numéraire (once the bank money, or florin banco, was taken as the unit of measurement for commodity prices):

Money of account…cannot be fixed to any material substance, the value of which may vary with respect to other things. The operations of trade, and the effects of a universal circulation of value, over the commercial world, can alone adjust the fluctuating value of all kinds of merchandize, to this invariable standard. This is a representation of the bank money of Amsterdam, which may at all times be most accurately specified in a determinate weight of silver and gold; but which can never be tied down to that precise weight for twenty-four hours, any more than to a barrel of herrings. (*ibid.*)

Steuart was aware of the special character of the Bank of Amsterdam, yet he seemed to suggest that the States of Holland were able to realize an objective that had long been sought with the separation between imaginary money and effective money:

The original intention of the States of Holland, in establishing the bank of Amsterdam, was to collect a large capital in coin within that city, which might there perpetually remain, buried in a safe repository for the purposes which we are now to explain. In order to accomplish this plan they established the bank upon the 31st January 1609. The method they fell upon to collect the coin, was to order, that all bills of exchange, for any sum exceeding 300 florins, should be paid in specie to the bank; and that the holder of such bills should, instead of receiving the coin, have the value of it written down in the books of the bank to his credit, at his command, to be transferred to any person he should appoint; but never more to be demandable from the bank to specie […] Now the credit in the books of the bank, which is every day transferable at the bank, answers every purpose of coin, either for *payment* or *loan*: and the proprietor has neither the trouble of receiving the species, nor any risk from robbery or false coin. [...] [The deposit at the bank] can only swallow up a sum equal to what is necessary for circulating the payments of the city of Amsterdam. Were a sum exceeding this be shut up in the bank, and were the credits written in the books of the bank to exceed this proportion, it is plain, that the value of the bank money would sink immediately. The reason is obvious: the credits transferable are of no use to those who have no occasion to transfer; that is, to pay, lend, or exchange at Amsterdam. So soon, then, as all demand of Amsterdam is satisfied, the proprietors of the overplus will seek to realize their superfluous credit, in order to invest the value arising from it, in some other place where a demand may arise. In order to realize, they must sell their bank credit for coin; because the bank pays in transfer only. Coin then would be demanded preferably to credit in bank; consequently, coin would rise in its proportional value to bank money, or bank money would lose, which is the same thing. (565–6)

The line of argument followed by James Steuart is part of a long tradition in European monetary thinking. For example, Gasparo Scaruffi, who was writing a couple of centuries before Steuart, advocated the introduction of a system of imaginary monetary units (the imperial lira and its subunits), on the grounds that similar arrangements were already in place among financial intermediaries (see Scaruffi, 1913 [1582]: 120). Geminiano Montanari, while critical of the monetary disturbances that could be associated with the dual money system, acknowledged that imaginary money could be useful in circumscribed trade networks involving repeated debt credit arrangements among members of the same social group:

An imaginary scute has currency in Padua in contracts involving horses, cattle and other animals, which is valued seven lire in Venetian currency (although foreigners, for their greater convenience, are more inclined to deal in terms of golden doubles), and that imaginary scute never changes in value from those seven lire, notwithstanding the changes in the value of gold and silver coins. Similarly in [Modena] the scute of 5.3 [lire], in Bologna the scute of 4, in Mantua that of 6, and in many other places other scutes, which are entirely imaginary. (Montanari, 1913 [1683]: 302)

The idea that imaginary money, while often impractical, may be of special value as a unit of account for transactions in a pure credit economy is a recurrent theme in the analysis of dual money systems. Luigi Valeriani, writing long after Montanari and about a century before Einaudi, expressed that view when he argued that the concept of imaginary money is rooted in the distinction between 'money as a simple measure of value derived in some way from the value of metals, and *money of account*' (Valeriani, 1821: 1; emphasis in original). In particular, Valeriani argued that money as a measure of value follows the principle that 'two quantities equal to a third be equal between themselves' (2). On the other hand, an appropriate money of account relative to contracts involving promises to pay in future periods 'measures the respective give and take between debtor and creditor, an obligation to be fulfilled by making use of any mix of the three metals according to the wish of the debtor *but without doing the creditor any harm*' (*ibid.*; emphasis added). This abstract requirement for an adequate money of account is seldom fulfilled in practice. This is because, so long as effective money is used side by side with imaginary money, commodity prices in terms of effective money may be subject to variation, which would bring about a change in the value of the imaginary unit of account. A special case in which imaginary money would be practically feasible is that of bank money:

And who is not acquainted with the Amsterdam Florin Banco? Entirely modelled on the Venitian Ducaton Banco, this is a money of account derived from a merely representative money. Such a representative money is generally defined as a credit entitlement drawn upon the respective state (considered either as the guarantor or as the principal debtor). The giver has the right to surrender, and the taker has the obligation to accept, such a credit entitlement as real money and pledge of value by decree of their respective Governments. (Valeriani, 1819: 177)

The relationship between imaginary money and *a particular type* of bank money (such as the Amsterdam florin banco) provides an important benchmark for the analysis of the dual money economy. Imaginary money may work in practice as an invariable standard of value so long as it is associated with a pure credit set-up such as the ones at Amsterdam or Venice. As soon as we move away from the pure credit set-up, and we consider the conditions of a multi-currency economy, some of the criticisms expressed above may become relevant. From this point of view, the contributions of Beccaria, Verri, and Einaudi call attention to the 'mixed' character of monetary governance in a dual money system. This is because, with dual money, stability targets (such as the stability of the general price level or the stability of foreign exchanges) are anchored to imaginary money (a system of pure proportions), but are also affected by the vicissitudes of monetary markets. Under these conditions, it is reasonable to conjecture that stability targets may be best achieved through a finely tuned monetary policy. Such a policy would presuppose the ability to identify objective standards of reference (such as Beccaria's 'European proportion' between gold and silver) and the capacity to adopt timely policy measures. In this way, it may be possible to prevent the speculative behavior associated with 'wrong' internal exchange values between account money and effective currencies, and to approximate the stability features of imaginary money.

Stylized historical analysis and monetary architectures

There is a duality between writers primarily interested in the general principles and prospects of the dual money system and writers whose primary interest is monetary disturbances and the means to avoid abuses of sovereign power. By and large, economists who emphasize the technicalities of bank money in financial transactions (such as Savary, Broggia, and Steuart) show a more positive attitude to imaginary money than economists whose primary concern is to reduce the volatility of currency and payments (such as Montanari and Valeriani). Einaudi's reconstruction of the vicissitudes of the dual money system holds a middle ground between the above two standpoints, as is the case with Beccaria in his analysis of the Milanese monetary disturbances. For example, Einaudi highlights at the same time the tight logic of imaginary money and its often poor practical performance. In order to overcome the unsatisfactory performance of imaginary money in a small multi-currency economy, Beccaria shifts the ground of discussion from the 'provincial' Milanese setting to the European level, and stresses that only a monetary benchmark anchored to a sufficiently wide monetary space may be effective.

Another feature of imaginary money that is worth emphasizing is that it is possible to conceive of dual money systems of different degrees of complexity. In the simplest case, dual money reduces to the separation between money as a standard of value (unit of account) and money as a means of payment. In other words, promises to pay are made in terms of a name different from that of the means of payment, independently of whether the *money of account* is of constant value or not. In a more complex case, promises to pay are made in terms of a monetary unit (*imaginary money* strictly speaking) having a constant gold or silver content, or keeping a fixed exchange value in terms of gold or silver metals. Finally, promises to pay may be made in terms of a monetary unit (sometimes called *ideal money*) whose metal (gold or silver) content maintains a constant exchange value with respect to all other commodities.[4]

Different concepts of dual money are associated with different points of view as to its feasibility. The mere separation between money of account and money of payment may occasionally serve a useful purpose and may be quite easy to achieve, but it is seldom of general relevance. Ideal money (as defined above) is an abstract benchmark whose realization may not be possible, except under certain special conditions (such as those of a

---

[4] The above taxonomy is discussed by Jannaccone (1954 [1946]), who points out that 'the three different properties...do not necessarily co-exist, but, on the contrary, may be incompatible with one another' (32).

'guaranteed' credit economy). The intermediate case (*imaginary money* strictly speaking) is the problem situation considered by Beccaria, Verri, and Einaudi. It is an *imperfect credit economy*, in which promises to pay are expressed in terms of a money of account, but actual transactions are carried out through multiple currencies.[5] In this type of economy, the constant exchange value of imaginary money removes the possibility of price variations due to changes in the purchasing power of money. At the same time, the need to fulfill monetary obligations through effective currencies of variable purchasing power makes it possible to deal with price level stability by a 'proclamation' (or a sequence of proclamations). Their objective will be to adjust the internal exchange rates of effective currencies so as to achieve the required constancy of the general price level. In a symmetrical way, the constancy of foreign exchanges may be achieved by letting 'effective money, in coins or bars' to be 'the only money accepted for settling international accounts' (Einaudi, 1937: 264). Foreign exchanges will be constant under the assumption that the weight and fineness of coins is unchanged (*ibid.*). On the other hand, monetary policy decisions may change the official exchange rate between effective currency and imaginary money, so that the internal exchange rates of all effective currencies (relative to one another) are also likely to change.

Monetary disturbances have a different character in different types of dual money economy. A dual money economy of the pure ('guaranteed') credit type is exposed to confidence crises as to the reliability of its ultimate pledge. A dual money economy of the multi-currency type is primarily exposed to currency crises and speculative trading, particularly if monetary policy is sluggish and unable to anticipate market changes through appropriate monetary policy (essentially, through appropriate changes in the internal exchange rates between effective currencies and imaginary money).

In this chapter, we have examined the conceptual benchmark of the dual money economy, and we have used such a benchmark in order to reconstruct the fundamental structure of imaginary money. We have found that imaginary money is not associated with any single set of monetary institutions. Rather, imaginary money points to a *continuum* of monetary arrangements, ranging from the mere distinction between account money and payment money to the 'ideal' set-up of a pure credit economy.

---

[5] In a recent contribution, Eduardo Loyo has also considered the case of a pure unit of account with a well-managed set of parities to the means of payment (see Loyo, 2002). Loyo explicitly links his own 'thought experiment' with the imaginary-money economy considered in Einaudi's article (Loyo, 2002: 1073).

The theory and history of imaginary money calls attention to a variety of monetary architectures and policy rules. The general principles and objectives of imaginary money are close to some of the central monetary developments in the second half of the twentieth century. To give but one example, the initial conception and subsequent history of the International Monetary Fund (IMF) point to an attempt to overcome a monetary set-up in which gold as a money of account coexists with the utilization of multiple currencies (the gold standard and subsequently the gold exchange standard) and to introduce a structure of imaginary money increasingly close to that of a pure credit economy (see Triffin, 1961, Fleming, 1964, and Horsefield, 1969). This interpretation of the need for monetary reform had already been expressed clearly in the report of the Financial Commission of the Genoa Conference, according to which 'an international convention to be adopted at a suitable time' would be essential in order to 'centralize and coordinate the demand for gold, and to avoid those wide fluctuations in the purchasing power of gold which might otherwise result from the simultaneous and competitive efforts of a number of countries to secure metallic reserves' (League of Nations, 1944: 28). The subsequent introduction of the gold exchange standard was only a temporary solution, as the combined holding of gold reserves and reserves of 'approved assets' collapsed in 1928 when France decided to accept only gold in settlement of international obligations (*ibid.*: 39).

The plan circulated by John Maynard Keynes on February 11, 1942 (*Proposal for an International Currency (or Clearing) Union*), shows a surprising similarity to the set-up of a credit economy anchored to imaginary money outlined above. For Keynes conceived of an international clearing bank, or currency union, whose function was

to keep banking accounts for central banks in exactly the same way as central banks in each country kept accounts for commercial banks. These amounts were to be denominated in an international currency, which...Keynes called bancor... Bancor was to be defined in terms of gold, but its value was not to be unalterable [...] The Union would have power to change the value of it if it deemed this desirable. Member countries could obtain bancor in exchange for gold but could not obtain gold in exchange for bancor. (Horsefield, 1969: 18)

A few years later, Robert Triffin proposed essentially the same plan (but with the important difference of a fixed standard of value) with the aim of removing the monetary disorders inherent in the gold exchange standard (see Triffin, 1961; see also Horie, 1964). The IMF's introduction in 1969 of 'special drawing rights' (SDRs) was a major attempt to steer the international monetary system into the direction of a credit economy (with nation states as partners with the mutual obligation to accept credit entitlements issued by the IMF).

John Hicks was acutely aware of these institutional developments. In *Managing without Money?* (Hicks, 1986b), he calls attention to the 'surplus of claims' condition that had allowed the success of the old gold standard before 1914, and that was subsequently at the root of the failure of the restored gold standard after 1925. He also notes the 'intimate relation between money and trade' (26), and points out that, 'in any country with a single government, a well-established government, and no trade going outside it, anything which that government liked to say was money would be money' (*ibid.*). It is reasonable to think that a similar condition would be satisfied in any network of trade relationships as long as participants in the network would recognize a single debt-clearing authority. Hicks comes close to this view in *A Market Theory of Money*, where he writes: 'We are on the way to a credit economy... Money remains of course a standard of value, in terms of which people do their calculations, and in terms of which debts are expressed. But money as means of payment is just a debt. The payment of a debt is an exchange of debts' (Hicks, 1989a: 104).

The conception of imaginary money and its manifold historical applications provide an intellectual benchmark for the analysis of current developments in monetary institutions and practices, and a significant guideline for monetary reform.

12 Hicks: money, prices, and credit management

Omar F. Hamouda

Introduction

Ever since economists have tried to find some kind of correlation between the level of prices and money, going back at least to Richard Cantillon and David Hume, they have come to some expression that relates a general price level to the 'quantity of money' (whatever that means) – as it were, an equation of exchange. The ultimate long-run effect of a one-to-one correlation of the level of price and the quantity of money, *ceteris paribus*, is then the definition of the quantity theory of money. In dynamics outside of equilibrium, however, many economists (such as Irving Fisher, Knut Wicksell, John Maynard Keynes, Friedrich Hayek, and John Hicks), in their pre-war writings, at least came to agree that this theory was not helpful. Wicksell sums it up as follows (see also Fisher, 1907):

> The Theory provides a real explanation of its subject matter, and in a manner that is logically incontestable; but only on assumptions that unfortunately have little relation to practice, and in some respects none whatsoever...
>
> The Quantity Theory is theoretically valid so long as the assumption of *ceteris paribus* is firmly adhered to. But among the 'things' that have to be supposed to remain 'equal' are some of the flimsiest and more intangible factors in the whole of economics – in particular the velocity of circulation of money, to which in fact all others can be more or less directly referred back. It is consequently impossible to decide *a priori* whether the Quantity Theory is *in actual fact* true – in other words, whether prices and the quantity of money move together in practice. (Wicksell, 1936: 41–2)

Over a span of sixty years, mainly as a pure theorist, Hicks grappled with all the controversial issues his predecessors and contemporaries addressed. An indication of the passionate views that have divided economists, the controversy following Keynes's *Treatise on Money* and Hayek's *Prices and*

This chapter has benefited from substantial comments made at the John Hicks Centenary Workshop in Bologna, October 2004, by Mauro Baranzini, Carlo Casarosa, Rainer Masera, Robert Solow, and Erich Streissler. An understanding of this essay will be immensely enhanced by an accompanying reading of the chapters by Masera (13), Solow (15), and Streissler (20) in this volume.

Production, described by Hicks as 'the thunderstorms of recent years' (the early 1930s), focused on what money is and the implications of its interpretation in dynamic models on monetary policy. Hicks attempted to come to terms with the controversy in two different ways. First, he used it as a springboard for his own emerging ideas on money and liquidity. Later, he put the debate into a more historical perspective and traced the major discrepancies all the way back to Henry Thornton and David Ricardo, representatives of two different schools on money, the banking and the currency schools respectively. One of the merits of Hicks's latter exercise is that it showed that the controversy was far more fundamental to the foundation of economic theory itself than a mere disagreement between two strong intellectuals.

Where, then, did Hicks stand on the concept of money, in terms of its nature and definition, its relationship to price levels and interest rates, its links to investment and savings, and, most importantly, the implications of it in policies? Aspects of these monetary discussions are found in many of his writings, starting with his ideas in 'A Suggestion for Simplifying the Theory of Money' (Hicks, 1935a – which he dated from 1933) and going all the way to his last work, *A Market Theory of Money* (1989a). In retrospect, Hicks's theory of money, such as it is, provides little by way of integrating money into a comprehensive general theory, whether through a theoretical analysis of money and prices, transmission mechanisms, money, savings and investment, and/or monetary directions for policymaking. Although there is much discussion here and there of the topic of money, in his major complete models – those of *Value and Capital* (1939a), *A Contribution to the Theory of the Trade Cycle* (1950a), *Capital and Growth* (1965), and *Capital and Time* (1973a) – Hicks managed almost completely to avoid having to integrate it in a mechanical way.

Hicks did not write on money in intellectual isolation; his contributions were always built upon his awareness of the debate at the time. His goal, like that of many economists of his stature, was undoubtedly to formulate a general theory that was able to integrate – among other things – money. In trying to relate his own contribution to those of other great economic theorists, Hicks always acknowledged the importance of the ideas of others in relation to his own, and this was no different in the sphere of monetary theory, where he noted those of Thornton, Thomas Tooke, Wicksell, Alfred Marshall, and Ralph Hawtrey. Curiously, he was particularly fascinated and absorbed by the work of Keynes, and the Cambridge economists, on the subject, and by the monetarist legacy of Hayek, which he had imbibed early on at the LSE. In monetary theory they became almost the benchmarks against which he measured his own ideas. Unlike the raging and almost disrespectful exchanges that occurred between

Keynes, Piero Sraffa, and Hayek, however, Hicks always chose a less confrontational, more syncretic approach to assessing the merits of the work of others in building his own theory. Admirable as this is, at the same time, however, it often leaves his readers with some difficulty in seeing, for example, in his discussions of Keynes or Hayek, where his interpretation of the other ends and his own ideas begin.

When Hicks entered the fray in 1932 the backdrop was the violent exchanges raised by the publication of Keynes's *Treatise on Money* (Keynes, 1930) and Hayek's *Prices and Production* (Hayek, 1931). There were the ensuing mutual reviews,[1] passionate advocacy for or against 'credit,' and opinions on the requisite attitude of the banking authorities as to alleviating or exacerbating economic fluctuations. While Keynes and Hayek had polarized positions with respect to the impact of credit and the role of monetary authorities, Hicks held a very difficult middle-of-the-road ground. Although he gave the explicit impression of being more Keynesian and less in agreement with Hayek,[2] in the end one can find evidence that the workings of his monetary system were probably as close to Hayek's as to Keynes's. Is this intermediate position between Keynes and Hayek not perhaps, however, due to the fact that Hicks had no theory of a cycle with an implicit money component on which to stand his own ground unambiguously?

As his mind was moving from the theoretical treatment of money needed for his *Value and Capital* to the monetary theory required for a credit economy (in the Wicksellian sense), Hicks did, however, seem to be engaged in a process of building up the elements of a monetary theory independent of those of Keynes and Hayek.[3] He came to realize, initiated perhaps by one of the traverse models in his *Capital and Growth* (Hicks, 1965), that his position was neither interventionist, in the sense of one institution – a central bank – dictating policy, nor laissez-faire, in the sense of a pure market outcome determining monetary policy. He stood between the two poles, envisaging an institutional framework in which monetary information emanates through 'rings' of financial players (the various monetary authorities, comprising a central bank and financial institutions as the lenders) to industry, the borrowing sector, which makes

---

[1] A collection of some of the most extensive components of this debate is to be found in volume IX of Hayek's *Collected Works* (Caldwell, 1995).

[2] This might be due to Hicks's IS-LM. That model, however, Hicks thought represented Keynes's *General Theory*, not his own monetary theory.

[3] Hicks himself writes in his *Collected Essays*, vol. II, that the 'substance of my later work on monetary theory … [was] scattered over several books,' noting 'chiefly in "The Two Triads" (*Critical Essays in Monetary Theory*, essays 1–3), in *Crisis in Keynesian Economics* (especially chapter 2) and in *Economic Perspectives* (essays 3 and 8)' (Hicks, 1982a: 236 footnote).

its own decisions. Hicks's intricate institutional framework is based on checks and balances, with safeguarding results both in the way gathered monetary information is disseminated, in that it reduces financial uncertainties, and in the manner the general public's interest as well as the functioning of the market economy are preserved.

The essential components of Hicks's own monetary theory, once credit came into play, were constructed as if they derived from the historical evolution of money and monetary theory itself. They are as follows:

  (i) an institutional framework in which credit might 'work smoothly';

 (ii) a quantity of available credit;

(iii) the need for credit management;

(iv) management strategy; and

 (v) the exercise of managerial responsibility,

      (a) by those who should exercise control and

      (b) according to how that control should be exercised.

Hicks's monetary theory: the institutional framework of the credit economy

Hicks's conception of money was undoubtedly a product of its time, but it was also 'consistent with the broad facts of monetary evolution' (Hicks, 1967a: 59). His monetary theory, encompassing credit, is, fundamentally, institutional. In virtually all Hicks's reflections on what money has been and is currently, there is recognition of the need for an institutional framework to support it (see Price, 2001: 127–8) and particularly 'in order for a credit system to work smoothly' (Hicks, 1967a: 158). Hicks would even go so far as to call money itself an institution, 'one of the most remarkable of human institutions' (*ibid.*: 59). In so doing he is alluding, it would seem, to the two sides of money: its existence as an object both of individual human practices and of social institutions. An illustration of his persuasion of this duality can be found in the context of his reflection on 'Friedman's interpretation of the statistical tendency towards an increase over time in the M/Y ratio (or fall in the income-velocity of circulation),' which Hicks finds not terribly compelling even though it is based on historical series data. For him, 'to seek for an explanation in terms of changes in monetary practices and monetary institutions, which is the recommendation which would follow from our present approach, looks like being more constructive' (*ibid.*: 16).

Hicks's assertions had much to do with the form of credit money, but not exclusively so. He felt that the functions of credit money had remained the same as those of earlier monetary forms. He observed, however, that, over time, in changing from a commodity, to metallic currency, to paper, to money deposits, and now to almost pure credit, something else about money had also been altered: its institutional connection. The essential role of a monetary institution in the existence of credit money 'is not in the nature of things; it is a consequence of the development of modern banking... It is the channel of money creation that is provided by the banking system which makes the difference' (Hicks, 1969a: 97).

For Hicks, credit money was just an extension of the existence of bank-issued metallic and then paper money, but with two important differences. First, it was not, strictly speaking, dependent on a physical resource for its creation: '[T]here is no more liquid asset into which claims on the bank can be turned' (Hicks, 1965: 285). 'A pure credit money, without commodity "backing", is analytically nothing else but a part of the general system of debits and credits that exist between "individuals" or "entities" that compose the economy, at any moment of time' (281). There was, in effect, a potentially infinite amount of realizable credit, since, without the constraints of metal or paper, the banks 'can always create money' (Hicks, 1967a: 158). In a closed economy, Hicks did not see any insurmountable problems presented by liquidity to the monetary authority; he believed that it might well have the means and power to increase liquidity at will, as long as 'the whole system of debits and credits' was in equilibrium. Second, the degree of trust or confidence in this form of money and in the institution that channeled its creation was more demanding and also therefore, perhaps, more fragile.

Quantity of available credit

According to Hicks, economic theorists had, in due course, come to the recognition that the quantity of monetary credit affects an economic system, but is also affected by that system. The actual way in which a quantity of available credit affects an economic system and is affected by it consumes, not surprisingly, a large part of the debate regarding credit theory. Especially relevant here historically is the fact that it was also the focus of the bulk of the discussion about money in the Keynes–Hayek controversy, with which Hicks was fully familiar. While discussion of the role of the quantity of credit was but a small part of the dynamic system of Hicks, it drew his wholehearted attention, as it had that of Keynes, and even Hayek. To Hicks, the entirety of Keynes's *Treatise* turns on what he called 'Stage One.' He did not find this surprising, since, when Keynes was writing the *Treatise*, the United Kingdom was in the midst of what he called 'years of semi-slump, or of a boom that misfired.' Thus, 'Stage One' drew Keynes's attention: '[I]n Stage One there is a rise in *flexible* prices (of capital goods and of consumer goods) without any change in output or in employment' (Hicks, 1967a: 191).[4]

Hayek, except perhaps according to Hicks's interpretation of his cycle, was also obsessed with the issue of the impact of credit. For him, however, its impact was felt most strongly in the last stages of his business cycle, when production is complete and goods are readily available to consumers.

The granting of credit to consumers, which has recently been so strongly advocated as a cure for depression, would in fact have quite the contrary effect; a relative increase of the demand for consumers' goods could only make matters worse... [In a depression] [t]he thing which is needed to secure healthy conditions is the most speedy and complete adaptation possible of the structure of production to the proportion between the demand for consumers' goods and demand for producers' goods as determined by voluntary saving and spending. If the proportion as determined by the voluntary decisions of individuals is distorted by the creation of artificial demand, it must mean that part of the available resources is again led into a wrong direction and a definite and lasting adjustment is again postponed. (Hayek, 1931: 85–6)

The backdrop to these discussions was the question of the source of the causal push or pull: is it credit or is it the real economy? Hicks was persuaded, like many others, that the inability of monetary policy prescriptions to contain disturbing economic situations[5] meant that their underlying monetary theory had to be rethought, particularly in light of a number of questions along the following lines.

(i) Can real events cause an increase or decrease in the quantity of money in the economic system? What sorts of events? How does their causal chain work?

(ii) Can a change in the quantity of money cause real positive results? How does such a change make its way into an economy? Does its effect reverberate (i.e. what is its transmission mechanism and what is the impact of changes in the quantity of money on other economic variables)?

The two diametrically opposed positions are: (i) that credit is the cause of real sector expansion and contraction, and (ii) that the real sector is the cause of credit expansion and contraction. Hicks started from Thornton, who, he says, recognized (as had Hume) that 'monetary causes may have real effects.' Hicks points out that, in Hayek's theory in *Prices and Production*, there are also the monetary effects of credit expansion whose

---

[4] 'The peculiarity of the treatment in the *Treatise* is the extreme concentration on what I have called Stage One. [...] It is Stage One alone that is closely analysed; it is Stage One alone to which the Fundamental Equations essentially refer' (Hicks, 1967a: 192).
[5] For example, unprecedentedly high levels of inflation and interest rates or persistently high unemployment.

impacts find their way through into the real sector: 'The initial effect of the expansion of credit – in "pure" terms, the reduction of the market rate below the natural rate of interest – is that the money value of Investment rises, implying a rise in the money prices of producers' goods' (Hicks, 1967a: 207). This inflationary rise in prices leads to shifts in real-sector production.

The other scenario, that the real sector is the cause of credit expansion and contraction, also derives from Thornton. Hicks identifies this reverse causality: '[R]eal causes can have monetary effects'; he goes on to note that this means that an expansion in the real sector will cause the credit system to expand 'automatically.' By 'an expansion' in economic activity, Hicks is referring, he writes, 'more or less' to 'what Keynes was later to call a rise in the marginal efficiency of capital.' Elsewhere, he sees the *Treatise*'s 'Natural Rate of Interest' reflecting that same role (*ibid.*: 198). As Hicks interprets Keynes, the 'Natural Rate of Interest' is the one that makes the value of investment equal to savings; a rise in this 'Natural Rate of Interest,' then, it is argued, would cause a rise in the quantity of available credit. The credit system will also 'contract automatically' if 'there are changes in the demand for capital which make for contraction' – foreign investment, perhaps, or panic surrounding the crediting institution. The panic would manifest itself in 'a sharp rise in Liquidity Preference,' or 'excess-bearishness,' to use the terminology of Keynes's *Treatise*, perhaps through increased consumer spending – a real-sector phenomenon.

From the conviction in the reciprocal impact of credit on the real sector and the real sector on credit, it was clear to Hicks that quantity correlations were going to have to be made. These could take a number of forms, all related to the quantity of credit, its increase, and its decrease.

Portfolio and liquidity theories

Much of Hicks's energies in monetary analysis were devoted to liquidity theory, from his portfolio approach to his scrutiny of voluntary and involuntary holdings. The discussion regarding the demand for money was the larger umbrella under which the debate about credit availability would figure prominently. In an economy in which the presence of credit was 'impure,' the characteristics of money in its different forms had direct bearing on the questions being asked about credit: for example, why would it or would it not be held in preference or deference to other currencies? What part did it play in the multiplier effect? What part did it play in the transmission effect? Hicks's earlier and later works definitely reflected a marked change in his conception of the demand for money. His early work was based on the straight application of the principle of value, to the point of his having interpreted Keynes's *Treatise* as having presented a marginal value theory of money, one of its three (!). In his later contributions he attempted, however, to recast his early liquidity theory and distance himself from the neo-quantitative conception of the demand for money.

In his earliest determinations of the demand for money, Hicks proposed the use of marginalist value theory in the same manner in which it is used in determining the ordinary demand for goods and services. In his portfolio approach, Hicks's demand for money was therefore dependent on only three factors: wealth, the cost of transferring assets from one form into another, and risk. Hicks made 'interest-bearing or not' the important distinction between the two forms of money in which an individual might choose to hold his or her wealth: non-interest-bearing money or interest-yielding capital assets (or both). He did not, however, link credit specifically to either form. In fact, throughout his career, like Wicksell, Hicks was content to see credit as either interest-bearing or non-interest-yielding, depending on the circumstance.[6] Hence, Hicks's early argument regarding the relationship of demand for money and wealth (that it increases but less than proportionately, because wealth will increase the demand for both non-interest-bearing money and capital investment assets) had nothing specifically to do with money in the form of credit.[7] Even his discussion of the demand for money as dependent on the cost of transferring assets from one form into another did not concern credit in particular.

While Hicks's fundamental innovation in his early liquidity theory was to associate the voluntary demand for money with the precautionary and speculative motives for holding money, rather than with the transactional 'motive' (as was the widespread practice[8]), the greatest impact of his ideas on credit theory came through his assertion that there was no necessary 'market clearing' for that voluntarily held 'commodity' of money. Having claimed early on that a volume of money exists as 'outstanding' – i.e. 'not absorbed by transactions' – Hicks would take two further important steps in credit theory. 'Outstanding' money, which reflects a disequilibrium situation, exists as a result of risk, uncertainty, and a lack of foresight,

---

[6] By 1965 he would drop this definitional (interest-bearing/non-interest-yielding) constraint on money entirely, abandoning the view that money is inherently non-interest-bearing. Hicks came to believe that it may or may not be (Hicks, 1965: 19).

[7] Hicks might have had a harder time holding such a position today, given the growing evidence for the 'proliferation of the rentier.'

[8] Hicks had detected that the transactional demand for money was not strictly speaking 'motivated,' and therefore not directly voluntary.

since each impacts demand. This assertion would open the door to a role for 'expectations,' in this aspect of monetary theory at least, and thereby lead to much contemplation on the question of how expectations affect the demand for credit, particularly by different groups (e.g. consumers, producers, financiers, funds). Secondly, with the link between the liquidity theory demand for money and disequilibrium established, Hicks moved to assert that credit could be analyzed in conjunction with economic cycles: the phases of the production/business/growth cycle in a closed economy, and those of the trade cycle in an open economy.

In the 1930s Hicks had turned to tackling the issue of the demand for money in specific theories of equilibrium and disequilibrium. Equilibrium theory involved a new step: the determination of the interest rate. While Hicks had developed all the ingredients for addressing the monetary component of any theory as a composite based on transactional demand and speculative demand, in his general equilibrium model the demand for money becomes emotionally sterile. The interest rate in the general equilibrium model can be defined simply as the price of money. While he had moved beyond pricing money according to the cost of obtaining it (like Nassau W. Senior), Hicks had not liberated it from determining its quantity as that quantity 'needed to "circulate" current output,' 'proportional to current output' (Hicks, 1965: 280). 'There is an equilibrium quantity of money and an equilibrium growth rate of the money supply, equal to the growth rate of everything else' (*ibid.*). Changes in the rate of interest would be determined only by the supply and demand for money based on liquidity preference theory, or the supply and demand for capital (the loanable funds theory).

Credit in relation to the real economy

Credit and prices

Hicks's discussions of money and liquidity preferences were only relative measuring sticks for the difficult issue of the effect of changes in the quantity of credit on the economy. Further, they treated the whole question as a 'monetary' one. The next difficult step was to extend these theories into the questions of the reciprocal impact of credit itself on the real sector and the real sector on credit. In all fairness, it raised its head many times in Hicks's discussions of demand for money and demand for liquidity. It can be seen in the guise of statements about prices and interest rate. Later in his career, however, Hicks might have considered them to be indexes one step removed from a direct discussion of the quantity of money in an economy.

There were, Hicks showed, the followers of Ricardo, who were convinced that the level of economic activity is determined by real factors alone and that the quantity of money acts only on the level of prices. A single unified theory from Hicks concerning the relationship of prices and credit is not easy to grasp nor to recount. He did, however, address the situation of a credit economy in growth equilibrium. Among the many dynamic models that Hicks developed to analyze the trade cycle, the only one in which he explicitly brought in money and credit to discuss them in relation to the phases of the cycle was his traverse analysis in *Capital and Growth* (see figure 12.1).

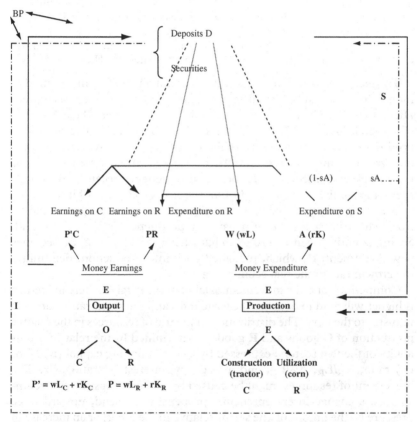

Notes: Model consists of: (1) price equations P and P'; (2) quantity equations $K = \forall R + aC$, $L = \exists R + bC$; and (3) saving equation $g = sr$.

$$G = F(A) \longrightarrow A = F(K_R/L_R, K_C/L_C, w/r).$$

Relative profitability determines the movement of resources from one sector into another.

Figure 12.1 Hicks's model in *Capital and Growth*: traverse I

Although Hicks dropped this 1965 model later,[9] for the purposes of the present topic it will serve, since it permits us to make a link between the phases of his trade cycle, money, and monetary policy. Hicks believed that, in a monetary economy in which money is commodity money, one could proceed with analyzing the real sector without its being affected by changes in the quantity of money. If, however, credit is introduced, variations in the quantity of money do affect prices, in such a way that they produce a set of money prices that is different from their relative 'real price' counterparts (determined by cost of production).

When we make comparisons of equilibria, the difference between the commodity money economy and the pure credit economy emerges at once... If there is commodity money, equilibrium money prices can only be different if there are differences in real costs (including the cost of obtaining money). But with credit money it is entirely possible that all *real* prices and quantities might be the same in the two economies, yet that money prices might be different. (Hicks, 1965: 282)

The technical aspect of the Traverse was initially built with commodity money in mind; thus, for all intents and purposes, money is ignored. Hicks's model is based on the production of consumer (**R**) and capital (**C**) goods, just like Wicksell's, Keynes's, and Hayek's. The factors of production are labor and capital; the factor payments are thus the wage bill, **W**, and entrepreneurs' profits, π. Workers are assumed to expend their entire wage income on **R** goods. Entrepreneurs, receiving the profit, spend part of their income on **C** goods and **R** goods; part of it they save. The earnings, **E**, from selling **C** and **R** goods in the market, are deposits, from which proceeds the firm pays for production in the next round. Saving is entirely out of profits. That saving, a net saving, **S**, becomes new investment, **I'**, which, ploughed back into production, determines the growth rate of the real economy, **g**.

Competition and the movement of labor and capital to where the return is higher will tend to equalize the wage rates and the profit rates from one industry to the next. The distribution of the use of resources in the relative production of **C** goods and **R** goods is determined by the relative profitability of the two sectors, expressed by a corresponding capital (**K**)/labor (**L**) ratio, K_R/L_R, K_C/L_C, and a wage (**w**)/interest (**r**) ratio, **w/r**. The movement of resources might be caused by one of at least three circumstances: a change in entrepreneurs' propensity to spend; upward wage pressure by the unions of one sector relative to the other; or an increase in the productivity of one sector over the other due to the introduction of

---

[9] Dissatisfied with that model, Hicks later developed another traverse model, Traverse II (Hicks, 1973a). He made no references to money in the latter formulation, however.

new technologies. All these may result in changes in the relative factor prices, and thus in the profitability of the economy.

Hicks discussed different scenarios, which depict an economy in various stages of growth. Credit money is discussed in isolation from the model itself. When there is resource movement from **R** goods to **C** goods production, there is a tendency to increase the capacity of the economy, and vice versa.

Hicks's attempts at integrating money into an equilibrium model, whether temporary or general, or even growth, seem at odds with some of his other reflections on the demand for money, but he was quick to point out that they are not at odds with his (demand for) credit theory. Even if, while building the temporary equilibrium model of *Value and Capital*, Hicks may have been too preoccupied with the technical aspects of value theory in a general equilibrium framework to contemplate the potential nuances of a credit 'monetization,' in the context of his equilibrium growth theory he lets it be known that he is not:

It is further possible with credit money (but not with commodity money) that an economy might be in Growth Equilibrium in real terms, while the money price-level was changing over time. Money prices could be rising over time, and everything else is as before: excepting that the rate of profit in money terms would have to be adjusted. If the real rate of profit (as previously calculated) were 10 per cent per annum, and prices were rising at 5 per cent per annum, the money rate of profit would have to be approximately 15 per cent. This (by now) is a familiar point; I do not think that I need to elaborate it. (1965: 282)

This is the situation in which, over time, within a single credit economy, the *real* price and the money price differ relative to one another. It is in effect parallel to another scenario, already identified above, in which Hicks noted the existence of money prices, possibly at different levels, for the same real price of the same commodity in two different economies. The important issue at hand, the relationship of prices and money in the credit economy, is explained generally as follows:

If it is pure credit money that is to be introduced into our equilibrium, we find (first of all) that there is no price equation to determine the value of money in terms of goods and services. It is impossible to determine the equilibrium price-level, as before, from the price side. On the quantity side we have to reinterpret the quantity equations, going into detail about the supplies and demands, from the individual entities, from which they are derived. [...] Thus we may generalize the conception of demand for money, and assert its equilibrium in the form of saying that the whole system of debits and credits must be in equilibrium. (*ibid.*: 281)

Hicks had already seen only modest implications, in the context of his demand for money theory, of viewing a credit economy as simply one of 'debits and credits.' Having distinguished voluntary from involuntary demands for money, in constructing a model of financial markets, once he had proceeded to define 'demand for liquidity,' and predominantly in terms of the precautionary demand for money, the potential differences in liquidity that 'debits and credits' afford would become a critical factor, even in price determination. Any shift in liquidity preference did not necessarily imply for Hicks a change in the demand for money. While he made distinctions in the relative liquidity of various forms of money, seeing 'bonds' or assets as fully liquid, more or less liquid, and non-liquid (a distinction he had already made in 'A Suggestion for Simplifying the Theory of Money' – 1935a), for him, within a given spectrum of assets, a change in liquidity preference could create a substitution between the various assets without necessarily changing the demand for money. The key feature of money in his growth model was, simply, its absolute liquidity. It was considered extremely important to investment decision-making, since great liquidity meant investment 'freedom'; a lack of liquidity might slow down one's 'ability to respond to future opportunities,' and potentially, in a competitive environment, to be economically viable (1979a: 94). As he writes:

All that needs to be said is that, in order to maintain this (inflationary) equilibrium, the whole system of debits and credits must be expanding (in money terms) at a rate which is correspondingly in excess of the real growth rate of the economy. If there is some part of the system – particular sorts of debts from government, or particular sorts of debts due by banks – which we dignify by the title of money supply, that money supply must be correspondingly expanding. (1965: 282)

Credit and the savings/investment relationship[10]

Did the monetary component, credit, play any particular role in Hicks's 'demand for liquidity' theory? One might, at the very least, say that it allowed for a differentiation in the roles of certain players in the economy. Take, for example, Hicks's linking of his classification of assets to a distinction between financial intermediaries, or financiers, and investors (the funds). The fund and the financier are going to make different liquidity preference choices, which, while they may not affect the demand for money, may alter the demand for 'credit.' For the fund, investment assets

---

[10] Curiously enough, this group of considerations is reflected on in Hicks's 'theory of the working of the Financial System,' which he described as 'stripped of all conventions, institutions [!] and institutional jargon.' He divided it into three parts: liquidity theory, which tells 'the story entirely in terms of financial running assets and financial reserve assets'; the theory of short and long interest rates; and the theory of 'speculative demand for money – the "Liquidity trap", or the "Speculative trap"' (Hicks, 1967a: 49).

(assets that are held for the sake of their yield and may serve either precautionary or speculative purposes) are crucial to the demand for liquidity. These same assets are regarded, by the financier, either as financial reserves (assets that, being easily marketable and profit-yielding, are kept for precautionary measures) or as running assets (assets held for the payment of everyday transactions). They reflect a liability to liquidity shifts on the part of the financier, since the same assets held for one reason by the fund are held for another two – emergencies or opportunities of doing financial business – by the financier. In this scenario, investors' needs are always the ones to cause changes in the demand for liquidity, since they require of the financier a substitution response among his or her various financial assets.

Hicks illustrated how changes in the demand for liquidity, due to the alternative means of financing the expansion of industry, create different liquidity pressures. In a closed economy, when industry is pushing for expansion in response to demand, there are different ways of securing financing. If industry is self-sufficient in liquidity, it can finance its expansion with its own resources. In so doing, it would not have to depend on an infusion from the financier. Undoubtedly, however, the decision to use some of its resources for expansion would entail changes in the liquidity of its reserves. Industry would have to exchange its less liquid reserve assets for those of sufficient liquidity in order for it to make the necessary acquisitions for expansion; this would presumably cause a 'debit' or decrease in its reserves of lesser liquidity, which, if withdrawn from the care of a financier, would create a 'debit' there. A second alternative for expansion would have industry receive 'credit' – i.e. borrow money from the financier. In that case, the liquidity of the financier would be diminished, while the liquidity of industry would increase. The third alternative would be for the financier to transmit a portion of an increase in the whole economy's quantity of money, as the channel of absolutely new liquidity, to industry. That liquidity would be matched by a 'debit' from industry to the immediate financier, which 'debit', however, particularly if does not reflect a 'debit' in the whole economy's liquidity, may well be 'in such a form as not to diminish the liquidity of industry' (1979a: 98).

Hicks was quite direct in talking about credit and interest rates when he turned to discussing a pure credit economy. He defined the amount of credit, or money supply, in a pure credit economy as 'some part of the system – particular sorts of debts from government, or particular sorts of debts due by banks' (1965: 282) Hicks came up with a sort of ceiling on the increase in credit, or expansion of debt by borrowers, that an economy could viably endure. At the root of all interest rates, in terms of their upper and lower limits, are expectations. The interest rate ceiling is determined by the 'profit rate expected by the firms,' the basement by the banks' or financial intermediaries' expectations of the 'firm's capacity to repay' (1965: 285). These expectations are rooted in the performance of the real sector.

The various liquidity pressures may affect the interest rates as well as the prices of securities, and probably differently, which effects in turn have their impact on investment decisions, and perhaps even economic stability. Hicks did not, however, want to read too much, nor too little, into the apparent fluctuations of these pressures. While interest rates seem to be the most obvious barometer for liquidity pressure, 'rates of interest, at most, are an index of liquidity; they are not by any means always a perfect index' (1979a: 96). Nonetheless, since monetary stability was as crucial to Hicks's analysis of the credit economy as it was to his and others' conception of earlier traditional monetary systems, he was on the lookout for signals – the market signals of demand, supply, and currency confidence, which he was persuaded, even on the international scale, could be read and effectively responded to, in order to maintain a form of monetary stability. Changes in liquidity preferences were one touchstone sign.

Need for credit management

Hicks was willing to take a next critical step in his monetary theory. Since there was, to his mind, enough empirical evidence and theory to link alterations in the quantity of available credit to potentially undesirable or desirable events, Hicks declared that 'a credit system must be *managed*' (1967a: 164; emphasis in original). It was to prevent 'those whose theory would allow them to contemplate a world in which the availability of credit to use as a monetary tool is a potentially positive instrument' being labeled 'those who would never use it' that Hicks developed the corollary about a credit system having to be managed. He fully recognized that it was not enough to be persuaded of the observation that, whatever the direction of the causal relationship of monetary or real expansions and contractions, they can be potentially undesirable or desirable (*ibid.*). This was the first nail in the coffin of his disassociation from the quantity theorists.

Economists have never been in agreement on the neutrality of money, but they have tended to one side or other of the spectrum. Hicks identified a group of followers of Ricardo as neo-quantity theorists, referring to them as the 'Currency School.' Hayek was interpreted by Hicks as having believed in 'the delusion (common to many economists, even the greatest economists) that with money removed "in a state of barter" everything would somehow fit' (Hicks, 1973a: 133). Hayek, often lumped together with such quantity theorists, agreed, however, with Hicks, that credit management is essential to stability 'if the "natural" movement of prices is disturbed by movements in the supply of money, whether by the injection of new money into circulation or by withdrawal of part of the money circulating' (Hayek, 1931: 75–6). Hayek thought the credit infusion scenario worth contemplating at least in theory, since 'it is at least possible that, during the acute stage of the crisis when the capitalist structure of production tends to shrink more than will ultimately prove necessary, an expansion of producers' credits might have a wholesome effect.' He went on to warn, however, that

this could only be the case if the quantity were *so regulated as exactly to compensate for* the initial, excessive rise of the relative prices of consumers' goods, and *if arrangements could be made to withdraw* the additional credits as these prices fall and the proportion between the supply of consumers' goods and the supply of intermediate goods adapts itself to the proportion between the demand for these goods. (Hayek, 1931: 86; emphasis added)

Although Hayek does seem to have been fairly accused of holding that acute cyclical disturbances had 'a monetary origin,' he was not beyond contemplating a credit theory in which 'an expansion of producers' credits might have a wholesome effect'!

Management strategy

The need for management was, once again, linked by Hicks back to the institutional framework of credit, to yield a central bank with certain responsibilities. As a theory-building step, he wedded the institution of the central bank, as credit manager, with a management strategy. While this begins to feel like policy formation, for yet a while longer it was still theory. The credit system, Hicks writes, 'must be *managed* by a Central Bank, whose *operations must be determined by judgement* and cannot be reduced to procedure by a mechanical rule' (Hicks, 1967a: 164; emphasis added). 'By judgement,' according to Hicks, theorists went on to develop a 'subtle appreciation of the "feel" of the market.' The credit management task was 'not one which can be performed in a mechanical fashion. It needs judgement and knowledge of business psychology much more than sustained logical reasoning' (1935a: 76).

Exercise of managerial responsibility

Of course, the notion of 'monetary policy' (1967a: 164) was very soon added to this sense of a need for a credit-managing institution, with managerial responsibility somehow transforming itself from the exercise of 'judgement' into the exercise of 'control.' For Hicks, the interest rate became 'the key instrument of monetary control' (1982a: 266). Managerial responsibility, broken down then into two parts, sees the interest rate as its focus: '[W]ho should exercise control over the interest rate/s' and 'how could/should that kind of control be exercised.' In short, Hicks contemplated a 'centre,' aided by close consultation with intermediaries, that orchestrates monetary policy through a form of monopolistic control with a primary goal: to narrow the gap between the monetary interest rate and the rate of return on marginal investment, in an effort to maintain the economy in a state of monetary equilibrium. This goal reflected his persuasion that the real challenge of a credit economy was to respond adequately to the credit needs of any sector; this would be the key to the maintenance of confidence in a nation's monetary strength and lead to its monetary stability.

Those who should exercise control   In general, Hicks's policy was to devise an institutional framework capable of both providing support and restraining credit availability 'in order for a credit system to work smoothly' (1965: 157). In principle, the objective of such a monetary framework was not to dictate interest rate policies, but to create a financial environment in which loans would be available to all with money rates of interest set as low as possible. To do so, Hicks constructed two models of the credit economy: the monocentric model, appropriate to a closed economy in which there is only one monetary authority; and the polycentric model, an economic system relevant to an open economy in which there are many monetary centers. In his basic monocentric model, Hicks expanded on the Wicksell one-bank model by letting financial institutions other than the bank borrow and lend, by allowing the bank to offer a deposit rate lower than its lending rate, and by introducing the financial intermediary so as to 'make use of specialized knowledge about the prospects of particular kinds of real investments, so that it can make advances to firms, or investments in the securities of the firms' (1989a: 108).

The bank, or the center, in Hicks's simple model refers both to the central bank and to the commercial banks. For Hicks, a nation's lending environment would take the form of concentric circles of lenders (making credit available to a perimeter of borrowers), emanating outward from a central bank. The credit available in an economy would filter from a national central bank through interdependent layers of lenders. Each layer would specialize in particular types of lending with particular risks, through a mechanism whereby the monetary and financial agents play the role of 'listening points' and act in gathering and making as much information as possible available to all. Thus, a highly regulated hierarchy would go from institutions dealing with lower-risk loans at a lower interest rate to those offering riskier loans at a higher interest rate. The working of such a structure would be under the regulation of the central bank, but the determination of the interest rates would be achieved through the market and the lenders' interdependence.

As in Wicksell's model, in Hicks's model the bank can, through interest rate policy, reduce the discrepancy between the money rate and the yield R, provided that the gap is narrow, and thus contain economic fluctuations.

How control should be exercised   Like Keynes, Hicks seems to have had in mind constraints on the efficacy of his contemporary lending environment, presented by limitations on the monetary authority to establish control over lending. Confidence in a national monetary system on the part of individuals engaged in market activity at the national level derived, Hicks felt, from a sense similar to that at work in the international market: that credit ought to be available as it is required in the production sector. Since the desired response on a national scale has to stem from the nation's central monetary authority, Hicks affirmed that the authority had to be aware of the needs of the real production sector at all times. Information would be the instrument to guarantee this awareness, since in a complex credit economy all kinds of general and specialized information are required to signal the state of an economy's production and multi-exchange trade. It is for this reason that Hicks attempted to devise his national hierarchical organization of Wicksellian rings of financial activity: to provide at all levels for the most direct access to information and the most efficient transmission of that information to the monetary authority.

The central bank cannot do without the assistance of specialized institutions, which Hicks called 'listening points,' to gather information about specific investments in response to liquidity pressures. In his monocentric financial sector, he argued, the functioning of financial institutions according to the market price mechanism would not necessarily be the most efficient way to see that information is collected and that the interests of the production sector are well understood. Instead, some concentration of institutions and information in the financial sector was, he believed, desirable (1989a: 110–11). More importantly, close collaboration between the specialized intermediaries and the center (which plays the role of 'lender of last resort') could better provide the desired stability in economic activity. In order to achieve, through the form of monopolistic control, a center aided by close consultation with the intermediaries to orchestrate monetary policy, it therefore seems that Hicks was advocating some strict regulation of the function of the banking system and the financial sector (for more detail on Hicks's monopolistic banking system, see Price, 2001: 131–4).

By the time Hicks reached the stage of recounting the state of the collective evolution of monetary theory up to his day, he was almost at the jumping-off point for his own policy position. There remained only Keynes's and Hayek's theories to integrate. Keynes, Hicks felt, had advanced matters on two fronts. His observations, that, while the bank can be an effective credit manager, 'against inflation and over-expansion, against over-contraction it is relatively powerless,' had shown that 'control through banking is one-sided.'

> Banks can restrict expansion by refusing to lend; but they cannot force expansion just by offering to lend, on whatever easy terms. It can be that business is feeling so dismal that even on the most favourable possible terms (which are consistent with the banking system making any sort of a profit) loans will not be taken up. (Hicks, 1967a: 169)

Within the institutional component, therefore, there had to be another control instrument: the government, specifically the government budget, which in times of over-contraction can boost activity again by its own spending. This sharing of the role of institutional control had its own implications for monetary policy. In effect, Hicks contemplated several possible scenarios: one overriding monetary policy deriving from the more powerful of the two institutions, the central bank or the national government; two distinct and counterbalancing policies; or two harmonized and reinforcing policies. Keynes had opted for the first scenario, which placed the burden of credit control and monetary policy in government hands and permitted its fiscal policy to use taxation.

> [T]he control of the State over the money supply, which for long ages was so imperfect, has become complete. [...] The power that thus passes into the hands of the State is very great, but by itself it is not unlimited. [...] [T]his is the point in our story when we come to the Age of Keynes, that new dispensation under which since 1936 we know that we have been living. The lesson that Keynes taught was of the existence of the power that I have just described. It had already existed, and Keynes had only to urge that it should be taken up... It did already exist when he was writing, but it had not existed for so very long. It is not in the nature of things; it is a consequence of the development of modern banking. (Hicks, 1969a: 96)

Hicks opted instead for the central bank to have the overriding control of credit, and therefore of monetary policy.[11] He defined the amount of

---

[11] Hicks went even further in proposing an international central bank with credit regulating control, 'since it is not in fact to the advantage of any single nation that it should be

credit, or money supply, in a pure credit economy as 'some part of the system – particular sorts of debts from government, or particular sorts of debts due by banks.' Hicks came up with a sort of ceiling on the increase in credit, or expansion of debt by borrowers, that an economy could viably endure. The liquidity preferences of the firms and risk, measured in terms of the bank's assessment of the firm's capacity to repay a loan, would determine the ceiling. 'Thus the bank's loans will be restricted, at any given rate of bank interest, by the bank's concern for the solvency of its debtors; and this will be reinforced by the concern of the borrowers for their own liquidity' (1965: 285).

It is clear that Hicks advocated some monetary policy in the form of bank intervention to increase the interest rate when an economy is heading toward a boom and developing inflation. Nowhere in his writings, however, did he advocate a monetary policy that could set up a specific interest rate level in order to target a certain level of prices or a certain level of economic activity.

Fluctuations can then be dampened by adjustment of timing of public investment.[12] On the other hand, some control can be exercised by monetary policy. This is a much less effective means of controlling the whole cycle, because its efficiency is much greater for purposes of checking the boom than for purposes of checking the slump; it is thus least efficient where it is most wanted. All the same, I do not think we ought to favour complete discarding of the weapon of monetary policy. There are two grounds on which it may be desirable to use it for checking a boom; one is to prevent the boom from eating too deeply into the supply of investment opportunities, and the other is to prevent too great a disturbance of price-levels, which may upset people's ideas of normal prices, and thus weaken a stabilising factor which will have a vital part to play later on. (1939a: 300–1)[13]

---

forgotten and left to look after itself; in the international economy of today (1967a: 171). As, therefore, the control of credit ought no longer to be conceived of solely on the national scale, policy for 'the kind of control that should be exercised' would also be conceptualized as operational at the international level. 'This extension of the credit environment must be left for another study' (*ibid.*).

[12] Hicks is making reference here to Ursula Hicks's *The Finance of British Government* (see Hicks, 1938).

[13] In a footnote to the above passage, Hicks writes: 'I am well aware that if the monetary authority were to abstain altogether from using interest as a brake, it might, in the end, cause the long-term rate of interest to fall to appreciably lower levels than it would otherwise have done. It is possible that this might assist recovery from future slumps. But I feel myself very doubtful whether, even in the breathing-space, one can count on a degree of confidence sufficient to make the difference between low and very low long-term rates a thing of great importance in promoting recovery. If this is so, the policy of total abstinence in all circumstances would mean risking the sense of normal prices in return for a very distant and very dubious advantage.'

Concluding remark

When it came to monetary theory and policy, Hicks's later stance derived from his sense that the world was moving toward a Wicksellian credit economy. Hicks's concerns with credit theory and policy management were, nonetheless, generated by his enduring belief in the importance of the real sector and real-sector causes of the production cycle. In this he resembled Hayek, who also believed that economic fluctuations are caused by real factors. When Hicks integrated a monetary aspect into his cycle theory, however, the influence of Keynes was also apparent, particularly in light of his conviction that, in addition to negative outcomes, credit can effect positive ones. Hicks's monetary policy stands out, therefore, as different from that of Hayek, in that Hicks felt that credit could be and had to be managed in order to alleviate the damaging aspects of inflation and deflation. Further, however, since Hicks felt that the financial management of credit ought to fall to currency market institutions rather than to the government, his position was decidedly different from that of Keynes, which relied predominantly on the government as the national monetary authority. However much a product of the ideas of his predecessors and contemporaries, John Hicks and his commitment to the role of the central bank in the dynamics of money and prices in the credit economy stood, after all, it would seem, decidedly apart.

13 Core, mantle, and industry: a monetary perspective of banks' capital standards

Rainer Masera

Introduction and summary

In addition to the stimulus that I derived from *Value and Capital* (Hicks, 1939a), I owed a fundamental debt in writing under John Hicks's guidance my Oxford DPhil thesis on *The Term Structure of Interest Rates* (Masera, 1972). In this chapter, however, I make particular reference to a book of Sir John's – *Economic Perspectives* (1977a) – that appeared after I had left Oxford for the monetary and economic department of the Bank for International Settlements in Basel.

In a brief yet very dense essay in *Economic Perspectives*, Hicks reconsiders the evolution of monetary experience and of the theory of money, starting from David Hume's *Essay on Money* (Hume, 1752). Four main models are presented and critically analyzed: the classical quantity theory; Knut Wicksell's (*Interest and Prices*, 1936 [1898]); John Maynard Keynes's (*A Treatise on Money*, 1930, and *The General Theory*, 1936); and Hicks's own approach ('Monetary Experience and the Theory of Money' 1977b).

I have read these essays on many occasions, finding every time new challenges, new insights, and new responses. Recently I went back to *Economic Perspectives*, to see what I could learn in my attempt to assess the analytical framework behind the current focus, both in the financial industry and in the regulatory environment, on the relationships between capital and risk. Beyond 'Monetary Experience,' I found extremely useful insights also in another essay in the book: 'Capital Controversies: Ancient and Modern' (Hicks, 1977d).

On rereading the essays, however, I convinced myself that Hicks's analysis of the classical model, and indeed of Keynes (*The General Theory*), had omitted two key variables, credit risk and the capital of the banking system, in its explanation of the interaction between industry and

I am grateful for suggestions and criticism on the first draft of this chapter to G. Mazzoni, R. Scazzieri, S. Zamagni, and an anonymous referee. The responsibility for any remaining errors and ambiguities is mine.

finance, and hence of the relationship between monetary impulses and macroeconomic activity. In Hicks's neoclassical interpretation of Keynes, industry finances its activities by issuing securities that, with the intermediation of the markets, are bought by banks. Therefore, there is not a clear distinction between banks' loans and bonds issued by industry. In this context, because of the implicit acceptance of the Modigliani–Miller (1958) theorem on the irrelevance of a firm's capital structure, monetary policy can be studied by considering exclusively shocks to the stock of money and/or to the level of interest rates.

Hicks's analysis does not highlight the crucial role played by the banking system in the transmission mechanism of monetary policy. Ben Bernanke and Alan Blinder (1988), working in terms of a consistent analytical approach and using an extended version of the IS-LM model with three assets (money, bonds, and bank loans), have pointed out that, in the analysis of monetary policy, it is necessary to consider a credit channel that is independent from the traditional monetary channel.

Recognition of the relevance of the banking system in the explanation of monetary impulses highlights the importance of regarding banks as firms. More specifically, banks cannot be analyzed without modeling the role of capital in their functioning. Banks' operations are, essentially, related to the absorption and transfer of risks. Capital can be considered as a cushion against unexpected losses, due primarily to credit risk. Well-established historical evidence in the United States, the United Kingdom, and Switzerland shows that capital funding has been a major characteristic of banks' operations, although common stock and contingency reserves appear relatively expensive compared to the other sources of funding, notably deposits.[1]

In Hicks's analysis of the Great Depression period of the late 1920s and early 1930s, these crucial factors are missing. Had they been taken into account, his interpretation (1977b: 84–5) would have been less mechanistic and less inclined to accept an excessive reliance on core money or 'monetary base' interpretations *à la* Friedman and Schwartz (1963).

Bernanke (1983), in his explanation of the Great Depression, shows that the reduction of the stock of money (in real terms) is not the key variable to be considered. He argues that it is necessary to consider the tightening of bank loans because of: (i) banks' defaults (and hence the destruction of their capital), (ii) the higher credit risk of borrowers (and hence their higher demand for bank capital), and (iii) the steeply higher cost of equity. The cost of equity is a function of the risk of a bank's assets

---

[1] On these points, which are developed in the second section of this chapter, see Lash (1987), Jackson (2001), and Berger, Herring, and Szego (1995).

and of the degree of leverage (see Miller, 1995), with obvious difficulties in the search for fresh capital resources.

Accordingly, this chapter is structured as follows. First, a brief overview of Hicks's interpretation of Keynes's approach is offered. In the next section attention is drawn to the missing link (banks' capital under conditions of credit distress). In doing so, I retrospectively use models that are now well accepted but that were already highly relevant throughout a period when banks were enterprises privately owned and facing default. Finally, the possible lessons of monetary history in evaluating the implications for banking and economic stability of the new international capital standards for banks (BIS, 2004) are briefly explored.

Hicks and monetary economics

Let us start by recalling Hicks's approach to economics and, more specifically, to monetary economics, by making a few quotations: 'The ideas of economics, the powerful ideas of economics, come from the marketplace, the "real world", and to the "real world" they go back. So there is a dialogue between economists and their subject matter' (1977d: 150). This is the case especially for monetary economics:

Monetary theory is less abstract than most economic theory; it cannot avoid a relation to reality, which in other economic theories is sometimes missing. It belongs to monetary history, in a way that economic theory does not always belong to economic history. [...] A large part of the best work on Money is topical... prompted by particular episodes, by particular experiences of the writer's own time. (1977b: 45)

To establish this point, Hicks makes reference to the works of David Ricardo and Keynes, prompted by their concern with monetary reconstruction – the former after Napoleon, the latter first with the return to the gold exchange standard, and then with the aftermath of the Great Depression. Moreover, in the case of Wicksell, Hicks's contention is that the formal theory was developed to explain a practical problem: economic growth at the same time as falling prices.

There is, in my assessment and recollection of Hicks's work, an even more fundamental reason why he was concerned with facts – both current and distilled through economic history. Hicks derives from the observation of economic facts over time and through space his basic tenet that 'a free market system is not automatically self-righting' (1977c: 119). In the same essay, 'Hawtrey,' he shows that the so-called Keynesian 'monetary instability of capitalism' is by no means a typical (and novel, at the time of *The General Theory*) Keynesian doctrine. Ralph Hawtrey (in *Currency and Credit*,

1919) anticipated this point through his analysis of the interaction between regressive and extrapolative expectations. To use Hicks's words again, 'Hawtrey and Keynes were surely right in holding that they were dealing with a system that had no automatic stabiliser: a system which needed to be stabilised by *policy*' (Hicks, 1977c: 120; emphasis in original).

To recall, according to Hawtrey, the instrument of policy necessary to stabilize the economy was the short-term rate of interest set by the central bank. This would affect the cost and availability of *bank lending*. Keynes, in the *Treatise*, developed a new approach, introducing as a fundamental link the relationship between the bank rate and the long-term rate of interest on bonds. If and only if the change in bank lending terms influenced the long-term rate of interest could the desired stabilizing impact of monetary policy and banking activity manifest itself.[2]

We also know that Keynes in *The General Theory* developed his ideas further, and came to the conclusion that, in conditions of major economic and monetary distress, it was only fiscal policy, and monetary demand created by government, that could act as an effective policy stabilizer. This also applied as a consequence of the 'liquidity trap,' from the monetary side.

What was Sir John's position on this issue?

I am certainly not contending that it is either possible, or desirable, that the Old King – Bank Rate – should be put back on his throne. We are living in the reign of his successor – the Government's Budget; that must be accepted. But the new reign, like the old, may not last forever; we can already see that the storm clouds are gathering round it. [...] The rate of interest – the short rate of interest[3] – when properly interpreted as a symbol of credit ease and credit stringency has a superiority...in that it gets the timing of its announcement effects just what they should be. (1977c: 131)

Hicks concludes by making a proposal – one that I find highly relevant for the current debate on economic policy in Europe, and on the golden rule:

[One possibility] which would...seem to be worth exploring, would be...the regulation of the investment expenditure of the Public Sector itself... An efficient Regulator must operate directly upon some key sector; the investment expenditure of the Public Sector...would seem to be a promising candidate. (*ibid.*: 132; see also Hawtrey, 1939a)

Let us look now at the view held by Hicks on overall economic policy. As has already been emphasized in this chapter, such a view should be at

---

[2] In retrospect, I suspect now that this was perhaps the main reason why Hicks was especially interested in my thesis on the term structure!

[3] Hicks clearly takes sides here in the debate on the policy role of the short versus the long rate of interest, and thus between the positions of Keynes in *The Treatise* and in *The General Theory*. Perhaps the work we did together helped to convince him that the short- and the long-term rates of interest cannot be divorced, as the institutional approach claimed.

the forefront of current debate on how to reshape the economic policy framework in the euro area.

This, perhaps, is a dream; I do not claim to be a judge of political possibilities: But I am not afraid to draw the moral, which emerges rather clearly from the line of thought I have tried to follow out, that the issue with which we have been concerned is political – even constitutional – as well as economic. There is the technical economic problem of the Instrument; but it is tied up with the political problem of how to secure that it is used decisively. This is a problem which Keynesian economics, so it seems to me, has refused to face; while the monetarists, who have seen it, have not faced the political implications. For myself, I would face it. I think we should say that monetary regulation is a major function of Government; but we should emphasize that if it is to be exercised decisively, it needs to be separated, in what is in fact the constitutional sense, from other functions. We need to remember the ancient doctrine of the Separation of Powers. The judicial function, in well-ordered states, is recognized to be a function of Government, but a function that is better *separated*: So it is with the monetary function. It is far too responsible a function to be handed over to a 'company of merchants' (Ricardo's pejorative expression for the Bank of England). Nevertheless it is harmful for it to be confused, as Keynesianism has led it to be confused, with the regular financing of the executive government. It belongs to the province of the executive government to further the maintenance of high employment and steady growth, within the framework of an economy that is monetarily well regulated. But it is a disaster that these things have got so mixed together. (1977c: 132–3)

It is by now clear that, according to Hicks, a monetary capitalist economy does not have any automatic stabilizer. This general belief and contention must, however, be applied in different ways, analytically and from the point of view of stabilization policies, according to the nature and workings of the markets of the economic system. Hicks introduces this distinction by making reference to economics and economic history, and thus to his interpretation of changing economic facts. He reviews Alfred Marshall's competitive market system (Hicks, 1965: chap. 5), with merchants who would keep the market atomistic. I might perhaps call them OTC (over-the-counter) markets. He then proceeds to Léon Walras and his 'organised markets.'

According to Hicks, as is well known, gradually over time unorganized, competitive (flex-price) markets for goods, services, and factors of production gave way to a combination of fix-price markets, in which producers are capable in the short run of setting prices, and of organized markets that retain flex-price characteristics, notably in the financial sector (Hicks, 1965: chap. 7, and 1969a). Hicks's view is that the transformation in Keynes's thought is along these lines, with the *Treatise* taking a Marshallian approach to price determination: monetary impulses make themselves felt first on prices and only subsequently, through price changes, on income and employment. In *The General Theory* the chrysalis had not fully burst open.

In the *General Theory* Keynes is moving towards a more modern world, though the transformation in his vision is not complete. He has not grasped that it is a change in market form that is at issue; though he does not draw, from the change, many of the consequences which follow from it. He sees, in particular, that in the fix-price system the direct effects of monetary changes are on output and employment; and that the effects on prices (including wages) follow from them, in ways that are much less automatic. And that, when one thinks it through, was perhaps the main thing that had to be said. Yet, if only it had been possible for Keynes to have set it in this context! We might then have been spared the excesses of those modern monetarists, who still live in their thinking in the old, universally flex-price, world; and who yet think that they can invoke Keynes's authority, or some part of his authority, for policies that still amount to 'leave it to the price-mechanism', policies which may well have been appropriate to that world but are not to its successor. And we might also have been spared the folly of some 'neo-Keynesians', who think only in terms of employment and output, and are prepared to let prices go hang! It is just because we do not live in a world of the old type that prices, money prices, do matter. *Not just wages, but many other prices also, have social functions as well as economic functions.* In a fix-price world, in which so many prices are administered, and have to be administered, the social functions have become more important, and more sensitive, than they were. If the *General Theory* had been set in this context, the model (or rather the principal model) that was used in it could have been represented as consisting of fix-price markets (for labour and for commodities) together with just one flex-price market, the market of bonds. On that arrangement, the single financial market must have a special relation with money. In reality, of course, there are many financial markets, and the relation between *them and money is less simple than it appears to be in Keynes.* Thus there was much in monetary theory (even in quite a narrow sense of a monetary theory) which Keynes left to be done. (Hicks, 1977a: xii–xiii; emphases added)

A key concern of Hicks was indeed the relation between short- and long-term rates of interest. In *Economic Perspectives* he goes as far as to say that the work he had done on it in *Value and Capital* was 'so incomplete as to be misleading' (1977a: xiii). The reason why he felt that the *single* rate of interest construction of *Value and Capital* was inadequate is explained in *Capital and Growth*:

As soon as we allow for uncertainty of expectation, such simple reductions fail us. They fail us in two ways. First, because of default risk, there will be no uniformity in the rates of interest that are established, at the same time, even on loans of the same maturity. Secondly (and more importantly), the amount that a business can borrow, at *any* fixed rate of interest, will be limited by its *credit*; but this barrier can be relaxed, to an extent which varies greatly with confidence, by the raising of funds in other markets, on equities and the like. (1965: 71)

As this quotation indicates, Hicks had already clearly identified by 1965 two crucial factors that limited the usefulness of his (and Keynes's) monetary analysis.

In *Economic Perspectives*, he states explicitly, on this fundamental issue: 'It is incumbent on one, as soon as one rejects the Money-Bonds [the *single* rate of interest] simplification, to construct a model of financial markets, showing, as explicitly as one can, the relations between them. I have made several attempts at such a model; that which is set out below is perhaps the most usable' (1977a: xv).

To this model we now turn. Hicks's aim is to broaden the basic scheme developed by Keynes in *The General Theory*, with a view to carrying the analysis further such that it covers the experience of the 1970s. Let us sketch the financial model and recall its basic assumptions (1977b: 72 ff.). To start with, money does not bear interest. The model explains the simultaneous holding of money and bonds, which bear (a long-term) interest.

We are thus confronted with a peculiar situation: the contemporary presence of a *developed financial system* and a *non-competitive banking system*. The advantage of this simplification is that it makes it possible to aggregate the central bank and the banking system: it is as if all money is hard money and the supply of money – which includes, of course, bank money – can be treated as exogenous. More specifically, the 'cartel' banking system, which offers a zero yield on its monetary liabilities, can be analyzed in terms of fixed-coefficient deposit and credit multipliers.

There are, however, disadvantages in this simplification. As Nicholas Kaldor has taught, one should spend at least a half of the time requested to develop a model in the identification, the monitoring, and the back-testing of his 'stylised facts'! An obvious disadvantage is that we go back to a simplified version of the classical quantity approach, and thereby neglect all the fundamental advances made by Wicksell and by Keynes himself in the *Treatise*. Other drawbacks will become clear shortly.

Three sectors are thus singled out in the model: the banks, which are called the core; the financial system, which is referred to as the mantle; and the rest of the economy – including the enterprise sector, households, and government. Hicks calls this aggregate industry. Further assumptions are as follows: the core does not lend directly to industry, but only indirectly by buying securities issued by the mantle. The mantle, in turn, issues financial securities and has as net assets industrial securities and money. Capital is neglected, both in the core and in the mantle.

It is the contention of this chapter that the three assumptions of (i) a non-competitive banking system (it is in the nature of a competitive system to offer interest on deposits), (ii) the uniformity of interest rates to industry, in spite of default risk, and the irrelevance of credit rationing in a situation of credit strain,[4] and (iii) a system in which capital liabilities are disregarded make it hard to interpret economic facts, above all when conditions of severe credit distress are examined.

The importance of the credit rationing phenomenon due to credit risk has been analyzed in a seminal paper by Donald Hodgman (1960), and then refined and developed by, among others, Marshall Freimer and Myron Gordon (1965) and Dwight Jaffee and Franco Modigliani (1969). In these papers it was underlined that previous explanations of credit rationing were fundamentally based on the stickiness of interest rates due to exogenous factors (not related to the borrower's risk), such as ceilings on interest rates.

On the other hand, credit rationing due to default risk is endogenously explained by explicitly modeling the positive relationship between (i) interest rates and default risk, and (ii) credit granted and default risk. The relevance of considering bank's capital in the analysis of the interaction between industry and finance is reinforced by recalling that *markets* require banks to hold capital ratios, which suggests that an optimal capital structure can be defined for banks.

Allen Berger, Richard Herring, and Giorgio Szego (1995) suggest that several departures from the frictionless world of Modigliani–Miller may help explain 'market capital requirements' for banks – i.e. why markets encourage banks to hold certain capital ratios, irrespective of regulatory capital requirements.

In particular, tax considerations tend to reduce market requirements, the expected costs of financial distress tend to raise these requirements, and transactions costs and asymmetric information problems may either increase or reduce capital held in equilibrium. Finally, they show that the federal safety net protects bank creditors from the full consequences of bank risk, and thus tends to reduce 'market capital requirements.' Support for this latter hypothesis may be inferred by analyzing the influence of the safety net on bank capital ratios over time (see figure 13.1).

It is, of course, paradoxical that Hicks should disregard the crucial role of capital in the workings of the banking system. In a splendid essay, also in *Economic Perspectives*, he surveys 'Capital Controversies: Ancient and Modern.' Perhaps the most interesting – and still highly relevant – part of the essay is represented by the distinction he makes between *fundists* and *materialists*: to the former, capital is a fund, embodied in real assets; to the latter, capital consists of physical goods, with the intrinsic difficulty of the

---

[4] As will be recalled, Hicks himself in *Capital and Growth* (1965) stresses the relevance of these factors.

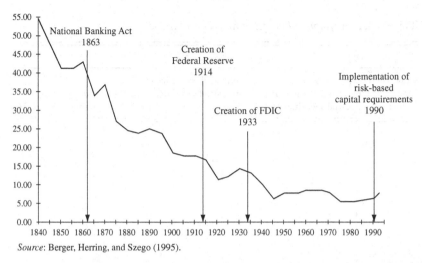

Source: Berger, Herring, and Szego (1995).

Figure 13.1 Equity as a percentage of assets for US commercial banks, 1840–1993

aggregation and measurement of real capital resulting from the fact that the utilities of capital goods are indirect, and thus the values of capital goods are capitalized values of future net products:

> If it is capital in the volume sense that is being measured, capital is physical goods, but in the value sense capital is not physical goods. It is a sum of values which may conveniently be described as a Fund. A Fund that may be embodied in physical goods in different ways. There are these two senses of Real Capital which need to be distinguished. (1977d: 152)

Hicks traces back to merchants, and therefore accountants, the origins of the fundist approach, to which all the British classical economists subscribed, and to which Hicks himself adhered in *Capital and Time* (1973a):

> Even to this day, accountants are Fundists. It is not true, accountants will insist, that the plant and machinery of a firm are *capital*; they are not capital, they are assets. Capital, to the accountant, appears on the liabilities side of the balance sheet; plant and machinery appear on the assets side. Capital, accordingly, is a Fund that is embodied in the assets. [...] These were the business terms which came naturally to the Classical Economists. (1977d: 154)

We are now ready to examine Hicks's monetary reinterpretation of Keynes's *General Theory*, with the aid of table 13.1 (see Hicks, 1977a: 76). As Hicks acknowledges, in this interpretation the Keynes monetary model is very close to the simplified classical quantity model. After all, Keynes was clearly more interested, at that point, in wages and employment. Keynes

Table 13.1 *A simplified model of financial markets*

	Liabilities	Assets
Core	Money $(M+m)$	Financial securities (F)
Mantle	Financial securities $(F+f)$	Industrial securities + money $(I+m)$
Industry	Industrial securities (I)	Real assets + financial securities + money $(R+f+M)$

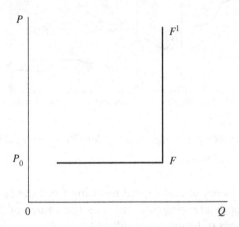

Figure 13.2 Aggregate supply with exogenous wage rates

works in terms of wage units: effective demand (PQ) is measured in terms of wage units. In the simplest case, the wage rate is taken to remain constant, as long as there is unemployment. If prices are related to labor costs through a fixed mark-up, the aggregate supply breaks into two parts: P_0F at less than full employment, and FF^1 at full employment (figure 13.2; 1977a: 82).

It is on the basis of this highly simplified approach that Hicks leans into a 'classical' (monetarist) interpretation of the financial side of the Great Depression. The total gold reserves of the main central banks represented the 'fundamental monetary base.' The return of the British pound to the old dollar parity in 1924, and the revaluation of other important currencies (such as the so-called 'quota 90' in the case of the Italian lira), had contributed to creating a monetary slump, precisely because prices and wages were inflexible downwards, as Keynes had argued.[5]

---

[5] His fight against Winston Churchill on the revaluation issue is well documented. Keynes had also warned against the risks of enforcing the real transfer of war repayments on Germany, which created further deflation in Europe, in a famous debate with Bertil Ohlin. These issues are analyzed in Masera and Triffin, 1984.

The pound fell in December 1931; a period of acute monetary and exchange rate turmoil followed. In April 1933 the United States left the gold standard. A fixed value of the dollar in terms of gold was re-established in January 1934, but with a large devaluation: the former parity was $20.67 per ounce, the new one $35 per ounce. In Hicks's words:

The dollar was reduced to about three-fifths of its previous gold value; when the dollar–sterling exchange appeared to settle at near its old parity, the pound could be reckoned to be devaluated, in terms of gold, in the same proportion. The new position could thus be described (approximately) as one in which the size of the monetary base had been written up by two-thirds. So the value of output, in the 'closed' international system, that could be financed without strain, seemed to be substantially increased.

The monetary brake had been taken off, but recovery, none the less, was tardy. These were the conditions in which Keynes was writing, so one can understand how it was that there was a turning-over, from monetary measures to more direct forms of stimulus. [...]

It should, however, be noticed that it would still have been possible, within the bounds of the theory, for the situation of that time to be read in another way. [...] If one had recognised, as Keynes (on his own principles) surely ought to have recognised, that there are liquidity elements which affect decisions in 'industry', not just in the financial markets (our 'mantle'), it could have been seen that there were similar reasons why real investment should react to monetary *and financial* [the long-term rate of interest] ease rather slowly. (1977b: 85–6; emphasis in original)

It is clear from this reconstruction of events that Hicks was conceding much to the 'monetarist' interpretation of the Great Depression. In his account, the monetary base brake is center stage in the process that transforms the recession into a depression.[6]

Let me therefore try to offer an alternative presentation of his model, by invoking some key factors, which Hicks himself had stressed in other works, as indicated above. I refer to a privately owned competitive banking sector, in which the capital of the banks plays a crucial role.[7] Additionally, the risk of default is explicitly recognized in the pricing mechanism, and credit availability is taken into account in the lending process.

Banks, risk, and capital

The existence and operation of banks can be explained from different points of view, which need not be mutually exclusive. Hicks underlined

---

[6] I cannot recall any other paper by Hicks in which even the term 'monetary base' is mentioned so frequently!

[7] On the specific point of markets in equities, Hicks makes an important contribution in *A Market Theory of Money* (1989a: 80 ff.).

the relevance of transaction costs in 'A Suggestion for Simplifying the Theory of Money' (1935a). Much later, those, such as myself, who work in a framework characterized by asymmetric information and agency costs[8] stress that banks play a fundamental role in facilitating the solution of problems of asymmetric information, both *ex ante* and *ex post*, for risk management and liquidity, in a context of principal–agent relationships. These processes are dynamic in nature, essentially because banks incorporate and foster technological and financial innovation, which reduces transaction and information costs.

In summary, the competitive bank enterprise (i) reduces transaction costs; (ii) manages and facilitates the solution of information asymmetries in specific markets; (iii) transforms intermediated financial resources over time and space; (iv) represents a central operator in the functioning of the monetary and payments system; (v) transmits monetary impulses generated by the central bank; and (vi) manages, allocates, transforms, and transfers risk.

These functions and characteristics overlap and are, basically, complementary. It is, however, the last point, the *absorption and management of risk*, which – in my view – is by far the most important feature of banks.

Risk management is the primary function of a competitive banking system. There are many risk factors: credit risk, market liquidity risk, operational risk, reputational risk, business risk, and strategic risk are the most relevant ones. To a bank, however, risk is ultimately unitary in nature, and its assessment and measure must be made consistent and homogeneous throughout risk factors and lines.

Several measures and definitions of risk have been proposed by both academics and the financial industry. Three main concepts can be identified: *volatility, value at risk*, (VaR), and *coherent risk measures*. Despite the different levels of complexity, all these indicators define risk in terms of probability theory, by allowing thereby its quantification. Technically, different types of risk can be thought of as different random variables, whose realizations represent all possible future values of a single position (or a portfolio of positions), subject to a given typology of risk.

Volatility was the first measure proposed, and it is still widely used for the quantification of risk, especially for market risk factors. The simplicity of this indicator also represents its weakness. In some cases volatility can be a misleading measure of risk, because of its high dependence on the assumption of normal-shaped (and, in general, symmetric) distributions for the risk factors (usually the rates of returns of financial assets, in market

---

[8] I have addressed these issues in Masera, 1991, 2001, and 2005.

risk applications). It can easily be demonstrated that, in the presence of asymmetric distributions with fat left tails, low volatility does not necessarily indicate low risk.

Value at risk, which is defined as the worst loss, for a given confidence interval, within a given time horizon, represents a standard framework used for the quantification of risk (and, as will be shown, of its dual aspect, *economic capital*). In terms of probability theory, VaR is the $(1 - p)\%$ quantile of the return distribution, where p is the confidence interval chosen for the analysis. VaR was initially developed for market risk, but its applications have been successively extended to other typologies of risks (as will be pointed out below, the extension to credit risk is not immediate). At least three different methods for its computation can be identified. Parametric approaches assume that the distribution functions of the risk factors are known (normal or normal-derived functional forms are usually modeled). Monte Carlo methods compute VaR by simulating the possible paths followed by risk factors (in this case a parametric form for the distribution function is also, however, assumed *ex ante*). Non-parametric models start from the idea that the true marginal and joint distributions of different risk factors are not known (for example, the historical approach generates the possible future paths by using distributions observed historically).

All VaR models, with their obvious methodological differences, compute the value of a portfolio at a given point in time and then quantify the sensitivity to changes in each underlying risk factor. The potential change in the various risk factors is also calculated, with the relevant confidence interval. VaR is finally computed with respect to an adverse move on both an individual and an aggregated basis (by considering the correlation among risk factors). We thus obtain the value of the maximum potential loss of the portfolio, over a given time period, with a defined level of statistical confidence.

The so-called axiomatic approach to coherent risk measurement, pioneered by Philippe Artzner, Freddy Delbaen, Jean-Mare Eber, and David Heath (1999), points out the limits of the VaR methodologies by showing that this measure, which, as indicated, represents a standard commonly accepted by both market participants and regulators, is a problematic (non-coherent) risk indicator. The two main drawbacks highlighted are its 'non-smoothness' (i.e. events with probability below the chosen confidence quantile are not considered at all) and its 'non-sub-additivity' (i.e. the VaR of a diversified portfolio could be higher than the sum of idiosyncratic VaR computed for each risk factor). Intuitively, it can therefore be said that VaR does not take into account the entire lower tail of the profit and loss (P&L) distribution, by just picking out one point (the quantile chosen).

To overcome these problems alternative risk measures, which take into account the lower tail of the returns distributions and satisfy the sub-additivity property, have been proposed. Among these new measures the expected shortfall (ES) is perhaps the most well known. In particular, this new metric measures the expected loss, conditional on VaR being violated. It must be recognized, however, that the theoretical attractiveness of this indicator is limited by the problems arising from its implementation in practice. In fact, it has been demonstrated (Yamai and Yoshiba, 2001) that, for back-testing purposes, ES requires much more data than VaR, which continues to represent the most generally used measure of risk. Integrated VaR-type measures of market and credit risk have been developed (such as, for instance, Barone, 1998) and are currently used.

For our present purposes, I shall focus the analysis, without losing in generality, by making reference only to credit risk, which is by far the most important one, in terms of the Hicks model under review. It is necessary, however, for a more immediate understanding of the concepts that will be developed, to draw attention to some key differences between credit and market risk that are not always fully appreciated.

Barring exceptional circumstances, the properly discounted mean value of a portfolio of financial assets, from the point of view of market risk, is the current market value. Probabilities that the market will go up or down should be broadly the same in a liquid, efficient market. The distribution curve is thus symmetric around the mean, although tail events tend to be fatter than in a normal curve. After standardization, market risk can therefore be approximated by a normal-type distribution, centered around the origin, with somewhat fatter tails (see figure 13.3, line 'Market risk').

The situation is very different with respect to credit risk. In particular, when the best scenario for the lender is realized (i.e. the solvency of all the borrowers is granted) losses will be equal to zero. When one or more borrowers are insolvent, however, losses can increase rapidly, reaching, in the extreme case of a zero recovery rate, the whole-face values of the loans granted: loss distributions are therefore highly skewed. It follows that they cannot be modeled as normal-shaped distributions (or, in any case, symmetric distributions). This last consideration has important consequences for the management of this risk. As has been indicated, this represents a drawback of VaR techniques, which rely strongly on the hypothesis of normality for the risk factors analyzed, and therefore cannot easily be used to quantify and to monitor credit risk.

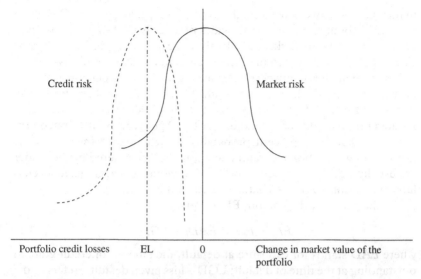

Figure 13.3 Credit and market risk: frequency distributions

When credit is granted an inherent cost has to be reckoned with: the expected loss (EL) on any given exposure, or a set (a portfolio) on any given exposure, or a set of exposures. There is a subtle point here. We use probabilities to assess expected losses. This first step does not capture the true risk component, however, which, as has been shown, is related to unexpected (unidentified) losses that may arise subsequently in the credit portfolio. *Risk* is, therefore, related to loss events that could happen, but have not been anticipated; the *expected loss* is the average level of credit losses that should be anticipated on the portfolio over a given time period. In statistical terms, given the frequency distribution of the portfolio of credit positions, the expected loss is the mean, and the unexpected loss is a function of the standard deviation – i.e. a volatility measure – of the distribution. A typical credit risk probability distribution is depicted by the line 'Credit risk' in figure 13.3; as can be seen, the curve is highly skewed. In general, credit losses (with a negative sign) below the average EL are relatively low. Sometimes, however, they can be very large: this is especially so when the cycle moves into a truly recessionary phase. The shape of the curve therefore takes into account the fact that, with a low frequency, severe losses can occur. The severity of the losses, in turn, depends on the effective diversification of the credit portfolio.

High skewness is mainly due to a large concentration of risks to a small number of counterparts. Here, too, there is a major difference with respect to market risk. As we know from the capital asset pricing model (CAPM), a holding of about twenty stocks provides practically all the possible diversification in terms of market risk. In the case of credit portfolio, there is virtually no end to gains from diversification in reducing credit risk.

In sum, default is relatively rare on average, but the dispersion of default probabilities across firms is very high: to recall, the probability that an AAA-rated firm defaults is less than two in 10,000 per annum, and an A-rated firm has odds of around one in 1,000 per year. A CCC-rated firm has more than a 10 percent probability of default over the same time horizon, however. When default occurs, the losses suffered by the lender are usually significant. The EL, both at individual and aggregated level, is largely determined by the characteristics of the specific contracts.

For the generic i-th position, EL is equal to

$$EL_i = PD_i \times EAD_i \times LGD_i \qquad (13.1)$$

where EAD stands for exposure at default, the amount of credit granted outstanding at the time of default; LGD – loss given default – refers to the amount of credit exposure that will effectively be lost taking into account all mitigant clauses and collateral held in the event of default; and PD is the probability of default – the probability that the borrower will default over the given time horizon.

Having defined EL, and explained that this is a cost to be anticipated over a given time horizon from lending activity, we must now turn to unexpected loss (UL), which is assumed to be a positive function of the standard deviation of the credit risk frequency distribution. As Chris Matten (2000) has pointed out, however, there is a close relationship between expected and unexpected loss for both the idiosyncratic and the portfolio positions held by the lender, as the following formula clarifies:[9]

$$UL_i = EAD_i \sqrt{EL_i(LGD_i - EL_i)}. \qquad (13.2)$$

Equation (13.2) relies on the joint implicit hypothesis that both EAD and LGD are non-stochastic. In some cases it may be unrealistic (and probably misleading) to assume a deterministic LGD. By allowing a stochastic LGD (more sophisticated models, not presented here, may also allow for a stochastic EAD) we may rewrite equation (13.2) as[10]

$$UL_i = EAD_i \sqrt{PD_i(1 - PD_i)\overline{LGD_i}^2 + vol_i^2 PD_i} \qquad (13.3)$$

[9] For the derivation of equation (13.2), see the appendix.
[10] For the derivation of equation (13.3), see the appendix.

where $\overline{LGD_i}$ and vol_i are, respectively, the average value and the standard deviation of the stochastic LGD

The total EL for a credit portfolio is the sum of the expected losses for the individual components:

$$EL_{portfolio} = \sum_{i=1}^{N} EL_i \qquad (13.4)$$

At the aggregated level the complication arises for the computation of UL when portfolio effects have to be taken into account, given the importance of diversification. As indicated, for simplicity's sake, we measure risk in terms of the standard deviation of outcomes. The issue is, therefore, to measure by how much the standard deviation of the sum is lower than the sum of the standard deviations. We can write

$$UL_{portfolio} = \sum_{i=1}^{N} UL_i \rho_{iP} \qquad (13.5)$$

where ρ_{iP} is the correlation of the i-th position and that of the portfolio as a whole. By substituting equation (13.2) or (13.3) in equation (13.5) for portfolios characterized respectively by deterministic or stochastic LGD, we can also write[11]

$$UL_{portfolio} = \sum_{i=1}^{N} EAD_i \sqrt{EL_i(LGD_i - EL_i)} \rho_{iP} \qquad (13.6)$$

or

$$UL_{portfolio} = \sum_{i=1}^{N} EAD_i \sqrt{PD_i(1 - PD_i)\overline{LGD_i}^2 + vol_i^2 PD_i \rho_{iP}} \qquad (13.7)$$

Arnaud de Servigny and Olivier Renault (2004) propose a simple measure to compute the (individual marginal) contribution of each position to the unexpected loss of the portfolio. Analytically, in their proposal, the risk contribution (RC) of the i-th position is given by

---

[11] Matten (2000) has proposed, in a simplified approach for the computation of unexpected loss in a portfolio, to substitute the individual correlations between the losses of each position and that of the portfolio as a whole with an average correlation of the loan losses, calculated historically, in one segment to the portfolio as whole. This simplification has two main drawbacks: (i) the implicit assumption that the portfolio remains unchanged, and (ii) it takes no account of concentration risks.

$$RC_i = \frac{\partial UL_{portfolio}}{\partial UL_i}\, UL_i \qquad (13.8)$$

In this formulation the idiosyncratic unexpected loss of the i-th position 'weighted' with the sensitivity of the portfolio's unexpected loss to its changes represents the marginal risk contribution of each position to the portfolio. This measure has also the desirable property of being additive,[12] so

$$UL_{portfolio} = \sum_{i=1}^{N} RC_i \qquad (13.9)$$

We should now complete our analysis by examining the implications in term of loan pricing. Let us start by considering a lending operation of a bank k to a client i, of the amount of €1. The euro lent costs to the bank:

$1 + i_k$ for the part $1 - a_i$ financed at the interbank rate; and

$1 + c_k$ for the part a_i financed at the cost of capital (a_i is obtained from PD_i, EL_i, and UL_i through the model by the determination of economic capital absorbed).

By equating the expected value of revenue to that of cost, we obtain one equation in one unknown (r_i):

$$(1 - PD_i)(1 + r_i) + PD_i R_i(1 + r_i) = (1 + i_k)(1 - a_i) + (1 + c_k)a_i \qquad (13.10)$$

where (R_i) is the recovery rate. From (13.10) we obtain

$$r_i = \frac{i_k + a_i(c_k - i_k) + PD_i LGD_i}{1 - PD_i LGD_i} \qquad (13.11)$$

As can easily be seen, r_i is an increasing function of i_k, LGD_i, PD_i, and a_i. Equation (13.11) makes it evident that loan pricing becomes highly sensitive to risk, not only through the direct impact of PD_i, but also indirectly, through a_i – i.e. economic capital absorption.

It can be shown that a_i is a *decreasing* function of credit quality, and an increasing function of correlation between the loss of the i-th facility and that on the portfolio as a whole (Matten, 2000). Applying equation (13.11) shows a very steep increase in risk-adjusted interest rates as PD_i and a_i increase. As has been indicated, unidentified, unexpected credit losses of large amounts can take place, with low probabilities.

How can a bank survive these highly damaging circumstances? This is the main role of capital in a bank. Capital is a buffer to absorb future unidentified (i.e. not expected on average) losses. Capital should ensure that the

---

[12] For a proof, see the appendix.

enterprise is able to continue to operate in the event of unexpected losses, thereby offering protection to creditors and avoiding deposit withdrawals.

We refer again to the credit distribution frequency; for ease of presentation we now consider portfolio credit losses with a positive sign (figure 13.4). The bank must hold enough capital to absorb unexpected losses up to a certain level of confidence: for instance, if a bank has an AA rating (0.03 percent probability of default in the following year) it is often decided to aim at a 99.97 percent of confidence level, with a view to maintain the existing credit rating.[13]

Given the skewness of the credit loss frequency curve, this may well imply that the confidence level will be positioned some ten standard deviations to the right of EL. The segment EL–R shows the area of unexpected losses that are covered by economic capital. If UL is above R the bank will default. Formally, it can therefore be said that the economic capital absorption (α) of a given portfolio is a positive function of its unexpected loss. De Servigny and Renault (2004) suggest a simple linear function,

$$\alpha_{portfolio} = m \times UL_{portfolio} \qquad (13.12)$$

where m is an appropriate multiplier. This formulation also allows an easy computation of the economic capital allocated to the i-th position; by exploiting (13.8) we can in fact write

$$\alpha_{portfolio} = m \times \sum_{i=1}^{N} RC_i = m \times \sum_{i=1}^{N} \frac{\partial UL_{portfolio}}{\partial UL_i} UL_i = m \times UL_{portfolio}$$

$$(13.13)$$

To sum up, risk and capital absorption are two sides of the same coin. From corporate financial theory we know that capital has two specific functions: (i) it permits the transfer of ownership, and (ii) it allows the funding of business, with a view to achieving the desired mix between debt and equity. In the case of banks, it is often held that capital should not be viewed as a significant source of financing, as banks can borrow at interest rates well below the cost of capital. In the extreme case, and notably in the traditional monetarist schemes, capital is totally disregarded, and the process of deposit and loan creation is, fundamentally, explained by means of mechanical applications of credit and money multipliers.[14]

---

[13] This is not completely consistent, since rating agencies do not rely exclusively on economic capital to attribute credit ratings to banks.

[14] The pitfalls of this approach are epitomized by Milton Friedman's 'explanation' of the work of the eurodollar market. On these points, see Masera, 1972. Hicks himself was uneasy about the exogeneity of the money supply (1977b: 60), but he did not fundamentally

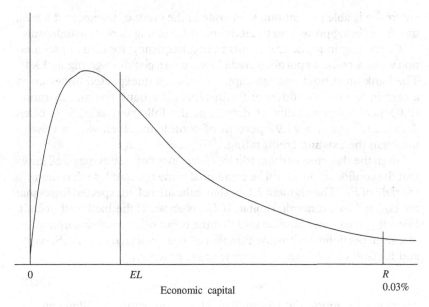

Figure 13.4 Portfolio credit losses

Banks are highly leveraged enterprises, and they can in principle borrow funds at interest rates lower than their cost of capital. A prudent bank also knows, however, that if excessive risk is taken, with insufficient capital buffers, the bank's soundness is impaired.

It is important to recognize that the Basel Capital Accords (1988 and 2004) shaped and directed these processes and set standards, but the process is fundamentally market-driven. This is especially so after the alignment by the supervisory authorities with the EL and UL methodologies in terms of Basel II (on this, see Masera, 2005).

This is not a novel experience. As has been anticipated, a careful examination of the historical experience of the banks shows, in fact, that they traditionally held significant amounts of capital in relation to risky assets. Available evidence dating back to the nineteenth century has been collected and analyzed by Patricia Jackson (2001). A graphical summary is offered here in figure 13.5.

question the issue. The approach outlined in this chapter indicates, instead, that the micro-foundations of the money supply and bank credit processes must be anchored to the concepts of EL and UL – i.e. risk-sensitive pricing and economic capital, respectively.

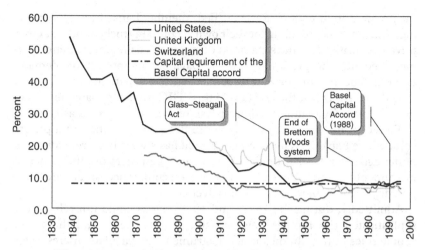

Figure 13.5 Capital/asset ratios of banking system in the United States, the United Kingdom, and Switzerland, 1830–2000

Competitive banking systems in the financially more advanced countries were characterized at the beginning of the twentieth century by average ratios of equity and capital as a percentage of total assets of around 15–20 percent. This was, so to speak, the conventional wisdom on the appropriate mix between equity and debt finance for a sound bank.

The crisis periods of the 1920s and 1930s saw a drastic lowering of these ratios. Clearly, this was not the result of desired portfolio choices, but mainly the consequences of the very large and significant credit losses and bank failures occurring in the period.[15] The creation of the Federal Deposit Insurance Corporation (FDIC) also reduced the demand for capital funding.

The stabilization, or even the further decline, in capital/asset ratios between 1940 and the end of the 1970s, can be viewed as a consequence of the various measures taken and regulations enacted to protect the banks, such as control of the issue of banking licenses, limits to competition, regulated interest rates on customer deposits, acceptance of cartel agreements, high reserve requirements, and lender-of-last resort facilities.

A look back at the enactment of the Banking (Glass–Steagall) Act of 1933 in the United States is illuminating: three features stand out. First,

[15] In the United States, the number of banks declined from around 31,000 to 25,000 in the period from 1920 to 1929, and from some 25,000 to 14,000 over the period from 1929 to 1933. In continental European countries, banking crises led to de facto nationalization of the banking systems. For an account of the Italian experience, see Masera, 2005.

the prohibition of Federal Reserve (Fed) member banks from underwriting, distributing, or dealing for their own account in stock, bonds, or other private securities (i.e. the separation of commercial and investment banking). Second, the prohibition of the payment of interest on demand deposits, and the authorization for the Fed to regulate interest rates on time deposits. Third, the creation of the FDIC, to insure bank deposit of up to $2,500 (for an illuminating analysis of these events, see Lash, 1987).

To recap, the argument developed in this section is that, in a private competitive banking system, equity capital has always been regarded as a buffer against risk – i.e. unidentified losses – and therefore the principal instrument to protect depositors, to maintain confidence, and to prevent a liquidity crisis from turning into insolvency.

Admittedly, during the 1920s and 1930s banks could not rely on the sophisticated risk models now available. Nonetheless, with the aid of simple rules of thumb, means and instruments to calculate interest rates adjusted for expected losses, and to assess the appropriate level of capital funding as a buffer against risk, were available and were utilized.

The simple pricing formulas recalled above also show that, when risk-adjusted rates become exceedingly high in comparison to the risk-free rate, their effective application is constrained. Customers would not accept, and banks themselves would find it difficult to charge, these lending rates, and to set aside very high ratios of capital funding. In these conditions, instances of market failure occur, and credit-rationing phenomena become relevant.

In conclusion, theories arise from experience and must necessarily be based on simplifications of the real world. Hicks, in *Capital and Growth*, correctly stressed the need to introduce in a financial model both default risk – and thus different rates of interest in respect of lending operations – and credit rationing. In 'Capital Controversies' he underlined the importance of capital, viewed as a fund, for firms in the market: there he went so far as to recognize that 'expected losses' should be taken into evidence from an accounting point of view (1977d: 158).

Unfortunately, in the simplification effort of his main monetary and financial model, as we saw, he chose to disregard these 'facts.' This limits the heuristic power of the model, especially in dealing with periods of severe credit distress. The alternative approach, based on expected loss, capital as a buffer, and risk viewed as unexpected loss, in a competitive banking system is definitely more appropriate and fruitful.

In particular, Sir John's simplification of Keynes does not do full justice to the Cambridge economist's diagnosis of and remedy for the Great Depression in the United States and in the rest of the world. The competitive banking model is consistent with the view that identified the main issue as a lack of effective demand. The decline in real economic activity may well have been amplified by the failure of the Federal Reserve to act decisively in terms of monetary base impulses, but the mechanical causal monetarist view, according to which over the 1929–33 period the halving of US Gross National Product (GNP) was caused by the drop by one-third in the money supply, can hardly be accepted. From a policy point of view, Keynes's argument that, to overcome idle money and idle labor, budgetary impulses were the most efficient instrument appears to be correct.

Referring to the Great Depression of the 1930s suggests the idea of concluding this chapter by briefly addressing the question of the relationship between capital standards in the banks and the cyclical behavior of the economy. Basel standards now apply worldwide, and cycles may well exhibit global connotations and acquire severe dimensions. The 2000–1 experience was a clear instance of this risk. Arguably, the specter of a new Great Depression was averted mainly as a result of the very strong (Keynesian?) fiscal and monetary stimuli imparted to the US economy.

Implications of (old and new) capital standards for banking and economic stability

Because of the positive correlation, and the non-linearity, between capital absorption and risk, notably credit risk, an inherent problem of *procyclicality* presents itself.[16] A possible solution to the problem is offered by Alan Greenspan (2000), who has developed the view of 'the spare tyre,' or the 'multiple intermediation shock absorbers' approach. The essence of this is that competitive, efficient, well-capitalized banks and deep and resilient financial markets can complement and substitute each other at times of stress, thereby preventing unique reliance on bank credit.

Such an explanation is essentially correct, but it may not be sufficient at times of acute distress when co-movements in the various markets amplify and reinforce themselves. Under these extreme conditions, I have made the suggestion (Masera, 2001) that banks should be exempted from securing incremental capital absorption needs in the presence of major systemic risks. A 'contract' would be made between banks and central banks, whereby the latter would offer a kind of 'catastrophe insurance.'

A more systematic approach has recently been indicated by Michael B. Gordy (2004). His suggestion is that, to preserve the integrity of the

---

[16] For a broad analysis of issue, see Masera, 2005. Historical perspectives on the long-term experience of banking crises in the United States and Italy, respectively, are contained in Jackson, 2001, and Martinez Oliva and Schlitzer, 2005.

system of capital requirements, even in the case of a cyclical downswing, in order to avoid procyclicality he would instead introduce a system that would rely on smoothing the input, rather than the output. In other words, dampening filters would be adopted for the translation of risk into capital absorption.

Arguably, however, this scheme could weaken the credibility of the banks' soundness, precisely when it has to be preserved. A different market-related approach is outlined here. Central banks could establish, on a regional or national basis,[17] a trust fund (financed in the market, using for instance gold and 'foreign' Treasury paper as collateral), which would invest in fresh capital for the banks at times of impending major systemic risk.

The fund(s) would be run independently on market principles and would replace direct and indirect forms of public support to individual banks. This would not preclude an active search for ways and means of fostering takeovers of ailing banks by sounder and stronger competitors. The fund(s) would therefore add to overall bank capital during severe recessionary periods, and sell back equity to the markets during the upswing of the cycle. If macroeconomic policies prevent the outset of major depressions, as they should, the operation of the fund(s) would be economical.

Appendix

Relationship between expected and unexpected losses for non-stochastic LGD

We impose

$$UL_i \equiv \sqrt{V[L_i]} \qquad (13.A1.1)$$

where L_i is the random variable 'loss on the i-th position.' It therefore follows that, for $EAD_i = 1$, we can write

$$V[L_i] = E[L_i^2] - E[L_i]^2 \qquad (13.A1.2)$$

We can note that

$$E[L_i^2] = LGD_i^2 \times PD_i \qquad (13.A1.3)$$

---

[17] For example, on a European Union (EU), US, Japanese, Chinese, or Latin American basis.

By substituting (13.A1.3) in (13.A1.2), we can write

$$V[L_i] = LGD_i^2 \times PD_i - LGD_i^2 \times PD_i^2 = E[L_i](LGD_i - E[L_i])$$

$$(13.A1.4)$$

By using (13.A1.1) and relaxing the hypothesis of $EAD_i = 1$, we finally obtain

$$UL_i = \sqrt{V[L_i]} = EAD_i \times \sqrt{V[L_i]}$$
$$= EAD_i \times \sqrt{E[L_i](LGD_i - E[L_i])}$$

$$(13.A1.5)$$

Relationship between expected and unexpected losses
for stochastic LGD

Let us assume, for the sake of easier computation, that the non-stochastic EAD_i is 1. We may therefore write

$$E[L_i] = E[LGD_i \times PD_i] = E[LGD_i] \times PD_i = \overline{LGD_i} \times PD_i \quad (13.A2.1)$$

where $E[LGD_i] \equiv \overline{LGD_i}$. By imposing also in this case

$$UL_i \equiv \sqrt{V[L_i]} \qquad (13.A2.2)$$

we can write

$$UL_i = \sqrt{E[L_i - E[L_i]]^2} = \sqrt{E\left[L_i^2 + \overline{LGD_i}^2 \times PD_i^2 - 2L_i \times \overline{LGD_i} \times PD_i\right]}$$
$$= \sqrt{E[L_i^2] + \overline{LGD_i}^2 \times PD_i^2 - 2E[L_i] \times \overline{LGD_i} \times PD_i}$$
$$= \sqrt{E[L_i^2] + \overline{LGD_i}^2 \times PD_i^2 - 2(PD_i \times \overline{LGD_i}) \times \overline{LGD_i} \times PD_i}$$
$$= \sqrt{E[L_i^2] - \overline{LGD_i}^2 \times PD_i^2}$$

$$(13.A2.3)$$

If we note that

$$E\left[\overline{LGD_i}^2\right] = vol_i^2 + \overline{LGD_i}^2 \qquad (13.A2.4)$$

where

$$vol_i = \sqrt{V[LGD_i]} \qquad (13.A2.5)$$

we can rewrite (13.A2.3) as

$$
\begin{aligned}
UL_i &= \sqrt{E\left[L_i^2\right] - \overline{LGD}_i^2 \times PD_i^2} \\
&= \sqrt{\left(V(LGD_i) + \overline{LGD}_i^2\right) \times PD_i - \overline{LGD}_i^2 \times PD_i^2} \\
&= \sqrt{\left(vol_i^2 \times PD_i\right) + \overline{LGD}_i^2 \times PD_i - \overline{LGD}_i^2 \times PD_i^2} \\
&= \sqrt{PD_i \times (1 - PD_i) + \overline{LGD}_i^2 + vol_i^2 \times PD_i}
\end{aligned}
\tag{13.A2.6}
$$

By relaxing the assumption of $EAD_i = 1$, (13.A2.6) can finally be written as

$$
UL_i = EAD_i \sqrt{PD_i \times (1 - PD_i) + \overline{LGD}_i^2 + vol_i^2 \times PD_i}
\tag{13.A2.7}
$$

Proof of the additive property of the risk contribution of the i-th position

By imposing respectively

$$
UL_i \equiv \sqrt{V[L_i]}
\tag{13.A3.1}
$$

and

$$
UL_{portfolio} \equiv \sqrt{V\left[L_{portfolio}\right]}
\tag{13.A3.2}
$$

we can write

$$
UL_{portfolio} = \sqrt{\sum_{i=1}^{N} \sum_{j=1}^{N} UL_i UL_j \rho_{ij}} = \sum_{i=1}^{N} UL_i \rho_{iP}
\tag{13.A3.3}
$$

By differentiating the left side of (13.A3.3) we obtain

$$
\frac{\partial UL_{portfolio}}{UL_i} = \frac{2UL_i + 2 \sum\limits_{j \neq 1}^{N} UL_j \rho_{ij}}{2UL_{portfolio}}
\tag{13.A3.4}
$$

If we define

$$
RC_i \equiv \frac{\partial UL_{portfolio}}{\partial UL_i} UL_i
\tag{13.A3.5}
$$

we can write

$$RC_i = \frac{2UL_i + 2\sum\limits_{j\neq 1}^{N} UL_j\rho_{ij}}{2UL_{portfolio}} UL_i = \frac{\sum\limits_{j\neq 1}^{N} UL_j \times UL_i \times \rho_{ij}}{UL_{portfolio}} \qquad (13.A3.6)$$

The additive property of individual RCs can easily be proved now:

$$\sum\limits_{i=1}^{N} RC_i = \frac{\sum\limits_{i=1}^{N} \left(\sum\limits_{j\neq 1}^{N} UL_j \times UL_i \times \rho_{ij} \right)}{UL_{portfolio}} = \frac{UL^2_{portfolio}}{UL_{portfolio}} = UL_{portfolio} \quad (13.A3.7)$$

14 A suggestion for simplifying the theory of asset prices

Riccardo Cesari and Carlo D'Adda

Introduction

In the opening pages of his essay 'A Suggestion for Simplifying the Theory of Money,' John Hicks (1935a) describes his uneasiness as a non-monetary economist trying to deal with a subject, the theory of money at that time, completely deprived of the basic result of the theory of value – i.e. 'that the relative value of two commodities depends upon their relative marginal utility': 'To an *ingénu*, who comes over to monetary theory,' he writes 'it is extremely trying to be deprived of this sheet-anchor. It was marginal utility that really made sense of the theory of value... What is wanted is a "marginal revolution"' (*ibid.*: 2).

The same feeling could be perceived by a non-financial economist trying to deal with the theory of asset prices and, more generally, the value of uncertain prospects.

At its very beginnings, in the seventeenth century, the value of an uncertain prospect (i.e. a random variable, in modern language) was defined by its expected value, or just 'value.' Christiaan Huygens's (1692 [1657]) book represented, coming as it did just after the years of the Pascal–Fermat correspondence, a milestone in theoretical development: 'He was trying to justify a method for pricing gambles which happens to be the same as what we call mathematical expectation' (Hacking, 1975: 95).

A few decades later the expectation as a valuation method was greatly undermined by the St. Petersburg paradox, in which a coin-tossing game produces an infinite expectation even if none would pay an infinite amount to play such a game. The name of the paradox is due to the solution, proposed by Daniel Bernoulli in 1731 (though not published until 1738), to a question posed by his cousin, Nicolas Bernoulli. In the words of Nicolas

We would like to thank Emilio Barone, Christopher Bliss, Umberto Cherubini, Sergio Ortobelli, Marcello Minenna, Fabio Panetta, Robert Solow, and Jerome Stein for their encouragement, comments, and critiques in connection with a previous version of this chapter. The authors bear responsibility for the contents, however. This work was partially supported by the Italian Ministry for Education, Universities and Research.

(dated September 9, 1713, and reported in Bernoulli, 1954 [1738]), the St. Petersburg game (or martingale strategy) is as follows:

Peter tosses a coin and continues to do so until it should land 'heads' when it comes to the ground. He agrees to give Paul one ducat if he gets 'heads' on the very first throw, two ducats if he gets it on the second, four if on the third, eight if on the fourth, and so on, so that with each additional throw the number of ducats he must pay is doubled. (Nicolas Bernoulli, as reported by Daniel Bernoulli in Bernoulli, 1954 [1738]: 31)

Paul is the player; if he obtains heads at the first flip he wins 1, at the second flip he wins 2, ..., at the n-th flip he wins 2^{n-1}, and so on. The challenge is to seek the fair price, G, to enter (or sell) the game. Clearly, the price must be at least 1 (the minimum gain), but the expected gain is infinite:

Flip	Probability of a head	Prize
1	½	1
2	¼	2
...	...	...
n	$1/2^n$	2^{n-1}
...	...	...

$$\sum_{n=1}^{\infty} 2^{n-1} \frac{1}{2^n} = +\infty$$

As Nicolas Bernoulli observed in stating the paradox, however, nobody would pay an arbitrary large amount to play the game: 'It has to be admitted that any fairly reasonable man would sell his chance, with great pleasure, for twenty ducats' (*ibid.*).

The Cramer–Bernoulli solution[1] provided a path-breaking device, introducing the concept of utility (moral expectation) and reducing the expectation to a finite value:

$$U(G) = \sum_{n=1}^{\infty} U(2^{n-1}) \frac{1}{2^n} < +\infty$$

[1] Daniel Bernoulli's solution, in terms of the log-utility of initial wealth plus prize, was presented to the St. Petersburg Academy of Sciences in 1730–1 and published in 1738. A similar solution, in terms of square-root utility, was independently proposed to Nicolas Bernoulli by Gabriel Cramer in a letter dated 1728.

Such a solution had two relevant consequences: first, probability instead of expectation became the primitive concept of any theory of uncertainty, from Pierre Simon Laplace (1814) to Andrei Kolmogorov (1933); second, the expected-utility approach became the fundamental framework for any valuation and decision theory, from Bernoulli (1738) to John von Neumann and Oskar Morgenstern (1947).

With respect to both consequences, it can be pointed out that the route undertaken by the theoretical mainstream was not the only possible route. With respect to the first consequence, the mathematical theory of uncertainty could be obtained by starting from an axiomatic definition of expectation.[2] With respect to the second consequence, a simpler solution would be to introduce, instead of the utility of money, additional moments of order greater than one as representative of different dimensions or characteristics of the uncertain prospects.

This was the attempt made by Hicks (1962b, 1967a), in his pure theory of portfolio selection. Having discarded expectation and expected utility, 'the third alternative is to look at the regular statistical parameters of the prospect, considered as a probability distribution – not just the first moment (E) but other moments also' (1967a: 106).

In the following, we consider this Hicksian line of reasoning, showing that it can greatly simplify the equilibrium theory of asset prices. Our hope is to have gone a bit further, in the sense of recognizing that, when a probability distribution is expressed by an appropriate number of parameters, these parameters represent quantities of joint products directly priced by the market.

The next section provides the simplest analysis in terms of mean and volatility. The theoretical foundations of ordinal utility are discussed in the following section. The subsequent two sections provide an outline of moment pricing theory and translate in our framework basic concepts such as non-satiation, risk aversion, certainty equivalence, etc. After that the present formulation is compared with the classical intertemporal asset pricing model, and the penultimate section makes use of moment pricing theory to solve several 'paradoxes' of value. The chapter ends with our conclusions.

---

[2] For such an alternative approach, going from expectation to probability instead of vice versa, see Peter Whittle (1992). He recognizes the similarity with the subjectivist approach adopted by both Bruno de Finetti (1970) and Leonard J. Savage (1972). In fact, the former obtains probability from expectation ('prevision'), the latter from primitive preferences over acts. A game-theory approach to probability, rooted back into the Blaise Pascal and Huygens pricing methods, has recently been proposed by Glenn Shafer and Vladimir Vovk (2001).

The simplest approach to asset prices: a naive analysis

In the theory of real commodity prices, the problem facing the optimizing consumer with just two goods available is represented by

$$(R) \begin{cases} \max_{x_1,x_2} V(x_1, x_2) & (two\ commodities) \\ B = x_1 p_1 + x_2 p_2 & (budget\ constraint\ in\ physical\ quantities) \end{cases}$$

where (ordinal) utility and the budget constraint are obtained from the physical quantities of the commodities. In the case of financial assets, the suggestion of using 'statistical parameters' implies, in the two-moment/two-asset case,

$$(F) \begin{cases} \max_{x_1,x_2} H(\mu, \sigma) & (two\ moments,\ two\ assets) \\ \mu \equiv x_1 \mu_1 + x_2 \mu_2 \\ \sigma \equiv \sqrt{x_1^2 \sigma_1^2 + x_2^2 \sigma_2^2 + 2x_1 x_2 \sigma_{12}} \\ W = x_1 P_1 + x_2 P_2 = \mu P_\mu + \sigma P_\sigma & (budget\ constraint\ in \\ physical\ quantities\ and\ in\ moment\ quantities) \end{cases}$$

where utility is obtained from moments and the budget constraint can be defined both in physical quantities and in moment quantities.

The first-order conditions (FOC) of the consumer's problem (R) give the 'sheet-anchor' result quoted by Hicks:

$$\frac{\partial V / \partial x_2}{\partial V / \partial x_1} = \frac{p_2}{p_1}$$

In the second problem we obtain, analogously,

$$\frac{\partial H / \partial \sigma}{\partial H / \partial \mu} = \frac{P_\sigma}{P_\mu}$$

In order to grasp such a pricing model based on 'statistical parameters,' let us suppose, first, that there is a single risky asset, along with an endogenous risk-free bond[3] maturing at the investment horizon T. Clearly, the risky asset is the market portfolio.

We assume, for the time being, that only two characteristics (moments) exist, the mean and the standard deviation: μ_0 and $\sigma_0 = 0$ for the risk-free asset, and μ_M and σ_M for the market portfolio. These two parameters may be conceived of in general as two 'joint products' accruing to the owner. Similarly to all products traded on the market, these two joint products have their own market prices: the price of *expected money* (for

---

[3] The term 'endogenous' means that its aggregate demand is zero.

example, the price of one euro that we expect next year) and the price of *risk* (loosely speaking, the risk of obtaining from *minus* to *plus* one euro). Note that saying this is not quite the same as saying that these parameters represent the result of *expected utility maximization*, as is usually done in financial models. We stress the fact that these two parameters are much like goods and services: they may be measured, have their own market price, and are to be thought of as arguments of an *ordinal utility function*.

Let us use the symbols P_μ and P_σ to indicate respectively the unit market price of expected money (the first characteristic) and the unit market price of risk (the second characteristic, or expected deviation, volatility, standard deviation, or any other name you wish to use). People like expected money, but are generally risk-averse. They would be happy if it were only possible to preserve the money expected from their asset and do without its risk. That risk is part of the asset, though: its market price wouldn't be the same if that risk were not there.[4]

The price of the market portfolio can be written as

$$P_M = \mu_M P_\mu + \sigma_M P_\sigma \qquad (14.1)$$

where P_μ is the market price of one unit of the first characteristic (expected value) and P_σ is the price of the second characteristic. Such a formula has the same value for a theory of asset prices as the bill in a restaurant has for a theory of commodity prices: it simply says that the total value is the sum of the prices times the quantities of each single component.

The risk-free asset is no exception:

$$P_0 = \mu_0 P_\mu \qquad (14.2)$$

and if the expected value is just one unit of money, $\mu_0 = 1$, then we can identify the market price of the mean with the price of the risk-free, unit, zero-coupon bond:

$$P_0 = P_\mu \qquad (14.3)$$

Therefore

$$P_M = \mu_M P_0 + \sigma_M P_\sigma \qquad (14.4)$$

saying that the price P_M is the discounted expected value, $\mu_M P_0$, plus an adjustment, $\sigma_M P_\sigma$, proportional to its risk. Note that if the price P_M and its moments are observable and the market reflects equilibrium values, then we can obtain

---

[4] A not too different situation is that of a production process from which both a desired product and pollution are obtained.

$$P_\sigma = \frac{P_M - \mu_M P_0}{\sigma_M} \qquad (14.5)$$

Risk aversion means that P_σ is negative – i.e. the market portfolio has a price less than its discounted expected value. For example,

$$P_\sigma = \frac{1 - 1.1 \cdot 0.97}{0.50} = -0.134$$

Analogously, first-order stochastic dominance (i.e. Maurice Allais's axiom of absolute preference or the non-satiation principle) implies a non-trivial condition on moment prices.

Let us suppose, now, that the market portfolio is a linear combination of n different risky assets. The price of any single risky asset P_j with outstanding quantity x_j is simply obtained from (14.4) as

$$P_j = \frac{\partial P_M}{\partial x_j} = \mu_j P_0 + \frac{\partial \sigma_M}{\partial x_j} P_\sigma \qquad (14.6)$$

with

$$\frac{\partial \sigma_M}{\partial x_j} = \frac{\sum\limits_{k=1}^{n} x_k \sigma_{jk}}{\sigma_M} = \frac{\mathrm{Cov}(\tilde{P}_j, \sum\limits_{k=1}^{n} x_k \tilde{P}_k)}{\sigma_M} = \frac{\mathrm{Cov}(\tilde{P}_j, \tilde{P}_M)}{\sigma_M}$$
$$= \frac{E\left[(\tilde{P}_M - \mu_M)(\tilde{P}_j - \mu_j)\right]}{\sigma_M}$$

so that, using (14.5),

$$P_j = \mu_j P_0 + \frac{\mathrm{Cov}(\tilde{P}_j, \tilde{P}_M)}{\sigma_M^2}(P_M - \mu_M P_0) \qquad (14.7)$$

which is clearly the CAPM of William F. Sharpe (1964) in price terms.

In fact, dividing both sides by P_0 and by P_j and rearranging,

$$\frac{\mu_j}{P_j} = \frac{1}{P_0} - \frac{P_M^2 \mathrm{Cov}\left(\dfrac{\tilde{P}_j}{P_j}, \dfrac{\tilde{P}_M}{P_M}\right)}{\sigma_M^2}\left(\frac{1}{P_0} - \frac{\mu_M}{P_M}\right) \qquad (14.8)$$

i.e.

$$\bar{R}_j = R_F + \frac{\mathrm{Cov}(\tilde{R}_j, \tilde{R}_M)}{\sigma_{RM}^2}(\bar{R}_M - R_F) \qquad (14.9)$$

This result means that the simple intuition we started with is in agreement with a basic model of the asset pricing theory. It may be worthwhile, therefore, trying to provide more sound foundations to our approach.

Theoretical foundations

It is well known that the theory of choice under uncertainty maps decisions into probability distributions, so that preferences and ordinal utility, V, are defined over the set of probability distribution functions.

In particular, let $\Im$ be the set of n-dimensional distribution functions with finite moments at least to order m, mapping R^n (the Euclidean space of n-dimensional real vectors) into $[0,1]$ and defined by at most $k \leq m$ real parameters:

$$F \in \Im, R^n \to [0, 1]$$

For simplicity, let us consider the case of univariate distributions ($n = 1$). We assume that the essential information concerning any distribution function F is contained in the m-dimensional vector of moments $\mathbf{M} \equiv (\mu, \mu^{(2)}, \mu^{(3)}, ..., \mu^{(m)})$, where μ is the mean and $\mu^{(s)}$ is the s-order central moment in original units.[5]

Definition of s-order modified central moment

$$\mu^{(s)} \equiv \begin{cases} 1 & s = 0 \\ \mu & s = 1 \\ \left(\int (x - \mu)^s dF \right)^{\frac{1}{s}} & s \geq 2 \end{cases} \qquad (14.10)$$

Note that $(\mu^{(s)})^s$ is the usual central moment of order $s \geq 2$.

Let $Q \subseteq R^m$ be a rectangular subset of R^m (the Cartesian product of m real intervals), whose elements are the m-dimensional vectors of moments, $\mathbf{M} \in Q$. By assumption, m is sufficiently large to include all relevant moments.[6]

According to Peter Fishburn (1970), we have the following results.

---

[5] It is always possible to pass from a distribution to its (possibly infinite) moments. The reverse, the so-called problem of moments, is not always guaranteed over infinite range. For a discussion, see Maurice Kendall and Alan Stuart (1977: chap. 4). Note that, instead of central moments, non-central moments could, equivalently, be used. Moreover, scale, location, and dispersion parameters can be considered in the case of distributions (e.g. stable) for which moments do not exist.

[6] In order to understand what 'relevant' means, we may consider an example used by Philip Dybvig and Jonathan Ingersoll (1982), showing that the classical two-moment asset pricing model (CAPM) in complete markets implies arbitrage opportunities. This is due to the fact that, if only the first two moments are priced, some derivative, non-linear assets have significant 'unpriced' higher-order moments, inducing arbitrage in the form of negative values to non-negative pay-offs.

Assumption of preference order

Let $\succ$ be a preference order – i.e. a binary relation defined by a subset $\Re$ of the Cartesian product QxQ, whose elements are the ordered pairs of vectors $(\mathbf{M_a},\mathbf{M_b})$. We write $\mathbf{M_a} \succ \mathbf{M_b}$ instead of $(\mathbf{M_a},\mathbf{M_b}) \in\Re$ and we say that '$\mathbf{M_a}$ is preferred to $\mathbf{M_b}$.'

Clearly, or $\mathbf{M_a} \succ \mathbf{M_b}$ or $\mathbf{M_a} \not\succ \mathbf{M_b}$, and both cannot hold: in fact, or $(\mathbf{M_a}, \mathbf{M_b}) \in\Re$ or $(\mathbf{M_a},\mathbf{M_b}) \notin\Re$.

I. Axiom of asymmetric preferences

We assume that $\succ$ is asymmetric:

$$\text{if } \mathbf{M_a} \succ \mathbf{M_b} \text{ then } \mathbf{M_b} \not\succ \mathbf{M_a} \tag{14.11}$$

Note that if $\mathbf{M_b} \not\succ \mathbf{M_a}$ then two alternative cases are possible: or $\mathbf{M_a} \succ \mathbf{M_b}$ or $\mathbf{M_a} \not\succ \mathbf{M_b}$. In the last case, we say that '$\mathbf{M_a}$ and $\mathbf{M_b}$ are equivalent' and we write $\mathbf{M_a} \sim \mathbf{M_b}$.

Definition of equivalence

$\mathbf{M_a} \sim \mathbf{M_b}$ if $\mathbf{M_a} \not\succ \mathbf{M_b}$ and $\mathbf{M_b} \not\succ \mathbf{M_a}$.

II. Axiom of transitive preferences

We assume that $\succ$ is transitive:

$$\text{if } \mathbf{M_a} \succ \mathbf{M_b} \text{ and } \mathbf{M_b} \succ \mathbf{M_c} \text{ then } \mathbf{M_a} \succ \mathbf{M_c} \tag{14.12}$$

Definition of weak order

The preference order $\succ$ is a weak order if it is asymmetric and transitive.

Definition of negatively transitive preferences

If $\mathbf{M_a} \not\succ \mathbf{M_b}$ and $\mathbf{M_b} \not\succ \mathbf{M_c}$ then $\mathbf{M_a} \not\succ \mathbf{M_c}$.

III. Axiom of continuity

There is a countable subset $D \subseteq Q|{\sim}$ that is $\succ$-dense in the set of equivalence classes $Q|{\sim}$. In other words, for every $\mathbf{M_A}, \mathbf{M_C} \in Q|{\sim}\backslash D, \mathbf{M_A} \succ \mathbf{M_C}$ there is $\mathbf{M_B} \in D$ such that:

$$\mathbf{M_A} \succ \mathbf{M_B} \text{ and } \mathbf{M_B} \succ \mathbf{M_C} \tag{14.13}$$

Note that the subset of rational numbers is $>$-dense and $<$-dense in the set of real numbers.

Theorem of ordinal utility

Under axioms I, II, and III there is a real function $H: Q \to R$ that represents the preferences $\succ$, such that for every $\mathbf{M_a}, \mathbf{M_b} \in Q$

$$\mathbf{M_a} \succ \mathbf{M_b} \text{ if and only if } H(\mathbf{M_a}) > H(\mathbf{M_b})$$

The function H is unique up to any order-preserving transformation Ψ:

$$H(\mathbf{M_a}) > H(\mathbf{M_b}) \text{ if and only if } \Psi(H(\mathbf{M_a})) > \Psi(H(\mathbf{M_b}))$$

Proof

Fishburn (1970: 27). Note that $\mathbf{M}_a \sim \mathbf{M}_b$ if and only if $H(\mathbf{M}_a) = H(\mathbf{M}_b)$, etc. The function H is called an ordinal utility because it just represents the given preference order $\succ$ in terms of otherwise arbitrary real numbers ('utils').[7]

Note that we have not introduced the highly questionable 'independence axiom' and its related expected utility theorem:[8] H is a utility of expectations and not an expectation of utilities.

Note also that such a solution is different from (and much simpler than) other generalizations suggested in the literature after Allais's (1953) contribution on the empirical critique of the von Neumann–Morgenstern (VNM) expected utility theory.

In fact, with most analysts, including Allais (1979), Daniel Kahneman and Amos Tversky (1979), Soo Hong Chew (1983), Fishburn (1983), Mark Machina (1982), and many others, the utility function is a function of moments of a Bernoullian utility U or a function of both Bernoullian utilities and subjective probabilities:

$$\sum_i U(x_i)\pi(p_i), \quad \frac{\sum_i U(x_i)p_i}{\sum_i T(x_i)p_i}, \quad \sum_i U(x_i)p_i + \left[\sum_i T(x_i)p_i\right]^2, \dots etc.$$

In our case, we obtain a more general result based on more intuitive elements:

$$H\left(\sum_i x_i p_i, (\sum_i x_i^2 p_i,)^{1/2}, \dots, (\sum_i x_i^m p_i)^{1/m}\right)$$

Moreover, it is well known that the expected utility can be approximated by a particular function of m central moments:

$$\sum_i U(x_i)p_i \approx U(\mu) + \frac{1}{2}U^{(2)}(\mu)\left(\mu^{(2)}\right)^2 + \dots + \frac{1}{m!}U^{(m)}(\mu)\left(\mu^{(m)}\right)^m$$

$$(14.14)$$

where $U^{(j)}$ is the j-th derivative of U, but this form is only a special case of H and it is not always able to account for observed phenomena (see below).

---

[7] An alternative ordinal utility theorem is obtained assuming that Q is a topological space and different axioms hold: see Gérard Debreu (1959: chap. 4) and J. Trout Rader (1963).

[8] For a review of the expected utility theory and its alternatives, see Machina (1987) and Fishburn (1982, 1988). The seminal work is in von Neumann and Morgenstern (1947: chap. 1, appendix).

One of the implications of the Hicksian ordinal utility function H $(\mu, \mu^{(2)}, \mu^{(3)}, \ldots, \mu^{(m)})$ is that, like consumption goods in Kelvin Lancaster's (1966) theory, any asset or portfolio, being a probability distribution, is essentially a bundle of different characteristics (moments). This has significant pricing implications.

Moment pricing theory

In the case of one risky and one risk-free asset and two moment distributions $(m = 2)$, we have, for the representative investor with current wealth W,

$$\begin{cases} \max_{x_0, x_M} H(\mu, \sigma) \\ \mu = x_0\mu_0 + x_M\mu_M \\ \sigma = x_M\sigma_M \\ W = x_0P_0 + x_MP_M \end{cases} \tag{14.15}$$

The first-order conditions are

$$\frac{\partial H}{\partial \mu}\mu_0 - \lambda P_0 = 0$$

$$\frac{\partial H}{\partial \mu}\mu_M + \frac{\partial H}{\partial \sigma}\sigma_M - \lambda P_M = 0 \tag{14.16}$$

so that, assuming without loss of generality $\mu_0 = 1$, and substituting for λ, we have

$$\frac{P_M}{P_0} = \mu_M + \frac{\partial H/\partial \sigma}{\partial H/\partial \mu}\sigma_M \tag{14.17}$$

In terms of characteristics, current wealth W can be equivalently expressed as

$$W = \mu P_\mu + \sigma P_\sigma \tag{14.18}$$

so that the FOC become

$$\frac{\partial H}{\partial \mu}\mu_0 - \lambda P_\mu\mu_0 = 0$$

$$\frac{\partial H}{\partial \mu}\mu_M + \frac{\partial H}{\partial \sigma}\sigma_M - \lambda(P_\mu\mu_M + P_\sigma\sigma_M) = 0$$

and substituting for λ we obtain the well-known relation of relative prices in terms of marginal utilities

$$\frac{\partial H/\partial \sigma}{\partial H/\partial \mu} = \frac{P_\sigma}{P_\mu} \tag{14.19}$$

and substituting

$$P_M = \mu_M P_0 + \frac{P_\sigma}{P_\mu} P_0 \sigma_M = \mu_M P_0 + \sigma_M P_\sigma \qquad (14.20)$$

the last equality coming from $P_0 = \mu_0 P_\mu = P_\mu$.

In the case of one risk-free and n risky assets, the problem becomes

$$\begin{cases} \max\limits_{x_0, x_1, \dots, x_k, \dots, x_n} \quad H(\mu, \sigma) \\[2mm] \mu = x_0 \mu_0 + \sum\limits_{k=1}^{n} x_k \mu_k \\[2mm] \sigma = \sqrt{\sum\limits_{h=1}^{n} \sum\limits_{k=1}^{n} x_h x_k \sigma_{hk}} \\[2mm] W = x_0 P_0 + \sum\limits_{k=1}^{n} x_k P_k = \mu P_\mu + \sigma P_\sigma \end{cases} \qquad (14.21)$$

with FOC

$$\frac{\partial H}{\partial \mu} \mu_0 - \lambda P_0 = 0$$

$$\frac{\partial H}{\partial \mu} \mu_j + \frac{\partial H}{\partial \sigma} \frac{\sum\limits_{k=1}^{n} x_k \sigma_{jk}}{\sigma} - \lambda P_j = 0 \qquad (14.22)$$

so that

$$\frac{P_j}{P_0} = \mu_j + \frac{\partial H / \partial \sigma}{\partial H / \partial \mu} \frac{\sum\limits_{k=1}^{n} x_k \sigma_{jk}}{\sigma} \sigma_M \qquad (14.23)$$

Under (14.18), however, we obtain again (14.19), so that, using $P_0 = P_\mu$,

$$P_j = \mu_j P_0 + \frac{\sum\limits_{k=1}^{n} x_k \sigma_{jk}}{\sigma} P_\sigma = \mu_j P_0 + \frac{\mathrm{Cov}(\tilde{P}_j, \sum\limits_{k=1}^{n} x_k \tilde{P}_k)}{\sigma} P_\sigma \qquad (14.24)$$

In equilibrium, $x_0 = 0$ and $\sigma = \sigma_M$ (the market portfolio volatility), so that (14.24) is equivalent to (14.6) – i.e. the CAPM: it says that the equilibrium asset price is the expected value μ_j discounted and adjusted by a risk measure proportional to the covariance between the asset price and the market portfolio.

Note that a risky asset having market price P_σ may occasionally exist in the real world as an asset with zero expected value. For example, in the case of a 'synthetic forward' contract (a long call and a short put position) written on an asset P_j with strike price equal to the expected value μ_j of the underlying asset, the price formula, applied to a future pay-off of $\tilde{P}_j - \mu_j$, gives

$$P_{FW} = P_\sigma \frac{\mathrm{Cov}(\tilde{P}_M, \tilde{P}_j)}{\sigma_M}$$

If the asset is the market portfolio itself, the result is simply that the price of the contract is P_σ times σ_M, a negative quantity.[9]

Elsewhere (Cesari and D'Adda, 2003), we have shown that the simple pricing procedure suggested above may be successfully applied to options, allowing the reproduction of the Black and Scholes equation and its possible generalizations.

Higher-order moments, risk aversion, stochastic dominance, and the like

If higher moments exist, beyond the mean and the standard deviation, the reasoning goes through as before.

The price of the market portfolio has the simple bell shape

$$P_M = \mu_M P_\mu + \sigma_M P_\sigma + \varsigma_M P_\varsigma + \kappa_M P\kappa + \dots \qquad (14.25)$$

ς_M, κ_M, etc. being respectively skewness, kurtosis, and higher moments of the market portfolio

$$\varsigma_M = \left[E\left(\tilde{P}_M - \mu_M\right)^3\right]^{\frac{1}{3}}$$

$$\kappa_M = \left[E\left(\tilde{P}_M - \mu_M\right)^4\right]^{\frac{1}{4}}$$

and the generic asset j has price

$$P_j = \frac{\partial P_M}{\partial x_j} = \mu_j P_0 + \frac{\partial \sigma_M}{\partial x_j} P_\sigma + \frac{\partial \varsigma_M}{\partial x_j} P_\varsigma + \frac{\partial \kappa_M}{\partial x_j} P_\kappa + \dots \qquad (14.26)$$

where, in addition to the covariance term, co-skewness and co-kurtosis of the asset with the market portfolio are included:[10]

---

[9] Note that, in this case, the strike is $\mu_M = \dfrac{P_M - P_\sigma \sigma_M}{P_0}$, greater than the forward price $\dfrac{P_M}{P_0}$ for which the contract has zero value.

[10] Note that co-skewness and co-kurtosis can be expressed in terms of covariance:

$$\mathrm{Cosk}(\tilde{P}_M, \tilde{P}_j) = \mathrm{Cov}(\tilde{P}_M^2, \tilde{P}_j) - 2\mu_M \mathrm{Cov}(\tilde{P}_M, \tilde{P}_j)$$

$$\mathrm{Coku}(\tilde{P}_M, \tilde{P}_j) = \mathrm{Cov}(\tilde{P}_M^3, \tilde{P}_j) - 3\mu_M \mathrm{Cov}(\tilde{P}_M^2, \tilde{P}_j) + 3\mu_M^2 \mathrm{Cov}(\tilde{P}_M, \tilde{P}_j)$$

$$\frac{\partial \sigma_M}{\partial x_j} = \frac{E\left[\left(\tilde{P}_M - \mu_M\right)\left(\tilde{P}_j - \mu_j\right)\right]}{\sigma_M} \equiv \frac{\text{Cov}(\tilde{P}_M, \tilde{P}_j)}{\sigma_M}$$

$$\frac{\partial \varsigma_M}{\partial x_j} = \frac{E\left[\left(\tilde{P}_M - \mu_M\right)^2\left(\tilde{P}_j - \mu_j\right)\right]}{\varsigma_M^2} \equiv \frac{\text{Cosk}(\tilde{P}_M, \tilde{P}_j)}{\varsigma_M^2}$$

$$\frac{\partial \kappa_M}{\partial x_j} = \frac{E\left[\left(\tilde{P}_M - \mu_M\right)^3\left(\tilde{P}_j - \mu_j\right)\right]}{\kappa_M^3} \equiv \frac{\text{Coku}(\tilde{P}_M, \tilde{P}_j)}{\kappa_M^3} \qquad (14.27)$$

Clearly, the general pricing formula (14.26) is linear: the value of a portfolio is the portfolio of values.

In addition, the usual definitions can be extended to our approach. Let F, G, be two probability distributions (i.e. two assets, under market completeness) with relevant moment vectors $\mathbf{M}_F \equiv (\mu_F, \mu_F^{(2)}, \mu_F^{(3)}, ..., \mu_F^{(m)})$ and $\mathbf{M}_G \equiv (\mu_G, \mu_G^{(2)}, \mu_G^{(3)}, ..., \mu_G^{(m)})$, respectively. Let $H(\mathbf{M})$ be a differentiable utility function.

Definition of non-satiation
The utility H is non-satiated if, for every $\delta > 0$,

$$H(\mu_F, \mu_F^{(2)}, \mu_F^{(3)}, ..., \mu_F^{(m)}) < H(\mu_F + \delta, \mu_F^{(2)}, \mu_F^{(3)}, ..., \mu_F^{(m)})$$

In differential terms, $\dfrac{\partial H}{\partial \mu} > 0$.

Definition of risk aversion
A utility H is risk-averse if, for every F,

$$H(\mu_F, 0, 0, ..., 0) > H(\mu_F, \mu_F^{(2)}, \mu_F^{(3)}, ..., \mu_F^{(m)})$$

Note that, for $m = 2$, risk aversion means $\dfrac{\partial H}{\partial \mu^{(2)}} < 0$; for $m \geq 3$, a negative marginal utility of volatility $\dfrac{\partial H}{\partial \mu^{(2)}} < 0$ does not imply risk aversion.

Definition of certainty equivalence
The certainty equivalent of F is defined as the amount C_F such that

$$H(\mu_F, \mu_F^{(2)}, \mu_F^{(3)}, ..., \mu_F^{(m)}) = H(C_F, 0, 0, ..., 0)$$

For the representative investor, the price equals the certainty equivalent $P_F = C_F$.

Definition of risk
Given two distributions F, G, with equal mean, $\mu_F = \mu_G$, we say that F is less risky than G if $H(\mathbf{M}_F) > H(\mathbf{M}_G)$ for every risk-averse utility H.

Definition of stochastic dominance
Given two distribution functions, F, G, defined over the same support, we have m-th-order stochastic dominance of F over G, $F \succ_m G$, $m \geq 1$, if $F \neq G$ and

$$F^{(m)}(x) \leq G^{(m)}(x) \quad \forall x$$

where

$$F^{(m)}(x) = \begin{cases} F(x) & m = 1 \\ \int\limits_{-\infty}^{x} F^{(m-1)}(y)dy & m \geq 2 \end{cases}$$

Clearly, if $F \succ_m G$ then $F \succ_{m+1} G$.

We recall a well-known result on stochastic dominance and Von Neumann–Morgenstern expected utility functions.

Theorem on stochastic dominance and expected utility
We have the following.
   (i) $F \succ_1 G \Leftrightarrow E_F(U(x)) \geq E_G(U(x))$ for every U with $U' \geq 0$.
  (ii) $F \succ_2 G \Leftrightarrow E_F(U(x)) \geq E_G(U(x))$ for every U with $U' \geq 0$, $U'' \leq 0$.
 (iii) $F \succ_3 G \Leftrightarrow E_F(U(x)) \geq E_G(U(x))$ for every U with $U' \geq 0$, $U'' \leq 0$, $U''' \geq 0$.

Proof
(i) By integration by parts:

$$E_F(U(x)) - E_G(U(x)) = \int U(x)dF(x) - \int U(x)dG(x)$$

$$= \int U(x)d(F(x) - G(x))$$

$$= -\int (F(x) - G(x))U'(x)dx \qquad (14.28)$$

Therefore, if $F(x) \leq G(x)$ then $E_F(U(x)) \geq E_G(U(x))$. Conversely, if $E_F(U(x)) \geq E_G(U(x))$ let I be an interval in which $F(x) > G(x)$ and let χ_I be the indicator function of I. Define

$$U(x) = \int \chi_I(x)dx$$

so that $U'(x) \equiv \chi_I(x) \geq 0$ and, inserted into (14.28), gives a contradiction.

For (ii) and (iii), see Peter Fishburn and Raymond Vickson (1978) and G. A. Whitmore (1970). As a result, first-order stochastic dominance means preferences with increasing VNM utilities; second-order stochastic dominance means preferences with increasing and concave VNM utilities. This is no longer true for the Hicksian utility.

Theorem on stochastic dominance and moments order

If $F \succ_m G$ then $\mathbf{M}_F \equiv (\mu_F, \mu_F^{(2)}, \mu_F^{(3)}, ..., \mu_F^{(m)}) \neq (\mu_G, \mu_G^{(2)}, \mu_G^{(3)}, ..., \mu_G^{(m)}) \equiv \mathbf{M}_G$ and $(-1)^{k-1}\mu_F^{(k)} > (-1)^{k-1}\mu_G^{(k)}$ for the smallest k for which $\mu_F^{(k)} \neq \mu_G^{(k)}$.

Proof

Apply Fishburn (1980: theorem 1) and the relation between central, μ, and non-central, ν, moments:

$$(\mu_F^{(s)})^s = \sum_{j=0}^{s} \binom{s}{j} \left(\nu_F^{(s-j)}\right)^{s-j}(-\mu_F)^j \quad \forall s \geq 2$$

As special cases we have:
  (i) if $F \succ_1 G$ then $\mu_F > \mu_G$;
  (ii) if $F \succ_2 G$ then $(\mu_F > \mu_G)$ or $(\mu_F = \mu_G$ and $\mu_F^{(2)} < \mu_G^{(2)})$; and
  (iii) if $F \succ_3 G$ then $(\mu_F > \mu_G)$, or $(\mu_F = \mu_G$ and $\mu_F^{(2)} < \mu_G^{(2)})$, or $(\mu_F = \mu_G$ and $\mu_F^{(2)} = \mu_G^{(2)}$ and $\mu_F^{(3)} > \mu_G^{(3)})$.

In the first case, in particular, it does not necessarily follow (even if it is plausible, however) that $H(\mathbf{M}_F) > H(\mathbf{M}_G)$ whenever higher-order moments are relevant.[11]

Moment pricing and intertemporal models

Our model extends the intertemporal general equilibrium asset pricing model. To see this, let us consider the classical intertemporal consumption-investment model (Merton, 1973) of a representative agent with additive, concave utility in consumption, $U(C_t, t)$, n financial assets with prices $P_j(t)$, and total returns $R_j(t)$ and wealth W_t at the beginning of period t, before the choice of the optimal consumption C_t and portfolio allocations $x_j(t)$ of residual wealth, with

$$\sum_{j=1}^{n} x_j(t) = 1.$$

---

[11] Allais (1953, 1979) *assumes* that $F \succ_1 G$ implies $H(F) > H(G)$ (the 'axiom of absolute preference'). In the expected utility approach it is equivalent to *assume* $U' > 0$ (non-satiation).

Following the Bellman approach to stochastic dynamic programming,[12] we have the constrained problem in terms of utility value function $\mathscr{J}$:

$$
\begin{cases}
\mathscr{J}(W_t, t) = \max_t(U(C_t, t) + E_t(\mathscr{J}(W_{t+1}, t+1))) \\[2mm]
W_{t+1} = (W_t - C_t)\left(1 + \sum_{j=1}^{n} x_j(t)R_j(t+1)\right) \\[2mm]
\sum_{j=1}^{n} x_j(t) = 1
\end{cases}
\tag{14.29}
$$

giving, for optimality, the envelope condition $\mathscr{J}_W(W_t, t) = U_C(C_t, t)$ and the stochastic Euler equation

$$
E_t\left[\frac{\mathscr{J}_W(W_{t+1}, t+1)}{\mathscr{J}_W(W_t, t)}(1 + R_j(t+1))\right] = 1
\tag{14.30}
$$

i.e.

$$
P_j(t) = E_t\left[\frac{\mathscr{J}_W(W_{t+1}, t+1)}{\mathscr{J}_W(W_t, t)}(P_j(t+1) + D_j(t+1))\right]
\tag{14.31}
$$

In the case of a one-period default-free zero-coupon bond we have

$$
P_0(t) = E_t\left(\frac{\mathscr{J}_W(W_{t+1}, t+1)}{\mathscr{J}_W(W_t, t)}\right)
\tag{14.32}
$$

so that, ignoring dividends and using the property that

$$
E(XY) = E(X)E(Y) + \text{Cov}(X, Y)
$$

the valuation equation (14.31) becomes

$$
P_j(t) = P_0(t)E_t(P_j(t+1)) + \text{Cov}_t\left(P_j(t+1), \frac{\mathscr{J}_W(W_{t+1}, t+1)}{\mathscr{J}_W(W_t, t)}\right)
\tag{14.33}
$$

Note that, from a Taylor expansion, the marginal utility can be written as

$$
\begin{aligned}
\mathscr{J}_W(W_{t+1}, t+1) = {} & \mathscr{J}_W(W_t, t+1) + \mathscr{J}_{WW}(W_t, t+1)(W_{t+1} - W_t) \\
& + \frac{1}{2}\mathscr{J}_{WWW}(W_t, t+1)(W_{t+1} - W_t)^2 + \cdots
\end{aligned}
$$

and the price (14.33) becomes

---

[12] According to the Bellman principle, the optimal consumption-investment path over the agent's time horizon must be such that, at any point in time, it must be optimal for the remaining period.

$$P_j(t) = P_0(t)E_t(P_j(t+1)) + F_2(t)\text{Cov}_t\big(P_j(t+1), W_{t+1}\big)$$
$$+ F_3(t)\text{Cov}_t\big(P_j(t+1), W_{t+1}^2\big) + \dots \qquad (14.34)$$

where W is both the aggregate wealth and the global market portfolio, and $F_k(t)$ is a market 'price of co-moments.' Clearly, equation (14.34) is equivalent to the moment-pricing function (14.6).

Is this a 'theory' of asset pricing? Viewed in these terms, the CAPM and its generalizations appear as a 'theory' of assets prices no more than the bill handed over to us before leaving a supermarket represents a theory of prices of consumer goods.

Of course, we can *interpret* the observed price of the market portfolio as the ultimate result of agents' expected utility maximization, supplemented by the execution of all possible arbitrages. Consequently, we may continue interpreting the CAPM as a theory based on expected utility maximization, provided that we are willing to accept all the critiques addressed to expected utility.

Solving paradoxes

The St. Petersburg paradox

Recall that, in the introduction, we mentioned the St. Petersburg game and Daniel Bernoulli's solution in terms of expected (log-)utility:[13]

Flip	Probability of a head	Prize
1	½	1
2	¼	2
...	...	...
n	$1/2^n$	2^{n-1}
...	...	...

$$U(G) = \sum_{n=1}^{\infty} U(2^{n-1})\frac{1}{2^n} < +\infty$$

---

[13] Note that Bernoulli's solution has limited validity, because, given U, it may be possible to find a lottery with prize w_n such that $U(w_n) = 2^{n-1}$ – i.e. $w_n = U^{-1}(2^{n-1})$ – so that the expected utility is infinite. This is the so-called Karl Menger superparadox (Menger, 1934), implying a limited U for the expectation to be finite. A different solution is provided by Whittle (1992: 65), using a discount factor.

Alternatively, the price G of the game can be obtained, in our approach, by considering the sequential game as a one-shot game (a lottery) with an infinity of tickets, identified by the natural numbers $(1, 2, ..., n, ...)$ with decreasing probability of extraction $(\frac{1}{2}, \frac{1}{4}, ..., 1/2^n, ...)$ and increasing prize $(1, 2, ..., 2^{n-1}, ...)$. This means that the original game is a portfolio of sub-games (one for each row in the table above) the first of which implies a prize of 1 if we get a head at the first flip and 0 otherwise, the second of which implies a prize of 2 if we get a head at the second flip and 0 otherwise, the n-th of which implies a prize of 2^{n-1} if we get a head at the n-th flip and 0 otherwise.

Clearly, each ticket could be sold separately at its price G_n, and the price of the lottery is the sum of the prices of its tickets. For each ticket, n, the expected value is always $\frac{1}{2}$ and the standard deviation is $0.5(2^n-1)^{0.5}$:

$$mean = 2^{n-1}\frac{1}{2^n} + 0(1 - \frac{1}{2^n}) = \frac{1}{2}$$

$$variance = (2^{n-1} - \frac{1}{2})^2\frac{1}{2^n} + (0 - \frac{1}{2})^2(1 - \frac{1}{2^n}) = \frac{2^n - 1}{4}$$

Ticket	Probability	Prize	Expected prize	Standard deviation
1	$\frac{1}{2}$	1	$\frac{1}{2}$	0.50
2	$\frac{1}{4}$	2	$\frac{1}{2}$	0.87
...	...	...	...	...
n	$\frac{1}{2}^n$	2^{n-1}	$\frac{1}{2}$	$0.5^*(2^n-1)^{0.5}$
...	...	...	...	...

Considering the first two moments and taking, for simplicity, the standard deviation as a proxy for the risk, the price of the n-th ticket is

$$G_n = \begin{cases} \frac{1}{2}P_0 + \frac{\sqrt{2^n - 1}}{2}P_\sigma & \text{if positive, i.e. if } \quad n < n° \equiv \dfrac{\ln\left(1 + \left(\frac{P_0}{P_\sigma}\right)^2\right)}{\ln 2} \\ 0 & \text{otherwise} \end{cases}$$

where the limited liability provision has been applied and the price of the game is just the sum of the (positive) prices of all tickets:

$$G = \sum_{n=1}^{\infty} G_n = \sum_{n=1}^{\infty} \max(\frac{P_0}{2} + \frac{P_\sigma}{2}\sqrt{2^n - 1}, 0)$$

For example, if $P_0 = 1$ and $P_\sigma = -0.134$ then $n° = 5.8$ and $G = 1.507$. This means that coin tosses beyond the fifth have no economic value.[14]

The Allais paradox

The Allais (1953) paradox was the first factual evidence against expected utility.

In fact, asking people to choose between games A and B, where A gives 1 million with certainty ($p_2 = 100\%$) and B gives 1 million with only 89 percent probability and 0 or 5 million with the remaining chances ($p_1 = 1\%$, $p_3 = 10\%$):

$$A = \begin{cases} 1 \quad 100\% \end{cases} \qquad B = \begin{cases} 0 \quad 1\% \\ 1 \quad 89\% \\ 5 \quad 10\% \end{cases}$$

people prefer in large majority A to B: $A \succ B$

Then, asking them to choose between A' and B', defined by

$$A' = \begin{cases} 0 \quad 89\% \\ 1 \quad 11\% \end{cases} \qquad B' = \begin{cases} 0 \quad 90\% \\ 5 \quad 10\% \end{cases}$$

the same people very often prefer B' to A': $B' \succ A'$.

The paradox stems from the fact that, from $A \succ B$, the expected utility approach deduces $A' \succ B'$, which is at variance with the experimental evidence (Allais reports that in 53 percent of cases there was a violation of the logical implication).

In fact, $A \succ B$ means $U(1) > 0.01U(0) + 0.89U(1) + 0.10U(5)$, but collecting $U(1)$ and adding to both members of the inequality $0.89U(0)$ you obtain, algebraically, $0.89U(0) + 0.11U(1) > 0.9U(0) + 0.10U(5)$ – i.e. $A' \succ B'$ – against the empirical evidence. According to Allais, either people in experimental situations do not use the rational thinking used in real-world decision-making,[15] or people do not follow the expected utility paradigm.

In fact, using our approach, the rationality of the choices actually made in the experiment may be recognized easily. Considering each lottery as an asset, the first four moments are:

---

[14] A refined price G could be also obtained using higher moments: the skewness of the n-th ticket is $[0.25(2^n - 1)(2^{n-1}-1)]^{1/3}$; the kurtosis is $[(2^n - 1)((2^n - 1)^3 + 1)/2^{n+4}]^{1/4}$.

[15] Savage (1972: chap. 5) himself makes the 'error' when asked to make his choices.

	A	B	A'	B'
Mean, μ	1.000	1.390	0.110	0.500
Standard deviation, σ	0	1.207	0.313	1.500
Skewness, ς	0	1.666	0.424	2.080
Kurtosis, κ	0	2.032	0.513	2.531

Assuming the following prices of the four moments,

$$P_0 = 1, P_\sigma = -0.34, P_\varsigma = 0.01, P_\kappa = -0.001$$

we obtain the prices of the lotteries, $P(A) = 1 > P(B) = 0.994$ and $P(A') = 0.007 < P(B') = 0.008$, in accordance with the Allais experiments.

This means that, using the Marschak triangle, as in Machina (1987), the indifference curves in our approach are non-linear in the probabilities and may display a 'fanning out' effect from the sure event A as implied in actual behavior.

The Kahneman and Tversky (1979) paradox

In a famous experiment, a systematic violation of the independence axiom has been documented: 80 percent of ninety-five respondents preferred A to B where

$$A = \{\, 3{,}000 \quad 100\% \qquad B = \begin{cases} 0 & 20\% \\ 4{,}000 & 80\% \end{cases}$$

65 percent preferred B' to A' where

$$A' = \begin{cases} 0 & 75\% \\ 3{,}000 & 25\% \end{cases} \qquad B' = \begin{cases} 0 & 80\% \\ 4{,}000 & 20\% \end{cases}$$

and more than 50 percent of respondents violated the independent axiom, given that, if Q pay 0 for certain, then[16]

$$A' = \begin{cases} Q & 75\% \\ A & 25\% \end{cases} \qquad B'' = \begin{cases} Q & 75\% \\ B = \begin{cases} 0 & 20\% \\ 4{,}000 & 80\% \end{cases} & 25\% \end{cases}$$

and B'' is considered equal to B' in terms of outcomes and probabilities.

---

[16] Note that treating lotteries as assets implies that linear combinations such as $0.75Q + 0.25A$ are meaningful and $P(0.75Q + 0.25A) = 0.25P(A) \neq P(A')$.

The point is that, in terms of valuation, B' and B'' are not the same asset, and B'' is equivalent to

$$B'' = \begin{cases} 0 & 75\% \\ P(B) & 25\% \end{cases} \neq B' = \begin{cases} 0 & 80\% \\ 4000 & 20\% \end{cases}$$

Using the first four moments:

	A'	B	B'
Mean, μ	750	3200	800
Standard deviation, σ	1299.04	1600	1600
Skewness, ς	1362.84	−1831.54	1831.54
Kurtosis, κ	1605.52	2148.28	2148.28

and assuming the following prices of the four moments:

$$P_0 = 1, P_\sigma = -0.2, P_\varsigma = 0.1, P_\kappa = -0.001$$

we obtain the prices of the lotteries: $P(A) = 3000 > P(B) = 2694.70$ and $P(A') = 624.87 < P(B') = 661.01$, in accordance with the experimental results. Note also that $P(B'') = 561.28 < P(A') < P(B')$.

The Tversky and Kahneman (1981) paradox

Most subjects, in face of the following alternatives – A versus B and A' versus B' – prefer B to A, but also A' to B' where

$$A = \begin{cases} 0 & 75\% \\ 30 & 25\% \end{cases} \qquad B = \begin{cases} 0 & 80\% \\ 45 & 20\% \end{cases}$$

$$A' = \begin{cases} 0 & 75\% \\ 30 & 25\% \end{cases} \qquad B' = \begin{cases} 0 & 75\% \\ B'' = \begin{cases} 0 & 20\% \\ 45 & 80\% \end{cases} & 25\% \end{cases}$$

The paradox (a 'reversal' or 'isolation' effect) stems from the fact that not only does $A = A'$ but also $B = B'$ in terms of ultimate outcomes and probabilities.

From the point of view of our theory of valuation and choice, however, the two-stage frame in B' is not irrelevant: in B, not 0 means 45; in B', not 0 means a new game B'', which can be sold for a certain price.

Using the first four moments:

	$A = A'$	B	B''
Mean, μ	7.5	9.0	36.0
Standard deviation, σ	12.99	18.00	18.00
Skewness, ς	13.628	20.605	−20.605
Kurtosis, κ	16.055	24.168	24.168

and assuming the following prices of the four moments:

$$P_0 = 1, P_\sigma = -0.2, P_\varsigma = 0.05, P_\kappa = -0.1$$

we obtain the prices of the lotteries: $P(A) = 3.98 < P(B) = 4.01$ and $P(A') = 3.98 > P(B') = 3.84$, being $30 > P(B'') = 28.95$. This result is in accordance with the Tversky and Kahneman (1981) experiment, showing that, in effect, no paradox is implied in the observed behavior.

In particular, note again that in terms of valuation

$$B' = \begin{cases} 0 & 75\% \\ B'' = \begin{cases} 0 & 20\% \\ 45 & 80\% \end{cases} & 25\% \end{cases} \quad \text{is} \quad B' = \begin{cases} 0 & 75\% \\ P(B'') & 25\% \end{cases} \quad \text{and not}$$

$$B = \begin{cases} 0 & 80\% \\ 45 & 20\% \end{cases}$$

and the risk-neutral probabilities for B'' are given by

$$B'' = \begin{cases} 0 & 1 - \dfrac{28.95}{45} \approx 36\% \\ 45 & \dfrac{28.95}{45} \approx 64\% \end{cases}$$

This observation also holds for Harry Markowitz's (1959) formulation of Allais's experiment:

$$B' = \begin{cases} 1 & 89\% \\ B'' = \begin{cases} 5 & 91\% \\ 0 & 9\% \end{cases} & 11\% \end{cases} \quad \text{is} \quad B' = \begin{cases} 1 & 89\% \\ P(B'') & 11\% \end{cases} \quad \text{and not}$$

$$B = \begin{cases} 1 & 89\% \\ 5 & 10\% \\ 0 & 1\% \end{cases}$$

For other examples of violation of the independence axiom, see Machina (1987) and Fishburn (1988 chap. 2).

Conclusions

According to a common point of view in finance, the CAPM (static as well as intertemporal) is a theory of asset pricing based on the maximization of the *expected utility* of future wealth. We have solved a simpler problem, by applying the observed market price of a unit of future expected money and the market price of a unit of risk to the amount of future money and risk borne by an asset, and we have obtained the CAPM. If it were possible, we would expect that John Hicks would consent to the procedure we have followed.

In fact, extending the Hicksian suggestion from the theory of money to the theory of asset prices, we have defined utility in terms of ordinal preferences on moments so that assets and portfolios, like Lancaster's (1966) consumption goods, are bundles of different measurable characteristics (moments). In such a way we have obtained a pricing formula without any assumption on expected utility maximization.

Asset prices are given in terms of one, two, and higher moments; moments are priced at the margin on the market, and the resulting pricing function is in agreement with previous results, such as CAPM and the Black and Scholes option-pricing model. The ordinal utility does not require any 'independence axiom,' and we are able, therefore, to solve straightforwardly the St. Petersburg, the Allais, the Kahneman and Tversky, and other paradoxes.

Commenting on their expected utility theorem, von Neumann and Morgenstern (1947: 28) wonder: 'Have we not shown too much?' Analogously (*si parva licet...*), we could ask: 'Have we not obtained too much generality?' Using the words of Yakov Amihud (1979): 'If no preference of any particular form is admitted what accounts for the violation? ...a more general formulation of the axioms takes its toll in a poorer predictive power.' Differently from Allais's (1979) construction, however, we used the von Neumann and Morgenstern set-up, but we stopped at the ordinal utility level.

The generality of the functional form of utility $H(.)$ has the same meaning as the passage from Bernoulli's log-utility to the Bernoullian $U(.)$. Moreover, the considered moments are, explicitly or implicitly, priced in the financial market (Carr and Madan, 1998), so the question of how many of them are to be included in the model is essentially an empirical one: we have to take into account all moments having non-zero market prices.

The fact that many people behave according to the expected utility theory and many others do not could be tackled in two different ways: (i) trying to show that some are wrong (or irrational or confused) and some are right; or (ii) trying to build, from first principles, a generalized approach that encompasses both types of behavior and is accessible to empirical measurement and test. We have followed the second route.

Part IV

Capital and Dynamics

15 'Distribution and Economic Progress' after seventy years

Robert M. Solow

Introductory remarks

The Theory of Wages, published in 1932, was John Hicks's first book. I was surprised to discover (from a later[1] 'Commentary') that he began professional life fresh out of Oxford as a labor economist whose first two published articles dealt with wages in the building trades and the history of industrial conciliation in the United Kingdom (Hicks, 1963: 318).

In his 'Commentary' on the original text, Hicks remarks that 1932 was the worst possible time to produce a rather classical book on the theory of wages. Edward Chamberlin's treatise on monopolistic competition and Joan Robinson's on imperfect competition came out in 1933, and John Maynard Keynes was already beginning to develop the ideas that became *The General Theory*. Hicks was unaware of any of this. He was 'out of tune' with Cambridge.

He tells an entertaining story about his first visit to the United States in 1946 (*ibid.*: 311). He found that he was being welcomed, not as the author of *Value and Capital* (1939a), of which he was proud, but as the author of *The Theory of Wages*, which he was in a mood to repudiate. He mentions a dinner at Harvard with a small group of 'eminent economists' unnamed except for Joseph Schumpeter, though I could make an educated guess at some of the others. '[W]e spent the evening, I trying to persuade them that [it] was a thoroughly bad book, they trying to persuade me that it was a good one.'

At that time I was a returned soldier, finishing my interrupted undergraduate degree at Harvard University and already taking some graduate

---

[1] The book was reissued in 1963, augmented by (i) Gerald Shove's adverse review in the *Economic Journal* (Shove, 1933), (ii) Hicks's short article called 'Wages and Interest: the Dynamic Problem' from *The Economic Journal* (Hicks, 1935c), (iii) Hicks's second shot at chapter 6, 'Distribution and Economic Progress: a Revised Version,' from *The Review of Economic Studies* (Hicks, 1936b), (iv) a long 'Commentary' on the text of the first edition, and (v) some 'Notes on the Elasticity of Substitution.' My references are all to this second edition, because these addenda are at the center of interest.

courses in economics. I would have enjoyed being a waiter at that dinner; all I can say is that my interpretation of the conversation would be a little different. Schumpeter was a famous flatterer, especially of anyone who could do some mathematics. And Wassily Leontief, who was certainly at that dinner, was already using part I of *Value and Capital* as the main text in his basic graduate course in economic theory; it was probably the first serious book on economic theory that I ever read. My guess is that some serious play-acting was going on in the Harvard faculty club that evening.

Economic progress and the distribution of national income

It is not my intention to survey the whole of *The Theory of Wages* in order to decide who was right at that dinner. My focus will be entirely on chapter 6, famously entitled 'Distribution and Economic Progress.' In it, Hicks takes up the question placed at the center of political economy by Thomas Malthus and David Ricardo: how does economic progress affect the distribution of the national income among the broad factors of production? The classical economists would have meant land, labor and capital, and of course they worried about rent; Hicks adopts the modern habit of omitting land – and thus natural resources – and I shall follow him. It is certainly simpler that way, though by now we have a better idea about how to deal with renewable and exhaustible natural resources.

By 'economic progress' Hicks means increases in working population and the stock of capital goods, and also invention, the advance of technology. Under the maintained assumption of universal constant returns to scale, he has to answer two questions. What is likely to happen to the equilibrium distribution of income as capital intensity – the capital/labor ratio – rises through time? And how can one classify inventions to highlight their distributional effects? On both these issues, Hicks's chapter 6 breaks new ground.

Equilibrium distribution and capital intensity

On the first distributional question, Hicks introduces into the literature the concept of the elasticity of substitution, and gives the standard formula for it (Hicks, 1963: 244, or, better, 245).[2] He uses this newly defined

---

[2] This gave rise to a flood of comments, mostly in *The Review of Economic Studies* from 1933 to 1936, by almost everyone who was anyone in English-speaking economics: Robinson, Paul Sweezy, Richard Kahn, Abba Lerner, Lorie Tarshis, James Meade, Arthur Pigou, David Champernowne, Fritz Machlup. It would be a different sort of exercise to go back and puzzle out what they were all up to.

parameter to provide a formula for the derived demand for a factor of production, and to discuss, in a now familiar way, how the relative shares of capital and labor in output will respond to a change in the capital/labor ratio. There is a lot to be said on this topic, and I intend to return to it.

Everyone is now familiar with the idea of a 'Hicks-neutral' technological change, and, by implication, the classification of inventions that goes along with it. Hicks says (*ibid.*: 121–2):

If we concentrate on two groups of factors of production, 'labour' and 'capital', and suppose them to exhaust the list, then we can classify inventions according as their initial effects are to increase, leave unchanged, or diminish the ratio of the marginal product of capital to that of labour. We may call these inventions 'labour-saving', 'neutral' and 'capital-saving' respectively. 'Labour-saving' inventions increase the marginal product of capital more than they increase the marginal product of labour; 'capital-saving' inventions increase the marginal product of labour more than that of capital; 'neutral' inventions increase both in the same proportion.

It is obvious, then, that a labor-saving invention increases the share of capital at the original capital/labor ratio, and so on for the other two cases.

It may be worth reminding a modern reader that *labor-augmenting* inventions are not necessarily labor-saving. They increase the ratio of 'effective' labor to capital and thus tend to increase the relative marginal product of capital; but the direct effect of the invention tends to increase the marginal product of a 'natural' unit of labor. The net effect depends on the elasticity of substitution: the relative share of capital will rise, stay the same, or fall according as the elasticity of substitution is less than, equal to, or greater than one. 'Labor-augmenting' equals 'labor-saving' only in the first case. Despite this additional complication, recent studies of the bias of technological change have tended to focus on relative factor augmentation, probably because it lends itself to econometric estimation and testing. (Indiscriminate use of the Cobb–Douglas production function, primarily for the sake of simplicity, tends to blur the whole issue.)

The induced bias of inventions

Hicks goes on to use this classification in an attempt to say something about the induced bias of inventions – that is, about endogenous forces that create a tendency at one time or another for inventions to be predominantly labor-saving or otherwise. Here he is not so successful.

He begins with the judgment that most inventions are in fact labor-saving. 'It is indeed difficult to find clear cases of important capital-saving inventions – wireless is, of course, the standard case, but beyond that, although there can be little doubt that capital-saving inventions occur, they are not easily identified. Obvious labour-saving inventions, on the other hand, are frequent' (1963: 123–4). That may have been a reasonable conjecture in 1932; it is far less obvious now in the heyday of computers, information technology, and telecommunications. It may, however, still be true.

Needless to say, Hicks does not want to attribute any such bias toward labor-saving invention to mere happenstance. Instead he proposes an endogenous mechanism. 'A change in the relative prices of the factors of production is itself a spur to invention, and to invention of a particular kind – directed to economising the use of a factor which has become relatively expensive' (*ibid.*: 124). As a matter of fact, capital accumulates more rapidly than the labor force grows. By itself, this would create a tendency for wage rates to rise relative to the price of capital services. The consequence is an induced bias toward labor-saving inventions that keeps this tendency in check.

There is probably something to this, but the case is not quite that simple. Most of the time – this is equilibrium economics, after all – the ratio of price to marginal product is approximately equalized across factors. It is not clear which factor price, if any, is out of line. One can imagine some sort of extrapolation going on, but the process would be fairly complicated, and inferences would be tenuous at best.

Hicks recognized from the start that some significant fraction of inventions would be autonomous, responsive not to current or anticipated factor prices, but to the internal logic of science – not to mention pure chance. The bias of autonomous inventions is likely, then, to be near-random, at least in the long run. This leaves Hicks with the presumption of some overall labor-saving bias in technical change. That is an extrapolation from facts, however, not a theoretical imperative. Hicks might have changed his mind after contemplating the computer revolution.

The elasticity of substitution: a broad view

I return now to the elasticity of substitution, beginning with the observation that the discussion of invention was not simply a digression. Nowadays it is customary to think of the elasticity of substitution as just a parameter of a production function. As early as the 1932 text, however, Hicks took a broader – and, in my opinion, more useful – view. He points out (1963: 120) that substitution between capital and labor can take any or all of three quite different forms. One of them, actually the second on his list, is the conventional movement along a known production function induced by a change in relative factor prices. This is what most contemporary economists have in mind. Another is the induced invention, the tendency of a rise in a factor's relative price to stimulate the search for inventions whose bias is precisely to economize on the use of that very factor. A gross look at aggregate time series would once have interpreted that as just another case of substitution, but we are more sophisticated now.

The third form, the first on his list, is potentially very important. When the price of factor X rises, goods and services that are currently especially X-intensive will rise in cost relative to the rest. If that cost change is reflected in prices, X-intensive goods will become more expensive than others. Buyers can be expected to shift their purchases from X-intensive goods to others. This is a force tending to make aggregate production less X-intensive even without any change in factor use within any industry.

Commodity elasticity of substitution and technical elasticity of substitution

There is, of course, a lot of general equilibrium machinery grinding away behind the scenes here, including the little matter of what made the relative price of X rise in the first place. If, for instance, it was an increase in the supply of non-X factors, then the process – if there is one – of getting the increment to non-X employed can be viewed as an economy-wide reduction in the X-intensity of production. The demand function side of this adjustment can be as important as the production function side, perhaps considerably more so. In a one-good economy, this process disappears from view, but it should leave traces in the economist's sense of the likely numerical value of the aggregative elasticity of substitution. This is not an obscure line of thought, but it is remarkable that it was clear to Hicks in 1932 at the moment of the invention of the elasticity of substitution.

He gets further with this issue in the 1963 'Revised Version' of chapter 6. (The enabling impulse may have been the working out, in 1934, of the famous 'A Reconsideration of the Theory of Value' with Roy Allen. Hicks liked to obliterate, as best he could, the rather elementary mathematics behind his results; Allen was not so shy.) The main result is a formula (Hicks, 1963: 298, footnote 2) for the 'commodity elasticity of substitution' that has to be added to the 'technical elasticity of substitution' to answer the canonical question mentioned earlier. I will not bother to reproduce this formula, as I have not bothered to reproduce the well-known formula for the technical elasticity. I do, however, want to quote part of the relevant passage (298–9).

In order for A's relative share to increase when its supply increases, it is only necessary that the combined elasticity of substitution should be greater than unity.

A qualification to this conclusion is, however, necessary. The changes in the relative demands for products may not be only due to the changes in relative price of the products. They may also be affected by any change in the size or distribution of the aggregate income which follows from the change in factor supply. If, in the new situation, consumers of relatively labour-using products have become richer relative to consumers who spend most of their money on products which need a great deal of capital, this is going to increase the relative share of capital. But this is not an effect about which much can be said.

The insight about income effects is excellent and potentially important. In the 1963 'Commentary' (341), Hicks remarks that very strong income effects can change the quantitative implications of his theory, and can even eliminate the possibility of equilibrium. My guess is that this sort of outcome is highly unlikely in a world with very many commodities. Edmond Malinvaud has quite recently come back to this question in a somewhat different model context (see below). His judgment is that distribution-induced income effects are not likely to play a major role in practice, and I share that intuition.

Multisectoral analysis

This whole range of questions has not had as much subsequent discussion as it deserves, probably because so much of modern growth theory lives in a one-sector model. I want to mention two valuable exceptions.

The first is by Ronald W. Jones (1965). He analyzes with great clarity a complete (real) two-factor/two-good model formulated so that it will fit neatly into a two-country model of international trade or a two-sector (consumer goods and capital goods) growth model. In a section on 'The Aggregate Elasticity of Substitution' he calculates the elasticity of the wage/rental ratio with respect to the relative endowments of labor and land or capital. (Obviously, this is enough to determine the response of relative shares to changes in factor supplies.) The answer is shown to depend on all the parameters of the model, including an economy-wide elasticity of substitution that is a weighted average of the technical elasticities in the two sectors and the commodity elasticity of substitution on the demand side. The underlying model is not exactly the one Hicks had in mind, so the formulas are not quite the same. Jones has clearly carried the Hicks idea much closer to direct applicability in growth theory, however.

The second recent contribution is by Malinvaud (2002). The setting here is quite different: a model with n sectors, each producing a single commodity from two inputs, namely skilled and unskilled labor. The market for unskilled labor has an exogenous wage, and thus the possibility of unemployment. The basic theoretical question – aimed squarely at an important practical issue – is this: how does the aggregate demand for unskilled labor respond to a change in the exogenous wage? Both the demand-side elasticities and the technical elasticities in the various sectors will be involved in the answer.

Malinvaud calculates both the exact answer and the answer one would get from the natural aggregative model, and thus the aggregation error involved. He isolates precisely the income-related effects described by Hicks in the paragraph quoted earlier. He points out that income effects could in principle reverse the presumption that the economy-wide elasticity of substitution is larger than the technical elasticity; but he doubts that this would be the case in practice. There is a further interesting question as to how much distortion is introduced into our intuitive rules of thumb by the casual tendency to focus on the technical elasticity, and more narrowly on Cobb–Douglas and therefore on the undoubted charms of the number one.

The two components of the economy-wide elasticity

These charms have both a theoretical and an empirical basis. Many sorts of modeling, and especially growth-theoretic modeling, are much simpler and user-friendly when the elasticity of substitution is exactly one. One well-known instance is that any pattern of factor-augmenting technical change is Hicks-neutral. (Incidentally, both versions of chapter 6 were written before the rebirth of growth theory; but Hicks observes in the 'Commentary' [1963: 336–7, 364–6] that much of what he has written fits very well in that context, at least in steady states.)

On the empirical side, it is one of the most familiar of all stylized aggregative facts that even fairly dramatic shifts in the relative supplies of labor and capital and (therefore?) in relative factor prices seem to be accompanied by rather minor changes in factor shares. (Hicks had an inkling of this from the work of Arthur Bowley.) An easy way to rationalize this regularity is through the Cobb–Douglas production function. Even more to the point, any attempt to estimate the elasticity of substitution using data that include or imply relative shares is pretty sure to come up with a number near one.

An interesting question of interpretation arises here. If the economy-wide elasticity of substitution, including the demand-side component, is actually near one, then the technical elasticity should be smaller than one, at least if the demand-side effect is not negligible. One way to look at this would be to compare estimates made using information on relative shares with estimates made strictly from 'physical' input-output data. Time-series estimates of this latter kind tend to be very uncertain, however, because of strong collinearity; and cross-section estimates tend to require implausible assumptions. I am not aware of any attempts to estimate the two components of the economy-wide elasticity simultaneously. It would certainly not be easy to do. Even 'the' technical elasticity of substitution is really an endogenously weighted average of the technical elasticities for each produced good, as mentioned in the report above on Ronald Jones's paper.

Substitution-driven growth

Hicks knew the Cobb–Douglas function, of course, but he did not know the formula for a production function with an arbitrary but constant elasticity of substitution(CES). It was not written out and discussed until 1964. A difficult question of judgment arises in the context of growth theory. Suppose I am using the conventional one-sector model to analyze some problem, understanding full well its metaphorical character. If I choose to represent the technology by a CES function, should I calibrate it – implicitly or explicitly – to the technical elasticity of substitution or to the economy-wide elasticity?

From all that has been said so far, the economy-wide version might be expected to give a better account of the distributional implications of a growth path. On the other side of the balance, however, we need the production function to translate inputs of labor and accumulated capital into output of the composite commodity, and that suggests the narrowly technical version. Nonetheless, that consideration does not seem to be decisive even on its own terms: the economy-wide elasticity should give a more accurate picture of the pace at which increasing capital intensity runs into diminishing returns, and that is an essential feature of any growth model. I do not know that there is a definite answer to this tactical question, which is why I referred to it as a matter of judgment. One possible inference, perhaps, is that we ought at least to think about the implications of a larger elasticity of substitution than we are used to considering.

Olivier de La Grandville and I have done exactly that in a paper that will appear as a chapter in a forthcoming book by him (de La Grandville and Solow, forthcoming). I will conclude this tribute to John Hicks by mentioning a few of our results that bear directly on the issues he pioneered in that famous chapter on 'Distribution and Economic Progress.'

It has long been understood that sustained neoclassical growth is feasible without technical progress, provided that the elasticity of substitution is sufficiently larger than one. A straightforward calculation tells us just how large. The condition is that $\sigma > \{1 + (\log \delta)/\log[s/(n+\lambda)]\}^{-1}$, where $0 < \delta < 1$ is the so-called distribution parameter in the CES function, s is the ratio of saving/investment to output, n is the rate of population growth, and λ is the rate of labor-augmenting technological change (and can be set at zero in the case without invention). This is for the CES case with elasticity of substitution equal to σ; more generally, the condition can be read as applying to the limiting value of the elasticity of substitution for very high capital intensity. When the threshold condition is met, growth is feasible without technical change (or, more generally, feasible at a rate definitely higher than the rate of labor-augmenting technical change). Moreover, the asymptotic rate of growth depends on the saving/investment rate s.

In words, this inequality says that the threshold value of the elasticity of substitution is smaller the less 'important' capital is as an input, the bigger the saving rate, and the smaller the population growth rate. The paper by de La Grandville and Solow provides some numerical values: for example, when $s = 0.2$, $n = 0.01$, and $\delta = 0.33$, the elasticity of substitution must exceed 1.58. That is larger than the numbers we are used to seeing in applications of growth theory; but it is not outlandishly larger, and certainly not if the Hicks–Jones–Malinvaud commodity elasticity is still to be factored into the computation. Evidently, it would be useful to have some approximate numerical range for this important and neglected elasticity.

This result has implications for the distributional issue that was central to Hicks's concerns in 1932. The threshold value of σ is clearly greater than one. If this sort of substitution-driven growth is occurring over and above technological progress, therefore, the share of capital must be increasing as the capital/labor ratio rises. What is more, the capital share tends eventually to one. The absolute wage bill may increase indefinitely, but the (competitively imputed) relative share of labor must dwindle to zero.

Is this a very bad thing? That depends on the ownership of capital (which has to be defined to include human as well as physical capital). What matters for good or ill is, presumably, the personal distribution of income, not the functional. If the ownership of capital were widely and equitably dispersed, one might argue that it would be a good outcome if income from work were to become a negligible part of total income. The only work that would get done then would be whatever pleased the doers of it, either for its own sake or in exchange for extraordinarily high wages. If, in the opposite case, most of the valuable capital were owned by a relatively small capitalist class who received almost all the national income, that would be a different story. Those of us with a taste for equality and democracy would not find the prospect pleasing.

Concluding remarks

As I stipulated at the beginning, I have paid careful attention only to chapter 6 of *The Theory of Wages*, and its various offshoots. I have laid no groundwork for an evaluation of Hicks's first book as a whole. Nevertheless, I will end with a few words about Hicks's 1963 statement (311) that, as of the late 1930s, 'I had reached a point when I should have been very happy if it could be forgotten.'

This is not an altogether atypical remark from Hicks. In the normal course of events, anything – especially a whole book – that an economic theorist writes is likely to be overtaken by the later work of others. That is no cause for regret; it is how any discipline makes progress. Hicks seemed to have a hard time reconciling himself to this inevitable process, however. He was forever chiding himself in public for not having seen this, or done that. He sometimes seemed to feel that no thought had been properly thought unless John Hicks had thought it, preferably first. That is not all bad; it reflects a liking for fundamentals.

In fact, *The Theory of Wages* was a good book for its time. That verdict certainly comes out of this inspection of 'Distribution and Economic Progress.' It was not perfect, and became less so as time went on. Hicks was evidently stung by Shove's review, because he realized that Shove had a point. (It was an honest and courageous act to reprint the review in the second edition of the book.) It was not a book in want of repudiation, though, just because macroeconomics was being reformed in Cambridge and elsewhere.

The analysis of the determination of wages and employment has remained contentious within economics up to and including today. Fashions come and go, partly as a result of changing intellectual styles and partly because the relevant facts and institutions evolve irreversibly. The process does not come back to where it was before, but traces out a sort of spiral. One hopes it spirals up, not down. *The Theory of Wages* played an honorable part in that story.

16   Flexible saving and economic growth

Mauro Baranzini

Macroeconomic income distribution, inequality, and growth

Christopher Bliss, himself a distinguished scientist in the finest Oxbridge tradition, in his authoritative entry on 'Hicks, John Richard' written for *The New Palgrave*, writes:

> Hicks's huge output...is all the more remarkable when one considers that he has seldom simply reacted to the works of others. There are no papers by Hicks pointing out mistakes by other writers and none which embody minor changes to or extensions of existing models. Naturally Hicks has produced work which follows paths opened up by others. [...] There is a streak of self-centredness and parochialism in Hicks which mirrors that to be found in other English economists of his generation and those before. It would be insufferable in an economist less gifted and genuinely self-critical. (Bliss, 1987: 642)[1]

Bliss's arguments are forceful, and they may not be entirely shared by a number of his younger colleagues in Oxford. One might argue that

I am grateful to Roberto Scazzieri, Daniele Besomi, Cristina Marcuzzo, and Caterina Mari for their helpful discussion and criticism of earlier drafts of this chapter. I am also grateful to Amalia Mirante for her precious editorial assistance. My colleague Simona Cain deserves a mention for her penetrating criticism and linguistic insights. All responsibility, of course, remains with the author.

[1] Paul Samuelson (2001) entirely subscribes to Bliss's entry in *The New Palgrave*, and concludes his touching contribution 'My John Hicks' by stating: 'To the end Sir John Hicks was as he had been throughout his life: a loner scholar, for whom the sun rose in the morning when first he opened his eyes. His works constitute his immortality' (Samuelson, 2001: 4). Earlier on, when recalling his last meeting with the former Drummond Professor at Salzesbaden near Stockholm in 1987, Samuelson had this to say (4, footnote): 'Wanting to square the books before it was too late, John Hicks in private at Salzesbaden expressed worry that he had been remiss in properly citing my works parallel to his. Long earlier I had made the optimal adjustment to his manner of composition and I could see no point in worrying a doughty warrior at that stage of life. Therefore I assured him that always I had learned much from him (a literal truth); and that indeed I had early known the brief 1937 French version of his developed 1939 classic. Reassured, he confided: "Now that I am old and working alone, getting the big books off the library shelf is quite a chore and that inhibits my bibliographical accuracy." When I told Bob Solow this story he added: "Those books were always heavy on Sir John's shelves."'

Hicks's apparent reclusiveness might have been enhanced by the Oxbridge collegial system, which was a tradition devised to facilitate discussions and exchanges with fellows of other disciplines. It is much easier to imagine Sir John having morning coffee, lunch, afternoon tea, or dinner at All Souls College in Oxford with fellow historians, philosophers, and men of letters, rather than with fellow economists at the twice-a-term sub-faculty meetings (which were mainly about the PPE – politics, philosophy and economics – honours school, Oxford's pride and joy, set up in 1923).[2]

When, at the beginning of Michaelmas term 1971, I joined the Queen's College as a research student (unaware that I would spend the next fifteen years there), a mere few yards from the mythic All Souls College, I was surprised by the relatively little regard paid to Hicks's work in some of Oxford's official economics circles, starting with the sub-faculty of economics. One might nevertheless argue that, on the whole, during the long and prolific period which followed his retirement in 1965, Hicks was held in much higher esteem by foreign scholars and students visiting Oxford. Even the award of the Nobel Prize in 1972 (see Hamouda, 1993: 36–7) did little to re-establish his prominence among Oxford economists, many of whom were being chosen for high-ranking appointments at a relatively young age and on the basis of highly mathematical papers in equally technical economic journals. Alas, the time of system builders was drawing to an end. Until the late 1970s Hicks chaired an important seminar at All Souls, in which he would expound various parts of his latest work, with a crescendo during his retirement period – his 'Risorgimento' as he once put it (Hicks, 1979b; reprinted in Hicks, 1983a: 362).

Since in those days my own field of interest was economic growth, I was attracted, long before coming to Oxford, to his *Capital and Growth*, first published in 1965. It may be of some importance to recall what Hicks wrote in the preface to this work:

Though I have been influenced, in many ways, by the 'growth models' that swarm in economic literature, I have allowed myself to make less reference to the work of contemporaries than the reader may well feel that he would have preferred. The field is vast; and I am well aware that my knowledge of it is only a sample. Now, as I write this Preface, but after the body of the book has gone to the printer, there comes into my hand the 'Survey' by Hahn and Matthews (*Economic Journal*, December, 1964). If I had had this earlier (but it would have to have been much

---

Samuelson may well be right, but in fact Sir John's study room at the 'Porch House' in Blockley, which I had the privilege to visit in the 1980s with Roberto Scazzieri and my oldest daughter Moira, had hundreds of years earlier been the back shop of a butcher's; it had a high ceiling, and its top shelves, were indeed very high.

[2] Omas Hamouda (1993: 30) informs us that in the 1950s, while at Nuffield College, Hicks lobbied 'for a bipartite or single course devoted to economics rather than PPE.'

earlier) I might have made an attempt to give further references. As it is, I must leave the reader – with their help – to fill the gap for himself. (Hicks, 1965: vii)

This attitude was typical of the man, since he always wrote his contributions to economic analysis with detachment from the 'fashions' that often have a derailing effect on the progress of economics. Sir John belonged to that rare breed of path-breaking scholars with a strongly independent mind, who never allow themselves to be distracted by futile controversies or dead-end research lines.

Sir John Hicks and the Cambridge School of Distribution

John Hicks's association with the English Cambridge, as he would put it, is somewhat mysterious. We know that from 1935 to 1938 he was a lecturer in economics and fellow of Gonville and Caius College, Cambridge. As we shall see, during his stay there he was mainly occupied with the writing of *Value and Capital*, which he had largely conceived and initially drafted at the London School of Economics. His stay on the river Cam is condensed in his paper 'The Formation of an Economist,' written as one of a series of recollections by major economists, and published by the *Banca Nazionale del Lavoro Quarterly Review* in September 1979. He writes as follows:

It was not because I was becoming Keynesian (as in a sense I was) that in the summer of 1935 I removed to Cambridge. I went there in consequence of an invitation from Pigou, and it was because of the friendship I had already formed with Robertson that I was attracted. Cambridge, however, was already riven by disputes by Keynesians and anti-Keynesians. I found myself regarded, at least by some Keynesians, as being in the 'anti' camp. The ISLM version of Keynes's theory,[3] which I myself produced, but which has never been highly regarded by orthodox Keynesians, did not help me. (Hicks, 1979b; reprinted in Hicks, 1983a: 359–60)

To my knowledge, the best account of Hicks's stay in Cambridge is that provided by Hamouda (1993) in his long chapter 'Hicks the Man' (1–41). It is a very detailed and reliable description, a sort of dictated autobiography that elucidates a number of grey areas of Sir John's life. It seems that initially it was Hicks's friendship with Dennis Robertson that attracted him to Cambridge; as Hamouda duly notes, however,

Hicks's invitation to a university lectureship at Cambridge came from Pigou, the examination commissioner for whom Hicks had served as an external examiner in 1934. It had, however, most certainly been backed, if not proposed, by Robertson. Thus, when it came, Hicks unhesitantly accepted the appointment and the

[3] Hicks duly notes: 'Mr Keynes and the "Classics,"' in *Econometrica* (1937a).

election to a fellowship at Gonville and Caius College, and moved to Cambridge in the summer of 1935. He was, however, very surprised to find Robertson distant and uncommunicative and was immediately to miss the physical closeness and collaboration of other economists he had had within the LSE seminar group. (Hamouda, 1993: 19–20)

This situation must have been difficult for Hicks to accept, especially because he was more inclined to work and argue with colleagues, rather than waste his time in internal struggles.

It seems that through his acceptance of the position Hicks had been caught in an internal power struggle to determine the appointment to the post. Keynes and his partisans had favoured Joan Robinson as a candidate, and looking back Hicks came to think in his last years that Pigou and Robertson had probably invited him in an effort to keep Joan Robinson out. As a consequence, unbeknown to Hicks when he arrived in Cambridge, Robertson, and to a lesser extent Pigou, did not want to associate with him much, for fear that it might appear that they had indeed recruited him for their purposes. By the time *The General Theory* came out in early 1936, during Hicks's second term in Cambridge, the sides had begun to draw their dividing lines very sharply. Clearly ill at ease with the situation, Robertson kept a very low profile throughout. (*ibid.*: 20)

In this chapter I concentrate on the few certain and largely evasive links between John Hicks and the Cambridge post-Keynesian group of scholars that would, especially after the early 1950s, provide the foundations for the long-term theory of income distribution, profit determination, and capital accumulation. It is beyond doubt, however, that during his three years of stay in Cambridge Hicks was more concerned with the welfare economics research program that, in Cambridge, had already established a strong tradition, especially through Arthur Pigou, that later on would be followed by James Meade, David Champernowne, Anthony Atkinson, and even Amartya Sen. A number of Hicks's writings, published during his stay on the Cam or immediately afterwards, may be considered in this tradition. They include, apart from *Value and Capital* (1939a), at least parts of the following works: the review of S. M. de Bernardi (ed.), 'De l'utilité et de sa mesure par Jules Dupuit: écrits choisis et republiés,' for *Economica* (1935d); the review of Pigou's *The Economics of Stationary States* for *The Economic Journal* (1936d); 'Distribution and Economic Progress: a Revised Version' for *The Review of Economic Studies* (1936b); 'Economic Theory and the Social Sciences' for the Institute of Sociology's publication *The Social Sciences: Their Relations in Theory and in Teaching* (1936c); 'The Foundations of Welfare Economics' for *The Economic Journal* (1939b); and 'The Valuation of the Social Income' for *Economica* (1940).[4]

---

[4] For a complete list, see Hamouda (1993: 292–301).

The general impression is that, at least initially during his stay in Cambridge and thereafter for several years, Hicks felt no particular reason to show sympathy for Keynes's pupils and their works. It is a state of affairs that was to continue at least until the Cambridge post-Keynesian school gathered momentum from the early 1950s onwards, when Sir John, after a spell in Manchester (1939–48), had already reached his final destination at Oxford. Nonetheless, apart from the internal struggle between Pigou and Robertson, on the one hand, and Keynes and his 'circus,' on the other, why is it that Hicks wasn't drawn directly into Keynes's sphere of influence, as had been, and was to be, the case with other distinguished scholars?[5] Indeed, as Hamouda (1993: 22) notes, if Keynes and his followers had been more 'receptive and attentive to Hicks, Keynesian economics would have probably gained a very powerful ally.' To illustrate the irony of events, Hamouda adds what follows (22–3):

While at the LSE, Hicks had given the impression in his work that his ideas were converging with those of the Cambridge School. Once in Cambridge, however, he was neither trusted nor given the chance to develop his thoughts along lines that would have been favourably received here. A window was perhaps beginning to open just as he had decided there was no point in staying among the Cambridge economists. Despite the apparent lack of support from his colleagues, Hicks was eventually elected to the faculty board. By that time, however, he was set on leaving Cambridge, especially after he heard that Robertson was also departing.

Two points may be mentioned in this respect. The first relates to the different personalities at play. On the one hand, there was a quite intolerant and 'vociferous' (to say the least)[6] group of scholars who had been part of Keynes's 1930–1 'circus',[7] a fairly close group including Kahn, Joan Robinson, and only to a certain extent Piero Sraffa, and much later Kaldor. On the other hand, there was Hicks, whose main preoccupation was to write his *Value and Capital*, with a clear touch of 'self-centredness' (see Bliss, 1987: 642). This wide difference between Hicks and the younger generation of Cambridge economists loyal to Keynes was clearly aggravated by the following events mentioned by Hamouda:

The fact that Hicks's way of thinking persisted from his LSE days well into his time in Cambridge is not surprising, since he remained very much on his own. All in all Hicks had minimal contact with Keynes or his most devoted followers, Joan

---

[5] With some reservations, we may mention the two Oxonians, Meade and Roy Harrod; and, later on, Nicholas Kaldor, who came to Cambridge from the LSE.

[6] On November 12, 1936, Keynes in a letter to Joan Robinson writes: 'Your fierceness may quite possibly land you in trouble in some quarters...' (Moggridge, 1973b: 147).

[7] On the exact meaning and timing of the 'Cambridge circus,' see Richard Kahn (1984, 1985) and E. A. G. Robinson (1977, 1985).

Robinson and Richard Kahn. When Hicks first arrived in Cambridge, he had called on Joan Robinson. She was so hostile, however, that Hicks was not encouraged to do so again. Although during his LSE period Hicks had corresponded with Keynes, he did not actually meet him until May 1935 when he was interviewed in Cambridge, over lunch, by Keynes and Pigou for the position of university lecturer. Hicks was subsequently invited several times by Keynes to lunch, but Keynes's work and his weak health during most of the time that Hicks was in Cambridge seemed to preclude much more serious intellectual contact. 'I only just knew him personally; we had very little conversation on theoretical matters.' (Hamouda, 1993: 22)

The second point relates to the harsh opinion that the master of them all, John Maynard Keynes, had expressed on Hicks's *Theory of Wages* (eventually published in 1932 by Macmillan).[8] Keynes was justly famous for his cutting judgments of those who did not go along with his views; and Hicks, on the other hand, was already known for his distinguished scientific standing, certainly when he arrived in Cambridge in 1935. Around 1932 or 1933 Samuelson (2001: 2) at Chicago was told by his tutor that Keynes was 'the greatest economist in the world,' while around 1935 an assistant professor at Harvard was claiming that Hicks was the greatest young economist at that time. It should come as no surprise that in Cambridge the two kept apart.

More than of a quarter of a century was to elapse before Hicks's attention turned to the way in which the Cambridge post-Keynesian school tackled the issue of income distribution and profit determination. It starts to emerge in the last part of the preface of *Capital and Growth*, and then is confirmed in chapter 12, 'The Model in Outline,' which I consider in some detail below. It is probably not the straight U-turn that Joseph Halevi (2001: 78) maintains – 'The way in which Hicks argues against the assumption of a given aggregate saving ratio takes him straight into the Kaldor–Pasinetti Cambridge Equation' – but this avenue is worth considering with attention (see Harcourt, 1969, 1972, and Sen, 1963, 1970). Hicks discusses at length the approaches, or methods, that may be applied to deal with economic growth (or 'economic dynamics,' as he calls it). Recalling that he himself used three different methods for *The Theory of Wages* (1932), *Value and Capital* (1939a), and the *Trade Cycle* (1950a) respectively, and explaining that he still wants to 'stand by them all' (1965: v), he goes on (vi):

---

[8] Harold Macmillan on April 15, 1932, invited Keynes to referee the manuscript of *The Theory of Wages*; Keynes replied on April 27. This is reported in Moggridge (1983: 861–2). See also Andrew Schuller's contribution to this volume (chapter 5).

There is, however, another method, which is perhaps entitled to be regarded as being, in a special sense, the method of Growth Theory, on which in my books I have hitherto had little to say. This is the method which uses as its central concept the equilibrium of an expanding economy – an equilibrium towards which (as towards the static equilibrium of economic statics) there is supposed to be some sort of (strong or weak) tendency. There is a sense in which this concept (in its original form, derived from Harrod and Domar) does appear in my Trade cycle; but its appearance there is mainly for illustrative purposes – I did not myself attach much importance to it. This, I suspect, was a principal reason why the earlier stages of the new developments (at the hands of Joan Robinson and Kaldor at the English Cambridge) rather passed me by.

As one can infer from this passage, Hicks's turn is certainly significant. He adds:

I am ready to recognize that (especially on the mathematical side) the new approach has major achievements to its credit. There are some fundamental issues (such as the perennial question of the working of factor substitution) that it can go a long way towards clearing up. On this level the new growth theory is important; but if its importance is to be assessed – neither over- nor under-assessed – it has to be set out systematically. That is not a thing that can be done in an article; yet since Joan Robinson's *Accumulation of Capital* (1956) there has been no full-scale treatment. Much has happened since then of which it is necessary to take account.

Such a statement is quite unusual for Hicks, and denotes the relevance that growth theory in general and the approach of the Cambridge school in particular seemed to have for him. Two stages might be identified in his approach: first, he rejects the classical and neoclassical approaches to growth and distribution, by considering the hypothesis of a flexible saving rate (i.e. of a different propensity to save and to consume for the classes of the system) by developing a fully fledged distributional model starting from Sraffa's framework; second, he considers a normative model in which the equilibrium values of the macro-variables are determined by the maximizing behavior of individuals or classes.

We might say that, in this latter case, Hicks's approach to growth and distribution represents, to a certain extent at least, a natural continuation and development of his earlier works on welfare economics. In this way he came to bridge, without perhaps being fully aware that that was what he was doing, two of the Cambridge main research programs of the twentieth century. The first, on welfare economics, was 'founded' by Pigou and pursued, as said above, by Meade, Champernowne, Atkinson, Sen, and other scholars (including even Hicks), whose works include the study of normative economics and the distribution of personal income and wealth, embodying concern for justice and the protection of the interests of the less fortunate in our society. The second research program concerned the so-called Cambridge post-Keynesian school, which focused on capital theory, income distribution, profit determination, structural dynamics, and fiscal policies, with a strong accent on aggregate, or semi-aggregate, variables and the bypassing of the neoclassical production or utility function.[9] Among the most important scholars engaged in this programme we find the direct pupils of Keynes, Kahn and Robinson, and to a certain extent Sraffa; their group would be joined later on by Kaldor, Richard Goodwin, Luigi Pasinetti, Geoffrey Harcourt, and other distinguished scholars. The 'bridge' between the two research programs is well represented by chapter 21 ('Optimum Saving') and appendixes D and E of *Capital and Growth*, where a (social) utility function is postulated in order to find the level of consumption that maximizes total utility and at the same time yields the levels of consumption and savings that allow the system to place itself on a given growth path with well-defined properties. In this sense, Hicks anticipated a wide literature on growth and optimal savings, which would proliferate in the late 1960s and 1970s, and later still.[10]

A number of scholars have pointed out that Hicks's *Capital and Growth* (1965) and the more recent *Methods of Dynamic Economics* (1985a) represent a critical rethinking of *Value and Capital* (1939a).

[T]he intellectual project of *Capital and Growth* up to chapter 16 dealing with the Traverse combines a critical rethinking of the method of *Value and Capital* with a dialogue with the theoretical evolution taking place in Cambridge. In so doing Hicks integrated Sraffa's approach to prices of production with the Kaldor–Pasinetti theory of growth and distribution. The adoption of the Cambridge theory of distribution and of Sraffa's prices represented only a stepping stone to build a model of structural disequilibrium. In this case imbalances cannot be corrected just by resorting to either a flexible distribution of income – *à la* Kaldor – or to flexible production coefficients – *à la* Solow. (Halevi, 2001: 80)

Hicks had the 'habit' of making little reference to other scholars' works, and when he did so it was 'mainly in footnotes' (Bliss, 1987: 642). As anticipated above, in the preface to *Capital and Growth* he writes that, though influenced by the huge literature on economic growth, he has allowed himself 'to make less reference to the work of contemporaries than the reader may well feel that he would have preferred' (Hicks, 1965: vii). This is why chapter 12 of *Capital and Growth*, entitled 'The Model in

---

[9] A reconstruction of the related controversies concerning the so-called 'paradoxes' of (neoclassical) capital theory may be found in Pasinetti and Scazzieri (1987, 2008), while the analytical foundation and outcome of the discussion are clearly set out in Sraffa (1960, chaps. 6 and 12) and Samuelson (1966).

[10] The first work in this field is, of course, that of Frank P. Ramsey (1928).

Outline,' where he grafts his growth model onto the Cambridge theory of distribution, arguably represents a remarkable exception.

Additionally, the convergence between Hicks's and the Cambridge theory of growth and distribution (Kaldor being a representative member) has also been pointed out by Kaldor himself. In fact, in his biographical essay 'Recollections of an Economist' (1988), Kaldor points out that his own and Hicks's 'intellectual work continued to converge at unexpected points as shown e.g. by Hicks's book on the Trade Cycle (Hicks 1950) or his book on Capital and Growth (Hicks 1965), or his most recent paper on "Monetary theory and Monetary Experience" (Kaldor, 1988: 30, footnote).

The Harrod–Domar 'knife-edge' and possible solutions of the 'dilemma'

Walter Eltis, himself one of the most distinguished pupils of Harrod, in *The New Palgrave* introduces the Harrod–Domar growth model as follows:

The Keynesian revolution led Roy Harrod and Evsey Domar to work out the implications of permanent full employment. In *The General Theory of Employment, Interest and Money* (1936) Keynes himself showed how full employment could be reached, but he made no attempt to work out the long-term conditions which must be satisfied before an economy can continue to produce at that level. Harrod's and Domar's analyses of this problem show that long-term full employment requires that two fundamental conditions be satisfied. (Eltis, 1987: 602)

Such conditions are that (i) the economy must invest full employment-saving every year, and (ii) the rate of growth of output must be equal to the sum of the rate of growth of the labor force and of the rate of increase in labor productivity. As has been pointed out many times,[11] the Harrod–Domar equilibrium condition may be written as

$$g_n = \frac{s}{v}$$

where g_n is the natural rate of growth of the system (which may include 'labor-saving' technical progress), s is the aggregate saving ratio of the system, and v is the capital/output ratio. If these three variables are all constant then it is unlikely that such conditions may be satisfied. Hence, in order to have a model in which the possibility of steady growth is assured, it is necessary to relax one or more of the assumptions.

[11] See, for instance, Hahn and Matthews (1964), Pasinetti (1974, chap. 6), Hicks (1985a, chap. 13), and Eltis (1987).

In his *Methods of Dynamic Economics*, in part based on his *Capital and Growth*, Hicks skillfully sums up the dilemma as follows:

> The chief thing which has emerged from the Harrod-type theory…is that an economy which has been in long-term equilibrium at fixed prices (which are to be maintained) cannot adjust to a change in its desired growth rate, unless the propensity to save is varied, or the capital–output ratio is varied. If (Kaldor's point, of which we took account when we came to it)[12] there is a difference between the propensities to save out of wages and out of profits, and it is these propensities that are fixed, a new equilibrium can be found, provided that there is a suitable change in the rate of profit.[13] Indeed if anything emerges to change the overall propensity to save out of income in the right direction, along any channel, the Harrod difficulty can be got over. And, of course, if the change in the growth rate affects the capital–output ratio in the right direction, that also will help. (1985a: 131)

More generally, the Harrod–Domar 'truism,' as Eltis (1987) defines it, implies one or the other of the following cases, or combinations of cases:

(i)   flexibility of v, the capital/output ratio (also referred to as the technology assumption);

(ii) flexibility of s (saving assumption); or

(iii) flexibility of g_n (labor market and/or labor supply assumption).

The above cases may, of course, be combined in various ways, as, for instance, in Paul Samuelson and Franco Modigliani's (1966a, 1966b) models, where (i) and (ii) apply simultaneously. As is well known, solution (i) was adopted by the neoclassical or marginalist school. Of course, this solution of the Harrod–Domar dilemma was merely the beginning, however, for if, on the one hand, it was necessary to provide a device ensuring equilibrium growth, on the other hand it was necessary to define income distribution exhaustively. Hence, in order to make income distribution determinate, several assumptions were added, so that the neoclassical economists ended up with a model incorporating a 'well-behaved' constant-returns-to-scale aggregate production function, perfect substitutability between labor and capital, profit-maximizing behavior, and perfect competition in the labor and capital markets – all within a single-commodity framework. In this way, whenever Euler's theorem applies, both shares are simultaneously determined, and no residual, by definition, can exist.

---

[12] Kaldor is quoted various times in *Capital and Growth* (Hicks, 1965): on pages 13, 124, 145, 156, 171–80, and 274–5. The first time is in the 'Introduction,' where Hicks mentions the Cambridge school of distribution.

[13] In fact, according to the Cambridge equation the profit rate is equal to the equilibrium rate of growth of the system divided by the propensity to save out of profits, or of the capitalists' class.

The second answer to the Harrod–Domar dilemma: the assumption of a flexible aggregate saving ratio

The second answer to the Harrod–Domar dilemma – i.e. the assumption of a flexible aggregate saving ratio – was primarily adopted by the post-Keynesian or Cambridge, England, school of economic analysis. Of course, there are many ways in which one may lend flexibility to the average propensity to save, s; but the hypothesis of a two-class society (namely wage-earners and profit-earners; or consumers and entrepreneurs; or workers and capitalists), each with different constant average and marginal propensities to save, has played the greatest role in the last fifty years or so. In this way there always exists a distribution of income between the two classes (or, indeed, many classes)[14] that produces precisely the saving ratio that will equal the value $g_n (K/Y)$, where g_n is the rate of growth and K/Y is the capital/output ratio – thus satisfying the Harrod–Domar equilibrium condition.

The reasons for this approach may be found in the following considerations that have emerged with the elaboration of successive 'generations' of post-Keynesian (as well as a number of mixed post-Keynesians and neoclassical) models of profit determination and income distribution.

(i) The assumption of a uniform rate of saving for the whole economic system ignores all possible differences in saving – and consumption – behavior among different classes of income recipients, or categories of income, or even different sectors of the economy.

(ii) The problem of savings aggregation might give rise to particular and unknown difficulties, so it may be safer to consider it in a disaggregated way, exactly as the post-Keynesian model does.

(iii) This assumption also receives empirical support from the observed high rates of saving out of corporate profits and lower rates out of labor income. See, for instance, Kaldor (1966), Burmeister and Taubman (1969), Murfin (1980), and Baranzini (1991a).

(iv) The nature itself of the savings differs from class to class (see, for instance, Horioka and Watanabe, 1997). Jan Kregel (1973, chap. 11) justifies the distinction not so much on grounds of class position as on grounds of different forms of income – for instance, between 'quasi-contractual incomes' (e.g. wages, fixed interest, and rent) and 'residual incomes' (e.g. corporate profits). It is worth noting that, for Kaldor (1961: 194–5), residual incomes are much more uncertain than contractual incomes, and they are subject to fluctuations.

---

[14] As James Tobin (1960) and Pasinetti (1962, 1974: chap. 6) have shown.

(v) Finally, it may be argued (as Kaldor, 1961: 194–5, has done) that the need to generate internal funding in order to carry out active investment requires a high propensity to save out of profits. This requirement will be even stronger in a lifecycle model on a steady-state growth path, where the capitalists' saving ratio has to allow for (a) life cycle wealth accumulation and (b) the gradual accumulation of intergenerational assets in order to let the capitalists' wealth stock grow at the same rate as that of the population.

On this Hicks states:

The simplest thing which has gone wrong is that we have carried the assumption of saving proportional to total income, over from the Harrod-type theory (where it belongs) to the present theory, where it is much less at home. As soon as we make a distinction between factor shares (as in the Harrod-type theory we did not have to do), the question must arise: will not the saving-income proportion be affected by income distribution? (1965: 145)

At this point Sir John reflects upon two kinds of savings differentiation to be found in the literature:

It may be affected in a 'classical' manner – that a lower rate of profit makes people less willing to save; in a Growth Equilibrium (which is quite different from Keynes's theory) that is by no means to be ruled out. But it is quite sufficient (as Kaldor has taught us)[15] to introduce a direct effect of income distribution on saving. We may call it 'a different propensity to save out of profits and out of wages'; or, since we do not have to go into detail about who does the saving, we may simply make saving proportional to some weighted average of profits and wages, not simply to their sum. (145–6)

Indeed, flexibility in the propensity to save may be conceived of in several different ways, as illustrated in Baranzini (1991a). We may note that, in more general terms, certain groups of people, or consumers' units, share a common behavior, such as a high propensity to consume and a low propensity to save; or a high propensity to endow their children with human capital and/or financial assets; or a high propensity to reinvest in the productive process; or again, in the case of pensioners, a very low income with a fairly high propensity to consume. There are, however, various parameters by which classes may be identified, aiming in particular at socio-economic phenomena. Among these we may consider:

---

[15] Here Hicks notes (1965: 145, footnote): 'See his [Kaldor's] "Alternative Theories of Distribution" (*Essays on Value and Distribution*, p. 209). I am entirely in agreement with Kaldor as long as we stick to the theory of Growth Equilibrium, in the sense I am here using that term. But it would appear that Kaldor would apply his principles more generally, and there I cannot follow him.'

(i)   different endowments (human and physical capital in particular);
(ii) different sources of income, or a predominance of a given type of income (from labor, capital, land, etc.);
(iii) different propensities to consume and to save (average and/or marginal);
(iv) the predominance of 'life cycle' or 'intergenerational' capital stock owned, which may be associated with different age groups, or indeed with other ways of considering different socio-economic behavior;
(v)   different propensities to leave a bequest to the next generation (in the form of human capital or education, physical or financial capital, and/or social contacts); and
(vi) different bargaining positions, which may lead to different economic rewards – e.g. income and/or wealth; this aspect is also related to the existence of residuals in certain functional theories of income distribution, where factors are not paid according to, say, their marginal productivity, but according to their particular role in the productive process.

Hicks picks up Kaldor's proposition (1956, 1957) as an 'extreme case,' and states (1965: 146):

The extreme case of Kaldor's assumption would make saving proportional to profits only.[16] This is a very convenient assumption, which simplifies things considerably, so that – purely in order to exhibit the properties of the model – it is one that I shall largely use.

It is important to stress that Hicks retains the 'Kaldorian' saving function as the more interesting one, since he indirectly confirms the approach of the classical and post-Keynesian economists, according to whom the distribution of income between factors of production depends uniquely on the capitalist's propensity to save and not on that of the other groups. (Nonetheless, the distribution of income, as well as wealth, among classes is a function of all parameters of the model, including the propensities to save and to consume of the classes.) Hicks goes on to specify (*ibid.*) that, by using Kaldor's saving assumption,

I do not mean to imply that 'saving out of wages' is practically unimportant. But the complications which it introduces are not matters of principle; they obscure our vision if we insist on taking them into account all the time.

[16] Hicks adds the following note (1965: 146, footnote): 'It has been maintained by L. Pasinetti (*Review of Economic Studies*, 1962) that this is the only assumption that we are entitled to make in a growth equilibrium model. If the model is considered as a long-period distribution theory there is much to be said for this view. But it does not seem to me that this is the only way of regarding it; it is not the aspect with which I am here principally concerned.'

If we make saving a fixed proportion (s_1) of profits, the saving equation is much simplified. For we then have

$$\text{saving} = px = pgK = s_1(rpK)$$

so that [where r stands for 'profits rate']

$$g = s_1 r$$

a relation that is becoming well known.

It is at this point that Hicks develops the rest of the model that he had formulated earlier on. Let us follow the development of his argument:

The whole structure of the model is then vastly simplified. For many purposes there are just two equations that we have to hang on to – this saving equation and the wage equation, which (if we now allow ourselves to take the consumption good – corn – as our standard of value) may be written

$$\frac{1}{w} = \beta + \frac{rab}{1 - ra}.$$

[...] If the real wage (w) is given, the rate of profit is determined from the wage equation, and the rate of growth is then determined from the saving equation. The higher the real wage, the lower the rate of profit, and the lower (therefore) the rate of growth.

This result may be compared with the outcome of the Sraffian and the general post-Keynesian models. While in Sraffa's model the distribution of income may be determined (but this is just one way of tackling the issue, as Sraffa points out)[17] by the exogenously given rate of interest (determined by the policy of the central bank), in the Kaldor–Pasinetti model the share of wages in national income is the residual and equal to $W/Y = 1 - (P/Y) = 1 - (P/K)(K/Y) = 1 - (g_n/s_c)(K/Y)$. The latter result means that the share of wages in national income is negatively associated with the share of profits as well as with the capital/output ratio. In other words, all other things being equal, the higher the level of the system's capitalization the lower the equilibrium of the share of wages in the economic system. Moreover, since in post-Keynesian models postulating a class of 'pure' capitalists (whose income is derived mainly from assets or capital) the profit rate is equal to g_n/s_c, it is clear that the share of wages in national income is positively associated with the propensity to save of the capitalists. Alternatively, this means that an increase in the entrepreneurial class's propensity to consume itself reflects positively on the share of

---

[17] On this point, see Pasinetti's (1988) paper 'Sraffa on Income Distribution.'

profits in national income. This reminds us of Michał Kalecki's statement, according to which 'capitalists spend what they earn' (Kalecki, 1942: 258).

Let us follow Hicks's argument further, however:

> If it is the rate of growth that is given, the same two equations work the other way round. The rate of profit (which is consistent with this rate of growth) is then determined by the saving equation [i.e. the so-called Cambridge equation], and the rate of real wage from the wage equation. The lower the rate of growth, the lower the rate of profit, and the higher the real wage. (Hicks, 1965: 146–7)

It is interesting to note that the causality chain may be reversed in the following way. Consider, for instance, the Cambridge equation $P/K = g_n/s_c$, which may be rewritten as $g_n = (P/K)s_c$. Suppose now that the rate of profits is a direct result, for instance, of the system's need to generate a given amount of profits or of the monetary policy of the central bank. In this case, the equilibrium rate of growth of the system may be determined by the rate of profits multiplied by the propensity to save of the capitalist class. Both parameters have a positive effect on the equilibrium rate of growth, which may include technical progress and the growth rate of the system's labor force. This is mainly due to the fact that, once either wages or profits are given, the second becomes a residual. It is also true that one of the main purposes of this kind of analysis is to define the kind of income distribution between wages and profits – or, indeed, among socio-economic classes – that guarantees that *ex post* savings are equal to *ex ante* full employment[18] investment (as it is determined by entrepreneurs). For this reason, it is more logical to take g_n and s_c as given, and to consider the rate of profits as well as the share of wages in national income as endogenous variables.

Let us see how Hicks brings his analysis to a close:

> The rate of growth is always less than the rate of profit (with $s_1 < 1$). The lowest growth that is consistent with equilibrium depends on the lowest profit that is acceptable; if the profit rate can fall to zero, the growth rate can fall to zero. The maximum possible growth rate is $s_1 \times$ the maximum possible profit rate; this, as we have seen, is limited by the technique and the limit (which must be presumed to exist) below which wages cannot fall. To compare these limits with the g_1 and g_2[19] at which we arrived under the other assumption about saving is not very meaningful; but there should certainly be more room, under the new assumption, at the lower end – and it is possible to argue, in a similar way, that there should be more room at the upper end (of the range of growth rates) also. (147)

---

[18] Or near-full employment, as Heinrich Bortis (1976) and Adrian Wood (1975) have argued.

[19] g_1 and g_2 represent the rate of growth for $r = 0$ and $w = 0$, respectively.

Hence Hicks considers the possibility of a differentiated rate of growth of the system – i.e. of a rate of growth of the consumption sector and of the capital sector. If we suppose that capitalists consume an irrelevant fraction of their total capital income and that workers have a much higher propensity to consume than the other classes, then this different propensity to grow may be transferred from the productive sector to the socio-economic classes, characterized by different behavior. Alternatively, one may posit that the same rate of growth may be obtained by assuming a different rate of interest or profits for the two classes. (This may be inferred from the relation $g = s_1 r$ obtained by Hicks above, which is the so-called Cambridge equation.) More generally, the distinction by classes may be rather wider than originally thought; and some reasons for their distinction, which may apply to various aspects of their economic behavior, have already been considered above. The hypothesis according to which classes can be differentiated on the basis of their behavior or of the way in which they confront economic rules is quite revealing, however. This is due to the fact that, on the one hand, a steady-state model (such as this one) requires that all variables grow at the same rate, while, on the other hand, the presence of different classes may explain different economic parameters.

The hypothesis of a differentiated interest rate on savings

What are the reasons for justifying a different rate of return on investment for the two classes? Several reasons may be put forward in support of a differentiated interest rate in a two- or multi-class model.

Property rights are fundamental determinants of distribution in post-Keynesian, as well as in classical and neo-Ricardian, theories, where the production process implicitly or explicitly requires some form of cooperation from individuals empowered to 'withdraw' (or at least 'condition') certain essential inputs. As in most classical theories, social classes remain crucial for post-Keynesian theories, and their distinctive feature is given by saving, consumption, and investment behavior. In more sophisticated theories (such as Pasinetti's, 1974: chap. 6, and Baranzini's, 1991b) the assumption of 'separate appropriation' of each production factor is no longer as drastic as in other models, although it hovers in the background, even if the income – or, indeed, wealth – of certain classes is made up by different types of income or, respectively, by accumulated wealth. For instance, in Pasinetti's (1962, 1974) models, workers' income is made up of wages and interests on accumulated savings. As a matter of fact, interest on accumulated savings may be linked only indirectly to the profit rate, as in the case of deposit and savings accounts having a predetermined rate of interest (which is not necessarily linked to the overall rate of profits of the economy). Of course, in general terms in post-Keynesian theories, different rates of saving are associated with different economic and social classes; and the distribution of savings among classes will be (or must be) such as to yield an overall saving equal to the desired level of full-employment investment. In this way, a differentiated interest rate may further redistribute income among the classes of the system; for this reason its analysis represents a key element in the determination of the overall equilibrium interest rate.

Considering specific points we might say the following.

(i) Historically and in most developed as well as developing countries, the interest rate has been considerably lower than the average profit rate, except for some periods characterized by recession or high inflation. In general, a ratio of 2:3 is more likely to reflect the world's realities than a ratio of 1:1. This observation implies one of two things: either the economy is not on an equilibrium growth path and there is no evident hope of ever achieving such a path, or it becomes necessary to incorporate a different hypothesis into the model. Such a hypothesis will have to take into account the observed difference between the rate of interest on normal life cycle savings and the overall profit rate.

(ii) One might argue that the act of saving and the act of investing are two separate operations. They refer, in fact, to two distinct acts of appropriation: one is closely connected with the wage rate and only indirectly with the average profit rate of the economy; the latter, in contrast, is more directly connected with capital and its profit rate. One might also say that saving is essentially passive, while investment is active. Not surprisingly, a higher remuneration is normally attached to (active) investment.

(iii) A different way of looking at the same phenomenon is to postulate that there is a risk factor associated with the act of investing. This risk should be reflected in the differential between the rate of interest on risk-free savings and the overall profit rate.

(iv) Finally, it may be said that, to be profitable, investment must be larger than a certain minimum. The wage-earners, taken individually, may not be able to exploit the profit opportunities of large investments. Accordingly, their saving is likely to carry a smaller reward. This, of course, does not mean that we would have to introduce the argument of increasing returns to scale on savings. One may simply maintain that the interest rate is not necessarily identical to the profit rate. It should be stressed, however, that in this context by 'interest rate' we mean the rate at which the workers place their savings in the hand of the entrepreneurial class (or in the hands of the state in a socialist country).

These points were originally considered in the late 1960s and early 1970s, when the hypothesis of a differentiated interest rate was for the first time explicitly considered; and that was immediately after the publication of *Capital and Growth* (see Laing, 1969, and Balestra and Baranzini, 1971). A large literature then followed. As a result, the hypothesis of a different rate of return on capital for the study of the steady-state growth of the system, and as it may be inferred from Hicks's analysis, appears very interesting indeed.

The generalization of class differences in a steady-state growth model

The above argument relating to a different rate of capital growth of the two classes, or relating to a different rate of return on their savings, may indeed open up new horizons in the field of steady-state growth analysis. In particular, the idea of differentiated endowments for different classes may be put forward: the entrepreneurial class, which owns mainly intergenerational capital (as well as human capital), and the workers' class, which owns mainly life cycle savings (as well as human capital). Alternatively, we might consider the case in which both classes own intergenerational capital, but are characterized by a different propensity to endow the next generation. This is not a completely new assumption. We know, in fact, that the entrepreneurial class has a higher propensity to save than the other classes (in particular, workers); and that one of the motives underlying saving is to endow the next generation with a physical or financial capital stock (see, for instance, Horioka and Watanabe, 1997). Hence a higher propensity to save will almost inevitably imply a stronger willingness to transmit physical or financial capital to the next generation.

One point about these various working hypotheses is that, in a steady-state situation, the capital stock of all classes present in the system must grow at the same overall rate. Secondly, the assumption of a long-term horizon may be associated with the presence in the model of different generations, either overlapping or clearly separated from one another. Hicks was never explicit on this point, though in many of his works indirect hints to various generations are obvious.

A model of wealth distribution and accumulation including all the elements quoted above has been considered (see Baranzini, 1991a: chaps. 5–7, and Kessler and Masson, 1988). The results obtained are interesting, since, within an original framework, the microeconomic pure exchange model (or utility maximization model, also following Hicks, 1965: chap. 21) is in turn encompassed by the post-Keynesian framework to define a more flexible approach to income and wealth distribution.

An analysis of this kind elicits two main conclusions.

(i) In a life cycle model where the transmission of intergenerational financial assets is a prerogative of the entrepreneurial class, the equilibrium rate of interest depends on the behavioral parameters of the capitalist class; it doesn't depend on those of other classes or of technology. The fact that the equilibrium rate of interest is independent of technological factors (i.e. of the capital/output ratio) is particularly relevant, and seems to reinforce the solution that was put forward by the Cambridge school and by Hicks.

(ii) When both classes are allowed to pass on intergenerational assets (excluding education) to their children, then, in order to have a steady-state path, capitalists must have a much stronger will to bequeath capital to their children than the other classes. It is only in such a situation that all classes will hold a positive share of the total capital stock.

The results obtained lead us to ask the following question: 'Can this analytical result be reconciled with economic reality and common sense?' To a certain extent the answer is positive, as (a) the workers' class, by definition, earns a high proportion of its income from human capital stock, so that it may be inclined to discount its intergenerational bequest at a rate lower than the average (on this point, see Flemming, 1969); and (b) it is not unrealistic to posit a situation in which, in general, low-income families give higher priority to life cycle consumption and consequently a lower one to the intergenerational capital stock. On the other hand, those classes that derive a high proportion of their income from intergenerational wealth (and the remaining part from life cycle savings) in a long-term perspective are bound to give weight to the accumulation of such wealth, by discounting it at a rate higher than average. As we have shown in this chapter, this different approach to the intergenerational bequest notwithstanding, there exists a real possibility for a balanced growth of the system, whereby each class maintains a constant relative economic strength and a constant share of the capital stock. Clearly, the system may well leave such a path; this would happen if the capitalists were to show too low a propensity to pass on bequests to their children, thereby diminishing their strength; similarly, a much stronger desire on the part of the workers to transmit intergenerational wealth would eventually achieve the same result.

The genesis of socio-economic classes: analysis and policy implications

The arguments developed above lead us to another important issue that is to be found in the background of long-term analysis: that of the formation, persistence, and dispersion of socio-economic classes at large. This issue is present in most of Hicks's works on economic growth, especially in his *Capital and Growth* as well as in his *Methods of Dynamic Economics*, but so far it hasn't been taken up by the vast literature in this field. There exist a number of elements that are continuously at work in the determination of the progressive concentration or dispersion of wealth, which is the very basis of the strength of a socio-economic class in the long run.

Various factors account for the dispersion of wealth. Some of them tend to level off life cycle savings, while others may reduce the relevance of intergenerational assets in total wealth. Their impact on the formation or dispersion of classes is the same, however, and may even be hard to identify once the process has been set in motion. Among these factors we may quote: (i) the fiscal policies of redistribution; (ii) a drop in the value of holdings; (iii) a gradual using up of savings; (iv) transfers in the donor's lifetime; and (v) dispersion at death. Among the factors contributing to the process of wealth concentration, we might mention instead: (i) a differentiated propensity to save, according to the level of income; (ii) different age cohorts, which account for different values of life cycle savings; (iii) a higher return for large capital stocks; (iv) a small number of children inheriting the intergenerational capital stock; (v) an unequal distribution of bequests; and (vi) selective mating, which tends to concentrate more and more wealth in the hands of a given socio-economic class.

Let us here dwell on a final point, concerning fiscal policies for redistribution (for a recent development in this area, see Teixeira, Suguhara, and Baranzini, 2002). This is an instrument of economic policy that has been used increasingly in recent decades. Atkinson and Joseph Stiglitz (1980: 63) indicate a variety of taxes on capital and/or return on capital that may be considered in this framework: (i) taxes on interest income, either at the same rate as other income – like labor – or at a differential rate (for instance, the UK investment income surcharge); (ii) taxes on (short-term or long-term) capital gains; (iii) wealth taxes on the net value of assets owned (with special provisions that reduce the effective rate – such as special treatment of housing, or life insurance and pensions, as well as certain tax-exempt bonds); and (iv) special taxes, for example those on houses, land, etc. The latter are labeled 'property taxes' in the United States, 'rates' and, later, 'community charge' in the United Kingdom, and 'municipal tax on property' in Italy. In certain cases the policies on redistribution and/or taxation have been successful in stopping or slowing down the progressive concentration of wealth. Such was the explicit goal of the various manifestos drafted by the Labour Party in the United Kingdom in the late 1960s and early 1970s. As a matter of fact, the aim was to limit to about £500,000 the personal wealth that could be inherited or accumulated in other ways by a single individual.

Many economists have given particular attention to the relevance of all the direct and indirect taxes to the process of wealth accumulation; their conclusions have often been ambiguous. Nevertheless, it seems clear that wealth taxes and estate duties have led to a lower concentration of wealth than one would otherwise have expected.

We may say that the conditions in which a class is born, consolidates itself, or even vanishes (the latter is the case with 'below-average' fertility or a 'low propensity to endow the next generation') are numerous, and can be studied only in the framework of a fairly complicated model. The traverse successfully studied by Hicks is surely a good starting point, but more work is needed in this direction. Recent works in the field of institutional change and structural analysis may also be of help in framing the whole issue (see Baranzini and Harcourt, 1993, and Pasinetti, 1993).

Conclusions

In this chapter I have tried to reconstruct how John Hicks came to stand halfway between his Cambridge mentors Pigou and Robertson, on the one hand, and Keynes and the heirs of his 'Cambridge circus' on the other. I have argued that Sir John has provided a sort of analytical bridge between the school of welfare economics based at the LSE and Cambridge, and the Cambridge post-Keynesian school of income distribution. In particular, I have focused on Hicks's contribution in the field of income distribution, profit determination, and class differentiation, which draws heavily on the Kaldor–Pasinetti approach. This contribution must also be judged against all his work. A number of analytical results obtained in Hicks's *Capital and Growth* confirm the validity of his approach, which was developed more or less at the same time as, or just after, that of the neoclassical economists, Meade, Samuelson, Modigliani, and Robert Solow, and that of the post-Keynesians, Kaldor, Robinson, Kahn, and Pasinetti.

A number of implications drawn from other parts of Hicks's *Capital and Growth* may, however, be inferred from, and successfully integrated into, steady-state growth theory. For instance, the hypothesis of a differentiated rate of growth for the capital stock of the two classes is particularly appealing in this context, or, indeed, other forms of differentiation between classes. This might sound strongly anti-neoclassical; but this is also one of the reasons why Hicks's analysis may be considered anti-conventional, and thus 'original' and stimulating. There is a lot to learn, a lot to be gained, by rereading Hicks, especially in connection with issues of long-term non-proportional growth. This is, in fact, a particularly demanding field of inquiry, but one that facilitates the analysis of trends, which in turn makes it possible to verify the conditions necessary for the creation or disappearance of nuclei of economic groups.

17 The economics of non-linear cycles

Piero Ferri

Introduction

John Hicks's contribution to dynamics has been particularly relevant. While *Capital and Growth* (1965) and *Capital and Time* (1973a) embrace a long-run perspective, *A Contribution to the Theory of the Trade Cycle* (1950a) is set in a medium-term framework. According to Robert Solow (2000), the adoption of such a perspective implies entering a 'no man's land.' Most of the literature on dynamics is concerned with either the short-run fluctuations of the economy or of its long-run tendencies. In a medium-run perspective, endogenous forces have to be identified because the lapse of time involved is such that the dynamics of the model cannot depend only on exogenous shocks. Hicks's contribution to the business cycle is an 'endogenous' explanation with two methodological characteristics:

  (i) a macro approach,
  (ii) based upon a piecewise linear technique.

Both the conclusion and the two characteristics of Hicks's analysis stand in strong contrast to the present 'mainstream' theories, which favor 'exogenous' interpretations based upon a stochastic approach, are micro-founded, and are linearized around the steady-state values. The dynamic stochastic general equilibrium approach, which is based upon these three tenets, is at the root of both the real business cycle and the so called 'New Keynesian' approach. In these models, it is very difficult to identify conclusions in keeping with Hicksian thought. In order to find them, one must look elsewhere. For instance, Hashem Pesaran and Simon Potter (1997) have recently reconsidered the 'ceiling and floor'

This chapter was written while I was honorary research professor at the Washington University (St. Louis, Missouri). I wish to thank Steve Fazzari and Ed Greenberg for intellectual support and the University of Bergamo for financial help. Furthermore, I wish to thank Robert Solow and Kumaraswamy Vela Velupillai for stimulating criticisms of a previous version of the chapter.

model in a time-series perspective. Ceilings and floors belong to the family of switching models. This chapter uses a variant of this technique (a Markov switching regression) to formulate expectations that are superimposed on a structural macro-model.

The objective of this chapter is to present a model in which the Hicksian tenets are not only maintained, but also possibly deepened, without abandoning the underlying philosophy of Hicks's original contribution. On the one hand, it tries to reconcile the economic and the time-series interpretations of ceilings and floors. In fact, agents are assumed to be boundedly rational: they do not possess all the information required by the assumption of rational expectations even though they are more sophisticated than the backward-oriented agents of the past (see Conlisk, 1996, Sargent, 1993, and Velupillai, 2003). They have probabilities of experiencing periods of good and bad times for growth and episodes of low and high inflation, and they form expectations accordingly. In particular, people are supposed to behave like econometricians whose expectations are expressed by a Markov regime-switching model and try to learn the parameters of the model (see Evans and Honkapohja, 2001). The only requirement is that agents' beliefs are consistent in the sense that, on average, their expectations match the outcomes of the economy.

On the other hand, the structural model reflects both the behavior of the agents and the impact of economic policy and is analyzed in a macro-perspective. It is within this perspective that a strong link between the real and the monetary aspects of the economy, as stressed by John Maynard Keynes (1936), is introduced. This interdependence depends not only on nominal rigidities in wage and price formation, but also on the presence of debt and cash flows in the investment function, as stressed by Hyman Minsky (1982). The benefit of this approach is that of showing a dual role for the rate of interest on both cash flows and debts. This dual role favors the presence of cycles and fluctuations that are different from both the 'real' variety and what Hicks (1989a) calls the 'old' cycle, based upon the working of mere financial aspects.

Finally, the structural equations present only some inevitable 'non-linearities,' which, according to Peter Flaschel, Gang Gong, and Willi Semmler (2001: 106), 'naturally arise from the growth rate formulation of certain laws of motion, certain unavoidable ratios and the multiplicative interaction of variables.' Since the model cannot remain small, the mathematical results becomes less straightforward. Furthermore, the non-linear nature of the model, which does not yield closed-form solutions, must be studied by simulation. Parameters are calibrated to reflect values estimated in the relevant literature. Simulations of the model show the persistence of oscillations even in the presence of perfect foresight. The cyclical dynamics are endogenous and robust to changes in the parameters of both the model and the learning process.

In the present framework, there are two main sources of endogeneity in the dynamics: (i) cash flows and debts are endogenously determined in the model and have a powerful influence on investment – a primary factor in the creation of business cycles, along with the working of the Phillips curve; and (ii) bounded rationality and learning. They are not the only determinants of the dynamics, as is the case in the self-fulfilling expectations literature (Farmer, 1999), but they are an additional source that contributes to making the cycle profile more irregular and therefore more realistic. In fact, the cycle can also be obtained in a purely deterministic model by referring to perfect foresight expectations.

The structure of the chapter is the following. The next section examines how the piecewise nature of ceilings and floors has been discussed in the literature. The following section introduces the structural model, starting from the labor and product markets. In the next section further interdependence between the monetary and real aspects is introduced through the investment function, after which the steady-state values of the model we presented. The non-linear nature of the model requires simulations to derive results. Starting from perfect foresight, these are presented in the following section, while the next discusses the results of a sensitivity analysis. In the following section expectations based upon a Markov regime-switching model are considered. The penultimate section presents a learning process, and finally there are some concluding remarks.

Ceilings, floors, and non-linearities

Ceilings and floors were introduced by Hicks in a slightly altered version of the Samuelson accelerator-multiplier model (see Ferri, 1997). Ceilings and floors are theoretical constructs postulated to check explosive patterns that are otherwise implied by linear difference equations. Because they introduce a particular case of non-linearity, they imply a richer menu of dynamics paths than simple linear models do. These paths are more consistent with historical experience than those implied by linear models, in which instability implies an explosive dynamic path or where harmonic oscillations can be obtained only in an Occam's razor kind of situation. The ceiling and floor theory of the business cycle is also in contrast with a view that attributes cycles to exogenous (stochastic) shocks. The apparently greater econometric support for the latter theory has discouraged the development of endogenous explanations. Enough contrary evidence to the thesis of the obsolescence of the business cycle has been presented recently, however, to revive interest in non-linear models, and hence in an endogenous explanation. Ceiling and floor models are piecewise linear models within the non-linear world. On dynamical mathematical grounds, Hicks's model is only sketched and lacks important details. In particular, Minsky (1959) has interpreted such floors and ceilings as imposing new initial conditions, so that the dynamic process could start anew whenever they become effective. Cars Hommes (1995) has generalized the model so that some mathematical theorems in the field of bifurcation can be applied, and the stability of the limit Hicks model has been deepened along different lines (see Saura, Vasquez, and Vegas, 1998).

The concepts of ceilings and floors have been questioned on several grounds (for example, by Robert Matthews, 1959). On empirical grounds, ceilings have been questioned because upper cyclical turning points often occur before full employment is reached. The floor concept is even more debatable, both empirically and theoretically. In order to overcome some of these objections, two different research strategies have been pursued. The first alternative consists in developing non-linear models whose parameters vary with system behavior. Richard Goodwin (1982), for instance, has developed models that could generate closed orbits (see also Velupillai, 1979) and, under more restrictive hypotheses, limit cycles toward which all possible paths of the variables converge. The other alternative consists in maintaining the piecewise approach but introducing changes in the interpretation of ceilings and floors. The overall results depend on the cocktail of assumptions made and the analytical devices put forward.

For instance, Hicks himself thought that ceilings and floors could be interpreted along financial lines, and these were particularly useful in interpreting the old cycle, when the Bank of England had to convert notes and deposits into gold at a fixed parity and this provided a firm ceiling for expansion. 'But this old style of financial cycle...thus came to an end' (Hicks, 1989a: 101) when the Federal Reserve started operating on a different basis. A different strand of literature has insisted that, if one abandons the 'fix-price' economy, the limitations to booms can derive more from inflation than from physical constraints. In this perspective, the concept of ceilings as a physical 'barrier' is replaced by that of a 'threshold' which imparts a piecewise change in the difference equation that governs the dynamics (see also Medio, 1979, and Minsky and Ferri, 1984). Ferri and Edward Greenberg (1989) present a regime switching mechanism in the Phillips curve capable of generating business cycles. In this case, the piecewise character of the analysis is preserved, while the possibility of generating cycles is maintained (see Ferri, Greenberg, and Day, 2001). Finally, Ferri and Minsky's (1992) interpretation of the ceiling and floor model is that of a metaphor of the interplay between the structural economic forces represented by the model and the role of institutions in checking their dynamics, which is explained by the presence of external barriers.

Recently, Pesaran and Potter (1997) have placed the 'ceiling and floor' model in a time-series perspective. This means that 'ceilings and floors' are just statistical phenomena. Their results suggest that the turning points of the business cycle provide new initial condition for the ensuing growth process, *à la* Minsky (1959), and also show important asymmetries in response to shocks. As the authors themselves recognize, however, 'we have left open the economic explanation of the nonlinear phenomena found' (Pesasan and Potter, 1997: 692).

In a time-series perspective, it is well known that regime-switching devices are a genus that covers the first two approaches. Regime-switching can be either deterministic (Ferri and Greenberg, 1989) or stochastic. Moreover, the devices can be classified as endogenous or exogenous. The endogenous variety includes the so-called threshold autoregressive models (TARs), in which regime-switching is endogenous but is generated by a fixed lag. In the case of Pesaran and Potter, the lag is endogenous. In contrast, the Hamilton model, based upon Markov regime-switching, is one of the most important examples of the exogenous category. In the present chapter, the Hamilton model is used for framing expectations, and therefore the time-series perspective is linked to the role of structural forces, dominated by the interplay between economic factors and the role of institutions.

The full employment barrier

The original Hicks model is based upon a 'fix-price' hypothesis. The supply side of the economy is exogenous and constrains the dynamics of demand. Later on, Hicks (1974b) reconsiders this hypothesis and discusses the impact of the presence of the Phillips curve on the working of a Keynesian system. In that case, supply (and therefore the ceiling) does not constrain demand directly but only through the inflationary channel (see also Ferri, 2000). In this way, the model becomes less mechanical and can overcome some of the criticism that has been made regarding the physical concept of a ceiling.

In the present model, prices and wages are determined in non-competitive markets (see Hicks, 1969a, and Layard, Nickell, and Jackman, 1991). Prices are set by firms on the basis of a mark-up on wage cost. Wage dynamics are based upon inflation expectations, the state of the labor market, and exogenous parameters. With a fixed mark-up, the inflation rate is

$$\pi_t = \pi_t^e - \sigma_1 u_{t-1} + \sigma_2$$

where π_t^e is the expected rate of inflation, u_{t-1} is the one-period lagged rate of unemployment, and σ_2 represents exogenous forces.

Outside the world of rational expectations, the crucial hypothesis for the NAIRU (non-accelerating inflation rate of unemployment) to exist is the presence of a unitary value of the coefficient on expectations (see Sargent, 1999). More generally, if expectations are generated by a vector of past prices, the sum of their coefficients must be one if the process generating inflation is stable with a unit root. In this case, a NAIRU – that is, the steady-state value of unemployment compatible with the steady-state rate of inflation – is equal to

$$u_0 = \sigma_2/\sigma_1$$

Given this definition, the above inflation equation can be generalized in the following way:

$$\pi_t = \alpha\pi_t^e - \sigma_1(u_{t-1} - u_0) + (1 - \alpha)\pi_{t-1} \qquad (17.1)$$

This equation has the form of an expectations-augmented Phillips curve. Depending on the hypotheses made about the nature of expectations and their timing, this equation can be compatible with different strands of the literature. For instance, the so called 'new' Phillips curve (see Woodford, 2003) implies that the expectations are forward-looking, while some older versions assume that expectations are formed by an adaptive process (or in a mixed way, as in Fuhrer and Moore, 1995).

According to George Akerlof, William Dickens, and George Perry (2000: 2), 'The inadequacy of such models has been demonstrated force-fully in recent years, as low and stable rates of inflation have coexisted with a wide range of unemployment rates. If there were a single, relatively constant natural rate, we should have seen inflation slowing significantly when unemployment was above the rate, and rising when it was below.' To remedy this inadequacy, they propose a non-linear inflation equation, in which the steady-state value of unemployment is a function of the inflation rate.

Since a constraint of the present analysis is that of avoiding unnecessary non-linearities and the focus is on the stability of the model, what matters in this framework is the specification of the whole system, not only the shape of the labor market. As will be made clear later on, the presence of a NAIRU does not necessarily create an inflation explosion, as happens when this equation is studied in isolation, because the result depends on the interaction with the remaining equations of the system. As a result, this specification of the supply curve can be tolerated.

To close the labor market, the definition of the rate of unemployment is introduced. Given a labor supply (normalized to one), unemployment is determined by the following difference:

$$u_t = 1 - e_t \qquad (17.2)$$

where e_t is the employment ratio. The dynamics of the employment ratio is determined from

$$e_t = e_{t-1}[(1 + g_t)/(1 + \tau)] \qquad (17.3)$$

The dynamics depends on the ratio between the growth rate of the product (g_t) and the productivity rate (τ).

An extended IS-LM

The labor market equations can generate a process of interdependence between real and monetary aspects that is a function of the nature of expectations. This process of interdependence can be strengthened by a particular specification of the investment equation that Hicks (1989a) names the 'balance-sheet' perspective. This perspective becomes very important when the business cycle is not based mainly on the process of stock decumulation but is generated by the whole process of accumulation. This specification, which is represented in intensive form (see also Fazzari, Ferri, and Greenberg, 2008), is based upon a real and a financial kind of accelerator and assumes the existence of asymmetric information and uncertainty (see Fazzari, Hubbard, and Petersen, 1988, Bernanke, Gertler, and Gilchrist, 1999, and Stiglitz and Greenwald, 2003):

$$i_t = \frac{I_t}{Y_{t-1}} = \eta_0 + \eta_1 g_t^e + \eta_2(1 - \omega)(1 + g_t^e) - \eta_2 \frac{R_t d_t}{(1 + \pi_t^e)} \qquad (17.4)$$

In fact, g_t^e represents the expected rate of growth, while the remaining terms represent the expected cash flows in real terms – i.e. the expected profit share (ω being the labor share) diminished by the debt service, where R_t is the nominal rate of interest, which appears in this expression because interest payments are fixed in nominal terms in a monetary economy, while $d_t = \frac{D_t}{p_{t-1}Y_{t-1}}$ is real debt in intensive form.

The dynamics of the debt is given by the following formula:

$$d_t = \frac{1 + R_{t-1}}{(1 + g_{t-1})(1 + \pi_{t-1})}d_{t-1} + \frac{1}{1 + g_{t-1}}i_{t-1} - (1 - \omega) \qquad (17.5)$$

while the nominal rate is determined from a version of the Taylor rule (see Clarida, Gali, and Gertler, 1999),

$$R_t = R_t^* + \psi_1(\pi_t^e - \pi_0) + \psi_2(g_t^e - g_0) + \psi_3 R_{t-1} \qquad (17.6)$$

which represents the stance of economic policy. Also in this area there has been a resurgence of interest in the themes of dynamics in general and of stability in particular. There is available now a large literature that shows how the most important results in the field are highly dependent on both the assumed economic environment and the technicalities according to which the Taylor rule is specified (see Woodford, 2003) or the process of learning is specified (see Bullard and Mitra, 2002). There are, however, three differences from the traditional Taylor rule that are more in keeping with the present model. The first is that it is written in terms of the rate of growth of output rather than the level (see Walsh, 2003). Second, the target variables are set equal to their steady-state values. Finally, while in the 'new neoclassical synthesis approach' put forward in the monetary debate (see Goodfriend and King, 1997) the parameters of the Taylor rule are usually the only relevant parameters that determine the stability of the system, in the present model the situation is different. In this more complex model, the system tends to oscillate not because of the violation of the Taylor principle that requires that the values of the coefficients remain within a certain range, but because other endogenous forces are at work.

To close the model the remaining equations must be introduced. First of all, the definition of the real rate of interest is given by means of the Fisher equation:

$$r_t = \frac{(1 + R_t)}{(1 + \pi_t^e)} - 1 \qquad (17.7)$$

Second, aggregate demand must be completed by introducing the consumption function. This depends on both expected and past disposable income, which includes the interests gained. Given this definition of consumption, along with the requirement that aggregate demand equals aggregate supply in dynamic (and intensive) terms, one obtains that

$$g_t = c_1(1 + g_t^e) + c_2 + c_3 \frac{R_t d_t}{(1 + \pi_t^e)} + i_t v_{t-1} - 1 \qquad (17.8)$$

Given g^e and π^e, it is possible to specify a temporary equilibrium for a system of eight equations in eight unknowns: $\pi_t, u_t, e_t, i_t, d_t, r_t, R_t,$ and g_t.

The steady state

The steady-state values (marked by the sign 0) can now be computed in a recursive way. Since the NAIRU equals $u_0 = \frac{a_2}{a_1}$, through equation (17.2) the employment ratio e_0 is determined. Equation (17.3) determines the rate of growth

$$g_0 = \tau$$

which is equal to the exogenous rate of productivity growth. The Taylor equation determines the nominal rate of interest, which is equal to

$$R_0 = \frac{R^*}{1 - \psi_3}$$

In turn, equations (17.4), (17.5), and (17.8) determine the investment ratio, the real rate of interest, and the debt ratio, which are equal to

$$\dot{i}_0 = \frac{c_3 B - \eta_2 C}{c_3 - \eta_2}$$

$$r_0 = \frac{(B - C)g_0 - D(i_0 - A)(\eta_2 - c_3)}{(B - C) + D(i_0 - A)(\eta_2 - c_3)}$$

$$d_0 = \frac{i_0 - A}{g_0 - r_0}$$

where $A = (1 - \omega)(1 + g_0)$, $B = \eta_0 + \eta_1 g_0 + \eta_2 A$, $C = g_0(1 - c_1) - c_1 - c_2 - 1$, $D = \frac{R_0}{1 + R_0}$.

In accordance with the no Ponzi game assumption, d_0 must be bounded to avoid an infinite amount of debt. Furthermore, the steady-state value must be greater than zero because we want to analyze an economy with debt. Finally, the Fisher equation (17.7) helps to determine the inflation rate.

Simulating the dynamics

To study the dynamics of the model it is necessary to specify how expectations are formed. One objection to the traditional Keynesian results based upon some form of autoregressive expectations is that a rational expectational agent, by anticipating the regular fluctuations, can destroy the cycle. In order to overcome this difficulty, let us abandon the hypothesis of autoregressive expectations and assume perfect foresight, so that one can write

$$g_t^e = g_t$$

$$\pi_t^e = \pi_t$$

Under this assumption, the model is simulated (the details are presented in the appendix). The system has some recursiveness, in the sense that inflation is first determined, than debts are fixed, while the nominal rate of interest, the investment rate, and the rate of growth are determined simultaneously. Finally, the remaining equations are solved. The results are illustrated in figure 17.1, where the data are quarterly annualized rates.

What emerges from the figure is rather interesting: the economy undergoes endogenous fluctuations. The engine of the cycle is the same as that discussed by Ferri (2007). It is based on interactions between the labor market and investment activity. The boom is accompanied by an increase

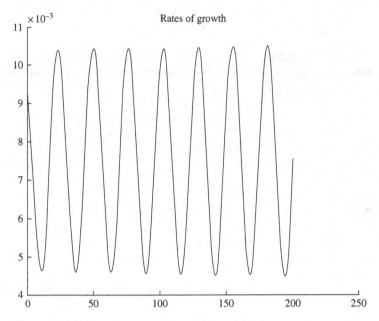

Figure 17.1 The endogenous fluctuations of the economy

of both investment and debt that eventually stops the mechanism, while the opposite happens in the recession phase.

Sensitivity analysis

Cyclical fluctuations of figure 17.1 are robust in at least two senses. First, if the system is subject to shocks, fluctuations persist for a very large number of successive values. In the second place, fluctuations persist in spite of changes in a significant constellation of parameters. In order to be more precise, the Jacobian of the model near the steady state has been calculated, while the parameters γ_1 and γ_2 in the investment equation have been used as a bifurcation device (see the appendix). Difference and differential equations are not the same in this regard. While the Hopf bifurcation generates limit cycles (see Benhabib, Schmitt-Grohé, and Uribe, 2002) in the differential equations, one must refer to the Neimark–Sacker theorem (see Medio and Lines, 2001) in the case of difference equations. For the latter case, some results are shown in table 17.1, where different values of the parameters are compatible with the modulus (i.e. the maximum absolute values of the complex

Table 17.1 *The impact of the accelerator parameters on the fluctuations*

γ_1	γ_2	Modulus
0	0.305	1
0.40	0.285	1
0.50	0.280	1
0.54	0.280	1

eigenvalues) equal to one, which is one of the conditions of the Neimark–Sacker theorem to generate cycles.

The table shows that the bifurcation values, at which the model generates cycles, can be obtained by various combinations of the parameters in the investment equation. Three observations are worth making. First, the strength of the real versus the financial accelerator must go in opposite directions in order to maintain fluctuations. Second, the model can also generate fluctuations when the real accelerator is absent, but the same does not hold true for the financial accelerator, which cannot assume the value zero because it would violate the constraints on debt that have been fixed for the steady-state values. Finally, in order to study the stability of the limit cycles, further investigations should be carried out (see Kuznetsov, 2004).

The 'bounded rationality' hypothesis

At this stage of the analysis, the hypothesis of perfect foresight is dropped and the hypothesis of bounded rationality is introduced. In other words, let us suppose that, over a medium-term perspective, people expect a dynamic pattern characterized by differences in performance between 'good times' and 'bad times.' This state of knowledge is specified as a two-state Markovian model with high-growth and low-growth states (see Hamilton, 1989) and periods of 'high' and 'low' inflation. In this perspective one supposes that agents form their expectations according to a particular form of bounded rationality (see Sargent, 1993, Conlisk, 1996, and Evans and Honkapohja, 2001).

At the end of period $t-1$, agents believe that the growth rate in period t will be (see also Clements and Hendry, 1999)

$$g_t^e = \alpha_1 + \beta_1 s_t + (\rho_1 + \mu_1 s_t)g_{t-1} + \epsilon_t$$

where ϵ is a random variable with the properties assumed by James Hamilton (1989) and s_t is a random variable that assumes the value zero in the low state and one in the high state. It evolves according to the following transition probabilities:

$$\Pr(s_t = 0|s_{t-1} = 0) = a_1$$
$$\Pr(s_t = 1|s_{t-1} = 0) = 1 - a_1$$
$$\Pr(s_t = 0|s_{t-1} = 1) = 1 - b_1$$
$$\Pr(s_t = 1|s_{t-1} = 1) = b_1$$

Since s_t is not known at time t, its expected value, conditioned on s_{t-1}, is taken as a forecast.

If $s_{t-1} = 0$, the conditional forecasting rule is

$$\hat{E}(g_t|s_{t-1} = 0) = \alpha_1 + (1 - a_1)\beta_1 + [\rho_1 + (1 - a_1)\mu_1]g_{t-1}$$

where the operator E is written as $\hat{E}$ to indicate its subjective character. For $s_{t-1} = 1$, one gets

$$\hat{E}(g_t|s_{t-1} = 1) = \alpha_1 + b_1\beta_1 + [\rho_1 + b_1\mu_1]g_{t-1}$$

The general forecasting rule is given by

$$\hat{g}_t = E(g_t|s_{t-1}) = \alpha_1 + \beta_1[b_1 s_{t-1} + (1 - a_1)(1 - s_{t-1})]$$
$$+ \{\rho_1 + \mu_1[(1 - a_1)(1 - s_{t-1}) + b_1 s_{t-1}]\}g_{t-1}$$

A similar forecasting rule can be applied to inflation, where the random-state variable is denoted by z_t; the forecast for this variable is

$$\hat{\pi}_t = E(\pi_t|z_{t-1}) = \alpha_2 + \beta_2[b_2 z_{t-1} + (1 - a_2)(1 - z_{t-1})]$$
$$+ \{\rho_2 + \mu_2[(1 - a_2)(1 - z_{t-1}) + b_2 z_{t-1}]\}\pi_{t-1}$$

The use of regime-switching can be interpreted as a convenient device to apply time-series analysis to the problem of forecasting, and, in view of its popularity among forecasters, it may reflect their practices. It is important to stress that s and z are unobserved (latent) random variables that introduce regime-switching. This does not imply that they have no economic meaning. The association with 'animal spirit' is made, for instance, by Peter Howitt and R. Preston McAfee (1992), or a correlation with other variables could be looked for.

In the spirit of bounded rationality, however, it is important to stress that these equations are accepted insofar as they work. The procedure must satisfy at least two constraints. First, as Hommes and Gerhard Sorger (1998) have argued, the expectations must be consistent with the data, in the sense that agents do not make systematic errors (see also Frydman and Phelps, 1983, and Grandmont, 1998). In other words, the forecasts and the data should have the same mean and autocorrelations. In the second place, the expectations must contribute

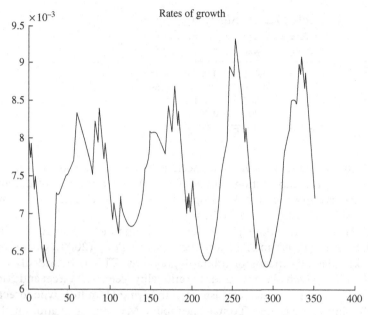

Figure 17.2 Endogenous cycles with bounded rationality

to the dynamics, though, in the present model, the fluctuations must be derived from the structural part of the model. The dynamics is represented in figure 17.2.

Note that the expectations mechanism does not create the cycle, which was present in the perfect foresight form of the model, but it does affect its dynamical profile. This is different from the literature on self-fulfilling expectations (see Farmer, 1999), in which there are no cycles unless they are triggered by some expectational mechanism. Unfortunately, in a non-linear model it is not possible to identify the separate contribution of the two forces (for the linear case, see Evans and Honkapohja, 2003, and Woodford, 2003). In this model, therefore, one can state that stochastic and deterministic forces interact without necessarily altering the endogenous mechanisms mentioned before, but expectations modify the time profile (see the appendix for the Jacobian in the present case).

The overall dynamics with learning

In order to make sure that the expectations are consistent with the data, a process of learning is introduced. In the previous analysis, two simplifications have been assumed. First, the special case $s_t = z_t$ was considered.

Table 17.2 *Consistent expectations*

Variable	Mean	σ	AR
π	0.0018	0.0018	0.91
π^e	0.0018	0.0018	0.89
g	0.0072	0.0012	0.90
g^e	0.0079	0.0014	0.79

Second, the regime-switching mechanism did not consider changes in the slope of the expectation functions ($\mu = 0$). At this stage of the analysis these assumptions can be dropped, and the more general case will be considered in the process of learning.

Agents learn about parameters in the manner assumed by Thomas J. Sargent (1999) and Akerlof, Dickens, and Perry (2000), where learning takes place by means of rolling regressions. This is boundedly rational learning, which places bounds to rationality (see also Marcet and Nicolini, 2003). The next stage consists of embodying Hamilton-type forecasts in the simulation model. To start the model, Markov expectations with fixed parameters are assumed for the first fifty periods. After these fifty periods, to make a forecast for period t, s_{t-1} is first determined. If, for example, it equals one, an autoregressive regression with a constant is fitted to the previous observations on g_t for which $s_{t-1} = 1$, but no more than fifty observations are utilized. Then the parameters estimated by the regression and the current value of g_{t-1} are used to compute $\hat{g}_t$. Analogous computations are used to forecast $\hat{g}_t$ when $s_{t-1} = 0$ and to forecast π_t.

To understand the overall dynamics, one cannot refer to the E-stability concept (see Evans and Honkapohja, 2001), as the non-linearity does not allow us to find closed-form solutions. Rather, one has to consider simulations. The results are presented in figure 17.2.

If one measures consistency by means of a triple statistical object (mean, standard error, and autoregression), then the results of table 17.2 are encouraging. It follows, therefore, that expectations contribute along with structural forces in determining the dynamics of the model, without violating the consistency assumption.

Concluding remarks

This chapter has revisited the 'ceiling and floor' tradition in business cycles that originated with Hicks's contribution. In particular, attention has been paid to the recent attempt to cast it in a time-series framework.

As is shown in the contribution by Pesaran and Potter (1997), it is possible to obtain models in which the effect of shocks varies over the business cycle and in which there are strong interactions between fluctuations and growth, both results being important. In this chapter, this time-series approach has undergone two major modifications. In the first place, since the 'ceiling and floor' device is a member of the regime-switching class of models, where the threshold is endogenous, I opted for a simpler option where the threshold is exogenous and stochastic. This Markov regime-switching device turns out to be particularly promising in shaping expectations. Second, I inserted this device within a structural model in which the equations for the various markets have been described.

Three constraints have been placed on the model. First, that the expectations must be consistent with the data, and the process of learning must guarantee this coherence. In the second place, non-linearities in the structural system have been limited. Finally, this boundedly rational approach must not be the exclusive source of fluctuations in the model, but it must enrich a dynamics that already fluctuates for endogenous reasons. Ascertaining whether models are truly deterministic is not important: they may have both stochastic and deterministic elements. What matters is identifying the particular kinds of non-linearities that are capable of generating cycles that have an economic meaning.

The following points need to be stressed.

(i) The tendency to oscillate endogenously is rather robust, in the sense that there is strong numerical evidence in favor of this conclusion.

(ii) The results depend very much on the interaction between real and financial variables.

(iii) These results are confirmed when one passes from perfect foresight to bounded rationality, in which a Markov process is introduced and learning is allowed. In this case, an additional source of dynamics is imposed on the model, resulting in greater complexity. When interacting with the structural forces of the system, the learning process generates patterns that are more consistent with the data. A switching mechanism increases the chances of obtaining business cycles, while learning can increase the frequency and the amplitude of the cycle.

These points, which are in keeping with Ferri and Minsky's (1992) interpretation of the ceiling and floor model as a metaphor for the interplay between the structural economic forces and the role of institutions in checking their dynamics, can be deepened. For instance, (i) more general features of actual economies (such as international and further financial aspects) must be considered in order to obtain more realistic results. Furthermore, (ii) policy considerations can be developed from this model. For instance, a control of the cycle by means of the Taylor rule can be enriched by a fiscal policy. Finally, (iii) the Hamilton model can be generalized in various ways. For example, the probabilities of the Markov scheme can be endogenized (see Filardo, 1994).

To deal with these problems, however, one has to confront a very radical objection. According to Buiter and Panigirtzoglou (2003: 740).

[T]here is only one way to be fully informed and rational. There are infinitely many ways of being 'reasonable', 'boundedly rational', etc. Any particular adaptive learning rule, such as recursive least squares, ...is ad-hoc and arbitrary, unless there is evidence, say from cognitive psychology, that empirically it is a reasonable representation of how agents tend to behave. [...] The adaptive learning of the 1990s does not appear to get us much beyond the adaptive expectations of the 1960s.

The results of the present chapter have shown that the latter part of this critique is not necessarily true. As far as the first part is concerned, a different route probably exists that consists in extending, in a world of uncertainty, boundedly rational assumptions from the realm of expectations to that of intertemporal behavior. In a world of uncertainty, the principles of behavioral macroeconomics can be used to justify both boundedly rational assumptions and the particular workings of markets in a macro-model (see Akerlof, 2002). This is what Hicks himself claimed – not so much in his famous IS-LM (1937a) article as in 'Micro and Macro' (1983b: 352), where he states that micro-foundation should be of a particular kind: 'Monetary institutions, certainly; but also a look at other markets, labour markets, and product markets to see how they really work, and can work. Not in the same way in all times and places.'

Appendix

(The absence of the government and the international trade sectors implies that the results of the exercises are only indicative, although the parameters are not unreasonable from an econometric point of view.)

Simulations generating figure 17.1 and table 17.1

Parameter values:

$\tau = 0.0075$	$\sigma_1 = 0.03$	$\sigma_2 = 0.04\sigma_1$	$\omega = 0.812$	$\eta_0 = 0.152$	$\eta_1 = 0.15$
$\eta_2 = 0.293$	$c_1 = 0.40$	$c_2 = 0.40$	$c_3 = 0.1$	$\psi_1 = 1.1$	$\psi_2 = 0.9$
$\psi_3 = 0;$	$R^* = 0.01$	$\alpha = 0.6$	$N = 1000$		

A linearized version of the previous model has been obtained in the following way. The symbol $\sim$ denotes deviations of the various variables from steady-state values. Constant values have been omitted. The system

has been made compact through substitution of the variables into six
equations,

$$
\begin{pmatrix}
1 & 0 & 0 & 0 & 0 & 0 \\
0 & 1 & 0 & 0 & 0 & 0 \\
-\psi_1 & 0 & 1 & 0 & -\psi_2 & 0 \\
-I_4 & I_3 & I_2 & 1 & -I_1 & 0 \\
G_4 & -G_3 & -G_2 & -G_1 & 1 & 0 \\
0 & 0 & 0 & 0 & -L_1 & 0
\end{pmatrix}
\begin{pmatrix}
\tilde{\pi}_t \\
\tilde{d}_t \\
\tilde{R}_t \\
\tilde{i}_t \\
\tilde{g}_t \\
\tilde{l}_t
\end{pmatrix}
$$

$$
=
\begin{pmatrix}
1 & 0 & 0 & 0 & 0 & P_1 \\
-D_4 & D_1 & D_5 & D_2 & -D_3 & 0 \\
0 & 0 & \psi_3 & 0 & 0 & 0 \\
0 & 0 & 0 & 0 & 0 & 0 \\
0 & 0 & 0 & 0 & 0 & 0 \\
0 & 0 & 0 & 0 & 0 & 1
\end{pmatrix}
\begin{pmatrix}
\tilde{\pi}_{t-1} \\
\tilde{d}_{t-1} \\
\widetilde{R_{t-1}} \\
\tilde{i}_{t-1} \\
\tilde{g}_{t-1} \\
\widetilde{l_{t-1}}
\end{pmatrix}
$$

where the coefficients of the matrices represent the following partial
derivatives (all variables are defined as deviations from the steady-state
values):

$$
D_1 = \partial d_t / \partial d_{t-1} = \frac{1 + R_0}{(1 + g_{k_0})(1 + \pi_0)}
$$

$$
D_2 = \partial d_t / \partial i_{t-1} = \frac{1}{1 + g_0}
$$

$$
D_3 = \partial d_t / \partial g_{t-1} = \frac{(1 + r_0)d_0 + i_0}{(1 + g_0)^2}
$$

$$
D_4 = \partial d_t / \partial \pi_{t-1} = \frac{(1 + R_0)d_0}{(1 + g_{k_0})(1 + \pi_0)^2}
$$

$$
D_5 = \partial d_t / \partial R_{t-1} = \frac{d_0}{(1 + g_{k_0})(1 + \pi_0)}
$$

$$
I_1 = \partial i_t / \partial g_t = \eta_1 + \eta_2(1 - \omega)
$$

$$
I_2 = \partial i_t / \partial R_t = \frac{\eta_2 d_0}{(1 + \pi_0)}
$$

$$
I_3 = \partial i_t / \partial d_t = \frac{\eta_2 R_0}{(1 + \pi_0)}
$$

$$
I_4 = \partial i_t / \partial \pi_t = \frac{(\eta_2 R_0 d_0)}{(1 + \pi_0)^2}
$$

$$G_1 = \partial g_t / \partial i_t = \frac{1}{1 - c_0}$$

$$G_2 = \partial g_t / \partial R_t = \frac{c_3 d_0}{(1 - c_1)} \frac{1}{(1 + \pi_0)}$$

$$G_3 = \partial g_t / \partial d_t = \frac{c_3}{(1 - c_1)} \frac{R_0}{(1 + \pi_0)}$$

$$G_4 = \partial g_t / \partial \pi_t = \frac{R_0 d_0}{(1 + \pi_0)^2} \frac{c_3}{(1 - c_1)}$$

$$L_1 = \partial l_t / \partial g_t = \frac{l_0}{\tau}$$

$$P_1 = \frac{\sigma_1}{1 - \alpha}$$

It is possible to obtain a system of the form

$$x_t = A^{-1^*} B x_{t-1}$$

where the eigenvalues and the eigenvector of the system can be computed. A couple of eigenvalues are complex and their modulus with the above parameters is one. This is a necessary condition in order to have a Neimark–Sacker kind of bifurcation. For the other conditions, along with the dynamic property of the invariant curve, see Yuri Kuznetsov (2004).

Simulations generating figure 17.2 and table 17.2

Parameter values:

$a = 0.8$	$\tau = 0.0075$	$\sigma_2 = 0.04^* \sigma_1$	$\sigma_1 = 0.03$	$\omega = 0.808$	$\eta_0 = 0.152$
$\eta_1 = 0.15$	$\eta_2 = 0.3$	$c_1 = 0.40$	$c_2 = 0.40$	$c_3 = 0.01$	$\psi_1 = 1.05$
$\psi_2 = 0.9$	$\psi_3 = 0.05$	$R^* = 0.01$	$N = 1000$		

The parameters of the stochastic components are the following:

$$a_1 = g_0[1 - (\rho_1 + \mu_1 b_1)] - \beta_1 b_1$$

$$a_2 = \pi_0[1 - (\rho_2 + \mu_2 b_2)] - \beta_2 b_2$$

These are obtained by setting $s = z = 1$ (respectively $s = z = 0$) and solving from the steady-state expectation formula. The other parameters are

$a_1 = 0.3$	$a_2 = 0.5$	$b_1 = 0.9$	$b_2 = 0.9$	$\beta_1 = 0.001$
$\beta_2 = 0.002$	$\rho_1 = 0.95$	$\rho_2 = 0.95$	$\mu_1 = 0$	$\mu_2 = 0$

The Jacobian can also be considered in the present case. There are two alternatives. The first consists in introducing three more variables – i. e. π_t^e, g_t^e, and s_t – to the matrices A and B. The second is to substitute out the expectations with their formulas and only add the variable s_t. According to Hamilton (1994), this variable can be expressed as

$$s_t = (1 - b_1) + (a_1 - (1 - b_1))s_{t-1}$$

18 A perspective on a Hicksian non-linear theory of the trade cycle

Kumaraswamy Vela Velupillai

Preamble

The great advances that have been made in recent years in our understanding of the Trade Cycle have consisted chiefly of the successful application of economic theory (and especially monetary theory) to the problem of fluctuations. The application was itself both the cause and the consequence of new developments in the field of pure theory; for one of the chief things that had to be done was to bring monetary theory into a closer relation with general (non-monetary) economics. The development in our knowledge of the Cycle was thus, from one point of view, *a purely theoretical development*. (Hicks, 1982a [1933] 28–9; emphasis added)

My main topic on this occasion is an aspect of *non-linear trade cycle theory*, and the major portion of my chapter is set against the backdrop provided by the contents of *A Contribution to the Theory of the Trade Cycle* (Hicks, 1950a; hereafter *CTTC*). I doubt that Hicks ever really, wholly, repudiated any of his early works, even when he had some misgivings that hindsight confers. In his later years his greatest reservations were directed at the analytical and conceptual limitations of 'Mr Keynes and the "Classics"' (1937a) and *CTTC*.[1] In a letter to me, dated February 14,

I can claim the pleasure and embarrassing privilege of having had three pioneering theorists of non-linear trade cycle theory as my direct doctoral supervisors: first, in Lund, Björn Thalberg; then, in Cambridge, first Nicholas Kaldor and, finally and decisively, Richard Goodwin. I suspect their influences, most obviously the Goodwinian ones, left indelible marks, possibly reflected here in the way I have interpreted Hicks. To that extent the interpretations may be unoriginal but not necessarily ungenerous or unfair. *It is inconceivable that anyone can be ungenerous or unfair to John Hicks*. I am greatly indebted to Björn Thalberg for detailed comments, and to Bob Clower, Geoff Harcourt, Rainer Masera, and Stefano Zambelli for encouraging remarks, on the first draft of this chapter. Their comments reinforced my convictions on the validity of its main themes. The usual caveat, of course, applies.

[1] Andrew Schuller, economics editor at Oxford University Press, during the presentation of his contribution to the Hicks Centennial Colloquium reminded us that OUP wanted to let *CTTC* go out of print in the late 1960s. Sir John had voiced objections against such a decision, however, and, as a result, the book continued to be available in its Clarendon imprint from OUP: 'When he objected to our 1977 proposal to put *Trade Cycle* out of print we relented and reprinted' (see chapter 5, by Schuller, in this volume).

1984, he wrote: 'The part of my own work which comes nearest to Dick Goodwin's is of course my *Trade Cycle* (1950); but of all my books that is the one from which I nowadays feel most remote.'

His reservations about IS-LM are recorded in 'IS-LM: an Explanation' (1983c), but the misgivings about both 'Mr Keynes and the "Classics"' and *CTTC* are stated in a broader context in his contribution to the Nicholas Georgescu-Roegen Festschrift (Hicks, 1976b). It is, therefore, with some trepidation that I seek to pay homage to this great economic theorist via a reflection on the analytical contents of *CTTC*. I am unsure whether this form of homage would have appealed to Sir John. *CTTC* continues to be a source of inspiration for work in macrodynamics (and mathematical dynamics), however, and celebrating it is a way of paying homage to their imaginative creator.

John Hicks contributed to the *theory* of aggregate economic fluctuations in many ways; he interpreted the *history* of fluctuations in almost as many ways; moreover, his macro-theoretical constructions have been used by legions of economists to theorize and interpret the stylized facts of fluctuations in a number of fertile ways. His earliest contribution to the theory of business cycles was produced when he was squarely in the Robbins–Hayek stables, in 1933; his last published work on the theory of cycles, 'Real and Monetary Factors in Economic Fluctuations' (1974d), suggests that he had found a Robertsonian theoretical corner most comfortable – having traversed, for long periods, a Keynesian path.

Hicks knew, and others pointed out almost ad nauseam, that the two main economic and technical infelicities in the mathematical model of *CTTC* were his handling of the definition of *autonomous investment* and the economic underpinnings of the lower turning point, the so-called *floor*; they are, of course, tightly connected. I discuss a way of remedying this infelicity regarding autonomous investment in Velupillai (2008). Like all classics, *CTTC* merits reading and rereading, if not for the ostensible subject matter, then for its supremely elegant prose. One reviewer is reputed to have referred to it as a *lyrical poem*. In my rereading of it I was pleasantly surprised to discover insights and suggestions that seem to have escaped formalizations by earlier students of the book. In the next section this 'discovery' is explained and formalized, and a solution suggested.

One of the most imaginative suggestions to circumvent the technical problems of having to rely on a rigid floor was given by Richard Goodwin in his illuminating review of *CTTC*. This technical suggestion led to the formulation of a new kind of dynamical system, one of those rare occasions when a purely economic hypothesis suggested, to an innovative economic theorist, a particular formalism that resulted in the discovery of a new kind of non-linear differential equation. This is the subject matter of the penultimate section. I conclude with reflections on the experience of reading and interpreting Hicksian writings.

In rereading Hicks, whilst preparing this chapter, there were occasions when I was puzzled by some of his more critical mathematical reflections, particularly on stability, existence, non-linearity, and dynamics. Thus, I am, at first, perplexed when I read a statement such as the following:

> My equilibrium path is the same as Harrod's warranted path, and (for the same reason as his) it is unstable. But (as I say) 'mathematical instability does not itself elucidate fluctuations. *A mathematically unstable system does not fluctuate; it just breaks down*'. A fluctuating model, even if it is unstable in the large, must be stable in the small, in order that the path which it actually follows should be determinate. In order to get that *local* stability, I had to introduce lags. (1982c: 173; first emphasis added)

A part of the above 1982 'Prefatory Note' to his 1949 review of Roy Harrod's *Towards a Dynamic Economics* (Harrod, 1948) reads suspiciously like a mathematically incorrect statement. Whenever I suspect that an intellectual giant has made a mistake, however, I remind myself of fallible gods and the Buddha's wise response to the hair-splitting Subuhti's perplexed question on whether the 'venerable Solow' might have 'made a mistake': 'Forsake fear, Subhuti. Venerable Solow may make peculiar assumptions, but *he never makes a mistake*' (Sen, 1974: 40; emphasis added).

On the whole, this precept has been helpful in guiding my rereading of the maestro on trade cycle theory, and other things.

A neglected basin of attraction in *CTTC*

> Of all the concepts which are used in [*CTTC*], that which has caused the most trouble is *Autonomous Investment*; and here I must admit to having brought the trouble upon myself, for I do not think that I was entirely consistent in the use which I made of the term. [...] I am afraid that I do occasionally talk as if one could tell whether a particular piece of investment was autonomous just by looking at it; this is quite wrong. (Hicks, 1950a: vi–vii [preface to the third impression])

CTTC was copiously reviewed almost within a few months of its publication by some of the most eminent trade cycle theorists of the time: James Duesenberry (1950), Rendings Fels (1951), Goodwin (1950), Kaldor (1951), Erik Lundberg (1950), just to mention a few of the more notable reviews.[2] There were three fundamental criticisms of the conceptual and technical underpinnings of the *CTTC* model in these reviews:

---

[2] A few years ago I had occasion to correspond with Robert Solow about Goodwin. I took the chance to ask him whether he was aware of any discussion that took place between

(i) the unsatisfactory definition, heavy burden placed on, and the imprecise role of autonomous investment, particularly in its action in the neighborhood of the floor;

(ii) the mathematical sufficiency of *one* of the 'constraints,' either the ceiling or the floor (but not of both), for the cycle implied in *CTTC*; and

(iii) the unsatisfactoriness, in inducement to invest, of relying on the *acceleration principle*.

Kaldor emphasized the latter; Lundberg and Duesenberry the first; Duesenberry, Fels, and Goodwin the second. I shall return to the proposition on the sufficiency of one 'constraint' for the existence of maintained oscillations in the next section. My concern here is on the imprecise role and definition of autonomous investment. With this in mind, it might be useful to reflect on the objections to its definition made by Duesenberry and Lundberg. Duesenberry points out, quite directly, that:

Hicks's argument and many similar ones are based on a division of investment into three classes: autonomous investment, induced investment, and replacement investment. Like many other concepts in business cycle theory the above classification is somewhat poorly related to the underlying micro-theory of investment. [...]

In fact, we cannot make a clear distinction between these three types of investment except in certain rather special cases. (Duesenberry, 1950: 473)

Lundberg was even more disturbed about the assumption of observable, measurable, differences between identifiable categories of *induced* and *autonomous* elements in total (gross) investment:

[There] is the question of the distinction between induced and non-induced ('autonomous') investment. Hicks gives an extremely unsatisfactory description of the latter, and all that we can discover is that it is not determined by the increase in production from year to year, and that it is a necessary condition for continuous expansion that autonomous investment should increase in step with national income. [...] But as far as I can see there is no firm basis for dividing total investment into these two categories. ...[T]his division [into induced and autonomous investment] can be expected to vary during the course of expansion. I consider, therefore, that this division of investment activity into categories, which is used by Harrod and

Goodwin and Duesenberry on their respective reviews of *CTTC*. Solow wrote back, on December 22, 1997, as follows (emphasis added): 'To answer your question about Jim Duesenberry, I called him up. He said yes, of course, he had many discussions with Dick about business cycles, about dynamic modelling, and about Hicks's book. [...] He could not remember details of their talks about Hicks. Except in one respect. Duesenberry did not like the *Trade Cycle* book, found it mechanical. He ended his review with a remark that Arthur Smithies liked, because he interpreted it as a sarcastic dig at Hicks. But Dick said: "*How could you be unkind to a nice man like Hicks?*" So Jim deleted or changed the offending comment.'

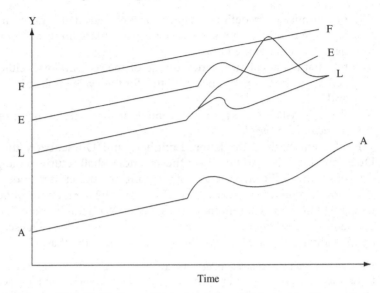

Figure 18.1 Multiple equilibria in *A Contribution to the Theory of the Trade Cycle*

Hicks, is a useless method for empirical investigation, and therefore probably an unfruitful hypothesis for a business cycle model. (Lundberg, 1950: 107)

Note, however, that neither Duesenberry nor Lundberg (nor anyone else who has pronounced on this issue) denies the existence of different categories of investment, at least two of which can be defined as induced and autonomous investment respectively. The objections are to the assumption of observable, empirically measurable, *additive* definitions of their *levels* as identifiable and distinguishable national accounting categories. I consider these to be valid and serious objections, and to the best of my knowledge no one has dealt with them satisfactorily within the framework of a (non-linear) *CTTC* model. These objections must also be viewed against the backdrop of a neglected aspect of the role of autonomous investment in a complete model of *CTTC*, at least as envisaged by Hicks (see figure 18.1, which is figure 13, page 121, in *CTTC*):

[T]he actual course of autonomous investment cannot possibly be so very regular – it must experience autonomous fluctuations on its own account. These fluctuations, and their consequences, are superimposed upon the cycle which we have been studying. [...]

Fluctuations in autonomous investment will be reflected in corresponding fluctuations in the equilibrium lines – both in the upper equilibrium line *EE* and in the lower equilibrium line *LL*. With this amendment [to the original model, as described in figure 12, page 97], the theory stands; it will still be true that *the upper equilibrium is unstable, the lower stable* – so that a cycle of the kind we have been describing can still be generated. (Hicks, 1950a: 120–1; emphasis added)

In other words, the complete *CTTC* model is one of *multiple equilibria*, in which there is a locally stable equilibrium coexisting with a separate unstable equilibrium, the former coming into play at the lower turning point when the 'floor' is subject to 'autonomous' fluctuations of a particular kind of intensity:

The discovery of a new investment opportunity is itself likely to be followed by a stream of net investment with the characteristic time-shape of the hump and the tail. Thus, if such a discovery becomes effective in a period of depression, there will be a hump in the *AA* line, and a corresponding hump in the *LL* line, as shown in [figure 18.1]. Output is following along the *LL* line, and it will follow it up the hump. If the hump is *large enough*, or comes *late enough*, the mere following-over of the hump *will raise output to such an extent that the accelerator will come back into action* – and will do so at an earlier date than if no hump had occurred. But, if the hump is only a small one, or comes too early, the expansion in output *may never reach this critical point*. Output would then fail to leave the *LL* line until after the hump was completed. What had happened would then look like a weak boom – an expansion in output which fell away again without reaching the ceiling. But theoretically considered, it would not be a boom at all; *the economy would have remained in its depression equilibrium all the time*. (*ibid.*: 121–2; emphasis added)

So far as I know, this Hicksian refinement to his basic model has never been discussed in the vast literature on *CTTC*.

To put in perspective the above point and the following discussion, it will be useful to point out that the standard interpretation of the *CTTC* model as a second-order, unforced, non-linear differential equation was initiated in Takuma Yasui's classic paper (Yasui, 1953). Goodwin had shown that the interaction of the non-linear accelerator and the dynamic multiplier could be reduced, under highly plausible economic assumptions, to a *forced*[3] Rayleigh-like equation in output y (see Goodwin, 1951: 12, equation 5e):

$$\ddot{y} + \vartheta\dot{y} - \frac{\varphi(\dot{y})}{\epsilon\theta} + \left[\frac{(1-\alpha)}{\epsilon\theta}\right]y = \frac{O^*(t)}{\epsilon\theta} \qquad (18.1)$$

Yasui, using this as a starting point and observing that the general economic hypotheses underpinning the Hicks model in *CTTC*, particularly the reliance on a non-linear acceleration principle, even though it was formulated in discrete time, were substantially equivalent to those in the Goodwin model, began a tradition of referring to the Hicks–Goodwin

---

[3] The forcing term comes about because Hicks and Goodwin introduced autonomous investment in a *linearly additive way* into their system. More on this below.

model as being represented by the (*forced*) Rayleigh equation. In contrast, there was the non-linear Kaldor model, relying on an investment function depending on the level of income and the stock of capital. Yasui, by the way, was the pioneer who reduced it to the (*unforced*) van-der-Pol-type equation in income, y (see Yasui, 1953: 232, equation 2.17):

$$\ddot{y} + \frac{1}{\epsilon}[\epsilon(\mu + \delta) + s - f'(y)]\dot{y} + \frac{s}{\epsilon}(\mu + \delta)y - \delta f(y) = 0 \qquad (18.2)$$

It will be immediately clear to any perceptive reader that the above equations are special cases of the generalized Liénard equation:

$$\ddot{y} + g(y, \dot{y})\dot{y} + h(y) = r(t) \qquad (18.3)$$

This was still an era of deriving special equations and showing the existence of limit cycles. It was not yet the era of formal dynamical systems formulations and (non-constructive) proofs of existence of limit cycles in planar dynamical systems using the Poincaré–Bendixson theorem. It was an era that came to an end with its high point: a demonstration, by construction, of specific equations – that economic hypotheses could lead to equations of the van der Pol type or Rayleigh type (they are *formally* equivalent) and then to harness results on such equations to show the existence of economic cycles with the required characteristics.

Let us now go back to the suggestive but neglected ideas in *CTTC*, encapsulated in figure 18.1, and substantiated by the two Hicks quotes. To be modeled, as has come to be standard in the mathematical macro-dynamic literature on *CTTC*, as a Rayleigh-like equation involves serious reconsiderations of the original non-linear investment function, $\psi(\dot{y})$. This, in its classic formalizations, consisted only of the induced part of investment, to which autonomous investment, L, was tagged on as an additive component (see Goodwin, 1951: 9; Morishima 1958: 167; or Ichimura, 1955: 200):

$$\dot{K} = \psi(\dot{y}) + L \qquad (18.4)$$

It is this kind of additive, separable, assumption that leads to the forced Rayleigh-like equation for the non-linear dynamics of output. Such non-linear equations, without simple assumptions on the forcing function, are impossible to solve or characterize. All the pioneers of non-linear trade cycle theory who analyzed the *CTTC* model assumed that autonomous investment was *constant* to reduce the non-homogeneous, forced equation to a homogeneous, second-order, non-linear, differential equation of the Rayleigh type, for which there were known methods of solution. On the other hand, if we take seriously some of the implications of the criticisms by Duesenberry, Lundberg, and others on the possible formalizations of autonomous investment, it is almost clear that a *multiplicative* assumption to include it inseparably in the functional form $\psi(.)$ might be a way out of some of the definitional infelicities. I opt, therefore, to include a parameter, say λ, to encapsulate the effects of autonomous investment, as the simplest alternative, as $\psi(\dot{y}; \lambda)$. With this formulation (18.1) can be rewritten, in generalized form, as (see Goodwin, 1951: 13, equation 7b or 7c):

$$\ddot{y} + \chi(\dot{y}; \lambda)\dot{y} + \zeta(y) = 0 \qquad (18.5)$$

In this form, it is easy to make sense of Hicks's desiderata for his generalized model to encapsulate multiple equilibria of the type described above: *a locally stable equilibrium coexisting with a separate unstable equilibrium giving rise to maintained oscillations*. Hicks is not explicit about the geometry of the locally stable equilibrium – i.e. he does not suggest a characterization of the *basin of attraction* of the locally stable attractor: it could be a *stable focus* or a *stable node*, although, reading between the lines, it appears as if there is a preference for the former. Making only those assumptions that have been made in the standard literature on the canonical *CTTC* model, the following proposition summarizes the main result for the generalized Hicks model with the required *two equilibria*.

For the following formalization of the *CTTC* model,

$$\ddot{y} + \vartheta\dot{y} - \frac{\varphi(\dot{y}; \lambda)}{\epsilon\theta} + \left[\frac{(1-\alpha)}{\epsilon\theta}\right]y = 0 \qquad (18.6)$$

where the dynamical system depending on the scalar parameter, λ, denotes the equivalent C^3 first-order system as

$$\dot{x}_1 = F_1(x_1, x_2; \lambda) \qquad (18.7)$$
$$\dot{x}_2 = F_2(x_1, x_2; \lambda) \qquad (18.8)$$

Let the vector-matrix representation of this system be (explicitly separating the linear and non-linear parts)

$$\dot{x} = A(\lambda)x + F(x; \lambda) \qquad (18.9)$$

such that

$$F(0; \lambda) = 0 \text{ and } D_x F(0; \lambda) = 0, \ \forall \ |\lambda| \text{ sufficiently small} \qquad (18.10)$$

Assumption 1
At the origin $A(\lambda)$ has the eigenvalues $\alpha(\lambda) \pm i\beta(\lambda)$, with $\alpha(0) = 0$ and $\beta(0) \neq 0$.

Assumption 2
The eigenvalues cross the imaginary axis with non-zero speed – i.e.

$$\frac{d\alpha}{d\lambda}(0) \neq 0 \qquad (18.11)$$

From this we have the following.

Proposition 1
In any neighborhood $N_{\{0\}}$ of the origin in the plane and for any given $\lambda_0 > 0, \exists \bar{\lambda} < \lambda_0$, such that (18.9) (or (18.6)) with the value $\bar{\lambda}$ has a non-trivial periodic orbit.

Remark 1
The assumptions are entirely consistent with those in CTTC (and implicit in Goodwin, 1951).

Remark 2
It is, in fact, possible, if given explicit functional forms and values for the constants, to determine a bifurcation diagram to compute the radius of the relevant periodic orbit. Moreover, it is also possible to derive a formal proposition on the value of the radius of the 'corridor' within which the locally stable attractor contains its dynamics (see Swinnerton-Dyer, 1977).

The 'dead' accelerator and the 'one-sided' oscillator!

The setting up of dynamic systems of equations and the discussion of their solutions in the form of explosive and cyclic processes, is undoubtedly a valuable branch of economic research. [...] The danger with dynamic theory is that, as with Hicks, the logic of the mechanism is unproductive, and the beauty of the model seduces the researcher into attaching an unreasonably exaggerated weight to the results. (Lundberg, 1950: 105)

In their detailed reviews of *CTTC*, Duesenberry (1950), Kaldor (1951), Fels (1951), Lundberg (1950), and Sho-Chieh Tsiang (1951) all take issue with the assumptions on, and the role of, the acceleration principle in the cyclical process of the model developed by Hicks. Duesenberry couples that discussion and critique with the observation that the hypothesis of the 'ceiling' may be redundant; but he does not suggest that a real cycle of the kind Hicks tried to construct (at least for all but the last two chapters of *CTTC*), with the tools of piecewise-linear difference equations, is a feasible technical enterprise. Lundberg, Fels, and Tsiang are more concerned with the variability of the accelerator coefficient, even in its tranquil region – the variability at the extremes was taken care of by means of non-linearities.

It is in Goodwin's review, however, that one finds a critique, and a remedy to the critique, of the role of the accelerator when the system approaches the 'floor.' For purely *economic reasons*, he objects to the role of the accelerator in the lower reaches of the downturn. His objections are, perhaps, best expressed in his own appreciative piece on Hicks in *The Legacy of Hicks* (Hagemann and Hamouda, 1994):

When output has fallen, leaving general excess capacity, there is no reason to invest and *the accelerator is dead*: it can take 15, 50 or more years for the excess capacity to disappear, so that the cycle would be spending most of its time in depression. (Goodwin, 1994: 77; emphasis added)

To this he, too, like the other reviewers, couples his objections to the *deus ex machina* of autonomous investment, which, together with a *dead accelerator*, was to revive the economy and set it on its recovery path. These considerations convinced him that, from a purely economic dynamic point of view, there was only justification for the assumption of the 'ceiling.' This left him in a quandary, however. To explain the quandary I will have to indulge in some minor circumlocution. In the review itself he has noted:

Since Professor Hicks proposes a theory which will explain *the maintenance of oscillations*, we can be sure, *on formal grounds*, that this *implies a non-linearity*. In fact, he assumes two – the lower limit of zero in gross investment and the upper limit of full employment in real income. […] It is evident that full employment constitutes a barrier because in order to get there we must have a rate of expansion, and hence a level of investment, of real income which cannot be maintained when once we have attained it. Hence induced investment must fall with consequent drops in income and employment. *This one barrier would suffice to maintain a steady oscillation*, but in fact there is a second barrier of a quite different sort form the first. (Goodwin, 1950: 318; emphasis added)

Goodwin's quandary was the formal one of devising a (second-order) non-linear dynamical system that would exhibit maintained oscillations without the need for a cubic characteristic! There was no known second-order planar dynamical system, at the time he was writing the review, that was capable of maintained oscillations – i.e. of generating limit cycles – without assuming a cubic-like characteristic. If this could not be avoided, then for a formal, second-order, non-linear differential equation economic model to be capable of maintained oscillations it was necessary to assume 'two barriers.'

This is where, proverbially, genius met with necessity and the result was serendipitous! Being the competent geometrist he was, he experimented with alternative characteristics; through a process of trial and error, but convinced that there was one to be found, he discovered, purely by construction, the feasibility of generating stable limit cycles in a planar dynamical system with a non-cubic characteristic that, to be consistent with the model in *CTTC*, had to be piecewise-linear and continuous. One of the first he experimented with was the following dynamical system:

$$\ddot{y} + \chi(\dot{y})\dot{y} + y = 0 \qquad (18.12)$$

with

$$\chi(\dot{y}) = \begin{cases} -m_1, & y < y_\alpha \\ m_2, & y \geq y_\alpha \end{cases} \qquad (18.13)$$

where, y_α, m_1, m_2 are positive constants and

$$4 > m_2^2 > \frac{4m_1}{(1 - m_1)^2} \qquad (18.14)$$

More generally, inspired by Goodwin's economically motivated construction of a one-sided oscillator, Philippe Le Corbeiller posed the general problem of proving the existence and uniqueness of a limit cycle for the above dynamical system with

Condition 1
$\chi(\dot{y})$: a real valued function having a piecewise continuous derivative.

One of the implications of the proof of existence of a limit cycle for such a system was that a particular condition in the Levinson–Smith theorem (Levinson and Smith, 1942) that the characteristic has to be an odd function became unnecessary. This was – and continues to be – assumed in many of the traditional non-linear macrodynamic models underpinning endogenous trade cycle theories.

The following dynamical system is one of the first that was discovered, in the sense of being formally defined (by Le Corbeiller), and, indeed, its characteristic was named (again by Le Corbeiller) a *Goodwin characteristic*:[4]

$$\dot{x}_1 = x_2 \qquad (18.15)$$

$$\dot{x}_2 = 0.5[(2x_2 - x_2 e^{x_2})] - x_1 \qquad (18.16)$$

The equation for the unimodal Goodwin characteristic is[5]

$$y = m(2x - xe^x) \qquad (18.17)$$

The graph of this equation is given in figure 18.2 and the stable limit cycle underpinned by this Goodwin characteristic is given in figure 18.3.

---

[4] Some of the personal aspects of this story I have already reported and narrated (Velupillai, 1990, 1998). Goodwin's two straight lines were 'smoothed' by Le Corbeiller, who correctly surmised that the key property that Goodwin wanted to encapsulate was unimodality rather than piecewise continuity.

[5] For years I had been trying to graph this function with a negative exponent, because that was how it was written down in Le Corbeiller's letter to Goodwin. Then, a chance simulation with a colleague at UNAM (the National Autonomous University of Mexico) led me to try a simulation with a plus sign!

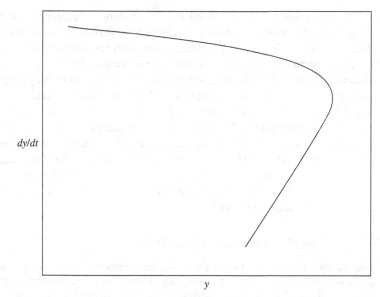

dy/dt

y

Figure 18.2 The Goodwin characteristic

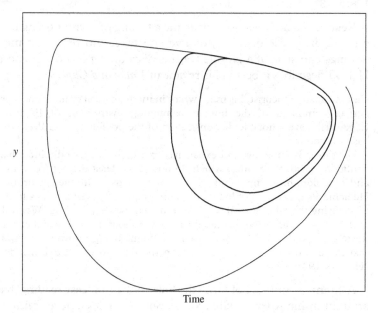

y

Time

Figure 18.3 Stable limit cycle for the Goodwin characteristic

Thus was born the one-sided oscillator, which resolved Goodwin's quandary. His economic intuition rebelled against the assumption of the dead accelerator reviving, in conjunction with an unacceptable autonomous investment component, a prostrate economy. He had absorbed the Harrodian precept of the inescapable one upper bound of fully employed resources and, hence, the acceptability of the 'ceiling.' He was, however, a 'modeler'; and needed a handle on a feasible dynamical system that would generate maintained oscillations to make the theory stand on its own feet, rather than invoke monetary rigidities and other 'exogenous' factors for the economic system to live without one or the other of the 'barriers.' The serendipitous result of a conjunction of these considerations resulted in the discovery and construction of the Goodwin characteristic, *directly inspired by a reading of CTTC*.

The pleasures of reading Hicks

John Hicks is an economist in the great classical tradition… He is a pure economist in the sense that his interest is in developing general economic theory by improving the framework of assumptions whenever the case for such an improvement is established, and in exploring their implications as fully as logical reasoning, *aided by mathematics*, makes possible. Unlike others, whose interest in economics is more pedestrian, Hicks' main aim is the pursuit of knowledge as such. (Kaldor, 1986a: 187–8; emphasis added)

Reading Hicks has always given me a feeling of a writer trying to engage a reader in gentle dialogue, of give and take, and reminded me of the writings and style of a Neville Cardus discoursing on cricket and music. Harrod describes it best in his review of *Value and Capital*:

Can the austere theorist, his mind wrapt in mathematical symbolism, ever obtain perfect command of the human palpitating instrument of English prose? Edgeworth gave a notable demonstration of the possibility, and Professor Hicks has now confirmed it.

His mood is a mellow and expansive one; there are friendly interchanges of confidence with the reader, which do not in the least detract from his dignity and precision; his companionly relation never lapses into the coy or the hearty. He achieves great feats of lucidity in many passages, even at times to the point of arousing the false hope that his volume will be easy reading. When the light grows dimmer, as it does sometimes, one feels that it is because there are some unstated though doubtless important problems being resolved by implication, that there is matter to be read between the lines to which one has no clue… (Harrod, 1939: 294)

A countless number of times the 'false hope's of 'easy reading' has been aroused in me when tackling a new book by Hicks, never raising alarm bells simply because each of the books conveyed that 'mellow and expansive mood' and lulled me into yet another somnambulant confidence that mastery of a difficult subject was close at hand.

Nonetheless, the first three of his more important books received vitriolic reviews[6] – even for the style and the tone they contained and conveyed – by eminent theorists: Gerald Shove on *The Theory of Wages*; Oskar Morgenstern on *Value and Capital* (Morgenstern, 1941); and Lundberg on *CTTC*. Indeed, Lundberg's remarkable comments on *Value and Capital*, in his review of *CTTC*, suggest something close to total incomprehension of a book that owed much to 'Swedish' concepts, tools and method:[7] '[H]is *Value and Capital* [is] to my mind a much overrated book. Its sterile problems and its dead logic have already bored to tears ten generations of students and a generation of teachers' (Lundberg, in Henriksson, 1994: 109).

Then there are those who harp and carp and cavil about the lack of attention to this or that work on the same subject; or the lack of references to anyone since Vilfredo Pareto or Léon Walras, or Henry Thornton or David Ricardo. These are the latterday reincarnations of that nitpicking Subuthi who cavil about Piero Sraffa reinventing the von Neumann wheel or Goodwin paraphrasing Felix Klein without acknowledgment. In the case of *CTTC*, it may well be remarkable that there are no references to Joseph Schumpeter's monumental *Business Cycles* or to Michał Kalecki's *Theory of Economic Fluctuations*, or even to Friedrich Hayek's writings on the cycle, which had inspired Hicks to write his very first article on business cycle theory (Hicks, 1933a), and, above all, the absence of serious references to Robertson's two classics on the trade cycle. Johan Åkerman

---

[6] Successful books have, not infrequently, received less than generous reviews by eminent contemporaries. Whether there is a particular pattern to be detected by an exhaustive case study of a decent sample I do not know. My mind goes back, almost routinely, to George J. Stigler's review of Paul Samuelson's *Foundations of Economic Analysis* (Stigler, 1948; interestingly, *The Journal of the American Statistical Association* reviewed Samuelson's book *twice*, an earlier one by Gerhard Tintner appearing in the issue previous to the one in which Stigler's appeared – and, in its conclusions, more diplomatically couched, but almost equally negative!) and to Arthur Pigou's ultra-brief and largely negative review of Knut Wicksell's *Lectures on Political Economy* (volume I), in *The Economic Journal*: 'In general character it is a critical exposition rather than an independent contribution to learning. [...] The somewhat laborious character of the exposition, coupled with the general familiarity of the ground covered, makes it unlikely that this new text-book will find many English readers – unless, indeed, an English as well as a German translation is produced' (Pigou, 1913).

Pigou must, surely, have been deceived by Wicksell's humble style, whereby he went out of his way, usually, to find predecessors to whatever he discovered or devised. Wicksell, Hicks, Samuelson – at the hands of Pigou, Morgenstern, Stigler – and many prior and subsequent classics have been savaged in equal measure by equally eminent luminaries, almost contemporaneously. I suppose the lesson I have drawn is that reviews are best left for a later stage in the life of a book; let a book make its own way and be at the mercy of the larger audience and not be subverted by the idiosyncrasies of singular reviewers!

[7] Perhaps *because* of it?

and Lundberg point out, caustically, and Goodwin in a mild-mannered way, the absence of any reference to Schumpeter, and Lundberg (in Henriksson, 1994: 109), laments:

> It is unfortunate and typical of Hicks' early 'static isolation', that in his book [*CTTC*] he does not even mention the name of Schumpeter, the man who since 1910 devoted the larger part of his great research work to the study of the cycle as a consequence of economic development (expansion).

I recall, with pleasure, Hicks's lecture (Hicks, 1991) on the occasion of the celebrations to commemorate the fiftieth anniversary of Bertil Ohlin's papers that codified, for the 'outside world,' the work that was being done in 'Stockholm.' The title of the lecture was 'The Swedish Influence on *Value and Capital*.' In spite of fading memories, even at that time, I was still able to remember that *Value and Capital* had absolutely no references whatsoever to any of the more important works of the Swedes who had influenced Hicks, right through the 1930s: Erik Lindahl, Gunnar Myrdal, Ohlin, Dag Hammarskjöld, and, no doubt, Lundberg himself. I also remembered, however, that over the many subsequent years he had found ways to pay tribute to the way their influences had been decisive in the development of his own thought and writings – in particular, the influences of Lindahl and Myrdal. A future historian of economic thought would find meticulously detailed documentation and indications of the exact nature, almost with precise datings, of 'Swedish influences,' not just on *Value and Capital* but on the genesis and evolution of Hicksian contributions to monetary, capital, and methodological issues over the whole span of his life.

The same story could easily be repeated, with exact and detailed references, for the influences of Dennis Robertson, Keynes, Hayek, Ralph Hawtrey, and, of course, the Continental neoclassical masters, and their English contemporaries, Francis Edgeworth and Alfred Marshall. That Lundberg and others find it mysterious that a book on trade cycle theory, written scarcely over a decade after Schumpeter's monumental two-volume opus on the same subject, does not refer to it – or to many of the other classics of the 1930s, except, of course, to Harrod's book – does seem justifiable.[8] As Hicks acknowledges in the preface to the third impression

---

[8] My own lack of mystification on these fronts may have a great deal to do with the fact that I read Goodwin's review of *CTTC before* I became familiar with the book itself. Goodwin's opening paragraph, after listing five of the significant theoretical 'accomplishments' of *CTTC*, goes on to observe that (Goodwin, 1950: 316; emphasis added) '[s]uch a theoretical offering, so well written, in such narrow compass (168 pages), for so little ($2.25), is most welcome, especially if we compare it with the ponderous, uninspired, expensive texts which are continually being hurled at us. [...] *Professor Hicks launches his model with a humility rare amongst economists...*'

of *CTTC* (1950a: v), however, 'It is an exercise in a particular method, and if I were to adopt a different method...I should have to write a different book.'

Moreover, even in the preface to the original version of *CTTC*, Hicks is explicit on the 'provisional' nature of the contents of the book:

Even on the purely theoretical side, I am very conscious that much remains to be done. If *a provisional answer* is given to the main question, that answer raises further questions, and many of these are left unexplored. The main argument itself has got some weak links, which need strengthening. [...] At the point where I leave it, the inquiry looks like branching out in many directions. That is a good point at which to write *a progress report, which is all that this 'contribution' claims to be.* (xi; emphasis added)

A 'progress report on an exercise in a particular method' and an implicit catalogue of unexplored questions suggest, in my opinion, a challenge to extend the method and attempt to answer the unanswered questions – using, if necessary, the wisdom of those whose contributions were not harnessed in *CTTC*, such as Schumpeter and Lundberg, or those whose work on trade cycle theory were given only a casual nod, such as Kalecki and Jan Tinbergen. Legions of imaginative non-linear trade cycle theorists have used *CTTC* in exactly this constructive way, to extend economic methodology in its conceptual, mathematical, and empirical frontiers, as I have tried to indicate, no doubt inadequately, in this chapter.

There is another aspect to this business of lack of reference to all and sundry. It is not very likely that I would read in a book by some of the contemporary theorists of mathematical business cycle theory that they 'could kick themselves for not having seen it before,' say in Schumpeter; Hicks was 'kicking himself' for 'not having seen' what Harrod helped him see (1950a: 7). This is the style that Harrod so poignantly outlined above. One reads Hicks and does not wonder why he does not refer to Schumpeter or Lundberg; one takes part in a dialogue and leaves, at the end, with a cleared mind and fresh attitudes to old problems, perhaps even with one or two answers to them. The pleasant conversations of enlightened intellectual discourse are not about footnotes to pioneers and precursors; they are about 'dis and dat,' without that proverbial 'rhyme or reason.'

What is the moral of the story – of not paying adequate attention to prior work? I had the personal experience of asking Hicks whether, in writing *Capital and Time*, he had prepared himself first by going back to look at Eugen von Böhm-Bawerk's classics and Irving Fisher's *Rate of Interest*. His answer was illuminating. He told me that he no longer had easy access to such works and his style of working was, as it always had been, to read the classics but then put them aside and think about a problem that preoccupied his mind at any particular point in time with such readings as the backdrop. What he wrote on any particular topic would, of course, have been colored by what he had read but, on the whole, he would try to work out the solutions to the problems he had posed for himself on his own and with his own intrinsic resources. Later, however, when the time came to reflect upon his own work, and go beyond it, he would try to organize the influences that had inspired a particular method of attack or a particular way of viewing history. I was witness to the same kind of method of working by Goodwin. This is, of course, quite the opposite to my own method of working; I am a lesser mortal and rely heavily on the work of others, not only for the problems I pose for myself but also for finding methods to solve them. I am rarely able to formulate original problems and even more rarely to find solutions to them, or if, indeed, I do find solutions, more often than not, do not recognize them as solutions without help from others. Hence I am forced to pepper my writings with umpteen references in which poor readers are drowned, as witness this very chapter!

Thus, in rereading several of the writings on trade cycles by John Hicks, written by him over a period of almost fifty years, I recall his own words in *Capital and Time* (1973a: v):

[W]herever one starts, it is hard to bring more than a few [aspects of a large subject] into view. It is just as if one were making pictures of a building; though it is the same building, it looks quite different from different angles. As I now realize, I have been walking round my subject, taking different views of it. Thus that which is presented here is just another view, it turns out to be quite useful in fitting the others together.[9]

It has helped me avoid rash conclusions about inconsistency or incoherence in Hicksian writings on trade cycles. Even more importantly, his remarkably humble 'confession,' in the Georgescu-Roegen Festschrift (Hicks, 1976b: 299–300; emphasis in original) was crucial for me to remember whenever I felt carried away by mathematical niceties and tended to forget the economic and historical contexts within which, and from which, Hicks was 'making pictures of a building':

For my part, I am very ignorant of science;[10] though I have dabbled in mathematics my spiritual home is in the Humanities. It is because I want to make economics more human that I was approaching the task from that end and I am content with a more earthy way of going about it. [...] It is the *new* things that humanity has discovered which makes its history exciting; and the new things that may be found in the future, before humanity blows itself up, or settles down to some ghastly 'equilibrium', make a future worth praying for, and worth working for.

[9] Although Hicks, in this passage, is talking about his changing views of *capital*, I have come to believe that this particular attitude permeates his methodology and philosophy of theorizing in economics in general.

[10] That the author of *Causality in Economics* (1979a) can 'confess' to be 'ignorant of science' is severely humbling to contemplate.

In all my many readings of *CTTC* I have always found it a refreshingly 'earthy' book, capable of being polished in various ways – sometimes with newer mathematics, at other times by deepening the tentative conceptual definitions of economic ideas or institutions, at still other times by reflections on method and methodology. In each of these ways *CTTC* and the other Hicksian visions and vignettes on non-linear trade cycle theories have furnished macrodynamic theorists with suggestions for the 'new things that may be found in the future' and for avoiding settlements in 'some ghastly equilibrium,' whilst squarely staying within the fold of the humanities.

19 Capital, growth, and production disequilibria: on the employment consequences of new technologies

Harald Hagemann

Capital, growth, and unemployment

Throughout his professional life John Hicks maintained a deep interest in capital theory, as is shown by his famous trilogy *Value and Capital* (1939a), *Capital and Growth* (1965), and *Capital and Time* (1973a). In his view, '[C]apital...is a very large subject, with many aspects; wherever one starts, it is hard to bring more than a few of them into view' (1973a: v). In the third volume on capital the unemployment consequences of new technologies are at the very center of Hicks's analysis. Implicit in *Capital and Time* is the concept of the *impulse*, which is developed in his 1973 Nobel lecture 'The Mainspring of Economic Growth' (1973c), and particularly in the essay on 'Industrialism' (1977a: chap. 2). The mainspring of economic progress is invention, which causes an impulse that works its way through the profit mechanism. The investigation of the macroeconomic consequences of such impulses on output and employment is at the focus of the *traverse* – i.e. the analysis of an economy whose initial equilibrium is disturbed by a change in one of the determinants of growth, such as technical progress. The necessary adjustment path requires both time and costs; in other words, in traverse analysis it is historical time, and no longer logical time, that is decisive.

By the late 1960s Hicks had become fascinated by the *Ricardo machinery effect* – i.e. the employment consequences of a different, more mechanized method of production. Hicks defended what he considered the core of David Ricardo's analysis: namely that there exist important cases in which the introduction of a new type of machinery might reduce both real output and employment in the short run, the detrimental effects continuing for a while, but higher investment activity, due to the higher profits resulting from the greater efficiency of the new production methods as they generate more savings and thereby a higher rate of growth for the economy as a whole, should eventually lead to a path of output and employment above the reference path (the growth path that would have been achieved with the old production process).

346

Hicks based his traverse analysis on a *neo-Austrian* representation of production structures, which 'recognizably descended from the "Austrian theory of capital" – the theory of Böhm-Bawerk, that was subsequently elaborated by Wicksell and Hayek' (Hicks, 1973a: 6–7). The long debate on the machinery problem had shown the importance of the time dimension in the diffusion process of a new technology, as well as for the compensation of technological unemployment. In Hicks's neo-Austrian theory, time is the essence of capital, which enters production in a double way: as the duration of the process by which labor inputs are converted into consumption goods; and in the sequence of final output at different dates generated by the fixed capital goods, which thus do not completely disappear in the production process but cause intertemporal joint production. Capital is a medium for sequential production. By dealing explicitly with fixed capital goods, Hicks's neo-Austrian theory considers production processes to be of the flow input/*flow* output type, and thus differs from that of Eugen von Böhm-Bawerk and the Friedrich Hayek of *Prices and Production* (Hayek, 1931a), who confined their models to working or intermediate capital and, therefore, could deal only with production processes of the flow input/*point* output type.

The real nature of business cycles

It was one of Hayek's major contributions to have shown the importance of the temporal structure of production processes for cyclical fluctuations. Hicks quite often emphasized how much he had been influenced by Hayek to think of the production process as a process in time when he participated in his seminar at the London School of Economics in the years from 1931 to 1935. Hayek's elaboration of the monetary explanation of business cycles owed a considerable debt to Knut Wicksell's analysis of cumulative processes caused by discrepancies between the money (market) rate of interest and the natural (equilibrium) rate of interest (Wicksell, 1907), and to Ludwig von Mises's theory of money and credit (Mises, 1981 [1912]). Wicksell's ideas on the dis- and re-equilibrating mechanism of divergences between the two rates of interest had provided an important building block for Austrian business cycle theory as it was developed by Mises and Hayek (see also Hagemann, 1994d, and Hagemann and Trautwein, 1998). In particular, the latter combined Wicksell's analysis of the cumulative processes with the doctrine of 'forced saving' to generate a monetary theory of the business cycle in which injections of money or bank credit lead to overinvestment and thereby to a distortion in the time structure of production that is not sustainable.

Two major impulses causing a divergence between the two rates of interest can be distinguished: (i) an improvement in profit expectations due to technical inventions, which raise the natural rate of interest and thereby investment demand; and (ii) a too generous granting of credit by the banking system, which leads to a fall in the money rate of interest below the natural rate. Whereas the first impulse is a real and 'natural' one, the second impulse is a monetary one and, in the view of Mises and Hayek, an 'artificial' one, causing disproportionalities in the structures of relative prices and production, thereby necessarily implying later corrections. Although Wicksell developed his analysis of cumulative processes mainly for a better understanding of changes in the price level, he essentially held a *real* theory of the business cycle, which treated monetary aspects as subordinate. Wicksell emphasized technology shocks, and perceived in real factors that lead to an increase in the natural rate of interest the essential reason for business cycles. In his article 'A New Theory of Crises' (Wicksell, 2001 [1907]), he clearly identified (the unsteady stream of) inventions as the 'deepest cause of changes in economic conditions.'[1]

Like Wicksell, Hicks always treated the business cycle as fundamentally a real phenomenon, reflecting technological change and the consequential fluctuations in investment that accompanied them (see Hicks, 1974d). In his *Contribution to the Theory of the Trade Cycle* he emphasizes 'the real (non-monetary) character of the cyclical process' (Hicks, 1950a: 136). Since his early participation in Hayek's seminar at the LSE, Hicks remained skeptical about Hayek's claim that the economy would be in equilibrium if there were no monetary disturbances. Although he took over from Hayek the idea that the impact of an impulse on the real structure of production is of decisive importance, he clearly disagreed with Hayek as to whether the divergence from equilibrium and the dynamic adjustment process are caused by monetary factors or by real factors, particularly technological change. This is shown in section 11.6 of *Capital and Time* ('The Contribution of Professor Hayek'), which concludes with the statement: 'Monetary disorders may indeed be superimposed upon other disorders; but the other disorders are more fundamental' (1973a: 134). Hicks's position marks a decisive difference from Hayek, for whom the business cycle is essentially caused by monetary factors even though real phenomena constitute it.

Hicks's position in the debate with Hayek thus has much in common with that of Adolph Lowe in the German debate on business cycles in the late 1920s and early 1930s. Lowe was the main opponent of Hayek, among other issues on the different basic causal factor endogenous to

---

[1] See Wicksell (2001 [1907]: 339), and, for more analysis, the discussions in Boianovsky and Trautwein (2001) and Hagemann (2001).

the economic system that distorts the rigid interrelations implied in static equilibrium, namely technological change versus money and credit (see Hagemann, 1994a). Another core issue in the Lowe–Hayek debate, which is of modern significance and relevant also for Hicks's work, was the emphasis on the importance of the structure of production. Whereas Hayek's *vertical* treatment of economic structure, in the Austrian tradition of von Böhm-Bawerk, focused on the relationships between the fund of productive resources and the production of final output highlighting the time aspect of production and adjustment processes, Lowe's *horizontal* approach, on the other hand, in the tradition of François Quesnay and Karl Marx, and later Wassily Leontief and Piero Sraffa, focused on the circular character of economic relationships and was characterized by a completely different treatment of the durable means of production.[2]

The analysis of the consequences of process innovations on sectoral structures is the strength of the horizontal approach, which does, however, have some difficulties in dealing adequately with product innovations and with the exact time profile of the inter-industry adjustments in the economic system. Hicks saw the decisive advantage of the Austrian approach in its ability to cope with the important fact that process innovations in most cases imply the introduction of *new* capital goods.

It is here undeniable that these goods should be physically specified, since there is no way of establishing a physical relation between the capital goods that are required in the one technique and those that are required in the other. The only relation that can be established runs in terms of costs, and of capacity to produce final output, and this is precisely what is preserved in Austrian theory. (1977a: 193)

Thus Hicks, the lifelong critic and modifier of Hayek's construction in business cycle theory, returned not only to (neo-)Austrian capital theory. He also reappraised the central message of Ricardo's machinery chapter in a way that seems to underline the basic role of the Ricardo effect in Hayek's business cycle theory: 'To industrialize, without the savings to support your industrialization, is to ask for trouble. That is a principle which practical economists have learned from experience. It deserves a place, a regular place, in academic economics also' (1973a: 99).[3]

---

[2] For a detailed analytical comparison of the 'vertical' and the 'horizontal' treatment of economic structure, see the contributions in Baranzini and Scazzieri (1990) and Landesmann and Scazzieri (1996).

[3] For a critical assessment of Hayek's adaptation of the Ricardo effect of a shortage of consumption goods on the production of investment goods and the role of the Ricardo effect in Hayek's business cycle theory, as well as a comparison with the original ideas of Ricardo, see Hagemann and Trautwein (1998). Interestingly, it had been Hicks's 'The Hayek Story' (Hicks, 1967c) that caused the latter to write his concluding 'Three Elucidations of the "Ricardo Effect"' (Hayek, 1969).

Inventions must increase the social dividend

Hicks recognized Ricardo as 'the greatest of the classical economists' who 'had candour and courage; he followed his reasoning where it led him, not just where he (or his friends) wanted it to go' (1969a: 151). Hicks's praise refers in particular to the new chapter 31, 'On Machinery,' in the third edition of Ricardo's *Principles*, published in 1821. In this chapter, which, according to Sraffa, marked 'the most revolutionary change in edition 3' (Sraffa, 1951: lvii), Ricardo retracts his previous opinion that the introduction of machinery is beneficial to all the different classes of society, and instead comes to the conclusion '[t]hat the opinion entertained by the labouring class, that the employment of machinery is frequently detrimental to their interests, is not founded on prejudice and error, but is conformable to the correct principles of political economy' (Ricardo, in Sraffa and Dobb, 1951: 392). By taking note of the labor-displacing effects of new machinery, the former confidence of classical economics in the steady growth of output and employment was lost. Ricardo thus removed the cornerstone from Adam Smith's edifice, in which the rate of growth in productivity is governed by the rate of growth of aggregate demand (the expansion of the markets), and the issue of reabsorbing displaced workers never came up because it was taken for granted that output expansion and cost reductions due to the introduction of new machinery were inseparably linked.

Ricardo gives the following rationale for his considerable reorientation to the machinery question:

My mistake arose from the supposition, that whenever the *net income* of a society increased, its *gross income* would also increase; I now, however, see reason to be satisfied that the one fund, from which landlords and capitalists derive their revenue, may increase, while the other, that upon which the labouring class mainly depend, may diminish, and therefore it follows, if I am right, that the same cause which may increase the net revenue of the country, may at the same time render the population redundant, and deteriorate the condition of the labourer. (Ricardo, in Sraffa and Dobb, 1951: 388; emphasis added)

As he explains in chapter 26, 'On Gross and Net Revenue,' of his *Principles*, gross income or gross revenue Y consists of the sum of wages, profits, and rent, whereas net income or net revenue S implies profits plus rent – i.e. the social surplus. Ricardo's statement as to the detrimental character of the introduction of new machinery to the interests of the labouring class thus implies a pattern that is marked by an increase in S with a simultaneous decrease in Y. The detriment of a declining wage bill shows itself either in a lower real wage per worker or, with the real wage being fixed, in a decline in employment. Ricardo did not analyse the question of whether and under what conditions technological change will lead to unemployment in terms of a supply and demand approach to the labour market. Thus he considered a fall in the real wage neither as a necessary consequence of the displacement of workers nor an effective remedy for a successful compensation process. In his numerical example, which he used to explain his new view on the machinery problem, Ricardo developed a sequential analysis based on a fix-wage model, in which labor supply is perfectly elastic and employment varies with circulating capital, to show that an introduction of improved machinery – i.e. the use of more fixed capital in order to economize on circulating capital – can negatively affect employment and the national (gross) income.

Wicksell, who was among the many great economists who came to be fascinated and stimulated by Ricardo's analysis of the machinery problem, was the first to apply the then new marginal productivity theory of distribution to the treatment of the effects of technological change on income shares. Wicksell recognized that Ricardo did not base his reasoning on a factor price/factor quantity mechanism and criticized him for the absence of it. From the viewpoint of marginal productivity theory the fall in real wages, on the one hand, is caused by the diminished demand for labor as a consequence of the introduction of new machinery, but, on the other hand, increases the profitability of old labor-intensive technology and thereby leads to the reabsorption of displaced workers. In the section 'The influence of technical inventions on rent and wages' in volume I of his *Lectures on Political Economy* (1934 [1913]), Wicksell's argument combines a flex-wage model with the possibility of substitution between the factors of production, which affects the extent to which a decrease in wages can act as a compensating factor. The negative impact of new machines then does not lie in unemployment but in lower wages.

Wicksell essentially restates his arguments in the article 'Ricardo on Machinery and the Present Unemployment,' which he submitted to *The Economic Journal* in 1923. That paper was then rejected by Keynes, but was published almost six decades later in the same journal (Jonung, 1981).[4] In that article, as in volume I of his *Lectures*, Wicksell emphasizes another basic disagreement with Ricardo:

I am myself the first who has pointed out that Ricardo's conclusion as to a possible diminution of the gross product is actually *wrong*, and that although the introduction of machinery may very often be detrimental to labourers, as a matter of fact it is never *necessarily* so. On the contrary, the machinery will always have the effect of

---

[4] For a detailed investigation of the development of Wicksell's views on technical change, real wages, and employment and a modern assessment, see Boianovsky and Hagemann (2004).

raising the gross produce of the country to its greatest possible amount, and in so far it will provide the *means* for bettering the economic conditions of the working men as well as their employers. (Wicksell, in Jonung, 1981: 201; emphasis in original)

Wicksell's queries about Ricardo's neglecting the impact of the displacement effect on real wages and the consequential compensation process, as well as about the effect of new machinery on output, have caused numerous economists to deal with these controversial issues. Among the most prominent modern commentators we find such diverse authors as Luigi Pasinetti and Paul Samuelson. Pasinetti criticizes Wicksell's first query harshly:

Suffice it to mention, as an example, the argument used by Wicksell, when trying to refute Ricardo's analysis of technological unemployment. For Wicksell, technical improvements and the introduction of machines may cause unemployment, but this unemployment is immediately re-absorbed because the wage rate will fall, and entrepreneurs will 'substitute' labour for capital, i.e. shift to more labour-intensive methods of production, so that more labour will be needed. If one follows this argument logically, one comes to the conclusion that a continuous process of technical progress is accompanied by a continuous process of decreasing wage rates! The conclusion is so absurd that it requires no comment. (Pasinetti, 1981: 230)

Samuelson (1988, 1989) set out to vindicate Ricardo's propositions, in particular the analytical question as to whether a viable invention can reduce total real output after all competitive prices adjust to clear all markets, and comes to the conclusion: 'Ricardo is right, Wicksell (and Kaldor and...) are wrong' (Samuelson, 1989: 52). Samuelson makes his case very clear: 'By thus ruling for Ricardo, the judge is ruling against the plaintiff in the famous suit K. Wicksell vs. D. Ricardo – in which Knut Wicksell denied that a viable invention could reduce aggregate output. My title could therefore have been the less gracious one: Wicksell was wrong!' (48).

Samuelson's 'ramble through the literature' resulted in a long list of economists, led by Kaldor (1932), who followed Wicksell in his dismissal of Ricardo's claim that the real national income can be reduced by the introduction of machinery. Samuelson adds that 'J. R. Hicks [1969a] is perhaps an exception but his discussion does not address Wicksell's query about the inventions's effect on total output' (*ibid.*). Whereas Samuelson is right with regard to Sir John, it has escaped his attention that J. R. Hicks, who wrote his first book, *The Theory of Wages* (1932), as a labor economist at a time when he was thoroughly neoclassical (see chapter 3, by Pasinetti and Mariutti, and chapter 15, by Solow, in this volume), expressed a clear view sharing Kaldor's position. In the famous chapter 6, 'Distribution and

Economic Progress,' which gave birth to the concepts of the elasticity of substitution and 'Hicks-neutral,' 'labour-saving' and 'capital-saving' inventions we also find the passage 'Inventions must increase the social dividend':

Under the assumption of competition, it inevitably follows that an invention can only be profitably adopted if its ultimate effect is to increase the National Dividend. For if it is to raise the profits of the entrepreneur who adopts it, it must lower his costs of production – that is to say, it must enable him to get the same product with a smaller amount of resources. On balance, therefore, resources are set free by the invention; and they can be used, either to increase the supply of the commodity in whose production the invention is used (if the demand for it is elastic), or to increase the supply of other commodities (if the demand for the first is inelastic). In either case, the total Dividend must be increased, as soon as the liberated resources can be effectively transferred to new uses. (Hicks, 1932: 121)

For a fuller elaboration of this argument, Hicks refers explicitly to Kaldor's 'A Case against Technical Progress?' (Kaldor, 1932) and the German edition of Wicksell's *Lectures*, which at that time were not yet translated into English. Although J. R. Hicks thus shared Wicksell's and Kaldor's statement that Ricardo's view that the introduction of new machinery can result in a reduction of gross income is erroneous, there is not necessarily a contradiction with the views of Sir John from the late 1960s onwards. The last sentence of the passage that inventions must increase the social dividend already indicates that this increase will take place under the assumption that employment is maintained – i.e. a successful compensation process has taken place. This conclusion in no way contradicts Ricardo's one of a diminution of gross income in his numerical example of an embryonic form of traverse analysis in which the introduction of new machinery causes a decline in the demand for labor and the output of consumption goods, but, due to a stop after four periods, the long-run time paths of employment and output are left in the dark. 'Ricardo's theory is a theory of the working of the individual impulse' (Hicks, 1983a: 38). Since it is a characteristic feature of Ricardo's example that it abstracts from capital accumulation, his theory contains a kind of *capital shortage* theory of temporary technological unemployment. Nevertheless, Ricardo deserves merits for pointing out that a process of additional saving and investing is necessary to assure the compensation of displaced workers.

Lederer and Neisser on Wicksell's analysis of Ricardo's machinery problem

Wicksell's critique of Ricardo's analysis of the machinery problem was re-examined by two German economists, Emil Lederer and Hans

Neisser, whose contributions are unduly neglected in the modern debate. Rapid labor-saving technical progress was regarded by Lederer as a decisive factor in explaining the severity of unemployment in the early 1930s. Lederer published numerous articles and two monographs on this issue, of which *Technical Progress and Unemployment: An Enquiry into the Obstacles to Economic Expansion* (Lederer, 1938) is a widely extended and modified version of his earlier German monograph on *Technical Progress and Unemployment* (1931). The latter book had been the focus of attack in the scathing review article 'A Case against Technical Progress?' by Kaldor, who, at that time, was a thoroughly neoclassical economist and had come to the conclusion: 'The fundamental objection against Professor Lederer's argument is that it is based on a case which cannot take place in a competitive society, i.e. where technical invention has the effect of diminishing the national dividend (i.e. it diminishes production in all industries from which capital is withdrawn without increasing it in those firms where more capital is now employed)' (Kaldor, 1932: 185–6). Kaldor explicitly refers to Wicksell, as well as to Arthur Pigou and Hicks's essay 'Distribution and Economic Progress,' which became chapter 6 of *The Theory of Wages*, '[f]or an analysis that the adoption of technical inventions must increase the national dividend' (186, footnote 7).

Lederer's analysis of the employment consequences of technological change combines central ideas of Karl Marx's theory of accumulation with Joseph Schumpeter's ideas of innovation and credit in capitalist development. Like Schumpeter, Lederer held the view that capitalist economies are normally in a dynamic disequilibrium. For Lederer, capitalist dynamics implied not only development but also destruction. Despite the impression given by Kaldor, however, he did not make a case against technical progress, because he never denied that technical progress offers enormous possibilities for the most rapid expansion of production and increasing employment with growing real income of the masses (see, for example, the end of the introduction in Lederer, 1931: vi), even when focusing on the negative aspects.

In contrast to Ricardo (and Neisser), Lederer did not share the view that a process of real capital accumulation is a necessary condition for a successful compensation process. On the contrary, he emphasizes 'that capital formation on its own does not guarantee growth in the number of jobs. If the speed of the increase in the organic composition becomes so fast that despite the capital accumulation the demand for workers falls permanently behind the supply of workers, then unemployment becomes *structural*' (Lederer, 1931: 72, footnote; emphasis added). The basic factor to cause disequilibrium identified by Lederer is the profit-motivated drive of the large firms to realize economies of scale, which leads to a growing tendency to concentration and cartelization. The similarity of Lederer's theory of structural unemployment with Marx's 'general law of capitalist accumulation' is clearly visible.

The young Kaldor, still awaiting his 'Keynesian enlightenment' in those days, also argued against Lederer: 'The existence *of permanent* unemployment will depend in any case upon the assumption of rigidity of money-wages and not on the nature of the invention' (Kaldor, 1932: 189). For Kaldor, technical changes and unemployment did not stand in a clear relation of cause and effect. Arguing from the basis of marginal productivity analysis, he could identify only one villain causing unemployment, namely 'monopolistic interference with the price system, either from the side of capital or from the side of labour' (195). Lederer, on the other hand, argued strongly against the orthodox statement according to which there is only one reason for persistent unemployment, namely that real wages are too high and too inflexible downwards. According to Lederer (1931: 11–16), one can neither blame the wage level if unemployment is the consequence of rapid technical progress nor cure technological unemployment by a forced reduction of wages. 'The greater the miracle of rationalization, the more absurd the claim that technical progress is a function of the wage level' (15). 'The mechanical loom does not owe its origin that hand-weavers lived too luxurious and that their pieces of work became too expensive. On the contrary: one cannot imagine any wage level which could have prevented the breakthrough of the mechanical loom' (14).[5]

Lederer took up the question as to whether wage reductions can increase the compensation for unemployment and reduce the extent of displacement in a longer section in *Technical Progress and Unemployment* (1938: 198–214), in which he also makes extensive comments on Wicksell's treatment of the issue of a decline in the marginal productivity of labor as a consequence of technical progress. Here one passage sounds like a direct reaction to the fundamental objection made by Kaldor (1932) (who is not explicitly mentioned), when Lederer states: 'It is also true that, in spite of the decline in marginal productivity and the consequent reduction in all labour income (real incomes as well as money incomes), the national dividend must rise because total output has expanded' (1938: 201, footnote 1). This statement stands in remarkable contrast to the numerical examples constructed in

---

[5] A similar argument has been made by Leontief in the modern debate: 'A drastic general wage cut might temporarily arrest the adoption of labor-saving technology, even though dirt-cheap labor could not compete in many operations with very powerful or very sophisticated machines. The old trend would be bound to resume, however, unless special barriers were erected against labor-saving devices' (Leontief, 1986 [1982]: 369).

chapter 4 of Lederer's earlier book (1931), which are characterized by a loss in the total value of the national output with a net increase in profits and interest being smaller than the decline in wage income. Thus, on the analytical question of whether a viable invention can reduce the total of real output after all competitive prices have adjusted to clear all markets, the later Lederer (1938) sided with Wicksell and Kaldor, whereas the earlier Lederer (1931) had sided with Ricardo.[6]

Although he was somehow skeptical concerning the practical relevance of Wicksell's assumption of diminishing physical returns, Lederer was now in basic agreement with Wicksell's denial that technical progress could reduce aggregate output. The feeling of a 'paradoxical technical development' remains, which leads, on the one hand, to an increase of average labor productivity but, on the other hand, to a decline of the marginal productivity of labor. Nevertheless, Lederer concludes the sub-section discussing Wicksell's views with the statement that 'the total income of the community will increase, first, because of the expansion of output in the dynamic firms, and secondly, because of the extra output of the displaced workers' (1938: 202). For good reasons, however, he remained skeptical concerning Wicksell's new equilibrium between the dynamic and static firms, since the latter might also try to introduce the new method of production under more realistic assumptions, such as additional investment activity as a requirement for obtaining the extra profits from technical improvements, which then may lead to an even greater reduction of the wage level. Like Neisser, Lederer thus referred to a weakness of Wicksell's analysis in which capital accumulation is not sufficiently integrated into the investigation of Ricardo's machinery problem. Most important for Lederer is the following conclusion:

Wicksell's analysis actually shows how difficult, and often even impossible, it is for the principle of marginal productivity to operate in the case of rapid technical progress. In any case, it cannot be advanced as an argument to prove that wage reduction is an effective practical remedy against the difficulties raised by technical progress, and one which will rapidly restore a stable equilibrium. (*ibid.*: 202, footnote)

With his famous 1932 paper 'The Wage Rate and Employment in Market Equilibrium,' available in English in an abridged version from

---

[6] Lederer even emphasizes that in 'our examples, in which the gross output of the dynamic firms does not decline, total production must expand more rapidly than in Wicksell's scheme, in which there was a fall in the gross output of the dynamic firms (according to Ricardo's example) which was not made up again until the displaced workers were again re-engaged. Moreover, it is only under our assumptions that an increase in gross returns is certain, because in Wicksell's example the gross returns of the whole economic system would fall if marginal productivity diminished faster than he assumes (1938: 205, footnote 1).

1990, Neisser not only made a seminal contribution to the theory of general equilibrium (see Hagemann, 1990) but also critically inspected Wicksell's basic objection to Ricardo's analysis of the problem of technological unemployment. Particular emphasis was given to the role of physical capital in classical theory: 'The hypothesis of the present essay is that the employment of workers can only be increased if the amount of physical capital is increased at the same time' (Neisser, 1990 [1932]: 141). According to Neisser, Ricardo had already provided the key to the modern view of the problem insofar as he referred to the fact that machinery is used more often in countries with high wages than in low-wage countries. Neisser (144) explicitly refers to Ricardo's statement: 'Machinery and labour are in constant competition, and the former can frequently not be employed until labour rises.'[7] Unfortunately, Neisser stops his quotation just before Ricardo's anticipation of Marx's idea of the tendency of the 'organic composition of capital' to rise: 'The demand for labour will continue to increase with an increase of capital, but not in proportion to its increase; the ratio will necessarily be a diminishing ratio' (*ibid.*).

The central question Neisser addressed is the extent to which additional workers can be employed on a given capital stock when wages are flexible downwards. An answer to that question depends primarily on the technologically determined shapes of the revenue curves. In his closer inspection, Neisser distinguishes two basic types of changes in the capital/labour ratio: a change in the economic lifetime of machinery, which is positively (negatively) correlated with the wage rate (interest or profit rate) but does not alter the size of the gross product; and a variation of capital intensity, due to the introduction of a new machine, that is associated with a change in the net and gross product. It is this second type that is more complex and interesting with regard to Wicksell's discussion of Ricardo's machinery problem. Neisser makes it clear that there may always exist different types of technical progress that shift the marginal productivity curves for labor, as is shown in figures 19.1 and 19.2, where the horizontal axis denotes the level of employment N and the vertical axis the value of the marginal product of labor or real wage. Figure 19.1 depicts a case in which the marginal productivity curves for the two methods of production do not intersect. If curve II represents the new method of production and a certain amount of labor is given at N_1, efficient production may either

---

[7] Ricardo, in Sraffa and Dobb, 1951: 395. This quotation is the leitmotif in the first article on 'The Ricardo Effect' by Hayek (1942), who had introduced this effect into his business cycle theory to explain the upper turning point. Hayek (1942: 128) refers explicitly to Neisser (1932) for the fullest discussion of 'the familiar Ricardian proposition that a rise in wages will encourage capitalists to substitute machinery for labour and vice versa.'

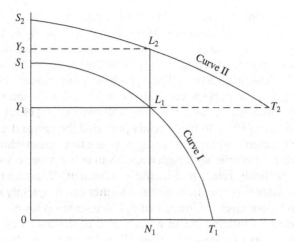

Figure 19.1 Effects of technological progress on the marginal product of labor (without displacement)

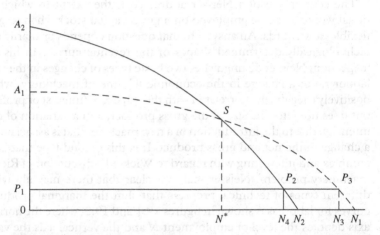

Figure 19.2 Effects of technological progress on the marginal product of labor (with displacement)

raise profits from the area $S_1 Y_1 L_1$ to $S_2 Y_1 L_1 L_2$ (at a constant real wage) or finally raise the wage level from Y_1 to Y_2 (which would imply a reduction of profits to $S_2 Y_2 L_2$), or lead to an increase in employment (and of profit) with the expansion of output if labor supply were elastic ($S_2 Y_1 T_2$). Since technique II is dominant, entrepreneurs would not go back to technique I nor would there be a coexistence of the old and the new method of production, as in Wicksell.

Figure 19.2, however, shows that there exists another important type in which the revenue curves for the old and the new method of production do intersect. Here, curve A_1N_1 represents the old and A_2N_2 the new technique of production. Suppose the old employment level has been somewhere between N_2 and N_1, say at N_3, then it would be impossible to keep that employment after a switch to the new production method. If, on the other hand, the initial employment level has been between N^* and N_2, then, however, it would be possible to keep the employment level after a switch to the new technique – at the expense of a lower wage rate. Since profit maximization is the decisive criterion for the choice of technique, the new method will be chosen if the area A_1A_2S is larger than the area SN_1N_2, independently of the initial wage rate. If we take P_3N_3 as the original wage, then profit would go up from $A_1P_3P_1$ to $A_2P_2P_1$ as a consequence of the switch from the old to the new method of production.

Neisser emphasizes the great theoretical and practical relevance of the case of two intersecting revenue curves for clarifying the exact conditions under which technical progress causes a displacement of workers that cannot be compensated for by mere adjustments. First, he points out that such a displacement will not occur in all cases of technical progress, not to mention all those cases of technical change that represent pure capital-intensive growth. He then distinguishes genuine displacement, which is sustained in market equilibrium, from non-genuine displacement, which originates from a remuneration of production factors exceeding the marginal product or from transitory problems and disappears with a slow variation of data. He agrees fully with Ricardo that certain cases of displacement exist which under conditions of market-clearing competition may reduce the gross product below its maximum. Neisser stresses that 'such a reduction is only possible if there is a minimum wage' (1990 [1932]: 160). Thus, with a zero wage, the area $0A_2N_2$ must be greater than the area $0A_1N_1$ if the new technique is more profitable than the old one – i.e. 'a smaller number of workers could produce a larger total product on a physical capital equipment of given size' (ibid.).

Neisser distinguishes two cases in which the level of production remains below its maximum level: (i) either the area A_1A_2S is greater than P_2SP_3 but smaller than N_2SN_1, making it possible that a return to the old system A_1N_1 would lead to an increase in the wage sum $N_4P_2P_3N_3$ that exceeds the reduction in overall profits; (ii) or even when A_1A_2S exceeds N_2SN_1, if the revenue curve of the new method between N_4 and N_2 is flatter than that of the old method between N_3 and N_1, in which case it is possible that the product represented by the area $0A_2P_2N_4$ is smaller than that represented by the area $0A_1P_3N_3$. According to Neisser, Wicksell could challenge Ricardo's conclusion as to a possible diminution of the gross product only because 'first, he assumes that the displaced workers would always have a positive marginal productivity and secondly he only considered the very special case of intersecting revenue curves in which the areas A_1A_2S and SN_1N_2 (or SP_2P_3 respectively) are just equal' (1932: 451).

Neisser was aware that Wicksell regarded a decline in wages as a necessary condition for gross production to reach its maximum amount. Nonetheless, Neisser probably made the most elucidating contribution on Wicksell's critique of Ricardo's treatment of the machinery problem before Samuelson in demonstrating that Ricardo was right that the introduction of new methods of production can lead, under certain conditions, to a reduction in the gross product. Thus, in contrast to the contemporary contribution by Kaldor (1932), 'and other important modern economists [who] have used the dogma that perfect competition is Pareto optimal to indict Ricardo for necessary error in his machinery chapter' (Samuelson, 1988: 48), it is clear that we have an important counter-example in Neisser.

Neisser elaborated Ricardo's argument that the demand for labor will continue to increase with an increase of capital only.[8] He emphasized, however, that wage capital must be understood as a part of money capital and not of real or physical capital. The latter consists of fixed capital and of circulating capital (intermediate goods). For Neisser, it 'is not surprising that the analysis of the wage fund theory of employment, on the whole, gave negative results. For this approach…is purely algebraic and does not indicate the causal mechanism, neither the motives of entrepreneurs nor the technical possibilities of re-employment' (1942: 61). In his assessment of different theories of technological unemployment he clearly states: 'It never has been doubted by any theorist of rank that accumulation of capital in the form of fixed equipment raises the demand for labor' (70). Therefore, he definitely cannot be accused of what Samuelson (1994) half a decade later has called the 'Classical Classical Fallacy' – i.e. that *fixed capitals* are prejudicial to wages and the demand for labor whereas *circulating capitals* are favorable.

A theory of economic history

Whereas abstract theoretical reasoning had been a distinguishing mark of the young J. R. Hicks, the older Sir John stressed the mutual relationship between economic theory and economic history as one of fundamental

---

[8] See section 3 of Neisser (1990 [1932]) and, for a complementary critique of the classical wage fund theory of employment, Neisser (1942: 58–62).

methodological significance (for a more detailed examination, see Scazzieri, 1994). In that context it has to be emphasized that the core of Hicks's message in his neo-Austrian theory of *Capital and Time* is already incorporated in his *A Theory of Economic History* (1969a), particularly in the culminating chapter 9 on 'The Industrial Revolution.' In a key passage, in which he reflects on the effect of the Industrial Revolution on real wages, Hicks comes to the following conclusion:

There is no doubt at all that industrialism, in the end, has been highly favourable to the real wage of labour. Real wages have risen enormously, in all industrialized countries, over the last century; and it is surely evident that without the increase in productive power that is due to industrialization the rise in real wages could not possibly have occurred. The important question is why it was so long delayed... It is the lag of wages behind industrialization which is the thing that has to be explained. (Hicks, 1969a: 148)[9]

The passage makes clear that Samuelson's verdict that '[p]urely on factual grounds, Ricardo (and, later, Hicks) probably exaggerated the wage-reducing effects of innovation' (Samuelson, 1989: 7) certainly does not hold for Hicks in general, who is in perfect agreement with Samuelson's statement that 'historically, the longer-run trend of productivity change seems to have been strongly in the direction of raising real wage rates' (*ibid.*). There were periods, however, in which the labor supply was fully elastic at a constant real wage due to high population growth and hidden unemployment in agriculture, and employment varied positively with saving (investment). Hicks dates these periods for the United Kingdom from 1780 to 1840 and 1800 to 1850, respectively (Hicks, 1969a: 148, 1977a: 185). The fix-wage model of *Capital and Time* therefore provides an exact replication of the assumptions adequate for the period in which Ricardo investigated the machinery problem.

It is a central message of Hicks, as it had been of Ricardo and all serious economists, that a successful compensation process is conditional on a process of real capital formation. Ricardo is quite clear on that issue toward the end of his machinery chapter when he observes that

the increase of net incomes..., which is always the consequence of improved machinery, will lead to new savings and accumulations. These savings...must soon create a fund, much greater than the gross revenue, originally lost by the discovery of the machine, when the demand for labour will be as great as before, and the situation of the people will be still further improved by the increased savings which the increased net revenue will still enable them to make. (Ricardo, in Sraffa and Dobb, 1951: 396)

---

[9] See also Hicks (1977a: 184–90).

So 'we have two forces at work on the growth of circulating capital and they are pulling in opposite directions' (Hicks, 1969a: 152). On the one hand, the introduction of new machinery can have a negative effect on employment in the *short run*; on the other hand, an increase in the rate of accumulation increases the demand for labor in the *long run*. The expansion of the demand for labor, however, is checked time and again by further innovations, particularly of the labor-saving type.

Hicks in this passage of his history book comes close the famous metaphor of Neisser, who, in discussing the Marxian analysis of Ricardo's machinery problem, regards 'the capitalistic process as a race between displacement of labor through technological progress and reabsorption of labor through accumulation...; displacement and accumulation are two largely *independent* factors, and it is impossible to predict the outcome of the race between the two on purely theoretical grounds' (Neisser, 1942: 70). Thus there is a special dialectics at work. An increase in the rate of accumulation raises the demand for labor, but accompanying changes in technology, which lead to a higher capital/labor ratio, can neutralize this favorable effect on employment. Neisser's conclusion therefore is clear: the outcome of the 'race' is open, and differs with time and across countries. The race becomes even more complex because of the fact that its two contestants are *not* entirely independent; on the contrary, there is a strong mutual correlation between capital accumulation and technical progress. In a qualifying remark, Neisser refers to the fact that a rise in aggregate income due to technical progress also raises the rate of accumulation and thereby the reabsorption of labor. It has to be added however, that this dependency also exists the other way round, as has been shown by modern approaches of induced or endogenous technical progress as they were first developed by Kaldor and Kenneth Arrow. A higher rate of capital accumulation will increase the rate of technical progress.

A fix-wage traverse with a strongly forward-biased innovation

Hicks's classification concept of 'neutral,' 'labour-saving,' and 'capital-saving' inventions in *The Theory of Wages* was developed primarily to analyze the impact of technological change on distribution shares. It was not designed with a view to the unemployment problem. For that purpose he had to develop a new classification concept of technological change, in which the time pattern of technological change plays the crucial role (see Hicks, 1973a: 75–7; Burmeister, 1974: 430–2; Faber, 1979: chap. 9; and Hagemann, 1994a: 207–8). In *Capital and Time*, he distinguishes three types of innovations:

(i) a *neutral* or unbiased innovation with $h = H$;

(ii) a *forward-biased* innovation with $H > h$; and

(iii) a *backward-biased* innovation with $h > H$,

where $h > 1$ indicates a saving in construction costs and $H > 1$ a saving in utilizational or running costs.

In contrast to these two indexes h and H, which are determined exclusively by technical labor/input coefficients, Hicks's new *Index of Improvement in Efficiency*, except in the case of a neutral innovation, depends also on distributional parameters – i.e. the rate of profit (interest rate) and the real wage rate. Whereas in cases of weakly biased innovations, with both h and H greater than unity, the new (old) technique would be dominant (inferior), an economic choice problem arises only with a strongly backward-biased innovation $h > 1 > H$, or a strongly forward-biased innovation $H > 1 > h$. It is the latter that gives rise to the Ricardo machinery effect.[10] Since construction costs of the new type of machine are higher before a saving in labor inputs can be obtained during the utilizational phase, a strongly forward-biased innovation must be profitable at sufficiently low rates of profit (see also the diagrammatic exposition in Faber, 1979).

With the 'classical' or Ricardian assumption of an exogenously given wage rate, employment varies positively with saving. The introduction of a strongly forward-biased innovation is the most complex and interesting case. It is profitable when the savings in running costs dominate, but during the constructional period of the new machines at first a higher input of labor is required. This implies that in the second year of the traverse a smaller number of (new) machines is available for the production of consumption goods compared with the same period on the reference path. The number of workers who are producing consumption goods with the machines of the new technique decreases even more because of the saving in utilizational labor. Although this saving in running costs implies an increase in profits, which, supposedly, are completely invested in the construction of new machines, the existence of temporary technological unemployment is inevitable. Hicks's fix-wage model is similar to the one discussed by Ricardo, namely an increase in mechanization – i.e. the use of more fixed capital in order to economize on circulating capital.[11]

---

[10] 'The *introduction* of machinery must, almost inevitably, be a switch with a strong forward bias. May it not be that this is what Ricardo (mainly) meant?' (Hicks, 1973a: 99; emphasis in original).

[11] Roberto Violi (1984, 1985), however, has shown that all types of innovations can lead to temporary unemployment when neo-Austrian production processes with more general profiles are considered (although the case of a strong forward bias combined with a lengthened construction period is the one that leads to it with the highest probability), and that the

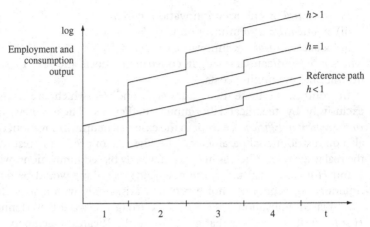

Figure 19.3 The fix-wage path

Figure 19.3 shows the preparatory phase – i.e. period 1, in which employment and consumption output are unchanged but workers are now constructing new machines that are not yet producing any consumption goods. This changes with the early phase, of which the first three periods are shown,[12] and during which both modern and old machines coexist. The paths of employment and output mainly depend on the parameter h – i.e. the relation of the labor input coefficients in the construction period between the old and the new techniques. Whereas, with $h \geq 1$, employment and consumption output exceed their magnitudes on the old equilibrium growth (reference) path, with $h < 1$ an initial decline in output and employment is unavoidable, if consumption out of profits is unaffected by the change in technology (Q-assumption). This implies that savings and investment are lower the higher h is – i.e. the traverse initially falls below the reference level. In contrast to Hicks's exposition, in which from the third period onward overall output and employment will start to recover,[13] and finally (beyond period 4) rise above the reference level, it can well happen that output and employment continue to fall for quite a while. This

crucial condition for technological unemployment to occur is not the specific form of the innovation but the effect on the development of the 'gross produce,' a point that had already been grasped by Ricardo.

[12] See figure 10 in Hicks (1973a: 92), which aims at providing an almost exact replica of Ricardo's numerical example.

[13] This implies that the number of new machines entering their utilization phase in period 3 must exceed the reference level by more than the decline in the number of new machines produced in period 2.

is caused by the fact that as long as the rate of starts remains below the reference level, the number of old machines leaving the utilization department is still higher than the number of new machines entering it. [...] Only when the number of machines in the utilization department...reaches the reference level the fall of output and employment comes to an end. (Kraus and Wirth, 2000: 7)

Thus technological unemployment can become a relatively persistent phenomenon.

Structural economic dynamics: complementary analytical perspectives

Traverse analysis is concerned with the effects of impulses or sequences of such impulses on productive structures, output, employment, and the resulting growth paths. Hicks moved back and forth between the vertical (Austrian) and the horizontal (circular) view of production, dismissing the latter after Charles Kennedy's critique of the neglect of the role of time in production and adjustment processes in *Capital and Growth*. By treating fixed capital as if it were working capital, Hicks did not recognize the need for a special machine tools sector in his neo-Austrian theory. An important consequence of this procedure is that the neo-Austrian approach does not show the effects of innovation on industrial interrelationships. An analysis of feedback processes is not possible, as is required for multiplier analysis, for example. Hicks's Austrian representation did, however, lead immediately to a 'stages' analysis of the adjustment process. The horizontal and the vertical approaches both enjoy comparative advantages in the analysis of traverses, and thus a complementary perspective should be followed (see also Zamagni, 1984: 136–7). Consequently, Hicks, after giving priority to the vertical approach in his *Capital and Time* period, finally converged to a more synthetic perspective in *Methods of Dynamic Economics* (Hicks, 1985a), in which he explored both analytical routes that can be followed to study a productive system's response to an exogenous impulse (chaps. 13 and 14).

In his traverse analysis, Hicks employed a scenario analysis in which (sometimes extraordinarily strong) assumptions about technology and behavior[14] are made and their implications for the adjustment processes are studied. In this scenario technique, which still falls into the realm of positive analysis, elements of older business cycle theories, such as 'forced savings,' are alluded to. Hicks focused on the short- and medium-run effects of an innovation, the 'early phase,' and played down the problem of

---

[14] Such as the Q-assumption, or the problematic assumption of static expectations in the case of the full-employment traverse.

the convergence of the traverse to a new equilibrium or steady-state growth path, which can be assured only under very special conditions (see Nardini, 1990, 1993).

Reflecting on his personal 'Keynesian Revolution,' Hicks came to the conclusion that '[t]he *General Theory* is a brilliant squeezing of dynamic economics into static habits of thought' (Hicks, 1977a: 148). Traverse analysis genuinely deals with dynamic issues, but all the complexities involved imply how difficult the analysis is without making simplifying assumptions or retaining fragments of static habits of thought. Innovations should not be made exogenous but, rather, should result as the outcome of economic factors. This point of view is at the center of modern endogenous growth theory, which, however, has mainly neglected structural analytical perspectives. Nevertheless, the most important part of *Capital and Time* is its theory of the traverse, which is as much inspired by Ricardo's analysis of the machinery problem as by the Austrians' attempt to clarify the role of time in economics: 'So where we have come to on this Austrian route, is close to Ricardo...to his latest insights, which he did not live to follow up. The Austrian method is indeed a Classical method' (Hicks, 1985a: 156). Whereas the switch from one representation of production processes to another is often regarded as a discontinuity in Hicks's thought, in fact we find a lot of continuity in the central economic themes discussed from *The Theory of Wages* to *Methods of Dynamic Economics*. For more than half a century John Hicks struggled for better perspectives in order to gain deeper insights, and thus he remained willing to reflect continuously and to change his analytical approaches on his own evolutionary path.

20 Capital and time

Erich W. Streissler

The time structure of decisions

'My education has been mostly in the non-monetary parts of economics, and I have only come to be interested in money because I found that I could not keep it out of my non-monetary problems,' John Hicks declares early on in his 'A Suggestion for Simplifying the Theory of Money' (Hicks, 1935a: 1). This is perhaps one of his most original publications, the foundation of several later Nobel Prizes, in particular that of Harry Markowitz. Already in that seminal paper, the time structure of decisions was prefigured: the 'decision to hold money...is always made at a point of time' (4). Hicks locates the critical problem in the 'preference for holding money rather than capital goods' (5). Then he announces the necessity of modeling money – or, rather, the riskiness of holding it – in a two-dimensional space: one has to specify a 'mean value, and some appropriate measure of dispersion' (8). Only 'the appearance of...safe investments will act as a substitute for money,' and 'banks...are enabled to go further than other concerns in the creation of money substitutes' (10). Finally, Hicks provides us with one of the main ideas of Keynes's *The General Theory*, a year before that work was published: 'The whole problem of applying monetary theory is largely one of deducing changes in anticipations from the changes in objective data which call them forth' (13).

'A Suggestion' is probably the most 'Austrian' of Sir John's essays; much more so than *Capital and Time* (1973a), which alone is expressly called 'A Neo-Austrian Theory.'[1] 'A Suggestion' refers to Eugen von Böhm-Bawerk: 'One understands that most economists have now read Böhm-Bawerk; yet whatever that union has bred, it has not been concord' (1935a: 1). Nor had it with Sir John. Probably the most important of

---

[1] What the 'neo' in neo-Austrian theory denotes is hardly explained, apart from on page 7, where the word refers to the analysis of *'separable elementary processes.'* Perhaps what is meant is merely that the date of publication of *Capital and Time* is some forty, or ninety, or even 100 years later than the 'old' Austrians?

Hicks's ideas in 'A Suggestion,' namely the relevance of the variance in returns for behavior toward risk, had actually been prefigured in Böhm-Bawerk's thesis of habilitation (Böhm-Bawerk, 1881) in his extensively discussed and famous lottery example – later, via Oskar Morgenstern, to become the foundation of the utility concept in game theory.[2] It cannot be said for certain, however, that Hicks knew Böhm-Bawerk. Hicks also mentions Ludwig von Mises (*ibid.*: 2), if only to dismiss him right away, as with his 'money is a ghost of gold,' nothing more. What is to be found in the 'Suggestion' – though no longer in *Capital and Time* – are the most important and most relevant ideas of Hayek: the more than short-run relevance of money for the equilibrium of the real economy in the sense of a 'preference for holding money rather than capital goods'; and the importance of anticipations or expectations. This may have to do with the fact that Hayek and Lionel Robbins, who was the great outside admirer of 'Austrian' economics, were the most influential professors for their still very junior colleague Hicks at the London School of Economics (five and six years of seniority count for much early in life).

By 1967 Hicks has already decided that money – or, at least 'a "demand for money for transactions purposes"' – 'is a disequilibrium, not an equilibrium phenomenon' (1967c: 15); but *Capital and Time* is mainly an equilibrium theory with just a few glances at disequilibrium phenomena. The only Austrian element left in *Capital and Time* is the time dimension of production. But is the consideration of a mere time dimension in economic analysis, and, in particular, time in an equilibrium framework, already 'Austrian'? Are we convinced by the claim made for *Capital and Time* (vi) that 'it is descended, as I emphasize in my sub-title, from the "Austrian" theory of Böhm-Bawerk and Hayek – a theory which had gone out of fashion'?

In addition to Hayek and Böhm-Bawerk, Hicks was familiar with Carl Menger. He seems to have been one of those rarest of birds in economics, those who have actually read Menger's *Principles* – or at least read in them. Moreover, in his early article on Léon Walras (Hicks: 1934), his first for the then new *Econometrica*, Hicks makes the highly perceptive remark: 'If a reader who is acquainted with the work of Böhm-Bawerk and Wicksell approaches Walras's theory of capital, the first thing which will strike him is that it is purely a theory of fixed capital' (345), while Böhm-Bawerk and Hayek used a model with circulating capital only, as Hicks was to note later on (Hicks, 1973a: 8). Hicks continues: 'It is only in a stationary state that we can get any sensible sort of equilibrium, so long as people expect the prices of products to remain unchanged in the future (as

---

[2] Böhm-Bawerk himself veered away from the full consequence of both mean and variance in returns by assuming risk neutrality.

Walras tacitly assumes they do)' (1934a: 346). From then on, Hicks never dropped the assumption of fixed capital, but was willing to assume that 'people expect the prices of products to remain unchanged in the future' (*ibid.*).

It is exactly the 'un-"Austrian"' combination of both fixed and circulating capital at different points in time that makes *Capital and Time* so fiendishly complex. Hicks assumes: 'There is an initial *construction period*, with large inputs but no final output; it is followed by a *running-in period*, in which output rises from zero to a normal level... There follows a period, probably a long period, of *normal utilization*. Finally, as a result of a fall in the output curve..., the process comes to an end' (1973a: 15; emphasis added). What a tricky time structure! Yet Hicks calls it the 'simple form' – the '*Simple Profile*' (41).

Earlier he had written:

One of the chief contributors to that blaze [the controversy of the 1930s] was Professor Hayek (*Prices and Production*). To one who like myself felt the full impact of that work on its first appearance, it has long appeared as one of the mysteries of economics. Something, one has long realized, had gone wrong with it; but just what? The question has been nagging at me. (1967c: ix)

As I have had the misfortune of being assigned the duty to make sense out of *Prices and Production* (Hayek, 1931) for a forthcoming survey article, I have to make up my mind what 'had gone wrong with it.' Apart from the impossibilities of a pure 'circulating capital' model – and that in a stationary framework while simultaneously describing *change* – the fault with that dubious classic is that it *always* uses the word 'always' when describing highly special (and really unusual) situations that depend on at least a dozen very specific assumptions. In contrast, *Capital and Time* never uses the little word 'always,' but fully shows up the extreme complexity of a wide range of possible economic constellations.

In *Capital and Time*, another work of Hayek is cited, namely *The Pure Theory of Capital* (Hayek, 1941), a much more mature and, indeed, highly convoluted tome. (Sir John must be one of the very few, to be numbered probably in single figures, who have ever read that volume.) The most important influence of Hayek on Hicks probably lies somewhere else, however. I knew both Hicks and Hayek well, having lunched with the latter about three times a week for the best part of five years. Hayek used to say in conversation, 'Did you know that it was I who told Hicks that it might be a good idea to look into general equilibrium theory and to study Pareto in particular?'

The remark, made very much in hindsight, may contain a kernel of truth. For neither *The Theory of Wages* (Hicks, 1932) nor 'A Suggestion for

Simplifying the Theory of Money' (1935a) shows as yet any traces of the general equilibrium approach. After 'Léon Walras' (Hicks, 1934a), general equilibrium (except in the labor market) clearly surfaces with Hicks in 'Mr Keynes and the "Classics"' (oral presentation in September 1936, publication April 1937 in *Econometrica*). As suggested above, moreover, what Hicks has totally dropped by then are anticipations or expectations: we are presented with a futureless, one-period model without any expectations. With Hicks this happened again and again: though frequently stating that he would look into the question of 'anticipations' or 'expectations,' in the end he leaves them out. That what he provides in 1937 was not Keynes can be seen from studying Keynes's own summary in chapter 18, section 2, of *The General Theory*, where we are treated to a complex sequence model in time, depending on expectations from the outset. Hicks, however, has won out in the textbook world, which presents only what I like to call 'Kicksianism,' a mixture containing little of Keynes and much more of Hicks. The full general equilibrium version of Hicks is, of course, his Nobel-Prize-winning *Value and Capital* (1939a), which shows some traces of anticipations, though not many. These have more or less dropped out once more, however, by the time of *Capital and Time* (1973a). Certainly, we are not treated to Hayek's disequilibrium interest rates, which are in his treatment expected by agents to continue for a long period of time, but cannot do so. The fact that Hicks's 'education has been mostly in the non-monetary parts of economics' comes once more to the fore, and Hicks does seem to find that he can 'keep [money] out of [his] non-monetary problems' after all.

In what sense can *Capital and Time* be said to be 'Austrian'?

Is *Capital and Time* 'Austrian' – 'neo' or otherwise? Certainly, the introduction of a long-run time structure of production is an Austrian idea. It goes back to the founder of the school, Carl Menger, who presented it in his thesis of habilitation, the *Principles of Economics* of 1871.[3] What Hicks discusses, though, is a fully foreseen time structure. The essence of Menger on time, on the other hand, is his chapter 'Time – Error' ('Zeit – Irrthum') – i.e. time equals error: the producers of the 'complementary goods…of higher order,' or of capital goods for short, take time to produce these goods. When they start their production processes, however,

---

[3] It is perhaps the only point taken over by all the sixty or so 'certified' members of the school – certified by their habilitation examination before older members of the school as academic judges.

they do not then know whether demand conditions at the distant moment of completion will justify the taking up of production; and they will know it less and less well the further in time the goods they produce are from final demand. None of this can be found in *Capital and Time*. Neither can there be found traces of Menger's prepublication attempt (1888) to refute Böhm-Bawerk, the essence of which is that the (own) rates of interest will typically differ from one process to another, while with Hicks they are equalized. Menger and Böhm-Bawerk did not at all agree on capital theory, as becomes most evident to anyone who reads Menger's scathing obituary evaluation of the academic merits of the president of the Academy of Sciences, Böhm-Bawerk, published in the Academy's yearbook (Menger, 1970 [1915]).

Again and again, Hicks makes much of his dependence on Böhm-Bawerk, which is, however, difficult to discern. Let us quote Joseph Schumpeter, who intimately knew both Böhm-Bawerk and the man's *magnum opus*, on the *Positive Theory of Capital*:

Work on [it]...had to be curtailed and the volume had to be hurried through the press in parts as the author wrote it... Distinct ideas are but imperfectly welded together; in essential respects the author changed his standpoints while writing; different currents of his own thought run side by side; the decisive later chapters are frankly provisional...and as he was *able* to make them, not as he *wanted* to make them. (Schumpeter, 1954: 845)

It has to be remembered that Böhm-Bawerk was in full-time academic duty only from 1881 to 1889 and then once more, briefly, from early 1905 to the middle of 1907. For most of his life he was a highly competent and hard-working civil servant, high court judge, and Cabinet minister; and it is his great success[4] in this that even Menger praised unstintingly.

Böhm-Bawerk gave three reasons for explaining the rate of interest in every capital-using economy – and not only, as he stressed, in a 'capitalistic' system, but also in a 'socialist' one. According to him, all these reasons are subjective valuations on the part of the final consumers. They are thus *demand*-side considerations, while *Capital and Time* presents us with purely *supply*-side explanations of the rate of interest. The 'three reasons' are the following. First, in the present there is a generally lower supply relative to the future, which leads to a higher valuation of present goods. (This would probably be expressed in modern economics as a positive rate of

---

[4] For his last seven years Böhm-Bawerk was at first vice-president, then president, of the Imperial Academy of Sciences in Vienna – i.e. holding highly influential, but certainly full-time, jobs. As such he was until recently pictured on the most common bank note of Austria, the 100-schilling note, the building at his back being the Academy of Sciences building, *not* that of the University of Vienna.

time preference.) Second, the underestimation of future needs due to a lack of knowledge and a deficiency in willpower. Third, roundabout methods of production are assumed to lead to higher returns. That this third reason, and possibly also the first, were considered by many actually to be supply-side arguments is immaterial. Böhm-Bawerk was adamant that he thought of them as purely subjective valuations on the demand side. As a pure 'supply-sider,' Hicks cannot be said to follow Böhm-Bawerk.

That J. R. Hicks had been no closer to Böhm-Bawerk than Sir John later proved to be had already been remarked upon by Schumpeter (1954: 909, footnote 49) in his inimitably outright way: 'A recent constructive reinterpretation of Böhm-Bawerk...is presented in J. R. Hicks, *Value and Capital*, chapter 17. It is not in Böhm-Bawerk's spirit. But it proves that Böhm-Bawerk's ideas worried Professor Hicks.'

It has already been argued that there is nothing in *Capital and Time* that is close to Hayek's *Prices and Production* in any way: Hayek asserted that the rate of interest, as set by commercial banks, is a 'wrong' price in terms of long-run general economic equilibrium, and for a considerable period at that. Possibly one might interpret Hayek as providing a temporary general equilibrium model of the 'second-best' type, as one price is fixed from 'outside' the model. There is no indication that Hicks considered such a model seriously, however. Certainly, Hayek assumed an ongoing stream of bank money creation, which leads to a longer-run disequilibrium rate of interest, as he made explicitly clear in an argument with Hicks (Hayek, 1969), as well as in a letter to him in late 1967. Furthermore, Hayek (1942, 1969) explicitly assumed a rising supply curve for credit, rising in the rate of interest and defined individually for each borrower. Nowadays we would probably use instead the 'credit-rationing' argument, perhaps in the Nobel-Prize-winning version of Joseph Stiglitz and Andrew Weiss (1981), who assume not only a rising but a backward-bending supply curve. In any event, the modeling structure differs between Hicks and Hayek, and this quite apart from 'the mysteries in economics' that Hicks could not figure out in Hayek (and that, to my mind, are not 'mysteries' but obvious mistakes of Hayek's).

As to *The Pure Theory of Capital* (1941), Hayek told me that he had tried to cast it in mathematical terms, but had been discouraged by the mathematicians he consulted, as the subject was mathematically much too difficult. In a sense, *Capital and Time* may be considered the mathematical version of certain simplified aspects of Hayek's *Pure Theory* by the trained mathematician Hicks. Even so, Sir John picked and chose, justifying the original mathematical advisers of Hayek. All the same, the argument of Hicks ends in the casuistry of suggestive, but overabundant examples.

My conclusion is, therefore: apart from the time dimension, there is very little 'Austrian' – 'neo' or otherwise – in Hicks's *Capital and Time*. This must not be read as a criticism but, rather, as a compliment from one who is mainly his student and, though Austrian by nationality, certainly not 'Austrian' in his economics. The only scientific likeness I can claim with all the old 'Austrians' is that they were all trained lawyers – in contrast to the American tribe that, very dubiously, claims descent from them. In the social sciences a lawyer is by profession eclectic, an adherent of ad hoc treatments, fitted to the occasion. In that respect Böhm-Bawerk and the early Hayek were poor lawyers. (In the 1964 Festschrift for Sir Karl Popper, the later Hayek, a thoughtful lawyer by then, gave his epistemological reason why all our economic models have by necessity to remain ramshackle and makeshift.)

What I cannot explain is why J. R. Hicks – and even Sir John – should have admired (from a safe distance!) Böhm-Bawerk.[5] Why should Hicks, long after Böhm-Bawerk's death, have shown such respect, though wisely an unspecified respect, to a man who was certainly an eminent administrator but, as to his theoretical economics, merely the Grand Master of Muddles (shot through, it is true, with flashes of intuitive insights)? The awe of Böhm-Bawerk might have lingered in Hayek; but even he had not known him personally.

---

[5] Böhm-Bawerk was a political and social power-monger, capable – and very willingly, too – of spreading more awe than light. He was a vicious scientific critic who could – and did – use his pen like a cat-o'-nine-tails in order to mar a reputation; and his position as a member of the Austrian House of Lords from relatively early on and as 'His Excellency' (*Wirklicher Geheimer Rat*) from 1900 on made his criticism telling. He was well known to have crossed even the emperor, Francis Joseph, repeatedly. When the University of Graz did not nominate his candidate to a professorial chair he made the emperor overrule the faculty's choice – I know of no other case when this happened – and appoint his own candidate, Joseph Schumpeter, in the teeth of university opposition. Furthermore, when Schumpeter shortly afterwards – wisely, only after definite appointment – published views that Böhm-Bawerk did not like, without, of course, daring to criticize Böhm-Bawerk outright, the reaction of the then president of the Academy of Sciences was their immediate refutation in a sixty-two-page (!) article (Böhm-Bawerk, 1913) that does not read very nicely. Even in the Academy of Sciences Böhm-Bawerk's influence was more negative than positive. All the Austrian economists, including Böhm-Bawerk while in office as minister of finance, had been elected at the energetic initiative of an eminent economic historian, Karl Theodor von Inama-Sternegg, Honorary Doctor of Vienna, Cambridge, Kracow, and Czernowitz, and member of the Lincei (Rome), Prussian and Bavarian Academies of Science. In contrast to Böhm-Bawerk, Inama was wide-ranging and inclusive in his choices, but he died early, just before succeeding in getting Alfred Marshall elected to the Vienna Academy. It was Inama whom the University of Vienna had originally wanted to appoint as professor of economics instead of Menger, who was also, though less obviously, appointed at the will of the emperor because he had been tutor to the Crown prince. So it is understandable that none of the 'Austrians' ever dared to criticize the scientific theories of His Excellency Böhm-Bawerk outright. Many 'earned merit' by defending them to outsiders; and it is quite possible that, by an application of the theory of cognitive dissonance, they even convinced themselves that they believed them – more or less.

The many dimensions of capital and economic transitions

Capital and Time is actually the last part of a trilogy that Hicks wrote on the subject of – according to him – a more or less 'Austrian' capital theory; a trilogy to which has to be added the correspondence between Hicks and Hayek, also published in the meantime (in Kresge, 1999). In this correspondence, dated November 27, 1967, Hicks writes:

> We have (a) full employment, (b) static expectations, (c) 'equilibrium' at every stage, so that demand = supply in every market, prices being determined by current demand and supply... [W]e clearly find that if there are no lags, the market rate of interest cannot be reduced below the natural rate in an equilibrium position; though it may indeed be so reduced in the disequilibrium position, while the economy is passing from one equilibrium to another. If we describe the process as a sequence of equilibria, then in each equilibrium the rate of interest is the same. [...] Relative prices will continue to be determined by real causes. [...] I insist that the position in which the rate of interest is *really* lowered is a disequilibrium position... I hold that one can only analyse such positions by dropping one or other of the assumptions with which I began. We can drop the Full Employment assumption (Keynes or Robertson); we can drop the static expectation assumption (Lindahl); but I was convinced by you that neither of these would fit your argument. One is left with the possibility of modifying the 'current' demand and supply assumption, so as to allow for lags. (Hicks, in Kresge, 1999: 100)

As I am not primarily concerned with Hayek's different type of analysis, it will suffice to point out that Hayek replied that he was thinking not only of a single, but of a continuous stream of bank money injections, all at a rate of interest below the 'natural' rate (see already Hayek, 1942). Therefore a relatively long-run 'disequilibrium' results, compounded by a complex lag structure. Hayek actually prefers to express what Hicks terms 'lags' as follows: 'I compare the speed with which the effect of one single act of additional expenditure [spreads] with the speed at which successive injections (at a rate growing with the growth of the total money stream) follow each other' (Hayek, in Kresge, 1999: 103).

Returning to *Capital and Time*, I would rather express this somewhat differently. Quite naturally for a long-run, production-based equilibrium model, Hicks assumed *perfect price information* – i.e. every agent knows and avails him- or herself of the equilibrium prices – and that not only for the old equilibrium situation, but just as well in case of a switch to a new technique or a new factor price structure. This is not what most Austrians had assumed, either implicitly (as Hayek) or explicitly (as Menger): Menger had suggested that the producers of capital goods would typically not know the prices that would rule for their capital goods, when after the period of production they would come on the market. Furthermore, in the long chapter 5, 'On Prices' ('Die Lehre vom Preise'; Menger, 1871: 172–212), Menger had discussed perfectly competitive prices as a limiting case only. More usually, isolated exchange or monopolistic pricing would rule. So, in its – very appropriate – pricing assumptions, *Capital and Time* once more is basically un-'Austrian.'

'The Hayek Story,' as told by Hicks (1967c), pre-dates the above-mentioned correspondence, which already refers to it. It is a reworking of Hayek's analysis of (mainly) the 1930s, which is surprisingly faithful to Hayek. In fact, upon rereading it recently, it seems to me more faithful to Hayek than I used to think thirty-five years ago (Streissler, 1969). Hicks writes: 'Hayek's model does engender a process; some kind of lag (or lags) must therefore be implicit in it' (Hicks, 1967c: 207). Indeed, this is so: a lag structure in the production sequence from capital goods to final consumption is clearly evident in Menger's original version, and then also in Hayek, who more or less followed him. Indeed, an explicit lag structure pervades the whole of the analysis of *Capital and Time*, which models a 'time profile' of a 'construction period' being followed by a 'utilization' period (Hicks, 1973a: 15). The lag structure assumed is best visualized by looking at figure 1 on page 15 of *Capital and Time*. Moreover, the construction period is one of '*m* weeks' and utilization accounts for 'a further *n* weeks' (41), time spans of possibly different lengths. In fact, this explicit time profile makes the mathematically simple model of Hicks highly complicated, and, indeed, quite indefinite in its large choice of possible conclusions. *Some* lag structure in production can, therefore, for once actually be said to be an 'Austrian' feature, though no Austrian would ever have even faintly thought of the complications of the lag structure introduced by Sir John, in particular as the 'Austrians' had never thought of distinguishing between fixed and circulating capital.

Hicks (1967c) proceeds as follows: 'Granted the initial change in the producer-price/consumer-price ratio, and granted that *it can be maintained*, the effect on the production process will be of the kind that Hayek describes' (1967c: 208–9; emphasis added). Hicks then thinks it better to modify Hayek a little: 'Suppose that one keeps the rest of Hayek's assumptions, but instead of the consumption lag, which is so implausible, one introduces a wage-lag: a lag of money wages behind the balance of supply and demand in the market for labour' (209). I believe this to be no modification at all but, rather, what Hayek actually assumed: prices of commodities change more rapidly than wages, which are fixed by trade unions for a period of a year or two. Hicks concludes (and here I am in full agreement with him and think he has discovered the nub of Hayek's argument): 'The Hayek theory is not a theory of the credit cycle, the *Konjunktur*, which need not work in the way he describes, nor is it, in fact, at all likely to do so. It is an analysis – a very interesting analysis – of the adjustment of an economy to change in the rate of genuine saving' (210).

We shall see that *Capital and Time* once more glosses over this point. 'If saving does not rise, this system of relative prices will be inconsistent with the maintenance of supply–demand equilibrium in the markets' (213). This is what Hayek actually says; in fact, he asserts that saving will have to rise over time in order merely to stabilize the same level of disequilibrium between the ruling supply rate of interest relative to its demand price (or the rate of profit, different from interest). That it is the saving behavior that is at fault is a contention Hayek shares with the Keynes of *The General Theory*; only the political conclusions of Hayek and Keynes differ widely, though in both cases these do not necessarily follow from the theories. And it had been exactly Hicks, in 'Mr Keynes and the "Classics"' (1937a), who had memorably drawn an IS curve that need not intersect the LL (*sic*) curve at the full employment level. In *Capital and Time*, however, *saving does not figure at all*; thus it may be 'Austrian,' but it certainly is not, on Hicks's own earlier analysis, 'Hayekian' – nor, of course, Keynesian.

'A Neo-Austrian Growth Theory' (1970) is the second part of Hicks's 'Austrian' trilogy. It differs very little from the third part, *Capital and Time*, as the *Economic Journal* article in question is a full-scale preview of the later book, announcing nearly all the main ideas of the latter. The article tells us, for the first time clearly, what is meant by 'Austrian' in all these publications: 'The characteristic device of the Austrian theory is that it conceives of the *technique* as a time-profile of inputs and outputs' (*ibid*.: 258). In Menger or Böhm-Bawerk or Hayek, perhaps; but neither Friedrich von Wieser, nor Schumpeter, nor Mises, to name only a few 'Austrians,' would have recognized themselves in that characterization. Should Sir John not perhaps have called his theory 'Fisherian' instead, as Irving Fisher is the authority most often named in the 1970 article? As the main reason for his choice of terms, Hicks points out: 'It is a main strength of the Austrian theory that it is rather good at dealing with transitions' (267) – or the 'Traverse,' as Hicks usually calls a transition. Hayek had completely bungled such 'transitions,' however, thinking that the transition from one stationary state to another can itself be a stationary process; and as for Böhm-Bawerk, had he ever even understood the problem at hand? We are treated to the surprising revelation that 'Jevons and Wicksell' should be taken 'as "Austrians"' (276). William Stanley Jevons at least might have objected.

The only 'real "Austrian"' mentioned is Hicks's former professor, Hayek: it is possible that new processes which have already begun cannot be finished. If they are to be finished there must be additional saving – or a fall in real wages. Is not this, again, a story we have heard before? It is the story of Hayek's *Prices and Production* – though it was mixed up, in that exciting work, with monetary considerations that do not really belong. We may justifiably label it the *Hayek effect*. (277)

That 'monetary considerations...do not really belong' is a view very much in the eye of the beholder – Hicks being the beholder. The intimate fusion of monetary aspects with 'real' problems is, indeed, a hallmark of most 'Austrians' from Menger onwards, with the exception perhaps of the Grand Master of Muddles. (Menger's theory of money is once more very much to the fore; see Kiyotaki and Wright, 1989.) Hicks concludes: 'It will...be noticed that we could not do...without making assumptions about the movement of prices that is *expected*, at each moment, to occur in the future. In an Austrian theory past and future must always be distinguished' (Hicks, 1970: 279; emphasis in original). Expectations in any essential sense, it has already been noted, are the only aspect that Hicks then leaves out of the final version of his trilogy, *Capital and Time*. He concludes the 1970 article as follows: 'Capital, all our investigation has tended to show, is not one-, but many-dimensional' (281). That is, indeed, the central idea of *Capital and Time*. It had already been the main idea of Hayek's *Pure Theory of Capital*. Hayek had been unable to make much of it, though. In that respect, therefore, Hicks did develop, more or less to its feasible limits, an important notion of at least one undoubted 'Austrian.'

Production as a profile of inputs and outputs and as a profile of capital values

A very brief review of the major themes in *Capital and Time* (1973a) will have to suffice. In contrast to the usual way of modeling capital, using production as a 'point-output' process (with either a point-input or a sequence of input streams preceding it), *Capital and Time* models 'a sequence (or stream) of inputs into a sequence of outputs' (*ibid.*: 8). Not only that, 'not simply (a) profile of inputs and outputs...but also a profile of capital values' (18). 'The capital value profile, unlike the input-output profile, depends on the rate of interest... [A] fall in the rate of interest will raise the capital value curve of any process...throughout' (19).

Hicks models one technique as follows:

Since we are working with goods as standard, b_t can be used, either to represent the quantity of the goods that are produced in week t of a unit process, or the value of those goods; for these come to the same thing. But if, as will now be convenient, we use a_t to denote the *quantity* of the labour input, the value of that input, in terms of goods, is wa_t. So the net output (positive or negative), which we shall still call q_t, is $b_t - wa_t$. The (initial) capital value of the unit process

$$k_0 = \sum q_t R^{-t} = \sum (b_t - wa_t)R^{-t} \text{ [sums over : 0 to } n]$$

now depends on w. (38)

w is the wage rate and $R = 1 + r$ the interest factor, with r the rate of interest. 'In an "Austrian" theory, the rate of interest is not the price of a "factor"' (39), Hicks points out in a footnote, giving once more an implicit definition of 'Austrian': the rate of interest makes different time points comparable.

This deceptively simple quantitative model allows for a very complex array of cases. In the case of the *simple* form (41 ff.) – using a terminology slightly inconsistent with the above – Hicks assumes a construction period of m weeks, with input coefficients the same for all these m weeks at the level a_c, while the output coefficient is zero, followed by a utilization period of n weeks with a constant input coefficient of a_n and output at unit level ($b = 1$). Previously, Hicks had already remarked that there would be 'modern' processes in use, earning the market rate of interest, but possibly also 'obsolescent' processes that earn a lower rate of return, but are nonetheless still viable when original cost, which is a bygone, has been written off. The continuation of obsolescent processes provides an interesting insight into the fact that actually measured average rates of return are often rather low.

This model is then taken through its paces; first for the 'full performance and full employment' case; then, in a chapter called 'Steady States,' in particular for a case Hicks calls the 'fix-wage economy,' thus contrasting flexible and constant wage cases in a fashion that, to my knowledge, he had first used – though later changing the terminology – in the *25 Economic Essays in Honour of Erik Lindahl* (Hicks 1956a), in order to model the different scenarios in Keynes's *General Theory*.

The 'Steady States' chapter also starts to analyze changes in techniques; and, be it noted, there are different techniques in *Capital and Time*, but no technical progress in the sense of a discussion as to why new technologies arise. The chapter closes with the distinction (Hicks, 1973a: 77; emphasis in original) between forward-biased technical change 'when the main cost-saving comes *late*' in terms of the length of the production process and backward-biased change when it comes early. At the end there are three chapters on 'Controversy': 'The Measurement of Capital,' 'The Accumulation of Capital,' and 'The Production Function.' In conclusion there is a long – very useful – and slightly more technical appendix, titled 'The Mathematics of Traverse.'

Within this bare framework there are also many fascinating asides for the historian of economic thought; for, as time went on, John Hicks in a sense turned more and more into an historian of thought. In *Capital and Time*, we find a stimulating defence of the wage fund theory of John Stuart Mill and the suggestion that Mill should not have recanted – in fact, 'that by 1868 he was much less interested in economics,' to the point of not to be taken really seriously as an economist (1973a: 58–60).

Harrod neutrality in technical advance is defended (74–6), while – most characteristically – Hicks thinks next to nothing of 'the "Hicks's classification"' and does not think he can find 'anything which corresponds to "Hicks-neutrality"' (183).

David Ricardo and 'the famous chapter "On Machinery", which he added to his third and last edition of the *Principles* (Ricardo, 1821 [1817]),' is taken up: 'It may nevertheless be asked: in associating his exception with "machinery" was not Ricardo overstating his case? On our analysis, the exception does not arise from any "improved machinery"; only from such improvements as have a strong forward bias' (Hicks, 1973a: 98).

Hayek is the only Austrian who is discussed seriously: 'The relevance, to economic fluctuations, of the time-structure of production was the discovery of Professor Hayek' (133). Note that, by using the vague term 'fluctuations,' Hicks sidesteps the issue of whether such an analysis was appropriate for the analysis of rather short-run *Konjunktur*, or not more so for unequal phases of growth. Hicks also distances himself from Hayek: 'Where…I do not go along with him (or with what he said in 1931) is in the view that the disturbances in question have a monetary origin' (*ibid*.). Hicks adds that it is not true 'that with money removed "in a state of barter" everything would somehow fit. One of my objects in writing this book has been to kill that delusion' (*ibid*.).

Finally, Hicks is highly critical of the concept of a 'production function' (177 ff.): 'So static a concept does not fit at all readily into our present line of thought' (177). A production function uses fixed capital only – what an 'Austrian' criticism! 'I shall henceforth call it not "capital" but *equipment*' (*ibid*.; emphasis in original). 'New Equipment, the increment of Equipment, is among the least suitable of all macro-economic magnitudes to be treated as an independent variable. That is really what is wrong with the Production Function' (182) – a criticism that is extended in a footnote to 'the quantity of money.' Was Hicks transmuted into a 'closet Cambridge don'? Reswitching, which is frequently taken up, is, on the other hand, less kindly treated as something of a curiosity: 'It seems safe to regard the exception…as so extreme that it can be disregarded' (118).

A very extended and totally persuasive impossibility theorem

In conclusion, I should like to make some brief remarks of evaluation. Hayek had assumed a disequilibrium situation of the rate of interest (for bank credit) being set independently of the rate of profit on real capital invested. We have *no theoretical* problem with this model any more: it just assumes credit rationing by banks, very much of the type of the Nobel-Prize-winning Stiglitz and Weiss (1981) analysis. (In fact, Hayek had made that clear himself, in 1942 and 1969, with the variant that he assumed a rising supply curve for credit relative to the individual customer of the bank, while Stiglitz and Weiss basically assumed a backward-bending total credit supply curve.) To my mind, the problem with Hayek's analysis is *empirical*, rather: he assumes long-run expectations as to an unchanging rate of interest and, on the other hand, rapid price adjustments in a complex interdependent production structure. This is a very unusual reaction structure over time; it can occur, but rarely so.

I see a corresponding problem in the time structure that Sir John assumes in *Capital and Time*. He basically assumes *unchanging techniques* for decades, not only when a technique first becomes ubiquitous, but even in case of replacements. There is no *induced* technical progress. Techniques are long-run givens. This does not take account, however, of the fact that firms buying new equipment usually experience a long span of 'learning by doing' (Arrow, 1962) until they find out how to use their new equipment most efficiently; or that, as a colleague of mine has found out, they defer start-ups of operations until they have learned how to comply with the numerous impositions of the regulating authorities. Imagined production functions may be of some use in order to rationalize *ex ante* decisions of firms in taking up production; once production is taken up they are rapidly changed by adaptations. Or, as John Enos (1962) described the situation decades ago: original inventions do not have a predetermined and specified capital intensity; once they are taken up, however, they are rapidly developed further in accordance with perceived relative factor prices and factor scarcities.

I think Adam Smith (1776) was factually correct in not yet separating given production functions and technical advances, but thinking of an inseparable mixture of both, apart from the fact of economies of scale. This brings me to the point: *I think it is the ruling rate of interest that is predetermined* (with production adapting) and not the other way around. In the developed world, the long-run real rate of interest has been more or less constant at least from the early eighteenth century onwards, for nearly 300 years by now in the case of the United Kingdom and the Netherlands.

After deducting inflation, interest has been constant on the average at around 3 or 4 percent annually, rising only for very rapidly developing nations to a real rate of 5 percent during some decades. If we look at the demand conditions that keep it so, it is not industrial production that counts; it is government borrowing that is the dominant force by far. I would rely more strongly, however, on the supply conditions: the risk aversion of lenders; the not inconsiderable risk, in the long run, of governments defaulting or (only in the twentieth century) just inflating away; and the loss of short-run opportunities of being able to pick up fleeting bargains because one has tied up one's financial capital in long-run investment.

Thus, it is then the rate of interest to be earned that is predetermined. In industry, this is, by a rule of thumb, about twice the safe rate of return on government bonds, because of the much higher risks in business. One has merely to find a technique that will yield this return more or less – if it exists. And then one will constantly have to modify that technique in order to retain the ruling rate of return, because of relatively rapid changes in the demand conditions for one's final products. (Do these demand conditions shift at all in the case of *Capital and Time*?) Techniques prove to be extremely malleable, if necessity arises, and labor can evidently be shed without changing output. Where it is not so, firms go under. The very complexity of *Capital and Time* convinces me that, if we add the further complexities of business life, in part mentioned above, it is quite impossible that the real world should function even faintly in the manner suggested by this great book. To me the book is nothing but a very extended and totally persuasive impossibility theorem. Even for an Austrian immersed from early youth in capital theory as a subject, that capital theory is too complex to use. Time marches on, but differently.

21 Sequential analysis and out-of-equilibrium paths

Mario Amendola and Jean-Luc Gaffard

Introduction: single period theory and continuation theory

In his last paper, John Hicks (1990) throws light on a fundamental issue for dynamic analysis: the nature and definition of economic activities and, behind this, the time structure of production. The insights thus provided, together with the reference to other contributions by the author, allow important steps forward in the analysis of processes of economic change interpreted as sequential processes. This, as is well known, consists of two analytical moments: the 'single period theory' and the 'continuation theory' – that is, the analysis of the way in which successive periods are linked in a sequence.

Hicks's article is essentially a critical review of Adam Smith and John Maynard Keynes in an attempt at what he calls a 'unification of macro-economics.' The focus is on the time articulation of economic activity; this makes it possible to stress the shortcomings of the analyses of both authors, but also to show that these analyses are, in a way, complementary: in fact, each of them lacks precisely what the other has, so that, together, they comprise a basis for a coherent system of thought.

Hicks proceeds from the consideration that 'Smith, like Keynes, is working with analysis of the behaviour of an economy during a period... a period which has a past and a future, which are not to be assumed to be just like itself carrying on in a static manner' (Hicks, 1990: 532); a viewpoint that depends on him being interested in growth – in the course of which specialization comes into existence – rather than in the comparison between the wealth of different nations, like his predecessors. The argument has a bearing on the Smithian definition of productive and unproductive labor, and, from this, on the interpretation of the role of investment and consumption.

The main point stressed by Hicks is that, if Smith had considered a period of finite length with a beginning and an end (as in the 'single period theory') and hence characterized by an initial and a final stock (of capital) – and not, as he actually seems to do, a time divided into periods of infinitesimal duration – he would have naturally defined productive labor as that devoted to increasing, in the period considered, the stock of capital, and hence unproductive labor as that employed during the period whose product was consumed within the period. Then the 'unproductive consumption' and 'production' of Smith would have obviously transformed into the consumption and investment of Keynes.

Something more, however, would have also come out within the structure of Smithian economics, Hicks argues: the possibility of hoarding. That is, the possibility of using the initial stock neither for production nor for unproductive consumption (i.e. for an unproductive use different from consumption, such as, for example, the piling up of reserves of whatever kind). Then parsimony, as opposed to industry, could not be reckoned to be the immediate and automatic cause of an increase of capital, as stressed by Smith (because it could result in the piling up of reserves); nor the only source, as there would be the possibility of drawing on reserves.

The conclusion is that, in this light, to consider consumption as being flatly opposed to investment – a view that comes from basing the distinction between 'productive' and 'unproductive' on the nature of the activity carried on (with the focus on producer goods industries as opposed to consumer goods industries – the same idea behind the distinction between basic and non-basic goods) – is not correct. The problem is more complex: Keynes's analysis of the multiplier, stressing the role of consumption in helping a given investment to bring about output and employment, is indicative in this sense.

A more accurate consideration of the time articulation of production, however, reveals not only the shortcomings of Smith's analysis – that is, opposing consumption to investment – but also those of Keynes's analysis. These, according to Hicks, are just the opposite, namely the consideration of consumption and investment as being on a par, as perfectly interchangeable components of demand – which is possible only if we overlook the time dimension of these magnitudes. This is a theme that Hicks had already developed, with reference to the multiplier, in *The Crisis in Keynesian Economics* (1974b). If production takes place over a period of finite length, labor must be applied at the beginning of that period while the product will be obtained only at the end of it. Thus for the multiplier actually to work – and for the results in terms of output and employment to be obtained – 'the goods on which the wages of that labour will be spent must also be available, and these cannot be provided out of the product of the labour which is newly employed, for that is not yet ready' (1990: 535). Either there must exist real reserves or the required goods must be released from the existing productive processes, by an increase in saving. This, according to Hicks, is where Smith comes to the rescue: his statement about parsimony, qualified by the possibility of hoarding, and hence of drawing on reserves, complements the analysis perfectly.

Failing that, the only way for an expansionary policy to be successful is to transmute the capital that was embodied in the late stages of old processes into capital embodied in the early stages of new processes – that is, a disruption of other economic activities, which 'is bound to be a strain' (*ibid.*). To identify this strain, and why its consideration is at the heart of the analysis of sequential dynamic processes, requires extending the consideration of the time articulation of production beyond the 'single period'; in other words, to 'continue with continuation – into the future' (538), a task to which Hicks himself calls others at the end of his paper. This chapter is an attempt to answer Hicks's call.

Harmonizing the phases of construction and utilization: the framework of a monetary economy

Our first step in the above direction is, again, reference to Hicks, namely to his neo-Austrian model (1970, 1973a). A neo-Austrian representation of production reflects the change from the hypothesis of a sectoral disintegration of the production process, which naturally evokes a substitution relationship, to that of full vertical integration, which stresses instead a complementarity relation over time. This different viewpoint makes it possible for us to reinterpret the issue of investment versus consumption in terms of a harmonization of the phases of the construction and utilization of production processes; that is, given the sequence of periods over which these phases take place, to consider the implications of the time articulation of production not only within a period of finite length, as done by Hicks, but also *between* periods. The problem of 'continuation – into the future' can then be placed in the right perspective, with focus on the 'form in which the terminal stock of a period is left.' When this form is not what is required, in fact, there is a distortion of productive capacity whose disequilibrium effects will be felt over time. These effects, we shall see, are likely to be amplified and become cumulative, so as to hamper the very viability of the path followed by the economy.

In equilibrium, a given and stable relation between the relevant magnitudes of the economy (such as output, capital, and employment) also implies a given relation between processes in the (different stages of the) phase of construction and processes in the phase of utilization, which assures complementarity over time of investment and consumption. When this is so, the time dimension of production is left somewhat in the shade. We can, in fact, abstract from the productive capacity that underlies the given functioning of the economy and concentrate on its utilization moment; inputs and output, costs and proceeds then become, analytically and from an accounting viewpoint, contemporaneous.

The time structure of production instead comes to light again when a shock of whatever type results in a change in the balance between processes in the phase of construction and processes in the phase of utilization. Inputs are then dissociated in time from output, and costs from proceeds, with important analytical consequences. The adjustment required to re-establish a new equilibrium can take place smoothly, however, with processes gradually transmuted into different ones as resources are gradually freed, as in the traverse to a superior technique analyzed by Hicks (1973a). Suitable hypotheses – such as the existence of a single, homogeneous final product, and 'full performance,' which imply that all output that is not consumed is invested, except for a constant 'take-out' – reduce the process to a sequence that can be fully traced out *ex ante* and in which expectations play no role. The supply and demand for final output are then kept in equilibrium in each period of the sequence through which the traverse is accomplished, and there is no room for cumulative and/or explosive processes. The difference with the standard analysis of transition – although a significant one – is that, here, focus on the distinction between 'investment at cost and investment of output capacity' and on the intertemporal complementarities of production makes it possible to explain phenomena such as David Ricardo's 'machinery effect' – the adverse effect of the introduction of machinery on employment in the short run (1973a: 98). Within the context considered, however, this appears as a transitory phenomenon, which does not involve a viability issue.

This is no longer the case when we are dealing with a process of change whose evolution and point of arrival cannot be predetermined, as they depend on the decisions taken step after step by the agents – that is, when we add the consideration of the intertemporal complementarity of the decision process to that of the production process. We are then dealing with a real sequence of 'constraints–decisions–constraints' (Amendola and Gaffard, 1988, 1998). A change in the balance of production processes can then be the expression of a distortion of productive capacity that implies a disruption of economic activity (the scrapping of some production processes not planned beforehand) and that comes from successive decisions taken in a context in which plans are not systematically fulfilled. In this 'out of equilibrium' context, investment and consumption are no longer harmonized over time, supply and demand no longer match, and, via expectations, cumulative processes set in.

Reference to 'hoarding,' another important insight of Hicks's paper, is fundamental for understanding dynamic processes of this kind. Both in the form of the accumulation of physical stocks or, much more so, in that of monetary idle balances, it is in fact the typical expression of a disruption of economic activity. Without hoarding we would have an automatic (change in the) distribution of resources between investment and consumption over time with no distortion of productive capacity.

Within this context, reference to a monetary economy is essential. One can certainly assert, with Hicks (1973a: 52–5), that a barter economy can also experience fluctuations, if we make the assumption that excess supplies are storable and can pile up in surplus stocks. This is only true, however, if it is not a perfect barter economy – that is, an economy where physical goods are perfectly liquid as they have all the properties of money, like the one in which Hicks's traverse takes place. Stocks (if any) could then always be used to increase the wage fund in successive periods; they would be desired stocks that appear as a means to liquidity in the presence of uncertainty, not as a sign of disequilibrium. Introducing money explicitly, instead, makes it possible to distinguish clearly between money itself (liquidity) and goods, and hence to take into account the appearance of involuntary stocks – be they physical goods or idle balances – reflecting distortions of productive capacity and the setting in of an out-of-equilibrium process that might hamper the viability of the path followed by the economy. There is more to it, though. While both physical and money stocks can account for a disruption of economic activity, money (now being used up instead of being kept as an idle balance) is, instead, essential for harmonizing construction and utilization (and hence investment and consumption, supply and demand) over time. It is essential for the viability of processes of change (such as innovation) that are in the nature of out-of-equilibrium processes (Amendola and Gaffard, 1988, 1998).

In order to show the analytical and policy implications of reinterpreting the issue of investment versus consumption in terms of the harmonization of the phases of the construction and utilization of production processes in an out-of-equilibrium context, we use a model that exhibits the above-mentioned basic Hicksian features but that, at the same time, makes it possible to 'continue – into the future' the argument just sketched out by Hicks. The simulations performed throw light both on the appearance of distortions of productive capacity (in particular, we show that a decrease in unproductive consumption may be as bad as its increase for the viability of a process of economic change) and on the conditions required for reabsorbing these distortions and ensuring the viability of the process itself.

The model of the economy[1]

Let us consider an economy with two classes of agents: firms and households.

Productive capacity

A homogeneous final output is obtained from a *primary* input (labor) by means of production processes of a neo-Austrian type. An elementary production process is defined by the input vector

$$\mathbf{a} = [a_k]; k = 1, .., n^c + n^u$$

whose elements represent the quantities of labor required in the successive periods of the phase of construction c (from 1 to n^c) and, following it, of the phase of utilization u (from $n^c + 1$ to $n^c + n^u$) of the productive capacity and by the output vector

$$\mathbf{b} = [b_k]; k = 0, ..., 0, n^c + 1, ..., n^c + n^u$$

At each given moment t, productive capacity is represented by the intensity vector

$$\mathbf{x}(t) = [\mathbf{x}^c(t), \mathbf{x}^u(t)]$$

each element of which is a number of elementary production processes of a particular age, still in the construction phase or already in the utilization phase.

Productive capacity is subject to aging and to modifications due to investment and scrapping. The scrapping of production processes occurs when resource constraints are so stringent as not to allow all the processes inherited from the past to be carried on.

Resource constraints

In each period the firms' level of activity (both investment and current production) depends on its wage fund $\omega(t)$, which is constrained by available financial resources $F(t)$ or, alternatively, by available human resources $\psi(t)$:

$$\omega(t) = \min[F(t), w(t)\psi(t)]$$

The available financial resources $F(t)$ are

$$F(t) = m(t-1) + h(t-1) + f(t) - c(t)$$

---

[1] This section is derived essentially from the model presented in Amendola and Gaffard, 1998.

where the internal financial resources are given by $m(t-1)$ the money proceeds from the sales of final output, the idle money balances involuntarily accumulated in the past and ready for use by $h(t-1)$, the external financial resources by $f(t)$, and the take-out by $c(t)$, which is the current resources withheld from the financing of production (consumption by producers, transfers, and so forth).

Within the sequential setting considered, prices are fixed within each given period and can change only at the junction between one period and the next. As a consequence, money proceeds are given by

$$m(t) = \min[p(t)d(t), p(t)s(t)]$$

Real stock changes $\Delta o(t)$ are substitutes for the price changes, which cannot take place within the period. Excess supply (if any) results in an accumulation of undesired stocks for the firms:

$$\Delta o(t) = o(t) - o(t-1) = p(t)\max[0, s(t) - d(t)]$$

where $s(t)$ and $d(t)$ are current real supply and real demand respectively, while excess demand for final output (if any) results in the appearance of undesired idle balances for households:

$$h(t) = p(t)\max[0, d(t) - s(t)]$$

External financial resources are such that

$$f(t) = \min[f_s(t), f_d(t)]$$

where $f_s(t)$ stands for the borrowing power of the firm, and $f_d(t)$ is the demand for external financing resulting from the production and investment decisions actually taken.

External financial constraints are formally exogenous in the model. Different financing scenarios, which imply considering the relation between external finance and the viability of innovation processes, can be explored. Available human resources depend on a natural growth rate of population and on wage elasticity:

$$\psi(t) = (1+g)^t L(0)w(t)^\vartheta$$

where g is the natural growth rate, w the wage rate, and ϑ the wage elasticity of the labor supply. When the human constraint is more stringent than the financial constraint, money balances are involuntarily accumulated:

$$h(t) = \max[0, \omega(t) - \tilde\omega(t)]$$

where $\tilde\omega(t)$ is the constrained wage fund.

Aggregate demand

Households are presumed to spend all their revenues – both wages and social revenues (the take-out) – unless they are rationed on the final good market. This corresponds to a behaviorist, and not to an optimizing, view of the decision process. Accordingly, the money value of current households' final demand is determined by their financial constraint:

$$y(t) = p(t)d(t) = \omega(t) + c(t) + h^h(t-1)$$

where $h^h(t-1) = \max[p(t-1)(d(t-1) - s(t-1)), \ 0]$ are the monetary idle balances of households, which pile up when the value of final demand exceeds the value of current supply.

Production decisions

Current final production is given by

$$q(t) = \hat{d}(t) - \eta o(t-1)$$

where the expected final demand $\hat{d}$ is such that

$$p(t)\hat{d}(t) = \frac{m(t-1)^2}{m(t-2)}$$

that is, the expected final demand is made to depend on the past trend of money proceeds, and η represents the fraction of accumulated real stocks put back on the market.

Produced quantity is subject to an inherited productive capacity constraint:

$$q(t) \leq \mathbf{bx}(t-1)'$$

In case of excess capacity the vector of processes in utilization, $\mathbf{x}^u(t)$, is scaled down by scrapping.

Investment decisions

The desired investment expresses the belief that the necessary condition for maintaining a stable and viable economy is to prevent any distortion in the structure of productive capacity. The investment that can actually be carried out, however, is constrained by the availability of productive resources, so that, in general, the actual evolution of the economy will diverge from that desired.

The investment actually realized will be determined as the minimum between the investment desired by firms and the whole of the financial resources not required to carry out current production:

$$i(t) = \min\left[\omega(t) - \omega^u(t), w(t)\mathbf{a}^c\mathbf{x}^c(t)'\right]$$

where $\omega(t) = w(t)\mathbf{a}^u\mathbf{x}^u(t)'$. The investment desired, $w(t)\mathbf{a}^c\mathbf{x}^c(t)'$, reflects a rate of starts of new production processes,

$$x_1(t) = x_{n^c}(t)[1 + g^*(t)]^{n^c}$$

where g^* is a steady-state growth rate that makes it possible to prevent distortions in the age structure of productive capacity.

Employment

Total employment at time t will be

$$E(t) = \mathbf{a}^c\mathbf{x}^c(t)' + \mathbf{a}^u\mathbf{x}^u(t)'$$

which results from current production and investment determined as shown above.

Price and wage changes

The price of final output and wages adjust step by step to oncoming disequilibria in the respective markets. The price reacts to net excesses of demand observed in the previous period:

$$g_p(t) = \kappa\Phi(t - 1)$$

where $g_p(t)$ is the rate of change of the price, $\Phi(t-1)$ the rate of excess demand for final output, and κ a reaction coefficient. An alternative price adjustment rule states that the price of final output can be adjusted in reaction to changes in the unit cost:

$$g_p(t) = \gamma Y(t - 1)$$

where $Y(t-1)$ is the rate of change of the unit cost, and γ a reaction coefficient.

The labor market works in the same way. Wages are changing from one period to the next in relation to labor market disequilibria (whose effects are more or less mediated according to the value of the parameter v):

$$g_w(t) = v\Psi(t - 1)$$

where $g_w(t)$ is the rate of change of the wage rate, and $\Psi(t-1)$ the rate of excess demand for labor.

Monetary policy

External money demand is matched with money supply $f^s(t)$ exogenously determined by the monetary authority:

$$f^s(t) = f^s(t-1)\big\{(1-\varsigma)(1+g^*) + \varsigma\big[1 + \xi g_{f^d} - (1-\xi)g_p(t-1)\big]\big\}$$

where g^* is the steady-state growth rate of the economy, g_{f^d} is the growth rate of money demand, which may be higher than g^* (when restructuring calls for additional financial means to sustain the required investment), and g_p is the expected growth rate of the price level. With $\varsigma = 0$, a sort of Friedman (money growth target) rule is applied. With $\varsigma = 1$ instead, monetary policy reacts to output and the inflation rate. In the latter case, ξ and $(1-\xi)$ are the weights of growth and inflation objectives, respectively. This simple formulation, 'helicopter' money, is enough in this framework to show the effect of monetary policy on liquidity constraints and hence on investment decision.

Take-out or saving policy

The 'take-out' – i.e. the resources subtracted from production and given back to the households as indirect revenues – is determined as a part of the global revenue. This ratio is the opposite of the saving rate.

Once explicitly formulated with given values for the parameters, the relations of the model determine the time path of the various variables for all future dates. The evolutionary path followed by the economy is actually determined by the behavior of the control variables $f(t)$ and $c(t)$ and by the adjustment mechanisms represented by price and wage changes, which stand for different hypotheses as to the availability and the allocation of productive resources in the economy.

Out-of-equilibrium economic paths: consumption-driven and investment-driven scenarios

We are interested in the 'out of equilibrium' behavior of the economy portrayed by the above-sketched model. To explore this behavior we start by considering a steady-state economy at a constant growth rate of 2 percent, and then proceed to disturb it, by assuming a fall (and, alternatively, an increase) in the growth rate of the 'take-out' (unproductive consumption), so as to be able to test both Smith's and Keynes's viewpoints in a sequential dynamic context.

Both in the case of a decrease and in that of an increase of the growth rate of the 'take-out,' the phases of construction and utilization are brought out of balance and there is a distortion of productive capacity. This generates an out-of-equilibrium process that the numerical calculations performed track for 300 successive periods (or fewer if the path followed is not viable), with specific reference to: the growth rate of the economy (mean and variance); a measure of the distortion of productive capacity, via a measure of the distortion of the x's (mean and variance); the rate of unemployment; and the level of productivity.

A decrease in the growth rate of the 'take-out' (through a reduction of the ratio c/m from 0.3 to 0.28 at $t = 20$, in the case portrayed in the simulation of figures 21.1) implies that investment is gradually being substituted for consumption. In a standard Smithian perspective this should result in a greater growth rate for the economy as a whole since what is reduced is unproductive consumption. This is possible, however, only if we can count on idle labor to start with (and even in this case it is not sufficient, as we shall see in what follows). With full employment, a shift of existing financial resources toward investment cannot, in the same period, bring about the construction of more production processes than in the original steady state. In the first period after the reduction in the growth rate of the 'take-out' the wage fund is unchanged, as wages cannot change within the period itself, and the greater resources available for investment, which cannot actually be used up because of the labor constraint, result in involuntary idle balances accumulated by the firms. A reduction in the 'take-out' resulting in idle balances (or in greater idle balances), on the other hand, necessarily implies a decrease in final demand, excess supply, the accumulation of stocks of final output, and hence a fall in money proceeds. This leads to a downward revision of short-term expectations determining current production decisions, and hence, in the following period, the scrapping of some production processes in the utilization phase and the shifting of workers from utilization to construction – a distortion of productive capacity. On the other hand, the smaller proceeds realized in the previous period will not make it possible to finance the shifting to the construction sector of all the workers released, which would lead to unemployment were not this countered by a decision on the part of the firms to reabsorb the existing idle balances immediately.

So much for productive capacity; what about demand? Final demand comes from consumption out of profits and from wage-earners. We have seen it to go down in the first period because of the reduction of consumption out of profits given an unchanged wage fund, and this to cause a fall in proceeds. Less in the way of proceeds in the first period, on the other hand, implies a reduction of consumption out of wages to be added to the reduction of consumption out of profits in the following period $t = 21$;

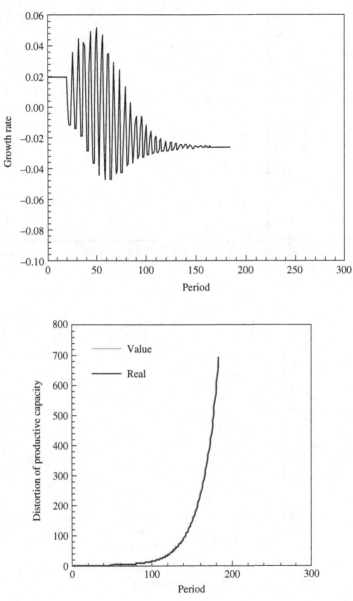

Figure 21.1a The evolution of the economy with a decreasing growth rate of 'take-out': the overall growth rate and productive capacity

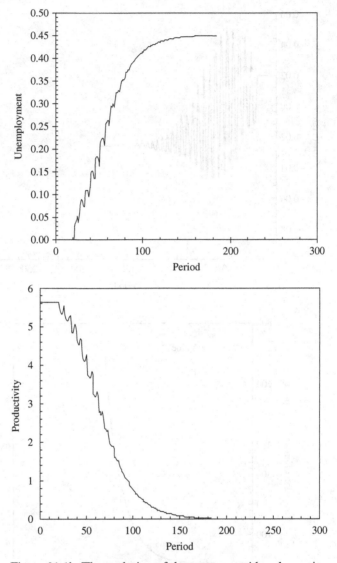

Figure 21.1b The evolution of the economy with a decreasing growth rate of 'take-out': unemployment and productivity

whatever happens to the wage rate (this, in the simulations, we assume to be market-determined), final demand on the whole, and hence proceeds, will still be falling. Moreover, since their fall will precede that of output, prices will also fall. In the following period ($t = 22$) the scrapping of processes in the phase of utilization (and hence the fall in final output), and the transfer of workers to construction, will go on. Final demand, however, determined by the production level of the preceding period (it is, in fact, the proceeds associated with the latter that make it possible to finance consumption both out of profits and out of wages), will result in excess, in the current period, with respect to a final output that keeps falling. This will cause prices, and proceeds, to start going up again in the following period ($t = 23$) in a sort of fluctuation of excesses of supply and excesses of demand, which, via expectations, feeds the disequilibrium and transmits it from one period to the next, leading sooner or later to unemployment.

Figures 21.1 illustrate the evolution of the economy. As a result of the decrease in the growth rate of the 'take-out,' the growth rate fluctuates, but it always remains lower than before the increase in investment; this implies a greater scrapping of production processes with respect to the original steady path. This is accompanied by the appearance of continuously increasing unemployment and continuously decreasing productivity. This clearly confirms the Hicksian argument that the consideration of 'hoarding' (the appearance of idle balances in the simulation of the evolutionary path of the economy) does not allow for an automatic change in the distribution of resources between investment and consumption over time with no distortion of productive capacity, and hence contradicts the Smithian conclusion that a shift of resources from unproductive consumption to production results automatically in more growth. The real problem is that this shift of resources brings about a distortion of productive capacity that, when a related sequence of periods is taken into account, results in imbalances and disequilibria that are passed on down the sequence, resulting in a threat to the viability of the economy. In the case considered, the distortion of productive capacity becomes so strong as to make the path followed by the economy no longer viable. This is so because the increasing variance in the age structure of productive capacity brings about fluctuations in current money proceeds that become more and more pronounced as time goes by, resulting in a shortage of financial resources that brings about a complete abandonment of the construction of new production processes – that is, a collapse of the economy – after some 200 periods.

This result is not confined to the particular evolution path considered. Figures 21.2 – in which alternative mean values and variances of the growth rate and of the distortion of productive capacity in the evolution paths (runs) associated with twenty-five increases in investment (reductions of the ratio c/m) of increasing magnitudes are considered – not only confirm the results of figures 21.1; they also show that the decrease of the growth rate and the distortion of productive capacity is monotonic, and the stronger the greater the increase in investment.

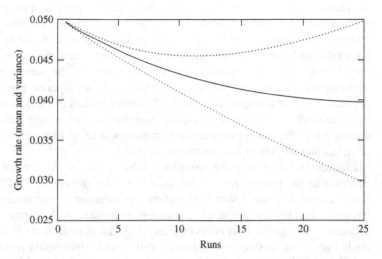

Figure 21.2a Increasing investment and monotonically decreasing growth rate

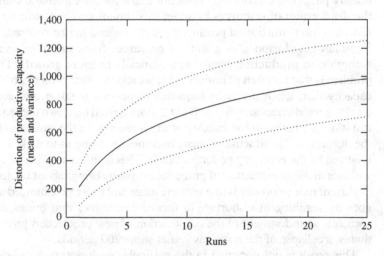

Figure 21.2b Increasing investment and increasing distortion of productive capacity

The opposite case – an increasing growth rate of the 'take-out,' implying a gradual substitution of consumption for investment – should cause no change for the economy as a whole from a standard Keynesian viewpoint, which looks at this process as a simple substitution between

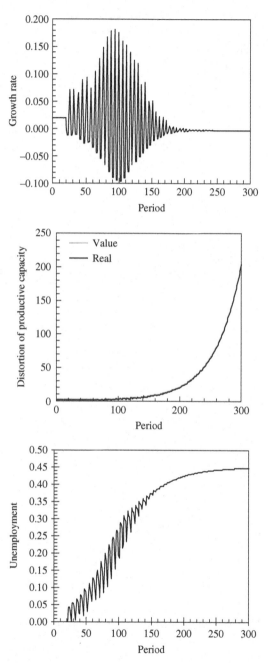

Figure 21.3a The evolution of the economy with an increasing growth rate of 'take-out'

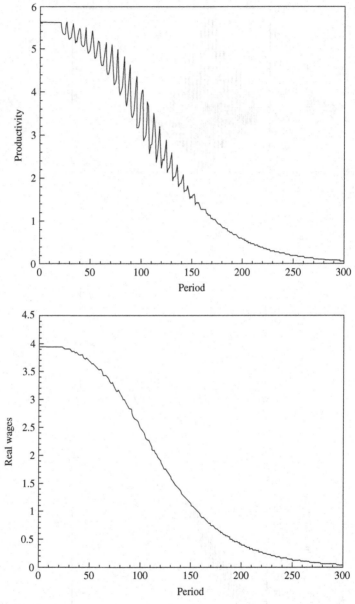

Figure 21.3b The evolution of productivity and real wages with an increasing growth rate of 'take-out'

components of final demand. In our analysis, carried out along the lines hinted at by Hicks by focusing on the different nature of consumption and investment, the simulation shows instead that an increase in the 'take-out' (an increase in the ratio c/m from 0.3 to 0.32 in the case considered in figures 21.3) is associated with a fall in the growth rate of the economy, a growing rate of unemployment, and continuously falling productivity. The reduction of the wage fund associated with an increasingly large 'take-out,' in fact, implies a reduction in the rate of start-ups for new production processes and, eventually, a scrapping of processes still in the construction phase. There will then be a shrinking of the productive capacity of the economy – after a period corresponding to the length of the construction phase – that will result in a shortage of supply, in falling money proceeds for the firms, and hence in a reduction of the wage fund in the following period. An excess of supply may then be the next step, with the setting in of strong fluctuations in economic activity. The stabilization of the growth rate after 150 periods is the result of real wages falling to zero – clearly, an unsupportable state for the economy.

The 'continuation' analysis carried out shows that, in both the cases considered, a change in the balance between unproductive consumption and investment brings about coordination problems that originate in a distortion of productive capacity. It also shows that, for Smithian and Keynesian results to be obtained in a sequential context, coordination mechanisms are required to re-establish the complementarity over time of investment and consumption.

Consider the case of a decrease in the growth rate of the 'take-out' – that is, of an attempt to carry out an expansionary policy. The appearance of idle balances is the expression of a distortion of productive capacity. This results from a break in the complementarity of productive resources, as the greater resources available for investment cannot actually be used up because of the labor constraint. The first thing that is required, therefore, is the removal of this constraint, as would be the case if we could count on an external inflow of labor. This would not be enough, however. We would also need additional final demand, at the end of the phase of construction, in connection with the greater number of new production processes made possible by the increase in investment; otherwise, the additional production processes carried on with respect to the original steady state would have to be scrapped sooner or later, as in the case of a labor constraint.[2] On the other hand, this additional demand can only be an external demand.

---

[2] This is a point that has already been touched upon by Thomas Malthus, according to whom a process of investment cannot sustain itself unless there is an external source of additional effective demand (see Amendola, Froeschlé, and Gaffard, 1993).

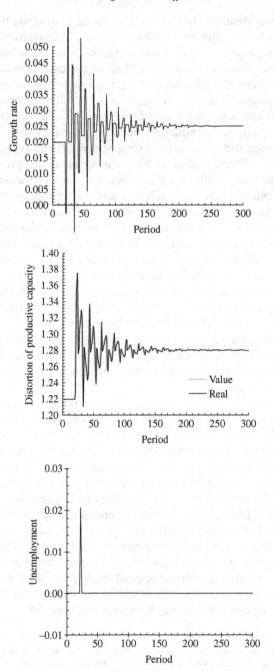

Figure 21.4a The evolution of the economy with coordination mechanisms and a decreasing growth rate of 'take-out'

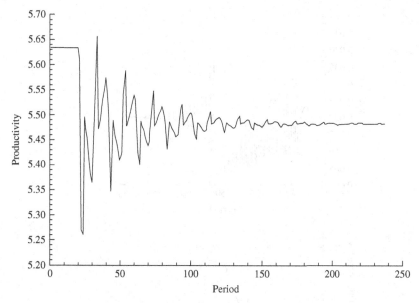

Figure 21.4b The evolution of productivity with coordination mechanisms and a decreasing growth rate of 'take-out'

We have, therefore, brought in an external inflow of labor – immigration, say – raising the growth rate of the latter from 2 percent to 2.5 percent, to match from the beginning the higher investment. We have also introduced at $t = 30$ – i.e. at the end of the phase of construction for the additional productive capacity – an additional demand (credit to consumption say), rendered in the model by the ratio c/m going back from 0.32 to the original value of 0.3. Finally, we have brought in fixed prices and wages, so as to smooth the fluctuations of the alternating excesses of supply and demand. The introduction of these coordination mechanisms makes it possible to re-establish the complementarity over time of investment and consumption, generating a higher stable growth rate after the initial period of turbulence (figures 21.4). The distortion of productive capacity, as well as the resultant unemployment, are fully reabsorbed. The expansionary policy has been successful.

In the opposite case, of an increase in the growth rate of the 'take-out,' the problem, we have seen, is a reduction in the rate of start-ups of production processes with respect to the original steady state and a short- age of financial resources to sustain the latter. We have, therefore, intro- duced an investment function that does not take into account the

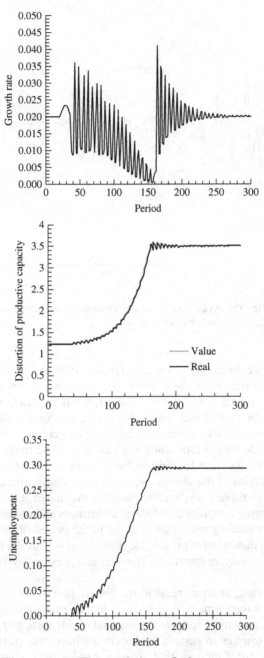

Figure 21.5a The evolution of the economy with coordination mechanisms and an increasing growth rate of 'take-out'

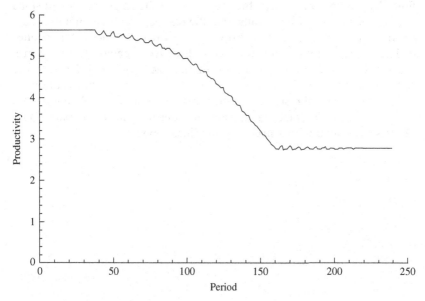

Figure 21.5b The evolution of productivity with coordination mechanisms and an increasing growth rate of 'take-out'

reduction of resources due to the increase in the 'take-out' but is aimed instead at maintaining the rate of start-ups of the original steady state, and allowed this investment policy actually to be carried out by postulating an accommodating monetary policy – that is, an external inflow of financial resources sufficient to be able always to realize the intended investment. Figures 21.5 show that, after the initial turbulence, the rate of growth and the distortion of productive capacity are stabilized and unemployment stops increasing.

Conclusions: the intertemporal complementarity of investment and consumption

When we move from the consideration of the behavior of an economy during a given period to a process taking place over time, investment and consumption are more realistically interpreted as the construction and utilization of processes of production that take place over a sequence of related periods, and hence their relation is considered to be one of intertemporal complementarity rather than of substitution. John Hicks's conclusions concerning Smith and Keynes with reference to a single period of finite length are confirmed, but other, more illuminating, conclusions can also be reached. Specifically, that the reallocation of financial resources from unproductive consumption to investment (or vice versa) sooner or later brings about a distortion of productive capacity, resulting in a breakdown of the coordination of economic activity and a threat to the viability of the economy. Different kinds of external interventions – concerning financial resources, human resources, and final demand – are then required to interact dynamically in order to make the expansionary process associated with a structural modification viable.

References

Adams, G. P., Jr. (1947) 'The Social Framework of the American Economy: An Introduction to Economics, by J. R. Hicks and A. G. Hart,' American Economic Review, 37 (3, June), 428–9.

Akerlof, G. A. (2002) 'Behavioral Macroeconomics and Macroeconomic Behavior,' American Economic Review, 92 (3, June), 411–33.

Akerlof, G. A., W. T. Dickens, and G. L. Perry (2000) 'Near-rational Wage and Price Setting and the Long-run Phillips Curve,' Brookings Papers on Economic Activity, 1 (2000), 1–60.

Allais, M. (1943) A la recherche d'une discipline économique, vol. I, L'économie pure, Paris, Atelier Industria.

(1953) 'Le comportement de l'homme rationnel devant le risque: critique des postulats et axiomes de l'école américaine,' Econometrica, 21 (4, October), 503–46.

(1979) 'The So-called Allais Paradox and Rational Decisions under Uncertainty,' in M. Allais and O. Hagen (eds.) Expected Utility Hypotheses and the Allais Paradox: Contemporary Discussions of Decisions under Uncertainty with Allais' Rejoinder, Dordrecht, Reidel, 437–681.

Allen, R. G. D. (1932) 'The Foundations of a Mathematical Theory of Exchange,' Economica, 12 (May), 197–226.

Allen, R. G. D., and J. R. Hicks (1934a) 'A Reconsideration of the Theory of Value I,' Economica, new series, 1 (1, February), 52–76.

(1934b) 'A Reconsideration of the Theory of Value II,' Economica, new series, 1 (2, May), 196–219.

Amendola, M., and J.-L. Gaffard (1988) The Innovative Choice, Oxford, Basil Blackwell.

(1998) Out of Equilibrium, Oxford, Clarendon Press.

Amendola, M., C. Froeschlé, and J.-L. Gaffard (1993) 'Sustaining Structural Change: Malthus' Heritage,' Structural Change and Economic Dynamics, 4 (1, June), 65–79.

Amihud, Y. (1979) 'A Critical Examination of the New Foundation of Utility,' in M. Allais and O. Hagen (eds.) Expected Utility Hypotheses and the Allais Paradox: Contemporary Discussions of Decisions under Uncertainty with Allais' Rejoinder, Dordrecht, Reidel, 149–60.

Ando, A., L. Guiso, and I. Visco (eds.) (1994) Saving and the Accumulation of Wealth, Cambridge, Cambridge University Press.

Arrow, K. J. (1951a) Social Choice and Individual Values, New York, Wiley.

(1951b) 'An Extension of the Basic Theorems of Classical Welfare Economics,' in J. Neyman (ed.) *Proceedings of the Second Berkeley Symposium on Mathematical Statistics and Probability*, Berkeley, University of California Press, 507–32.

(1962), 'The Economic Implications of Learning by Doing,' *Review of Economic Studies* 29 (3, June), 155–73.

Arrow, K. J., and F. H. Hahn (1971) *General Competitive Analysis*, San Francisco, Holden-Day [republished (1979), Amsterdam, North-Holland].

Artzner, P., F. Delbaen, J.-M. Eber, and D. Heath (1999) 'Coherent Measures of Risk,' *Mathematical Finance*, 9 (November), 203–28.

Ashton, T. S. (1971) [1946] 'The Relation of Economic History to Economic Theory,' in N. B. Harte (ed.) *The Study of Economic History*, London, Cass, 161–80.

Atkinson, A. B., and J. E. Stiglitz (1980) *Lectures on Public Economics*, New York, McGraw-Hill.

Balestra, P., and M. Baranzini (1971) 'Some Optimal Aspects in a Two-class Growth Model with a Differentiated Interest Rate,' *Kyklos*, 24 (2, May), 240–56.

Baranzini, M. (1991a) *A Theory of Wealth Distribution and Accumulation*, Oxford, Clarendon Press.

(1991b) 'The Pasinetti and Anti-Pasinetti Theorems: a Reply to K. Miyazaki and P. A. Samuelson,' *Oxford Economic Papers*, new series, 43 (2, April), 195–8.

Baranzini, M., and G. C. Harcourt (eds.) (1993) *The Dynamics of the Wealth of Nations: Growth, Distribution and Structural Change: Essays in Honour of Luigi Pasinetti*, London, Macmillan.

Baranzini, M., and R. Scazzieri (eds.) (1990) *The Economic Theory of Structure and Change*, Cambridge, Cambridge University Press.

Barone, E. (1998) 'A Unified VaR Approach,' available at http://ssrn.com/abstract=512544.

Barro, R. J. (1974) 'Are Government Bonds Net Wealth?,' *Journal of Political Economy*, 82 (6, November/December), 1095–117.

Bauer, P. (1971) 'Economic History as Theory', *Economica*, new series, 38 (May), 163–79.

Baumol, W. J. (1972) 'John R. Hicks' Contribution to Economics', *Swedish Journal of Economics* 74 (4, December), 503–27.

(1990) 'Sir John versus the Hicksians, or Theorist malgré Lui?,' *Journal of Economic Literature* 28 (4, December), 1708–15.

Beccaria, C. (1986) [1762] *Del disordine e de' rimedi delle monete nello stato di Milano nell'anno 1762*, in A. Quadrio Curzio and R. Scazzieri (eds.) *Sul disordine delle monete a Milano nel Settecento: Tre saggi di Cesare Beccaria e Pietro Verri*, Milan, Electa, 49–100.

Bell, P. W. (1976) '*The Crisis in Keynesian Economics* by John R. Hicks,' *Journal of Economic Literature*, 14 (1, March), 68–70.

Benetti, C., G. O. Dostaler, O. F. Hamouda, M. Rosier, and C. Tutin (2001) 'Presentation,' in *Cahiers d' Economie Politique: Histoire de la pensée et théories*, vol. XXXIX, *J. R. Hicks: Une oeuvre multi-dimensionnelle*, Paris, L'Harmattan, 7–8.

Benhabib, J., S. Schmitt-Grohé, and M. Uribe (2002) 'Avoiding Liquidity Traps,' *Journal of Political Economy*, 110 (3, June), 535–63.

Berger, A. N., R. J. Herring, and G. P. Szego (1995) 'The Role of Capital in Financial Institutions,' *Journal of Banking and Finance*, 19 (3–4, June), 393–430.

Berlin, I. (1958) *Two Concepts of Liberty: An Inaugural Lecture Delivered before the University of Oxford on 31 October 1958*, Oxford, Clarendon Press.

Bernanke, B. S. (1983) 'Non-monetary Effects of the Financial Crisis in the Propagation of the Great Depression,' *American Economic Review*, 73 (3, June), 257–76.

Bernanke, B. S., and A. S. Blinder (1988) 'Credit Money and Aggregate Demand,' *American Economic Review*, 78 (2, May), 435–9.

Bernanke, B. S., M. Gertler, and S. Gilchrist (1999) 'The Financial Accelerator in a Quantitative Business Cycle Framework,' in J. B. Taylor and M. Woodford (eds.) *Handbook of Macroeconomics*, vol. I, Amsterdam, Elsevier, 1342–93.

Bernoulli, D. (1954) [1738] 'Specimen theoriae novae de mensura sortis,' in *Commentarii Academiae Scientiarum Imperialis Petropolitanae*, vol. V, *1730–1731*, 175–92, trans. L. Sommer, 'Exposition of a New Theory on the Measurement of Risk', *Econometrica*, 22 (1, January), 23–36.

Besomi, D. (2000) 'On the Spread of an Idea: the Strange Case of Mr Harrod and the Multiplier,' *History of Political Economy*, 32 (2, Summer), 347–79.

(2003) 'Editorial Introduction,' in D. Besomi (ed.) *The Collected Interwar Papers and Correspondence of Sir Roy Harrod*, vol. I, Cheltenham, Edward Elgar, xxxi–xliv.

BIS (2004) *International Convergence of Capital Measurement and Capital Standards*, Basel, Bank for International Settlements.

Bliss, C. (1987) 'Hicks, John Richard,' in J. Eatwell, M. Milgate, and P. Newman (eds.) *The New Palgrave: A Dictionary of Economics*, vol. II, London, Macmillan, 641–6.

(1994) 'Hicks on General Equilibrium and Stability,' in H. Hagemann and O. F. Hamouda (eds.) *The Legacy of Hicks: His Contributions to Economic Analysis*, London, Routledge, 87–95.

Böhm-Bawerk, E. von (1881) *Rechte und Verhältnisse vom Standpunkte der Volkswirthschaftlichen Güterlehre*, Innsbruck, Wagnersche Universitätsbuchhandlung.

(1913) 'Eine "dynamische" Theorie des Kapitalzinses,' *Zeitschrift für Volkswirtschaft, Sozialpolitik und Verwaltung*, 22, 1–62 and 640–56.

Boianovsky, M., and H. Hagemann (2004) 'Wicksell on Technical Change, Real Wages and Employment,' in M. Bellet, S. Gloria-Palermo, and A. Zouache (eds.) *Evolution of the Market Process: Austrian and Swedish Economics*, London, Routledge, 69–93.

Boianovsky, M., and H.-M. Trautwein (2001) 'Wicksell's Lecture Notes on Economic Crises (1902/05),' *Structural Change and Economic Dynamics*, 12 (3, September), 343–66.

Boland, L. A. (1980) '*Causality in Economics*, John Hicks,' *Canadian Journal of Economics*, 13 (4, November), 740–3.

Bortis, H. (1976) 'On the Determination of the Level of Employment in a Growing Capitalist Economy,' *Revue Suisse d'Economie Politique et de Statistique*, 112 (1, March), 67–93.

Boulding, K. E. (1939) 'Review of John R. Hicks, *Value and Capital: An Inquiry into Some Fundamental Principles of Economic Theory*, and Henry Schulz, *The Theory of Measurement of Demand*,' *Canadian Journal of Economics and Political Science*, 5 (4, October), 521–8.

Bowley, A. L. (1938) '*Théorie mathématique de la valeur en régime de libre concurrence*: J. R. Hicks,' *Economic Journal*, 48 (September), 513–15.

Bridel, P., and B. Ingrao (2005) 'Managing Cambridge Economics: the Correspondence between Keynes and Pigou,' in M. C. Marcuzzo and A. Rosselli (eds.) *Economists in Cambridge: A Study through Their Correspondence, 1907–1946*, London, Routledge, 149–66.

Broggia, C. A. (1743) *Trattato delle Monete…*, in *Trattato de' Tributi, delle Monete, e del governo politico della Sanità*, Naples, Presso Pietro Palombo, 174–436.

Brown, A. J. (1960) '*Essays in World Economics*, J. R. Hicks,' *Economic History Review*, new series, 13 (2, May) 303–4.

(1988) 'A Worm's Eye View of the Keynesian Revolution,' in J. Hillard (ed.) *J. M. Keynes in Retrospect: The Legacy of the Keynesian Revolution*, Aldershot, Edward Elgar, 18–44.

Brunner, K. (1981) '*The Crisis in Keynesian Economics* by Sir John R. Hicks,' *Journal of Political Economy*, 89 (5, October), 1052–4.

Buiter, W. H., and N. Panigirtzoglou (2003) 'Overcoming the Zero Bound on Nominal Interest Rates with Negative Interest on Currency: Gesell's Solution,' *Economic Journal*, 113 (October), 723–47

Bullard, J., and K. Mitra (2002) 'Learning about Monetary Policy Rules,' *Journal of Monetary Economics*, 49 (6, September), 1105–29.

Burmeister, E. (1974) 'Synthesizing the Neo-Austrian and Alternative Approaches to Capital Theory: a Survey,' *Journal of Economic Literature*, 12 (2, June), 413–56.

Burmeister, E., and T. Taubman (1969) 'Labour and Non-labour Income Saving Propensities,' *Canadian Journal of Economics*, 2 (1, February), 78–89.

Caldwell, B. (ed.) (1995) *The Collected Works of F. A. Hayek*, vol. IX, *Contra Keynes and Cambridge: Essays, Correspondence*, London, Routledge.

Carr, P., and D. Madan (1998) 'Toward a Theory of Volatility Trading,' in R. Jarrow (ed.) *Volatility*, London, Risk Books, 417–27.

Cesari, R., and C. D'Adda (2003), 'A Simple Approach to the Theory of Asset Pricing,' available at http://papers.ssrn.com/sol3/papers.cfm?abstract_id=519443.

Chew, S. H. (1983), 'A Generalization of the Quasilinear Mean with Applications to the Measurement of Income Inequality and Decision Theory Resolving the Allais Paradox,' *Econometrica*, 51 (4, July), 1065–92.

Ciocca, P. (ed.) (2002) *Le vie della storia nell'economia*, Bologna, Il Mulino.

Clarida, R., J. Gali, and M. Gertler (1999) 'The Science of Monetary Policy: a New-Keynesian Perspective,' *Journal of Economic of Literature*, 37 (4, December), 1661–707.

Clay, H. (1933) 'Review of *The Theory of Wages* by J. R. Hicks,' *Economica*, new series, 41 (August), 329–32.

Clements, M. P., and D. F. Hendry (1999) *Forecasting Non-stationary Economic Time Series*, Cambridge, MA, MIT Press.

Clower, R. (1970) 'Critical Essays in Monetary Theory by John Hicks,' Journal of Political Economy, 78 (3), 608–11.

Coase, R. H. (1937) 'The Nature of the Firm,' Economica, new series, 4 (November), 386–405.

(1982) 'Economics at LSE in the 1930s: a Personal View,' Atlantic Economic Journal, 10 (1, March), 31–4.

Coddington, A. (1980) 'Causality in Economics by John Hicks,' Economic Journal, 90 (June), 395–7.

Coleman, D. C. (1971) 'A Theory of Economic History by John Hicks,' English Historical Review, 86 (July), 596.

Conlisk, J. (1996) 'Why Bounded Rationality?,' Journal of Economic Literature, 34 (2, June), 669–700.

Cramp, T. (1990) 'A Market Theory of Money, John Hicks,' Economic Journal, 100 (March), 251–2.

Dahrendorf, R. (1995) A History of the London School of Economics and Political Science, 1895–1995, Oxford, Oxford University Press.

David, W. L. (ed.) (1973) Public Finance, Planning and Economic Development: Essays in Honour of Ursula Hicks, London, Macmillan.

Debreu, G. (1959) Theory of Value: An Axiomatic Analysis of Economic Equilibrium, Cowles Foundation Monograph no. 17, New Haven, CT, Yale University Press.

De Finetti, B. (1970) Teoria della probabilità, Turin, Einaudi.

de la Grandville, O., and R. Solow (forthcoming) 'Capital–Labour Substitution and Economic Growth', in O. de la Grandville (ed.) Economic Growth: A Unified Approach, Cambridge, Cambridge University Press, chap. 5.

De Servigny, A., and O. Renault (2004) Measuring and Managing Credit Risk, New York, McGraw-Hill.

De Turri, R. (1641) Tractatus de cambijs, Genoa, Petrus Joannes Calenzanus.

Dewey, D. (1966) 'Capital and Growth by John R. Hicks,' Journal of Finance, 21 (3, September), 568–9.

Director, A. (1935) 'Review of The Theory of Wages by J. R. Hicks,' Journal of Political Economy, 43 (1, February), 109–11.

Dobb, M. (1946) Studies in the Development of Capitalism, London, Routledge and Kegan Paul.

Dornbusch, R. (1976) 'Expectations and Exchange Rate Dynamics,' Journal of Political Economy, 84 (6, December), 1161–76.

Dostaler, G. 2001. 'De J. R. à John ou les metamorphoses de Hicks, elements de biographie intellectuelle,' in Cahiers d'Economie Politique: Histoire de la pensée et théories, vol. XXXIX, J. R. Hicks: Une oeuvre multi-dimensionnelle, Paris, L'Harmattan, 9–23.

Duesenberry, J. J. (1950) 'Hicks on the Trade Cycle,' Quarterly Journal of Economics, 64 (3, August), 464–76.

Dybvig, P. H., and J. E. Ingersoll, Jr. (1982) 'Mean-variance Theory in Complete Markets,' Journal of Business, 55 (2, April), 233–51.

Ebenstein, A. (2001) Friedrich Hayek: A Biography, New York, Palgrave.

Einaudi, L. (1936a) 'Teoria della moneta immaginaria nel tempo da Carlomagno alla rivoluzione francese,' Rivista di Storia Economica, 1 (1–4), 1–35.

(1936b) 'Intorno alla funzione della moneta immaginaria' [reply to Loria, 1936], *Rivista di storia economica*, vol. 1 (1–4), 302–6.

(1937) 'The Medieval Practice of Managed Currency,' in A. D. Gayer (ed.) *The Lessons of Monetary Experience: Essays in Honor of Irving Fisher*, New York, Ferrar and Rinehart, 259–68.

Eltis, W. A. (1987) 'Harrod–Domar Growth Model,' in J. Eatwell, M. Milgate, and P. Newman (eds.) *The New Palgrave Dictionary of Economics*, vol. II, London, Macmillan, 602–4.

Endemann, W. (1874–83) *Studien in der romanisch-kanonistischen Wirtschafts- und Rechtslehre bis gegen ende des 17. Jahrhunderts*, 4 vols., Berlin, Guttentag.

Enos, J. R. (1962) 'Invention and Innovation in the Petroleum Refining Industry,' in R. R. Nelson (ed.) *The Rate and Direction of Inventive Activity: Economic and Social Factors*, Princeton, NJ, Princeton University Press, 299–321.

Evans, G. C. (1930) *Mathematical Introduction to Economics*, New York, McGraw-Hill.

Evans, G. W., and S. Honkapohja (2001) *Learning and Expectations in Macroeconomics*, Princeton, NJ, Princeton University Press.

(2003) 'Expectational Stability of Stationary Sunspot Equilibria in a Forward-looking Linear Model,' *Journal of Economic Dynamics and Control*, 28 (1, October), 171–81.

Faber, M. (1979) *Introduction to Modern Austrian Capital Theory*, Berlin, Springer.

Farmer, R. E. A. (1999) *Macroeconomics of Self-fulfilling Prophecies*, Cambridge, MA, MIT Press.

Fazzari, S., P. Ferri, and E. Greenberg (2008) 'Cash Flow, Investment and Keynes–Minsky Cycles,' *Journal of Economic Behavior and Organization*, 65 (3–4, March), 555–72.

Fazzari, S., G. R. Hubbard, and B. C. Petersen (1988) 'Financing Constraints and Corporate Investment,' *Brookings Papers on Economic Activity*, 1 (1988), 141–206.

Fels, R. (1951) 'Methodology of Research on the Business Cycle,' *Southern Economic Journal*, 17 (4, April), 397–408.

Ferri, P. (1997) 'Ceilings and Floors,' in D. Glasner (ed.) *Business Cycles and Depressions: An Encyclopedia*, New York, Garland, 86–8.

(2000) 'Ceilings and Floors, Growth and the Nairu,' in R. Bellofiore and P. Ferri (eds.) *Financial Fragility and Investment in the Capitalist Economy: The Economic Legacy of Hyman Minsky*, vol II, New York, Edward Elgar, 53–68.

(2007) 'The Labor Market and Technical Change in Endogenous Cycles,' *Metroeconomica*, 58 (4, November), 609–33.

Ferri, P., and E. Greenberg (1989) *The Labor Market and Business Cycles*, New York, Springer-Verlag.

Ferri, P., E. Greenberg, and R. Day (2001) 'The Phillips Curve, Regime Switching and the NAIRU,' *Journal of Economic Behavior and Organization*, 46 (1, September), 23–37.

Ferri, P., and H. P. Minsky (1992) 'Market Forces and Thwarting Systems,' *Structural Change and Economic Dynamics*, 3 (1, June), 79–91.

Filardo, A. (1994) 'Business-cycle Phases and Their Transitional Dynamics,' *Journal of Business and Economic Statistics*, 12 (3, July), 299–308.

Fine, B., and K. Fine (1974a) "Social Choice and Individual Ranking I," *Review of Economic Studies*, 41 (3, July), 303–22.

(1974b) "Social Choice and Individual Rankings II," *Review of Economic Studies*, 41 (4, October), 459–75.

Firth, G. G. (1939) 'An Excursion in Dynamic Theory,' *Economic Record*, 15 (June), 68–73.

Fishburn, P. C. (1970) *Utility Theory for Decision Making*, New York, Wiley.

(1980), 'Stochastic Dominance and Moments of Distributions,' *Mathematics of Operations Research*, 5 (1, February), 94–100.

(1982) *The Foundations of Expected Utility*, Dordrecht, Reidel.

(1983), 'Transitive Measurable Utility,' *Journal of Economic Theory*, 31 (2, December), 293–317.

(1988) *Nonlinear Preference and Utility Theory*, Brighton, Wheatsheaf.

Fishburn, P. C., and R. G. Vickson (1978) 'Theoretical Foundations of Stochastic Dominance,' in G. A. Whitmore and M. C. Findlay (eds.) *Stochastic Dominance: An Approach to Decision-making under Uncertainty*, Lexington, MA, D. C. Heath, 37–113.

Fisher, I. (1907) *The Rate of Interest: Its Nature, Determination and Relation to Economic Phenomena*, New York, Macmillan.

Flaschel, P., G. Gong, and W. Semmler (2001) 'A Keynesian Macroeconometric Framework for the Analysis of Monetary Policy Rules,' *Journal of Economic Behavior and Organization*, 46 (1, September), 101–36.

Fleming, J. M. (1964) 'The Fund and International Liquidity,' *International Monetary Fund Staff Papers*, 11 (2, July), 177–215.

Flemming, J. S. (1969) 'The Utility of Wealth and Utility of Windfalls,' *Review of Economic Studies*, 36 (1, January), 55–66.

Fontana, G. (2004) 'Hicks on Monetary Theory and History: Money as "Endogenous Money,"' *Cambridge Journal of Economics*, 28 (1, January), 73–88.

Freimer, M., and M. Gordon (1965) 'Why Bankers Ration Credit,' *Quarterly Journal of Economics*, 79 (3, August), 397–416.

Friedman, M., and A. J. Schwartz (1963) *A Monetary History of the United States, 1867–1960*, Princeton, NJ, Princeton University Press.

Frydman, R., and E. S. Phelps (eds.) (1983) *Individual Forecasting and Aggregate Outcomes: Rational Expectations Examined*, Cambridge, Cambridge University Press.

Fuhrer, J., and G. Moore (1995) 'Inflation Persistence,' *Quarterly Journal of Economics*, 110 (1, February), 127–59.

Gardenfors, P. (1973) 'Positionalist Voting Functions,' *Theory and Decision*, 4 (1, September), 1–24.

Georgescu-Roegen, N. (1936) 'The Pure Theory of Consumer's Behavior,' *Quarterly Journal of Economics*, 50 (4, August), 545–93.

Gerschenkron, A. (1971) 'Mercator Gloriosus', *Economic History Review*, new series, 24 (4, November), 653–66.

Godelier, M. (ed.) (1970). *Sur les sociétés précapitalistes*, Paris, Editions Sociales.

Goethe, J. W. (1976) [1821] *Maximen und Reflexionen*, Frankfurt, Insel Verlag [originally published in *Kunst und Alterthum*, 1821, IV, 1].

Goodfriend, M., and R. G. King (1997) 'The New Neoclassical Synthesis and the Role of Monetary Policy,' in B. S. Bernanke and J. J. Rotemberg (eds.) *NBER Macroeconomic Annual*, Cambridge, MA, MIT Press, 231–83.

Goodwin, R. M. (1950) 'A Non-linear Theory of the Cycle,' *Review of Economics and Statistics*, 32 (4, November), 316–20.

(1951) 'The Nonlinear Accelerator and the Persistence of Business Cycles,' *Econometrica*, 19 (1, January), 1–17.

(1982) 'A Growth Cycle,' in R. M. Goodwin *Essays in Economic Dynamics*, London, Macmillan, 165–70 [originally published in C. H. Feinstein (ed.) (1967) *Socialism, Capitalism and Economic Growth: Essays Presented to Maurice Dobb*, Cambridge, Cambridge University Press, 54–8].

(1994) 'A Reformulation and Extension of Hicksian Dynamics,' in H. Hagemann and O. F. Hamouda (eds.) *The Legacy of Hicks: His Contributions to Economic Analysis*, London, Routledge, 75–86.

Gordy, M. B. (2004) 'Address' in the panel session on the role of rating systems in the credit process, conference on 'Validation of Credit Risk Models,' Ca' Foscari University of Venice, October 1.

Grandmont, J.-M. (1976) 'Théorie de l'équilibre temporaire général,' *Revue Economique*, 27 (5, September), 805–43.

(1977) 'Temporary General Equilibrium Theory,' *Econometrica*, 45 (3, April), 535–72.

(1998) 'Expectations Formations and Stability of Large Socioeconomic Systems,' *Econometrica*, 66 (4, July), 741–81.

Greenspan, A. (2000) 'Global Challenges,' speech given at the Financial Crisis Conference, Council on Foreign Relations, New York, July 12.

Grendi, E. (1971) 'Review of John Hicks, *A Theory of Economic History*,' *Rivista Storica Italiana*, 83, 197–201.

Grice-Hutchinson, M. (1952) *The School of Salamanca: Readings in Spanish Monetary Theory, 1544–1605*, Oxford, Clarendon Press.

Guillebaud, C. W. (1943) '*The Social Framework: An Introduction to Economics*, by J. R. Hicks,' *Economica*, new series, 10 (May), 190–1.

Haberler, G. (1937) *Prosperity and Depression*, Geneva, League of Nations.

Hacking, I. (1975) *The Emergence of Probability*, Cambridge, Cambridge University Press.

Hagemann, H. (1990) 'Neisser's "The Wage Rate and Employment in Market Equilibrium": an Introduction,' *Structural Change and Economic Dynamics*, 1 (1, June), 133–9.

(1994a) 'Employment and Machinery,' in H. Hagemann and O. F. Hamouda (eds.) *The Legacy of Hicks: His Contributions to Economic Analysis*, London, Routledge, 200–24.

(1994b) 'Hayek and the Kiel School: Some Reflections on the German Debate on Business Cycles in the Late 1920s and Early 1930s,' in M. Colonna and H. Hagemann (eds.) *Money and Business Cycles: The Economics of F. A. Hayek*, vol. I, Aldershot, Edward Elgar, 101–20.

(2001) 'Wicksell's "New Theory of Crises": an Introduction,' *Structural Change and Economic Dynamics*, 12 (3, September), 331–4.

Hagemann, H., and O. F. Hamouda (eds.) (1994) *The Legacy of Hicks: His Contributions to Economic Analysis*, London, Routledge.

Hagemann, H., and H.-M. Trautwein (1998) 'Cantillon and Ricardo Effects: Hayek's Contributions to Business Cycle Theory,' *European Journal of the History of Economic Thought*, 5 (2, May), 292–316.

Hahn, F. H. (1966) '*Capital and Growth*, by Sir John Hicks,' *Economic Journal*, 76 (March), 84–7.

(1984) '*Classics and Moderns: Collected Essays on Economic Theory*, vol. 3, by John Hicks,' *Economic Journal*, 94 (December), 960–2.

(1990) 'John Hicks the Theorist,' *Economic Journal*, 100 (June), 539–49.

(1991) '*A Market Theory of Money*, by John Hicks,' *Economica*, new series, 58 (August), 410–11.

Hahn, F. H., and R. C. O. Matthews (1964) 'The Theory of Economic Growth: a Survey,' *Economic Journal*, 74 (December), 779–902.

Halevi, J. (2001) 'Capital and Growth: Its Relevance as a Critique of Neoclassical and Classical Economic Theories,' in K. Puttaswamaiah (ed.) *John Hicks: His Contributions to Economic Theory and Application*, New Brunswick, NJ, Transaction, 78–97.

Haley, B. F. (1939) '*Value and Capital: An Inquiry into Some Fundamental Principles of Economic Theory*, by J. R. Hicks,' *American Economic Review*, 29 (3, June), 557–60.

Hamilton, J. D. (1989) 'A New Approach to the Economic Analysis of Nonstationary Time Series and the Business Cycle,' *Econometrica*, 57 (March), 357–84.

(1994) *Time Series Analysis*, Princeton, NJ, Princeton University Press.

Hamouda, O. F. (1993) *John R. Hicks: The Economist's Economist*, Oxford, Basil Blackwell.

Harcourt, G. C. (1969) 'Some Cambridge Controversies in the Theory of Capital,' *Journal of Economic Literature*, 7 (2, June), 369–405.

(1972) *Some Cambridge Controversies in the Theory of Capital*, Cambridge, Cambridge University Press.

(1979) '*Economic Perspectives: Further Essays on Money and Growth*, by John Hicks,' *Economic Journal*, 89 (March), 144–6.

(1983) '*Money, Interest and Wages: Collected Essays on Economic Theory*, vol. II, John Hicks,' *Economic Journal*, 93 (March), 215–17.

Harrod, R. F. (1937) 'Mr Keynes and Traditional Theory,' *Econometrica*, 5 (1, January), 74–86 [reprinted in S. Harris (ed.) (1948) *The New Economics: Keynes' Influence on Theory and Public Policy*, London, Dennis Dobson, 591–605].

(1939) '*Value and Capital*, J. R. Hicks', *Economic Journal*, 49 (2, June), 294–300.

(1948) *Towards a Dynamic Economics*, London, Macmillan.

Hawtrey, R. G. (1919) *Currency and Credit*, London, Longmans Green.

(1939a) *A Century of Bank Rate*, London, Longmans Green.

(1939b) ' Review: *Value and Capital: An Inquiry into Some Fundamental Principles of Economic Theory*, by J. R. Hicks,' *Journal of the Royal Statistical Society*, 102 (2), 307–12.

Hayek, F. A. (1931a) *Prices and Production*, London, Routledge and Kegan Paul.

(1941) *The Pure Theory of Capital*, London, Macmillan.

(1942) 'The Ricardo Effect,' *Economica*, new series, 9 (May), 127–52.

(1969) 'Three Elucidations of the "Ricardo Effect,"' *Journal of Political Economy*, 77 (2, March–April), 274–85.

(1995) [1963] 'The Economics of the 1930s as Seen from London,' in B. Caldwell (ed.) *The Collected Works of F. A. Hayek*, vol. IX, *Contra Keynes and Cambridge: Essays, Correspondence*, London, Routledge, 49–63.

Helm, D. R. (1984) 'Introduction,' in J. R. Hicks *The Economics of John Hicks: Selected Papers*, Oxford, Basil Blackwell, 1–20.

Henriksson, R. G. M. (ed.) (1994) *Erik Lundberg: Studies in Economic Instability and Change*, Stockholm, SNS Forlag.

Hicks, J. R. (1931) 'The Theory of Uncertainty and Profit,' *Economica*, 32 (May), 170–89.

(1932) *The Theory of Wages*, London, Macmillan.

(1933a) 'Gleichgewicht und Konjunktur,' *Zeitschrift für Nationalökonomie*, 4, 441–55, [trans. 'Equilibrium and the Cycle,' *Economic Enquiry*, 18 (4, October), 1980, 523–34; reprinted in J. R. Hicks (1982a) *Collected Essays on Economic Theory*, vol. II, *Money, Interest and Wages*, Oxford, Basil Blackwell, 28–41].

(1934a) 'Léon Walras,' *Econometrica*, 2 (October), 338–48.

(1935a) 'A Suggestion for Simplifying the Theory of Money,' *Economica*, new series, 2 (5, February), 1–19 [reprinted in J. R. Hicks (1967a) *Critical Essays in Monetary Theory*, Oxford, Clarendon Press, 61–82].

(1935b) 'Annual Survey of Economic Theory: the Theory of Monopoly,' *Econometrica*, January, 1–20 [reprinted in J. R. Hicks (1983a) *Collected Essays on Economic Theory*, vol. III, *Classics and Moderns*, Oxford, Basil Blackwell, 131–52].

(1935c) 'Wages and Interest: the Dynamic Problem,' *Economic Journal*, 45 (September), 456–68.

(1935d) 'De l'utilité et de sa mesure, par Jules Dupuit: écrits choisis et republiés par Mario de Bernardi (Turin: La Riforma Sociale),' *Economica*, new series, 2 (7, August), 341–2.

(1936a) 'Mr Keynes's Theory of Employment,' *Economic Journal*, 46 (June), 238–53.

(1936b) 'Distribution and Economic Progress: a Revised Version,' *Review of Economic Studies*, 4 (1, October), 1–12.

(1936c) 'Economic Theory and the Social Sciences,' in Institute of Sociology *The Social Sciences: Their Relations in Theory and in Teaching*, London, Le Play House Press, 129–40.

(1936d) 'Review of A. C. Pigou, *The Economics of Stationary States*,' *Economic Journal*, 46 (March), 98–102.

(1937a) 'Mr Keynes and the "Classics": a Suggested Interpretation,' *Econometrica*, 5 (2, April), 147–59.

(1937b) *La Théorie mathématique de la valeur en régime de libre concurrence*, Paris, Hermann.

(1939a) *Value and Capital: An Inquiry into Some Fundamental Principles of Economic Theory*, Oxford, Oxford University Press.

(1939b) 'The Foundations of Welfare Economics,' *Economic Journal*, 49 (December), 696–712 [reprinted in J. R. Hicks (1981a) *Collected Essays on Economic Theory*, vol. I, *Wealth and Welfare*, Oxford, Basil Blackwell, 59–77].

(1940) 'The Valuation of the Social Income,' *Economica*, new series, 7 (May), 105–24 [reprinted in J. R. Hicks (1981a), *Collected Essays on Economic Theory*, vol. I, *Wealth and Welfare*, Oxford, Basil Blackwell, 78–99].

(1941a) 'Education in Economics,' *Bulletin of the Manchester Statistical Society*, April, 1–20.

(1941b) 'Rehabilitation of Consumer's Surplus,' *Review of Economic Studies*, 8 (2, February), 108–16.

(1942a) 'Maintaining Capital Intact: a Further Suggestion,' *Economica*, new series, 9 (34, May), 174–9.

(1942b) '"Consumer's" Surplus and Index Numbers,' *Review of Economic Studies*, 9 (2, Summer), 126–37 [reprinted in J. R. Hicks (1981a) *Collected Essays on Economic Theory*, vol. I, *Wealth and Welfare*, Oxford, Basil Blackwell, 114–32].

(1942c) *The Social Framework: An Introduction to Economics*, Oxford, Clarendon Press.

(1944) 'The Interrelations of Shifts in Demand: Comment,' *Review of Economic Studies*, 12 (1, January), 72–5.

(1945a) *The Social Framework of the American Economy* (adapted by A. G. Hart), New York, Oxford University Press.

(1945b) 'The Generalised Theory of Consumer's Surplus,' *Review of Economic Studies*, 13 (2, January), 68–74.

(1946) *Value and Capital: An Inquiry into Some Fundamental Principles of Economic Theory*, 2nd edn., Oxford, Clarendon Press.

(1949) 'Mr Harrod's Dynamic Theory,' *Economica*, May, 106–21.

(1950a) *A Contribution to the Theory of the Trade Cycle*, Oxford, Clarendon Press.

(1950b) 'Demand,' in *Chambers's Encyclopedia*, new rev. edn., vol. IV, Oxford, Pergamon Press, 432–4.

(1950c) 'Interest,' in *Chambers's Encyclopedia*, new rev. edn., vol. VII, Oxford, Pergamon Press, 619–23.

(1950d) 'Rent,' in *Chambers's Encyclopedia*, new rev. edn., vol. XI, Oxford, Pergamon Press, 596–7.

(1950e) 'Value,' in *Chambers's Encyclopedia*, new rev. edn., vol. XIV, Oxford, Pergamon Press, 211–17.

(1950f) 'Wages, Theory of,' in *Chambers's Encyclopedia*, new rev. edn., vol. XIV, Oxford, Pergamon Press, 370–2.

(1952) *The Social Framework: An Introduction to Economics*, 2nd edn., Oxford, Clarendon Press.

(1956a) 'Methods of Dynamic Analysis,' in *25 Economic Essays in Honour of Erik Lindahl*, Stockholm, Ekonomisk Tidskrift. 139–51 [reprinted with addendum in J. R. Hicks (1982a) *Collected Essays on Economic Theory*, vol. II, *Money, Interest and Wages*, Oxford, Basil Blackwell, 219–35].

(1956b) *A Revision of Demand Theory*, Oxford, Oxford University Press.

(1957) 'A Rehabilitation of "Classical" Economics?,' *Economic Journal*, 67 (June), 278–89.

(1959a) 'A *Value and Capital* Growth Model,' *Review of Economic Studies*, 26 (3, June), 159–73.

(1959b) *Essays in World Economics*, Oxford, Clarendon Press.

(1959c) 'Preface – and a Manifesto,' in J. R. Hicks *Essays in World Economics*, Oxford, Clarendon Press, v–xv [published as a separate essay, with an appendix, in J. R. Hicks (1981a) *Collected Essays on Economic Theory*, vol. I, *Wealth and Welfare*, Oxford, Basil Blackwell, 135–41.

(1960) 'Linear Theory,' *Economic Journal*, 70, (December), 671–709 [reprinted in J. R. Hicks (1966) *Surveys of Economic Theory*, vol. III, *Resource Allocation*, London, Macmillan, 75–113].

(1961a) *A Contribution to the Theory of the Trade Cycle*, 2nd edn., Oxford, Clarendon Press.

(1961b) 'The Measurement of Capital in Relation to Other Economic Aggregates,' in F. A. Lutz and D. C. Hague (eds.) *The Theory of Capital: proceedings of a Conference held by the International Economic Association (Corfu, September 4–11, 1958)*, London, Macmillan, 18–31.

(1962a) 'Economic Theory and the Evaluation of Consumers' Wants,' *Journal of Business*, 35 (3, July), 256–63.

(1962b) 'Liquidity,' *Economic Journal*, 72 (December), 787–802.

(1963) *The Theory of Wages*, 2nd edn., London, Macmillan.

(1965) *Capital and Growth*, Oxford, Clarendon Press.

(1967a) *Critical Essays in Monetary Theory*, Oxford, Clarendon Press.

(1967b) 'The Pure Theory of Portfolio Selection,' in J. R. Hicks *Critical Essays in Monetary Theory*, Oxford, Clarendon Press, 103–25.

(1967c) 'The Hayek Story,' in J. R. Hicks *Critical Essays in Monetary Theory*, Oxford, Clarendon Press, 203–15.

(1969a) *A Theory of Economic History*, Oxford, Clarendon Press.

(1969b) 'Automatists, Hawtreyans and Keynesians,' *Journal of Money, Credit and Banking*, 1 (3, August), 307–17.

(1970) 'A Neo-Austrian Growth Theory,' *Economic Journal*, 80 (3, June), 257–81.

(1972) Prize lecture, Nobel banquet, Stockholm, December 10.

(1973a) *Capital and Time: A Neo-Austrian Theory*, Oxford, Clarendon Press.

(1973b) 'On the Measurement of Capital,' *Economic Science*, Nagoya University, Japan.

(1973c) 'The Mainspring of Economic Growth,' *Swedish Journal of Economics*, 75 (December), 336–48.

(1973d) 'Recollections and Documents,' *Economica*, new series, 40 (February), 2–11 [reprinted in J. R. Hicks (1977a) *Economic Perspectives: Further Essays on Money and Growth*, Oxford: Clarendon Press, 134–48].

(1974a) [1939] *Value and Capital: An Inquiry into Some Fundamental Principles of Economic Theory*, Oxford, Clarendon Press.

(1974b) *The Crisis in Keynesian Economics*, Oxford, Basil Blackwell.

(1974c) 'Capital Controversies: Ancient and Modern,' *American Economic Review*, May, 307–16.

(1974d), 'Real and Monetary Factors in Economic Fluctuations,' *Scottish Journal of Political Economy*, 21 (3, November), 205–14.

(1974e) 'Review of D. C. North and R. P. Thomas, *The Rise of the Western World: A New Economic History*,' *Economic History Review*, 27 (4, November), 692–4.

(1975a) 'The Scope and Status of Welfare Economics,' *Oxford Economic Papers*, new series, 27 (3, November), 307–26 [reprinted in J. R. Hicks (1981a) *Wealth and Welfare: Collected Essays on Economic Theory*, vol. I, Oxford, Basil Blackwell, 218–39.

(1975b) 'Revival of Political Economy: the Old and the New (a Reply to Harcourt),' *Economic Record*, 51 (September), 365–7.

(1975c) 'What Is Wrong with Monetarism?,' *Lloyds Bank Review*, 118 (October), 1–13.

(1976a) '"Revolutions" in Economics,' in S. J. Latsis (ed.) *Method and Appraisal in Economics*, Cambridge, Cambridge University Press, 207–18.

(1976b) 'Some Questions of Time in Economics,' in A. Tang, F. M. Westfield, and J. S. Worley (eds.) *Evolution, Welfare and Time in Economics: Essays in Honour of Nicholas Georgescu-Roegen*, Lexington, MA, D. C. Heath, 135–51.

(1977a) *Economic Perspectives: Further Essays on Money and Growth*, Oxford, Clarendon Press.

(1977b) 'Monetary Experience and the Theory of Money,' in J. R. Hicks *Economic Perspectives: Further Essays on Money and Growth*, Oxford, Clarendon Press, pp. 45–109.

(1977c) 'Hawtrey,' in J. R. Hicks *Economic Perspectives: Further Essays on Money and Growth*, Oxford, Clarendon Press, 118–34.

(1977d) 'Capital Controversies: Ancient and Modern,' in J. R. Hicks *Economic Perspectives: Further Essays on Money and Growth*, Oxford, Clarendon Press, 149–65.

(1979a) *Causality in Economics*, Oxford, Basil Blackwell.

(1979b) 'The Formation of an Economist,' *Banca Nazionale del Lavoro Quarterly Review*, September, 195–204 [reprinted in J. R. Hicks (1983a) *Collected Essays on Economic Theory*, vol. III, *Classics and Moderns*, Oxford, Basil Blackwell, 355–64, and in J. R. Hicks (1984a) *The Economics of John Hicks: Selected Papers* (introd. D. R. Helm), Oxford, Basil Blackwell, 282–90].

(1980) 'IS-LM: an Explanation,' *Journal of Post Keynesian Economics*, Winter 1980–81, 139–54.

(1981a) *Collected Essays on Economic Theory*, vol. I, *Wealth and Welfare*, Oxford, Basil Blackwell.

(1981b) 'The Rationale of Majority Rule,' in J. R. Hicks *Collected Essays on Economic Theory*, vol. I, *Wealth and Welfare*, Oxford, Basil Blackwell, 283–99.

(1982a) *Collected Essays on Economic Theory*, vol. II, *Money, Interest and Wages*, Oxford, Basil Blackwell.

(1982b) 'Introductory: LSE and the Robbins Circle,' in J. R. Hicks (1982a) *Collected Essays on Economic Theory*, vol. II, *Money, Interest and Wages*, Oxford, Basil Blackwell, 3–10.

(1982c) 'Prefatory Note' to chapter 15: 'Harrod's Dynamic Theory,' in J. R. Hicks (1982a) *Collected Essays on Economic Theory*, vol. II, *Money, Interest and Wages*, Oxford, Basil Blackwell, 173–4.

(1982d) 'A Note on Robertson,' in J. R. Hicks (1982a) *Collected Essays on Economic Theory*, vol. II, *Money, Interest and Wages*, Oxford, Basil Blackwell, 127–31.

(1983a) *Collected Essays on Economic Theory*, vol. III, *Classics and Moderns*, Oxford, Basil Blackwell.

(1983b) 'Micro and Macro,' in J. R. Hicks (1983a) *Collected Essays on Economic Theory*, vol. III, *Classics and Moderns*, Oxford, Basil Blackwell, 349–52.

(1983c) 'IS-LM: an Explanation,' in J.-P. Fitoussi (ed.) *Modern Macroeconomic Theory*, Oxford, Basil Blackwell, 49–63.

(1984a) *The Economics of John Hicks: Selected Papers* (introd. D. R. Helm), Oxford, Basil Blackwell.

(1984b) 'Is Economics a Science?,' *Interdisciplinary Science Reviews*, 9(3), 213–19.

(1985a) *Methods of Dynamic Economics*, Oxford, Clarendon Press.

(1985b) 'Sraffa and Ricardo – a Critical View,' in G. A. Caravale (ed.) *The Legacy of Ricardo*, Oxford, Basil Blackwell, 305–19.

(1986a) 'Is Economics a Science?,' in M. Baranzini and R. Scazzieri (eds.) *Foundations of Economics: Structures of Inquiry and Economic Theory*, Oxford, Basil Blackwell, 91–101.

(1986b) *Managing without Money?*, Chung-Hua Series of Lectures by Invited Eminent Economists 11, Institute of Economics, Academia Sinica, Taipei.

(1988) Introductory remarks at the International Economic Association conference '*Value and Capital* – Fifty Years Later,' mimeo, University of Bologna.

(1989a) *A Market Theory of Money*, Oxford, Clarendon Press.

(1989b) 'The Assumption of Constant Returns to Scale,' *Cambridge Journal of Economics*, 13 (1, March), 9–17.

(1990) 'The Unification of Macroeconomics,' *Economic Journal*, 100 (June), 528–38.

(1991) 'The Swedish Influence on *Value and Capital*,' in L. Jonung (ed.) *The Stockholm School of Economics Revisited*, Cambridge, Cambridge University Press, 369–76

Hicks, J. R., and A. G. Hart (1945) *The Social Framework of the American Economy: An Introduction to Economics*, New York, Oxford University Press.

Hicks, U. K. (1938) *The Finance of British Government, 1920–1936*, London, Oxford University Press.

Hirai, T., M. C. Marcuzzo, T. Nishizawa, and E. Sanfilippo (eds.) (2005) *The Letters between John Hicks and Ursula Webb September–December, 1935*, Working Paper no. 207, Institute for Economic and Business Administration Research, University of Hyogo, Tokyo.

Hobsbawm, E. J. (1964) 'Introduction' to K. Marx, *Pre-capitalist Economic Formations*, London, Lawrence and Wishart, 9–65.

Hodgman, D. R. (1960) 'Credit Risk and Credit Rationing,' *Quarterly Journal of Economics*, 74 (2, May), 258–78.

Hommes, C. H. (1995) 'A Reconsideration of Hicks' Non-linear Trade Cycle Model,' *Structural Change and Economic Dynamics*, 6 (4, December), 435–59.

Hommes, C. H., and G. Sorger (1998) 'Consistent Expectations Equilibria,' *Macroeconomic Dynamics*, 2 (3, September), 287–321.

Horie, S. (1964) *The International Monetary Fund: Retrospect and Prospect*, London, Macmillan.

Horioka, C. Y., and W. Watanabe (1997) 'Why Do People Save? A Micro-analysis of Motives for Household Saving in Japan,' *Economic Journal*, 107 (May), 537–52.

Horsefield, K. (1969) *The International Monetary Fund 1945–1965: Twenty Years of International Monetary Cooperation*, vol. I, *Chronicle*, Washington, DC, International Monetary Fund.

Hotelling, H. (1932) 'Edgeworth's Taxation Paradox and the Nature of Demand and Supply Functions,' *Journal of Political Economy*, 40 (5, October), 577–616.

  (1935) 'Demand Functions with Limited Budgets,' *Econometrica*, 3 (1, January), 66–78.

Howitt, P., and R. P. McAfee (1992) 'Animal Spirits,' *American Economic Review*, 82 (3, June), 493–507.

Howson, S. (2005) 'The Robbins Circle,' draft paper presented at the American Society for the History of Economics annual conference, Tacoma, WA, June 24–7.

Hughes, J. R. T. (1972) '*The Unbound Prometheus: Technological Development in Western Europe from 1750 to the Present*, by David L. Landes and *A Theory of Economic History*, by John Hicks,' *Journal of Interdisciplinary History*, 2 (3, Winter), 263–80.

Hume, D. (1752) 'Of Money,' in D. Hume, *Political Discourses*, Edinburgh, R. Fleming.

Huygens, C. (1692) [1657] *De ratiociniis in ludo aleae*, trans. J. Arbuthnot, *Of the Laws of Chance, or, A Method of Calculation of the Hazards of Game*, London, Benjamin Motte.

Ichimura, S. (1955) 'Toward a General Nonlinear Macrodynamic Theory of Economic Fluctuations,' in K. K. Kurihara (ed.) *Post-Keynesian Economics*, London, Allen and Unwin, 192–226.

Jackson, P. (2001) 'A Central Banker's Perspective on Basel II,' paper presented at the conference 'Managing Capital for Financial Institutions,' Bank of England, London, November 29.

Jaffee, D., and F. Modigliani (1969) 'A Theory and Test of Credit Rationing,' *American Economic Review*, 59 (5, December), 850–72.

Jannaccone, P. (1954) [1946] *Moneta e lavoro*, Turin, Utet.

Jones, R. W. (1965) 'The Structure of Simple General Equilibrium Models,' *Journal of Political Economy*, 73 (6, December), 557–72.

Johnson, H. G. (1960) '*Essays in World Economics*, by J. R. Hicks,' *Economica* (new series), 27 (August), 279–80.

  (1965) *The World Economy at the Crossroads: A Survey of Current Problems of Money, Trade and Economic Development*, Oxford, Clarendon Press.

  (1975) '*The Crisis in Keynesian Economics* by John Hicks,' *Journal of Political Economy*, 83 (3, June), 671–3.

Jonung, L. (1981) 'Ricardo on Machinery and the Present Unemployment: an Unpublished Manuscript by Knut Wicksell,' *Economic Journal*, 91 (March), 195–205.

Kahn, R. F. (1931) 'The Relation of Home Investment to Unemployment,' *Economic Journal*, 41 (June), 173–98.

(1984) *The Making of Keynes' General Theory*, Cambridge, Cambridge University Press.

(1985) 'The Cambridge "Circus" (1),' in G. C. Harcourt (ed.) *Keynes and His Contemporaries*, London, Macmillan, 42–51.

Kahneman, D., and A. Tversky (1979) 'Prospect Theory: an Analysis of Decision under Risk,' *Econometrica*, 47 (2, March), 263–91.

Kaldor, N. (1932) 'A Case against Technical Progress?,' *Economica*, 12 (May), 180–96.

(1951), 'Mr. Hicks on the Trade Cycle,' *Economic Journal*, 61 (December), 833–47.

(1956) 'Alternative Theories of Distribution,' *Review of Economic Studies*, 23 (2, March), 83–100.

(1957) 'A Model of Economic Growth,' *Economic Journal*, 67 (December), 591–624.

(1961) 'Capital Accumulation and Economic Growth,' in F. A. Lutz and D. C. Hague (eds.) *The Theory of Capital*, London, Macmillan, 177–222.

(1966) 'Marginal Productivity and the Macro-economic Theories of Distribution,' *Review of Economic Studies*, 33 (4, October), 309–19.

(1986a) 'Limits on Growth' [Oxford Hicks Lecture 1985], *Oxford Economics Papers*, new series, 38 (2, July), 187–98.

(1986b) *Ricordi di un economista* (ed. M. C. Marcuzzo), Milan, Garzanti.

(1988) 'Recollections of an Economist,' in J. A. Kregel (ed.) *Recollections of Eminent Economists*, vol. I, Basingstoke, Macmillan, 11–35.

Kalecki, M. (1942) 'A Theory of Profit,' *Economic Journal*, 52 (June–September), 258–67.

Kane, E. J. (1969). '*Critical Essays in Monetary Theory*, by Sir John Hicks and *Essays in Monetary Economics*, by Harry G. Johnson,' *Canadian Journal of Economics*, 2 (February), 141–4.

Kendall, M., and A. Stuart (1977) *The Advanced Theory of Statistics*, vol. I, *Distribution Theory*, 4th edn., London, Griffin.

Kessler, D., and A. Masson (eds.) (1988) *Modelling the Accumulation and Distribution of Wealth*, Oxford, Clarendon Press.

Keynes, J. M. (1923) *A Tract on Monetary Reform*, London, Harcourt, Brace.

(1930) *A Treatise on Money*, London, Macmillan.

(1936) *The General Theory of Employment, Interest and Money*, London, Macmillan [reprinted in D. E. Moggridge (ed.) (1973) *The Collected Writings of John Maynard Keynes*, vol. VII, *The General Theory of Employment, Interest and Money*, London, Macmillan].

(1937a) 'The General Theory of Employment,' *Quarterly Journal of Economics*, 51 (2, February), 209–23 [reprinted in D. E. Moggridge (ed.) (1973b) *The Collected Writings of John Maynard Keynes*, vol. XIV, *The General Theory and After: Defence and Development*, London, Macmillan, 109–23].

(1937b) Letter to J. R. Hicks,' in D. E. Moggridge (ed.) (1973b) *The Collected Writings of John Maynard Keynes*, vol. XIV, *The General Theory and After: Defence and Development*, London, Macmillan, 79–81.

(1971) [1930] *A Treatise on Money*, vol. I, *The Pure Theory of Money*, London, Macmillan.

Kindleberger, C. P. (1980) '*Causality in Economics* John Hicks; *Looking into the Seeds of Time: Social Mechanisms in Economic Development* Y. S. Brenner,' *Journal of Economic Literature*, 18 (3, September), 1086–8.

King, R. G. (1983) '*Money, Interest and Wages*, John Hicks,' *Journal of Economic Literature*, 21 (4, December), 1497–9.

Kirman, A. (1989) 'The Intrinsic Limits of Modern Economic Theory: the Emperor Has no Clothes,' *Economic Journal*, 99, Conference Issue, 126–39.

Kiyotaki, N., and R. Wright (1989) 'On Money as a Medium of Exchange,' *Journal of Political Economy*, 97 (4, August), 927–54.

Kolmogorov, A. N. (1933) *Grundbegriffe der Wahrscheinlichkeits* [*Foundations of the Theory of Probability*], Berlin, Springer.

Kraus, M., and S. Wirth (2000) *Savings, Expectations and Technological Unemployment: A Generalization of Assumptions for the Hicksian Fixwage Traverse*, Discussion Paper no. 00–29, Centre for European Economic Research, Mannheim.

Kregel, J. A. (1973) *The Reconstruction of Political Economy: An Introduction to Post-Keynesian Economics*, London, Macmillan.

Kresge, S. (ed.) (1999) *The Collected Works of F. A. Hayek*, vol. VI, *Good Money*, part 2, 'Correspondence between Hayek and John Hicks,' London, Routledge, 100–5.

Kruger, A. (1965) '*The Theory of Wages*, second edition, J. R. Hicks,' *Canadian Journal of Economics and Political Science*, 31 (1, February), 164.

Kuznetsov, Yu. A. (2004) *Elements of Applied Bifurcation Theory*, New York, Springer.

Lachmann, L. M. (1989) [1973] 'Sir John Hicks as a Neo-Austrian,' in J. Cunningham Wood and R. N. Woods (eds.) *Sir John Hicks: Critical Assessments*, vol. II, London, Routledge, 262–77 [originally published in *The South African Journal of Economics*, 41 (3, September), 1973, 195–207].

Laidler, D. (1983) '*Money, Interests and Wages: Collected Essays on Economic Theory* John Hicks,' *Journal of Money, Credit and Banking*, 15 (3, August), 385–9.

Laing, N. F. (1969) 'Two Notes on Pasinetti's Theorem,' *Economic Record*, 45 (September), 373–85.

Lancaster, K. (1966) 'A New Approach to Consumer Theory,' *Journal of Political Economy*, 74 (2, April), 132–57.

Landesmann, M. A., and R. Scazzieri (eds.) (1996) *Production and Economic Dynamics*, Cambridge, Cambridge University Press.

Lane, F. C. (1970) '*A Theory of Economic History* by John Hicks,' *Journal of Economic Literature*, 8 (3, September), 821–3.

Laplace, P. S. (1814) *Essai philosophique sur les probabilités*, Paris, Courcier.

Lash, N. A (1987) *Banking Laws and Regulations: An Economic Perspective*, Upper Saddle River, NJ, Prentice-Hall.

Layard, R., S. Nickell, and R. Jackman (1991) *Unemployment*, Oxford, Oxford University Press.

League of Nations (1944) *International Currency Experience: Lessons of the Interwar Period*, Geneva, Economic, Financial and Transit Department, League of Nations.

Lederer, E. (1931) *Technischer Fortschritt und Arbeitslosigkeit*, Tübingen, J. C. B. Mohr.

(1938) *Technical Progress and Unemployment: An Enquiry into the Obstacles to Economic Expansion*, London, P. S. King and Son.

Leijonhufvud, A. (1979) 'Economic Perspectives: Further Essays on Money and Growth by John Hicks,' *Journal of Economic Literature*, 17 (2, June), 525–8.

Leontief, W. (1986) [1982] 'The Distribution of Work and Income,' in W. Leontief *Input-Output Economics*, 2nd edn., New York, Oxford University Press, 363–78.

Lerner, A. P. (1940) 'Professor Hicks' Dynamics,' *Quarterly Journal of Economics*, 54 (2, February), 298–306.

(1951) '*A Contribution to the Theory of the Trade Cycle*. J. R.Hicks,' *Econometrica*, 19 (4, October), 472–4.

Levinson, N., and O. E. Smith (1942) 'A General Equation for Relaxation Oscillations,' *Duke Mathematical Journal*, 9 (2, June), 382–403.

Lindahl, E. (1933) 'The Concept of Income,' in *Economic Essays in Honour of Gustav Cassel*, London, Allen and Unwin, 399–407.

(1939) *Studies in the Theory of Money and Capital*, London, Allen and Unwin.

Loria, A. (1936) 'Intorno alla funzione della moneta immaginaria,' *Rivista di Storia Economica*, 1 (1–4), 299–301.

Loyo, E. (2002) 'Imaginary Money against Sticky Relative Prices,' *European Economic Review*, 46 (6, June), 1073–92.

Lundberg, E. (1950) 'Den Ekonomiska Expansionens Stabilitet,' *Ekonomisk Tidskrift*, 52 (September), 196–215 [trans. in R. G. H. Henriksson (ed.) (1994) *Erik Lundberg: Studies in Economic Instability and Change*, Stockholm, SNS Forlag].

Machina, M. J. (1982) '"Expected Utility" Analysis without the Independence Axiom,' *Econometrica*, 50 (2, March), 277–324.

(1987) 'Choice under Uncertainty: Problems Solved and Unsolved,' *Journal of Economic Perspectives*, 1 (1, Summer), 121–54.

Machlup, F. (1940) 'Professor Hicks' Statics,' *Quarterly Journal of Economics*, 54 (2, February), 277–97.

McCloskey, D. (1990) 'Ancients and Moderns,' *Social Science History* 14 (3, Fall), 289–303.

McCormick, B. J. (1992) *Hayek and the Keynesian Avalanche*, London, Harvester Wheatsheaf.

McFadden, D. (1968) 'On Hicksian Stability,' in J. N. Wolfe (ed.) *Value Capital and Growth: Papers in Honour of Sir John Hicks*, Edinburgh, Edinburgh University Press, 329–51.

McKenzie, L. W., and S. Zamagni (1991) 'Introduction', in L. W. McKenzie and S. Zamagni (eds.) *Value and Capital Fifty Years Later*, London, Macmillan, xviii–xxix.

Maine, H. S. (1905) [1861] *Ancient Law: Its Connection with the Early History of Society and its Relation to Modern Ideas*, London, John Murray.

Malinvaud, E. (2002) 'Sur l'agrégation des demandes de travail non-qualifié,' *Annales d'économie et de statistique*, 66 (April–June), 41–80 [together with some unpublished notes].

Marcet, A., and J. P. Nicolini (2003) 'Recurrent Hyperinflations and Learning,' *American Economic Review*, 93 (5, December), 1476–98.

Marcuzzo, M. C. (2002) 'The Collaboration between J. M. Keynes and R. F. Kahn from the *Treatise* to the *General Theory*,' *History of Political Economy*, 34 (2, Summer), 421–47.

(2005) 'Piero Sraffa at the University of Cambridge,' *European Journal of the History of Economic Thought*, 12 (3, September), 425–52.

Marcuzzo, M. C., and A. Rosselli (eds.) (2005) *Economists in Cambridge: A Study through Their Correspondence, 1907–1946*, London, Routledge.

Markowitz, H. M. (1952) 'Portfolio Selection,' *Journal of Finance*, 7 (1, March), 77–91.

(1959) *Portfolio Selection: Efficient Diversification of Investments*, Cowles Foundation Monograph no. 16, New York, Wiley.

Marshall, A. (1920) *Principles of Economics*, 8th edn., London, Macmillan.

Martinez Oliva, J. C., and G. Schlitzer (2005) *Le Battaglie della Lira*, Florence, Le Monnier.

Marty, A. L. (1980) '*The Crisis in Keynesian Economics* by John Hicks,' *Journal of Money, Credit and Banking*, 12 (2, March), 253–5.

Masera, R. S. (1972) *The Term Structure of Interest Rates*, Oxford, Clarendon Press.

(1991) *Intermediari, Mercati e Finanza d'Impresa*, Bari, Laterza.

(2001) *Il Rischio e le Banche*, Milan, Il Sole24Ore.

(2005) *Rischio, Banche, Imprese*, Milan, Il Sole24Ore.

Masera, R. S., and R. Triffin (eds.) (1984) *Europe's Money: Problems of European Monetary Co-ordination and Integration*, Oxford, Clarendon Press.

Matten, C. (2000) *Managing Bank Capital*, Chichester, John Wiley.

Matthews, R. C. O. (1959) *The Trade Cycle*, Cambridge, Cambridge University Press.

(1989) *John Richard Hicks Kt., M.A., F.B.A. [...] A Memorial Address Delivered in the University Church of St. Mary the Virgin on 28th October 1989*. Oxford, All Souls College.

(1994) '*In Memoriam*,' in H. Hagemann and O. F. Hamouda (eds.) *The Legacy of Hicks: His Contributions to Economic Analysis*, London, Routledge, 12–15.

(2004) 'Hicks, Sir John Richard (1904–1989),' in H. C. G. Matthew and B. Harrison (eds.) *Oxford Dictionary of National Biography: From the Earliest Times to the Year 2000*, vol. XXVII, Oxford, Oxford University Press (in association with the British Academy), 32–3 [online edition: www.oxford-dub.com, accessed May 27, 2007]

Meade, J. E. (1936) *An Introduction to Economic Analysis and Policy*, Oxford, Oxford University Press.

(1937) 'A Simplified Model of Mr Keynes' System,' *Review of Economic Studies*, 4 (2, February), 98–107 [reprinted in S. Harris (ed.) (1948) *The New Economics: Keynes' Influence on Theory and Public Policy*, London, Dennis Dobson, 606–18].

Meade, J. E., and C. Hitch (1938) *An Introduction to Economic Analysis and Policy* (introd. A. Hansen), New York, Oxford University Press.

Medio, A. (1979) *Teoria Nonlineare del Ciclo Economico*, Bologna, Il Mulino.

Medio, A., and M. Lines (2001) *Nonlinear Dynamics: A Primer*, Cambridge, Cambridge University Press.

Menger, C. (1871) *Grundsätze der Volkswirthschaftslehre*, Vienna, Braumüller [2nd edn. reprinted in F. A. Hayek (ed.) (1968) *Carl Menger: Gesammelte Werke*, vol. I, Tübingen, Mohr-Siebeck, 1–116].

(1888) 'Zur Theorie des Kapitals,' *Jahrbücher für Nationalökonomie und Statistik*, 17, 1–49 [reprinted in F. A. Hayek (ed.) (1970) *Carl Menger: Gesammelte Werke*, vol. III, Tübingen, Mohr-Siebeck, 133–83].

(1970 [1915]) 'Eugen von Böhm-Bawerk,' in F. A. Hayek (ed.) *Carl Menger: Gesammelte Werke*, vol. III, Tübingen, Mohr-Siebeck, 293–307.

Menger, K. (1934) 'Das Unsicherheitsmoment in der Wertlehre: Betrachtungen in Anschluss an das sogenannte Petersburger Spiel,' *Zeitschrift für Nationalökonomie*, 5 (4, October), 459–85.

Merton, R. C. (1973) 'An Intertemporal Capital Asset Pricing Model,' *Econometrica*, 41 (5, September), 867–87.

Meyers, A. L. (1946) '*The Social Framework of the American Economy: An Introduction to Economics*, by J. R. Hicks and Albert Gailord Hart,' *Journal of Political Economy*, 54 (3, June), 275.

Miller, M. (1995) 'Do the M&M Propositions Apply to Banks?,' *Journal of Banking and Finance*, 19 (3–4, June), 483–9.

Minsky, H. P. (1959) 'A Linear Model of Cyclical Growth,' *Review of Economics and Statistics*, 41 (2, May), 133–45.

(1982) *Can it Happen Again?*, New York, M. E. Sharpe.

Minsky, H. P., and P. Ferri (1984) 'Prices, Employment, and Profits,' *Journal of Post Keynesian Economics*, 6 (4, Summer), 489–99.

Mises, L. von (1981) [1912] *The Theory of Money and Credit*, trans. H. E. Batson, Indianapolis, Liberty Fund.

Mitchell, B. R. (1970) '*A Theory of Economic History*, by Sir John Hicks,' *Economic Journal*, 80 (June), 350–2.

Mizen, P., and J. R. Presley (1998) 'Keynes, Hicks and the Cambridge School,' *History of Political Economy*, 30 (1, Spring), 1–16.

Modigliani, F., and M. Miller (1958) 'The Cost of Capital, Corporate Finance and the Theory of Investment,' *American Economic Review*, 48 (3, June), 261–97.

Moggridge, D. E. (ed.) (1973a) *The Collected Writings of John Maynard Keynes*, vol. XIII, *The General Theory and After: Preparation*, London, Macmillan.

(ed.) (1973b) *The Collected Writings of John Maynard Keynes*, vol. XIV, *The General Theory and After: Defence and Development*, London, Macmillan.

(1983) *The Collected Writings of John Maynard Keynes*, vol. XII, *Economic Articles and Correspondence: Investment and Editorial*, London, Macmillan.

Moggridge, D. E. (1992) *Maynard Keynes: An Economist's Biography*, London, Routledge.

Montanari, G. (1913) [1683] *La Zecca in Consulta di Stato...*, in A. Graziani, (ed.) *Economisti del Cinque e Seicento*, Bari, Laterza, 237–379.

Morgenstern, O. (1941) 'Professor Hicks on Value and Capital,' *Journal of Political Economy*, 49 (3, June), 361–93.

Morishima, M. (1958) 'A Contribution to the Nonlinear Theory of the Trade Cycle,' *Zeitschrift für Nationalökonomie*, 18 (1–2, May), 165–73.

(1994) 'Capital and Growth,' in H. Hagemann and O. F. Hamouda (eds.) *The Legacy of Hicks: His Contributions to Economic Analysis*, London, Routledge, 28–44.

Morrison, L. A. (1933) '*The Theory of Wages*, by J. R. Hicks,' *American Economic Review*, 23 (December), 686–7.

Murfin, A. J. (1980) *Saving Propensities from Wage and Non-wage Income*, Warwick Economic Research Paper no. 174, Department of Economics, University of Warwick, Coventry.

Naldi, N. (2005) 'Robertson and the Great Divide: the Correspondence between Kahn, Kaldor, J. Robinson and Sraffa,' in M. C. Marcuzzo and A. Rosselli (eds.) *Economists in Cambridge: A study through Their Correspondence, 1907–1946*, London, Routledge, 371–87.

Nardini, F. (1990) 'Cycle-trend Dynamics in a Fixwage Neo-Austrian Model of Traverse,' *Structural Change and Economic Dynamics*, 1 (1, June), 165–94.

(1993) 'Traverse and Convergence in the Neo-Austrian Model: the Case of a Distributive Shock,' *Structural Change and Economic Dynamics*, 4 (1, June), 105–25.

Natoli, S. (1937) 'C. A. Broggia e la moneta immaginaria,' *Giornale degli Economisti e Rivista di Statistica*, 52 (1, January), 192–6.

Neisser, H. (1932) 'Lohnhöhe und Beschäftigungsgrad im Marktgleichgewicht,' *Weltwirtschaftliches Archiv*, 36 (2, October) 415–55.

(1942) '"Permanent" Technological Unemployment, Part I,' *American Economic Review*, 32 (1, March), 50–71.

(1990) [1932] 'The Wage Rate and Employment in Market Equilibrium,' *Structural Change and Economic Dynamics*, 1 (1, June), 141–63.

Neri, P. (1804) [1751] *Osservazioni sopra il prezzo legale delle monete*, in P. Custodi (ed.) *Scrittori classici italiani di economia politica*: Parte antica, vol. VI, Milan, Destefanis, 1–233.

Newlyn, W. T. (1962) *Theory of Money*, Oxford, Clarendon Press.

North, D. C., and R. P. Thomas (1973) *The Rise of the Western World: A New Economic History*, Cambridge, Cambridge University Press.

Onofri, P., and A. Stagni (1984) 'Rate of Profit and Return on Financial Assets in Italian Industry 1951–1981,' in D. M. Holland (ed.) *Measuring Profitability and Capital Cost: An International Study*, Lexington, MA, Lexington Books, 465–80.

Pantaleoni, M. (1925). 'L'atto economico' ['The Economic Act'], in M. Pantaleoni *Erotemi di economia*, Bari, Laterza, 67–155

Pareto, V. (1943) *Corso di economia politica*, 2 vols., Turin, Einaudi.

Parker, W. N. (1972) 'John Hicks, *A Theory of Economic History*, and Jonathan Hughes, *Industrialization and Economic History: Theses and Conjectures*,' *American Historical Review*, 77 (4, October), 1087–8.

Pasinetti, L. L. (1960) 'Cyclical Fluctuations and Economic Growth,' *Oxford Economic Papers*, new series, 12 (2, June), 215–41.

(1962) 'The Rate of Profit and Income Distribution in Relation to the Rate of Economic Growth,' *Review of Economic Studies*, 29 (4, October), 267–79.

(1974) *Growth and Income Distribution: Essays in Economic Theory*, Cambridge, Cambridge University Press.

(1981) *Structural Change and Economic Growth: A Theoretical Essay on the Dynamics of the Wealth of Nations*, Cambridge, Cambridge University Press.

(1988) 'Sraffa on Income Distribution,' *Cambridge Journal of Economics*, 12 (1, March), 135–8.

(1993) *Structural Economic Dynamics: A Theory of the Economic Consequences of Human Learning*, Cambridge, Cambridge University Press.

(2002) *Due modi diversi di fare teoria economica: L'influenza recondita della storia*, in P. Ciocca (ed.) *Le vie della storia nell'economia*, Bologna, Il Mulino, 183–90.

Pasinetti, L. L., and R. Scazzieri (1987) 'Capital Theory: Paradoxes,' in J. Eatwell, M. Milgate, and P. Newman (eds.) *The New Palgrave Dictionary of Economics*, vol. I, London, Macmillan, 363–8.

(2008) 'Capital Theory: Paradoxes,' in S. N. Durlauf and L. E. Blume (eds.) *The New Palgrave Dictionary of Economics*, 2nd edn., vol. I, London, Palgrave Macmillan, 675–84.

Patinkin, D. (1959) 'Keynesian Economics Rehabilitated: a Rejoinder to Professor Hicks,' *Economic Journal*, 69 (September), 582–7.

(1968) '*Critical Essays in Monetary Theory*, by J. R. Hicks,' *American Economic Review*, 58 (December), 1435–8.

Patinkin, D., and J. C. Leith (eds.) (1977) *Keynes, Cambridge and The General Theory*, London, Macmillan.

Pesaran, M. H., and S. M. Potter (1997) 'A Floor and Ceiling Model of US Output,' *Journal of Economic Dynamics and Control*, 21 (4, May), 661–95.

Phoonsen, J. (1715) *Les Lois et les coutumes du change des principales places de l'Europe* (trans. J. P. Ricard), Amsterdam, Estienne Roger.

Pigou, A. C. (1913) 'Review of K. Wicksell, *Vorelesungen uber Nationalökonomie auf Grundlage des Marginalprinzipes*,' *Economic Journal*, 23 (December), 605–6.

(1933) *The Theory of Unemployment*, London, Macmillan.

(1935) *The Economics of Stationary States*, London, Macmillan.

Plumptre, A. F. W. (1947) 'Keynes in Cambridge,' *Canadian Journal of Economics and Political Science*, 13 (3, August), 366–71.

Pontryagin, L. S., V. G. Boltyanskii, E. Gamkrelidze, and E. F. Mishchenko (1962) *Mathematical Theory of Optimal Processes*, New York, Interscience.

Posner, M. V. (1976) '*The Crisis in Keynesian Economics*, by Sir John Hicks,' *Economic Journal*, 86 (March), 122–3.

Postan, M. M. (1944) 'The Rise of a Money Economy,' *Economic History Review*, 14 (2, May), 123–34.

Price, B. B (2001) 'The Function of the Hicksian Economic Institution,' in K. Puttaswamaiah (ed.) *John Hicks: His Contributions to Economic Theory and Application*, New Brunswick, NJ, Transaction, 111–37.

Puttaswamaiah, K. (ed.) (2001) *John Hicks: His Contributions to Economic Theory and Application*, New Brunswick, NJ, Transaction.

Puviani, A. (1973) [1903] *Teoria dell'illusione finanziaria*, Milan, ISEDI.

Quadrio Curzio, A., and R. Scazzieri (1986) 'Governo della moneta ed economia politica: su tre saggi di Cesare Beccaria e di Pietro Verri,' in A. Quadrio Curzio and R. Scazzieri (eds.) *Sul disordine delle monete a Milano nel Settecento: Tre saggi di Cesare Beccaria e Pietro Verri*, Milan, Electa, 9–43.

(1992) 'Dall'economia politica al governo dell'economia: riflessioni sul contributo di Cesare Beccaria e Pietro Verri sulla teoria e pratica della moneta,' in Nicola Acocella, Guido Rey, and Mario Tiberi (eds.) *Scritti in onore di Federico Caffè*, Milan, Angeli, 141–81.

Rader, J. T. (1963) 'The Existence of a Utility Function to Represent Preferences,' *Review of Economic Studies*, 30 (3, October), 229–32.

Radford, R. A. (1945) 'The Economic Organization of a P.O.W. Camp,' *Economica*, 12 (November), 189–201.

Radner, R. (1972) 'Existence of Equilibrium of Plans, Prices, and Price Expectations in a Sequence of Markets,' *Econometrica*, 40 (2, March), 289–303.

Ramsey, F. P. (1928) 'A Mathematical Theory of Savings,' *Economic Journal*, 38 (December), 543–59.

Reder, M. W. (1965) '*The Theory of Wages*, second edition, by J. R. Hicks,' *Economica*, new series, 32 (February), 88–90.

Ricardo, D. (1821 [1817]) *On the Principles of Political Economy and Taxation*, 3rd edn., London, John Murray.

Richardson, G. (1960) *Information and Investment*, Oxford, Clarendon Press.

Robbins, L. (1971) *Autobiography of an Economist*, London, Macmillan.

Robertson, D. H. (1931) 'Mr Keynes' Theory of Money,' *Economic Journal*, 41 (September), 395–411.

Robinson, E. A. G. (1943). '*Economic Analysis*, by Kenneth Boulding, and *The Social Framework: An Introduction to Economics*, by J. R. Hicks,' *Economic Journal*, 53 (December), 387–92.

(1977) 'Keynes and his Cambridge Colleagues,' in D. Patinkin and J. C. Leith (eds.) *Keynes, Cambridge and The General Theory*, London, Macmillan, 25–38.

(1985) 'The Cambridge "Circus" (2),' in G. C. Harcourt (ed.) *Keynes and His Contemporaries* London, Macmillan, 52–7.

Robinson, J. (1933) *The Economics of Imperfect Competition*, London, Macmillan.

(1937) *Essays in the Theory of Employment*, London, Macmillan.

(1951) *Collected Economic Papers*, vol. I, Oxford, Basil Blackwell.

(1978a) *Contributions to Modern Economics*, Oxford, Basil Blackwell.

(1978b) 'Keynes and Ricardo,' *Journal of Post Keynesian Economics*, 1 (1, Fall), 12–18.

(1979) *Collected Economic Papers*, vol. V, Oxford, Basil Blackwell.

Rosselli, A., and D. Besomi (2005) 'The Unlooked for Proselytiser: J. Robinson and the Correspondence with Sraffa, Harrod and Kaldor,' in M. C. Marcuzzo and A. Rosselli (eds.) *Economists in Cambridge: A Study through Their Correspondence, 1907–1946*, London, Routledge, 309–23.

Rymes, T. K. (1974) '*Capital and Time: A Neo-Austrian Theory* by John Hicks,' *Canadian Journal of Economics*, 7 (4, November), 705–6.

Samuelson, P. A. (1947) *Foundations of Economic Analysis*, Cambridge, MA, Harvard University Press.

(1948) *Economics*, New York, McGraw-Hill.

(1966) 'A Summing Up,' *Quarterly Journal of Economics*, 80 (4, November), 568–83.

(1988) 'Mathematical Vindication of Ricardo on Machinery,' *Journal of Political Economy*, 96 (2, April), 274–82.

(1989) 'Ricardo was Right!,' *Scandinavian Journal of Economics*, 91 (1, March), 47–62.

(1994) 'The Classical Classical Fallacy,' *Journal of Economic Literature*, 32 (2, June), 620–39.

(2001) 'My John Hicks,' in K. Puttaswamaiah (ed.) *John Hicks: His Contributions to Economic Theory and Application*, New Brunswick, NJ, Transaction, 1–4.

Samuelson, P. A., and F. Modigliani (1966a) 'The Pasinetti Paradox in Neoclassical and More General Models,' *Review of Economic Studies*, 33 (4, October), 269–301.

(1966b) 'Marginal Productivity and the Macro-economic Theories of Distribution: Reply to Pasinetti and Robinson,' *Review of Economic Studies*, 33 (4, October), pp. 321–30.

Sanfilippo, E. (2005) 'Keynes's Valuable Opponent and Collaborator: the Correspondence between Keynes and Robertson,' in M. C. Marcuzzo and A. Rosselli (eds.) *Economists in Cambridge: A Study through Their Correspondence, 1907–1946*, London, Routledge, 58–76.

Sargent, T. J. (1993) *Bounded Rationality in Macroeconomics*, Oxford, Clarendon Press.

(1999) *The Conquest of American Inflation*, Princeton, NJ, Princeton University Press.

Saura, D., F. J. Vasquez, and J. M. Vegas (1998) 'Non-chaotic Oscillations in Some Regularized Hicks Models: a Restatement of the Ceiling and Floor Conditions,' *Journal of Economic Dynamics and Control*, 22 (5, May), 667–78.

Savage, L. J. (1972) *The Foundation of Statistics*, 2nd edn., New York, Dover.

Savary, J. (1749) [1679] *Le Parfait Négociant, ou Instruction Générale pour ce qui regarde le Commerce*, Paris, Veuve Estienne et Fils.

Scarfe, B. L. (1984) '*Collected Essays on Economic Theory*, vol. III, *Classics and Moderns*,' *Journal of Economic Literature*, 22 (4, December), 1633–4.

Scaruffi, G. (1913) [1582] *L'Alitinonfo*, in A. Graziani (ed.) *Economisti del Cinque e Seicento*, Bari, Laterza, 1–140.

Scazzieri, R. (1993a) *A Theory of Production: Tasks, Processes and Technical Practices*, Oxford, Clarendon Press.

(1993b) 'Actions, Processes and Economic Theory,' in A. Heertje (ed.) *The Makers of Modern Economics*, vol. I, London, Harvester Wheatsheaf, 84–114.

(1994) 'Economic Theory and Economic History,' in H. Hagemann and O. F. Hamouda (eds.), *The Legacy of Hicks: His Contributions to Economic Analysis*, London, Routledge, 225–40.

Scitovsky, T. (1982) '*Wealth and Welfare, Collected Essays on Economic Theory*, vol. I, John Hicks,' *Journal of Economic Literature*, 20 (3, September), 1062–4.

Schumpeter, J. A. (1954) *History of Economic Analysis*, London, Allen and Unwin.

Sen, A. (1963) 'Neo-classical and Neo-Keynesian Theories of Distribution,' *Economic Record*, 39 (March), 53–64.

(1970) 'Introduction,' in A. K. Sen (ed.) *Growth Economics (Selected Readings)*, Harmondsworth, Penguin Books, 9–40.

(1974) 'On Some Debates in Capital Theory,' *Economica*, new series, 41 (August), 328–35 [reprinted in A. Mitra (ed.) *Economic Theory and Planning: Essays in Honour of A. K. Das Gupta*, Calcutta, Oxford University Press, 39–48].

(1993) 'Markets and Freedoms,' *Oxford Economic Papers*, new series, 45 (4, October), 519–41.

Shafer, G., and V. Vovk (2001) *Probability and Finance: It's Only a Game!*, New York, Wiley.

Sharpe, W. F. (1964) 'Capital Asset Prices: a Theory of Market Equilibrium under Conditions of Risk,' *Journal of Finance*, 19 (3, September), 425–42.

Shehadi, N. (1991) 'The LSE and the Stockholm School in the 1930s,' in L. Jonung (ed.) *The Stockholm School of Economics Revisited*, Cambridge, Cambridge University Press, 377–89.

Shove, G. F. (1933) 'A Review of *The Theory of Wages* by J. R. Hicks,' *Economic Journal*, 43 (September), 460–72.

Simkin, C. (2001) 'John and Ursula Hicks: a Personal Recollection,' in K. Puttaswamaiah (ed.) *John Hicks: His Contributions to Economic Theory and Application*, New Brunswick, NJ, Transaction, 5–15.

Skidelsky, R. (1992) *John Maynard Keynes: The Economist as Saviour 1920–1937*, London, Macmillan.

Smith, A. (1776) *An Inquiry into the Nature and Causes of the Wealth of Nations*, London, Strahan and Cadell.

Snowdon, B., and H. R. Vane (2005) *Modern Macroeconomics: Its Origins, Development and Current State*, Cheltenham, Edward Elgar.

Solow, R. M. (1966) '*Capital and Growth*, by John Hicks,' *American Economic Review*, 56 (December), 1257–60.

(1974) '*Capital and Time: A Neo-Austrian Theory*, by John Hicks,' *Economic Journal*, 84 (March), 189–92.

(1984), 'Mr Hicks and the Classics,' in D. A. Collard, N. H. Dimsdale, L. L. Gilbert, D. R. Helm, M. F. G. Scott, and A. K. Sen (eds.) *Economic Theory and Hicksian Themes*, Oxford, Oxford University Press, 13–25.

(2000) 'Toward a Macroeconomy of the Medium Run,' *Journal of Economic Perspectives*, 14 (1, Winter), 151–8.

Sonnenschein, H. (1972) 'Market Excess Demand Functions,' *Econometrica*, 40 (3, May), 549–63.

(1973) 'Do Walras' Identity and Continuity Characterize the Class of Community Demand Functions?,' *Journal of Economic Theory*, 6 (4, August), 345–54.

Sraffa, P. (1951) 'Introduction,' in P. Sraffa and M. H. Dobb (eds.) *The Works and Correspondence of David Ricardo*, vol. I, *On the Principles of Political Economy and Taxation*, Cambridge, Cambridge University Press, xiii–lxii.

(1960) *Production of Commodities by Means of Commodities: Prelude to a Critique of Economic Theory*, Cambridge, Cambridge University Press.

Sraffa, P., and M. H. Dobb (eds.) (1951) *The Works and Correspondence of David Ricardo*, vol. I, *On the Principles of Political Economy and Taxation*, Cambridge, Cambridge University Press.

Steuart, J. (1966) [1767] *An Inquiry into the Principles of Political Economy*, ed. and introd. A. S. Skinner, Edinburgh, Oliver and Boyd.

Stigler, G. J. (1946) *The Theory of Price*, New York, Macmillan.

(1948) 'Review of *Foundations of Economic Analysis* by Paul Samuelson,' *Journal of the American Statistical Association*, 43 (December), 603–5.

(1952) *The Theory of Price*, 2nd edn., New York, Macmillan.

(1957) '*A Revision of Demand Theory*, J. R. Hicks,' *Journal of Political Economy*, 65 (2, April), 169–70.

Stiglitz, J. E., and B. Greenwald (2003) *Towards a New Paradigm in Monetary Economics*, Cambridge, Cambridge University Press.

Stiglitz, J. E., and A. Weiss (1981) 'Credit Rationing in Markets with Imperfect Information,' *American Economic Review*, 71 (3, June), 393–410.

Stokes, C. J. (1960) '*Essays in World Economics*, by J. R. Hicks,' *American Economic Review*, 50 (June), 483–5.

Streissler, E. (1969) 'Hayek on Growth: a Reconsideration of his Early Theoretical Work,' in E. Streissler, G. Haberler, F. A. Lutz, and F. Machlup (eds.) *Roads to Freedom: Essays in Honour of Friedrich A. von Hayek*, London, Routledge and Kegan Paul, 245–85.

Swinnerton-Dyer, P. (1977) 'The Hopf Bifurcation Theorem in Three Dimensions,' *Mathematical Proceedings of the Cambridge Philosophical Society*, 82 (3, November), 469–83.

Teixeira, J. R., R. N. Suguhara, and M. Baranzini (2002) 'On Micro-foundations of the Kaldor–Pasinetti Growth Model with Taxation on Bequest,' *Brazilian Journal of Business Economics*, 2 (1, January), 9–23.

Tew, B. (1968) '*Critical Essays in Monetary Theory*, by Sir John Hicks,' *Economic Journal*, 78 (March), 108–10.

Thirlwall, A. P. (1987) *Nicholas Kaldor*, Brighton, Wheatsheaf Books.

Tobin, J. (1960) 'Towards a General Kaldorian Theory of Distribution,' *Review of Economic Studies*, 27 (2, February), 119–20.

Toulmin, S. (1972) *Human Understanding: The Collective Use and Development of Concepts*, Oxford, Clarendon Press.

Triffin, R. (1961) *Gold and the Dollar Crisis*, New York, Yale University Press.

Tsiang, S.-C (1951) 'Accelerator Theory of the Firm and the Business Cycle,' *Quarterly Journal of Economics*, 65 (3, August), 325–41.

Tversky, A., and D. Kahneman (1981) 'The Framing of Decisions and the Psychology of Choice,' *Science*, 211 (January), 453–8.

Valeriani, L. (1819) *Ricerche critiche ed economiche sull'Agostaro di Federico II, sul Ducato detto del Senato, sul Fiorino d'oro di Firenze, sul ragguaglio fra l'Agostaro e questi, e con cio' sulle monete di conto in genere*, vol. I, Bologna, Annesio Nobili.

(1821) *Contro la sentenza del celebre inglese giuspubblicista-economico Adam Smith che l'unità monetaria di conto traggasi nella colta Europa dall'argento piuttosto per particolari consuetudini che per universali cagioni*, Bologna, Annesio Nobili.

Velupillai, K. V. (1979) 'Some Stability Properties of Goodwin's Growth Cycle,' *Zeitschrift für Nationalökonomie*, 38 (3–4, October), 245–57.

(1990) 'The (Nonlinear) Life and Economic Times of Richard M. Goodwin,' in K. V. Velupillai (ed.) *Nonlinear and Multisectoral Macrodynamics: Essays in Honour of Richard M. Goodwin*, London, Macmillan, 7–27.

(1998) 'Richard Goodwin: 1913–1996,' *Economic Journal*, 108 (September), 1436–49.

(2003) *Essays on Computable Economics, Methodology and the Philosophy of Science*, Discussion Paper no. 8, Department of Economics, University of Trento.

(2008) 'Japanese Contributions to Nonlinear Cycle Theory in the 1950s,' *Japanese Economic Review*, 59 (1, March), 54–74.

Verri, P. (1986a [1762]) *Dialogo sul disordine delle monete nello Stato di Milano nel 1762*, in A. Quadrio Curzio and R. Scazzieri (eds.) *Sul disordine delle monete a Milano nel Settecento: Tre saggi di Cesare Beccaria e Pietro Verri*, Milan, Electa, 101–18.

(1986b [1772]) *Consulta su la riforma delle monete dello Stato di Milano [...] presentata al Magistrato Camerale da inoltrarsi alla R.I. Corte il 20 aprile 1772*, in A. Quadrio Curzio and R. Scazzieri (eds.) *Sul disordine delle monete a Milano nel Settecento: Tre saggi di Cesare Beccaria e Pietro Verri*, Milan, Electa, 119–35.

Violi, R. (1984) 'I processi dinamici di transizione indotti dall'innovazione tecnologica,' *Annali della Fondazione Luigi Einaudi*, 18, 53–95.

(1985) 'Sentiero di traversa e convergenza,' *Giornale degli Economisti e Annali di Economia*, new series, 44 (3–4, March–April), 153–78.

Von Neumann, J., and O. Morgenstern (1947) *Theory of Games and Economic Behavior*, Princeton, NJ, Princeton University Press.

Walsh, C. E. (2003) 'Speed Limit Policies: the Output Gap and Optimal Monetary Policy,' *American Economic Review*, 93 (1, March), 265–78.

Weintraub, E. R. (1979) *Microfoundations: The Compatibility of Microeconomics and Macroeconomics*, Cambridge, Cambridge University Press.

Whitmore, G. A. (1970) 'Third-degree Stochastic Dominance,' *American Economic Review*, 60 (3, June), 457–9.

Whittle, P. (1992) *Probability via Expectation*, 3rd edn., New York, Springer-Verlag.

Wicksell, K. (1907) 'The Influence of the Rate of Interest on Prices,' *Economic Journal*, 17 (June), 213–20.

(1934) [1913] *Lectures on Political Economy*, vol. I, London, Routledge.

(1936) [1898] *Interest and Prices*, London, Macmillan.

(2001) [1907] 'A New Theory of Crises,' *Structural Change and Economic Dynamics*, 12 (3, September), 335–42.

Wolfe, J. N. (ed.) (1968) *Value, Capital and Growth: Papers in Honour of Sir John Hicks*, Edinburgh, Edinburgh University Press.

Wood, A. (1975) *A Theory of Profits*, Cambridge, Cambridge University Press.

Woodford, M. (2003) *Interest and Prices*, Princeton, NJ, Princeton University Press.

Yamai, Y., and T. Yoshiba (2001) *Comparative Analyses of Expected Shortfall and VaR: Their Estimation Error, Decomposition, and Optimization*, IMES Discussion Paper no. 2001-E-12, Institute for Monetary and Economic Studies, Bank of Japan, Tokyo.

Yasui, T. (1953) *Self-excited Oscillations and the Business Cycle*, Cowles Commission Discussion Paper no. 2065, Cowles Foundation for Research in Economics, Yale University, New Haven, CT.

Young, W. (1987) *Interpreting Mr Keynes*, Boulder, CO, Westview Press.

(1991) 'The Early Reactions to *Value and Capital*: Critics, Critiques and Correspondence in Comparative Perspective,' *Review of Political Economy*, 3 (3, July), 289–308.

Young, W. and F. Lee (1993) *Oxford Economics and Oxford Economists*, London, Macmillan.

Zamagni, S. (1984) 'On Ricardo and Hayek Effects in a Fixwage Model of Traverse,' in D. A. Collard, D. R. Helm, M. F. G. Scott, and A. K. Sen (eds.) *Economic Theory and Hicksian Themes*, Oxford, Clarendon Press, 135–51.

(1991) 'Hicks on Capital and Growth,' *Review of Political Economy*, 3 (3, July), 249–67.

Zollino, F. (2001) 'Personal Saving and Social Security in Italy: Fresh Evidence from a Time Series Analysis,' *Temi di discussione*, 417 (August) (available at www.bancaditalia.it).

Name index

The name index does not include the references to John Hicks as these are too numerous through the volume

Acocella, N. 427
Adams, G. P. Jr. 113, 124, 405
Akerlof, G. A. 314, 322, 324, 405
Åkerman, J. 341
Alighieri, D. 90
Allais, M. 26, 50, 257, 260, 266, 270, 273–4,
    405, 408
Allen, R. G. D. 50, 75–6, 78, 111, 134,
    281, 405
Allen, W. M. 78
Alston, L. 79
Amendola, M. 33, 35, 382, 385–7,
    399, 405
Amihud, Y. 274, 405
Ando, A. 166, 405
Andrews, J. 105
Andrews, V. 105
Aquinas, T. 129
Araùjo, J. T. 430
Arbuthnot, J. 419
Arestis, P. 405
Arrow, K. J. 20, 41–3, 46, 49, 62, 66,
    123, 133, 138, 141, 149, 362, 380,
    405–6
Artzner, P. 237, 406
Ashton, T. S. 13, 14, 150, 406
Atkinson, A. B. 290, 293, 306, 406
Atsumi, H. 406
Aubrey, H. G. 103

Backhouse, R. 72
Balestra, P. 304, 406
Baranzini, M. 27–8, 72, 204, 287, 297–8,
    302, 304, 306, 349, 406, 418,
    427, 430
Baranzini, Moira 288
Barone, E. 238, 252, 406
Barro, R. J. 169, 406

Bauer, P. T. 2, 80, 118, 125, 148, 406
Baumol, W. J. 2–3, 67, 406, 422
Beach, E. F. 406
Beaud, M. 406
Becattini, G. 148
Beccaria, C. 186–93, 199–201, 406,
    426–7, 431
Bell, P. W. 119–20, 125, 406
Bellet, M. 407
Bellman, R. 267
Bellofiore, R. 410
Bendixson, I. 334
Benetti, C. 5, 406
Benhabib, J. 318, 406
Bensusan-Butt, D. M. 81, 86, 103
Berger, A. N. 226, 232, 407
Berlin, I. 9, 407
Bernanke, B. S. 226, 315, 407, 412
Bernoulli, D. 252–3, 254, 268, 407
Bernoulli, N. 252–3, 268
Besomi, D. 72, 73, 77, 84, 87, 287, 407, 427
Beveridge, W. H. 75, 78
Black, F. 274
Blinder, A. S. 226, 407
Bliss, C. 19–20, 129, 130, 136, 252, 287,
    291, 294, 407
Blume, L. 426
Böhm-Bawerk, E. von 34, 110, 141, 142, 143,
    144, 343, 347, 349, 367–73, 376, 407, 424
Boianovsky, M. 348, 351, 407
Boland, L. A. 121, 125, 407
Boltyanskii, V. G. 137, 426
Borda, J.-C. 44
Bortis, H. 301, 407
Boulding, K. E. 111, 113, 124, 408, 427
Bourguignon, F. 146
Bowley, A. L., 19, 111–12, 124, 283, 408
Brady, M. E. 408

Brenner Y. S. 421
Bridel, P. 79, 408
Britto, R. 408
Broggia, C. A. 195–6, 200, 408, 425
Brown, A. 78, 115, 124, 408
Brunner, K. 119–20, 125, 408
Bryce, R. 81
Buiter, W. H. 324, 408
Bullard, J. 316, 408
Bunge, M. 414
Burmeister, E. 297, 362, 408
Byron, G. G. N, Lord Byron 99

Caffè, F. 427
Cain, S. 287
Caldwell, B. 414
Cantillon, R. 204, 413
Caravale, G. A. 418
Cardus, N. 340
Carli, G. 408
Carr, P. 274, 408
Casarosa, C. 204
Cassel, G. 422
Cassells, J. 49
Cesari, R. 26, 263, 274, 408
Chamberlin, E. 277
Champernowne, D. G. 86, 278,
    290, 293
Cherubini, U. 252
Chew, S. H. 260, 408
Chick, V. 72
Chomsky, N. 51
Churchill, W. 234
Ciocca, P. 20–1, 146, 148, 408,
    426
Clarida, R. 315, 408
Clark, G. C. 79
Clay, H. 110, 124, 408
Clements, M. P. 319, 408
Clower, R. 19, 116–17, 122, 125,
    328, 409
Coase, R. H. 74, 160, 409
Cobb, C. 279, 283–4
Coddington, A. 19, 121, 125, 409
Cole, G. D. H. 150
Coleman, D. C. 118, 125, 148, 409
Collard, D. A. 429, 432
Colonna, M. 412
Condorcet, J.-A.-N.-C., Marquis de 44
Conlisk, J. 310, 319, 409
Cordy, J. 103, 105
Courakis, A. 102, 104, 105
Cournot, A. A. 135
Cramer, G. 253
Cramp, T. 122, 126, 409

Craven, J. 409
Cunningham W. J. 421

D'Adda, C. 26, 263–74, 408
Dahrendorf, R. 73–4, 409
Dalton, H. 75
Dalziel, P. C. 430
Dasgupta, A. K. 42, 73, 429
Datta, B. 42
David, W. L. 90, 409
Day, R. 410
de Bernardi, M. 290, 414
de Cecco, M. 21–2, 148, 157
de Finetti, B. 254, 409
de La Grandville, O. 284–5
De Servigny, A. 241, 243, 409
De Turri, R. 194, 409
Debreu, G. 20, 46, 49, 123, 133, 138, 141,
    149, 260, 409
del Vecchio, G. 18, 94
Delbaen, F. 237, 266
Dennison, S. 81
Dewey, D. 116, 125, 409
Dickens, W. T. 322, 405
Director, A. 110, 124, 409
Dobb, M. H. 42, 79, 153, 409, 427, 429
Domar, E. D. 293, 295, 410
Donne, J. 90
Dornbusch, R. 137, 409
Dostaler, G. 5, 406, 409
Douglas, P. 279, 283, 284
Duesenberry, J. J. 62, 113, 124, 330, 331–2,
    334, 336, 409
Dupuit, J. 290
Durbin, E. F. 75, 78
Durlauf, S. N. 426
Dybvig, P. H. 258, 409

Eatwell, J. 407, 426
Ebenstein, A. 78, 409
Eber, J. 237, 406
Edelberg, V. G. 86
Edgeworth, F. Y. 342
Einaudi, L. 186, 188, 189–90, 192–4,
    198–201, 409–10
Einstein, A. 7, 51
Eltis, W. A. 295–6, 410
Endemann, W. 194, 410
Enos, J. R. 380, 410
Erreygers, G. 72
Euler, L. 296
Evans, G. C. 50, 310, 319, 321–2, 410

Faber, M. 363, 410
Farmer, R. E. A. 311, 321, 410

Farmiloe, T. 94–6, 105
Fay, C. R. 79
Fazzari, S. 309, 315, 410
Feinstein, C. H. 412
Fels, R. 330–1, 336, 410
Fenoaltea, S. 146
Ferri, P. 31, 309, 311–13, 315, 317, 323, 410, 424
Filardo, A. 324, 410
Findlay, M. C. 431
Fine, B. 44, 411
Fine, K. 44, 411
Firth, G. G. 111, 124, 411
Fishburn, P. C. 258, 260, 266, 273, 411
Fisher, I. 204, 316–17, 343, 376, 410–11, 430
Fitoussi, J.-P. 418
Flaschel, P. 310, 411
Fleming, A. G. 86, 202
Fleming, J. M. 411
Flemming, J. S. 305, 411
Folloni, M. 164
Fontana, G. 64, 411
Foxwell, H. 75
Franz Joseph, Emperor of Austria-Hungary 373
Frederick II, Holy Roman Emperor 430
Freimer, M. 232, 411
Friedman, M. 50, 62, 140, 148, 226, 243, 391, 411
Frisch, R. 30, 97
Froeschlé, C. 399, 405
Frydman, R. 320, 411
Fuhrer, J. 314, 411

Gaffard, J. L. 33, 35, 382, 385–7, 399, 405
Gali, J. 315, 408
Galilei, G. 135
Gamkrelidze, E. 137, 426
Gardenfors, P. 44, 411
Gayer, A. D. 410
Georgescu-Roegen, N. 50, 344, 411, 417
Gerschenkron, A. 118, 125, 411
Gertler, M. 315, 407–8
Gilchrist, S. 315, 407
Gini, C. 147
Glasner, D. 410
Glass, C. 245
Gloria-Palermo, S. 407
Godelier, M. 151, 411
Goethe, J. W. 2, 411
Gong, G. 310, 411
Goodfriend, M. 316, 412

Goodwin, R. M. 19, 32, 49, 114, 124, 294, 312, 328–31, 333–42, 344, 412, 430
Gordon, M. 232, 411
Gordy, M. B. 247, 412
Gram, H. 431
Grandmont, J.-M. 11, 320, 412
Graunt, J. 146
Graziani, A. 424
Greenberg, E. 309, 312–13, 315, 410
Greenspan, A. 247, 412
Greenwald, B. 315, 430
Grendi, E. 148, 412
Gresham, T. 192
Grice-Hutchinson, M. 103, 412
Guillebaud, C. W. 79, 113, 124, 412
Guiso, L. 166, 405

Haberler, G. 84, 87, 412
Hacking, I. 252, 412
Hagemann, H. 5, 32–3, 347–9, 351, 366, 407, 412–13, 423, 425, 428
Hagen, O. 405
Hague, D. C. 416, 420, 422
Hahn, F. H. 10, 19, 46, 115–16, 122–3, 125–6, 288, 295, 406, 413
Hakamata, Y. 72
Halevi, J. 292, 294, 413
Haley, B. F. 111, 124, 413
Hamilton, J. D. 130, 313, 319, 322, 324, 327, 413
Hammarskjöld, D. 342
Hamouda, O. F. 4, 5, 24–5, 56, 72, 74, 79, 84, 89, 204, 288–92, 406–7, 412–13, 423, 425, 428
Hansen, A. 60, 423
Harcourt, G. C. 19, 65, 120, 122, 125, 294, 328, 406, 413, 417, 420, 427
Harrington, S. E. 413
Harris, D. J. 413
Harris, S. 414, 423
Harrison, A. J. 406
Harrison, B. 423
Harrod, R. F. 50, 58, 63, 73, 81–2, 84, 87, 111, 117, 124, 291, 293, 295–7, 298, 330–1, 340, 342–3, 407, 410, 414, 417, 427
Hart, A. G. 113, 405, 415, 418, 424
Harte, N. B. 406
Hawtrey, R. G. 75, 81, 111, 124, 205, 227–9, 342, 414, 417
Hayek, F. A. von 32, 34, 50, 53, 73–6, 84, 86–7, 119, 144–5, 204–6, 208–10, 214, 219, 222, 224, 329, 341–2, 347–51, 357, 368–70, 372–7, 379–80, 412–14, 416, 422, 429–30, 432

Heath, D. 237, 406
Heertje, A. 406, 428
Heisenberg, W. 11
Helm, D. R. 8, 102, 105, 414,
　418, 432
Henderson, D. 103
Hendry, D. F. 319, 408
Henriksson, R. G. H. 148, 422
Herring, R. J. 226, 232, 407
Hicks, E. 64
Hicks, U. K., Lady Hicks 17, 57, 72, 75–8,
　80–2, 84–90, 96–8, 105, 164, 409, 418,
　426, 429
Higgs, H. 75
Hillard, J. 408
Hirai, T. 72, 105, 418
Hitch, C. J. 78, 95, 113, 423
Hobsbawm, E. J. 151, 418
Hodgman, D. 232, 418
Holland, D. M. 425
Hollond, M. see Tappan Hollond, M.
Hommes, C. H. 312,
　320, 418
Honkapohja, S. 310, 319,
　321–2, 410
Hopf, H. 318
Horie, S. 202, 419
Horioka, C. Y. 297, 304, 419
Horsefield, K. 202, 419
Hotelling, H. 50, 419
Howitt, P. 320, 419
Howson, S. 72–3, 419
Hubbard, G. R. 315, 410
Hughes, J. R. T. 118, 125, 148,
　419, 425
Hume, D. 204, 225, 419
Huygens, C. 252, 254, 419

Ichimura, S. 334, 415, 419
Inama-Sternegg, K. T. von 373
Ingersoll, J. E. Jr. 258, 409
Ingrao, B. 79, 408

Jackman, R. 313, 421
Jackson, P. 226, 244–7, 419
Jaffee, D. 419
James, E. 105
Jahnsson, Y. 65
Jannaccone, P. 194, 200, 419
Jarrow, R. 408
Jevons, W. S. 376
Johnson, H. G. 103, 115, 119, 124–5,
　419–20
Jones, R. W. 282, 284–5, 419
Jonung, L. 418, 431

Kahn, R. F. 17, 50, 63, 74, 76–7,
　79, 81–2, 84, 87, 278, 287,
　291–2, 294, 307, 413–14, 420,
　423, 425
Kahneman, D. 26, 260, 271–4,
　420, 430
Kaldor, N. 19, 33, 51, 63, 74–8,
　85, 114, 124, 131, 231, 291–300,
　307, 328, 330–1, 334, 336, 340,
　352–6, 360, 362, 406, 420, 425,
　427, 430
Kalecki, M. 63, 301, 343, 420
Kane, E. J. 116–17, 125, 420
Kendall, M. 258, 420
Kennedy, C. 365
Kessler, D. 304, 420–1, 424, 430–1
Keynes, J. M. 2, 8, 9, 12–13, 16–18, 30,
　49, 50, 52–4, 62–4, 66, 68, 70, 71,
　73–7, 79–85, 87, 93, 95–6, 100–1,
　104, 117, 119, 121, 133–5, 139–40,
　150, 158–60, 185, 202, 204–6,
　208–9, 210–11, 214, 221–2, 224–31,
　233–5, 246, 277, 289–92, 294–6,
　298, 307, 310, 328, 342, 351, 367,
　370, 374, 376, 378, 382–3, 403,
　408, 410, 413–14, 420–1, 423–4,
　426–9, 431
Kindleberger, C. P. 121,
　125, 421
King, G. 146
King, R. G. 19, 122–3, 125, 316,
　412, 421
Kirman, A. 130, 421
Kiyotaki, N. 377, 421
Klamer, A. 421
Klein, F. 341
Klein, L. 62
Knight, F. H. 421
Kolmogorov, A. N. 254, 421
Koopmans, T. 50
Kotlikoff, L. J. 421
Kraus, M. 365, 421
Kregel, J. A. 297, 420, 421
Kresge, S. 416
Kruger, A. 110–11, 124, 421
Kuhn, I. 411
Kuhn, T. 421
Kurihara, K. K. 419
Kuznets, S. 146, 155
Kuznetsov, Yu. A. 319, 326, 421
Kydland, F. E. 123

Lachmann, L. M. 11, 421
Laidler, D. 19, 122, 125, 421
Laing, N. F. 304, 413, 421

Lamberti Zanardi, M. 86
Lancaster, K. 274, 421
Lander, B. 75
Landes, D. L. 419
Landesmann, M. A. 349, 421
Lane, F. C. 118, 125, 148, 421
Lange, O. 117, 415
Laplace, P. S. 11, 254, 421
Lash, N. A. 226, 245, 421
Laski, H. 75, 90
Latsis, S. J. 417
Layard, R. 313, 421
Le Corbellier, P. 338
Lederer, E. 33, 353–6, 422
Lee, F. 116, 432
Leijonhufvud, A. 19, 120–3, 125, 422
Leith, J. C. 74, 424, 426–7, 430
Leontief, W. 278, 349, 355, 422
Lerner, A. P. 19, 74, 76, 85, 87, 111, 114, 124, 278, 422
Levinson, N. 338, 422
Liakopoulou, I. 72, 105
Liénard, A. 334
Lindahl, E. 10, 84, 92, 342, 374, 415, 422
Lines, M. 318, 424
Little, I. M. D. 102
Long, J. B. 123
Loria, A. 189, 410, 422
Lowe, A. 32, 348–9
Loyo, E. 201, 422
Lucas, R. 13, 122–3
Lundberg, E. 330–2, 334, 336, 341–3, 422
Lutz, F. A. 416, 420, 422

McAfee, R. P. 320, 419
McCloskey, D. 14, 422
McCormick, B. J. 75, 422
McFadden, D. 137, 422
McKenzie, L. W. 2, 49, 422
Machina, M. J. 260, 271, 273, 422
Machlup, F. 19, 111–12, 124, 278, 422
Macmillan, H. 17–18, 92–3, 96, 292
Macmillan, M. 96
Macmillan, P. 105
Madan, D. 274, 408
Maddison, A. 146
Maine, H. S. 22, 162–3, 422
Mair, J. 75
Majumdar, T. 42
Malestroit, J. C., Seigneur de 188–9
Malinvaud, E. 282–3, 285, 422
Malthus, T. R. 278, 399, 405
Marcet, A. 322, 423

Marcuzzo, M. C. 17, 72, 77, 85, 88–9, 105, 287, 408, 418, 420, 423, 425, 427, 428
Mari, C. 287
Mariutti, G. 16–17, 52, 426
Markov, A. A. 310, 313, 322–4
Markowitz, H. M. 50–1, 273, 367, 423
Marshall, A. 2, 13, 20, 50, 75, 83, 88, 123, 131–2, 135–8, 205, 229, 342, 373, 423
Marschak, J. 271
Martinez Oliva, J. C. 247, 423
Marty, A. L. 119–20, 125, 423
Marx, K. 20–1, 60, 65, 146, 150–1, 153–4, 349, 354–5, 357, 418
Masera, R. S. vi, 25–6, 204, 225, 234, 236, 243–7, 328, 423
Masson, A. 304, 420–1, 424, 430, 431
Matten, C. 240–2, 423
Matthews, R. C. O. 4, 89, 102, 148, 288, 295, 312, 413, 423
Maw, M. 105
Mazzoni, G. 225
Meade, J. E. 50, 58, 62, 76, 113, 117, 278, 290–1, 293, 307, 423
Medio, A. 312, 318, 423–4
Menger, C. 34, 77, 268, 368, 370–1, 373, 374–7, 424
Merton, R. C. 266, 424
Meyers, A. 113, 124, 424
Milgate, M. 407, 426
Mill, J. S. 18, 100, 379
Miller, M. 169, 226, 228, 232, 424
Millikan, M. F. 80
Minenna, M. 252
Minsky, H. P. 310, 312–3, 323, 410, 424
Mirrlees, J. A. 420
Mises, L. von 347–8, 368, 376
Mishchenko, E. F. 137, 426
Mitchell, B. R. 118, 125, 148, 424
Mitra, A. 429
Mitra, K. 316, 408
Miyazaki, K. 406
Mizen, P. 83, 424
Modigliani, F. 60, 62, 169, 226, 232, 296, 307, 405, 419, 423–4, 427–8
Moggridge, D. E. 72, 74–5, 79, 104, 420–1, 424
Montanari, G. 198, 200, 424
Moore, G. 314, 411
Morgenstern, O. 19, 111, 124, 254, 260, 265, 274, 341, 368, 424, 431
Morishima, M. 102, 143, 334, 424, 425
Morrison, L. A. 110, 124, 425
Mulgan, J. 95, 97

Murfin, A. J. 297, 425
Muth, J. 123
Myint, H. 102
Myrdal, G. 84, 342, 414

Naldi, N. 72, 79, 425
Napoleon Bonaparte, Emperor 227
Nardini, F. 366, 425
Natoli, S. 195, 425
Neimark, Y. 319, 326
Neisser, H. 33, 353–4, 356–62,
    412, 425
Neri, P. 194–5, 425
Netto, E. 50
Newlyn, W. T. 103, 425
Newman, P. 407, 426
Newton, I. 135
Neyman, J. 406, 414
Nickell, S. 313, 421
Nicolini, J. P. 322, 423
Niehaus, G. R. 413
Nishizawa, T. 72, 105, 418
Nobel, A. 49, 66, 68
Norrington, T. 98
North, D. C. 148, 417, 425

Occam, W. 311
Olivieri, R. 102, 105
Onofri, P. 22–3, 164, 169, 425
Ortobelli, S. 252

Panetta, F. 252
Panigirtzoglou, N. 324, 408
Pantaleoni, M. 5–6, 425
Pareto, V. 2, 20, 50, 55, 112, 131–2, 149,
    157, 341, 360, 369, 425
Parker, W. N. 118, 125, 148, 425
Pascal, B. 254
Pasinetti, L. L. 16–17, 52, 61, 63, 148,
    155, 292, 294–5, 297, 299, 300,
    302, 307, 352, 406, 421, 425–6,
    428, 430
Patinkin, D. 62, 74, 116–17, 125, 424,
    426–7, 430
Peacock, A. 426
Pearsall, C. W. 78
Perry, G. L. 314, 322, 405
Pesaran, H. M. 309, 313, 323, 426
Petersen, B. C. 315, 410
Phelps, E. S. 320, 411
Phillips, A. W. 311, 313–14, 405, 410
Phoonsen, J. 196, 426
Pigou, A. C. 17, 56, 61, 79, 81, 83, 86,
    87–8, 278, 289–93, 307, 341, 354, 408,
    414, 426

Pirenne, H. 148–9, 153
Plosser, C. I. 123
Plumptre, A. F. W. 74, 426
Poincaré, H. 334
Polanyi, K. 162–3
Pontryagin, L. S. 137, 426
Ponzi, C. 317
Popper, K. R. 373, 414
Posner, M. V. 120, 125, 426
Postan, M. M. 149, 150, 426
Potter, S. M. 309, 313, 323, 426
Power, E. 150
Prescott, E. C. 123
Presley, J. R. 83, 424
Price, B. B. 222, 426
Puttaswamaiah, K. 5, 408, 413, 426, 429
Puviani, A. 166, 169, 426

Quadrio Curzio, A. 23–4, 185, 186, 406,
    426, 431
Quesnay, F. 349

Raffaelli, T. 72
Rader, T. 260, 427
Radford, R. A. 427
Radner, R. 11, 427
Ramsey, F. P. 294, 427
Rayleigh, Lord see Strutt, J. W., Lord
    Rayleigh
Reddaway, W. B. 117
Reder, M. W. 110–11, 124, 427
Renault, O. 241, 243, 409
Rey, G. 427
Ricard, J. P. 195, 426
Ricardo, D. 18, 33, 100, 146, 150, 154, 205,
    213, 218, 227, 229, 278, 341, 346,
    349–54, 356–7, 359–60, 361–2, 363–4,
    366, 379, 382, 385, 406, 413, 414, 427–9,
    431–2
Richardson, G. 98, 102, 105, 427
Robbins, L. 17, 53, 56, 73–6, 78,
    85, 87, 92, 105, 131, 329, 417,
    419, 427
Roberts, S. C. 98
Robertson, D. H. 17, 18, 42, 47, 56,
    75–7, 79–80, 82–4, 87–9, 93, 96,
    289–91, 307, 341–2, 374, 415, 418,
    425, 427, 428
Robinson, E. A. G. 51, 74, 76, 79, 88, 113,
    124, 291, 427, 428
Robinson, J. V. 17, 50, 56, 63, 66, 76–9,
    81–2, 85–8, 277–8, 290–4, 307,
    425, 427
Roncaglia, A. 72
Roosevelt, F. D. 159

Rosier, M. 5, 406
Rosselli, A. 72, 77, 87–9, 408, 423, 425, 427, 428
Rostas, L. 105
Rostow, W. W. 102
Rotemberg, J. J. 412
Rothschild, M. 427
Rowe, J. 79
Russell, B. 129
Rymes, T. K. 19, 119, 125, 427

Sacker, R. 319, 326
Samuelson, P. A. 10, 15–16, 49, 50, 59, 62–3, 89, 130, 134–6, 148, 287–8, 292, 307, 311, 341, 352, 360–1, 406, 427–8, 430
Sanders, A. 105
Sanfilippo, E. 17, 72, 80, 105, 418, 428
Sargent, T. J. 310, 314, 319, 322, 428
Saunders, A. 72
Saura, D. 312, 428
Savage, L. J. 254, 270, 428
Savary, J. 195, 200, 428
Scarfe, B. L. 122, 126, 428
Scaruffi, G. 198, 428
Scazzieri, R. 1, 6, 23–4, 185–6, 225, 287–8, 294, 349, 361, 406, 418, 421, 426–7, 428
Schlitzer, G. 247, 423
Schmitt-Grohé, S. 406
Scholes, M. 274
Schuller, A. L. 17–18, 108, 292, 328, 428
Schulz, H. 408
Schumpeter, J. A. 159, 277–8, 341–3, 354, 371–3, 376, 428
Schwartz, A. J. 226, 411
Scitovsky, T. 121, 125, 428
Scott, M. F. G. 429, 432
Sedaghat, H. 428
Seers, D. 103
Semmler, W. 310, 411
Sen, A. 15, 41–2, 46, 102, 290, 293, 330, 428–9, 432
Shackle, G. L. S. 75
Shafer, G. 254, 429
Sharpe, W. F. 257, 429
Shehadi, N. 74, 80, 89, 429
Shell, K. 116
Shove, G. F. 79, 110, 124, 277, 286, 341, 429
Simkin, C. 89, 429
Simon, R. 81
Singer, H. W. 86

Sisam, K. 98, 104
Skidelsky, R. 60, 73–5, 429
Skinner, A. S. 429
Skouras, T. 405
Slutsky, E. 50
Smith, A. 6, 34, 103, 146, 148, 150, 350, 380, 382–4, 403, 429, 430
Smith, O. E. 338, 422
Smithies, A. 331
Snowdon, B. 60, 429
Solow, R. M. 19, 26–7, 62, 66, 102, 115, 119, 125, 204, 252, 277, 285–7, 294, 307, 309, 330, 413, 429
Sommer, L. 407
Sonnenschein, H. 130, 429
Sorger, G. 320, 418
Spengler, O. 150
Sraffa, P. 17, 42, 51, 75–7, 79, 82, 85–8, 291, 293–4, 300, 341, 349–50, 423, 425–7, 429
Stagni, A. 22–3, 164, 169, 425
Staley, E. 49
Steagall, H. B. 245
Stein, J. 252
Steuart, J. 194, 196–8, 200, 429
Stigler, G. J. 114–15, 124, 341, 430
Stiglitz, J. E. 306, 315, 372, 380, 406, 427, 430
Stokes, C. J. 115, 124, 430
Stone, R. 81, 86
Streissler, E. W. 33–5, 204, 367, 375, 430
Strutt, J. W., Lord Rayleigh 333–4
Stuart, A. 258, 420
Subhuti 330, 341
Suguhara, R. N. 306, 430
Summers, L. H. 421
Sweezy, P. M. 278
Swinnerton-Dyer, P. 336, 430
Sylos Labini, P. 148
Szegö, G. P. 226, 232, 407, 430

Tang, A. 417
Tappan Hollond, M. 75, 79
Tarshis, L. 74, 81, 278, 430
Taubman, T. 297, 408
Taylor, J. B. 267, 315–16, 323, 407, 430
Teixeira, J. R. 306, 430
Tew, B. 116, 125, 430
Thalberg, B. 328
Thatcher, W. 79
Theil, H. 147
Thirlwall, A. P. 74, 84, 430
Thomas, R. P. 148, 417, 425
Thornton, W. T. 150, 205, 210, 341

Tiberi, M. 427
Tinbergen, J. 343
Tintner, G. 86–7, 341
Tobin, J. 60, 62, 159, 297, 430
Tooke, T. 205
Toulmin, S. 18, 109, 430
Toynbee, A. J. 150
Trautwein, H.-M. 347–9, 407, 413
Triffin, R. 202, 234, 423, 430
Troeltsch, E. 150
Tsiang, S. C. 336, 430
Tutin, C. 5, 406
Tversky, A. 26, 260, 271–4, 420, 430

Uribe, M. 406

Valeriani, L. 198–200, 430
van der Pol, B. 334
Vane, H. R. 60, 429
Vasquez, F. J. 428
Vaughan, R. 430
Vegas, J. M. 428
Velupillai, K. V. 31–2, 309–10, 312, 328–9,
    338, 418, 429, 430–1
Venditelli, E. 72
Verri, P. 186, 190–1, 193, 199, 201,
    426–7, 431
Vickson, R. G. 266, 411
Violi, R. 363, 431
Visco, I. 166, 405
von Neumann, J. 16, 36, 51, 254, 260, 265,
    274, 341, 431
Vovk, V. 254, 429

Walras, L. 2, 20, 129, 131, 135, 149, 341,
    368–9, 370, 414, 429

Walsh, C. E. 316, 431
Watanabe, W. 297, 304, 419
Webb, U. K. see Hicks, U. K.
Weber, M. 150, 162–3
Weintraub, E. R. 59, 431
Weiss, A. 372, 380, 430
Westfield, F. M. 417
Whale, B. 55
Whitmore, G. A. 266, 431
Whittle, P. 254, 268, 431
Wicksell, K. 33, 50, 83–4, 92, 123, 132–4,
    137, 141, 143, 204–5, 211, 214,
    220–1, 225, 227, 231, 341, 347–8,
    351–4, 355–60, 368, 376, 407, 412,
    426, 431
Wieser, F. von 376
Wirth, S. 365, 421
Wolfe, J. N. 5, 410, 422, 431
Wolff. E. N. 431
Wood, A. 301, 431
Woodford, M. 314, 316, 321, 407, 431
Woods, R. N. 421
Worley, J. S. 417
Wright, R. 377, 421

Yamai, Y. 238, 431
Yasui, T. 333–4
Yoshiba, T. 238, 431
Young, W. 18–19, 109, 111, 116–17,
    431–2

Zamagni, S. 1, 2, 8, 225, 365, 422, 432
Zambelli, S. 328
Zeno 43
Zollino, F. 166, 432
Zouache, A. 407

Subject index

accelerator, 63, 331, 336–7
  financial, 319
  'dead,' in Hicks's theory of the trade
    cycle, 337
  non-linear, 333
  real, 319
account money, 24, 195,
    197–200, 202
accumulation, of capital, *see* capital
    accumulation
accumulation, of stock, 388–9, 392
adjustment, 13, 35, 67, 144, 365
  lagged, 13, 136, 374
  lagged, of out-of-market prices, 20,
    136, 212
  out-of-equilibrium, 35, 119, 212,
    368, 374
    Keynesian phase of, 391–403
    Smithian phase of, 391–403
adjustment mechanism (horizontal and
    vertical), 84n
adjustments, differentiated, in Hicks,
    13, 365
aggregate demand, 316, 350, 389
aggregate supply, 316
Allais paradox, 270–1
Allais's axiom (non-satiation
    principle), 257
Amsterdam Bank (and bank money), 24,
    195–7
arbitrage conditions, 139
Arrow–Debreu model, of general
    economic equilibrium, 133,
    138, 141
Arrow's impossibility theorem, 43–4
assets, 26, 266–8
  composition of, 8, 12
  inter-generational, 298, 305
associations of concepts, and the history of
    economic theory, 6
asymmetric preferences, axiom of, 259

asymmetry, between contemporaneous
    goods (in Hicks), 143
Austrian capital theory, 2, 118–19, 347
averages, and norms, 21, 150

backward-biased technical change, 378
bank money, 24, 186, 194, 199–200,
    372, 374; *see also* state
    money
Banking School, 205
banking system, 231
banks' loans, 226, 228
barter economy, and economic
    fluctuations, 386
Basel Capital Accords, 244, 247
beliefs, 310
bequest propensity, 28, 299,
    304, 305
bifurcation values, and the generation of
    cycles, 319, 336
bonds, 226, 228, 231
book review
  purposive, 18, 109, 116, 119, 123
  substantive, 18, 109, 114, 116–17
booms, in the trade cycle, 317
bounded rationality, *see* rationality, bounded
business accounting, and dynamic
    analysis, 22
business practice, and economic
    conceptualization, 1

'Cambridge circus,' 17, 55, 85, 291, 307
'Cambridge equation,' 296
Cambridge Graduate Seminar, 75, 85
Cambridge post-Keynesian theories of
    income distribution, 295–6, 307
Cambridge–London School of Economics
    'Joint Seminar,' 75, 78, 86
capital, 1, 25, 131, 344, 346–7,
    354, 377
  absorption of, 243–4, 247

capital (cont.)
of the banking system, 225–6
of the banks, 25, 226–7, 242, 246; *see also*
capital standards.
cost of, 172–3
measurement of, 140, 377–8
organic composition of, 357
ownership of, 285
capital accumulation, 3, 14, 29,
142, 290, 353–6, 360, 362,
378, 386
first phase of, 29
late phase of, 29–30
middle phase of, 29
capital/assets ratios, evolution of, 245–6
capital/output ratio, 295, 296
flexible, 296
capital goods, 27, 29, 349, 370, 374
capital intensity, or capital/labor ratio, 27,
285, 359, 362, 380
capital-saving inventions, 279,
353, 362
capital shortage, and technological
unemployment, 353
capital standards (for banks), 25, 247
capital stock, 170, 304, 307, 334, 357
depreciation of, 140
final, 382, 384
initial, 382, 383
of the intergenerational type, 299, 304
of the life cycle type, 299, 304
capital theory, 4, 20, 51, 63, 110, 132–3,
139–41, 143, 246, 294, 346, 349,
368, 371
paradoxes of, 294
capital value profile, 377–8
Capital and Growth, 18, 19, 42, 63, 99, 101,
115–16, 143–4, 205–6, 229–30, 232,
246, 288–9, 292, 294, 296, 304,
306–7, 309, 346, 365
Capital and Time, 8, 18–19, 65, 99–100,
118–19, 144, 205, 309, 343, 344,
346, 348, 361–2, 365–81
as a 'modernization not only of the
Austrians, but also of the English
classics', 18, 367–8
capital-intensive growth, 278, 362
capitalism, 21, 146–50, 229, 354
dynamics of, 147–9, 159, 162, 354–5
instability of, 22, 147, 227, 311
late, in Hicks's analysis, 158
cash flows, 315
and debts, 310–11
casual labor, versus regularly employed
labor, 154

catastrophe insurance, 247
causal process, as distinguished from a
system of coordinated conditions, 5
causal processes, in Hicks, 1, 2, 6, 7–10,
12–13, 68, 118
causal structures, 3, 5–9, 14, 121
causality, 6, 9, 33, 77, 121
contemporaneous, 7, 12
ex ante, 7, 11–12
ex post, 7, 12
'new,' in Hicks, 6, 10
'old,' in Hicks, 6, 10
sequential, 7, 8, 11–12
Causality in Economics, 18–19, 121,
147, 344
causation principles, and the trade cycle, *see*
trade cycle and causation principles
ceiling and floor model, of the trade cycle,
30–1, 63, 309–13, 322–3
ceilings, in trade cycle theory, 312, 331,
336–7, 340
central bank, international, 222
central banking, 25, 206, 219–22, 224, 228,
231, 236, 301
certainty equivalence, 254, 264
choice, 3, 5–9
rational, 1
circulating, or working, capital, 153, 351,
360, 363, 365, 368–9, 375
Clarkian neoclassical marginalism, 16, 51
classical economists, 278
clearing bank, international, and Keynes's
proposal, 202
closed orbits, in non-linear models, 312
command economies, 146, 153
commercial banks, 220
communication, slowness of, 14
comparative statics, 129, 134, 137
compensation effects and the machinery
problem, 347, 351–5, 359,
361–2
competitive advantage
and production, 155
and trade, 155
competitive bank enterprise, 236, 245–6
complementarity and complements, 134,
142, 144
complementarity over time, 3, 6–7, 10–11,
384–5, 399, 401, 403–4
of investment and consumption,
384, 399
complex dynamics, 7–11
concentration of attention, in economic
analysis, 1–4
conceptual integration, in Hicks, 36

constant elasticity of substitution (CES)
    production function, 284–5
construction costs, 363, 392
construction period, of capital goods, *see*
    construction period, of production
    process
construction period, of production process,
    29, 35, 363–4, 369, 375, 378, 384–7,
    392, 399–401, 403
  lengthening of, 363
consumer goods industries, 383
consumption, 383
  unproductive, 383, 386, 392, 395,
    399, 404
consumption function, in macroeconomics,
    61, 316
consumption lag, 375
constraints, intertemporal, 4
contexts, and causal relationships, in Hicks,
    3–4
contingent markets, 133
continuation theory, 382, 384, 399
*Contribution to the Theory of the Trade Cycle,
    A*, 19, 63, 99, 101, 113, 205, 292,
    309, 328–9, 331, 341–2, 345, 348
cooperation, 146
coordinated conditions, system of (as
    distinguished from a causal process),
    5, 9
coordination mechanisms, 399, 401, 404
coordination policies, 35–6, 404
coordination problems, and out-
    of-equilibrium paths, 399
cost equity, 226
cost of capital, and inflation, 172
credit, 24, 207–8, 213, 216–18, 354
  supply curve of, 372, 380
credit cycle, 375
credit distress, 227, 232, 242, 246, 247
credit economy, 25, 123, 189, 198, 199,
    201–2, 206, 215, 217, 220, 224
  imperfect, 201
  monocentric model of, 220–2
  polycentric model of, 220
  Wicksellian, 224
credit management, 218–19, 224
  and governmental activity in Keynes, 224
  and market institutions in Hicks, 218, 224
credit money, 207–8, 215
credit rationing, 372, 380
credit risk, 25, 225–6, 232, 238, 247
Crisis in Keynesian Economics, The, 101,
    119–20, 206, 383
Critical Essays in Monetary Theory, 19, 63,
    100–1, 116–17, 206

cumulative processes, 347–8, 384–5
currency school, 205, 218
custom, 146
custom and command economies,
    151, 153
cycles, 114, 310–12, 317, 321–3, 329,
    333–4, 337
  see also fluctuations, economic
cycles of indecision, and pair-wise majority
    voting, 43–4

debt, dynamics of, in the trade cycle, 315,
    317–18
decisions, 121, 389
  sequence model of, 7, 11
  time structure of, 4, 367
default, 240
demand theory, 114–15, 134
destruction, of productive capacity, and
    capitalist dynamics, 354
diagonal dominance, 137
diminishing returns, in Wicksell, 356
displacement of workers, and technical
    progress, 356, 359, 362
distortion, of productive capacity, *see*
    productive capacity, distortion of
distribution, Cambridge theory of, 288–9
distribution of income, functional, 7, 12,
    26–7, 154, 278, 285, 287–90, 292–4,
    296, 362
distribution of income, personal, 26–7, 147,
    154, 285, 287–9, 293
double vision, and decision-making, in
    Hicks, 7, 10–11, 14, 23
dual money system, 24, 186, 189–94,
    198–201
dynamic theory, as theory of a process, 7, 10

early phase, of traverse, 365; *see also*
    traverse
Economic Club, the 75, 86
economic dynamics, 3–4, 8, 12, 20, 130,
    138, 144–5, 227, 284, 292
  in Cournot, 135
  Hicks's definition of, 137–8
  in Marshall, 13, 136
  in Walras, 135
economic freedom
  and efficiency, 46
  and liberty, 41
  and markets, 46
economic history, 51, 64, 68, 118, 148, 227,
    229, 360
  and economic theory, 64–5, 148, 150,
    162–6, 360

Economic Perspectives, 100–1, 120–1, 206, 230, 231
economic policy, Hicks's view of, 47–8, 228–9
economic progress, 118, 278
economic theorizing, 1–5
economies of scale, and concentration of capital, 354, 380
effective demand, 234, 247, 399
    principle of, 58
efficiency, 15, 41, 46, 363
efficiency improvement, index of, 363
elasticity of substitution, 27, 54, 278–81, 284–5, 353
    aggregate, 282–4
    and aggregation error, 283
    between commodities, 27, 281–2
    technical, 27, 281–3
elementary production process, defined, 387
employment, 154, 286, 337, 346, 350–4, 357–9, 362, 364, 390
    casual, 154
    regular, 154
    theory of, 8, 12, 58
endogeneity, of trade cycles, in medium-term dynamics, 31, 311, 321, 323
endogenous growth theory, 366
equilibrium, xiii, 68, 70, 117, 212, 374
    equilibrium, in the long-run, *see* long-period equilibrium
    equilibrium, in the market period, *see* market-period equilibrium
    equilibrium, in the short-run, *see* short-period equilibrium
    equilibrium, monetary, *see* monetary equilibrium
equilibrium concepts, 84, 139
equipment, versus capital, in Hicks, 379
equity to capital ratio, in banks, 245–6
errors, and time, in Menger, 370
Essays in World Economics, 100, 115
European proportion, of gold to silver currencies, in Beccaria, 191, 193
evolution, in history, 70, 118
ex ante income, 172
ex post income, 172
exchange rates, between abstract money and national currency, *see* exchange rates, internal
exchange rates, between real currencies, 191, 193
exchange rates, internal (and imaginary money), 190–3, 199, 201

expansionary policy, and distortion of productive capacity, 384, 399, 401
expectations, 20, 34, 58, 83–4, 114, 116, 121, 139, 141–3, 145, 161, 165–6, 212, 217, 230, 254, 310–11, 314–15, 317, 319–23, 327, 370, 374, 377, 380, 385, 392
    in de Finetti's approach, 254
    elasticity of, 114, 143, 161
    of interest rates, 165
    of price, 138–9, 141, 143, 161, 165, 377
    static, 365, 374
expectations formation, 145, 311, 322
expected loss, 239, 240–1, 246, 248–51; *see also* unexpected loss
expected shortfall, as a measure of risk, 238
expected utility, 26, 253–4, 256, 260, 265–6, 274
expected value, 252
explosive pattern, in Hicks's trade cycles, 31; *see also* trade cycle

factor prices, relative, 215
    and substitution, 280
final demand, expected, 389
finance, international, 123
financial assets, 170–1
financial development, and the sinking of capital, 154
financial intermediaries, as listening points in Hicks's monocentric model, 220–1
financial markets, 231
financial players, rings of, in Hicks, 206, 220–1
fiscal illusion, 23, 169
fixed capital, 154, 170, 351, 360, 363, 365, 368–9, 375
fix-price assumption, and fix-price method, 8–9, 13, 27, 139, 401
fix-price markets, 13, 21–2, 144, 157, 164, 229, 312–13
fix-price and flex-price markets
    coexistence of, 157, 159–13
    in Keynes, 230
fix-price/flex-price distinction, and econometric models, 164
fix-wage assumption, 351, 361, 401
fix-wage path, of traverse, 361–3, 378
flex-price markets, 13, 21–2, 117, 157, 162, 164, 208, 229

flex-wage model, and Wicksell's analysis of the machinery problem, 351
floors, in trade cycle theory, 312, 329, 331, 333, 337
flow input/flow output production process, 347, 377
flow input/point output production process, 347, 377
flow equilibrium, 67, 139–40
flows, 67, 139
fluctuations, economic, 63, 206, 209, 212, 221, 224, 247, 309–10, 317–19, 321, 323, 328–9, 331–3, 347–9, 399; see also cycles
focus external (in book reviews), 18, 114, 120, 122–3
focus internal (in book reviews), 18, 114, 117, 120–1, 123
forced saving, 365; see also saving, forced
foreign exchanges, 190, 192–3
foresight, perfect, 122, 311, 319, 321, 323
formal connections, and conceptual integration, in Hicks, 36
forward-biased technical change, 363, 378–9
forward markets, 133, 138–9, 143
free will and determinism, 7, 10
freedom, 9, 41
  of choice, 5–11
  and efficiency, 15, 46
  and markets, 46–8
  negative, 5
  positive, 5
full employment, and out-of-equilibrium path, 392
full employment path, of traverse, 365, 374, 378
full performance path, of traverse, 378, 385
fund, of productive resources, 349
fundism, in Hicks's theory of capital, 25, 232–3, 246; see also materialism, in Hicks's theory of capital

general economic equilibrium, 8, 12, 20, 46, 116, 129, 131–3, 136, 140, 215, 266–8, 370, 372
  of the dynamic type, 122, 129, 130
  existence of, 129, 135
  ontology of, 129–30
  of the simultaneous type, 136
  stability of, 130, 135, 137

of the static type, 129, 134
  uniqueness of, 129
general economic equilibrium theory, 19, 46–7, 49, 52, 117, 129, 130, 132–4, 136, 266–8, 357, 369, 370
gold exchange standard, 202
golden rule, of economic policy, 228
Goodwin characteristic, 338
Goodwin's full employment barrier, 337
government borrowing, and the long-run real rate of interest, 381
gross income, and Ricardo's machinery effect, 350–1, 352–3, 356–7
gross substitutability, 137
growth (economic), 1, 63, 287–308, 323, 382
  natural rate of, 295
  natural rate of (flexible), 296
  neoclassical, 284
  non-proportional, 308
  rate of, 296, 316–17, 319, 346, 392, 399
  as substitution driven, 27, 284–5
growth equilibrium, in Hicks, 115–16, 213, 215, 298
growth rate, and monetary policy, in Hicks, 35–6, 391–403
growth rates, differentiated, in Hicks, 302
growth theory, 284–5, 288, 293, 295, 366
  method of, 293

harmonizing, of construction and utilization phases, 35, 384–6
Harrod instability, 63
Harrod neutrality, of technical progress, 379
Harrod–Domar knife-edge problem, 295
Hayek effect, 377
Hayek seminar, 75
Hayek's lag structure of production stages, 34
Hicks curve, of long-run combinations of inflation and real growth rates, 120
Hicks-neutral technological change, 279, 353, 379
Hicksian correction, and disposable income measurement, 164, 168, 170, 174
Hicksian income, 140
Hicksian ordinal utility function, and Lancaster's theory of the demand of characteristics, 261
Hicksian 'week,' and temporary equilibrium, 28, 141, 161
higher-order moments, and moment pricing theory, 263–6
history, and economic theory, xiii, 1, 3, 68
history, of economic theory, 6, 9
hoarding, of stock, in Smith and Hicks, 35, 383–4, 386, 395

horizontal representation, of economic
　　structure, 32–3, 349, 365
horizontal and vertical bottlenecks, in
　　Hicks's dynamic theory, 30, 33
hump, in Hicks's trade cycle theory, 32, 333

ideal money, and imaginary money, 200
idle balances, 392, 395, 399
imaginary money, 24, 186–91, 193–5,
　　197–203
　　origins of, in trade fairs, 194
imperfect competition, 77
impulse, in Hicks's dynamic analysis, 8,
　　346, 353, 365
income, 61, 164, 302, 354–5
　　concepts of, 164
　　definitions of, 22, 165
　　disposable, 164–6, 168, 316
　　expected, 316
　　gross, 350–3, 357, 364, 391
　　national, 350–4, 356
　　net, 350–2, 357
income effects, 54, 134, 137
income measurements, 22, 140, 172
independence axiom, 26
index of improvement, in efficiency, 363
indifference curves, 81, 134
　　convexity of, 134
industrial interrelationships, 365
Industrial Revolution, 146, 361
'industrialism,' in Hicks's analysis,
　　153–4, 361
inflation, 23, 123, 164, 166, 168,
　　172–3, 209, 310, 313–14, 317,
　　320, 391
　　ex ante, 168
　　expected, 166, 168
　　ex post, 166, 168
inflationary expectations, 313
innovation, 354, 361, 363
　　backward-biased, 363
　　forward-biased, 362–3
　　neutral, 363
innovations, capital-using, 119
institutions
　　in economics, 1, 3, 21, 151
　　and the trade cycle, 31
integrable demand structures, 50
integrated VAR-type measures of risk, 238
interest, 131
interest, rate(s) of, 34, 83, 120, 139–40,
　　142, 205, 209, 212, 218, 220, 228,
　　231–2, 246, 310, 371–2, 377–8,
　　380–1; see also interest rates
　　long-run, 216, 228, 230, 235, 380

market, 210, 347
monetary, 139, 235, 315, 317,
　　347–8
natural, 210, 347–8, 374
real
　　and the Fisher equation, 316–17, 348
　　in the long-run, 164
short-run, 216, 228, 230
interest, supply rate of, 376
interest rate ceiling, 217
interest rate floor, 217
interest rate policy, 221
interest rates
　　differentiated, and equilibrium growth,
　　　302–3, 304
　　and disequilibrium, 370
　　expectations of, 165
intergenerational assets, 298
intermediate items, in a collection of capital
　　goods, 51
international finance, see finance,
　　international
intertemporal joint production, 347
inventions, 27, 348, 354–5
　　induced-biased of, 27, 279–80, 362
　　labor-saving, 350, 352–6, 362
investment, 210, 214, 317–18, 331, 383,
　　395, 399, 404
　　at cost, 385
　　at output capacity, 385
　　autonomous, and 'floor' in Hicks's
　　　trade cycle theory, 31, 329–32,
　　　334–5, 337
　　desired, 390
　　induced, 331–2, 334, 337
　　net, 140
　　realized, 390
　　of the replacement type, 331
investment decisions, 172, 174,
　　205, 389
investment freedom, 216
investment function, 61, 310–11, 315,
　　318, 334
　　non-linear, 334
irreversibility, 5–11, 67, 118
IS and LM curves, 8, 12, 16, 50, 55, 59,
　　60–1, 66, 70, 226, 329

joint determination, of outcomes, 5,
　　7–11, 12

Kahneman and Tversky paradoxes, 271–4
Keynes's macroeconomics, 2, 117
Keynes's political economy seminar,
　　73–5, 87

labor-augmenting inventions, 279
labor-displacing effect, of new
    machinery, 350
labor markets, 157–60
labor-saving inventions, 110, 279–80,
    353–5, 362
lagged adjustment, see adjustment,
    lagged
lags and reserves, 7, 11, 374–5, 383–4
laissez-faire, 24
Lausanne school, of economic theory, 131–4
learning, 311, 316, 321–3
learning by doing, 380
lengthening, of construction period, 363
liberty
    and freedom, 9, 41
    and majority rule, 44–5
life cycle model of saving, 305
limit cycles, 312, 319, 334, 337–8
limits, of economic theory, according to
    Hicks, 2
liquid reserves, 35
    and material goods, 35
liquidity, 7, 11, 14, 16, 35, 205, 210, 212,
    216–18, 228, 386
    constraints, 391
    theory, 210–12, 216–18, 223
liquidity preference, theory of, 56, 61, 117,
    210, 212, 216
loan markets, 139, 142
loanable funds theory, 212
London Political Economy Club, 75, 86–7
long-period equilibrium, 136, 372
long-run tendencies, 309

Machiavellism, in economics, 36
machine tool sector, 365
machinery, 146, 349, 350–1, 357
machinery problem, 347, 349, 350–1, 361,
    362, 366; see also Ricardo machinery
    effect
macroeconomics, unification of, in Hicks, 382
maintaining capital intact, 169
majority rule, 15, 43–4
    arbitrariness of, 43–4
marginal efficiency of capital, 58, 210
marginal productivity, theory of income
    distribution, 351, 355
market, rise of, in history, 2, 51, 149–50,
    153, 155
Market Theory of Money, A, 18–19, 102,
    104, 109, 122–3, 147, 205, 235
markets, 14, 16, 19–21, 120, 146,
    162, 207
    and freedoms, 74

fix-price, 13, 21–2, 144, 157, 164, 229,
    312–13
flex-price, 13, 21–2, 117, 157, 162, 164,
    208, 229
    historical dynamics of, 20, 51, 151
Markov expectations, 322
Marshall's method, of lagged factor input
    adjustment, 20
Marshall's period analysis, 136
Marshallian economics, 2, 20, 131
martingale strategy, 253
materialism, in Hicks's theory of capital,
    25, 232; see also fundism, in Hicks's
    theory of capital
means of payment, 188–9, 192, 194, 196,
    200–1
medium term, dynamics of, 28, 309, 365
medium-term perspective, in dynamic
    analysis, 319
Menger's time structure of production, 34
merchant law (lex mercatoria), 152
merchants, and economic progress, 118
methods, of dynamic analysis, 16, 115
Methods of Dynamic Economics, 18, 101–2,
    306, 365–6
'Minister of Money,' in Beccaria, 191–3
minority rights, and majority rule, 44–5
Modigliani–Miller theorem, 169
moment pricing, and intertemporal
    moments, 26, 266–8
moment pricing theory, 26, 254, 261–3,
    266–8; see also higher-order
    moments
monetary authorities, role of, 206, 221, 223
monetary base, 226
monetary disorders, 24, 185–91, 193,
    200–1, 348
monetary economy, 23, 35, 67, 117, 186,
    188–9, 206, 384–6
monetary equilibrium, 25
monetary history, 16, 23, 64, 193–4, 227
monetary institutions, 24, 185, 187, 194,
    203, 207–8, 231, 246
monetary obligations, and the flexibility of
    monetary arrangements, 187
monetary policy, 7, 12, 23–5, 186, 190–1,
    193, 201, 205–6, 214, 219, 220, 222,
    223, 224, 226, 228, 391
    accommodating, 403
    and the separation of powers, 229
monetary reform, 185, 191–2, 194, 202–3
monetary theory, 4, 7, 11–13, 16, 23–4, 56,
    64, 117, 122, 185–6, 190, 193,
    205–7, 212, 218, 222, 224–5, 227,
    231, 328, 377

money, 1, 3, 34, 67, 68, 70, 117, 185, 204,
    205, 207, 213, 214, 231, 252, 368
  demand for, 7, 12, 61, 143, 210, 211, 212,
    215, 216, 391
  outstanding, 211
  quantity of, 204, 209, 212, 213, 214
  quantity theory of, 218, 225, 231, 233
    in Wicksell, 204
  as store of value, 67
  supply of, 391
money bonds, 231
money loans, 139
money prices, as distinct from real
    prices, 215
moral expectation, 253; see also expected
    utility
'Mr Keynes and the "Classics",' 54, 58, 61
multi-class, growth model, 302
multi-currency economy, 186–7, 189, 192,
    199, 200–2
multiple equilibria, and the trade cycle, 333
multiple equilibria, in trade cycle theory,
    31, 335
multiplicative assumption, and autonomous
    investment, 32, 335
multiplier, 63, 210, 365, 383
  dynamic, 333

negative freedom, 5–6, 9; see also positive
    freedom
neutrality, and non-neutrality, of technical
    change, 54, 362
neo-Austrian capital theory, 349
neo-Austrian growth theory, 119, 144, 347,
    365, 376–7
neoclassical synthesis, 59, 62
'new causality,' in Hicks, see causality, 'new,'
    in Hicks
non-integrable demand structures, 50
non-linear trade cycles, 49
non-market organizations, in Hicks,
    151, 153
non-proportional economic growth, 308
non-satiation, principle of, 254, 257, 264
non-steady-state analysis, 116
non-terminable processes, 144; see also
    terminable processes
numéraire, in price theory, 189, 191

obsolescent processes, 378
'old causality,' in Hicks, see causality, 'old,'
    in Hicks
optimum growth, in Hicks, 115
'order of being,' in Pantaleoni, 5–11
'order of doing,' in Pantaleoni, 5–11

ordinal utility, theorem, 26, 259–61
organic composition, of capital, see capital,
    organic composition of
oscillations, maintenance of, 337, 340
oscillator, one-sided, and Goodwin
    characteristic, 338
out-of-equilibrium, adjustment, see
    adjustment, out-of-equilibrium
out-of-equilibrium, state of the economy,
    368, 374, 380, 385–6, 391–403
outstanding money, 211; see also money,
    outstanding
own rates of interest, 371

parsimony, and hoarding, in Smith, 383–4
partial equilibrium, 136–7
period analysis, 137
Phillips curve, 313–14
pluralism, in economic analysis according to
    Hicks, 4, 8, 12
Pontryagin's maximum principle, 137
portfolio, 23, 26, 210
  diversification of, 241–2
portfolio selection, theory of, 211, 254
positive freedom, 5, 6, 9; see also negative
    freedom
preparatory phase, of traverse, 364
price expectations, 138–9, 141, 143, 161,
    165, 377
  sensitivity of, 22
price information, 374
price and wage changes, on sequential
    adjustment paths, 390–1
prices, perfectly competitive (a limiting case
    in Menger), 375
prices, social functions of, 230
primitive preferences, in Savage's
    approach, 254
process innovations, 349
producer goods industries, 383
production, 146, 389
  coordination, 21
  and the economy of markets, 152–3
production coefficients, flexible, 294
production function, 68, 280, 294,
    378–80; see also constant elasticity
    of substitution (CES) production
    function
production monetary economy, and the
    division of labor, 67
production period, 110, 374
production process
  duration of, 3, 14, 28, 347, 375
  elementary, 387
  stage structure of, 3, 347, 368, 375, 379

production planning
  intertemporal, 141
  static, 141
productive capacity, 170, 387, 392, 399
  age structure of, 395
  distortion of, 384–6, 392, 395, 399, 401, 403–4
productive and unproductive labor, 382–3
productivity, 119, 356, 392, 399
  growth of, 316, 350
profit share, 315
profits, 214, 290, 292, 294, 296, 299
  rate of, 170–1, 214, 296, 302, 363, 380
    differentiated, and equilibrium growth, 302
public debt, 164, 168, 169
public sector regulation, 228

rate of starts, of new production processes, 399, 401, 403
rationality, xiii, 5, 9
  bounded, 310–11, 319, 320, 323, 324
real and financial variables, interaction of in trade cycle, 323
real prices, as distinguished from money prices, 215
reference path, in Hicks's traverse analysis, 346, 363–5
regime-switching, 312–13, 320, 322–3
research traditions, in economics, xiii
reserves, and economic dynamics, 383–4
resource constraints, and out-of-equilibrium paths, 387–8; see also horizontal and vertical bottlenecks, in Hicks's dynamic theory
return
  rate of (on financial assets), 169–74
  real rate of, 164, 170–1
Revision of Demand Theory, A, 114–15
'revolutions,' in economics, 17, 52–3, 69, 74, 122
Ricardo machinery effect, 32–3, 346, 349, 351–3, 356–63, 366, 385; see also machinery problem
risk, 25, 122, 236, 242–4, 246–7, 256, 303, 368
  absorption, 25, 236
  aversion, 254, 256–7, 263–6
  definitions of, 236–64
  management, 236
  measurement, coherent, 237–8
  neutrality, 368n
Robbins' seminar, 73–5
roundabout methods of production, 372
'running-in' period, of utilization, 363, 369

St. Petersburg paradox, 252, 268–70
Samuelson's accelerator-multiplier model, 311
Samuelson's correspondence principle, 134
saving; see also savings
  flexible, 27–8, 287–308
  forced, 347
  net, 140, 214
saving behavior, 23, 28, 35, 116, 174, 285
saving decisions, 174–5, 205
saving function, 61
  Kaldorian, 299–300
  Kaldorian, and growth equilibrium in Hicks, 300–1
saving policy, 391
saving propensity, 27, 164, 175, 293, 296, 298
saving rate, 391
savings, 210, 214, 285, 292, 295, 297, 376–7, 384
  aggregation of, 297
  differentiation of, 297–8
  distribution of, 303
  optimal, 294
saving/investment relationship, 23, 77, 216–17
scrapping, of production processes, 387
sectoral disintegration, of the production process, 384
separation of powers, and monetary policy, in Hicks, 229
sequence economies, 7, 10, 370, 374
sequential analysis, of economic fluctuations, in Robertson, 82–3
sequential causality, see causality, sequential
sequential determination, of outcomes, 7, 11–12
sequential processes, of change, 35, 382, 384, 391
sequential production, 347
shock, and the balance between construction and utilization processes, 385
short-period equilibrium, 136
simple profile, of the production process, in Hicks, 369, 378
single-period theory, 382
slowness, of communication, see communication, slowness of
Smithian phase, of out-of-equilibrium adjustment, 391–403
social accounting, 113
social choice theory, 15, 41–2, 49

socio-economic classes, 28, 302–3,
        306–7
    dispersion of, 27–8
    dynamics of, 27–8, 307
    formation of, 27–8
    and saving behavior, 28
Special Drawing Rights (SDRs), 202
specialization, and sequential analysis, in
        Smith, 382
speculative currency flows, in a multiple
        currency arrangement, 187
speculative specie flows, 188–9
speculative trap, 216
stability, 112, 130, 134, 136–7, 160, 218,
        311–12, 316, 333, 338, 356
    factors of, 161
    in Hicks's trade cycle theory,
        330, 335
    monetary, 218
stagnation, in the long run, 83
static equilibrium, 112, 129
stationary process, and transitions, 376
stationary state, 132, 138,
        368–9, 376
stationary states, in Pigou, 86
statistical uniformities, and Hicks's theory
        of economic history, 2–3
status and contract, in Maine, 162
steady-state analysis, 116, 119, 143, 316,
        318, 324–5, 378, 391
stochastic dominance, and expected utility,
        263–6
stock equilibrium, 67, 139, 140
stocks, 7, 12, 67, 139, 386, 388
    final, 382, 384
    initial, 382; see also capital stock
strongly forward-biased invention, in
        Hicks, 33
structural economic dynamics, 294,
        365–6; see also viability, of structural
        change
subjective value, 34, 371–2
substitutability, gross, 137
substitution, 6, 10, 16, 134, 142, 144, 280,
        352, 384, 396
    intertemporal, 119, 144
substitution effect, 54, 137
'Suggestion for Simplifying the Theory of
        Money, A,' 158–9, 205, 214, 236,
        252, 367, 369
supply curve, for credit, see credit, supply
        curve of
supply demand equilibrium, 376
supply rate of interest, see interest, supply
        rate of

'surplus of claims,' and debt-clearing in
        Hicks, 203
Swedish economists, their influence on
        Hicks, 2, 92, 342

'take-out,' in Hicksian time structure
        models, 385, 389, 391–2, 395–6,
        399, 401, 403
technological change, 119, 140, 154, 214,
        284–5, 346, 348, 351, 353–7, 359,
        362, 380
technological disequilibria
    and horizontal representations of the
        production system, 349
    and vertical representations of the
        production system, 349
technological unemployment, and Ricardo
        machinery effect, 33, 352–3
temporary equilibria, sequence of, 141–2
temporary equilibrium, 7, 8, 11–12, 28, 139,
        141, 144, 161–2, 215, 316, 372
term structure, of interest rates, 228
terminable processes, 144; see also
        non-terminable processes
theoretical pluralism, in economics, 4
Theory of Economic History, A, 65, 117–18,
        147, 155, 162, 229, 361
Theory of Wages, The, 17–19, 49, 53–5,
        62–3, 92–6, 101, 104, 109, 110,
        163, 277–86, 292, 341, 352, 362,
        366, 369
    second edition, 277, 282–3, 286
time, xiii, 4, 5–9, 33, 70, 373
    in economics, 7, 8, 10, 12, 16, 34, 70,
        366, 373, 382
time preference, 372
time profile, of inputs and outputs, 375–6
time structure of production, 20, 33–4, 368,
        370, 382–5
    between periods, 110, 384
    within a period of finite length, 384
trade advantage, one-off, 155
trade cycle, 30, 63, 83, 114, 213–14, 247,
        310–13, 315, 317–18, 322–3, 328,
        347–8
trade cycle theory, 224, 329, 331, 343, 347,
        349, 357
    non-linear, 328, 334, 343
trade fairs, and imaginary money, 194
trade networks, circumscribed, 198
transaction cost, removal policies of, 21
transaction money, 24, 211
transitional paths, 33
transitions, and economic dynamics,
        119, 376

transitive preferences, axiom of, 259
traverse, 3, 8, 13, 32–4, 144, 213–14,
    294, 307, 346–7, 353, 363–6, 378,
    385, 386
trust fund, and major systemic risk, 26, 248
two-class, or multi-class, growth model, 302

uncertainty, 7, 12, 67, 133, 143, 386
unemployment, 60, 117, 314, 346, 351,
    354–5, 359, 365, 392, 395,
    399, 401
  permanent, 355
  structural, 354–5, 357, 360, 363–4
  temporary, 362–3, 365
unexpected loss, 239, 241–3, 246,
    248–51; *see also* expected loss
unit of account, 186, 190–4, 196, 198–201
utility, 114–15
  measurement of, 80
utility function
  individual, 114–15, 134, 294
  social, 294
utilization period, of capital goods, *see*
    utilization period, of production
    process
utilization period, of production process, 35,
    363–5, 369, 375, 378, 384–7, 392,
    395, 403
utilizational cost, 363

value, 1, 4
value, subjective, *see* subjective value
Value and Capital, 18–19, 28, 30, 41, 50,
    57, 62–3, 65, 81, 92, 95–6, 99,
    101, 104–5, 109, 110–12, 129,
    131–4, 136–8, 140, 143–4, 155,
    160–1, 164, 205–6, 215, 225, 230,
    277–8, 289–92, 294, 340–2, 346,
    370, 372

'*Value and Capital* growth model,' 115
value at risk (VaR), as a measure of risk,
    237–8
Venice Banco, 195
Venice bank money, 24, 199
vertical integration, of production
    processes, 365, 384
vertical representation, of economic
    structure, 32–3, 349, 365
viability, of structural change, 404
volatility, as a measure of risk, 236–7
von Neumann technology, 16, 51
voting rules, and social choice
    outcomes, 44

wage, monetary, 355
wage capital, 360
wage fund, 360, 379, 386–7, 392, 399
wage rate, 234, 363
wage rigidity, 160, 234, 355,
    357, 375
wage units, 234
wages, 119–20, 122, 154, 157, 214, 277,
    282, 286, 296, 313, 351, 355–6, 377,
    383, 389–90, 392
Walrasian statics, 2
wealth, 23, 166, 168, 293, 302
  concentration of, 306
  dispersion of, 306
  financial, 166
wealth–income ratio, 116
wealth redistribution
  and fiscal policies, 306–7
  and inflation, 169, 174
welfare, 1, 4, 15, 53, 290
welfare economics, and the Cambridge
    tradition, 290
welfare theory, 53, 121, 293
Wicksell's cumulative process, 347